This
Sunday
at
4:00

LK PS

FINANCIAL
ACCOUNTING
EDITION 8

Financial Accounting, 8e, by W. Steve Albrecht, James D. Stice, Earl K. Stice, and K. Fred Skousen

Publisher: Dave Shaut
Acquisitions Editor: Sharon Oblinger
Developmental Editor: Leslie Kauffman, Litten Editing and Production, Inc.
Production Editor: Kara ZumBahlen
Manufacturing Coordinator: Doug Wilke
Marketing Manager: Dan Silverburg
Promotions Manager: Jon Schneider
Photo Research: Fred Middendorf
Photo Manager: Cary Benbow
Cover Design: Lamson Design/Cincinnati
Cover Photography: Greg Grosse Photography/Cincinnati
Internal Design: Michael H. Stratton
Production House: Peggy Shelton, Litten Editing and Production, Inc.
Compositor: GGS Information Services
Printer: R.R. Donnelley, Willard

Printed in the United States of America
3 4 5 04 03 02

For more information contact South-Western, 5191 Natorp Blvd, Mason, Ohio, 45040 or find us on the Internet at http://www.swcollege.com

For permission to use material from this text or product, contact us by
• **telephone: 1-800-730-2214**
• **fax: 1-800-730-2215**
• **web: http://www.thomsonrights.com**

ISBN: 0-324-06670-8 (text and CD)
ISBN: 0-324-11165-7 (text only)
ISBN: 0-324-06760-7 (CD only)

Library of Congress Cataloging-in-Publication Data

Financial accounting/W. Steve Albrecht ... [et al.] — 8th ed.
    p. cm.
    Includes bibliographical references and index.
    ISBN 0-324-06670-8
    1. Accounting I. Albrecht, W. Steve.

HF5635 .S618 2001
657—dc21   00-067078

photo credits

brief contents

contents

PART f2
Operating Activities   235

expanded material

expanded
material

The Best Team

Authors W. Steve Albrecht, James D. Stice, Earl K. Stice, and K. Fred Skousen are all key players in the curriculum change process at Brigham Young University. Individually and as a team, the authors feel passionately about making this the most relevant and useful book you will ever use.

W. Steve Albrecht is the Arthur Andersen & Co. Alumni Professor of Accountancy and the Director of the School of Accountancy & Information Systems at Brigham Young University. He received a bachelor's degree in accounting from Brigham Young University and MBA and Ph.D. degrees from the University of Wisconsin at Madison. Dr. Albrecht, a certified public accountant, certified internal auditor, and certified fraud examiner, came to BYU in 1977 after teaching at Stanford and at the University of Illinois. Earlier in his career, he worked as a staff accountant for Deloitte & Touche. Dr. Albrecht has received numerous awards and honors, including the BYU School of Management's Outstanding Faculty Award and the BYU Outstanding Researcher Award, and was recognized, as part of Utah's Centennial Celebration, as one of 131 Utahians who have made outstanding contributions or brought unusual recognition to the state. Dr. Albrecht has served as President of the American Accounting Association, the Administrators of Accounting Programs Group, and the Association of Certified Fraud Examiners and is currently president-elect of Beta Alpha Psi.

James D. Stice is the Distinguished Teaching Professor of Accounting at Brigham Young University. He is also the Associate Director of BYU's MBA program. He holds bachelor's and master's degrees from BYU and a Ph.D. from the University of Washington, all in accounting. He has been on the faculty at BYU since 1988. During that time, he has been selected by graduating accounting students as "Teacher of the Year" on numerous occasions, selected by his peers in the Marriott School of Management at BYU to receive the "Outstanding Teaching Award," and received the University's top award for teaching excellence, the Maeser Award, in 1999. Professor Stice has published articles in *The Accounting Review, Decision Sciences, Issues in Accounting Education, The CPA Journal*, and other academic and professional journals.

Earl K. Stice is the PricewaterhouseCoopers Professor of Accounting in the School of Accountancy & Information Systems at Brigham Young University. He holds bachelor's and master's degrees from Brigham Young University and a Ph.D. from Cornell University. Dr. Stice has taught at Rice University, the University of Arizona, Cornell University, and the Hong Kong University of Science and Technology (HKUST). He won the Phi Beta Kappa teaching award at Rice University and was twice selected at HKUST as one of the ten best lecturers on campus. Dr. Stice has also taught in a variety of executive education and corporate training programs in the United States, Hong Kong, and South Africa. He has published papers in the *Journal of Financial and Quantitative Analysis, The Accounting Review, Review of Accounting Studies,* and *Issues in Accounting Education,* and his research on stock splits has been cited in *Business Week, Money,* and *Forbes.*

K. Fred Skousen is Advancement Vice President at Brigham Young University. Previously, he was Dean of the Marriott School of Management and Director of the School of Accountancy at BYU. He earned a bachelor's degree from BYU and master's and Ph.D. degrees from the University of Illinois. Dr. Skousen taught at the University of Illinois and the University of Minnesota prior to joining the faculty at Brigham Young University. In 1983, Dr. Skousen was awarded the Peat Marwick Professorship at BYU. In 1984, Dr. Skousen was elected to the AICPA Council, and in 1985, he received the UACPA Outstanding Faculty Award.

How the Best got Better.

edition 8

A Benchmark Text—Raising the Bar Even Higher

Through each successful edition, **Financial Accounting** has come to be the text by which all others are judged. With the perfect blend of procedure and concepts, the text gives students an inside, realistic view of how accounting is done in leading companies across the nation and around the world. Now in its eighth successful edition, the book takes the bar up a notch by offering a combination of new and proven features that make the best even better:

 ▪ An enhanced integration of real company financial statements and real-world examples in every chapter gives students a clear picture of how to use accounting information

 ▪ A completely integrated learning system that includes elements for classroom learning, technology-assisted learning, and distance learning

▪ An organization that focuses on the principal activities of a business— financing, investing, and operating

 ▪ A cumulative spreadsheet assignment that reinforces each chapter's topics

▪ Specialized customer service through trained and personal consultants

How the Best got Better

The Best Language for Business

In order for today's student to be the best, they must have a complete understanding of the numbers. Understanding what the numbers reveal, and what they do not reveal, allows business managers and investors to make every type of business decision: expand, merge, close, launch, subcontract, downsize, invest, reposition, lease, replace. As the basis for all these decisions, accounting is the universal language of business. This edition makes it even easier to understand what the numbers mean.

Take, for instance, the case of Safeway, a major supermarket chain, as examined in the opening vignette of **Chapter 2: Financial Statements: An Overview**. In the last twenty years, Safeway has experienced, at various times: falling market share, challenging union demands, high overhead, significant job cuts, an aggressive construction and remodeling program, a leveraged buyout, and reintroduction of the firm as a public company.

Safeway has the third largest sales of major supermarket chains today. Its current net income is higher than that of Kroger and Albertson's stores, which have higher sales volumes. What does the Safeway experience tell us? It tells us that to truly comprehend what is going on in a business, whether in the grocery store or in the corporate boardroom, one must understand accounting data—both how it is prepared and why it is meaningful.

Changing for the Better

The past few years have seen many calls for improving accounting education. This call for change drove past editions of **Financial Accounting** to be the best book on the market. The central themes in all these calls for change have been (1) that the business world and accounting professions are changing rapidly, (2) that accountants of the past must become the premier information professionals of the future, and (3) that accounting and business graduates need new skills and knowledge if they are to effectively meet tomorrow's professional demands. We answered those calls by creating a textbook that teaches students both how to prepare financial statements and how to use that accounting information to make smart business decisions.

In creating this Eighth Edition, we crafted a textbook that does an even better job of addressing the needs of an ever-changing world of accounting education. **Financial Accounting**, Eighth Edition is written and organized in a manner that allows students and instructors at all institutions to capitalize on our positive curriculum development experience and strive to make the best education even better.

The Best Approach
Real Numbers, Real Understanding

Today's business students need to have an understanding of the basics of accounting, no matter what their future career plans include. Most will be business managers that use accounting information to make business decisions, but even then, in order to make sound decisions, one must understand how the accounting information was derived. And, of course, those students who plan an accounting career need a strong foundation upon which to build. Financial Accounting has built a reputation as the best balance of these attributes by using real company financials in every chapter to give students an understanding of why and how accounting works. Our approach to this book is to introduce students to basic accounting concepts, excite them by using lots of real-world examples (both U.S. and international), provide them with some basic accounting knowl-

edge, and then show them how accounting is used and analyzed in actual case situations.

The Eighth Edition continues this rich tradition and makes it better. The authors have taken great care to fully integrate the use of each chapter's real company financials within the content of that chapter. For instance, in Chapter 2 *(Financial Statements: An Overview)*, the Setting the Stage opening vignette focuses on Safeway. Safeway's balance sheet and income statement are analyzed within the chapter. Also, several basic ratio calculations are taught in the chapter, and examples are shown using Safeway's numbers. In the CEO material at the end of the chapter, one of the *Analyzing Real Company Information* exercises centers on Safeway and further analysis of its financial statements.

The Best Business is Real Business

On the road from better to best, every company, regardless of its industry or type, must manage its business to acquire and sell products or services, make financing decisions, and invest in assets that will help the company generate growth and income. One of the reasons that Financial Accounting is the best is that we use an organizational format that is consistent with business activities and cycles (as opposed to the more traditional financial statement organization). This same approach was used in the last edition of the book, which was well received by reviewers

and adopters. Specifically, after introducing and explaining financial reporting and the accounting cycle in Part f1 (Chapters 1-5), we discuss the operating activities of a business in Part f2 (Chapters 6-8) and the investing and financing activities in Part f3 (Chapters 9-12). We conclude the financial portion of the text by discussing the statement of cash flows in Part f4 (Chapter 13). This focus on business activities helps students understand functions of business and see accounting as a tool to assist in making business decisions, not as an end in itself.

Ahead of the Curve

With the Best Technology

Today's students learn in more visual and interactive ways than ever before. These are students that have grown up in a multimedia- and technology-enhanced world. In order to educate these students, technology must be employed as an efficient means for both teaching and learning accounting. Educators now have the opportunity to bring more information to students in more media than ever before. **Financial Accounting** takes full advantage of these possibilities with the best technology package that fills a variety of needs.

The technology package consists of three distinct elements that can effectively be woven together. The three elements are *Product Web Site, Personal Trainer,* and the *Personal Web Tutor.* Some key facets to this package include:

- Lecture Replacement/Enhancement
- Concept Reinforcement
- Application
- Competency/Testing/Quizzing
- Remediation

Flexible Coverage
Brings out the Best in Instructors

Because the authors know that the best instructors continually try to make their classrooms better, we have preserved the text's innovation of dividing most chapters into two parts. This flexibility allows the instructor the chance to easily alter what they cover in class to fit the needs of their particular students. The first part includes material that needs to be covered to understand essential accounting concepts, while the second part features "expanded material" dealing

with additional topics to be covered at the instructor's discretion.

This strategy of dividing chapters into basic and expanded material was universally applauded by users of our last edition. It allows significant flexibility in covering desired material, without the disruption of skipping to appendices for more advanced material. Also note that end-of-chapter materials are divided and labeled to coincide with the essential/expanded division in the chapters.

The Best of the Best

Outstanding Features

This edition makes the connection to real-life business even better with the use of many insightful pedagogical features and real-world examples. As real companies and current events are examined, the focus is not only on how business managers collect and record data, but also why the information is important as the basis for decisions. For example, Microsoft's annual report is provided at the end of the text and referenced throughout.

Other Pedagogy

Special Margin Features

LEARNING OBJECTIVES Each chapter begins with specific learning objectives to guide students in their study of the chapter. Where applicable, chapters include expanded learning objectives.

SETTING THE STAGE An interesting, real-life scenario sets the stage for each chapter. These scenarios tie directly to materials covered in the chapter and help students relate chapter topics to actual business happenings. For example, Chapter 6 begins with a discussion of Yahoo!, and many examples using Yahoo!'s financial data are featured throughout the chapter.

BUSINESS ENVIRONMENT ESSAYS The text contains numerous real-world vignettes, adapted from financial newspapers and business publications, which illustrate important concepts being discussed. These examples enable students to see how the accounting topics they are studying are applied and interpreted in real-world situations.

KEY TERMS Throughout each chapter, key terms are defined in the margins. A list of key terms (with page references) is presented at the end of each chapter, and all key terms are defined in a comprehensive glossary at the end of the book.

SUMMARIES Several concise summaries are presented within each chapter to help students remember the important points just discussed, and each chapter concludes with a comprehensive summary, organized by learning objectives.

FYI
FYI features provide relevant information for students, drawing from real business events or situations.

STOP & THINK
Students are encouraged to take a step back occasionally to consider thought-provoking issues.

CAUTION
These reminders speak directly to students, helping them avoid common mistakes or misconceptions.

NET WORK
These exercises give students practice in seeking out information on the Internet.

More Outstanding Features

REVIEW PROBLEMS A review problem is provided at the end of each chapter (where applicable). These review problems (with solutions) demonstrate the application of the major concepts and procedures covered in the chapter.

CUMULATIVE SPREADSHEET PROJECT The cumulative spreadsheet project builds in each chapter. It is based on cash flow difficulties faced by The Home Depot at the end of 1985, but a fictitious name (Handyman) is used. The early assignments simply have the students construct a spreadsheet balance sheet and do a couple of simple manipulations, ratio calculations, and so forth. By the end of the text, the spreadsheet grows to a five-year forecast of operating cash flows that depends on assumptions about different operating parameters (speed of receivables collection, inventory efficiency, interest rates, sales growth, profitability).

COMPREHENSIVE PROBLEMS Three comprehensive problems, integrating multiple issues and methods, are found throughout the text.

FOCUS ON GLOBAL ECONOMY As mentioned, the focus in today's business world is on a global economy. To help students develop this global perspective, many international examples are provided throughout the Eighth Edition. In addition, there is at least one International Case provided at the end of each chapter.

FOCUS ON ETHICS Ethical considerations are increasingly important in all aspects of business. A section in Chapter 1 introduces the topic of ethics. Each chapter contains an Ethics Case relating to the topics covered in the chapter. These cases present ethical dilemmas that require students to think about behavioral and moral issues in business and accounting. We believe these ethics cases will provide a basis for rich classroom discussions and more responsible business conduct by students exposed to them.

Practice Makes the Best Better

The old adage *"practice makes perfect"* holds true in accounting. This book has all the traditional end-of-chapter assignments which has rendered it the best. Before describing the traditional material, however, we want you to understand our excitement for what makes this book even better: the **Competency Enhancement Opportunities** (CEO) that are included in the end-of-chapter material. Responding to well-justified calls for changes in accounting education, this material is included to help students develop critical thinking, ethical perspectives, oral and written communication skills, experience with electronic research, and team skills.

In each chapter's assignments, the CEO section begins with *Analyzing Real Company Information* exercises, based on actual company annual reports and data. CEO also includes:

- *International cases*, focusing on businesses that operate across international borders
- *Ethics cases*, examining issues of personal and business responsibilities

- *Writing assignments*, to be completed individually or in groups
- *Debates*, requiring two teams to argue the opposing sides of an accounting issue
- *Cumulative spreadsheet project*, building from one chapter to the next
- *Internet search exercises*, requiring students to find specific information on the Net

We believe students will find these assignments very relevant, interesting, and beneficial in their business careers.

Users have responded favorably to the traditional end-of-chapter assignments in previous editions. The discussion questions are intended to refine students' understanding of specific accounting terms and concepts. Discussion cases encourage classroom discussion of real-world business situations. Exercises deal with single concepts, and each can be completed fairly quickly. Problems probe for a deeper level of understanding. Those problems identified as "Unifying Concepts" and those with "Interpretive Questions" require students to analyze or interpret the computed results.

The Best Support, the Best Service

Because we know how difficult Financial Accounting can be to both teach and learn, we are not satisfied with merely offering the best textbook. We take it one step better by offering the most comprehensive and carefully prepared educational package available today. The package accompanying **Financial Accounting** consists of more than simple "supplements." Taken in whole, it is a comprehensive teaching and learning system that incorporates the Internet, powerful multimedia, and exceptional printed materials—all

coming together to create an educational experience unlike any other. Using the text in combination with these well-designed ancillaries makes it simple—and smart—to integrate technology into your course and makes it easy to be the best that you can be.

For more information on any of these supplements, don't hesitate to contact your South-Western/Thomson Learning™ sales representative. They are committed to providing you with unparalleled service and support.

Ancillary Materials

Thomson Learning is committed to providing you, our educational partners, with the best educational resources available. Because we prepare our instructor resources with a variety of teaching environments in mind, it is likely that you will need only a portion of these for your course. Before you request an item, we ask that you please read thoroughly the description of each resource. If you still need more information about resources, we urge you to contact your local Thomson Learning sales representative or visit our Web site at http://albrecht.swcollege.com. Many teaching and learning resources can be downloaded directly from this site.

Instructor's Resource CD This CD contains all the resources listed below (except the videos) in an easily accessible format. No longer will you have to lug heavy print items from school to home back to school again. This CD is your one-stop resource for assistance in teaching your course.

Web Site This site, http://albrecht.swcollege.com, contains downloadable supplements, interactive quizzes, Internet exercises and related URLs, accounting career information, lecture enhancement slides, and numerous other teaching resources.

Solutions Manual   (Prepared by W. Steve Albrecht, James D. Stice, and Earl K. Stice) This manual contains independently verified answers to all end-of-chapter discussion questions, discussion cases, exercises, problems, and Competency Enhancement Opportunities (CEO). Suggested solutions to the Stop & Think questions are also included.

Instructor's Manual   (Prepared by Michael Shapeero, Bloomsburg University) This manual contains learning objectives, chapter outlines, topical overviews of end-of-chapter materials, and assignment classifications with level of difficulty and estimated completion time. Transparency masters for each chapter are also provided.

Test Bank   (Prepared by Dick Wasson, Southwestern College) The revised and expanded test bank contains a collection of more than 1,100 examination problems, multiple-choice questions, true-false questions, and matching exercises, all accompanied by solutions.

ExamView® Computerized Testing Software   This supplement contains all of the questions in the printed test bank. This program is an easy-to-use test creation software compatible with Microsoft Windows®. Instructors can add or edit questions, instructions, and answers, and select questions (randomly or numerically) by previewing them on the screen. Instructors can also create and administer quizzes online, whether over the Internet, a local area network (LAN), or a wide area network (WAN).

Solutions Transparencies   Acetate transparencies of solutions for all end-of-chapter exercises and problems are available to text adopters.

PowerPoint™ Slides   (Prepared by Michael Blue, Bloomsburg University) Selected teaching transparency slides of key concepts and exhibits are available in PowerPoint presentation software, improving lecture organization and reducing preparation time.

Teaching Transparencies   Acetate transparencies of key concepts and exhibits are available to text adopters.

BusinessLink™ Video   A financial accounting video features segments of actual companies illustrating key accounting concepts. An Instructor's Manual is available to assist in the use of the video and the optional student workbook.

Personal Trainer Online   This Internet-based resource is designed to help students complete end-of-chapter assignments with helpful hints and interactive tips. By giving students this additional assistance in applying the concepts of the course you are ensuring their understanding of complex topics. (Hints and Tips prepared by Suneel Maheshwari, Marshall University)

Study Guide   (Prepared by W. Steve Albrecht, James D. Stice, and Earl K. Stice)

The study guide provides a means for students to re-examine the concepts and procedures in each chapter from several different perspectives. This publication includes learning objectives; detailed chapter summaries; discussions of topics that typically cause problems for students and suggestions for overcoming those problems; and tests for student self-assessment.

Working Papers   Forms for solving end-of-chapter problems are perforated for easy removal and use.

Homework Assistant and Tutor (HAT) Software   (Prepared by Rayman Meservy, Brigham Young University) This user-friendly software for Windows visually teaches the relationships among journals, ledgers, and financial statements. A built-in tutor function offers numerous hints and help screens. The software can be used to solve selected end-of-chapter exercises and problems, identified with the HAT icon. It is also an ideal teaching aid.

General Ledger Software   (Prepared by Warren Allen and Dale Klooster) This best-selling educational general ledger package may be used to solve selected end-of-chapter problems, which are identified with the general ledger icon.

Spreadsheet Templates   (Prepared by Michael Blue, Bloomsburg University) Excel templates are provided for solving selected end-of-chapter exercises and problems, which are identified with the spreadsheet icon.

BusinessLink™ Video Workbook   This workbook enriches understanding of the BusinessLink video through questions and related activities.

Personal Finance Resource CD-ROM   This supplement helps students understand how the concepts they learn in the textbook can assist them in making better personal financial decisions. Topics have been chosen and ordered to correlate with the chapters in the textbook.

Related Products

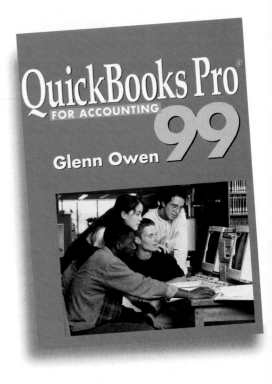

Annual Report Project and Readings (0-324-02473-8)

This highly popular project by Bruce Baldwin of Arizona State University West is designed for use by either learning teams or individual students. It is tailored to reinforce the concepts presented in the text. Students work with annual reports of real companies to understand, interpret, and analyze the information. The project guides them through this process. Interesting readings from publications like *The Wall Street Journal* along with supporting Questions for Consideration provide additional material for discussion.

INTACCT (rama.swcollege.com)

This software and on-line tutorial by Dasaratha Rama reviews each major step in the accounting cycle in a short, user-friendly manner that is easily integrated into classroom use. It is designed for use in a financial accounting course or any course where a review of the accounting cycle is desired.

Using QuickBooks Pro '99 for Accounting (0-324-02831-8)

Written by Glenn Owen of Alan Hancock College, this book provides a self-paced environment where students use commercial software to analyze, interpret, and investigate accounting information to make business decisions.

Financial Accounting Albrecht, Stice, Stice, Skousen

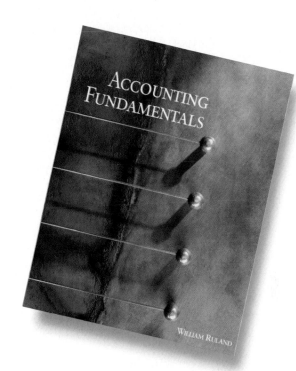

Hazzard Travel (0-538-86552-0)

With this computerized simulation, students maintain an accounting system for the first two months of operation of Hazzard Travel, a small service business. Created by Donna Ulmer, St. Louis Community College at Meramec, and M. Robert Carver, Southern Illinois University–Edwardsville, this practice set familiarizes students with basic accounting documents, procedures, and concepts. Students make investing, financing, and operating decisions that may result in a different financial outcome from their class-mates. The problems are unstructured, encouraging creativity and individual judgment.

Excel Applications for Accounting Principles (0-538-88887-3)

These text-workbooks, by Gaylord Smith, Albion College, include a software tutorial and accounting application with an accompanying template disk. Preprogrammed problems require students to develop formulas and enter data to complete partially constructed spreadsheet models. Model-building problems give students experience in developing their own spreadsheet models.

Accounting Fundamentals 2nd Edition (0-324-02361-8)

William Ruland, CUNY-Baruch College, has designed this self-paced workbook to help financial statement users who may have had little or no exposure to the accounting system understand accounting procedures.

Acknowledgements

Throughout the textbook, relevant publications of standard-setting and professional organizations are discussed, quoted, or paraphrased. We are indebted to the American Accounting Association, the American Institute of Certified Public Accountants, and the Financial Accounting Standards Board for material from their publications.

The 8th edition of **Financial Accounting** reflects many comments and suggestions from colleagues and students, all of which are deeply appreciated. In particular, we wish to thank the following accounting educators who have served as reviewers, diary keepers, and focus group participants:

Anwer Ahmed	Syracuse University
Matthew J. Anderson	Michigan State University
James W. Bannister	University of Hartford
Benjamin W. Bean	Utah Valley State College
Patricia A. Doherty	Boston University
Janice Glatt	North Dakota State University
Jeri Griego	Laramie County Community College
Gerald Lobo	Syracuse University
Robert L. Putman	University of Tennessee at Martin
Donald J. Raux	Sienna College
Lola Rhodes	Southern Methodist University
Frederic M. Stiner, Jr.	University of Delaware
Cynthia VanGelderen	Aquinas College

We would like to thank Cathy Xanthaky Larson, Middlesex Community College, for checking the accuracy of the text and solutions manual. Her meticulous review contributed to a more concise, higher-quality product. We would also like to thank James Emig, Villanova University, who served as verifier for the test bank and study guide.

Steve Albrecht
Jim Stice
Kay Stice
Fred Skousen

FINANCIAL
ACCOUNTING
EDITION 8

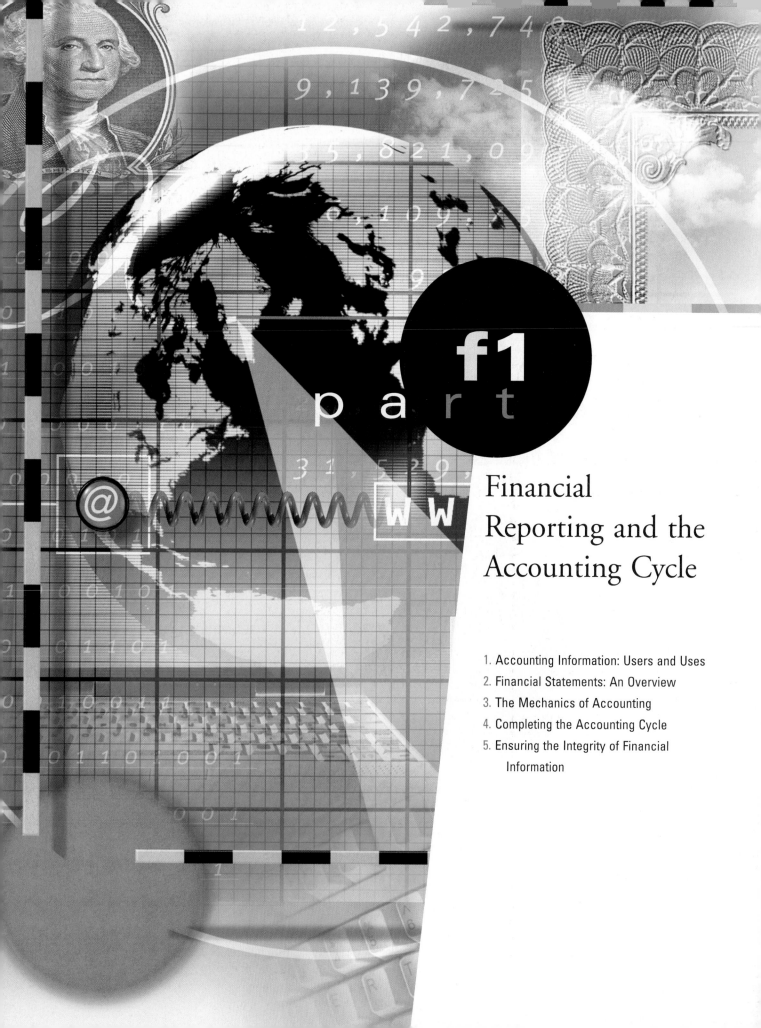

f1 part

Financial Reporting and the Accounting Cycle

Accounting
Information:
Users and Uses

c h a p t e r

f1

learning objectives After studying this chapter, you should be able to:

1 Describe the purpose of accounting and explain its role in business and society.

2 Identify the primary users of accounting information.

3 Describe the environment of accounting, including the effects of generally accepted accounting principles, international business, ethical considerations, and technology.

4 Analyze the reasons for studying accounting.

In 1987, IBM was the most valuable company in the world, worth an estimated $105.8 billion. By the end of 1992, IBM had an estimated value of $28.8 billion. This decline in value can be traced to a strategic error made by IBM in the early 1980s. Prior to 1981, IBM was the major player in the computer market and was the primary provider of computers for government, universities, and businesses. At this time, believe it or not, virtually no computers were available at an affordable price for individuals. Then, in 1981, IBM introduced its personal computer (IBM PC), and it quickly established the standard by which other PCs would be measured. However, IBM elected to leave the software development for PCs to other companies. Instead of developing its own disk operating system (DOS), IBM elected to use a DOS developed by a small company located in Seattle—MICROSOFT.[1]

Microsoft was founded in 1975 by Bill Gates and Paul Allen.[2] When they founded Microsoft, Gates and Allen envisioned that computers would eventually find their way into everyday life (contrary to IBM's prediction in the 1950s when one IBM executive forecast the total worldwide demand for computers to be about five). While IBM's performance floundered in the mid- and late-1980s, Microsoft demonstrated an amazing ability to become a major player in practically every aspect of the computer software market—from operating systems to the Internet to networks to spreadsheets and word processors.

With Microsoft's many accomplishments comes the question: "Just how successful is the company?" The answer to that question depends on how you define "success." Measured in terms of number of employees, Microsoft has grown from just 32 employees in 1981 when IBM elected to use Microsoft's DOS to 31,575 as of the June 30, 1999, fiscal year. In terms of social impact, Microsoft and its employees donate millions of dollars each year to such charitable causes as Special Olympics, Boys and Girls Clubs, and the United Negro College Fund. Microsoft also supports elementary and high schools throughout the country in their efforts to incorporate technology into the curriculum, and the company has established scholarship programs to encourage minorities and women to pursue careers in computer science and related technical fields. In addition, Bill Gates and his wife Melinda have started a foundation dedicated primarily to health and education. Thus far they have contributed several billion dollars to their foundation.

In terms of stock price, Microsoft's per share stock price (adjusted for stock splits) has gone from $0.17 in 1986 to over $70 in April of 2000 (see Exhibit 1-1). On virtually every dimension you can think of, Microsoft has succeeded. But most of these dimensions are a by-product of Microsoft's ability to produce products that are valued by the market. If Microsoft were unable to produce and sell quality products, the company would not be in a position to employ so many people, to give so much money to charities, to dominate (some would say monopolize) its markets, or to experience such an incredible increase in stock price. And this is where accounting enters the picture.

fyi

In fact, many people are of the opinion that Microsoft has succeeded too well. Several of Microsoft's competitors allege that Microsoft is involved in monopolistic practices that stifle competition. As this book goes to press, the government is considering several options relating to Microsoft's business practices including breaking the company into several smaller entities.

setting the stage

---

1 The decision to have another company develop the software for its personal computer was not IBM's only strategic error. At the same time, IBM decided to use another company's microprocessors—the "brains" of the computer. As a result, another successful company was born—INTEL. IBM lost the opportunity to dominate the software market as well as the computer chip market. By May 2000, Microsoft, Intel, and IBM had market values exceeding $364 billion, $398 billion, and $195 billion, respectively.

2 Everybody knows Bill Gates, but few people know about Paul Allen. Allen was Microsoft's head of research and new product development until 1983 when a serious illness caused him to leave the company. He still remains on the company's board of directors and is Microsoft's second largest shareholder. He now spends much of his time investing in technology companies and watching the Seattle Seahawks, a professional football team, and the Portland Trailblazers, a professional basketball team—both of which he owns.

exhibit 1-1   History of Microsoft's Stock Price Per Share

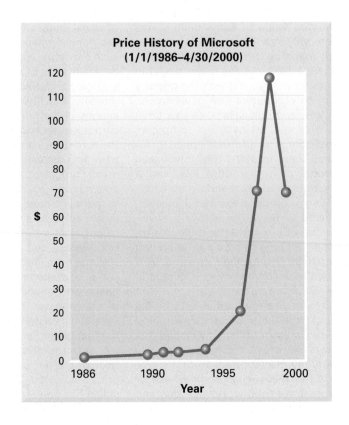

In this textbook, you will begin your study of accounting. You will learn to speak and understand accounting, "the language of business." Without an understanding of accounting, business investments, taxes, and money management will be like a foreign language to you. In brief, an understanding of accounting facilitates the interpretation of financial information, which allows for better economic decisions.

The major objectives of this text are to provide you with a basic understanding of the language of accounting and with the ability to interpret and use financial information prepared using accounting techniques and procedures. With the knowledge you obtain from this exposure to accounting, you will be able to "read" the financial statements of companies such as Microsoft, understand the information that is being conveyed, and use accounting information to make good business decisions. Also, through discussion of the business environment in which accounting is used, you will increase your understanding of general business concepts such as corporations, leases, annuities, leverage, derivatives (the financial kind, not the calculus kind), and so forth.

You will become convinced that accounting is not "bean counting." Time after time you will see that accountants must exercise judgment about how to best summarize and report the results of business transactions. As a result, you will gain a respect for the complexity of accounting and develop a healthy skepticism about the precision of any financial reports you see.

Finally, you will see the power of accounting. Financial statements are not just paper reports that get filed away and forgotten. You will see that financial statement numbers, and, indirectly, the accountants who prepare them, determine who receives loans and who doesn't, which companies attract investors and which don't, which managers receive salary bonuses and which don't, and which companies are praised in the financial press and which aren't.

So, let's get started.

<table>
<tr><td>caution</td></tr>
<tr><td>Don't be too concerned with all the new and unfamiliar terms you see in the first chapter of the book. Learning a "new language" takes time. Be patient. Before too long, you will be speaking the "language of business" (accounting) quite fluently.</td></tr>
</table>

1

Describe the purpose of accounting and explain its role in business and society.

bookkeeping The preservation of a systematic, quantitative record of an activity.

WHAT'S THE PURPOSE OF ACCOUNTING?

Imagine a long distance telephone company with no system in place to document who calls whom and how long they talk. Or a manager of a 300-unit apartment complex who has forgotten to write down which tenants have and have not paid this month's rent. Or an accounting professor who, the day before final grades are due, loses the only copy of the disk containing the spreadsheet of all the homework, quiz, and exam scores. Each of these scenarios illustrates a problem with bookkeeping, the least glamorous aspect of accounting. **Bookkeeping** is the preservation of a systematic, quantitative record of an activity. Bookkeeping systems can be very primitive—cutting notches in a stick to tally how many sheep you have or moving beads on a string to track the score in a billiards game. But the importance of routine bookkeeping cannot be overstated; without bookkeeping, business is impossible.

To evaluate the importance of bookkeeping records, we'll use a thought experiment. Suppose that sometime during the night, every copy of every novel ever written were to disappear. Could life proceed normally the next day? While the cultural loss would be incalculable, the normal activities of the next day would not be noticeably affected. What if television were suddenly gone when we woke up? While we might wander around wondering what to do with our time, life would go on. But what if we woke up tomorrow morning to find the bookkeeping records of all businesses worldwide destroyed during the night? Businesses that rely on up-to-the-minute customer account information, such as banks, simply could not open their doors. Retailers would have to insist on cash purchases, since no credit records could be verified. Manufacturers would have to do a quick count of existing inventories of raw materials and components to find out whether they could keep their production lines running. Suppliers would have to call all their customers, if they could remember who they were, to renegotiate purchase orders. Attorneys would find themselves in endless arguments about their fees because they would have no record of billable hours. Routine and dry as bookkeeping may seem, the world simply could not function for one day without it.

Rudimentary bookkeeping is ancient, probably predating both language and money. The modern system of double-entry bookkeeping still in use today (described in Chapter 3) was developed in the 1300s–1400s in Italy by the merchants in the trading and banking centers of Florence, Venice, and Genoa. The key development in accounting in the last 500 years has been the use of the bookkeeping data, not just to keep track of things, but to evaluate the performance and health of a business.

This use of bookkeeping data as an evaluation tool may seem obvious to you, but it is a step that is often not taken. Let's consider a bookkeeping system with which most of us are familiar—a checking account. Your checking account involves (or should involve) careful recording of the dates and amounts of all checks written and all deposits made, the maintenance of a running account total, and reconciliations with the monthly bank statement. Now, assume that you have a perfect checking account bookkeeping system. Will the system answer the following questions?

- Are you spending more for groceries this year than you did last year?
- What proportion of your monthly expenditures are fixed, meaning that you can't change them except through a drastic change in lifestyle?
- You plan to study abroad next year; will you be able to save enough between now and then to pay for it?

In order to answer these kinds of evaluation questions, each check must be analyzed to determine the type of expenditure, your checks must then be coded by type of expenditure, the data must be boiled down into summary reports, and past data must be used to forecast future patterns. How many of us use our checking account data like this? Not many. We do the bookkeeping (usually), but we don't structure the information to be used for evaluation.

accounting system The procedures and processes used by a business to analyze transactions, handle routine bookkeeping tasks, and structure information so it can be used to evaluate the performance and health of the business.

In summary, an **accounting system** is used by a business to (1) analyze transactions, (2) handle routine bookkeeping tasks, and (3) structure information so it can be used to evaluate the performance and health of the business. Exhibit 1-2 illustrates the three functions of the accounting system.

exhibit 1-2   Functions of an Accounting System

Analysis	Bookkeeping	Evaluation
		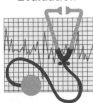
Analyze business events to determine if information should be captured by the accounting system	Day-to-day keeping track of things	Use summary information to evaluate the financial health and performance of the business

accounting A system for providing quantitative, financial information about economic entities that is useful for making sound economic decisions. Accounting is often called the "language of business" because it provides the means of recording and communicating business activities and the results of those activities.

Accounting is formally defined as a system for providing "quantitative information, primarily financial in nature, about economic entities that is intended to be useful in making economic decisions."[3] The key components of this definition are:

- *Quantitative.* Accounting relates to numbers. This is a strength because numbers can be easily tabulated and summarized. It is a weakness because some important business events, such as a toxic waste spill and the associated lawsuits and countersuits, cannot be easily described by one or two numbers.
- *Financial.* The health and performance of a business are affected by and reflected in many dimensions—financial, personal relationships, community and environmental impact, and public image. Accounting focuses on just the financial dimension.
- *Useful.* The practice of accounting is supported by a long tradition of theory. U.S. accounting rules have a theoretical conceptual framework. Some people actually make a living as accounting theorists. However, in spite of its theoretical beauty, accounting exists only because it is useful.
- *Decisions.* Although accounting is the structured reporting of what has already occurred, this past information can only be useful if it impacts decisions about the future.

Making good decisions is critical for success in any business enterprise. When an important decision must be made, it is essential to use a rational decision-making process. The process is basically the same no matter how complex the issue. First, the issue or question must be clearly identified. Next, the facts surrounding the situation must be gathered and analyzed. Then, several alternative courses of action should be identified and considered before a decision is finally reached. This decision-making process is summarized in Exhibit 1-3.

One must be careful to make a distinction between a good decision and a good outcome. Often, many factors outside the control of the decision maker affect the outcome of a decision. The decision-making process does not guarantee a certain result; it only ensures that a good decision is made. To illustrate this process, let's consider an example. It's Friday afternoon, the sun is shining, your homework is done, and you have the rest of the afternoon and evening ahead of you. What to do? You check the movie listings in the newspaper to see if there are any new movies you haven't seen, you call several of your friends to see what they are doing, and you review your list of "things you always wanted to organize around your apartment but never had the time." With this information, you decide that you could either (1) go to the new Tom Hanks movie with a group of friends or (2) go over to your friend's house and watch TV. (Spending time at home organizing your sock drawer on a Friday night is out of the question.) You

3 Statement of the Accounting Principles Board No. 4, "Basic Concepts and Accounting Principles Underlying Financial Statements of Business Enterprises," New York: American Institute of Certified Public Accountants, 1970, par. 40.

exhibit 1-3   The Decision-Making Process

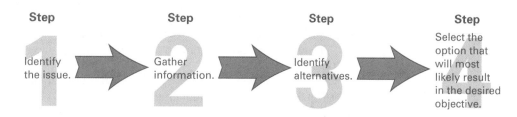

decide to go to the movies. You get to the movie theater, buy your ticket, your popcorn, and your drink, then select a seat. The lights dim, the movie starts, and the only empty seat left in the theater is right in front of you. It turns out you have the best seat in the house—until Shaquille O'Neal (7′2″, 300 pounds) comes in and sits in that seat. Good decision, bad outcome.

The four steps of the decision-making process lead to the best decision under the circumstances, but the outcome always has an element of chance. Part of business is learning how to protect yourself against bad outcomes. The first step in achieving a favorable outcome begins with making a good decision.

Accounting plays a vital role in the decision-making process. An accounting system provides information in a form that can be used to make knowledgeable financial decisions. The information supplied by accounting is in the form of quantitative data, primarily financial in nature, and relates to specific economic entities. An economic entity may be an individual, a business enterprise, or a nonprofit organization. A **business**, such as a grocery store or a car dealership, is operated with the objective of making a profit for its owners. The goal of a **nonprofit organization**, such as a city government or a university, is to provide services in an effective and efficient manner. Every entity, regardless of its size or purpose, must have a way to keep track of its economic activities and to measure how well it is accomplishing its goals. Accounting provides the means for tracking activities and measuring results.

Without accounting information, many important financial decisions would be made blindly. Investors, for example, would have no way to distinguish between a profitable company and one that is on the verge of failure; bankers could not evaluate the riskiness of potential loans; corporate managers would have no basis for controlling costs, setting prices, or investing the company's resources; and governments would have no basis for taxing income. No list of examples could fully represent the pervasive use of accounting information throughout our economic, social, and political institutions. When accounting information is used effectively as a basis for making economic decisions, limited resources are more likely to be allocated efficiently. From a broad perspective, the result is a healthier economy and a higher standard of living.

The value of accounting information can also be illustrated on a personal level. Since very few of us will ever make more money than we can spend, we each will be making choices as to what to do with our limited incomes. For example, assume you have a job that results in take-home pay of $2,000 per month. What do you do with the money? If you are making monthly payments on a home and/or an automobile, you previously made choices to use part of your monthly income for these two items. How about a trip around the world, season tickets for your favorite basketball team, or a new home entertainment system? You could spend your money on these items, but that might not be the best use of your income. After all, you haven't eaten yet. Routine expenditures for food, clothing, and utilities must be made. How much money will you need for these and other everyday expenditures? By collecting financial information relating to prior months' inflows and outflows of cash, you will be able to approximate how much money you will need for this month. This process—called *budgeting* (discussed later)—is often used by individuals (and businesses) to ensure that monthly income is used in the best manner possible. While it is true that budgeting is not necessary, budgeting is part of good decision making.

business An organization operated with the objective of making a profit from the sale of goods or services.

nonprofit organization An entity without a profit objective, oriented toward providing services efficiently and effectively.

The Relationship of Accounting to Business

Business is the general term applied to the activities involved in the production and distribution of goods and services. Accounting is used to record and report the financial effects of business activities. Thus, as mentioned earlier, accounting is often called the "language of business." It provides the means of recording and communicating the successes and failures of business organizations.

All business enterprises have some activities in common. As shown in Exhibit 1-4, one common activity is the acquisition of monetary resources. These resources, often referred to as "capital," come from three sources: (1) investors (owners), (2) creditors (lenders), and (3) the business itself in the form of earnings that have been retained. Once resources are obtained, they are used to buy land, buildings, and equipment; to purchase materials and supplies; to pay employees; and to meet any other operating expenses involved in the production and marketing of goods or services. When the product or service is sold, additional monetary resources (revenues) are generated. These resources can be used to pay loans, to pay taxes, and to buy new materials, equipment, and other items needed to continue the operations of the business. In addition,

e x h i b i t 1 - 4   Activities Common to Business Organizations

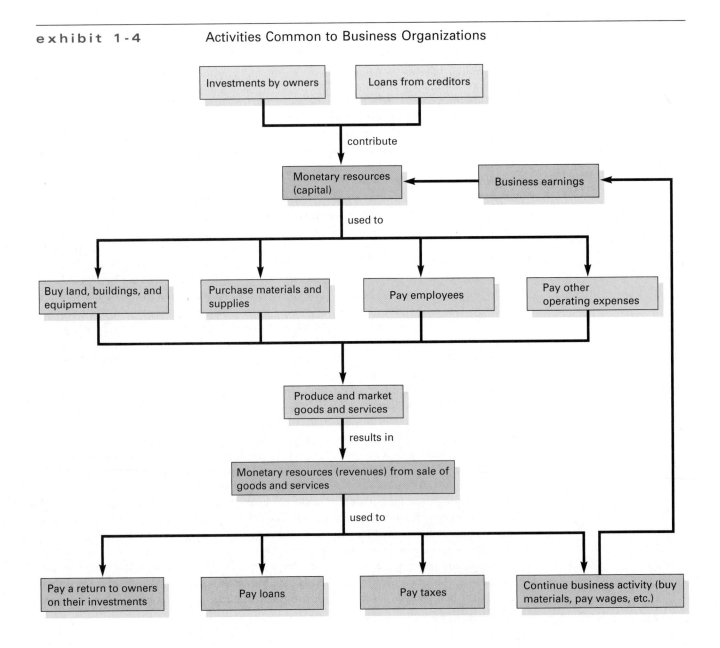

some of the resources may be distributed to owners as a return on their investment. MICROSOFT, for example, uses the earnings from its operations to fund research and development and to purchase other companies. The developed (or purchased) products can then be sold at a profit under the Microsoft name. This produces more funds that can then be used to purchase more companies or develop more products. Microsoft currently does not distribute its resources back to its owners. Owners receive a return on their investment through the growth in value of the stock.

Accountants measure and communicate (report) the results of these activities. In order to measure these results as accurately as possible, accountants follow a fairly standard set of procedures, usually referred to as the **accounting cycle**. The cycle includes several steps, which involve analyzing, recording, classifying, summarizing, and reporting the transactions of a business. These steps are explained in detail in Chapters 3 and 4.

> **accounting cycle** The procedure for analyzing, recording, classifying, summarizing, and reporting the transactions of a business.

---

to summarize

Accounting is a service activity designed to accumulate, measure, and communicate financial information about economic entities—businesses and non-profit organizations. Its purpose is to provide information used to make informed decisions about how to best use available resources. Accounting is often called the "language of business" because it provides the means of recording and communicating business activities and the results of those activities.

2

Identify the primary users of accounting information.

> **management accounting** The area of accounting concerned with providing internal financial reports to assist management in making decisions.

> **annual report** A document that summarizes the results of operations and financial status of a company for the past year and outlines plans for the future.

> **financial statements** Reports such as the balance sheet, income statement, and statement of cash flows, which summarize the financial status and results of operations of a business entity.

> **financial accounting** The area of accounting concerned with reporting financial information to interested external parties.

WHO USES ACCOUNTING INFORMATION?

The accounting system generates output in the form of financial reports. As shown in Exhibit 1-5, there are two major categories of reports: internal and external. Internal reports are used by those who direct the day-to-day operations of a business enterprise. These individuals are collectively referred to as "management," and the related area of accounting is called **management accounting**. Management accounting focuses on the information needed for planning, implementing plans, and controlling costs. Managers and executives who work inside a company have access to specialized management accounting information that is not available to outsiders. For example, the management of McDONALD'S CORPORATION has detailed management accounting data on exactly how much it costs to produce each item on the menu. Further, if BURGER KING or WENDY'S starts a local burger price war in, say, Missouri, McDonald's managers can request daily sales summaries for each store in the area to measure the impact.

Other examples of decisions made using management accounting information are whether to produce a product internally or purchase it from an outside supplier, what prices to charge, and which costs seem excessive. Consider those companies that produce computers. Most computers are shipped with an operating system already installed. Approximately 85% of computers have MICROSOFT's Windows pre-installed. The computer makers must decide whether to develop their own operating system or pay Microsoft a licensing fee to use Windows. Most computer manufacturers have determined it is cost effective to license from Microsoft. Companies such as SEARS and RADIO SHACK often use products produced by outside suppliers rather than manufacture the products themselves. The products are then labeled with the "Kenmore" or "Realistic" brand names and sold to customers. These are just two examples of decisions that must be made by management given available financial information.

External financial reports, included in the firm's **annual report**, are used by individuals and organizations that have an economic interest in the business but are not part of its management. Information is provided to these "external users" in the form of general-purpose **financial statements** and special reports required by government agencies. The general-purpose information provided by **financial accounting** is summarized in the three primary financial

e x h i b i t   1 - 5   Output of the Accounting Cycle

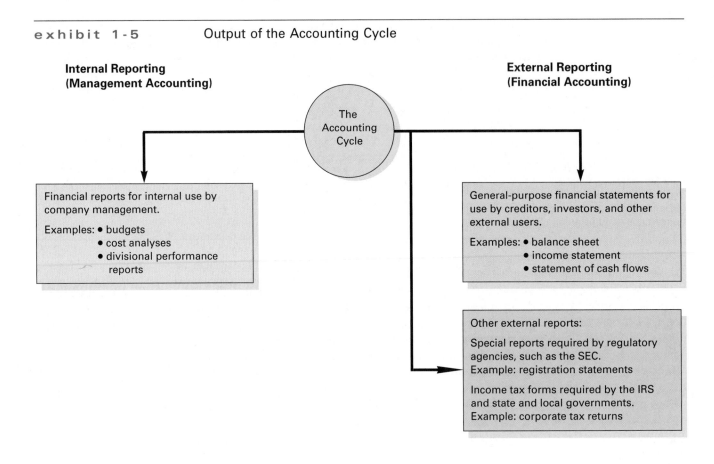

statements: balance sheet, income statement, and statement of cash flows (more formally introduced in Chapter 2).

- The *balance sheet* reports the resources of a company (the assets), the company's obligations (the liabilities), and the owners' equity, which represents the difference between what is owned (assets) and what is owed (liabilities).
- The *income statement* reports the amount of net income earned by a company during a period, with annual and quarterly income statements being the most common. Net income is the excess of a company's revenues over its expenses; if the expenses are more than the revenues, then the company has suffered a loss for the period. The income statement represents the accountant's best effort at measuring the economic performance of a company.
- The *statement of cash flows* reports the amount of cash collected and paid out by a company in the following three types of activities: operating, investing, and financing. The types of activities in each of these three categories will be explained in Chapter 2. The statement of cash flows is the most objective of the financial statements because, as you will see in subsequent chapters, it involves a minimum of accounting estimates and judgments.

Examples of external users of the information contained in these three financial statements, along with other available information, are described in the following paragraphs.

Lenders

Lenders (creditors) are interested in one thing—being repaid, with interest. If you were to approach a bank for a large loan, the bank would ask you for the following types of information in order to evaluate whether you would be able to repay the loan:

- A listing of your assets and liabilities
- Payroll stubs, tax returns, and other evidence of your income

- Details about any monthly payments (car, rent, credit cards, etc.) you are obligated to make
- Copies of recent bank statements to document the flow of cash into and out of your account

In essence, the bank would be asking you for a balance sheet, an income statement, and a statement of cash flows. Similarly, banks use companies' financial statements in making decisions about commercial loans. The financial statements are useful because they help the lender predict the future ability of the borrower to repay the loan.

In the case of Microsoft, a review of its balance sheet indicates that the company has no formal lenders. It does, however, report a balance in its "accounts payable" account. This amount represents amounts owed to vendors from whom Microsoft has purchased on credit. Considering Microsoft's reputation, this "lending" is very low risk.

Investors

Investors want information to help them estimate how much cash they can expect to receive in the future if they invest in a business now. Financial statements, coupled with a knowledge of business plans, market forecasts, and the character of management, can aid investors in assessing these future cash flows. Many companies have broad ownership with a few individuals owning a large portion of the company's stock. At Microsoft, Bill Gates owns 787,055,600 shares (15.3% of total shares outstanding); Paul Allen, Microsoft's co-founder, owns 260,723,896 shares (5.1%); and Steve Ballmer, Microsoft's chief executive officer, owns 239,626,854 shares (4.7%).

Obviously, millions of Americans invest in McDonald's, Microsoft, CISCO SYSTEMS, and GENERAL ELECTRIC without ever seeing the financial statements of these companies. Investors can feel justifiably safe in doing this because large companies are followed by armies of financial analysts who would quickly blow the whistle if they found information suggesting that investors in these companies were at serious risk. But what about investing in a smaller company, one that the financial press doesn't follow, or in a local family business that is seeking outside investors for the first time? In cases such as these, investing without looking at the financial statements is like jumping off the high dive without looking first to see if there is any water in the pool.

Management

In addition to using management accounting information available only to those within the firm, managers of a company can use the general financial accounting information that is also made available to outsiders. Company goals are often stated in terms of financial accounting numbers, such as a target of sales growth in excess of 5%. Also, reported "net income" is frequently used in calculating management bonuses. Finally, managers of a company can analyze the general-purpose financial statements (using the techniques introduced in Chapter 2) in order to pinpoint areas of weakness about which more detailed management accounting information can be sought. Microsoft uses internally produced accounting reports to evaluate such things as the profitability of product lines, the success of international operations, and the performance of product and management teams.

Other Users of Financial Information

There are many other external users of financial information, including suppliers, customers, employees, competitors, government agencies, and the press. These are described below.

SUPPLIERS AND CUSTOMERS In some settings, suppliers and customers are interested in the long-run staying power of a company. On the supplier side, if BOEING receives an order from an airline for 30 new 747s over the next 10 years, Boeing wants to know whether the airline will be around in the future to take delivery of and pay for the planes. On the customer side, a homeowner who has foundation repair work done wants to know whether the company making the repairs will be around long enough to honor its 50-year guarantee. Financial statements provide information that suppliers and customers can use to assess the long-run prospects of a company. Each version of a software release has a limited life, and part of Microsoft's success has been its ability to provide product upgrades. Microsoft's customers can use financial information to help them ascertain the company's ability to survive and have the resources to fix glitches and provide upgrades as the technology improves.

EMPLOYEES   Employees are interested in financial accounting information for a variety of reasons. As mentioned earlier, financial statement data are used in determining employee bonuses. In addition, financial accounting information can help an employee evaluate the likelihood that the employer will be able to fulfill its long-run promises, such as pensions and retiree health-care benefits. Financial statements are also important in contract negotiations between labor and management.

COMPETITORS   If you were a manager at PEPSICO, would you be interested in knowing the relative profitability of COCA-COLA's operations in the United States, Brazil, Japan, and France? Of course you would, because that information could help you identify strategic opportunities for marketing pushes where potential profits are high or where your competitor is weak. Microsoft can use the information in financial statements to track its competitors and identify new opportunities to grow and use its market share in operating systems to increase its revenues in other software ventures. For example, Microsoft's recent antitrust troubles relate, in large part, to its competition with NETSCAPE, an Internet-browser alternative to Microsoft's Explorer. In 1997 (the last year that Netscape provided publicly available financial information), Netscape lost over $115 million on sales of almost $534 million. During that same period, Microsoft was earning a profit of almost $3.5 billion on sales of almost $12 billion.

GOVERNMENT AGENCIES   Federal and state government agencies make frequent use of financial accounting information. For example, to make sure that investors have sufficient information to make informed investment decisions, the Securities and Exchange Commission monitors the financial accounting disclosures of companies (both U.S. and foreign) whose stocks trade on U.S. stock exchanges. The International Trade Commission uses financial accounting information to determine whether the importation of Ecuadorian roses or Chinese textiles is harming U.S. companies through unfair trade practices. The Justice Department uses financial statement data to evaluate whether companies (such as Microsoft) are earning excess monopolistic profits. In Microsoft's case, from 1994 through 1999, it reported profits of $0.34 on every dollar of sales. During that same period, General Electric, one of America's most admired companies, generated profits of $0.09 on every dollar of sales.

THE PRESS   Financial statements are a great place for a reporter to find background information to flesh out a story about a company. For example, a story about Microsoft can be enhanced by using the sales data shown in its annual report. In addition, a surprising accounting announcement, such as a large drop in reported profits, is a trigger for an investigative reporter to write about what is going on in a company. When the Justice Department proposed the breakup of Microsoft, *The Wall Street Journal* reported analysts' estimates of the value of the company's various parts based on past revenue figures. For example, one analyst estimated that Microsoft's consumer business would be worth 50 times its revenue.[4]

In summary, who uses financial accounting information? Everyone does, or at least everyone should. External financial reports come within the area of accounting referred to as financial accounting. Most of the data needed to prepare both internal and external reports is provided by the same accounting system. A major difference between management and financial

---

4 Gregory Zuckerman, "Figuring Worth of a Split-Up, Microsoft Leaves Analysts Scattered All Over Map," *The Wall Street Journal*, May 2, 2000, p. C1.

accounting is the types of financial reports prepared. Internal reports are tailored to meet the needs of management and may vary considerably among businesses. General-purpose financial statements and other external reports, however, follow certain standards or guidelines and are thus more uniform among companies. The first thirteen chapters of *Accounting: Concepts and Applications* focus on financial accounting, specifically on the primary financial statements (discussed and illustrated in Chapter 2). The remaining chapters, 14 through 23, focus on management accounting.

to summarize

Two major categories of reports are generated by the accounting cycle: internal and external. Management accounting focuses on providing reports for internal use by management to assist in making operating decisions and in planning and controlling a company's activities. Financial accounting provides information to meet the needs of external users. General-purpose financial statements are used by investors, creditors, and other external parties who are interested in a company's activities and results.

3

Describe the environment of accounting, including the effects of generally accepted accounting principles, international business, ethical considerations, and technology.

WITHIN WHAT KIND OF ENVIRONMENT DOES ACCOUNTING OPERATE?

Accounting functions in a dynamic environment. Changes in technology as well as economic and political factors can significantly influence accounting practice. Four particularly important factors are the development of "generally accepted accounting principles" (GAAP), international business, ethical considerations, and technology.

The Significance and Development of Accounting Standards

Imagine a company that compensates a key employee in the following ways:

- Paying a cash salary of $80,000.
- Giving a new car with a value of $30,000.
- Offering the option to become, a year from now, a 10% owner of the company in exchange for an investment of $200,000.

If the company does well in the coming year, the company will increase in value, the $200,000 price tag for 10% ownership will look like a great deal, and the employee will exercise the option. If the company does poorly, it will decline in value, the $200,000 price will be too high, and the employee will throw the option away and forget the whole thing. Assume the company then sells the ownership option to interested outside investors for $25,000.

The accounting question is how to summarize in one number the company's compensation cost associated with this employee. We would probably all agree to include the $110,000 ($80,000 + $30,000) compensation cost from the cash salary and the new car. What about the option? Both of the following arguments could be put forward:

1. If the employee were to buy the option from the company, just like any other outside investor, the employee would have to pay $25,000. Therefore, giving the option to the employee is just like paying him or her $25,000 cash. The $25,000 value of the option should be added to compensation cost.
2. The option doesn't cost the company a thing. In fact, the option merely increases the probability that the employee will invest $200,000 in the company in the future. The option doesn't add a penny to compensation cost.

The Evolution of Accounting It can be argued that accounting as a profession is very young; as a service activity, however, it dates back several thousand years. Long before numerical figures were invented, people designated possessions and debts through natural means. Collections of pebbles, shells, or bones were used to represent exchanges between people. Some maintained records of debt by carving notches in rods or canes. The ancient Peruvians used knotted strings before numerical symbols were invented. Regardless of the rudiments put into practice through the generations, it is obvious that accounting for ownership between parties drove ancient peoples to invent new methods of record keeping and communication. In fact, in his book *The Temper of Our Times*, Eric Hoffer argues that accounting was the driving force behind written language:

> We are often told that the invention of writing in the Middle East about 3000 B.C. marked an epoch in man's career because it revolutionized the transmission of knowledge and ideas. Actually, for many centuries after its invention, writing was used solely to keep track of the intake and outgo of treasuries and warehouses. Writ-

ing was invented not to write books but to keep books. (Hoffer, p. 196)

Among the earliest known records are those of the Egyptians and Babylonians (from approximately 3000 B.C.), who recorded on clay tablets such transactions as the payment of wages and taxes. Multiple clay tablets listing valuable items in treasuries and temples have been found at excavation sites in Sumeria and Babylon. It makes sense that accountants of old would only take the time to carve in these clay tablets instead of writing on papyrus if they regarded the information to be of great importance. As a result, we have accurate knowledge of the wealth maintained in the treasuries, but little information relating to the persons who actually owned them.

With the development of a written language came the ability to represent measures of tallied items with a single symbol. Different numerical systems existed throughout the world. As empires gained and lost power, advances in culture and science spread among the different nations. In order to maintain their empires, rulers would dictate the use of more unified communication methods. Under Roman rule, people living in territories in Europe, Africa, the Middle East, and parts of Asia were forced to write and maintain business communications in Latin. During the Roman period (which lasted from approximately 500 B.C. to 500 A.D.), detailed tax records were maintained.

So, which argument is right? Should each company decide for itself whether to include the $25,000 option value as part of compensation cost, or should there be an overall accounting standard followed by all companies? And if there is a standard, who sets it?[5]

There are many situations in business, such as the option compensation case just described, in which reasonable people can disagree about how certain items should be handled for accounting purposes. And, since financial accounting information is designed to be used by people outside a company, it is important that outsiders understand the rules and assumptions used by the company in constructing its financial statements. This would be extremely difficult and costly for outsiders to find out if every company formulated its own set of accounting rules. Accordingly, in most countries in the world there exists a committee or board that establishes the accounting rules for that country.

The Financial Accounting Standards Board

Financial Accounting Standards Board (FASB) The private organization responsible for establishing the standards for financial accounting and reporting in the United States.

In the United States, accounting standards are set by the **Financial Accounting Standards Board (FASB)**. The FASB is based in Norwalk, Connecticut, and its seven full-time members

5 The answer to this surprisingly controversial question of the accounting for option compensation is given in Chapter 8. Just to show how influential accounting can be, this exact issue was debated on the floor of the U.S. Senate.

After the fall of Rome, trade continued to increase around the Mediterranean Sea. Italy found itself positioned between European consumers and Asian and Arabian producers. As trade increased in Italy's port cities, the need to borrow and purchase on credit also increased. In fact, the first bank of importance, Casa di San Georgio, was founded in Genoa, Italy, during the 12th century. During and after the era of the crusades from 1096 to about 1270, money from Italy's European neighbors streamed into and out of Italian cities. Credit transactions rose in volume as traders in Florence, Pisa, and Venice became merchant-bankers. Although accounting did not originate in Italy, its geographic location facilitated the formalization of a system of recording business transactions. In 1494, an Italian Franciscan monk, Luca Pacioli, published a treatise containing a small section titled "Particularis de Computis et Scripturis [Details of Accounting and Recording]," which contained the essential elements of the double-entry accounting system that is still in use today.

But accounting has not remained static. The Industrial Revolution brought about changes in business, and therefore in accounting. Beginning in England in the mid-1800s, manufacturing processes started to evolve from individualized, handicraft systems to mass-production, factory systems. Technological advances not only provided new machinery but required new types of expenditures as well. Cost accounting systems had to be developed to analyze and control the financial operations of these increasingly complex manufacturing processes.

Governmental laws and requirements also have caused changes in the business environment and have stimulated the growth of accounting services. For example, the Companies Act in England in the 1850s established compulsory independent audits by chartered accountants. In the United States, the 1913 Revenue Act instituted the personal federal income tax, which created a need for income tax accounting. The 1934 Securities Exchange Act established the Securities and Exchange Commission, which monitors the reporting procedures of companies that sell stock publicly.

These and other factors have produced changes in the types of accounting services needed, and in many instances they have affected the accounting procedures themselves. Thus, the profession of accounting has evolved to meet the needs of the people it serves in an ever-changing and increasingly complex business environment.

As this brief history makes clear, accounting is not a static science. It is constantly evolving, changing to meet the needs of users and adapting itself to the economic environment in which it operates.

Source: Eric Hoffer, *The Temper of Our Times* (New York: Harper & Row, 1966).

are selected from a variety of backgrounds—professional accounting, business, government, and academia. The FASB receives about one-third of its $20 million annual operating budget through donations from the accounting profession and from businesses. The remaining two-thirds is generated through sales of publications and other services (e.g., a CD-ROM version of all the existing accounting standards). An important thing to note about the FASB is that it is not a government agency; the FASB is a private body established and supported by the joint efforts of the U.S. business community, financial analysts, and practicing accountants. Because the FASB is not a government agency, it has no legal power to enforce the accounting standards it sets. The FASB gets its authority to establish rules from the Securities and Exchange Commission (discussed later).

The FASB maintains its influence as the accounting standard setter for the United States (and the most influential accounting body in the world) by carefully protecting its prestige and reputation for setting good standards. In doing so, the FASB must walk a fine line between constant improvement of accounting practices to provide more full and fair information for external users and practical constraints on financial disclosure to appease businesses that are reluctant to disclose too much information to outsiders. To balance these opposing forces, the FASB seeks consensus by requesting written comments and sponsoring public hearings on all its proposed standards. The end result of this public process is a set of accounting rules that are described as being **generally accepted accounting principles (GAAP)**. Without general acceptance by the

generally accepted accounting principles (GAAP) Authoritative guidelines that define accounting practice at a particular time.

business community, FASB standards would merely be theoretical essays by a powerless body, and the FASB would be disbanded. This may sound overly dramatic, but the FASB was created in 1973 to replace the previously existing accounting standards body (the Accounting Principles Board or APB), which had lost credibility with the business community because it was seen as being completely controlled by accountants.

STOP & THINK Why is it important for the FASB to remain completely independent?

As you study this text, you will be intrigued by the interesting conceptual issues the FASB must wrestle with in setting accounting standards. The FASB has deliberated over the correct way to compute motion picture profits, the appropriate treatment of the cost of dismantling a nuclear power plant, the best approach for reflecting the impact of changes in foreign currency exchange rates, and the proper accounting for complex financial instruments such as commodity futures and interest rate swaps. And since U.S. companies are always suspicious that any change in the accounting rules will make them look worse on paper, almost all FASB decisions are made in the midst of controversy.

Other Organizations

In addition to the FASB, several other organizations affect accounting standards and are important in other ways to the practice of accounting. Some of these organizations are discussed below.

Securities and Exchange Commission (SEC) The government body responsible for regulating the financial reporting practices of most publicly owned corporations in connection with the buying and selling of stocks and bonds.

SECURITIES AND EXCHANGE COMMISSION In response to the Stock Market Crash of 1929, Congress created the **Securities and Exchange Commission (SEC)** to regulate U.S. stock exchanges. Part of the job of the SEC is to make sure that investors are provided with full and fair information about publicly traded companies. The SEC is not charged with protecting investors from losing money; instead, the SEC seeks to create a fair information environment in which investors can buy and sell stocks without fear that companies are hiding or manipulating financial data.

As part of its regulatory role, the SEC has received from Congress specific legal authority to establish accounting standards for companies soliciting investment funds from the American public. For now, the SEC refrains from exercising this authority and allows the FASB to set U.S. accounting standards. The SEC has generally been content to be publicly supportive of the FASB and to work out any disagreements privately. Remember, however, that the SEC is always looming in the background, legally authorized to take over the setting of U.S. accounting standards should the FASB lose its credibility with the public.

certified public accountant (CPA) A special designation given to an accountant who has passed a national uniform examination and has met other certifying requirements.

American Institute of Certified Public Accountants (AICPA) The national organization of CPAs in the United States.

AMERICAN INSTITUTE OF CERTIFIED PUBLIC ACCOUNTANTS The label "CPA" has two different uses—there are individuals who are CPAs and there are CPA firms. A **certified public accountant (CPA)** is someone who has taken a minimum number of college-level accounting classes, has passed the CPA exam administered by the **American Institute of Certified Public Accountants (AICPA)**, and has met other requirements set by his or her state. In essence, the CPA label guarantees that the person has received substantial accounting training. Not all CPAs work as accountants, however. CPAs work in law firms, as business consultants, as corporate managers, for the government, and even some as accounting professors.

The second use of the label "CPA" is in association with a CPA firm. A CPA firm is a company that performs accounting services, just as a law firm performs legal services. Obviously, a CPA firm employs a large number of accountants, not all of whom have received the training necessary to be certified public accountants. CPA firms also employ attorneys, information technology specialists, experts in finance, and other business specialists. CPA firms help companies establish accounting systems, formulate business plans, redesign their operating procedures, and just about anything else you can think of. A good way to think of a CPA firm is as a freelance business-advising firm with a particular strength in accounting issues.

fyi

Other tasks accountants perform are planning for acquisitions and mergers, measuring efficiency improvements from new technology, managing quality, and developing accounting software.

f y i

Other accounting-related certifications also exist. Examples include the Certified Management Accountant (CMA), Certified Internal Auditor (CIA), and the Certified Fraud Examiner (CFE).

CPA firms are also hired to perform independent audits of the financial statements of a company. The important role of the independent audit in ensuring the reliability of the financial statements is discussed in Chapter 5.

INTERNAL REVENUE SERVICE   Imagine that you have a contract to design a computerized accounting system for a local business. Your fee is $100,000, which will be paid in full when the job is finished. By the end of the year, you have collected nothing, but you estimate that you have completed 80% of the work on the contract.

If you are asked by a potential business partner how much money you have earned during the past year, what will you say? To say that you made $0, the amount you've collected on the contract, significantly understates the value of the work you have completed. If the 80% estimate is a fair reflection of the work you've done, it would seem reasonable for you to report to the potential partner that you've earned $80,000 ($100,000 × 0.80) during the year. And, as you'll see later in the text, this is exactly what you would report according to financial accounting rules.

Now, if you are asked by the **Internal Revenue Service (IRS)** to state your income for the year, how much should you report? You don't have much leeway in the matter, because the IRS has very specific rules about what is considered taxable income. Assume that IRS rules state that you must pay income tax on the $80,000 income from the estimated amount of the contract that you have completed. Two practical problems would arise:

1. You don't have the money to pay the tax. You won't be able to pay the tax until the job is completed and you have collected your entire fee.
2. You could have endless arguments with the IRS about the completion percentage. The IRS could send an agent to dispute your estimate. The whole thing might end up in Tax Court.

This example illustrates that what works for financial accounting purposes does not necessarily work for income tax purposes. Financial accounting reports are designed to provide information about the economic performance and health of a company. Tax rules are designed to tax income when the tax can be paid and to provide concrete rules to minimize inefficient arguing between taxpayers and the IRS. Accordingly, the IRS rules would probably allow you to report $0 income and delay paying income tax until you have actually collected the cash and could thus pay the tax.

The implication of this separation between financial accounting and tax accounting is that companies must maintain two sets of books—one set from which the financial statements can be prepared and the other set to comply with income tax regulations. There is nothing shady or underhanded about this. Financial accounting and tax accounting involve different sets of rules because they are designed for different purposes.

Internal Revenue Service (IRS) A government agency that prescribes the rules and regulations that govern the collection of tax revenues in the United States.

International Business

One of the significant environmental changes in recent years has been the expansion of business activity on a worldwide basis. As consumers, we are familiar with the wide array of products from other countries, such as electronics from Japan and clothing made in China. On the other hand, many U.S. companies have operating divisions in foreign countries. Other American companies are located totally within the United States but have extensive transactions with foreign companies. The economic environment of today's business is truly based on a global economy. As an example, in 1999 over 65% of MICROSOFT'S sales were to individuals and companies located outside the United States.

Accounting practices among countries vary widely. Attempts are being made to make those practices more consistent among countries. In an attempt to harmonize conflicting national standards, the **International Accounting Standards Board (IASB)** was formed in 1973 to develop worldwide accounting standards. This body now represents more than 142 accountancy bodies from 103 countries (including the United States). Like the FASB, the IASB develops proposals, circulates them among interested organizations, receives feedback, and then issues a final pronouncement.

The accounting standards produced by the IASB are referred to as International Accounting Standards (IAS). IAS are envisioned to be a set of standards that can be used by

International Accounting Standards Board (IASB) The committee formed in 1973 to develop worldwide accounting standards.

f y i

Since international accounting standards often differ from GAAP, foreign companies may be required to adjust their books to be listed on the New York Stock Exchange. For example, when Germany's DAIMLER-BENZ (makers of Mercedes Benz) became a NYSE-listed company in 1994, its GAAP-adjusted books showed a loss of $748 million, whereas its German standard books reported earnings of $636 million. Note: Daimler-Benz subsequently merged with CHRYSLER to become DAIMLER-CHRYSLER.

Do You Have What It Takes? There are many opportunities in the field of accounting. The Bureau of Labor Statistics forecasts that the demand for accounting graduates will increase 10 to 20 percent over the next decade. Accounting graduates use their education to obtain jobs in public accounting, for federal, state and local governments (including the Internal Revenue Service), and in commercial banking. In addition to becoming accountants, many accounting students use their undergraduate accounting education as a stepping-stone to law school or investment banking or to obtain other graduate degrees (like an MBA).

Many accounting students who go on to become accountants pursue the CPA designation. To be a CPA, specific requirements must be met. First, CPAs are re-

 **Why is it so difficult to make international accounting standards consistent?**

all companies regardless of where they are based. In the extreme, IAS could supplement or even replace standards set by national standard setters such as the FASB. IASB standards are gaining increasing acceptance throughout the world. For example, in April 2000, the IASB Web site (http://www.iasb.org.uk) listed more than 958 companies around the world that prepare financial statements according to IAS. Of these companies, 161 are located in Germany and 121 are located in China. Thus far, however, the SEC has not recognized IASB standards and has barred foreign companies from listing their shares on U.S. stock exchanges unless those companies agree to provide financial statements in accordance with U.S. accounting rules. Disclosure requirements in the United States are the strictest in the world, and foreign companies are reluctant to submit to the SEC requirement. This conflict will be interesting to watch in the coming years: Will the SEC maintain a hard line and ultimately force U.S. accounting rules on the rest of the world? Or will the IASB standards gain increasing acceptance and become the worldwide standard? We'll see.

At numerous points throughout this text, we will point out certain international applications of accounting as well as some differences that might exist in accounting rules between the United States and other countries. In addition, each chapter includes a case in the end-of-chapter material dealing with an international accounting issue.

Because of the expansion of international business, consumers are familiar with products from other countries, such as Hong Kong.

quired to have a formal education. For example, although individual state laws vary, as of April 17, 2000, 27 states require students to have completed 150 hours of college education to become CPAs. An additional 19 states have enacted legislation that will require 150 hours at some future date. Currently, only California, Delaware, New Hampshire, and Vermont have not enacted the 150-hour requirement. Next, aspiring CPAs must pass an examination based on the skills obtained from their education. This ensures that accountants are competent to perform independent services for the community. In addition to the examination, field experience requirements must be met to satisfy state licensing laws for CPAs.

If you are interested in someday working in a business environment, a degree in accounting can help you understand business issues, analyze accounting information, and make business decisions.

Ethics in Accounting

Another environmental factor affecting accounting, and business in general, is the growing concern over ethics. This concern was highlighted in a speech given by the chairman of the SEC, Arthur Levitt, in September 1998. In that speech, entitled "The Number's Game," Chairman Levitt identified several major accounting techniques that he believed were being used to undermine the integrity of financial reporting. As you will find, accounting involves significant judgment. Chairman Levitt expressed concern that this accounting judgment was giving way to pressure to "meet the numbers." In other words, Wall Street's expectations about a company, rather than the company's actual business performance, were driving the reported accounting numbers.

> **fyi**
>
> The AICPA's Code of Professional Conduct can be found on its Web site at www.aicpa.org. The Code of Conduct spells out what CPAs are famous for—they are required to be independent of their clients, to be good at what they do, and to keep client information confidential.

In his speech, Chairman Levitt mentioned the standards of objectivity, integrity, and judgment in reporting accounting numbers. These standards are an integral part of the public accounting profession's Code of Professional Conduct and form the foundation upon which audited financial statements are compiled and interpreted.

The ethical dilemmas facing businesses and their accountants often revolve around pressures placed on companies by investors, creditors, and potential investors and creditors. As Chairman Levitt mentioned, these pressures can sometimes cause company officials to become involved in "accounting hocus-pocus." Because accounting involves judgment, the reported accounting numbers can differ significantly depending on the assumptions made by those preparing the financial statements. As a simple example of how this can occur, consider again the case of Microsoft. When a customer buys a Microsoft product, part of the purchase price relates to promised customer service and future product upgrades. So the question is this: How much of the sales price should Microsoft report as a "sale" on the date of the sale, and how much relates to future services to be provided? As you can imagine, that is a difficult question to answer, and any answer will involve an estimate.

To quote again from Chairman Levitt's speech, accounting principles "allow for flexibility to adapt to changing circumstances." It is this flexibility that creates many of the ethical dilemmas faced by accountants. As businesses come under pressure to report favorable performance, accountants may also come under pressure to "flex" the rules just a little too far.

Fortunately, the public accounting profession is guided by a Code of Professional Conduct. Many other accounting organizations also have codes of conduct to provide guidance for their members.

Don't let yourself naively think that ethical dilemmas in business are rare. Such issues arise quite frequently. To help prepare you to enter the business world and to recognize and deal with ethical issues, we have included at least one ethics case at the end of each chapter. Ethics is an important topic that should be considered carefully, with the ultimate goal of improving individual and collective behavior in society.

Technology

Few developments have changed the way business is conducted as much as computers have. Computer technology allows businesses to do things that 20 years ago were unimaginable. Consider being able to use your desktop computer to track the status of a package shipped from Los Angeles to New York. Companies such as UPS and FEDEX incorporate this type of technology as an integral part of their business. Financial institutions use computer technology to wire billions of dollars each day to locations around the world.

So how have computers changed the way accounting is done? That question can be addressed on several levels. First, computer technology allows companies to easily gather vast amounts of information about individual transactions. For example, information relating to the customer, the salesperson, the product being sold, and the method of payment can be easily gathered for each transaction using computer technology. Prior to today's technology, the cost of gathering this information was prohibitive.

Second, computer technology allows large amounts of data to be compiled quickly and accurately, thereby significantly reducing the likelihood of errors. As you will soon discover, a large part of the mechanics of accounting involves moving numbers to and from various accounting records as well as adding and subtracting a lot of figures. Computers have made this process virtually invisible. What once occupied a large part of an accountant's time can now be done in an instant.

Third, in the precomputer world of limited analytical capacity, it was essential for lenders and investors to receive condensed summaries of a company's financial activities. Now, lenders and investors have the ability to receive and process gigabytes of information, so why should the report of Microsoft's financial performance be restricted to three short financial statements? Why can't Microsoft provide access to much more detailed information online? In fact, why can't Microsoft allow investors to directly tap into its own internal accounting database? Information technology has made this type of information acquisition and analysis possible; the question accountants face now is how much information companies should be required to make available to outsiders. Ten years ago, the only way you could get a copy of Microsoft's financial statements was to call or write to receive paper copies in the mail. Now you can download those summary financial statements from Microsoft's Web site. How will you get financial information 10 years from now? No one knows, but the rapid advances in information technology guarantee that it will be different from anything we are familiar with now.

Finally, and most importantly, although technology has changed the way certain aspects of accounting are carried out, on a fundamental level the mechanics of accounting are still the same as they were 500 years ago. People are still required to analyze complex business transactions and input the results of that analysis into the computer. Technology has not replaced judgment.

So if you are asking "Why do I need to understand accounting—can't computers just do it?"—the answer is a resounding "No!" You need to know what the computer is doing if you are to understand and interpret the information resulting from the accounting process. You need to understand that since judgment was required when the various pieces of information were put into the accounting systems, judgment will be required to appropriately use that information. We have included numerous end-of-chapter opportunities for you to experience how technology helps in the accounting process. These opportunities will illustrate the important role that technology can play in the accounting process as well as emphasize the critical role that the accountant plays as well.

net work

Access Microsoft's Web site at http://www.microsoft. com. Identify the different kinds of information found on Microsoft's home page, e.g., marketing, product information, etc. Can you find any financial information?

to summarize

Accounting functions in a dynamic environment. Generally accepted accounting principles (GAAP) have developed over time. The primary standard-setting body for the private sector is the Financial Accounting Standards Board (FASB). The accounting environment includes business activity that is conducted on an international basis. Consequently, accounting practices often must be modified to reflect the accounting standards of different countries. Attempts are being made to establish comparable international accounting practices. There is increasing concern in society over ethics. High standards of ethical conduct are important, especially for accountants who assume a special responsibility to the public. CPAs have adopted standards of conduct that contain principles and rules as guidelines for the performance of accounting services. Technology has changed the way accounting information is collected, analyzed, and used. The use of computers in the accounting process has increased significantly, and although they allow more information to be gathered and used, computers have not replaced the accountant nor eliminated the need for qualified decision makers.

4

Analyze the reasons for studying accounting.

SO, WHY SHOULD I STUDY ACCOUNTING?

You may still be asking, "But why do I need to study accounting?" Even if you have no desire to be an accountant, at some point in your life you will need financial information to make certain decisions, such as whether to buy or lease an automobile, how to budget your monthly income, where to invest your savings, or how to finance your (or your child's) college education. You can make each of these decisions without using financial information and then hope everything turns out okay, but that would be bad decision making. As noted in the discussion of Exhibit 1–3, a good decision does not guarantee a good outcome, but a bad decision guarantees one of two things—a bad outcome or a lucky outcome. And you cannot count on lucky outcomes time after time. On a personal level, each of us needs to understand how to collect and use accounting information.

Odds are that each of you will have the responsibility of providing some form of income for yourself and your family. Would you prefer to work for a company that is doing well and has a promising future or one that is on the brink of bankruptcy? Of course we all want to work for companies that are doing well. But how would you know? Accounting information will allow you to evaluate your employer's short- and long-term potential.

When you graduate and secure employment, it is almost certain that accounting information will play some role in your job. Whether your responsibilities include sales (where you will need information about product availability and costs), production (where you will need information regarding the costs of materials, labor, and overhead), quality control (where you will need information relating to variances between expected and actual production), or human resources (where you will need information relating to the costs of employees), you will use accounting information. The more you know about where accounting information comes from, how it is accumulated, and how it is best used, the better you will be able to perform your job.

Everyone is affected by accounting information. Saying you don't need to know accounting doesn't change the fact that you are affected by accounting information. Ignoring the value of that information simply puts you at a disadvantage. Those who recognize the value of accounting information and learn how to use it to make better decisions will have a competitive advantage over those who don't. It's as simple as that.

review of learning objectives

1 **Describe the purpose of accounting and explain its role in business and society.** Accounting is a service activity designed to assist individuals and organizations in deciding how to allocate scarce resources and reach their financial objectives. It is used to accumulate, measure, and communicate economic data about organizations and to assist in the decision-making process.

2 **Identify the primary users of accounting information.** The primary users of accounting information are lenders, investors, management, and other interested individuals and organizations. Management accounting deals primarily with the internal accounting functions of planning, implementing, and control. Financial accounting is concerned with reporting business activities and results to external parties. The objectives of both areas of accounting are measurement and communication of information for decision-making purposes.

3 **Describe the environment of accounting, including the effects of generally accepted accounting principles, international business, ethical considerations, and technology.** Accounting functions in a dynamic environment. The principles of accounting have evolved over time to meet the changing demands of the business environment. They are therefore not absolute. Only if they prove useful do they become generally accepted. Accounting principles provide comparable data for external users and need to be applied with judgment.

Since the 1930s, several organizations have been involved in the development of accounting principles in the United States. The American Institute of Certified Public Accountants (AICPA), the Securities and Exchange Commission (SEC), and the Financial Accounting Standards Board (FASB) are among the most prominent. The FASB is currently the primary standard-setting body for accounting principles in the private sector.

Accounting is practiced in an international environment. Accounting procedures in the United States sometimes must be modified to accommodate foreign operations. Attempts are being made to establish consistent and comparable accounting practices throughout the world, primarily through the efforts of the International Accounting Standards Board (IASB).

Ethical considerations affect society and are particularly important for accountants, who have a special responsibility to the public. CPAs have adopted standards of conduct to guide them in the performance of their duties.

Technology has changed the way accounting information is accumulated and analyzed. What once occupied a large part of an accountant's time is now done quickly by computers, thereby freeing the accountant to be involved in more productive tasks. But computer technology has not removed the accountant from the decision-making process. Accounting judgment is still essential.

4 **Analyze the reasons for studying accounting.** Knowing how to use accounting information will help individuals make better decisions in their personal life as well as in their employment. Whatever the job, it is likely that accounting information plays a part. Knowing where information comes from, how it is accumulated, and how it is best used will result in better decision making.

key terms and concepts

accounting 6

accounting cycle 9

accounting system 5

American Institute of Certified Public Accountants (AICPA) 16

annual report 9

bookkeeping 5

business 7

certified public accountant (CPA) 16

financial accounting 9

Financial Accounting Standards Board (FASB) 14

financial statements 9

generally accepted accounting principles (GAAP) 15

Internal Revenue Service (IRS) 17

International Accounting Standards Board (IASB) 17

management accounting 9

nonprofit organization 7

Securities and Exchange Commission (SEC) 16

discussion questions

1. What are the three functions of an accounting system?
2. What are the essential elements in decision making, and how does accounting fit into the process?

3. What types of personal decisions have required you to use accounting information?
4. What does the term *business* mean to you?

5. Why is accounting often referred to as the "language of business"?

6. In what ways are the needs of internal and external users of accounting information the same? In what ways are they different?

7. What are generally accepted accounting principles (GAAP)? Who currently develops and issues GAAP? What is the purpose of GAAP?

8. Why is it important for financial statements and other external reports to be based on generally accepted accounting principles (GAAP)?

9. What are the respective roles of the Securities and Exchange Commission (SEC) and the Internal Revenue Service (IRS) in the setting of accounting standards?

10. For you as a potential investor, what is the problem with different countries having different accounting standards? For you as the president of a multinational company, what is the problem with different countries having different accounting standards?

11. Ethical considerations affect all society. Why are ethical considerations especially important for accountants?

12. Given significant technological advances, can we expect to see less demand for accountants and accounting-type services?

13. Other than that it is a requirement for your major or that your mom or dad is making you, why should you study accounting?

discussion cases

CASE 1-1

TO LEND OR NOT TO LEND—THAT IS THE QUESTION

Sam Love is vice president and chief lending officer of the Meeker First National Bank. Recently, Bill McCarthy, a new farmer, moved to town. Sam has not dealt with Bill previously and knows little about the Mountain Meadow Ranch that Bill operates. Bill would like to borrow $100,000 to purchase some equipment and yearling steers for his ranch. What information does Sam need to help make the lending decision? What type of information should Bill collect and analyze before even requesting the loan?

CASE 1-2

INFORMATION NEEDS TO REMAIN COMPETITIVE

In an article in *U.S. News & World Report*, Dan McGraw described how two computer giants, DELL and COMPAQ, were poised to do battle in the personal computer market. Compaq had 13.2% of the U.S. market share for personal computers to Dell's 8.8%. However, Dell's market share had more than doubled in the last four years while Compaq's share had increased less than 1%. What type of information, accounting or otherwise, do you think the management of Compaq may have wanted and needed as they competed with Dell and the other PC companies?

Source: Dan McGraw, "Shootout at PC Corral," *U.S. News & World Report*, June 23, 1997, pp. 37–38.

CASE 1-3

INTERNATIONAL HAPPENINGS

July 1, 1997, marked a historic date as Hong Kong reverted to political and economic control by mainland China. The Stock Exchange of Hong Kong offers the opportunity to invest in both local Hong Kong companies and in "red-chip offerings," which are stocks of companies that are listed in Hong Kong but controlled by mainland China interests. As an international investor, what accounting information might be helpful as you consider investing in the Hong Kong stock market? For which variables in this situation is accounting information unlikely to be very helpful?

exercises

EXERCISE 1-1

THE ROLE AND IMPORTANCE OF ACCOUNTING

Assume that you are applying for a part-time job as an accounting clerk in a retail clothing establishment. During the interview, the store manager asks how you expect to contribute to the business. How would you respond?

EXERCISE 1-2

BOOKKEEPING IS EVERYWHERE

Describe how bookkeeping is applied in each of the following settings:

a.   Your college English class.
b.   The National Basketball Association.
c.   A hospital emergency room.
d.   Jury selection for a major murder trial.
e.   Four college roommates on a weekend skiing trip.

EXERCISE 1-3

ACCOUNTING INFORMATION AND DECISION MAKING

You are the owner of Automated Systems, Inc., which sells APPLE computers and related data processing equipment. You are currently trying to decide whether to continue selling the Apple computer line or to distribute the Windows-based computers instead. What information do you need to consider in order to determine how successful your business is or will be? What information would help you decide whether to sell the Apple or the Windows-based personal computer line? Use your imagination and general knowledge of business activity.

EXERCISE 1-4

USERS OF FINANCIAL INFORMATION

Why might each of the following individuals or groups be interested in a firm's financial statements? (a) The current stockholders of the firm; (b) the creditors of the firm; (c) the management of the firm; (d) the prospective stockholders of the firm; (e) the Internal Revenue Service (IRS); (f) the SEC; (g) the firm's major labor union.

EXERCISE 1-5

STRUCTURING INFORMATION FOR USE IN EVALUATION

You work in a small convenience store. The store is very low-tech; you ring up the sales on an old-style cash register that merely records the amount of the sale. The store owner uses this cash register tape at the end of each day to verify that the correct amount of cash is in the cash register drawer.

In addition to verifying the cash amount, how else could the information on the cash register tape be used to evaluate the store's operation? What additional bookkeeping procedures would be necessary to make these additional uses possible?

EXERCISE 1-6

INVESTING IN THE STOCK MARKET

Assume your grandparents have just given you $20,000 on the condition that you invest the money in the stock market. As you contemplate making your investment choices, what accounting information do you want to help identify companies that will have high future rates of return?

EXERCISE 1-7

ALLOCATION OF LIMITED RESOURCES

Assume you are a small business owner trying to increase your company's profits. How can accounting information help you efficiently allocate your limited resources to maximize your business profit?

EXERCISE 1-8

MANAGEMENT VERSUS FINANCIAL ACCOUNTING

This chapter discusses two areas of accounting: management and financial accounting. Contrast management and financial accounting with respect to the following:

- Overall purpose
- Type of financial reports used (i.e., external, internal, or both)
- Users of the information

Also, in what ways are these two fields of accounting similar?

EXERCISE 1-9

THE ROLE OF THE SEC

It is not often that the federal government has allowed the private sector to govern itself, but that is exactly what has happened with the field of accounting. The SEC has delegated the responsibility of rule making to the FASB, a group of seven individuals who are hired full-time to discuss issues, research areas of interest, and determine what GAAP is and will be. What are the advantages of allowing the private sector to determine accounting standards? Identify any advantages that the SEC might gain if it established the rules that govern the practice of accounting.

EXERCISE 1-10

WHY TWO SETS OF BOOKS?

This past year you were married. This coming April you will be faced with preparing your first tax return since mom and dad said "you are now on your own." As you review the IRS regulations, you notice several differences from what you learned in your accounting class. It appears that businesses must keep two sets of books: one for the IRS and one in accordance with GAAP. Why aren't GAAP and IRS rules the same?

EXERCISE 1-11

DIFFERENCES IN ACCOUNTING ACROSS BORDERS

In the United States, accounting for inventory is a difficult issue. Inventory is comprised of those items either purchased or manufactured to be resold at a profit. Numerous methods are available to account for inventory for financial reporting purposes. A very commonly used method—called LIFO (last-in, first-out)—minimizes a company's tax obligation. In the United Kingdom, however, LIFO is not permitted for tax purposes and thus is not used very often for financial reporting. In Turkey, the use of LIFO is severely restricted, and in Russia, LIFO is a foreign term. Only in Germany, where the tax laws have been modified to allow the use of LIFO, is LIFO being adopted. Different accounting methods are available for numerous other issues in accounting. Identify some major problems associated with comparing the financial statements of companies from different countries.

EXERCISE 1-12

ETHICS IN ACCOUNTING

The text has pointed out that ethics is an important topic, especially for CPAs. Derek Bok, former law professor and president of Harvard University, has suggested that colleges and universities have a special opportunity and obligation to train students to be more thoughtful and perceptive about moral and ethical issues. Other individuals have concluded that it is not possible to "teach" ethics. What do you think? Can ethics be taught? If you agree that colleges and universities can teach ethics, how might the ethical dimensions of accounting be presented to students?

EXERCISE 1-13

CAREER OPPORTUNITIES IN ACCOUNTING

You are scheduled to graduate from college with a degree in accounting, and your mother would like to know what you plan to do with the rest of your life. She assumes that your only option is to be a bookkeeper like Bob Cratchit in the story *A Christmas Carol*. What can you tell Mom regarding the options available to you with your degree in accounting?

EXERCISE 1-14

WHY DO I NEED TO KNOW ACCOUNTING?

One of your college friends recently graduated from school with a major in music (specifically piano). He has told you that he is going to start his own piano instructional business. He plans to operate the business from home. You ask him how he is going to account for his business, and his reply is, "I graduated in music, not accounting. I am going to teach music, not number crunching. I didn't need accounting in college and I don't need it now!" Is your friend right? What financial information might he find useful in operating his business?

EXERCISE 1-15

CHALLENGES TO THE ACCOUNTING PROFESSION

As the business world continues to change the way in which business is conducted, accountants are faced with the challenge of accounting for these changes. Who, for example, could have anticipated the risks associated with asbestos? Or the decline of communism? Or the increasingly litigious environment in the United States? Each of these events, and many more, has influenced business—which has, in turn, influenced accounting. From your general understanding of accounting and the current business environment, what are some of the challenges you see facing the accounting profession?

competency enhancement opportunities

▶ Analyzing Real Company Information ▶ The Debate
▶ International Case ▶ Internet Search
▶ Ethics Case
▶ Writing Assignments

The following additional assignments provide opportunities for students to develop critical thinking, ethical perspectives, oral and written communication skills, experience with electronic research, and teamwork through group and business activities.

▶ ## ANALYZING REAL COMPANY INFORMATION

• Analyzing 1-1 (Microsoft)

In the Appendix at the back of this text is MICROSOFT's complete annual report for the year ended June 30, 1999. Review the annual report and identify its major areas. How many pages of the report are devoted to a narrative of the prior three years' performance? How many pages focus on explaining technical accounting and business-related issues and procedures? In your opinion, given your limited knowledge of accounting, what is the most interesting part of the annual report? What is the least interesting?

• Analyzing 1-2 (General Motors)

Below is a condensed listing of the assets and liabilities of GENERAL MOTORS as of December 31, 1999. All amounts are in millions of U.S. dollars.

Assets		*Liabilities*	
Cash	$ 21,250	Loans payable	$187,059
Loans receivable	80,627	Pensions	3,339
Inventories	10,638	Other retiree benefits	34,166
Property & equipment	69,186	Other liabilities	28,708
Other assets	92,572		
Total assets	$274,273	Total liabilities	$253,272

1. Among its assets, General Motors lists more than $80 billion in loans receivable. This represents loans that General Motors has made and expects to collect in the future. This is exactly the kind of asset reported among the assets of banks. Given what you know about General Motors' business, how do you think the company acquired these loans receivable?
2. The difference between the reported amount of General Motors' assets and liabilities is $21.001 billion ($274.273 − $253.272). What does this difference represent?

▷ **INTERNATIONAL CASE**

• *Should the SEC choose the FASB or the IASB?*
The SEC has received from Congress the legal authority to set accounting standards in the United States. Historically, the SEC has allowed the FASB to set those standards. In addition, the SEC has refused to allow foreign companies to seek investment funds in the United States unless they agree to provide U.S. investors with financial statements prepared using FASB rules.

The number of foreign companies seeking to list their shares on U.S. stock exchanges is increasing. Even more would likely sell stock to the American public if the SEC were to agree to accept financial statements prepared according to usually less stringent IASB standards.

Why do you think the SEC has so far insisted on financial statements prepared using FASB rules? Do you agree with its policy? Explain.

▷ **ETHICS CASE**

• *Disagreement With the Boss*
You recently graduated with your degree in accounting and have accepted an entry-level accounting position with BigTec, Inc. One of your first responsibilities is to review expense reports submitted by various executives. The expense reports include such items as receipts for taking clients to dinner and hotel receipts for business travel. In conducting this review, you note that your boss has submitted for reimbursement several items that are clearly outside the established guidelines of the corporation. In questioning your boss about the items, he told you to process the items and not worry about them. What would you do?

▷ **WRITING ASSIGNMENTS**

• *The Language of Business*
Accounting is known as the "language of business." Prepare a one- to two-page paper explaining why all business students should have some accounting education. Also include a discussion of how accounting applies to at least five different types of businesses, such as a grocery store, a university, or a movie theater.

• *Visiting an Accounting Professional*
Select a field of accounting you are interested in. Visit a professional who works in that area and discuss the career opportunities available in that specific accounting field. After the visit, prepare a one- to two-page paper summarizing what you learned from your discussion with the accounting professional.

▷ **THE DEBATE**

• *Insulate the FASB*
As mentioned in the text, the FASB conducts public hearings concerning any new accounting standards that it is considering. In addition, the FASB invites

interested parties (businesses, trade groups, user groups, accounting professors) to send in written comments on proposed standards. This "due process" system occasionally exposes the FASB to intense lobbying pressure for and against proposed standards. For example, when the FASB was deliberating over the proper accounting for option compensation (see the example in the chapter), some companies, upset at the FASB's proposed approach, appealed to Congress to pass a bill outlawing the FASB's standard. Can the FASB establish good accounting standards in such a heated, public environment?

Divide your group into two teams.

- One team represents the "Open Door Policy." Prepare a two-minute oral argument supporting the continuation of the FASB's policy of adopting accounting standards only after public debate.
- The other team represents the "Insulate the FASB Movement." Prepare a two-minute oral argument outlining why it is impossible for the FASB to design conceptually correct accounting standards while being bombarded with the complaints and threats of self-interested companies and lobbyists.

▶ **INTERNET SEARCH**

• The Financial Accounting Standards Board
The FASB's Web address is http://www.fasb.org. Sometimes Web addresses change; so if this address is out of commission, access the Web site for this textbook (http://albrecht.swcollege.com) for an updated link.

Once you have gained access to the site, answer the following questions.

1. What is the mission of the FASB?
2. How many FASB statements are there? When was the most recent statement issued?
3. When was the first statement issued and what is it about? What other statements are related to Statement No. 1?
4. In what ways are the following three types of FASB pronouncements different: (1) Statements of Financial Accounting Standards (SFAS), (2) Interpretations of SFAS, and (3) Statements of Financial Accounting Concepts?

Financial Statements: An Overview

chapter

f2

learning objectives After studying this chapter, you should be able to:

1 Understand the basic elements and formats of the three primary financial statements—balance sheet, income statement, and statement of cash flows.

2 Recognize the need for financial statement notes and identify the types of information included in the notes.

3 Describe the purpose of an audit report and the incentives the auditor has to perform a good audit.

4 Use financial ratios to identify a company's strengths and weaknesses and to forecast its future performance.

5 Explain the fundamental concepts and assumptions that underlie financial accounting.

In addition to founding the brokerage firm of MERRILL LYNCH, in 1926 Charles Merrill was instrumental in the consolidation of several grocery store chains in the western United States to form one big holding company called SAFEWAY. In 1955, control of Safeway passed to Robert Magowan, Merrill's son-in-law. Under Magowan's leadership, Safeway expanded to become the second largest supermarket chain in the United States. Shortly after Magowan retired in 1971, Safeway passed THE GREAT ATLANTIC AND PACIFIC TEA COMPANY (A&P) to become the largest supermarket chain.

During the 1970s, Safeway became too cautious and conservative (in the view of many). It was whispered that Safeway would become the A&P of the West—a fallen giant no longer willing to make the bold moves that had created its success in the first place. In 1980, Robert Magowan's 37-year-old son, Peter (who had started out in Safeway as a teenager bagging groceries), became chairman of the board of directors. As he assumed leadership of Safeway, Magowan faced a host of problems: an overall decrease in the size of the grocery market due to an increased tendency by Americans to eat at fast-food restaurants; union contracts that resulted in higher labor costs for Safeway than many of its competitors; high corporate overhead; and stores that were too small and too close together. As a result of these problems, between 1976 and 1980 Safeway lost market share in 9 of the 14 major markets in which it operated. As one executive put it, "[Losing market share] in the food business [is] a hell of an indicator you're not giving the customer what he wants." By 1981, Safeway's financial performance had hit disappointing lows.

Under Peter Magowan's leadership, Safeway eliminated 2,000 office and warehouse jobs and embarked upon an impressive program of new construction and remodeling. During much of the early 1980s, Safeway spent more on capital expenditures than any other U.S. company, averaging nearly $600 million per year. In November 1986, Safeway was acquired by KOHLBERG, KRAVIS, ROBERTS & CO. (KKR) for $5.3 billion in what was then the second-largest leveraged buyout (LBO) of all time. In an LBO, a group of private investors, sometimes joined by company managers, supply only a small amount of the money needed to buy an entire corporation. The bulk of the purchase price is provided by banks and other lenders, with the assets of the acquired company serving as collateral for the loans. As an indication of how leveraged the Safeway buyout was, the KKR investors put only $130 million of their own money into the $5.3 billion deal.

So, how is Safeway doing today? In the 1999 Fortune 500 survey, Safeway, with 1999 sales of $28.9 billion, ranks as the third-largest food and drug chain in the United States, behind KROGER ($45.3 billion in sales) and ALBERTSON'S ($37.5 billion in sales).[1] In fact, Safeway's 1999 sales increased 18% to reach this peak. Sales volume isn't the only financial measure that can be used to evaluate a company, however. For example, Safeway's net income in 1999 was $971 million, higher than the net income for both Kroger and Albertson's. Also, Safeway's cash income ("cash from operations") was $1,488.4 million. Further, Safeway earned 23.8 cents of profit for every dollar invested by its stockholders—a decent one-year return on investment (a dollar invested in a certificate of deposit during the same period would have earned only about 4 cents).

setting the stage

To adequately answer the question of how Safeway is doing today, one must have a working knowledge of financial statements. In this chapter, you will learn that the financial statements are summary reports that show how a business is doing and where its successes and failures lie. The financial statements covered in this chapter are the same as those used every day by millions of business owners, investors, and creditors to evaluate how well or poorly organizations are doing.

You will also be introduced to the use of financial ratios, which are the tools of financial statement analysis. You will learn how to compute and interpret ratios such as return on equity, asset

1 In 1999, Albertson's merged with AMERICAN STORES to form what was, at the time, the largest supermarket chain in the United States. Coincidentally, American Stores traces its roots back to the Skaggs family, whose stores also formed the backbone of the original Safeway chain organized by Charles Merrill in 1926.

turnover, and price-earnings (PE) ratio. Hopefully, you will come away from this chapter convinced that the purpose of accounting is not to fill out dull reports that are then filed away in dusty cabinets, but rather to prepare summary financial performance measures to be used as the basis for thousands of economic decisions every day.

THE FINANCIAL STATEMENTS

1

Understand the basic elements and formats of the three primary financial statements—balance sheet, income statement, and statement of cash flows.

The job of a mortgage loan officer is to evaluate each mortgage applicant to determine the likelihood that he or she will repay the mortgage loan. A key piece of evidence in each applicant's file is the financial information included as part of the loan application. A loan officer can use this information to evaluate whether an applicant will generate enough income to make the monthly mortgage payments and continue to make the required payments on other obligations. In fact, it is difficult to imagine how a mortgage loan officer could make an informed decision without this financial information.

Gaining access to an applicant's financial information clearly helps the mortgage lender make a better loan decision, but the applicant also benefits from making these financial disclosures. If no financial disclosures were provided, lenders would be forced to make loan decisions in the absence of reliable financial information about applicants. With greater uncertainty about applicants' ability to repay loans, a lender's risk would increase, causing the lender to raise the interest rate charged on loans. Thus, disclosure of financial information allows a lender to make better lending decisions and also allows an applicant to reduce the lender's uncertainty, leading to a lower interest rate on the loan.

primary financial statements The balance sheet, income statement, and statement of cash flows, used by external groups to assess a company's economic standing.

The financial statements prepared by companies yield the same benefits as do the financial disclosures provided by mortgage applicants. Financial statement information provides potential lenders and investors with a reliable basis for evaluating the past performance and future prospects of a company. Because financial statements are used by so many different groups (investors, creditors, managers, etc.), they are sometimes called *general-purpose financial statements*. The three **primary financial statements** are the balance sheet, the income statement, and the statement of cash flows. These statements provide answers to the following questions:

1. What is the company's current financial status?
2. What were the company's operating results for the period?
3. How did the company obtain and use cash during the period?

balance sheet (statement of financial position) The financial statement that reports a company's assets, liabilities, and owners' equity at a particular date.

The **balance sheet** (or **statement of financial position**) reports the resources of a company (assets), the company's obligations (liabilities), and the difference between what is owned (assets) and what is owed (liabilities), called owners' equity. The **income statement** (or **statement of earnings**) reports the amount of net income earned by a company during a period, with annual and quarterly income statements being the most common. (Net income is discussed later in the chapter.) The income statement represents the accountant's best effort at measuring the economic performance of a company. The **statement of cash flows** reports the amount of cash collected and paid out by a company in the following three types of activities: operating, investing, and financing. As an illustration, the 1999 financial statements from MICROSOFT are reproduced in Appendix A at the end of the book. The Microsoft statements are referred to throughout this chapter and the rest of the book.

income statement (statement of earnings) The financial statement that reports the amount of net income earned by a company during a period.

statement of cash flows The financial statement that reports the amount of cash collected and paid out by a company during a period of time.

The Balance Sheet

In the movie *The Princess Bride*, the hero, Wesley, was "mostly dead all day" until being revived by a miracle pill. Wesley was immediately challenged to come up with a plan to stop the imminent marriage of his true love, Buttercup, to the evil Prince Humperdinck. In formulating his plan, Wesley's first question to his conspirators was "What are our liabilities?" followed by "What are our assets?" In essence, the recently revived hero was saying, "Let me see a balance sheet." Similarly, the first questions asked about any business by potential investors and credi-

assets Economic resources that are owned or controlled by a company.

liabilities Obligations to pay cash, transfer other assets, or provide services to someone else.

owners' equity The ownership interest in the net assets of an entity; equals total assets minus total liabilities.

net assets The owners' equity of a business; equal to total assets minus total liabilities.

stockholders (shareholders) The owners of a corporation.

stockholders' equity The owners' equity section of a corporate balance sheet.

tors are "What are the resources of the business?" and "What are its existing obligations?" The balance sheet answers these questions.

The three categories of the balance sheet—assets, liabilities, and owners' equity—are each explained below.

ASSETS **Assets** are economic resources that are owned or controlled[2] by a company. Assets for a typical company include cash, accounts receivable (amounts owed to the company by customers), inventory (goods held for sale), land, buildings, equipment, and even intangible items, such as copyrights and patents. To be summarized and aggregated on a balance sheet, each asset must be assigned a dollar amount. A balance sheet wouldn't be very useful with the following asset listing: one bank account, two warehouses full of goods, three trucks, and four customers who owe us money. As emphasized throughout this text, the monetary measurement and valuation of assets is an area in which accountants must exercise considerable professional judgment.

LIABILITIES **Liabilities** are obligations to pay cash, transfer other assets, or provide services to someone else. Your personal liabilities might include unpaid phone bills, the remaining balance on an automobile loan, or an obligation to complete work for which you have already been paid. Some common liabilities of a company are accounts payable (amounts owed by the company to suppliers), notes payable (amounts owed to banks or others), and mortgages payable (amounts owed for purchased property, such as land or buildings). Like assets, liabilities must be measured in monetary amounts. And, as with assets, quantifying the amount of a liability can require extensive judgment. As one example, consider the difficulties faced by a company to quantify its obligation to clean up a particular toxic waste site when the cleanup will take years to complete; the exact extent of the environmental damage at the site is still in dispute; and legal responsibility for the toxic mess is still debated in the courts. Properly valuing a company's liabilities is one of the biggest (if not *the* biggest) challenges that an accountant faces.

OWNERS' EQUITY The remaining claim against the assets of a business, after the liabilities have been deducted, is **owners' equity**. Thus, owners' equity is a residual amount; it represents the **net assets** (total assets minus total liabilities) available after all obligations have been satisfied. Obviously, if there are no liabilities (an unlikely situation, except at the start of a business), then the total assets are exactly equal to the owners' claims against those assets—the owners' equity.

In order to get a business started, investors transfer resources, usually cash, to the business in return for part ownership. Ownership of a company can be restricted to one person (a sole proprietorship), to a small group (a partnership), or to a diffuse group of owners who often don't even know one another (a corporation). When owners initially invest money in a corporation, they receive evidence of their ownership in the form of shares of stock, represented by stock certificates. These shares of stock may then be privately traded among existing owners of the corporation, privately sold to new owners, or traded publicly on an organized stock exchange such as the New York Stock Exchange (NYSE) (where SAFEWAY's shares are traded) or the NASDAQ exchange (where Microsoft's shares are traded). The owners of a corporation are called **stockholders** or **shareholders**, and the owners' equity section of a corporate balance sheet is sometimes referred to as **stockholders' equity**.

Owners' equity is increased when owners make additional investments in a business or when the business generates profits that are retained in the business. Since business profits belong to the owners, retaining the profits in the business is equivalent to giving the profits to the owners and then having them immediately reinvest that amount back into the business.

---

2 An example of an asset that a company technically does not own, but does economically control, is a building that the company uses under a long-term, noncancelable lease agreement.

Should I Incorporate? Pick up just about any business newspaper or magazine, look in the classified section, and you are sure to see advertisements offering to help you set up a corporation. "Incorporate in USA by Fax or Phone!!!" "Incorporate: All 50 States and Offshore." "Typical Incorporating Fees: Delaware, $199; Wyoming, $285; the Bahamas, $500; Isle of Man, £250." With all this eagerness to incorporate, there must be some advantages. To understand these advantages, as well as the disadvantages, it is necessary to review the three major types of business entities: proprietorships, partnerships, and corporations.

1. *Proprietorship.* A proprietorship is a business owned by one person. Almost always, the owner of the business also manages the operation. For example, many owners of small businesses (especially those that provide personal services) manage the day-to-day activities of, and receive the profits

directly from, those businesses. Legally, a proprietorship is merely an extension of the owner. The owner is personally responsible for all the activities and obligations of the business.

2. *Partnership.* A partnership is a business association of two or more individuals. As in a proprietorship, the partners generally own and manage the business and are personally responsible for all the obligations of the business. A partnership organization makes sense when the workload and financial requirements associated with starting and operating a business are too much for one person.

3. *Corporation.* A corporation is a business that is chartered (incorporated) as a separate legal entity under the laws of a particular state or country. With a proprietorship or a partnership, the owners are the business. With a corporation, the operations and obligations of the business are legally separated from the personal affairs of the owners. Typically, stockholders in a corporation can freely buy and sell their interests, thus allowing the corporate ownership to change without dissolving the business. The stock-

---

dividends Distributions to the owners (stockholders) of a corporation.

retained earnings The amount of accumulated earnings of the business that have not been distributed to owners.

capital stock The portion of a corporation's owners' equity contributed by owners in exchange for shares of stock.

accounting equation An algebraic equation that expresses the relationship between assets (resources), liabilities (obligations), and owners' equity (net assets, or the residual interest in a business after all liabilities have been met): Assets = Liabilities + Owners' Equity.

Owners' equity is decreased when the owners take back part of their investment. If the business is a corporation, distributions to the owners (stockholders) are called **dividends**. Owners' equity can also be decreased if operations generate a loss instead of a profit. In the extreme, very poor performance can result in the loss of all the assets originally invested by the owners. For a corporation, the amount of accumulated earnings of the business that have not been distributed to owners is called **retained earnings**. The portion of owners' equity contributed by owners in exchange for shares of stock is called **capital stock**. The amount of retained earnings plus the amount of capital stock equals the corporation's total owners' equity.

ACCOUNTING EQUATION   The balance sheet presents information based on the basic **accounting equation**:

Assets = Liabilities + Owners' Equity

In fact, the name *balance sheet* comes from the fact that a proper balance sheet must always balance—total assets must equal the total of liabilities and owners' equity. The accounting equation is not some miraculous coincidence; it is true by definition. Liabilities and owners' equity are just the sources of funding used to buy the assets; that is, they are the claims (creditors' claims and owners' claims) against the assets. So, another way to view the accounting equation is that the total amount of the assets is equal to the total amount of funding needed to buy the assets. The total resources, therefore, equal the claims against those resources. This is illustrated in Exhibit 2-1.

The accounting equation is presented here merely to give you a glimpse of **double-entry accounting**. Chapter 3 gives an in-depth discussion of the equation elements and the mechanics of double-entry accounting.

holders elect a board of directors, which then hires executives to manage the corporation. The managers, as employees of the corporation, may or may not be stockholders. Thus, in a corporation there is a separation of ownership from management.

The primary advantages of incorporation are:

- Investment funds can be accumulated from many different individuals, allowing for the development of larger, more efficient companies.
- Individual owners can buy and sell their ownership shares without getting the permission of the other owners.
- The liability of the owners is limited. If the business does not flourish, the worst that can happen to the owners is that they lose their investment; their other personal assets are not at risk.

The primary disadvantages of incorporation are:

- Corporate income is taxed twice: once when it is earned by the corporation and again when it is paid out to shareholders in the form of dividends.

- Management of the business is separated from ownership. The owners must be cautious in monitoring the activities of their hired managers.

As shown below, the majority of business activity in the United States is conducted by corporations, although the actual number of proprietorships is greater.

Type of Business	Number of Businesses	Sales
Sole proprietorships	16.955 million	$ 843 billion
Partnerships	1.654 million	1,042 billion
Corporations	4.631 million	14,890 billion

Source: U.S. Bureau of the Census, *Statistical Abstract of the United States: 1999* (Washington, D.C., 1999). Data are based on IRS information for 1996.

---

exhibit 2-1   Elements of the Accounting Equation

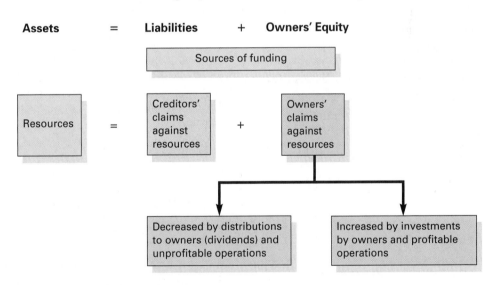

double-entry accounting A system of recording transactions in a way that maintains the equality of the accounting equation.

THE FORMAT OF A BALANCE SHEET   A simple balance sheet, adapted from Microsoft's 1999 balance sheet reproduced in Appendix A at the end of the book, is shown in Exhibit 2-2.

Note that a balance sheet is presented for a particular date because it reports a company's financial position at a point in time. The balance sheet in Exhibit 2-2 presents Microsoft's financial position as of June 30, 1999.

exhibit 2-2   Simplified Balance Sheet for Microsoft

Microsoft Corporation
Balance Sheet
June 30, 1999
(amounts in millions)

Assets		Liabilities	
Cash and short-term		Accounts payable	$ 874
investments	$17,236	Accrued compensation	396
Accounts receivable	2,245	Income taxes payable	1,607
Other current assets	752	Unearned revenue	4,239
Property, plant, and		Other current liabilities	1,602
equipment	1,611	Long-term loans	0
Equity and other investments	14,372	Total liabilities	$ 8,718
Other assets	940		
		Owners' Equity	
		Capital stock	$14,824
		Retained earnings	13,614
		Total liabilities and	
Total assets	$37,156	owners' equity	$37,156

As illustrated, the balance sheet is divided into the three major sections we have described: assets, liabilities, and owners' equity. The asset section identifies the types of assets owned by Microsoft (cash, for example) and the monetary amounts associated with those assets. The liability section defines the extent and nature of Microsoft's debts (income taxes not yet paid, for example).

Remember that the balance sheet is not merely a report to be prepared and forgotten; it is a summary of important information that is useful to investors and creditors. For example, if you were a banker, would you give a loan to Microsoft based on the information from the June 30, 1999, balance sheet? Of course you would, because you see that Microsoft already has enough cash on hand ($17 billion) to be able to pay off all existing liabilities ($8.7 billion) almost two times over. Based on the balance sheet information, you can see that any loan to Microsoft could be easily repaid.

STOP & THINK Actually, the Microsoft balance sheet is quite unusual. Very few companies have the large amount of cash ($17 billion) and low amount of long-term debt ($0) that Microsoft has. Is it good for a company to have so much cash?

Owners' equity completes the balance sheet. This section identifies the portion of Microsoft's resources that were contributed by owners, either in exchange for shares of stock or as undistributed earnings since Microsoft's inception. Together with liabilities, owners' equity indicates how a company is financed (whether by borrowing or by owner contributions and operating profits). You can see that Microsoft has been financed primarily through owner investment. Almost half of this owner investment ($13.6 billion) has been in the form of retained earnings.

CLASSIFIED AND COMPARATIVE BALANCE SHEETS   Imagine that two people each owe you $10,000. You ask to see the balance sheets of each. Borrower A has assets of $10,000 in the form of cash. Borrower B has assets of $10,000 in the form of undeveloped land. If you need to collect the loan in the next two weeks, which of the two borrowers is more likely to be able to pay you back? Borrower A is more likely to be able to repay you quickly because the assets of A are more *liquid*, meaning that they are in the form of cash or can be easily converted into cash. Assets such as undeveloped land are said to be *illiquid* in that it takes time and effort to convert them into cash. This illustration shows that not all assets are the same. For some purposes, it is very important to distinguish between current assets, which are generally more liq-

classified balance sheet A balance sheet in which assets and liabilities are subdivided into current and long-term categories.

current assets Cash and other assets that can be easily converted to cash within a year.

liquidity The ability of a company to pay its debts in the short run.

long-term assets Assets that a company needs in order to operate its business over an extended period of time.

comparative financial statements Financial statements in which data for two or more years are shown together.

market value The value of a company as measured by the number of shares of stock outstanding multiplied by the current market price of the stock; the current value of a business.

book value The value of a company as measured by the amount of owners' equity; that is, assets less liabilities.

uid, and long-term assets. A balance sheet that distinguishes between current and long-term assets is called a **classified balance sheet**.

To illustrate a classified balance sheet, we consider the balance sheet for Safeway, the supermarket chain described in the opening scenario of this chapter. In Exhibit 2-3, Safeway's assets are classified as current, or short-term, and long-term.

Current assets include cash and other assets that are expected to be converted to cash within a year. Current assets generally are listed in decreasing order of **liquidity**; cash is listed first, followed by the other current assets, such as accounts receivable. **Long-term assets**, such as land, buildings, and equipment, are those that a company needs in order to operate its business over an extended period of time.

Like assets, liabilities usually are classified as either current (obligations expected to be paid within a year) or long-term. Accounts payable, for example, usually would be paid within 30 to 60 days, whereas a mortgage may remain on the books for 20 to 30 years before it is fully paid.

Safeway's balance sheet in Exhibit 2-3 includes financial information for both the current year and the preceding year. Most companies prepare such **comparative financial statements** so that readers can identify any significant changes in particular items. For example, notice that Safeway's total assets increased by $3,510.7 million ($14,900.3 million − $11,389.6 million) from 1998 to 1999. Where did the money come from to finance this increase in assets? Most of it came from an increased amount of loans (liabilities increased by $2,507 million).

LIMITATIONS OF A BALANCE SHEET Although the balance sheet is useful in showing the financial status of a company, it does have some limitations. The primary limitation of the balance sheet is that it does not reflect the current value or worth of a company. Refer back to the balance sheet numbers for Microsoft in Exhibit 2-2. If the balance sheet were perfect, meaning that it included all economic assets reported at their current market values, then the amount of owners' equity would be equal to the market value of the company. In the case of Microsoft, the value of the company would be $28.438 billion, which is the amount of assets that would remain after all the liabilities were repaid. The actual market value of Microsoft on May 18, 2000, however, was $348 billion. How could the balance sheet be so wrong?

The discrepancy between recorded balance sheet value and actual market value is the result of the following two factors:

1. Accountants record many assets at their purchase cost, not at their current market value. **Market value** is the price that would have to be paid to buy the same asset today. For example, if land was obtained ten years ago, it would still be reported on the balance sheet at its original cost, even though its market value may have increased dramatically.
2. Not all economic assets are included in the balance sheet. For example, important economic assets of Microsoft are its proven track record of successful products, the genius of Bill Gates, and a strong, established position in the marketplace (ask NOVELL, WORDPERFECT, LOTUS, and NETSCAPE what it is like to compete against Microsoft). These intangible factors are all very valuable economic assets. In fact, they are by far the most valuable assets Microsoft has. Nevertheless, these important economic assets are outside the normal accounting process.

Because the balance sheet can underreport the value of some long-term assets, and not report other important economic assets, the accounting **book value** of a company (measured by the amount of owners' equity) is usually less than the company's market value, measured by the market price per share times the number of shares of stock. This is illustrated in Exhibit 2-4 using data for the ten largest companies (in terms of market value) in the United States.

Despite its deficiencies, the balance sheet is a useful source of information regarding the financial position of a business. A lender would never loan a company money without knowing what assets the company has and what other loans the company is already obligated to repay. An investor shouldn't pay money in exchange for ownership in a company without knowing something about the company's existing resources and obligations. When a balance sheet is classified, and when comparative data are provided, the balance sheet provides an informative picture of a company's financial position.

exhibit 2-3 Classified Balance Sheets for Safeway

Safeway, Inc.
Comparative Balance Sheet
December 28, 1999 and December 30, 1998
(amounts in millions)

	1999	1998
Assets		
Current assets:		
Cash	$ 106.2	$ 45.7
Accounts receivable	292.9	200.1
Merchandise inventories	2,444.9	1,856.0
Prepaid expenses and other current assets	208.1	218.1
Total current assets	$ 3,052.1	$ 2,319.9
Property:		
Land	$ 996.2	$ 794.1
Buildings	2,502.3	2,069.9
Leasehold improvements	1,784.3	1,498.3
Fixtures and equipment	3,852.4	3,282.6
Property under capital leases	591.4	379.2
Total property	$ 9,726.6	$ 8,024.1
Less accumulated depreciation and amortization	3,281.9	2,841.5
Total property, net	$ 6,444.7	$ 5,182.6
Other assets:		
Goodwill	$ 4,786.6	$ 3,348.0
Prepaid pension costs	405.6	369.6
Investments in unconsolidated affiliates	131.6	115.2
Other assets	79.7	54.3
Total assets	$14,900.3	$11,389.6
Liabilities and Stockholders' Equity		
Current liabilities:		
Accounts payable	$ 1,878.4	$ 1,595.9
Accrued salaries and wages	387.7	348.9
Other current liabilities	1,316.5	948.8
Total current liabilities	$ 3,582.6	$ 2,893.6
Long-term debt:		
Notes and debentures	$ 5,922.0	$ 4,242.6
Obligations under capital leases	435.4	408.0
Total long-term debt	$ 6,357.4	$ 4,650.6
Deferred income taxes	379.1	216.9
Accrued claims and other liabilities	495.4	546.4
Total liabilities	$10,814.5	$ 8,307.5
Stockholders' equity:		
Common stock: par value $0.01 per share	$ 5.6	$ 5.5
Additional paid-in capital	1322.4	1,297.3
Unexercised warrants purchased	(126.6)	(126.0)
Cumulative translation adjustments	(11.5)	(19.7)
Retained earnings	2,895.9	1,925.0
Total stockholders' equity	$ 4,085.8	$ 3,082.1
Total liabilities and stockholders' equity	$14,900.3	$11,389.6

exhibit 2-4   Book Value and Market Value for the Ten Largest U.S. Firms

Rank	Company	Book Value*	Market Value*†
1	Microsoft	$28,438.0	$492,462
2	Cisco Systems	11,678.0	453,879
3	General Electric	42,557.0	417,175
4	Intel	32,535.0	391,817
5	ExxonMobil	63,466.0	268,598
6	AT&T	78,927.0	236,704
7	Oracle	3,695.3	217,258
8	Lucent Technologies	13,584.0	214,185
9	Wal-Mart Stores	25,848.0	212,666
10	International Business Machines (IBM)	20,511.0	193,810

*Accounting book value and market value are in millions of dollars.
†On a previous page we noted that Microsoft's market value was $348 billion on May 18, 2000. In this exhibit, Microsoft's value is listed as $492 billion as of March 14, 2000. The reason for the dramatic decrease in market value in two months is the government's theatened breakup of the company.

Source: Fortune 500 listing, 1999. Market values are as of March 14, 2000. Accounting book values are for the end of the immediately preceding fiscal year. Accessible at http://www.fortune.com.

to summarize

The balance sheet provides a summary of the financial position of a company at a particular date. It helps external users assess the financial relationship between assets (resources) and liabilities and owners' equity (claims against those resources). Assets and liabilities are usually classified as either current or long-term and are presented in descending order of liquidity. For a corporation, owners' equity consists of directly invested funds as well as retained earnings. Classified and comparative balance sheets provide useful information for readers of financial statements. Because not all economic assets are included on the balance sheet, the book value as shown in the balance sheet is usually less than the market value of the company.

The Income Statement

Almost every day, *The Wall Street Journal* includes a section called "Digest of Earnings Reports" that contains the net income, or earnings, figures announced by companies the day before. The stock prices of companies go up or down depending on whether their announced earnings meet the expectations of investors. For example, on April 19, 1997, Microsoft stock shot up from $98.125 to $107.625 per share in response to news of an 85% increase in Microsoft's net income as compared to the previous year. This high level of interest centered on net income makes it apparent that investors find this accounting number useful in evaluating the health and performance of a business.

Net income is reported in the income statement. The income statement shows the results of a company's operations for a period of time (a month, a quarter, or a year). The income statement summarizes the revenues generated and the costs incurred (expenses) to generate those revenues. The "bottom line" of an income statement is net income (or net loss), the difference between revenues and expenses. To help you understand an income statement, we must first define its elements—revenues, expenses, and net income (or net loss).

revenue Increase in a company's resources from the sale of goods or services.

REVENUES **Revenue** is the amount of assets created through business operations. Think of revenue as another way for a company to acquire assets. In the same way that assets can be acquired by borrowing or by owners' investment, assets can also be acquired by providing a product or service for which customers are willing to pay. Manufacturing and merchandising companies receive revenues from the sale of merchandise. For example, Safeway's revenue is the cash that customers pay in exchange for groceries. A service enterprise generates revenues from the fees it charges for the services it performs. For example, a portion of the sales price of Microsoft software is not payment for the software itself, but instead is an advance payment for the customer support service that Microsoft promises. Companies might also earn revenues from other activities, such as charging interest or collecting rent. When goods are sold or services performed, the resulting revenue is in the form of cash or accounts receivable (a promise from the buyer to pay for the goods or services by a specified date in the future). Revenues thus generally represent an increase in total assets. These new assets are not tied to any liability obligation; therefore, the assets belong to the owners and thus represent an increase in owners' equity.

expenses Costs incurred in the normal course of business to generate revenues.

EXPENSES **Expenses** are the amount of assets consumed through business operations. Expenses are the costs incurred in normal business operations to generate revenues. Employee salaries and utilities used during a period are two common examples of expenses. For Safeway, the primary expense is the wholesale cost of the groceries that it sells to its customers at retail. Just as revenues represent an increase in assets and equity, expenses generally represent a decrease in assets and in equity.

In considering revenues and expenses, remember that not all inflows of assets are revenues; nor are all outflows of assets considered to be expenses. For example, cash may be received by borrowing from a bank, which is an increase in a liability, not a revenue. Similarly, cash may be paid for supplies, which is an exchange of one asset for another asset, not an expense. The details of properly identifying revenues and expenses will be discussed further in Chapter 3.

net income (net loss) An overall measure of the performance of a company; equal to revenues minus expenses for the period.

NET INCOME (OR NET LOSS) **Net income**, sometimes called earnings or profit, is an overall measure of the performance of a company. Net income reflects the company's accomplishments (revenues) in relation to its efforts (expenses) during a particular period of time. If revenues exceed expenses, the result is called net income (revenues − expenses = net income). If expenses exceed revenues, the difference is called **net loss**. Because net income results in an increase in resources from operations, owners' equity is also increased; a net loss decreases owners' equity. Exhibit 2-5 lists the ten U.S. companies with the highest net incomes in 1999.

It is important to note the difference between revenues and net income. Both concepts represent an increase in the net assets (assets − liabilities) of a firm. However, revenues represent total resource increases; expenses are subtracted from revenues to derive net income or net loss. Thus, whereas revenue is a "gross" concept, income (or loss) is a "net" concept.

THE FORMAT OF AN INCOME STATEMENT Comparative income statements, which have been modified to a "multi-step format," for Safeway are presented in Exhibit 2-6. In contrast to the balance sheet, which is "as of" a particular date, the income statement refers to the "year ended." Remember, the income statement covers a period of time; the balance sheet is a report at a point in time. The multi-step format illustrated here highlights several profit measurements including gross profit, operating income, and net income.

The income statement usually shows two main categories, revenues and expenses, although several subcategories may also be presented (as illustrated). Revenues are listed first. Typical operating expenses for most businesses are employee salaries, utilities, and advertising. For Safeway, as with any retail firm, the largest expense is for cost of goods sold. The difference between sales and cost of goods sold represents the difference between the retail price Safeway receives from a grocery sale and the wholesale cost of the groceries that are sold. This difference (sales − cost of goods sold) is called **gross profit** or **gross margin**.

Expenses are sometimes divided into operating and nonoperating categories. The primary nonoperating expenses are interest and income taxes. These expenses are called nonoperating because they have no connection with the specific nature of the operation of the business. For ex-

gross profit (gross margin) The excess of net sales revenue over the cost of goods sold.

exhibit 2-5   Top Ten U.S. Companies, Ranked by Net Income

Company Name	Net Income*
General Electric	$10,717.0
Citigroup	9,867.0
SBC Communications	8,159.0
ExxonMobil	7,910.0
Bank of America Corporation	7,882.0
Microsoft	7,785.0
International Business Machines	7,712.0
E.I. du Pont de Nemours	7,690.0
Philip Morris	7,675.0
Intel	7,314.0

*Net income is in millions of dollars.

Source: Fortune 500 listing, 1999. Accessible at http://www.fortune.com.

gains (losses) Money made or lost on activities outside the normal operation of a company.

ample, Safeway and Microsoft deal with interest and income taxes in a similar way, even though the two companies operate in completely different industries.

Two other items that frequently appear in the income statement are **gains** and **losses**. Gains and losses refer to money made or lost on activities outside the normal business of a company. For example, when Safeway receives cash for selling groceries, it is called revenue. But when

exhibit 2-6   Adapted Comparative Income Statements for Safeway

Safeway, Inc.
Comparative Income Statement
For the Years Ended December 28, 1999
and December 30, 1998
(in millions)

	1999	1998
Revenues:		
Sales	$28,859.9	$24,484.2
Less: Cost of goods sold	20,349.2	17,359.7
Gross profit	$ 8,510.7	$ 7,124.5
Less: Operating and administrative expense	6,411.4	5,466.5
Goodwill amortization	101.4	56.3
Operating income	$ 1,997.9	$ 1,601.7
Add: Other income	38.3	30.2
Less: Interest expense	362.2	235.1
Less: Income tax expense	703.1	590.2
Net income	$ 970.9	$ 806.6
Basic earnings per share	$ 1.95	$1.67

Safeway makes money by selling an old delivery truck, the amount is called a gain, not revenue, because Safeway is not in the business of selling trucks.

Recently, companies have been providing an additional measure of income—comprehensive income. The wealth of a company is affected in a variety of ways that have nothing to do with the business operations of the company. For example, changes in exchange rates can cause the U.S. dollar value of a company's foreign subsidiaries to increase or decrease. **Comprehensive income** is the number used to reflect an overall measure of the change in a company's wealth during the period.

In addition to net income, comprehensive income includes items that, in general, arise from changes in market conditions unrelated to the business operations of a company. These items are excluded from net income because they are viewed as yielding little information about the economic performance of a company's business operations. Nevertheless, they do affect the value of assets and liabilities reported in the balance sheet, so they are reported as part of comprehensive income.

The most common examples of items included in comprehensive income include changes in foreign currency exchange rates, changes in the value of certain investment securities, and changes in the value of certain derivative financial instruments. Each of these items is affected by market conditions, affects a company's reported assets and liabilities, yet cannot be influenced in any large degree by the company. Therefore, they are reported as part of a firm's comprehensive income. To summarize, net income is a measure of a company's performance during the period; comprehensive income includes the net income performance measure plus other wealth changes resulting from changes in investment values and exchange rates.

One final bit of information required on the income statements of corporations is **earnings (loss) per share (EPS)**. This EPS amount is computed by dividing the net income (earnings or loss) for the current period by the number of shares of stock outstanding during the period. Earnings per share information tells the owner of a single share of stock how much of the net income for the year belongs to him or her.

Like the balance sheet, the income statement usually shows the comparative results for two or more periods, allowing investors and creditors to evaluate how profitable an enterprise has been during the current period as compared with earlier periods. For example, examination of Safeway's comparative income statements in Exhibit 2-6 shows that net income in 1999 was 20% higher [($970.9 − $806.6) ÷ $806.6] than in 1998. Further analysis of the income statement is introduced later in this chapter and reinforced throughout the text. (For another illustration of a comparative income statement, see the income statement for Microsoft in Appendix A at the back of the book.)

THE STATEMENT OF RETAINED EARNINGS   In addition to an income statement, corporations sometimes prepare a **statement of retained earnings**. This statement identifies changes in retained earnings from one accounting period to the next. As illustrated in Exhibit 2-7, the

comprehensive income A measure of the overall change in a company's wealth during a period; consists of net income plus changes in wealth resulting from changes in investment values and exchange rates.

earnings (loss) per share (EPS) The amount of net income (earnings) related to each share of stock; computed by dividing net income by the number of shares of stock outstanding during the period.

statement of retained earnings A report that shows the changes in retained earnings during a period of time.

---

exhibit 2-7   Illustrated Statement of Retained Earnings for Safeway

Safeway, Inc.
Illustrated Statement of Retained Earnings
For the Year Ended December 28, 1999
(in millions)

Retained earnings, January 1, 1999	$1,925.0
Add net income for the year	970.9
	$2,895.9
Less dividends	0
Retained earnings, December 28, 1999	$2,895.9

statement shows a beginning retained earnings balance, the net income for the period, a deduction for any dividends paid, and an ending retained earnings balance. For Safeway, which paid no dividends during 1999, its retained earnings would simply increase by the amount of reported net income.

Note how the accounting equation is affected by the elements reported in the statement of retained earnings. Net income results in an increase in net assets and a corresponding increase in Retained Earnings, which increases Owners' Equity.

Dividends reduce net assets (e.g., cash) and similarly reduce Retained Earnings, which reduces Owners' Equity.

Corporations sometimes present a *statement of stockholders' equity* instead of a statement of retained earnings. The statement of stockholders' equity, illustrated for Microsoft in Appendix A at the back of the book, is more detailed and includes changes in capital stock as well as changes in retained earnings.

---

to summarize

The income statement provides a measure of the success of an enterprise over a specified period of time. The income statement shows the major sources of revenues generated and the expenses associated with those revenues. The difference between those revenues and expenses is net income or net loss. Gains and losses refer to money made or lost on activities outside the normal activities of a business. The income statements of corporations must also include earnings per share figures. Comprehensive income includes net income as well as other wealth changes resulting from changes in investment values and exchange rates. Like balance sheets, income statements are usually prepared on a comparative basis. A statement of retained earnings or statement of stockholders' equity is often provided by corporations in their annual reports to shareholders.

The Statement of Cash Flows

Net income is the single best measure of a company's economic performance. However, anyone who has paid rent or college tuition knows that bills must be paid with cash, not with "economic performance." Accordingly, in addition to net income, investors and creditors also desire to know how much actual cash a company's operations generate during a period and how that cash is used. The statement of cash flows shows the cash inflows (receipts) and cash outflows (payments) of an entity during a period of time. As shown in Exhibit 2-8, companies receive cash primarily by selling goods or providing services, by selling other assets, by borrowing, and by receiving cash from investments by owners. Companies use cash to pay current operating expenses such as wages, utilities, and taxes; to purchase additional buildings, land, and otherwise expand operations; to repay loans; and to pay their owners a return on the investments that have been made.

In the statement of cash flows, individual cash flow items are classified according to three main activities: operating, investing, and financing.

exhibit 2-8   Cash Flows

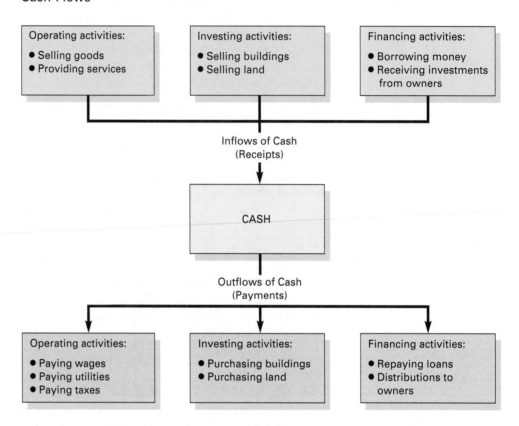

OPERATING ACTIVITIES   **Operating activities** are those activities that are part of the day-to-day business of a company. Cash receipts from selling goods or from providing services are the major operating cash inflow. Major operating cash outflows include payments to purchase inventory and to pay wages, taxes, interest, utilities, rent, and similar expenses.

INVESTING ACTIVITIES   The primary **investing activities** are the purchase and sale of land, buildings, and equipment. You can think of investing activities as those activities associated with buying and selling long-term assets.

FINANCING ACTIVITIES   **Financing activities** are those activities whereby cash is obtained from or repaid to owners and creditors. For example, cash received from owners' investments, cash proceeds from a loan, or cash payments to repay loans would all be classified under financing activities.

Conceptually, the statement of cash flows is the easiest to prepare of the three primary financial statements. Imagine examining every check and deposit slip you have written in the past year and sorting them into three piles—operating, investing, and financing. You would have to exercise some judgment in deciding which pile some items go into (for example, is the payment of interest an operating or a financing activity?). But overall, the three-way categorization of cash flows is not that difficult. In essence, this is all that is involved in the preparation of a statement of cash flows. As you will see in Chapter 13, however, actual preparation of a statement of cash flows can sometimes be challenging. The reason for this is that traditional accounting systems are designed to streamline the computation of net income. So, instead of preparing the statement of cash flows directly from the raw cash flow data, the process is as shown in Exhibit 2-9. The raw cash flow data are transformed into revenue and expense data using the accounting adjustments, assumptions, and estimates that you will learn about in this text. Then, to prepare the statement of cash flows, all of those adjustments must be undone to get back to the raw cash flow data. Challenging, but by the time we get to Chapter 13, you will be ready for it.

operating activities Activities that are part of the day-to-day business of a company.

investing activities Activities associated with buying and selling long-term assets.

financing activities Activities whereby cash is obtained from or repaid to owners and creditors.

exhibit 2-9   Cash Flow to Net Income to Cash Flow

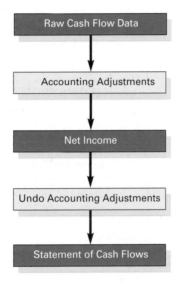

fyi

Notice that the Boston Celtics has chosen June 30 as the end of its fiscal year. About two-thirds of large U.S. companies choose December 31. The Boston Celtics uses June 30 because that coincides with a natural lull in its business (the playoffs are over and the next regular season is months away). Safeway chooses the last Saturday of the year to make sure that each fiscal year contains a whole number of weeks.

Exhibit 2-10 contains the statement of cash flows for the BOSTON CELTICS for the year ended June 30, 1996[3]. As sports fans know, the Boston Celtics is the NBA team with the most championships in history. What is not widely known is that ownership shares in the Boston Celtics could once be purchased by the general public and were traded on the New York Stock Exchange. Because the Celtics was a publicly traded company, it was required to make its financial statements publicly available, thus providing the information for Exhibit 2-10. As with balance sheets and income statements, companies usually provide comparative statements of cash flows. However, we have elected not to show comparative statements of cash flows in order to keep the Celtics illustration simple. (The Microsoft financial statements in Appendix A provide comparative statements of cash flows.)

One interesting item to note in the Celtics' cash flow statement is the $5.2 million payment for deferred compensation. This represents players' salaries that were earned (and reported as expenses) in prior years but not paid until 1996. Also notice the large amount of activity in buying and selling investment securities—$171 million in securities purchased and $157 million sold. And you thought that the Celtics only played basketball.

to summarize

The statement of cash flows is one of the three primary financial statements. It shows the significant cash inflows (receipts) and cash outflows (payments) of a company for a period of time. These cash flows are classified according to operating, investing, and financing activities. The statement of cash flows is discussed and illustrated in Chapter 13.

How the Financial Statements Tie Together

articulation The interrelationships among the financial statements.

Although we have introduced the primary financial statements as if they were independent of one another, they are interrelated and tie together. In accounting language, they "articulate." **Articulation** refers to the relationship between an operating statement (the income statement or the statement of cash flows) and comparative balance sheets, whereby an item on the operating statement helps explain the change in an item on the balance sheet from one period to the next.

---

3 Beginning in 1997, the Celtics were no longer publicly traded.

exhibit 2-10   Statement of Cash Flows for the Boston Celtics

BOSTON CELTICS LIMITED PARTNERSHIP
Statement of Cash Flows
For the Year Ended June 30, 1996

CASH FLOWS FROM OPERATING ACTIVITIES

Receipts:

Basketball regular season receipts:		
Ticket sales	$31,323,249	
Television and radio broadcast rights fees	19,908,800	
Other (principally promotional advertising)	8,424,038	
Basketball playoff receipts	360,895	
		60,016,982

Outflows:

Basketball regular season expenditures:		
Team expenses	26,066,875	
Game expenses	2,481,007	
Basketball playoff expenses	0	
General and administrative expenses	13,996,805	
Selling and promotional expenses	1,333,238	
		43,877,925
		16,139,057
Interest income		9,553,938
Interest expense		(4,624,043)
Ticket refunds paid		(504)
Proceeds from league expansion		4,490,673
Payment of income taxes		(4,973,883)
Payment of deferred compensation		(5,226,095)
Other operating cash outflows		(2,931,742)
NET CASH FLOWS FROM OPERATING ACTIVITIES		12,427,401

CASH FLOWS FROM INVESTING ACTIVITIES

Purchases of investment securities	(171,422,268)	
Proceeds from sales of investment securities	156,655,561	
Net cash proceeds from the sale of Boston Celtics		
Broadcasting Limited Partnership	77,597,929	
Capital expenditures	(796,424)	
Other investing receipts	293,503	
NET CASH FLOWS FROM INVESTING ACTIVITIES		62,328,301

CASH FLOWS (USED BY) FINANCING ACTIVITIES

Repayment of bank borrowings	(80,000,000)	
Repurchase of Boston Celtics Limited Partnership		
shares from owners	(1,941,450)	
Cash distributions to owners	(26,395,139)	
NET CASH FLOWS (USED BY) FINANCING ACTIVITIES		(108,336,589)
NET (DECREASE) IN CASH		(33,580,887)
Cash at beginning of period		39,563,015
CASH AT END OF PERIOD		$ 5,982,128

Exhibit 2-11 shows how the financial statements tie together. Note that the beginning amount of cash from the 1998 balance sheet is added to the net increase or decrease in cash (from the statement of cash flows) to derive the cash balance as reported on the 1999 balance sheet. Similarly, the retained earnings balance as reported on the 1999 balance sheet comes from the beginning retained earnings balance (1998 balance sheet) plus net income for the period (from the income statement) less dividends paid. As you study financial statements, these relationships will become clearer and you will understand the concept of articulation better.

NOTES TO THE FINANCIAL STATEMENTS

The three primary financial statements contain a lot of information. Still, three summary reports cannot possibly tell financial statement users everything they want to know about a company. Additional information is given in the **notes to the financial statements**. In fact, in a typical annual report, the notes go on for 15 pages or more, whereas the primary financial statements fill only 3 pages. The notes tell about the assumptions and methods used in preparing the financial statements and also give more detail about specific items.

The financial statement notes are of the following four general types:

1. Summary of significant accounting policies.
2. Additional information about the summary totals found in the financial statements.
3. Disclosure of important information that is not recognized in the financial statements.
4. Supplementary information required by the Financial Accounting Standards Board (FASB) or the Securities and Exchange Commission (SEC).

Summary of Significant Accounting Policies

As mentioned earlier, accounting involves making assumptions, estimates, and judgments. In addition, in some settings, there is more than one acceptable method of accounting for certain

---

2

Recognize the need for financial statement notes and identify the types of information included in the notes.

notes to the financial statements Explanatory information considered an integral part of the financial statements.

---

exhibit 2-11   How the Financial Statements Tie Together

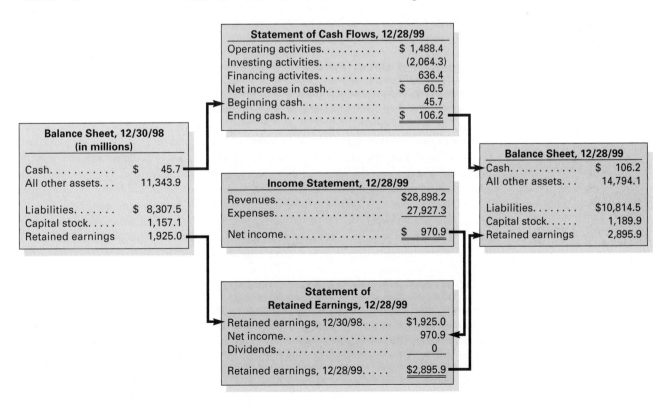

Statement of Cash Flows, 12/28/99

Operating activities..........	$ 1,488.4
Investing activities..........	(2,064.3)
Financing activites..........	636.4
Net increase in cash.........	$ 60.5
Beginning cash.............	45.7
Ending cash................	$ 106.2

Balance Sheet, 12/30/98 (in millions)

Cash..........	$ 45.7
All other assets...	11,343.9
Liabilities.......	$ 8,307.5
Capital stock.....	1,157.1
Retained earnings	1,925.0

Income Statement, 12/28/99

Revenues..................	$28,898.2
Expenses..................	27,927.3
Net income................	$ 970.9

Balance Sheet, 12/28/99

Cash...........	$ 106.2
All other assets...	14,794.1
Liabilities........	$10,814.5
Capital stock......	1,189.9
Retained earnings	2,895.9

Statement of Retained Earnings, 12/28/99

Retained earnings, 12/30/98.....	$1,925.0
Net income..................	970.9
Dividends..................	0
Retained earnings, 12/28/99.....	$2,895.9

b u s i n e s s   e n v i r o n m e n t   e s s a y

How to Get Your Own Copy of Microsoft's Financial Statements The complete Microsoft annual report containing the 1999 financial statements is reproduced at the end of this text. Is this secret information, available only to owners of this book? No. Anyone can get a copy of the most recent annual report of Microsoft or any other public corporation in the United States. Any of the following methods will work:

- Become an investor in Microsoft by buying shares of stock in the company. As a Microsoft investor, you are entitled to receive a copy of the annual report each year. In fact, according to U.S. government regulations, Microsoft is required to send a copy of the annual report to all of its investors within three months of the end of Microsoft's fiscal year on June 30.
- Call, write, fax, or e-mail Microsoft's Investor Relations department. The phone numbers and addresses are given in the Microsoft annual report re-

f y i

In its 1920 annual report, IBM included zero pages of notes (and the dollar amounts were carried out to the penny). In 1966, there were four pages of notes (and dollar amounts were rounded to the nearest dollar). In 1996, IBM's annual report included 26 pages of notes (and dollar amounts were rounded to the nearest million).

items. For example, there are a variety of acceptable ways of estimating how much a building depreciates (wears out) in a year. In order for financial statement users to be able to properly interpret the three primary financial statements, they must know what procedures were used in preparing those statements. This information about accounting policies and practices is given in the financial statement notes.

Additional Information about Summary Totals

For a large company, such as MICROSOFT or SAFEWAY, one summary number in the financial statements represents literally thousands of individual items. For example, the $5.922 billion in long-term notes and debentures included in Safeway's 1999 balance sheet (see Exhibit 2-3) represents loans of U.S. dollars, loans of Canadian dollars, mortgages, senior secured debentures, senior subordinated debentures, an unsecured bank credit agreement, and more. The balance sheet includes only one number, with the details in the notes.

Disclosure of Information Not Recognized

One way to report financial information is to boil down all the estimates and judgments into one number and then report that one number in the financial statements. This is called *recognition*. The key assumptions and estimates are then described in a note to the financial statements. Another approach is to skip the financial statements and just rely on the note to convey the information to users. This is called *disclosure*. Disclosure is the accepted way to convey information to users when the information is too uncertain to be recognized. For example, in July 1988, Safeway suffered a fire in one of its warehouses in Richmond, California. As of February 10, 2000, there were still 2,600 unsettled lawsuits against Safeway stemming from the fire. It is impossible to summarize the complexity of the potential outcome of these lawsuits in one financial statement number; so, Safeway describes the situation, in some detail, in the notes to the financial statements.

Supplementary Information

The FASB and SEC both require supplementary information that must be reported in the financial statement notes. For example, the FASB requires the disclosure of quarterly financial information and of business segment information. A sample of this type of disclosure can be seen in Microsoft's annual report in Appendix A. In the notes to its financial statements, Microsoft reports that 30% of its 1999 net income was generated outside of the United States.

produced at the back of this book. For promotional purposes, companies are happy to mail their annual report to anyone who asks.

- Download a copy of the annual report from Microsoft's Web site at microsoft.com. On the Web sites of most companies (Microsoft included), the annual report is not easy to find. You have to skirt past games, promotional material, and lots of nonfinancial information, but the annual report is usually there somewhere.

- Download a copy of the annual report (and lots of other information) from the U.S. government archives at sec.gov/edgarhp.htm. These government filings are pure text documents (no pictures) and are made available through the EDGAR (Electronic Data Gathering, Analysis, and Retrieval) system.

Now that you know how to get your own copy of the Microsoft annual report, make sure you study the rest of this book to learn how to use the report.

to summarize

The notes to the financial statements contain additional information not included in the financial statements themselves. The notes explain the company's accounting assumptions and practices, provide details of financial statement summary numbers and additional disclosure about complex events, and report supplementary information required by the SEC or the FASB.

3

Describe the purpose of an audit report and the incentives the auditor has to perform a good audit.

THE EXTERNAL AUDIT

Refer back to the opening scenario for this chapter. Following the November 1986 leveraged buyout by KOHLBERG, KRAVIS, ROBERTS & CO. (KKR), SAFEWAY decided to again issue shares to the public. In April 1990, Safeway issued shares at a price of $11.25 per share. The $11.25 price implied that the market value of KKR's initial investment had risen from $130 million to $731 million. The $11.25 price was determined by investment bankers and potential investors after examining the financial statements of Safeway. Now, consider the following questions:

- Who controlled the preparation of the Safeway financial statements used by investors in arriving at the $11.25 price? The owners and managers of Safeway, led by KKR.
- Did KKR have any incentive to bias the reported financial statement numbers? Absolutely. The better the numbers, the higher the stock offering price and the more money raised by KKR.
- Since KKR had control of the preparation of the financial statements and stood to benefit substantially if those statements looked overly favorable, how could the financial statements be trusted? Good question.

audit report A report issued by an independent CPA that expresses an opinion about whether the financial statements fairly present a company's financial position, operating results, and cash flows in accordance with generally accepted accounting principles.

This situation illustrates a general truth: the owners and managers of a company have an incentive to report the most favorable results possible. Poor reported financial performance can make it harder to get loans, can lower the amount that managers receive as salary bonuses, and can lower the stock price when shares are issued to the public. With these incentives to stretch the truth, the financial statements would not be reliable unless they were reviewed by an external party.

To provide this external review, a company's financial statements are often audited by an independent certified public accountant (CPA). A CPA firm issues an **audit report** that expresses an opinion about whether the statements fairly present a company's financial position, operating results, and cash flows in accordance with generally accepted accounting principles. Note that the financial statements are the responsibility of a company's management and not of the CPA. Although not all company records have to be audited, audits are needed for many purposes. For example, a banker may not make a loan without first receiving audited financial statements from a prospective borrower. As another example, most securities cannot be sold to the general public until they are registered with the SEC. Audited financial statements are required for this registration process.

Though an audit report does not guarantee accuracy, it does provide added assurance that the financial statements are not misleading since they have been examined by an independent professional. However, the CPA cannot examine every transaction upon which the summary figures in the financial statements are based. The accuracy of the statements must remain the responsibility of the company's management. An example of a typical audit report is found in Appendix A in Microsoft's 1999 annual report. Microsoft's financial statements were audited by DELOITTE & TOUCHE LLP, one of the large international audit firms.

One final question: Who hires and pays Deloitte & Touche to do the audit of Microsoft's financial statements? Microsoft does. At first glance, this situation appears to be similar to allowing students in an accounting class to choose and pay the graders of the examinations. However, two economic factors combine to allow us to trust the quality of the audit, even though the auditor was hired by the company being audited:

- *Reputation.* Deloitte & Touche, as one of the large accounting firms, has a reputation for doing high-quality audits (as do almost all independent auditors in the United States). It would be very reluctant to risk this reputation by signi ng off on a questionable set of financial statements.
- *Lawsuits.* Auditors are sued all the time, even when they conduct a perfect audit. Investors who lose money claim that they lost the money by relying on bogus financial statements that were certified by an external auditor. If even honest auditors get sued, then an auditor who intentionally approves a false set of financial statements is at great risk of losing a big lawsuit.

to summarize

An audit report is issued by an independent CPA firm attesting to the conformity of a set of financial statements with generally accepted accounting principles. CPA firms have an economic incentive to perform credible audits in order to preserve their reputations and to avoid lawsuits.

4

Use financial ratios to identify a company's strengths and weaknesses and to forecast its future performance.

financial statement analysis Examining both the relationships among financial statement amounts and the trends in those numbers over time.

FINANCIAL STATEMENT ANALYSIS

Financial statements are prepared so that they can be used. One important use is in analyzing a company's economic health. **Financial statement analysis** involves the examination of both the relationships among financial statement numbers and the trends in those numbers over time. One purpose of financial statement analysis is to use the past performance of a company to predict how it will do in the future. Another purpose of financial statement analysis is to evaluate the performance of a company with an eye toward identifying problem areas. Financial statement analysis is both diagnosis, identifying where a firm has problems, and prognosis, predicting how a firm will perform in the future.

Relationships between financial statement amounts are called **financial ratios**. For example, net income divided by sales is a financial ratio called "return on sales." Return on sales tells

financial ratios Ratios that show relationships between financial statement amounts.

you how many pennies of profit a company makes on each dollar of sales. The return on sales for MICROSOFT is 28.9%, meaning that Microsoft makes $0.289 worth of profit for every dollar of software sold. There are hundreds of different financial ratios, each shedding light on a different aspect of the health of a company. Some of the more common ratios are introduced in the following section. The numbers from the SAFEWAY balance sheet (Exhibit 2-3) and income statement (Exhibit 2-6) will be used to illustrate the ratio calculations.

Debt Ratio

debt ratio A measure of leverage, computed by dividing total liabilities by total assets.

Comparing the amount of liabilities to the amount of assets shows the extent to which a company has borrowed money to leverage the owners' investments and increase the size of the company. One frequently used measure of leverage is the **debt ratio**, computed as total liabilities divided by total assets. The debt ratio represents the proportion of borrowed funds used to acquire the company's assets. For Safeway, the 1999 debt ratio is computed as follows:

$$\text{Debt Ratio:} \frac{\text{Total Liabilities}}{\text{Total Assets}} = \frac{\$10,814.5}{\$14,900.3} = 72.6\%$$

In other words, Safeway borrowed 72.6% of the money it needed to buy its assets.

Is 72.6% a good debt ratio, a bad debt ratio, or is it impossible to tell? If you are a banker thinking of lending money to Safeway, you want Safeway to have a low debt ratio; a smaller amount of other liabilities increases your chances of being repaid. If you are a Safeway stockholder, you want a higher debt ratio; you want the company to add borrowed funds to your investment dollars to expand the business. There is some middle ground where the debt ratio is not too high for creditors, nor too low for investors. The general rule of thumb is that debt ratios should be around 50%. However, this general benchmark varies widely from one industry to the next. The 72.6% debt ratio for Safeway is not unusual for a supermarket chain.

Current Ratio

current (working capital) ratio A measure of the liquidity of a business; equal to current assets divided by current liabilities.

An important concern about any company is its *liquidity*. If a firm cannot meet its short-term obligations, it may not live to enjoy the long run. The most commonly used measure of liquidity is the **current** (or **working capital**) **ratio**, a comparison of the current assets (cash, receivables, and inventory) to the current liabilities. The current ratio is computed by dividing total current assets by total current liabilities. For Safeway, the 1999 current ratio is computed as follows:

$$\text{Current Ratio:} \frac{\text{Current Assets}}{\text{Current Liabilities}} = \frac{\$3,052.1}{\$3,582.6} = 0.852$$

Historically, a current ratio below 2.0 suggests the possibility of liquidity problems. However, advances in information technology have enabled companies to be much more effective in minimizing the need to hold cash, inventories, and other current assets. As a result, current ratios for successful companies are frequently less than 1.0. The 0.852 current ratio for Safeway is similar to that for other supermarket chains.

Minimum current ratio requirements are frequently included in loan agreements. A typical agreement might state that if the current ratio falls below a certain level, the lender can declare the loan in default and require immediate repayment. This type of minimum current ratio restriction forces the borrower to maintain its liquidity and gives the lender increased assurance that the loan will be repaid.

Asset Turnover

asset turnover A measure of company efficiency, computed by dividing sales by total assets.

The balance sheet of Safeway reveals total assets of $14,900.3 million at December 28, 1999. Are those assets being used efficiently? The **asset turnover** ratio gives an overall measure of company efficiency and is computed as follows:

$$\text{Asset Turnover:} \frac{\text{Sales}}{\text{Total Assets}} = \frac{\$28,859.9}{\$14,900.3} = 1.94$$

Safeway's 1999 asset turnover ratio of 1.94 means that for each dollar of assets, Safeway is able to generate $1.94 in sales. The higher the asset turnover ratio, the more efficient the company is at using its assets to generate sales.

Return on Sales

return on sales A measure of the amount of profit earned per dollar of sales, computed by dividing net income by sales.

As mentioned at the beginning of this section, Microsoft makes 28.9 cents of profit on each dollar of sales. This ratio is called **return on sales** and (using Safeway's 1999 numbers) is computed as follows:

$$\text{Return on Sales: } \frac{\text{Net Income}}{\text{Sales}} = \frac{\$970.9}{\$28,859.9} = 3.36\%$$

Clearly, the return on sales for Safeway of 3.36 cents per dollar is dramatically below that for Microsoft. As with all ratios, however, the return on sales value for Safeway must be evaluated within the appropriate industry. Return on sales in the supermarket industry is frequently between 1% and 2%; so, the Safeway value is very good indeed. In addition, Safeway's 1999 return on sales of 3.36% represents a small improvement over its 1998 return on sales of 3.29%.

Return on Equity

return on equity A measure of the amount of profit earned per dollar of investment, computed by dividing net income by equity.

What investors really want to know is how much profit they earn for each dollar they invest. This amount, called the **return on equity**, is the overall measure of the performance of a company. Return on equity for Safeway for 1999 is computed as follows:

$$\text{Return on Equity: } \frac{\text{Net Income}}{\text{Owners' Equity}} = \frac{\$970.9}{\$4,085.8} = 23.8\%$$

Safeway's return on equity of 23.8% means that 23.8 cents of profit was earned for each dollar of stockholder investment in 1999. If your intuition tells you that this seems high, you are right. Good companies typically have return on equity values between 15% and 25%. Safeway had a good year in 1999.

Price-Earnings Ratio

price-earnings (PE) ratio A measure of growth potential, earnings stability, and management capabilities; computed by dividing market price per share by earnings per share.

If a company earned $100 this year, how much should you pay to buy that company? If you expect the company to make more in the future, you would be willing to pay a higher price than if you expected the company to make less. Also, you would probably be willing to pay a bit more for a stable company than for one experiencing wild swings in earnings. The **price-earnings (PE) ratio** measures the relationship between the market value of a company and that company's current earnings. This ratio is computed by dividing the market price per share of stock by the earnings per share. Safeway's PE ratio at the end of 1999 was:

$$\text{PE Ratio: } \frac{\text{Market Price per Share}}{\text{Earnings per Share}} = \frac{\$35.75}{\$1.95} = 18.33$$

In the United States, PE ratios typically range between 5 and 30. High PE ratios are associated with firms for which strong growth is predicted in the future. Refer back to Exhibits 2-4 and 2-5 and notice that **CISCO SYSTEMS** and **ORACLE** are included in the list of companies with the highest market values but are not among those with high net incomes. The reason Cisco Systems and Oracle are valued so highly is that they are expected to continue to grow rapidly; their current incomes are small compared to what investors are expecting in the future. This expected future growth is reflected in the PE ratios for these companies, which, on August 9, 2000, were 123.6 for Cisco Systems and 39.5 for Oracle.

A summary of the financial ratios discussed in this section is presented in Exhibit 2-12. The values of financial ratios are most meaningful when they are compared with similar values for other companies. A comparison of ratio values for several large U.S. corporations is presented in Exhibit 2-13.

exhibit 2-12   Summary of Selected Financial Ratios

1. Debt ratio	$\dfrac{\text{Total liabilities}}{\text{Total assets}}$	Proportion of borrowed funds used to purchase assets.
2. Current ratio	$\dfrac{\text{Current assets}}{\text{Current liabilities}}$	Measure of liquidity; number of times current assets could cover current liabilities.
3. Asset turnover	$\dfrac{\text{Sales}}{\text{Total assets}}$	Number of dollars of sales generated by each dollar of assets.
4. Return on sales	$\dfrac{\text{Net income}}{\text{Sales}}$	Number of cents earned on each dollar of sales.
5. Return on equity	$\dfrac{\text{Net income}}{\text{Owners' equity}}$	Number of cents earned on each dollar invested.
6. Price-earnings ratio	$\dfrac{\text{Market price per share}}{\text{Earnings per share}}$	Amount investors are willing to pay for each dollar of earnings; indication of growth potential.

exhibit 2-13   Selected Ratios for Several Large U.S. Corporations for 1999

	Debt Ratio	Current Ratio	Asset Turnover	Return on Sales	Return on Equity	Price–Earnings Ratio
Microsoft	0.23	2.32	0.53	0.39	0.28	66.82
Cisco Systems	0.2	1.54	0.83	0.27	0.29	208.95
General Electric	0.92	1.09	0.15	0.12	0.27	48.33
Intel	0.26	2.51	0.67	0.25	0.22	62.53
ExxonMobil	0.56	0.8	1.26	0.043	0.125	34.67

to summarize

This overview of financial ratios is intended to emphasize that the preparation of the financial statements by the accountant is not the end of the process, but just the beginning. Those financial statements are then analyzed by investors, creditors, and management to detect signs of existing deficiencies in performance and to predict how the firm will perform in the future. Proper interpretation of a ratio depends on comparing a firm's ratio value to the value for the same firm in the previous year, as well as to values for other firms in the same industry.

FUNDAMENTAL CONCEPTS AND ASSUMPTIONS

5

Explain the fundamental concepts and assumptions that underlie financial accounting.

Certain fundamental concepts and assumptions underlie financial accounting practice and the resulting financial statements. These ideas are so fundamental to any economic activity that they usually are taken for granted in conducting business. Nevertheless, it is important to be aware of them because these assumptions, together with certain basic concepts and procedures, determine the rules and set the boundaries of accounting practice. They indicate which events will be accounted for and in what manner. In total, they provide the essential characteristics of the traditional **accounting model**.

accounting model The basic accounting assumptions, concepts, principles, and procedures that determine the manner of recording, measuring, and reporting a company's transactions.

This section will describe the separate entity concept, the assumption of arm's-length transactions, the cost principle, the monetary measurement concept, and the going concern assumption. The concept of double-entry accounting was already introduced on page 34 as the basis for the accounting equation. As noted, this concept will be explained in much more detail in Chapter 3. Additional concepts and assumptions will be covered in later chapters. Remember that accounting is the language of business, and it takes time to learn a new language. The terms and concepts we introduce here will become much more familiar as your study continues.

The Separate Entity Concept

entity An organizational unit (a person, partnership, or corporation) for which accounting records are kept and about which accounting reports are prepared.

Because business involves the exchange of goods or services between entities, it follows that accounting records should be kept for those entities. For accounting purposes, an **entity** is defined as the organizational unit for which accounting records are maintained—for example, IBM CORPORATION. It is a focal point for identifying, measuring, and communicating accounting data. Furthermore, the entity is considered to be *separate* from its individual owners.

separate entity concept The idea that the activities of an entity are to be separated from those of the individual owners.

We are all engaged in a variety of economic activities. For example, John Scott works for a large corporation, owns some real estate, is president of the local Little League baseball organization, and manages the family estate on behalf of his brothers and sister. The **separate entity concept** is the idea that, when John Scott is called upon to report the financial activities of the local Little League, he must make sure not to include any of his personal or family financial activities in the results. Similarly, the accounting records of a small business must be kept separate from the personal finances of the owner.

Applying the separate entity concept to large corporations can also be difficult. Large corporations, such as GENERAL ELECTRIC and IBM, own networks of subsidiaries (and those subsidiaries own subsidiaries) with complex business ties among the members of the group. A key part of the accounting process for such an organization is carefully defining what is part of General Electric and what is not. For example, one difficult accounting issue (covered in advanced accounting courses) is deciding how much of another company General Electric must own (20%? 45%? 51%? 100%?) before that other company is considered part of the General Electric reporting entity.

The Assumption of Arm's-Length Transactions

transactions Exchange of goods or services between entities (whether individuals, businesses, or other organizations), as well as other events having an economic impact on a business.

Accounting is based on the recording of economic transactions. Viewed broadly, **transactions** include not only exchanges of economic resources between separate entities, but also events that have an economic impact on a business independently. The borrowing and lending of money and the sale and purchase of goods or services are examples of the former. The loss in value of equipment due to obsolescence or fire is an example of the latter. Collectively, transactions provide the data that are included in accounting records and reports.

arm's-length transactions Business dealings between independent and rational parties who are looking out for their own interests.

Accounting for economic transactions enables us to measure the success of an entity. However, the data for a transaction will not accurately represent that transaction if any bias is involved. Therefore, unless there is evidence to the contrary, accountants assume **arm's-length transactions**. That is, they make the assumption that both parties—for example, a buyer and a seller—are rational and free to act independently; each trying to make the best deal possible in establishing the terms of the transaction.

To illustrate, assume you are preparing a personal balance sheet and want to list the value of your minivan. You bought the three-year-old minivan for $5,000. Of course, you should list

historical cost The dollar amount originally exchanged in an arm's-length transaction; an amount assumed to reflect the fair market value of an item at the transaction date.

cost principle The idea that transactions are recorded at their historical costs or exchange prices at the transaction date.

> **c a u t i o n**
>
> When reading accounting reports, remember that many reported values are historical costs, reflecting exchange prices at various transaction dates.

monetary measurement The idea that money, as the common medium of exchange, is the accounting unit of measurement, and that only economic activities measurable in monetary terms are included in the accounting model.

the minivan on your balance sheet at the $5,000 price you paid for it. That should be a good reflection of the value of the vehicle. But, what if you bought the minivan from your brother (who gave you a good deal) and the real market value of the minivan is $11,000? The problem here is that the $5,000 price negotiated between you and your brother is not a market price. Market prices can be thought of as prices negotiated between two strangers who are both competing to get the best deal possible. Thus, a necessary assumption for financial statements to be informative is that the reported financial results come from arm's-length transactions. Without this assumption, the numbers in the financial statements (like the $5,000 for the minivan you bought from your brother) do not reflect true values.

An illustration of the accounting problems that can arise from the lack of arm's-length transactions is provided by the labor problems of major league baseball. The team owners and the players are always arguing about the profitability of the teams. The players do not believe the numbers in the owners' financial statements; many important transactions reported are between the baseball teams and other businesses controlled by the owners, such as television stations.

Since the revenues received in these deals (between the baseball teams and related businesses) are not from arm's-length transactions, the players question whether the full value of the deals is reflected in the owners' financial reports.

The Cost Principle

To further ensure objective measurements, accountants record transactions at **historical cost**, the amount originally paid or received for goods and services in arm's-length transactions. The historical cost is assumed to represent the fair market value of the item at the date of the transaction because it reflects the actual use of resources by independent parties. In accounting, this convention of recording transactions at cost is often referred to as the **cost principle**.

The Monetary Measurement Concept

Accountants do not record all the activities of economic entities. They record only those that can be measured in monetary terms. Thus, the concept of **monetary measurement** becomes another important characteristic of the accounting model. For example, employee morale cannot be measured directly in monetary terms and is not reported in the accounting records. Wages

Major league baseball salary disputes are frequently in the news. The lack of arm's-length transactions may contribute to some of the friction between players and owners.

paid or owed, however, are quantifiable in terms of money and are reported. In accounting, all transactions are recorded in monetary amounts, whether or not cash is involved. In the United States, the dollar is the unit of exchange and is thus the measuring unit for accounting purposes.

As noted earlier in discussing the limitations of a balance sheet, the listed values may not be the same as actual market values for two reasons. The first is due to the cost principle. Because of such factors as inflation (an increase in the general price level of goods and services), the recorded amount of an item may be quite different from the amount required at a later time to buy or replace the item. The second reason results from the monetary measurement concept. Not all economic assets are recorded, because they are too difficult or impossible to measure in monetary amounts.

The Going Concern Assumption

going concern assumption
The idea that an accounting entity will have a continuing existence for the foreseeable future.

The SAFEWAY balance sheet in Exhibit 2-3 was prepared under the assumption that Safeway would continue in business for the foreseeable future. This is called the **going concern assumption**. Without this assumption, preparation of the balance sheet would be much more difficult. For example, the $2.4 billion inventory for Safeway in 1999 is reported at the cost originally paid to purchase the inventory. This is a reasonable figure because, in the normal course of business, Safeway can expect to sell the inventory for this amount, plus some profit. But if it were assumed that Safeway would go out of business tomorrow, the inventory would suddenly be worth a lot less. Imagine the low prices you could get on Safeway merchandise if it had to conduct a one-day, going-out-of-business sale! The going concern assumption allows the accountant to record assets at what they are worth to a company in normal use, rather than what they would sell for in a liquidation sale.

to summarize

In conducting economic activities, entities enter into transactions that form the basis of accounting records. An accounting model has been developed for recording, measuring, and reporting an entity's transactions. This model is founded on certain fundamental concepts and several important assumptions, principles, and procedures. First, the organizational unit being accounted for is a separate entity. The entity may be small or large, but it is the organizational unit for which accounting records are kept and financial reports prepared. Second, the transactions are assumed to be arm's-length. Third, transactions are recorded at historical cost. Fourth, transactions must be measurable in monetary amounts. Fifth, the accounting entity is assumed to be a going concern.

review of learning objectives

1 Understand the basic elements and formats of the three primary financial statements—balance sheet, income statement, and statement of cash flows. The balance sheet provides a summary of the financial position of a company at a particular date. It lists a company's assets, liabilities, and owners' equity. Assets and liabilities are usually classified as either current or long-term. For a corporation, owners' equity consists of directly invested funds as well as retained earnings.

The income statement shows the major sources of revenues generated and the expenses associated with those revenues. The difference between revenues and expenses is net income or net loss. The income statements of corporations must also include earnings per share.

The statement of cash flows shows the significant cash inflows (receipts) and cash outflows (payments) of a company for a period of time. These cash flows are classified according to operating, investing, and financing activities.

2 Recognize the need for financial statement notes and identify the types of information included in the notes. The notes to the financial statements contain additional information not included in the financial statements themselves. The notes explain the company's accounting assumptions and practices, provide details of financial statement summary numbers and additional disclosure about complex events, and report supplementary information required by the SEC and the FASB.

3 Describe the purpose of an audit report and the incentives the auditor has to perform a good audit. An audit report is issued by an independent CPA firm attesting to the conformity of a set of financial statements with generally accepted accounting principles. CPA firms have an economic incentive to perform credible audits in order to preserve their reputations and to avoid lawsuits.

4 Use financial ratios to identify a company's strengths and weaknesses and to forecast its future performance. Financial statements are analyzed by investors, creditors, and management to detect signs of existing deficiencies in performance and to predict how the firm will perform in the future. Proper interpretation of a financial ratio depends on comparing a firm's ratio value to the value for the same firm in the previous year, as well as to values for other firms in the same industry.

5 Explain the fundamental concepts and assumptions that underlie financial accounting. Certain fundamental concepts underlie the practice of accounting. First, a business must be accounted for as an economic entity separate from the personal affairs of the owners and separate from other businesses. Second, the transactions are assumed to be arm's-length, so that the negotiated prices reflect true market values at the dates of the transactions. Third, transactions are recorded at historical cost. Fourth, only those transactions and events that can be measured in monetary terms are reported. Fifth, the accounting entity is assumed to be a going concern.

key terms and concepts

accounting equation 34

accounting model 54

arm's-length transactions 54

articulation 45

asset turnover 51

assets 33

audit report 49

balance sheet (statement of financial position) 32

book value 37

capital stock 34

classified balance sheet 37

comparative financial statements 37

comprehensive income 42

cost principle 55

current assets 37

current (or working capital) ratio 51

debt ratio 51

dividends 34

double-entry accounting 34

earnings (loss) per share (EPS) 42

entity 54

expenses 40

financial ratios 50

financial statement analysis 50

financing activities 44

gains (losses) 41

going concern assumption 56

gross profit (gross margin) 40

historical cost 55

income statement (statement of earnings) 32

investing activities 44

liabilities 33

liquidity 37

long-term assets 37

market value 37

monetary measurement 55

net assets 33

net income (net loss) 40

notes to the financial statements 47

operating activities 44

owners' equity 33

price-earnings (PE) ratio 52

primary financial statements 32

retained earnings 34

return on equity 52

return on sales 52

revenue 40

separate entity concept 54

statement of cash flows 32

statement of retained earnings 42

stockholders (shareholders) 33

stockholders' equity 33

transactions 54

review problem

The Income Statement and the Balance Sheet

Shirley Baum manages The Copy Shop. She has come to you for help in preparing an income statement and a balance sheet for the year ended December 31, 2003. Several amounts, determined as of December 31, 2003, are presented below. No dividends were paid this year.

Capital stock (10,000 shares outstanding)	$ 40,000		Mortgage payable	$72,000
Retained earnings (12/31/02)	12,400		Accounts payable	6,000
Advertising expense	2,000		Land	24,000
Cash	17,000		Supplies	2,000
Rent expense	2,400		Salary expense	20,000
Building (net)	100,000		Revenues	42,000
Interest expense	700		Other expenses	1,300
			Accounts receivable	3,000

Required

1. Prepare an income statement for the year ended December 31, 2003, including EPS.
2. Determine the amount of retained earnings at December 31, 2003.
3. Prepare a classified balance sheet as of December 31, 2003.
4. Calculate the current ratio for The Copy Shop. What does the current ratio tell you about the company?

Solution

1. Income Statement
The first step in solving this problem is to separate the balance sheet items from the income statement items. Asset, liability, and owners' equity items reflect the company's financial position and appear on the balance sheet; revenues and expenses are reported on the income statement.

Balance Sheet Items	Income Statement Items
Capital stock	Advertising expense
Retained earnings	Rent expense
Cash	Interest expense
Building (net)	Salary expense
Mortgage payable	Revenues
Accounts payable	Other expenses
Land	
Supplies	
Accounts receivable	

After the items have been separated, the income statement and the balance sheet may be prepared using a proper format.

The Copy Shop
Income Statement
For the Year Ended December 31, 2003

Revenues		$42,000
Expenses:		
Advertising expense	$2,000	
Rent expense	2,400	
Interest expense	700	
Salary expense	20,000	
Other expenses	1,300	26,400
Net income		$15,600
EPS = $15,600 ÷ 10,000 shares = $1.56		

2. Retained Earnings

The amount of Retained Earnings at December 31, 2003, may be calculated as follows:

Retained earnings (12/31/02)	$12,400
Add: Net income for year	15,600
Subtract: Dividends for year	(0)
Retained earnings (12/31/03)	$28,000

Since no dividends were paid during 2003, the ending balance in Retained Earnings is simply the beginning balance plus net income for the year.

3. Balance Sheet

The Copy Shop
Balance Sheet
December 31, 2003

Assets			**Liabilities and Owners' Equity**		
Current assets:			**Current liabilities:**		
Cash	$ 17,000		Accounts payable. . .	$ 6,000	
Accounts receivable. .	3,000				
Supplies	2,000	$ 22,000	**Long-term liabilities:**		
			Mortgage payable . .	72,000	
Long-term assets:			Total liabilities.		$ 78,000
Land	$ 24,000				
Building (net).	100,000	124,000	**Owners' equity:**		
			Capital stock	$40,000	
			Retained earnings . .	28,000*	68,000
			Total liabilities and		
Total assets		$146,000	owners' equity		$146,000

*See item 2 for calculation.

4. Current Ratio

CR = Current Assets/Current Liabilities
CR = $22,000/$6,000 = 3.67

The current ratio shows the relationship of total current assets to total current liabilities. It indicates whether a company can pay its current obligations with its current assets and therefore helps short-term creditors assess a company's liquidity. The amount of The Copy Shop's current assets is almost four times its current liabilities (3.67:1). In other words, The Copy Shop has $3.67 of current assets for every $1 of current liabilities, which shows a favorable liquidity position.

discussion questions

1. As an external user of financial statements, perhaps an investor or creditor, what type of accounting information do you need?

2. What is the major purpose of:
   a. A balance sheet?
   b. An income statement?
   c. A statement of cash flows?

3. Assume you want to invest in the stock market, and your friends tell you about a company's stock that is "guaranteed" to have an annual growth rate of 150 percent. Should you trust your friends and invest immediately, or should you research the company's financial statements before investing? Explain.

4. Why are classified and comparative financial statements generally presented in annual reports to shareholders?

5. Why are owners' equity and liabilities considered the "sources" of assets?

6. Owners' equity is not cash; it is not a liability; and it generally is not equal to the current worth of a business. What is the nature of owners' equity?

7. What are the limitations of the balance sheet? Why is it important to be aware of them when evaluating a company's growth potential?

8. Some people feel that the income statement is more important than the balance sheet. Do you agree? Why or why not?

9. How might an investor be misled by looking only at the "bottom line" (the net income or EPS number) on an income statement?

10. Why is it important to classify cash flows according to operating, investing, and financing activities?

11. You are thinking of investing in one of two companies. In one annual report, the auditor's opinion states that the financial statements were prepared in accordance with generally accepted accounting principles. The other makes no such claim. How important is that to you? Explain.

12. Some people think that auditors are responsible for ensuring the accuracy of financial statements. Are they correct? Why or why not?

13. What are the four general types of financial statement notes typically included in annual reports to stockholders?

14. What are the primary purposes of financial statement analysis?

15. Indicate how each of the following financial ratios is computed and describe what the ratio is attempting to explain:
    a. Debt ratio
    b. Current ratio
    c. Asset turnover
    d. Return on sales
    e. Return on equity
    f. Price-earnings ratio

16. Explain why each of the following is important in accounting:
    a. The separate entity concept
    b. The assumption of arm's-length transactions
    c. The cost principle
    d. The monetary measurement concept
    e. The going concern assumption

discussion cases

CASE 2-1

CREDITOR AND INVESTOR INFORMATION NEEDS

Ink Spot is a small company that has been in business for two years. Wilford Smith, the president of the company, has decided that it is time to expand. He needs $10,000 to purchase additional equipment and to pay for increased operating expenses. Wilford can either apply for a loan at First City Bank, or he can issue more stock (1,000 shares are outstanding) to new investors. Assuming that you are the loan officer at First City Bank, what information would you request from Ink Spot before deciding whether to make the loan? As a potential investor in Ink Spot, what information would you need to make a good investment decision? What financial ratios might you consider as a potential lender or investor before making a decision?

CASE 2-2

ANALYZING TRENDS AND KEY FINANCIAL RELATIONSHIPS

An investor may choose from several investment opportunities: the stocks of different companies; rental property or other real estate; or savings accounts, money market certificates, and similar financial instruments. When considering an investment in the stock of a particular company, comparative financial data presented in the annual report to stockholders helps an investor identify key relationships and trends. As an illustration, comparative operating results for Prime Properties, Inc., from its 2003 annual report are provided. (Dollars are presented in thousands except for earnings per share.)

	Year Ended December 31		
	2003	**2002**	**2001**
Revenues:			
Property management fees	$ 58,742	$ 63,902	$ 66,204
Appraisal fees	55,641	60,945	62,320
Total revenues	$114,383	$124,847	$128,524
Expenses:			
Selling and advertising	$ 64,371	$ 75,403	$ 80,478
Administrative expenses	30,671	31,115	31,618
Other expenses	9,265	9,540	9,446
Interest expense	2,047	1,468	26
Total expenses	$106,354	$117,526	$121,568
Income before taxes	$ 8,029	$ 7,321	$ 6,956
Income taxes	2,409	2,196	2,087
Net income	$ 5,620	$ 5,125	$ 4,869
*Earnings per share	$2.25	$2.05	$1.95

*2.5 million shares outstanding

What trends are indicated by the comparative income statement data for Prime Properties, Inc.? Which of these trends would be of concern to a potential investor? What additional information would an investor need in order to make a decision about whether to invest in this company?

CASE 2-3

ACCOUNTING FOR THE PROPER ENTITY
You have been hired to prepare the financial reports for White River Building Supply, a proprietorship owned by Bill Masters. Upon encountering several payments made from the company bank account to a nearby university, you contact Bill Masters to find out how to classify these payments. Masters explains that those checks were written to pay his daughter's tuition and to purchase her textbooks and miscellaneous supplies. He then tells you to include the payments with other expenses of the business. "This way," he explains, "I can deduct the payments on my tax return. Why not, since it all comes out of the same pocket?" How would you respond to Masters?

exercises

EXERCISE 2-1

CLASSIFICATION OF FINANCIAL STATEMENT ELEMENTS
Indicate for each of the following items whether it would appear on a balance sheet (BS) or an income statement (IS). If a balance sheet item, is it an asset (A), a liability (L), or an owners' equity item (OE)?

1. Accounts Payable
2. Sales Revenue
3. Accounts Receivable
4. Advertising Expense
5. Cash
6. Supplies
7. Consulting Revenue
8. Land
9. Capital Stock
10. Rent Expense
11. Equipment
12. Interest Receivable
13. Mortgage Payable
14. Notes Payable
15. Buildings
16. Salaries & Wages Expense
17. Retained Earnings
18. Utilities Expense

EXERCISE 2-2

ACCOUNTING EQUATION

Compute the missing amounts for companies A, B, and C.

	A	B	C
Cash	$25,000	$ 9,000	$12,000
Accounts receivable	20,000	15,000	7,000
Land and buildings	50,000	?	40,000
Accounts payable	?	6,000	14,000
Mortgage payable	30,000	10,000	15,000
Owners' equity	55,000	30,000	?

EXERCISE 2-3

Spread-Sheet Software

COMPREHENSIVE ACCOUNTING EQUATION

Assuming no additional investments by or distributions to owners, compute the missing amounts for companies X, Y, and Z.

	X	Y	Z
Assets: January 1, 2003	$360	$?	$230
Liabilities: January 1, 2003	280	460	?
Owners' equity: January 1, 2003	?	620	150
Assets: December 31, 2003	380	?	310
Liabilities: December 31, 2003	?	520	90
Owners' equity: December 31, 2003	?	720	?
Revenues in 2003	80	?	400
Expenses in 2003	100	116	?

EXERCISE 2-4

COMPUTING ELEMENTS OF OWNERS' EQUITY

From the information provided, determine:
1. The amount of retained earnings at December 31.
2. The amount of revenues for the period.

Totals	January 1	December 31
Current assets	$ 5,000	$ 10,000
All other assets	150,000	160,000
Liabilities	25,000	30,000
Capital stock	50,000	?
Retained earnings	80,000	?

Additional data:
Expenses for the period were $35,000.
Dividends paid were $7,500.
Capital stock increased by $5,000 during the period.

EXERCISE 2-5

BALANCE SHEET RELATIONSHIPS

Correct the following balance sheet.

Canfield Corporation
Balance Sheet
December 31, 2003

Assets		Liabilities and Owners' Equity	
Cash	$ 55,000	Buildings	$325,000
Accounts payable	65,000	Accounts receivable	75,000
Interest receivable	20,000	Mortgage payable	150,000
Capital stock	200,000	Sales revenue	350,000
Rent expense	60,000	Equipment	85,000
Retained earnings	145,000	Utilities expense	5,000
		Total liabilities and	
Total assets	$545,000	owners' equity	$990,000

EXERCISE 2-6

Spread-Sheet Software

BALANCE SHEET PREPARATION

From the following data, prepare a classified balance sheet for Low Price Company at December 31, 2003.

Accounts payable	$ 46,500
Accounts receivable	99,000
Buildings	325,500
Owners' equity, 1/1/03	150,000
Cash	116,250
Distributions to owners during 2003	18,750
Supplies	2,250
Land	165,000
Mortgage payable	412,500
Net income for 2003	117,750
Owners' equity, 12/31/03	?

EXERCISE 2-7

INCOME STATEMENT COMPUTATIONS

Following are the operating data for an advertising firm for the year ended December 31, 2003.

Revenues	$175,000
Supplies expense	45,000
Salaries expense	70,000
Rent expense	1,500
Administrative expense	6,000
Income taxes (30% of income before taxes)	?

For 2003, determine:
1. Income before taxes.
2. Income taxes.
3. Net income.
4. Earnings per share (EPS), assuming there are 15,000 shares of stock outstanding.

EXERCISE 2-8

INCOME STATEMENT PREPARATION

The following selected information is taken from the records of Sel Tec Corporation.

Accounts payable	$ 25,000
Accounts receivable	49,000
Advertising expense	7,500
Cash	15,500
Supplies expense	23,000

(continued)

Rent expense	$ 5,000
Utilities expense	1,500
Income taxes (30% of income before taxes)	?
Miscellaneous expense	2,200
Owners' equity	125,000
Salaries expense	88,000
Fees (revenues)	242,000

1. Prepare an income statement for the year ended December 31, 2003. (Assume that 5,000 shares of stock are outstanding.)
2. Explain what the EPS ratio tells the reader about Sel Tec Corporation.

EXERCISE 2-9

CASH FLOW COMPUTATIONS

From the following selected data, compute:

1. Net cash flow provided (used) by operating activities.
2. Net cash flow provided (used) by investing activities.
3. Net cash flow provided (used) by financing activities.
4. Net increase (decrease) in cash during the year.
5. The cash balance at the end of the year.

Cash receipts from:	
Customers	$270,000
Investments by owners	54,000
Sale of building	90,000
Proceeds from bank loan	60,000
Cash payments for:	
Wages	$ 82,000
Utilities	3,000
Advertising	4,000
Rent	36,000
Taxes	67,000
Dividends	20,000
Repayment of principal on loan	40,000
Purchase of land	106,000
Cash balance at beginning of year	$386,000

EXERCISE 2-10

INCOME AND RETAINED EARNINGS RELATIONSHIPS

Assume that retained earnings increased by $240,000 from December 31, 2002, to December 31, 2003, for Miller Corporation. During the year, a cash dividend of $140,000 was paid.

1. Compute the net income for the year.
2. Assume that the revenues for the year were $920,000. Compute the expenses incurred for the year.

EXERCISE 2-11

RETAINED EARNINGS COMPUTATIONS

During 2003, Safe Lite Corporation had revenues of $180,000 and expenses, including income taxes, of $100,000. On December 31, 2002, Safe Lite had assets of $400,000, liabilities of $100,000, and capital stock of $250,000. Safe Lite paid a cash dividend of $40,000 in 2003. No additional stock was issued. Compute the retained earnings on December 31, 2002, and 2003.

EXERCISE 2-12

PREPARATION OF INCOME STATEMENT AND RETAINED EARNINGS STATEMENT

Prepare an income statement and a statement of retained earnings for Big Sky Corporation for the year ended June 30, 2003, based on the following information:

Capital stock (1,500 shares @ $100).		$150,000
Retained earnings, July 1, 2002		76,800
Dividends		6,500
Ski rental revenue		77,900
Expenses:		
Rent expense	$ 6,000	
Salaries expense	38,600	
Utilities expense.	2,400	
Advertising expense.	7,500	
Miscellaneous expense.	7,700	
Income taxes	2,100	64,300

EXERCISE 2-13

ARTICULATION: RELATIONSHIPS BETWEEN A BALANCE SHEET AND AN INCOME STATEMENT

The total assets and liabilities of Roloflex Company at January 1 and December 31, 2003, are presented below.

	January 1	December 31
Assets	$76,000	$112,000
Liabilities	26,000	28,800

Determine the amount of net income or loss for 2003, applying each of the following assumptions concerning the additional issuance of stock and dividends paid by the firm. Each case is independent of the others.

1. Dividends of $10,800 were paid and no additional stock was issued during the year.
2. Additional stock of $4,800 was issued and no dividends were paid during the year.
3. Additional stock of $62,000 was issued and dividends of $15,600 were paid during the year.

EXERCISE 2-14

CASH FLOW CLASSIFICATIONS

For each of the following items, indicate whether it would be classified and reported under the Operating Activities (OA), Investing Activities (IA), or Financing Activities (FA) section of a statement of cash flows:

a. Cash receipts from selling merchandise
b. Cash payments for wages and salaries
c. Cash proceeds from sale of stock
d. Cash purchase of equipment
e. Cash dividends paid
f. Cash received from bank loan
g. Cash payments for inventory
h. Cash receipts from services rendered
i. Cash payments for taxes
j. Cash proceeds from sale of property no longer needed as expansion site

EXERCISE 2-15

CURRENT RATIO

Using the data in Exercise 2-6, compute the current ratio for Low Price Company. What does the current ratio show?

EXERCISE 2-16

DEBT RATIO

Using the data in Exercise 2-6, compute the debt ratio for Low Price Company. What does the debt ratio explain?

EXERCISE 2-17

RETURN ON EQUITY AND PRICE-EARNINGS RATIO

Using the data in Exercise 2-6, and assuming 20,000 shares of stock outstanding and a market price per share of $36.00, compute the return on equity and PE ratios for Low Price Company. Does the PE ratio seem reasonable relative to other U.S. stocks?

EXERCISE 2-18

NOTES TO FINANCIAL STATEMENTS

Refer to **MICROSOFT**'s annual report in Appendix A at the end of the book. How important are the notes to financial statements? What are the major types of notes that Microsoft includes in its annual report?

EXERCISE 2-19

THE COST PRINCIPLE

On January 1, 2003, Save-More Construction Company paid $150,000 in cash for a parcel of land to be used as the site of a new office building. During March, the company petitioned the city council to rezone the area for professional office buildings. The city council refused, preferring to maintain the area as a residential zone. After nine months of negotiation, Save-More Construction convinced the council to rezone the property for commercial use, thus raising its value to $200,000.

For accounting purposes, what value should be used to record the transaction on January 1, 2003? At what value would the property be reported at year-end, after the city council rezoning? Explain why accountants use historical costs to record transactions.

EXERCISE 2-20

THE MONETARY MEASUREMENT CONCEPT

Many successful companies, such as **FORD MOTOR COMPANY**, **EXXONMOBIL**, and **MARRIOTT CORPORATION**, readily acknowledge the importance and value of their employees. In fact, the employees of a company are often viewed as the most valued asset of the company. Yet in the asset section of the balance sheets of these companies there is no mention of the asset Employees. What is the reason for this oversight and apparent inconsistency?

EXERCISE 2-21

THE GOING CONCERN ASSUMPTION

Assume that you open an auto repair business. You purchase a building and buy new equipment. What difference does the going concern assumption make with regard to how you would account for these assets?

problems

PROBLEM 2-1

BALANCE SHEET CLASSIFICATIONS AND RELATIONSHIPS

Tu'aa Corporation has the following balance sheet elements as of December 31, 2003.

Land	$ 69,000	Mortgage payable	$300,000
Cash	?	Capital stock	135,000
Building	178,000	Retained earnings	88,000
Accounts payable	100,000	Supplies	17,000
Notes payable (short-term)	105,000	Accounts receivable	88,000
Equipment	350,000		

Required: Compute the total amount of:
1. Current assets.
2. Long-term assets.
3. Current liabilities.
4. Long-term liabilities.
5. Stockholders' equity

PROB

PROBLEM 2-2

PREPARATION OF A CLASSIFIED BALANCE SHEET

Following are the December 31, 2003, account balances for Siraco Company.

Cash	$ 1,950
Accounts receivable	2,500
Supplies	1,800
Equipment	11,275
Accounts payable	3,450
Wages payable	250
Dividends paid	1,500
Capital stock	775
Retained earnings, January 1, 2003	12,000
Revenues	10,000
Miscellaneous expense	1,550
Supplies expense	3,700
Wages expense	2,200

Required:

1. Prepare a classified balance sheet as of December 31, 2003.
2. **Interpretive Question:** On the basis of its 2003 earnings, was this company's decision to pay dividends of $1,500 a sound one?

PROBLEM 2-3

BALANCE SHEET PREPARATION WITH A MISSING ELEMENT

The following data are available for Sunshine Products Inc., as of December 31, 2003.

Cash	$10,000
Accounts payable	14,000
Capital stock	35,200
Accounts receivable	20,000
Building	28,000
Supplies	1,200
Retained earnings	?
Land	10,000

PROB

Required:

1. Prepare a balance sheet for Sunshine Products Inc.
2. Determine the amount of retained earnings at December 31, 2003.
3. **Interpretive Question:** In what way is a balance sheet a depiction of the basic accounting equation?

PROBLEM 2-4

INCOME STATEMENT PREPARATION

Listed below are the results of Rulon Candies' operations for 2002 and 2003. (Assume 4,000 shares of outstanding stock for both years.)

	2003	2002
Sales	$300,000	$350,000
Utilities expenses	15,000	8,500
Employee salaries	115,000	110,000
Advertising expenses	10,000	20,000
Income tax expense	9,000	36,500
Interest expense	25,000	15,000
Cost of goods sold	115,000	85,000
Interest revenue	10,000	10,000

PRO

Required:

1. Prepare a comparative income statement for Rulon Candies, Inc., for the years ended December 31, 2003 and 2002. Be sure to include figures for gross margin, operating income, income before taxes, net income, and earnings per share.
2. **Interpretive Question:** What advice would you give Rulon Candies, Inc., to improve its profitability for the year 2004?

PRO

Dividends	$ 12,400
Retained earnings (6/1/02)	156,540
Income taxes	21,180
Consulting fees (revenues)	115,100
Administrative expense	7,250

Required:
1. Determine the net income for the year by preparing an income statement. (Assume that 3,000 shares of stock are outstanding.)
2. Compute the return on equity (ROE) for Streuling Company, assuming total owners' equity is $255,000.
3. **Interpretive Question:** What does the ROE ratio explain about Streuling's profitability?
4. **Interpretive Question:** Assuming an operating loss for the year, is it a good idea for Streuling to still pay its shareholders dividends?

PRC

PROBLEM 2-11

UNIFYING CONCEPTS: NET INCOME AND STATEMENT OF RETAINED EARNINGS

A summary of the operations of Stellenbach Company for the year ended May 31, 2003, is shown below.

Advertising expense	$ 2,760
Supplies expense	37,820
Rent expense	1,500
Salaries expense	18,150
Miscellaneous expense	4,170
Dividends	12,400
Retained earnings (6/1/02)	156,540
Income taxes	21,180
Consulting fees (revenues)	115,100
Administrative expense	7,250

Required:
1. Determine the net income for the year by preparing an income statement. (There are 2,000 shares of stock outstanding.)
2. Prepare a statement of retained earnings for the year ended May 31, 2003.
3. Prepare a statement of retained earnings assuming that Stellenbach had a net loss for the year of $25,000.
4. **Interpretive Question:** Assuming a loss as in (3), is it a good idea for Stellenbach to still pay its shareholders dividends?

PROBLEM 2-12

FINANCIAL RATIOS

The following information for High Flying Company is provided.

High Flying Company	
Current assets	$ 145,000
Long-term assets	750,000
Current liabilities	75,000
Long-term liabilities	300,000
Owners' equity	520,000
Sales for year	1,425,000
Net income for year	105,000
Average market price per share	145.00
Average number of shares outstanding	10,000

PR

Required:
1. Compute the current ratio, debt ratio, return on sales, return on equity, asset turnover, and price-earnings ratio.
2. **Interpretive Question:** What do these ratios show for High Flying Company?

PROBLEM 2-13

COMPREHENSIVE FINANCIAL STATEMENT PREPARATION

The following information was obtained from the records of Uptown, Inc., as of December 31, 2003.

Land.	$ 37,500
Buildings	145,050
Salaries expense	40,050
Utilities expense.	9,750
Accounts payable.	25,650
Revenues	397,800
Supplies.	69,450
Retained earnings (1/1/03)	272,550
Capital stock (1,000 shares outstanding)	45,000
Accounts receivable	46,500
Supplies expense	207,900
Cash.	?
Notes payable (long-term)	25,800
Rent expense	25,650
Dividends in 2003.	60,750
Other expenses	13,050
Income taxes	52,800

Required:

1. Prepare an income statement for the year ended December 31, 2003.
2. Prepare a classified balance sheet as of December 31, 2003.
3. Compute the current ratio as of December 31, 2003.
4. Compute the debt ratio as of December 31, 2003.
5. **Interpretive Question:** What does the current ratio tell about Uptown's liquidity?
6. **Interpretive Question:** What does the debt ratio tell about Uptown's leverage?
7. **Interpretive Question:** Why is the balance in Retained Earnings so large as compared with the balance in Capital Stock?

PROBLEM 2-14

ELEMENTS OF COMPARATIVE FINANCIAL STATEMENTS

The following report is supplied by Smith Brothers Company.

Smith Brothers Company
Comparative Balance Sheets
As of December 31, 2003 and 2002

Assets	2003	2002	Liabilities and Owners' Equity	2003	2002
Cash	$13,000	$15,000	Accounts payable.	$ 5,000	$ 4,000
Accounts receivable.	18,000	11,000	Salaries and commissions		
Notes receivable	11,000	10,000	payable.	8,000	8,000
Land	38,000	38,000	Notes payable	25,000	27,000
			Capital stock	20,000	20,000
			Retained earnings	22,000	15,000
			Total liabilities and		
Total assets.	$80,000	$74,000	owners' equity	$80,000	$74,000

Operating expenses for the year included utilities of $4,500, salaries and commissions of $44,800, and miscellaneous expenses of $1,500. Income taxes for the year were $3,000, and the company paid dividends of $5,000.

Required:

1. Compute the total expenses, including taxes, incurred in 2003.
2. Compute the net income or net loss for 2003.
3. Compute the total revenue for 2003.
4. **Interpretive Question:** Why are comparative financial statements generally of more value to users than statements for a single period?

▶ Analyzing Real Company Information
▶ International Case
▶ Ethics Case
▶ Writing Assignment
▶ The Debate
▶ Cumulative Spreadsheet Project
▶ Internet Search

The following additional assignments provide opportunities for students to develop critical thinking, ethical perspectives, oral and written communication skills, experience with electronic research, and teamwork through group and business activities.

▶ ## ANALYZING REAL COMPANY INFORMATION

• Analyzing 2-1 (Microsoft)

The 1999 annual report for MICROSOFT is included in Appendix A. Locate that annual report and answer the following questions:

1. Locate Microsoft's 1999 balance sheet. What percentage of its total assets consists of cash and short-term investments? Compute Microsoft's current ratio. How does its current ratio compare to yours? How much long-term debt does Microsoft have?
2. Find Microsoft's 1999 income statement. Have revenues increased or decreased over the last three years? Is the rate of increase rising? Compute Microsoft's return on sales. Is it increasing?
3. Compute Microsoft's return on equity. How does that return compare to the rate of return you might earn if you were to invest your money in a savings account at a local bank?
4. Review Microsoft's statement of cash flows. What activity generates most of Microsoft's cash? What is Microsoft doing with all its money—buying back its own stock, investing in other companies, or something else?

• Analyzing 2-2 (Safeway)

At the start of this chapter you learned a little about SAFEWAY and its history. Now let's take a look at the company's financial performance in recent years. Refer back to Safeway's income statement (on page 41) and balance sheet (on page 38).

Based on information contained in these financial statements, answer the following questions:

1. Compute Safeway's debt ratio for the past two years. Has this ratio increased or decreased? Why?
2. Compute the company's current ratio. Do you notice anything unusual about Safeway's current ratio? How can a company stay in business with a current ratio this low?
3. Compute Safeway's return on sales for 1999. Does the size of this number surprise you? Now compute the company's asset turnover. Considering return on sales and asset turnover together, what does the result indicate?

▶ **INTERNATIONAL CASE**

• *Diageo*

DIAGEO is a United Kingdom (UK) consumer products firm, best known in the United States for the following brand names: Smirnoff, Johnnie Walker, J&B, Gordon's, Guinness, Pillsbury, Häagen-Dazs, and Burger King. Diageo's 1998 balance sheet is shown below.

Diageo
Consolidated Balance Sheet
30 June 1998
(in millions of pounds)

Fixed assets		
Intangible assets		4,727
Tangible assets		3,006
Investments		1,244
		8,977
Current assets		
Stocks	2,236	
Debtors—due within one year	2,037	
Debtors—due after more than one year	999	
Debtors subject to financing arrangements (franchisee loans of £145 million, less non-returnable proceeds of £127 million)	18	
Investments	484	
Cash at bank and in hand	2,503	
	8,277	
Creditors—due within one year		
Borrowings	(4,724)	
Other creditors	(3,524)	
	(8,248)	
Net current assets		29
Total assets less current liabilities		9,006
Creditors—due after more than one year		
Borrowings	(2,894)	
Other creditors	(243)	
		(3,137)
Provisions for liabilities and charges		(705)
		5,164
Shareholders' funds		
Equity share capital		1,034
Non-equity share capital		105
Called-up share capital		1,139
Share premium account	1,121	
Revaluation reserve	190	
Profit and loss account	2,179	
Reserves attributable to equity shareholders		3,490
		4,629
Minority interests		
Equity	169	
Non-equity	366	
		535
		5,164

1. Can you identify any major differences between Microsoft's and Diageo's balance sheets in terms of the order in which major categories are displayed?
2. What is Diageo's total assets? Is it as easy to determine as Microsoft's total assets?
3. Take a look at the following list of accounts and identify, given your knowledge of assets, liabilities, and owners' equity, what the American equivalent of those accounts might be (you might want to reference Microsoft's balance sheet for comparison):

   - Stocks
   - Debtors
   - Called-up share capital
   - Profit and loss account

▶ **ETHICS CASE**

• Violating a Covenant

Often banks will require a company that borrows money to agree to certain restrictions on its activities in order to protect the lending institution. These restrictions are called "debt covenants." An example of a common debt covenant is requiring a company to maintain its current ratio at a certain level, say, 2.0.

Your boss has just come to you and asked, "How can you make our current ratio higher?" You know that the company has a line of credit with a local bank that requires the company to maintain its current ratio at 1.5. You also know that the company was dangerously close to violating this covenant during the previous quarter. The end of the fiscal period is next week, and some action must be taken to increase the current ratio. If the covenant is violated, the lending agreement allows the bank to significantly modify the terms of the debt (in the bank's favor) and also gives the bank a seat on the company's board of directors. Management would prefer not to have the bank involved in the day-to-day affairs of the business, nor do they want to alter the terms of the lending agreement.

Identify ways in which the current ratio can be increased. Would any of the alternatives you identify be good for the business, e.g., selling equipment might raise the current ratio but would that be good for the business? Should a company engage in these types of transactions?

▶ **WRITING ASSIGNMENT**

• The Most Important Financial Statement

As you have discovered, there are three primary financial statements—balance sheet, income statement, and statement of cash flows. In no more than two pages, answer the following question: If you could have access to only one of the primary financial statements, which would it be and why? As you provide support for the financial statement of your choice, also provide reasons as to why you would not pick the other two statements.

▶ **THE DEBATE**

• Save the Notes

As pointed out in the chapter, IBM's annual report in 1920 included zero pages of notes to the financial statements. In 1996, the notes had grown to 26 pages. While the number of financial statements has remained constant, the number of notes to the financial statements continues to grow.

Divide your group into two teams and prepare two-minute presentations representing the following points of view.

- The first team represents "Kill the Notes." You are to take the position that financial statements providing information relating to a firm's current asset and liability position, a summary of its operations, and its cash inflows and outflows are all that is needed to make good resource allocation decisions. The three primary financial statements are all that need to be provided to current and potential investors and creditors. In other words, the notes do not add value to the financial reports.
- The other team represents "Save the Notes." You are to argue that the notes represent essential information that must be used when interpreting the data contained in the financial statements themselves.

CUMULATIVE SPREADSHEET PROJECT

Starting with this chapter and continuing throughout the next twelve chapters, this text will include a spreadsheet assignment based on the financial information of a fictitious company named Handyman. The first assignments are simple—in this chapter you are asked to do little more than set up financial statement formats and input some numbers. In succeeding chapters, the spreadsheets will get more complex so that by the end of the course you will have constructed a spreadsheet that allows you to forecast operating cash flow for five years in the future and adjust your forecast depending on the operating parameters that you think are most reasonable.

So, let's get started with the first spreadsheet assignment.

1. The following numbers are for Handyman Company for 2003:

Short-term Loans Payable	$ 10	Long-term Debt	$207
Interest Expense	9	Income Tax Expense	4
Paid in Capital	50	Retained Earnings (as of 1/1/03)	31
Cash	10	Receivables	27
Dividends	0	Sales	700
Accumulated Depreciation	9	Accounts Payable	74
Inventory	153	Property, Plant, & Equipment	199
Cost of Goods Sold	519	Other Operating Expenses	160

Your assignment is to create a spreadsheet containing a balance sheet and an income statement for Handyman Company.

2. Handyman is wondering what its balance sheet and income statement would have looked like if the following numbers were changed as indicated:

	CHANGE	
	From	**To**
Sales	700	730
Cost of Goods Sold	519	550
Other Operating Expenses	160	165

Create a second spreadsheet with the numbers changed as indicated. Note: After making these changes, your balance sheet may no longer balance. Assume that any discrepancy is eliminated by increasing or decreasing Short-term Loans Payable as much as necessary.

▷ **INTERNET SEARCH**

• *Microsoft*

While you have a copy of MICROSOFT's annual report in Appendix A, let's go see what its most current financial statements look like. Access Microsoft's Web site at http://www.microsoft.com. Sometimes addresses change, so if this Microsoft address doesn't work, access the Web site for this textbook (http://albrecht.swcollege.com) for an updated link to Microsoft.

Once you have accessed Microsoft's Web site, answer the following questions (you may have to search a bit to answer some of these questions):

1. When was Micro-Soft founded? (That's right, the company's name originally had a hyphen.)
2. Make your way to the shareholder information and locate the company's most recent income statement. Detail the steps you had to take to find this financial statement.
3. How has the company done since its 1999 financial statements were issued? Are sales still increasing? Are profits still on the rise?
4. Microsoft was one of the first companies to provide an income statement in multiple languages. Take a look at Microsoft's income statement based on accounting principles accepted in the United Kingdom. Do you recognize any of the terms? Now look at the German version of the income statement. Even though you probably don't speak German, can you guess what the German word is for "revenues"?

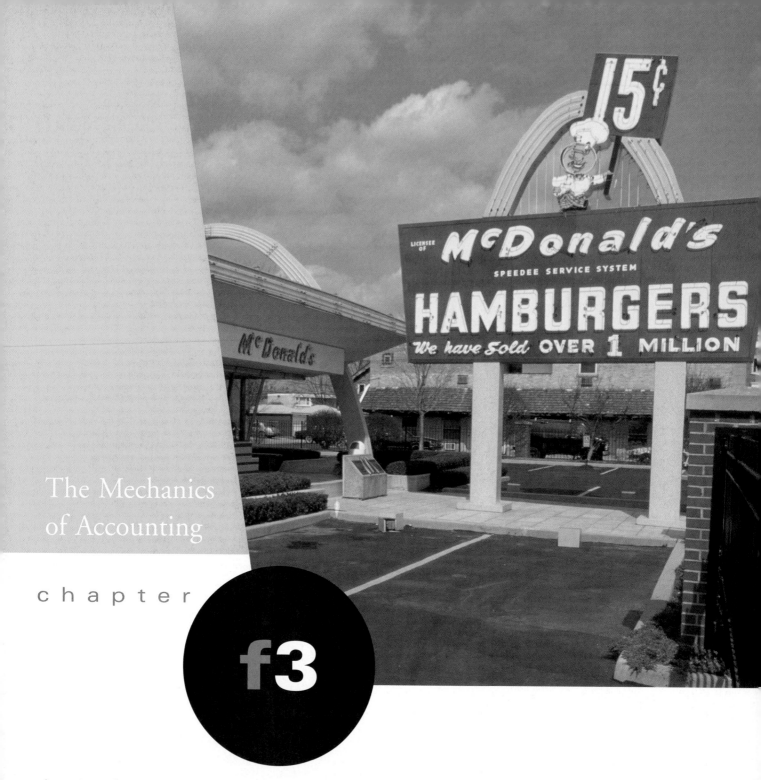

The Mechanics of Accounting

c h a p t e r

f3

learning objectives
After studying this chapter, you should be able to:

1 Understand the process of transforming transaction data into useful accounting information.

2 Analyze transactions and determine how those transactions affect the accounting equation (step one of the accounting cycle).

3 Record the effects of transactions using journal entries (step two of the accounting cycle).

4 Summarize the resulting journal entries through posting and prepare a trial balance (step three of the accounting cycle).

5 Describe how technology has affected the first three steps of the accounting cycle.

Ray Kroc, a 51-year-old milkshake machine distributor, first visited the McDonald brothers' drive-in (in San Bernardino, California) in July of 1954 because he wanted to know why a single "hamburger stand" needed ten milkshake machines. That first day, Kroc spent the lunch rush hour watching the incredible volume of business the small drive-in was able to handle. By the time he left town, Kroc had received a personal briefing on the "McDonald's Speedee System" from Dick and Mac McDonald and had secured the rights to duplicate the system throughout the United States.

In his first outlet in Chicago, Ray Kroc soon discovered that duplicating the McDonald's system involved more than just signing a licensing agreement. Kroc's french fries, for example, were mushy, even though he closely copied the McDonald brothers' process. Feverish detective work finally revealed that Dick and Mac McDonald had been storing their potatoes in an outside bin before turning them into french fries. This aging process allowed some of the natural sugars in the potatoes to turn into starch, resulting in fries that would cook all the way through without burning. Further research revealed the optimal temperature for the cooking oil, the best type of potato to use, and how to make frozen french fries that taste as good as fresh. The end product, the McDONALD'S french fry, was instrumental in establishing the McDonald's reputation for consistent quality.

As the number of McDonald's locations expanded (to 26,806 at the end of 1999), so did the menu. Originally, the McDonald's menu contained just 15-cent hamburgers, 12-cent french fries, 20-cent milkshakes, cheeseburgers, three flavors of soft drinks, milk, coffee, potato chips, and pie. The first addition to this menu was the Filet-O-Fish sandwich in the early 1960s. The Big Mac started in Pittsburgh in 1967, and the Egg McMuffin debuted in Santa Barbara in 1971. Not all of the McDonald's menu innovations caught on— the McLean Deluxe (a low-fat hamburger held together with a seaweed-based filler) and the Hulaburger, one of Ray Kroc's personal favorites (a cheeseburger with a big slice of pineapple), are among the items that are no longer offered.

The essence of McDonald's business seems fairly simple: revenues come from selling Big Macs, Happy Meals, Chicken McNuggets, etc.; operating costs include the costs of the raw materials to produce the food items, labor costs, building rentals, income taxes, and so forth. But the magnitude of McDonald's operations in terms of volume (sales average over $105 million per day) as well as geography (McDonald's has locations in 118 countries throughout the world) makes compiling this information a challenge. In order to prepare its year-end financial reports, McDonald's must accumulate financial information from its various locations throughout the world, summarize that information according to U.S. accounting standards, and make the report available to the public in less than four weeks. In fact, McDonald's annual report for the period ended December 31, 1999, was finished on January 26, 2000.

With the number of transactions that occur on a daily basis, the accounting for McDonald's would be impossible were it not for a systematic method for analyzing these transactions and collecting and recording transaction-related information. What is the process by which McDonald's and other entities transform raw transaction data into useful information? Certainly, shareholders and others would not understand how McDonald's has performed if the company merely published volumes of raw transaction data. How are millions of transactions summarized and eventually reported in the primary financial statements? This transformation process is referred to as the **accounting cycle**.

setting the stage

accounting cycle The procedure for analyzing, recording, summarizing, and reporting the transactions of a business.

In the first two chapters, we provided an overview of accounting. We discussed the environment of accounting and its objectives, some basic concepts and assumptions of accounting, and the primary financial statements. Now we begin our study of the "accounting cycle." This simply means that we will examine the procedures for analyzing, recording, summarizing, and reporting the transactions of a business. In this chapter, we describe the first three steps in the cycle. The remaining step (preparing reports for external users) is explained in Chapter 4.

1

Understand the process of transforming transaction data into useful accounting information.

HOW CAN WE COLLECT ALL THIS INFORMATION?

Suppose you were asked, "What was the total cost, to the nearest dollar, of your college education last year?" To answer this question would require that you (1) gather information (in the form of receipts, credit card statements, and canceled checks) for all your expenditures, (2) analyze that information to determine which outflows relate to your college education, and (3) summarize those outflows into one number—the cost of your college education. Once you have answered that question, answer this one, "How much did you spend on food last year?" Again you would have to go through the same process of collecting data, analyzing the information to identify those expenditures relating to food, and then summarizing those expenditures into one number. From these two examples you can see that, without a method for gathering and organizing day-to-day financial data, answers to seemingly routine questions can get quite complex.

Now you may be thinking, "Doesn't my checkbook allow me to easily answer these questions?" Your check register would certainly help, but it is limited in that it tracks only the transactions that go through your checking account. It does not track the cash in your pocket, in your savings accounts, or in other investment accounts. So, if any of your expenditures for food were made with cash, your check register would understate the amount you spent for food. In addition, you would still have to review each check and determine to what it related. Your check register provides good information for calculating exactly how much money you have in your checking account at any point in time, but it does not contain all the information necessary to determine exactly how your money was spent.

Now consider the dilemma for businesses. They typically have far more transactions than you, and the kinds of transactions are more varied. Businesses buy and sell goods or services; borrow and invest money; pay wages to employees; purchase land, buildings, and equipment; distribute earnings to owners; and pay taxes to the government. These activities are referred to as "exchange transactions" because the entity is actually trading (exchanging) one thing for another. A college bookstore, for example, exchanges textbooks for cash. **Business documents**, such as a sales invoice, a purchase order, or a check stub, are often used (1) to confirm that an arm's-length transaction has occurred, (2) to establish the amounts to be recorded, and (3) to facilitate the analysis of business events.

business documents
Records of transactions used as the basis for recording accounting entries; include invoices, check stubs, receipts, and similar business papers.

Businesses, such as a college bookstore, have many exchange transactions in which they trade one thing for another—like textbooks for cash.

To determine how well an entity is managing its resources, the results of transactions must be analyzed. The accounting cycle makes the analysis possible by recording and summarizing an entity's transactions and preparing reports that present the summary results. Exhibit 3-1 shows the sequence of the accounting cycle. Later, we will discuss these general categories and the specific steps of the cycle.

Keeping track of a company's transactions requires a system of accounting that is tailor-made to the needs of that particular enterprise. Obviously, the accounting system of a large multinational corporation with millions of business transactions each day will be much more complex than the system needed by a small Internet start-up company. The more complex and detailed the accounting system, the more likely it is to be automated. Historically, of course, all accounting systems had to be maintained by hand. The image of the accountant with green eye-shade and quill pen, sitting on a high stool, meticulously maintaining the accounting records, reflects those early manual systems. Today, few accounting systems are completely manual. Even small companies generally use some type of inexpensive accounting software. Such software helps reduce the number of routine clerical functions and improves the accuracy and timeliness of the accounting records.

Although a computer-based system is faster and requires less labor than a manual system, the steps in the process are basically the same for both: transactions are recorded on source documents; they are then analyzed, journalized, and posted to the accounts; and the resulting information is summarized, reported, and used for evaluation purposes. The difference lies in who (or what) does the work. With a computer-based system, the software transforms the recorded data, summarizes the data into categories, and prepares the financial statements and other re-

---

exhibit 3-1   Sequence of the Accounting Cycle

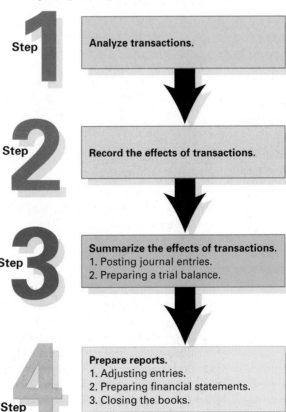

Exchange Transactions
(Businesses enter into exchange transactions signaling the beginning of the accounting cycle)

Step 1   **Analyze transactions.**

Step 2   **Record the effects of transactions.**

Step 3   **Summarize the effects of transactions.**
1. Posting journal entries.
2. Preparing a trial balance.

Step 4   **Prepare reports.**
1. Adjusting entries.
2. Preparing financial statements.
3. Closing the books.

ports. Nevertheless, human judgment is still essential in analyzing and recording transactions, especially those of a nonroutine nature.

Because a manual accounting system is easier to understand, we will use a manual system for the examples in this text. As you begin studying the steps in the accounting cycle, it is important that you understand the accounting equation and double-entry accounting more fully. This concept was briefly introduced in Chapter 2. You will recall that the accounting model is built on this basic equation. You now need to learn how to use the equation in accounting for the transactions of a business.

to summarize

Businesses enter into exchange transactions. Evidence of these transactions is provided by business documents. Accounting is designed to accumulate and report in summary form the results of a company's transactions, therefore transforming the financial data into useful information for decision making.

2

Analyze transactions and determine how those transactions affect the accounting equation (step one of the accounting cycle).

HOW DO TRANSACTIONS AFFECT THE ACCOUNTING EQUATION?

Suppose you are the keeper of the archives at MCDONALD'S assigned to protect the secret ingredient mix for the Big Mac special sauce. You came to work this morning only to hear that BURGER KING has cracked the secret ingredient recipe and plans to come out with a Big Mac clone at half the price. How would this event be reflected in the financial statements?

Often, the most difficult aspect of accounting is determining which events are to be reflected in the accounting records and which are not. In this example, the proliferation of Big Mac clones could have a serious impact on the future of the firm. However, as discussed in Chapter 2, events that cannot be measured in monetary terms will not be reflected in the financial statements. It would be virtually impossible to reliably quantify the impact that Big Mac clones could have on the future profitability of McDonald's, and thus, that information would not be reflected in the financial statements.

Now you may be saying to yourself, "We have an obligation to inform financial statement users about this attack on the Big Mac." We would all agree that this information should be shared, but the financial statements are not the place to do it. As you review MICROSOFT's annual report (in Appendix A), you'll notice that the financial statements are only one part of the information provided to users. Information relating to the competitive environment, product development, and marketing and sales efforts is included in the annual report, but not as part of the accounting information.

After quantifying an event's monetary impact, the event must be analyzed to determine if an arm's-length transaction has occurred. Accounting is concerned primarily with reflecting the effects of transactions between two independent entities. So a mining company's oil strike on the North Slope of Alaska would not be reflected in the financial statements until that oil is sold. Likewise, signing a promising young financial analyst directly out of college for a salary of $80,000 per year involves an exchange of promises. No accounting entry would be made until the analyst actually worked and received a paycheck.

Transactions between independent parties must be analyzed to determine their effect on the accounting equation. This analysis is often what separates an accountant from a bookkeeper. While many transactions are routine, some business events are quite complex and require a comprehensive analysis to determine how the event should be reflected in the financial statements. Consider the following examples:

net work

Access MCDONALD'S Web site (http://www.mcdonalds.com) and compare it to BURGER KING's (http://www.burgerking.com).

In your opinion, which Web site is easier to navigate? How easy is it to find information on, for example, nutrition? Which site provides easier access to the company's financial information?

- An employee works for one year, earning a base salary of $60,000. In addition, if the employee stays with the company for at least five years, the company promises to make a contribution to the employee's pension fund equal to 15% of salary. Approximately 60% of employees who start with the company stay for five years. Also, by working for one year, the employee earns 15 extra vacation days. Those vacation days can be saved and used any time in the future. How do we record compensation cost associated with this employee for the year?

- A company buys a building. In addition to paying $20,000 cash, the company agrees to pay $10,000 per year for the next ten years. The company will also pay a $2,000 property tax bill associated with the building from last year. As part of the purchase, the company gave the former owners of the building 500 shares of stock. Finally, the building will require $23,000 worth of repairs and renovations before it can be used. How much should be recorded as the cost of the building?

As these examples illustrate, transactions can become quite complex and the accounting for these types of transactions reflects that complexity. The good news is that the transaction analysis framework introduced in this chapter allows you to break complex transactions into manageable pieces and also provides a self-checking mechanism to ensure that you haven't forgotten anything. Once a transaction is properly analyzed and the affected accounts identified (along with the direction of those effects), the remainder of the accounting cycle can proceed without much difficulty.

The Accounting Equation

So let's begin our analysis of transactions by first reviewing some of the basics. Recall that the fundamental accounting equation is:

$$\textbf{Assets} \quad = \quad \textbf{Liabilities} \quad + \quad \textbf{Owners' Equity}$$

Assets	=	**Liabilities**	+	**Owners' Equity**
[Resources]		[Creditors' claims against resources]		[Owners' claims against resources]

Because the accounting equation is an equality, it must always remain in balance. To see how this balance is maintained when accounting for business transactions, consider the following activities:

Business Activity (Transaction)	**Effect in Terms of the Accounting Equation**
1. Investment of $50,000 by owners	Increase asset (Cash), increase owners' equity (Capital Stock): A ↑ $50,000 = OE ↑ $50,000
2. Borrowed $25,000 from bank	Increase asset (Cash), increase liability (Notes Payable): A ↑ $25,000 = L ↑ $25,000
3. Purchased $14,000 worth of inventory on credit. The inventory is to be resold at a later date.	Increase asset (Inventory), increase liability (Accounts Payable): A ↑ $14,000 = L ↑ $14,000
4. Purchased equipment costing $15,000 for cash	Decrease asset (Cash), increase asset (Equipment): A ↓ $15,000 = A ↑ $15,000

For each of the transactions, the terms in parentheses are the specific accounts affected by the transactions, as will be explained in the next section.

In each case, the equation remains in balance because an identical amount is added to both sides, subtracted from both sides, or added to and subtracted from the same side of the equation. Following each transaction, we can ensure that the accounting equation balances. Note how the following spreadsheet keeps track of the equality of the accounting equation:

TRANSACTION #	ASSETS		LIABILITIES		OWNERS' EQUITY
Beginning Balance	$ 0	=	$ 0	+	$ 0
1	+50,000				+50,000
Subtotal	$50,000	=	$ 0	+	$50,000
2	+25,000		+25,000		
Subtotal	$75,000	=	$25,000	+	$50,000
3	+14,000		+14,000		
Subtotal	$89,000	=	$39,000	+	$50,000
4	+15,000 −15,000				
Total	$89,000	=	$39,000	+	$50,000

Using Accounts to Categorize Transactions

In Chapter 2, the balance sheet and the income statement were introduced as two of the three primary financial statements, the third being the statement of cash flows. We learned that the elements of the balance sheet are assets, liabilities, and owners' equity; the elements of the income statement are revenues and expenses. Now we must learn how each of these elements is composed of many different accounts.

account An accounting record in which the results of transactions are accumulated; shows increases, decreases, and a balance.

An **account** is a specific accounting record that provides an efficient way to categorize transactions. Thus, we may designate asset accounts, liability accounts, and owners' equity accounts. Examples of asset accounts are Cash, Inventory, and Equipment. Liability accounts include Accounts Payable and Notes Payable. The equity accounts for a corporation are Capital Stock and Retained Earnings. You can think of an individual account as a summary of every transaction affecting a certain item (such as cash); the summary may be recorded on one page of a book, or in one computer file, or in one column of a spreadsheet (seen as follows).

business environment essay

Do Accountants Record the Most Important Events? Are all important economic events captured in a company's accounting records? No. In fact, the majority of events that affect the value of a company may fall outside the scope of traditional financial reporting. Consider the following selection of business events reported on the front page of *The Wall Street Journal* (Business and Finance column) on a typical day (Friday, August 11, 2000):

- DELL's earnings rose 19%, exceeding estimates, but revenue rose at its slowest rate in five years.

- AT&T's board of directors and management are considering breaking up the company by spinning off certain assets.
- FIRESTONE instigates the second biggest tire recall ever.
- The yield on 10-year Treasury notes fell to 5.754%, its lowest level this year.
- KMART and LAND'S END released operating results that fell short of already lowered market expectations.
- Brazil's PETROBAS began trading on the NYSE.

All of these events had impacts on the values of companies. For example, Dell's announcement caused the value of the company's shares to decrease by about

	ASSETS				LIABILITIES			OWNERS' EQUITY
Transaction #	Cash	Inventory	Equipment		Accounts Payable	Notes Payable		Capital Stock
Beginning Balance	$ 0	$ 0	$ 0	=	$ 0	$ 0	+	$ 0
1	+50,000							+50,000
Subtotal	$50,000	$ 0	$ 0	=	$ 0	$ 0	+	$50,000
2	+25,000					+25,000		
Subtotal	$75,000	$ 0	$ 0	=	$ 0	$25,000	+	$50,000
3		+14,000			+14,000			
Subtotal	$75,000	$14,000	$ 0	=	$14,000	$25,000	+	$50,000
4	−15,000		+15,000					
Total	$60,000	$14,000	$15,000	=	$14,000	$25,000	+	$50,000

Using the previous transactions, we can easily see how the accounting equation can be expanded to include specific accounts under the headings of assets, liabilities, and owners' equity. We can also see that after each transaction, the equality of the accounting equation can be determined simply by adding up the balances of all the asset accounts and comparing the total to the sum of all the liability and owners' equity accounts.

Now suppose that a company has 200 accounts and 10,000 transactions each month—this spreadsheet would quickly get very big. Today, computers help in compiling this massive amount of data. Five hundred years ago, when double-entry accounting was formalized, all the adding and subtracting was done by hand. You can imagine the difficulties of tracking multiple ac-

5%. And yet none of these value-relevant events would have been recorded in the accounting records of any company anywhere in the world.

Accounting academics have long been dismayed by the weak connection between a company's reported accounting numbers and the company's market value. In a famous paper, Professor Baruch Lev summarized this issue as follows:

The correlation between earnings and stock returns is very low, sometimes negligible.... [T]he possibility that the fault lies with the low quality ... of reported earnings looms large.

The challenge to accountants is to figure out how to bring more business events into the accounting model in order to increase the relevance of the financial statements. The risk of doing nothing to improve accounting is that potential investors and creditors will increasingly turn their backs on the financial statements when they can get more current, comprehensive, and relevant information merely by using an Internet search engine.

Source: Baruch Lev, "On the Usefulness of Earnings and Earnings Research: Lessons and Directions from Two Decades of Empirical Research," *Journal of Accounting Research*, Supplement 1989, p. 153.

counts, involving hundreds of transactions, using the spreadsheet method described above while doing all the computations by hand. Mixing "+" and "−" in one column would provide ample opportunity to make mistakes.

This problem was solved by separating the "+" and the "−" for each account into separate columns, totaling each column, and then computing the difference between the columns to arrive at an ending balance. The simplest, most fundamental format is the configuration of the letter T. This is called a **T-account**. Note that a T-account is an abbreviated representation of an actual account (illustrated later) and is used as a teaching and learning tool. The following are examples of T-accounts, representing the transactions described previously.

T-account A simplified depiction of an account in the form of a letter T.

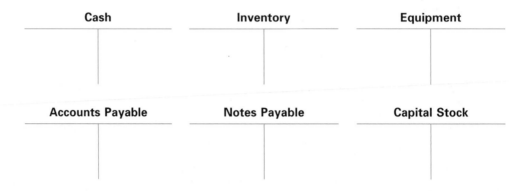

debit An entry on the left side of a T-account.

credit An entry on the right side of a T-account.

The account title (Cash, for example) appears at the top of the T-account. Transaction amounts may be recorded on both the left side and the right side of the T-account. Instead of using the terms left and right to indicate which side of a T-account is affected, terms unique to accounting were developed. **Debit** is used to indicate the left side of a T-account, and **credit** is used to indicate the right side of a T-account. Debit means left, credit means right—nothing more, nothing less.

Besides representing the left and right sides of an account, the terms *debit* (abbreviated DR) and *credit* (abbreviated CR) take on additional meaning when coupled with a specific account. By convention, for asset accounts, debits refer to increases and credits to decreases. For example, to increase the cash account, we debit it; to decrease the cash account, we credit it. Since we expect the total increases in the cash account to be greater than the decreases, the cash account will usually have a debit balance after accounting for all transactions. Thus, we can make this generalization—asset accounts will have debit balances. The opposite relationship is true of liability and owners' equity accounts; they are decreased by *debits* and increased by *credits*. As a result, liability and owners' equity accounts will typically have credit balances. The effect of this system is shown here, with an increase indicated by (+) and a decrease by (−).

Assets		=	Liabilities		+	Owners' Equity	
DR	CR		DR	CR		DR	CR
(+)	(−)		(−)	(+)		(−)	(+)

In addition to assets equaling liabilities and owners' equity, debits also equal credits. If you fully grasp the meaning of these two equalities, you are well on your way to mastering the mechanics of accounting. Debits and credits allow us to take a shortcut to ensure that the accounting equation balances. If, for every transaction, debits equal credits, then the accounting equation will balance.

To understand why this happens, keep in mind three basic facts regarding double-entry accounting:

1. Debits are always entered on the left side of an account and credits on the right side.
2. For every transaction, there must be at least one debit and one credit.
3. Debits must always equal credits for each transaction.

Now notice what this means for one of the business transactions shown earlier (page 83): investment by owners. An asset account (Cash) is debited; it is increased. An owners' equity account (Capital Stock) is credited; it is also increased. There is both a debit and a credit for the transaction, and we have increased accounts on both sides of the equation by an equal amount, thus keeping the accounting equation in balance.

Be careful not to let the general, nonaccounting meanings of the words *credit* and *debit* confuse you. In general conversation, credit has an association with plus and debit with minus. But on the asset side of the accounting equation, where debit means increase and credit means decrease, this association can lead you astray. In accounting, debit simply means left and credit simply means right. To make sure you understand the relationship between debits and credits, the various accounts, and the accounting equation, let us examine further the transactions listed on page 83.

Business Activity (Transaction)	Effect in Terms of the Accounting Equation					
	Assets		**=**	**Liabilities**	**+**	**Owners' Equity**
1. Investment by owners	Cash DR (+)					Capital Stock CR (+)
2. Borrowed money from bank	Cash DR (+)			Notes Payable CR (+)		
3. Purchased inventory on credit	Inventory DR (+)			Accounts Payable CR (+)		
4. Purchased equipment for cash	Equipment DR (+)	Cash CR (−)				

Note that every time an account is debited, other accounts have to be credited for the same amount. This is the major characteristic of the double-entry accounting system: *the debits must always equal the credits.* This important characteristic creates a practical advantage: the opportunity for "self-checking." If debits do not equal credits, an error has been made in analyzing and recording the entity's activities.

Before proceeding any further, let's stop for a moment and review the relationship between the various types of accounts and debits and credits. It is in your best interest not to go on until you understand these relationships.

Account Type			Debit or Credit?		Ending Balance
Asset	Increase	results in	Debit		Debit
	Decrease	results in	Credit		
Liability	Increase	results in	Credit		Credit
	Decrease	results in	Debit		
Owners' Equity	Increase	results in	Credit		Credit
	Decrease	results in	Debit		

Expanding the Accounting Equation to Include Revenues, Expenses, and Dividends

At this point, we must bring revenues and expenses into the picture. Obviously, they are part of every ongoing business. Revenues provide resource inflows; they are increases in resources from the sale of goods or services. Expenses represent resource outflows; they are costs incurred in generating revenues. Note that revenues are not synonymous with cash or other assets, but are a way of describing where the assets came from. For example, cash received from the sale of a product would be considered revenue. Cash received by borrowing from the bank would not be revenue, but an increase in a liability. By the same token, expenses are a way of describing how an asset has been used. Thus, cash paid for interest on a loan is an expense, but cash paid to buy a building represents the exchange of one asset for another.

How do revenues and expenses fit into the accounting equation? Remember that revenues minus expenses equals net income; and net income is a major source of change in owners' equity from one accounting period to the next. Revenues and expenses, then, may be thought of as *temporary* subdivisions of owners' equity. Revenues increase owners' equity and so, like all owners' equity accounts, are increased by credits. Expenses reduce owners' equity and are therefore increased by debits. As will be explained in Chapter 4, all revenue and expense accounts are "closed" into the retained earnings account at the end of the accounting cycle.

One other temporary account affects owners' equity. It is the account that shows distributions of earnings to owners. For a corporation, this account is called **Dividends**. Since dividends reflect payments to the owners, therefore reducing owners' equity, the dividends account is increased by a debit and decreased by a credit. The dividends account, like revenues and expenses, is also "closed" into the retained earnings account.

Just a warning here: students who have trouble grasping debits and credits usually get hung up on the revenue and expense accounts. Remember that revenues and expenses are subcategories of Retained Earnings. When you credit a revenue account, you are essentially increasing Retained Earnings. When you debit an expense account, you are increasing the amount of expense, which in turn reduces Retained Earnings.

Using the corporate form of business as an example, the accounting equation may be expanded to include revenues, expenses, and dividends, as shown in Exhibit 3-2.

Keep in mind that in actual business practice, when a manual accounting system is used, the T-account is an integral feature of a more formal and complete account. Exhibit 3-3 is an example of such an account. Note that in addition to the debits and credits in the T-account portion (drawn in heavy lines in this example), the account has a title, Cash; an account number, 101; and columns for a transaction date, an explanation of the transaction, a posting reference (a cross-reference to other accounting records), and a balance.

> **caution**
>
> We stated previously that owners' equity accounts will have credit balances. However, expenses, a component of Retained Earnings, will almost always have debit balances. Since revenues will usually exceed expenses, the net effect on Retained Earnings will result in a credit balance.

dividends Distributions to the owners (stockholders) of a corporation.

Why Should I Understand the Mechanics of Accounting?

If computers now take care of all the routine accounting functions, why does a businessperson need to know anything about debits, credits, journals, posting, T-accounts, and trial balances? Good question. First of all, even though computers now do most of the dirty work, the essence of double-entry accounting is unchanged from the days of quill pens and handwritten ledgers. Thus, understanding the process explained in this chapter is still relevant to a computer-based accounting system. In addition, with or without computers, the use of debits, credits, and T-accounts still provides an efficient and widely used shorthand method of analyzing transactions. At a minimum, all businesspeople should be familiar enough with the language of accounting to understand, for example, why a credit balance in Cash or a debit balance in Retained Earnings is something unusual enough to merit investigation. Finally, an understanding of the accounting cycle—analyzing, recording, summarizing, and preparing—gives one insight into how information flows within an organization. And great advantages accrue to those who understand information flow.

exhibit 3-2   Expanded Accounting Equation

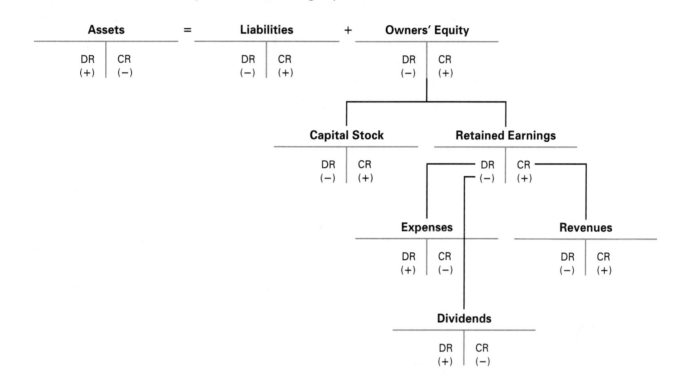

exhibit 3-3   Typical Account

ACCOUNT: Cash					ACCOUNT NO. 101
Date	Explanation	Post. Ref.	Debits	Credits	Balance

to summarize

Regardless of the size or complexity of a business, or the manner in which the records are maintained (manual or automated system), the steps of the accounting cycle are the same. The entire process is based on double-entry accounting and the basic accounting equation. Accounts accumulate the results of transactions. Debits are always entered on the left side of an account, and credits are always entered on the right side. Debits increase asset, expense, and dividend accounts and decrease liability, owners' equity, and revenue accounts. Credits decrease asset, expense, and dividend accounts and increase liability, owners' equity, and revenue accounts. Revenues increase owners' equity, whereas expenses and dividends decrease owners' equity. Therefore, under a double-entry system of accounting, it is always possible to check the accounting records to see that Assets = Liabilities + Owners' Equity and debits equal credits.

3

Record the effects of transactions using journal entries (step two of the accounting cycle).

journal An accounting record in which transactions are first entered; provides a chronological record of all business activities.

journalizing Recording transactions in a journal.

journal entry A recording of a transaction where debits equal credits; usually includes a date and an explanation of the transaction.

HOW DO WE RECORD THE EFFECTS OF TRANSACTIONS?

With our knowledge of the different types of accounts (assets, liabilities, and owners' equity) and the use of the terms *debit* and *credit* (debit means left and credit means right), we are now ready to actually record the effects of transactions.

The second step in the accounting cycle is to record the results of transactions in a **journal**. Known as "books of original entry," journals provide a chronological record of all entity transactions. They show the dates of the transactions, the amounts involved, and the particular accounts affected by the transactions. Sometimes a detailed description of the transaction is also included.

This chronological recording of transactions provides a company with a complete record of its activities. If amounts were recorded directly in the accounts, it would be difficult, if not impossible, for a company to trace a transaction that occurred, say, six months previously.

Smaller companies, such as a locally owned pizza restaurant, may use only one book of original entry, called a "general journal," to record all transactions. Larger companies having thousands of transactions each year may use special journals (for example, a cash receipts journal) as well as a general journal.

A specific format is used in **journalizing** (recording) transactions in a general journal. The debit entry is listed first; the credit entry is listed second and is indented to the right. Normally, the date and a brief explanation of the transaction are considered essential parts of the **journal entry**. (In the text, we often ignore dates and explanations to simplify the examples.) Dollar signs usually are omitted. Unless otherwise noted, this format will be used whenever a journal entry is presented.

General Journal Entry Format

Date Debit Entry xx
       Credit Entry xx
          Explanation.

Exhibit 3-4 is a partial page from a general journal, showing typical journal entries. Study this exhibit carefully because the entire accounting cycle is based on journal entries. If journal entries are incorrect, the resulting financial information will be inaccurate.

To give you additional exposure to analyzing transactions and recording journal entries, we are going to start our own business. Rather than spend the summer flipping burgers at the local hamburger house, you decide that you want to have an outdoor job—one that allows you to enjoy the summer sun, engage in rigorous physical activity, and sharpen your skills as an entrepreneur. You are going to start your own landscaping business. This business will involve mowing lawns, pulling weeds, trimming and planting shrubs, and so forth. We will use your new business to illustrate the journal entries used to record some common transactions of a business enterprise.[1]

---

1 Normally, a small business like this one would be started as a sole proprietorship or as a partnership. We assume a corporation here to show a complete set of transactions.

exhibit 3-4   General Journal

Date	Description	Post. Ref.	Debits	Credits
JOURNAL				**Page 1**
2003 July 1	Cash		2,000	
	Capital Stock			2,000
	Issued 200 shares of capital stock at $10 per share.			
5	Truck		800	
	Cash			800
	Purchased a used truck.			
5	Equipment		250	
	Accounts Payable			250
	Purchased a lawnmower on account.			
5	Supplies		180	
	Cash			180
	Purchased supplies for cash.			

These transactions fit into the following four general categories: acquiring cash, acquiring other assets, selling goods or providing services, and collecting cash and paying obligations. Obviously, we cannot present all possible transactions in this chapter. In studying the illustrations, strive to understand the conceptual basis of transaction analysis rather than memorizing specific journal entries. Pay particular attention to the dual effect of each transaction on the company in terms of the basic accounting equation (that is, its impact on assets and on liabilities and owners' equity). Remember that business activity involves revenues, expenses, and distributions to owners as well, and that these accounts eventually increase or decrease owners' equity (the retained earnings account for a corporation).

Acquiring Cash, Either from Owners or by Borrowing

Your first task in starting this business is to acquire cash, either through owners' investments or by borrowing. Your parents indicate that they will match any funds that you are going to put into your business. You have $1,000 in savings, and coupled with your parents' matching funds, you decide to issue 200 shares of stock.

EXAMPLE 1   The following transaction illustrates investments by owners:

assets (+)   Cash. 2,000
owners' equity (+)   Capital Stock.   2,000
                Issued 200 shares of capital stock at $10 per share.

This transaction increases cash as a result of capital stock being issued to investors, or stockholders. The cash account is debited, and the capital stock account is credited. The economic impact of this situation may be summarized as follows:

Transaction #	ASSETS					=	LIABILITIES		+	OWNERS' EQUITY
	Cash	Inventory	Equipment	Supplies	Truck		Accounts Payable	Notes Payable		Capital Stock
Beginning Balance	$ 0	$0	$0	$0	$0	=	$0	$0	+	$ 0
Invested money in the business	2,000	–	–	–	–		–	–		2,000
Subtotal	$2,000	$0	$0	$0	$0	=	$0	$0	+	$2,000

EXAMPLE 2 Suppose that in addition to coming up with the money yourself or from your parents, you went to a bank and convinced the loan officer to lend you the money. The journal entry for such a transaction would be:

assets (+)
liabilities (+)

Cash. 2,000
    Notes Payable. 2,000
       Borrowed $2,000 from First National Bank, signing a
       12-month note at 12% interest.

Here, the cash account is debited, and the notes payable account is credited. The accounting equation captures the economic impact of borrowing the money as follows:

Transaction #	ASSETS					=	LIABILITIES		+	OWNERS' EQUITY
	Cash	Inventory	Equipment	Supplies	Truck		Accounts Payable	Notes Payable		Capital Stock
Beginning Balance	$ 0	$0	$0	$0	$0	=	$0	$ 0	+	$ 0
Invested money in the business	2,000	–	–	–	–		–	–		2,000
Borrowed money from a bank	2,000	–	–	–	–		–	2,000		–
Subtotal	$4,000	$0	$0	$0	$0	=	$0	$2,000	+	$2,000

Acquiring Other Assets

Now that you have obtained the funds necessary to start your business, either from owner investment or by borrowing, you can use that money to acquire other assets needed to operate the business. Such assets include supplies (such as fertilizer), inventory (perhaps shrubs that you will plant), and equipment (for example, a lawnmower and a truck for hauling). These assets may be purchased with cash or on credit. Credit purchases require payment after a period of time, for example, 30 days. Normally, interest expense is incurred when assets are bought on a time-payment plan that extends beyond two or three months. (To keep our examples simple here, we will not include interest expense. We will show how to account for interest on page 98, where we discuss the payment of obligations.) Examples of transactions involving the acquisition of noncash assets follow.

EXAMPLE 1 The first thing you need is a lawnmower and some form of transportation. You find an old 1988 pickup truck for sale for $800, and you buy it paying cash.

	assets (+)	Truck	800	
	assets (−)	Cash		800
		Purchased a used truck.		

The accounting equation shows:

		ASSETS				=	LIABILITIES		+	OWNERS' EQUITY
Transaction #	Cash	Inventory	Equipment	Supplies	Truck		Accounts Payable	Notes Payable		Capital Stock
Beginning Balance	$ 0	$0	$0	$0	$ 0	=	$0	$ 0	+	$ 0
Invested money in the business	2,000	–	–	–	–		–	–		2,000
Borrowed money from a bank	2,000	–	–	–	–		–	2,000		–
Purchased a truck paying cash	−800	–	–	–	800		–	–		
Subtotal	$3,200	$0	$0	$0	$800	=	$0	$2,000	+	$2,000

Next, you drive to the local Sears store and purchase a Craftsman lawnmower and gas can for $250. Instead of paying for the mower with cash, you open a charge account, which will allow you to pay for the mower in 30 days with no interest charge. (If you wait and pay beyond this 30-day grace period, an interest charge will apply.) The journal entry to record this purchase is:

	assets (+)	Equipment	250	
	liabilities (+)	Accounts Payable		250
		Purchased a lawnmower and gas can on account.		

The accounting equation shows:

		ASSETS				=	LIABILITIES		+	OWNERS' EQUITY
Transaction #	Cash	Inventory	Equipment	Supplies	Truck		Accounts Payable	Notes Payable		Capital Stock
Beginning Balance	$ 0	$0	$ 0	$0	$ 0	=	$ 0	$ 0	+	$ 0
Invested money in the business	2,000	–	–	–	–		–	–		2,000
Borrowed money from a bank	2,000	–	–	–	–		–	2,000		–
Purchased a truck paying cash	−800	–	–	–	800		–	–		–
Purchased a mower on account	–	–	250	–	–		250	–		–
Subtotal	$3,200	$0	$250	$0	$800	=	$250	$2,000	+	$2,000

When you pay for the mower, cash will be reduced, and the liability, Accounts Payable, will also be reduced, thus keeping the equation in balance.

EXAMPLE 2 Off you go to the neighborhood Eagle Hardware & Garden Shop to purchase fertilizer, gloves, a rake, a shovel, and other assorted supplies. The total cost is $180, which you pay in cash; an increase in one asset (supplies) results in a decrease in another asset (cash).

assets (+)	Supplies...	180
assets (−)	Cash..	180
	Purchased supplies for cash.	

The accounting equation shows:

Transaction #	Cash	Inventory	Equipment	Supplies	Truck	=	Accounts Payable	Notes Payable	+	Capital Stock
			ASSETS			**=**	**LIABILITIES**		**+**	**OWNERS' EQUITY**
Beginning Balance	$ 0	$0	$ 0	$ 0	$ 0	=	$ 0	$ 0	+	$ 0
Invested money in the business	2,000	–	–	–	–		–	–		2,000
Borrowed money from a bank	2,000	–	–	–	–		–	2,000		–
Purchased a truck paying cash	−800	–	–	–	800		–	–		–
Purchased a mower on account	–	–	250	–	–		250	–		–
Purchased supplies for cash	−180	–	–	180	–		–	–		–
Subtotal	$3,020	$0	$250	$180	$800	=	$250	$2,000	+	$2,000

EXAMPLE 3 On your way home from the hardware store, you drive past a greenhouse and notice a big sign advertising a "50% off" sale on shrubs. Since you anticipate that planting shrubs will be part of your business, you stop and purchase for cash $150 worth of shrubs as inventory. You plan to make money in two ways with the shrubs: (1) revenue from the labor associated with planting them and (2) a profit on selling the shrubs for more than you paid. (This is fair; after all, you are saving your client the time and trouble of having to go to the greenhouse.)

assets (+)	Inventory...	150
assets (−)	Cash..	150
	Purchased inventory for cash.	

The accounting equation shows:

Transaction #	ASSETS					=	LIABILITIES		+	OWNERS' EQUITY
	Cash	Inventory	Equipment	Supplies	Truck		Accounts Payable	Notes Payable		Capital Stock
Beginning Balance	$ 0	$ 0	$ 0	$ 0	$ 0	=	$ 0	$ 0	+	$ 0
Invested money in the business	2,000	–	–	–	–		–	–		2,000
Borrowed money from a bank	2,000	–	–	–	–		–	2,000		–
Purchased a truck paying cash	−800	–	–	–	800		–	–		–
Purchased a mower on account	–	–	250	–	–		250	–		–
Purchased supplies for cash	−180	–	–	180	–		–	–		–
Purchased inventory for cash	−150	150	–	–	–		–	–		–
Subtotal	$2,870	$150	$250	$180	$800	=	$250	$2,000	+	$2,000

Selling Goods or Providing Services

Now that you have your lawnmower, your transportation, your supplies, and your inventory, it is time to go to work. The next category of common transactions involves the sale of services or merchandise. Revenues are generated and expenses incurred during this process. Sometimes services and merchandise are sold for cash; at other times, they are sold on credit (on account), and a receivable is established for collection at a later date. Therefore, revenues indicate the source not only of cash but of other assets as well, all of which are received in exchange for the merchandise or services provided. Similarly, expenses may be incurred and paid for immediately by cash, or they may be incurred on credit—that is, they may be "charged," with a cash payment to be made at a later date. Illustrative transactions follow. Note the effect of revenues and expenses on owners' equity is indicated in brackets for each transaction.

EXAMPLE 1 As soon as people find out that you are in the lawn care and landscaping business, your phone begins ringing off the hook. Although most of your clients pay you immediately when you perform the service, some prefer to pay you once a month. As a result, a portion of your revenues is received immediately in cash, while the balance becomes receivables. The journal entry to record your first week's revenue for lawn care services is:

assets (+)	Cash. 270	
assets (+)	Accounts Receivable 80	
revenues (+) [equity (+)]	Lawn Care Revenue	350
	To record revenue for lawn care services.	

compound journal entry A journal entry that involves more than one debit or more than one credit or both.

As the journal entry illustrates, more than two accounts can be involved in recording a transaction. This type of entry is called a **compound journal entry**.

Because revenues increase owners' equity, the accounting equation shows:

Assets	=	Liabilities	+	Owners' Equity (Revenues)
(increase $350)		(no change)		(increase $350)

The detailed effect of this transaction and of each of the following transactions is summarized in Exhibit 3-5 on page 100.

EXAMPLE 2   One of your customers asks if you will plant some shrubs in her backyard. You mention that you have some shrubs and describe them to her; she is thrilled that you have just the shrubs she wants, thereby saving her a trip to the greenhouse. You use one-half of your inventory of shrubs in this customer's yard, and it takes you three hours to complete the job. She pays you in cash. In this instance, we are dealing with two different types of revenue—profit from the sale of the shrubs and revenue from your labor. Let's deal with each type of revenue separately.

Sale of Shrubs   Sales, whether made on account or for cash, require entries that reflect not only the sale, but also the cost of the inventory sold. The "cost of goods sold" is an expense and, as such, is offset with the sales revenue to determine the profitability of sales transactions. The special procedures for handling inventory are described in Chapter 7. It is sufficient here to show an example of the impact of the transaction on the accounting equation.

In this example, you charged your customer $90 for one-half of the shrubs you purchased earlier.

assets (+)	Cash.	90	
revenues (+) [equity (+)]	Sales Revenue		90
	Sold inventory for cash.	
expenses (+) [equity (−)]	Cost of Goods Sold	75	
assets (−)	Inventory		75
	To record the cost of inventory sold and to reduce inventory for its cost.	

In this example, inventory costing you $75 is being sold for $90. The effect on the accounting equation for each transaction is:

Sales on Account

Assets	=	Liabilities	+	Owners' Equity (Revenues)
(increase $90)		(no change)		(increase $90)

Could the two journal entries relating to the sale of inventory be combined into one journal entry?

Cost of Goods Sold

Assets	=	Liabilities	+	Owners' Equity (Expenses)
(decrease $75)		(no change)		(decrease $75)

Labor for Planting   In addition to making a profit on the sale of the shrubs, you also generated revenue planting them. The journal entry to record this revenue is:

assets (+)	Cash.	45	
revenues (+) [equity (+)]	Landscaping Revenue.		45
	To record revenue for landscaping services.	

The effect of the transaction on the accounting equation is:

Assets	=	Liabilities	+	Owners' Equity (Revenues)
(increase $45)		(no change)		(increase $45)

EXAMPLE 3   In addition to expenses relating to the sale of inventory, other expenses are also incurred in operating a business. Examples include gas for your lawnmower and your truck and the wages you agreed to pay your little brother for working for you (Mom said you had to let him help). The following journal entries illustrate how these expenses would be accounted for:

expenses (+) [equity (−)]
assets (−)

Gasoline Expense..	50	
Cash..		50
Paid cash for gas for the truck and the mower.		

expenses (+) [equity (−)]
assets (−)

Wages Expense...	60	
Cash..		60
Paid wages expense.		

The effect on the accounting equation of the gasoline expense is:

Assets	=	Liabilities	+	Owners' Equity (Expense)
(decrease $50)		(no change)		(decrease $50)

The entry for Wages Expense affects the equation in the same manner, the only difference being the amount, $60.

Collecting Cash and Paying Obligations

Obviously, once merchandise or services are sold on account, the receivables must be collected. The cash received is generally used to meet daily operating expenses and to pay other obligations. Excess cash can be reinvested in the business or distributed to the owners as a return on their investment.

EXAMPLE 1   The collection of accounts receivable is an important aspect of most businesses. Receivables are created when you allow certain customers to pay for your services at a later date. When receivables are collected, that asset is reduced and cash is increased, as shown here.

assets (+)
assets (−)

Cash..	80	
Accounts Receivable................................		80
Collected $80 of receivables.		

The effect of collecting the receivables on the accounting equation is:

Assets	=	Liabilities	+	Owners' Equity
(increase $80; decrease $80)		(no change)		(no change)

Note that no revenue is involved here. Revenue is recorded when the original sales transaction creates the accounts receivable. The cash collection on account merely involves exchanging one asset for another.

EXAMPLE 2   Remember that lawnmower and gas can you purchased on account? Well, now you have to pay for them. The entry to record the payment of obligations with cash is:

liabilities (−)
assets (−)

Accounts Payable..	250	
Cash..		250
Paid $250 for the lawnmower and gas can previously purchased.		

After payment of accounts payable, the accounting equation shows:

Assets   =   Liabilities   +   Owners' Equity
(decrease $250)   (decrease $250)   (no change)

Remember that two parties are always involved in exchange transactions. What one buys, the other sells. When sales are on credit, the seller will record a receivable and the buyer will record a payable. The two accounts are inversely related. The seller of merchandise records a receivable and a sale, and simultaneously records an expense for the cost of goods sold and a reduction of inventory (as in Example 2 on page 96). The buyer records the receipt of the merchandise and, at the same time, records an obligation to pay the seller at some future time. When payment is made, the buyer reduces Accounts Payable and Cash (as in this example), whereas the seller increases Cash and reduces Accounts Receivable (as in Example 1).

EXAMPLE 3   On page 92, we showed the entry required when cash was borrowed from the bank. In that entry, you borrowed $2,000 to be paid over 12 months. Suppose you are required to make monthly loan payments of $178 with a portion of each payment being attributed to interest and a portion to reducing the liability—just like a mortgage on a house. As the following compound journal entry shows, a note payable or similar obligation requires an entry for payment, as well as for the interest due. Note that "interest" is the amount charged for using money, as will be more fully explained in later chapters.

liabilities (−)
expenses (+) [equity (−)]
assets (−)

Notes Payable	158	
Interest Expense..	20	
Cash..		178
Paid first monthly payment on note with interest		
($2,000 × 0.12 × 1/12).		

Analysis of this transaction reveals that assets have decreased for two reasons. First, a portion of a liability has been paid with cash. Second, interest expense at 12% for one month on the note payable has been paid. This relationship will generally be present in most long-term and some short-term liability transactions. Since the interest charge is an expense and decreases owners' equity, the impact of the entry on the accounting equation is:

Assets   =   Liabilities   +   Owners' Equity (Expense)
(decrease $178)   (decrease $158)   (decrease $20)

EXAMPLE 4   Recall that you obtained financing in two ways to start your business—investors (you, Mom, and Dad) and the bank. In the previous journal entry, we illustrated how the bank receives a return on its investment. Well, Mom and Dad would like a return as well. Corporations that are profitable generally pay dividends to their stockholders. "Dividends" represent a distribution to the stockholders of part of the earnings of a company. The following entry illustrates the payment of a cash dividend:

STOP & THINK   Why are dividends NOT considered to be an expense?

dividends (+) [equity (−)]
assets (−)

Dividends...	50	
Cash..		50
Paid a $50 cash dividend.		

As noted earlier, dividends, like revenues and expenses, affect owners' equity. Unlike revenues and expenses, dividends are a distribution of profits and, therefore, are not considered in determining net income. Because dividends reduce the retained earnings accumulated by a corporation, they decrease owners' equity. The payment of a $50 dividend affects the accounting equation as follows:

Assets   =   Liabilities   +   Owners' Equity (Dividends)
(decrease $50)   (no change)   (decrease $50)

See Exhibit 3-5 for a summary of the transactions shown in this chapter and their effect on the accounting equation.

A Note on Journal Entries

When preparing a journal entry, a systematic method may be used in analyzing every transaction. A journal entry involves a three-step process:

1. Identify which accounts are involved.
2. For each account, determine if it is increased or decreased.
3. For each account, determine by how much it has changed.

The answer to step 1 tells you if the accounts involved are asset, liability, or owners' equity accounts. The answer to step 2, when considered in light of your answer to step 1, tells you if the accounts involved are to be debited or credited. Consider the instance where $25,000 is borrowed from a bank. The two accounts involved are Cash and Notes Payable. Cash increased, and since Cash is an asset and assets increase with debits, then Cash must be debited. Notes Payable increased (we owe more money), and since Notes Payable is a liability and liabilities increase with credits, then Notes Payable must be credited. The answer to step 3 completes the journal entry. Cash is debited for $25,000, and Notes Payable is credited for $25,000.

This three-step process will always work, even for complex transactions. Consider the case where inventory costing $60,000 is sold on account for $75,000. Using the three-step process results in the following:

1. *Step 1:* What accounts are involved?
   - Accounts Receivable (an asset), Inventory (an asset), Cost of Goods Sold (an expense—part of owners' equity), and Sales Revenue (a revenue account—part of owners' equity).

2. *Step 2:* Did the accounts increase or decrease?
   - Accounts Receivable increased (customers owe us more money). Since Accounts Receivable is an asset, it is increased with a debit.
   - Inventory decreased (we don't have it anymore). Since Inventory is an asset, it is decreased with a credit.
   - Cost of Goods Sold increased (an expense causing owners' equity to decrease). Since owners' equity decreases with a debit, Cost of Goods Sold must be debited.
   - Sales Revenue increased (a revenue causing owners' equity to increase). Since owners' equity increases with a credit, Sales Revenue must be credited.

3. *Step 3:* By how much did each account change?
   - The answer to step 3 results in the following journal entries:

Accounts Receivable.	75,000	
Sales Revenue.		75,000
Cost of Goods Sold	60,000	
Inventory.		60,000

to summarize

Journal entries are used to summarize the effects of business transactions. Journal entries are prepared or analyzed by answering three questions: (1) What accounts are involved? (2) Did those accounts increase or decrease? (3) By how much did each account change? By correctly answering these three questions, transactions will be properly accounted for, and the accounting equation will always balance.

exhibit 3-5   Summary of Transactions

	Cash	Accounts Receivable	Inventory	Equipment	Supplies	Truck		Accounts Payable	Notes Payable
			ASSETS				**=**	**LIABILITIES**	
Balance	$2,870	–	$150	$250	$180	$800	=	$250	$2,000
Revenue from lawn care	270	80	–	–	–	–		–	–
Sold inventory for cash	90	–	–75	–	–	–		–	–
Revenue from landscaping	45	–	–	–	–	–		–	–
Paid for gasoline	–50	–	–	–	–	–		–	–
Paid wages	–60	–	–	–	–	–		–	–
Collected receivables	80	–80	–	–	–	–		–	–
Paid accounts payable	–250	–	–	–	–	–		–250	–
Paid loan payment	–178	–	–	–	–	–		–	–158
Paid dividend	–50	–	–	–	–	–		–	–
Total	$2,767	$ 0	$ 75	$250	$180	$800	=	$ 0	$1,842

A Bookkeeping Attack Starts a War Tom Clancy typed the first draft of his first novel, *The Hunt for Red October,* on an IBM Selectric typewriter while still holding down his full-time job as an insurance agent. The book was published in October 1984, and sales took off when it became known that the book was President Ronald Reagan's favorite. To date, Clancy has published a total of seven novels featuring the reluctant hero Jack Ryan, and the stories have been so popular that Clancy now commands a record $25 million advance per book.

In *The Hunt for Red October,* Jack Ryan, who was trained as a historian, is a part-time analyst for the CIA. By the sixth novel in the series, *Debt of Honor,* a well-earned reputation for being a "good man in a storm" has landed Ryan, against his wishes, in the position of serving as the president's National Security Adviser. Jack Ryan's abilities are tested as an international crisis is touched off when a group of Japanese businessmen gain control of their government and determine that the only way to save the Japanese economy is through neutralization of U.S. power in the Pacific.

The first act of war against the United States is an attack not on a military target but instead on the book-

+	OWNERS' EQUITY								
	Retained Earnings								
	Capital Stock	Lawn Care Revenue	Sales Revenue	Landscaping Revenue	Cost of Goods Sold*	Gasoline Expense*	Wages Expense*	Interest Expense*	Dividends*
+	$2,000	–	–	–	–	–	–	–	–
	–	350	–	–	–	–	–	–	–
	–	–	90	–	–75	–	–	–	–
	–	–	–	45	–	–	–	–	–
	–	–	–	–	–	–50	–	–	–
	–	–	–	–	–	–	–60	–	–
	–	–	–	–	–	–	–	–	–
	–	–	–	–	–	–	–	–	–
	–	–	–	–	–	–	–	–20	–
	–	–	–	–	–	–	–	–	–50
+	$2,000	$350	$90	$45	–$75	–$50	–$60	–$20	–$50

*Recall that an increase in these accounts actually decreases owners' equity, hence the – (minus sign).

keeping system used by U.S. stock exchanges. A computer virus, injected into the program used to record trades on all the major U.S. stock exchanges, is activated at noon on Friday. The records of all trades made after that time are eliminated with this result:

No trading house, institution, or private investor could know what it had bought or sold, to or from whom, or for how much, and none could therefore know how much money was available for other trades, or for that matter, to purchase groceries over

the weekend. (Tom Clancy, *Debt of Honor*, p. 312)

The uncertainty created by the destruction of the stock exchange bookkeeping records threatens to throw the U.S. economy into a tailspin and distract U.S. policy makers from other moves being made by Japan in the Pacific. Jack Ryan saves the world as we know it and restores the U.S. economy to sound footing by . . . well, it wouldn't be fair to say—you'll have to read the book. Suffice it to say that a key part of the restoration plan is the repair of the stock exchange bookkeeping system.

4

Summarize the resulting journal entries through posting and prepare a trial balance (step three of the accounting cycle).

posting The process of transferring amounts from the journal to the ledger.

ledger A book of accounts in which data from transactions recorded in journals are posted and thereby summarized.

chart of accounts A systematic listing of all accounts used by a company.

---

c a u t i o n

Common mistakes when manually posting include posting a debit to the credit side of an account, transposing numbers (e.g., a 45 magically becomes a 54), and posting to the wrong account (e.g., Supplies instead of Inventory). The lesson—be very careful or mistakes will creep into your work. Thankfully, posting is a task done almost exclusively by computers these days.

POSTING JOURNAL ENTRIES AND PREPARING A TRIAL BALANCE

Once transactions have been analyzed and recorded in a journal, it is necessary to classify and group all similar items. This is accomplished by the bookkeeping procedure of **posting** all the journal entries to appropriate accounts. As indicated earlier, accounts are records of like items. They show transaction dates, increases and decreases, and balances. For example, all increases and decreases in cash arising from transactions recorded in the journal are accumulated in one account called Cash. Similarly, all sales transactions are grouped together in the sales revenue account.

Posting is no more than sorting all journal entry amounts by account and copying those amounts to the appropriate account. No analysis is needed; all the necessary analysis is performed when the transaction is first recorded in the journal.

All accounts are maintained in an accounting record called the "general ledger." A **ledger** is a "book of accounts." Exhibit 3-6 shows how the three cash transactions in the general journal would be posted to the cash account in the general ledger, with arrows depicting the posting procedures. Observe that a number has been inserted in the "posting reference" column in both books. This number serves as a cross-reference between the general journal and the accounts in the general ledger. In the journal, it identifies the account to which the journal entry has been posted. In the ledger, it identifies the page on which the entry appears in the general journal. For example, the GJ1 notation in the cash account for the July 1 entry means that the $2,000 has been posted from page 1 of the general journal. As you will discover, these posting references are useful in tracking down mistakes. With a computer system, the software automatically generates these posting references.

A particular company will have as many (or as few) accounts as it needs to provide a reasonable classification of its transactions. The list of accounts used by a company is known as its **chart of accounts**. The normal order of a chart of accounts is assets (current and long-term), then liabilities (current and long-term), followed by owners' equity, sales, and expenses. Exhibit 3-7 shows some accounts that might appear in a typical company's chart of accounts.

Determining Account Balances

At the end of an accounting period, the accounts in the general ledger are reviewed to determine each account's balance. Asset, expense, and dividend accounts normally have debit balances; liability, owners' equity, and revenue accounts normally have credit balances. In other words, the balance is normally on the side that increases the account.

To illustrate how to determine an account balance, consider the following T-account depicting all the cash transactions from our landscaping business (with dates being added). The beginning cash account balance plus all Cash debit entries, less total credits to Cash, equals the ending balance in the cash account.

Cash			
Beg. Bal.	0		
7/1	2,000		
7/1	2,000	7/5	800
7/9	270	7/5	180
7/14	90	7/7	150
7/14	45	7/18	50
7/30	80	7/23	60
		7/31	250
		7/31	178
		7/31	50
	4,485		(1,718)
	(1,718)		
End. Bal.	2,767		

exhibit 3-6   Posting to the General Ledger

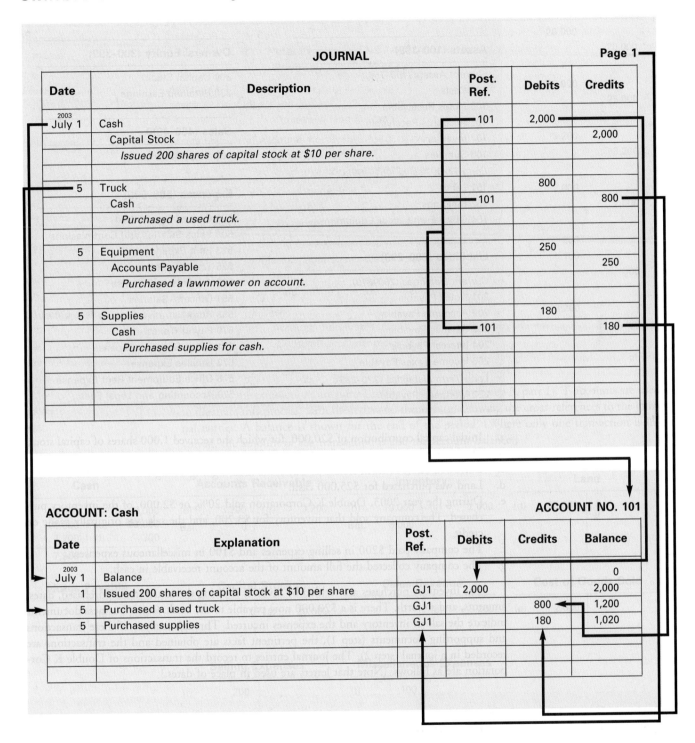

		JOURNAL			Page 1
Date		**Description**	**Post. Ref.**	**Debits**	**Credits**
2003 July 1	Cash		101	2,000	
	Capital Stock				2,000
		Issued 200 shares of capital stock at $10 per share.			
5	Truck			800	
	Cash		101		800
		Purchased a used truck.			
5	Equipment			250	
	Accounts Payable				250
		Purchased a lawnmower on account.			
5	Supplies			180	
	Cash		101		180
		Purchased supplies for cash.			

ACCOUNT: Cash   **ACCOUNT NO. 101**

Date	**Explanation**	**Post. Ref.**	**Debits**	**Credits**	**Balance**
2003 July 1	Balance				0
1	Issued 200 shares of capital stock at $10 per share	GJ1	2,000		2,000
5	Purchased a used truck	GJ1		800	1,200
5	Purchased supplies	GJ1		180	1,020

Illustration of the First Three Steps in the Accounting Cycle

We have introduced the first three steps in the accounting cycle. A simple illustration will help reinforce what you have learned about the relationship of assets, liabilities, and owners' equity, as well as revenues, expenses, and dividends, and the mechanics of double-entry accounting. Katherine Kohler established the Double K Corporation in 2003. The following transactions occurred.

exhibit 3-8   Effects of Business Transactions on the Accounting Equation

Transaction #	ASSETS				=	LIABILITIES	+	OWNERS' EQUITY					
	Cash	Inventory	Land	Accounts Receivable		Notes Payable		Capital Stock	Retained Earnings				
										Sales Revenue	Cost of Goods Sold*	Selling Expenses*	Misc. Expenses*
Beginning Balance	$ 0	$ 0	$ 0	$ 0	=	$ 0	+	$ 0	–	–	–	–
a	20,000	–	–	–		–		20,000	–	–	–	–
b	−10,000	10,000	–	–		–		0	–	–	–	–
c	20,000	–	–	–		20,000		–	–	–	–	–
d	−25,000	–	25,000	–		–		–	–	–	–	–
e	–	−2,000	–	3,200		–		–	3,200	−2,000	–	–
f	−300	–	–	–		–		–	–	–	−200	−100
g	3,200	–	–	−3,200		–		–	–	–	–	–
Total	$ 7,900	$ 8,000	$25,000	$ 0	=	$20,000	+	$20,000	$3,200	−$2,000	−$200	−$100

*Recall that an increase in these accounts actually decreases owners' equity, hence the − (minus sign).

ing a trial balance; additional analysis would be required. In this case, total debits equal total credits. Thus, the accounting equation is in balance. The balances are taken from each ledger account.

Students frequently mistake a trial balance and the balance sheet for one another. In fact, they are very different reports. A trial balance is strictly an internal document used to summarize all of the account balances (assets, liabilities, owners' equity, revenues, expenses, and dividends) in a company's accounting system. Few people outside a company's accounting department ever see the trial balance; most businesspeople never see a real trial balance during their

exhibit 3-9   Trial Balance

Double K Corporation
Trial Balance
December 31, 2003

	Debits	Credits
Cash..	$ 7,900	
Accounts Receivable...........................	0	
Inventory.....................................	8,000	
Land..	25,000	
Notes Payable.................................		$20,000
Capital Stock.................................		20,000
Sales Revenue.................................		3,200
Cost of Goods Sold............................	2,000	
Selling Expenses..............................	200	
Miscellaneous Expenses........................	100	
Totals....................................	$43,200	$43,200

entire business career. The balance sheet, on the other hand, is a summary document that is frequently provided to interested parties both inside and outside a company.

From the data in the trial balance, an income statement and a balance sheet can be prepared. Exhibit 3-10 shows these two financial statements for Double K Corporation. Notice that there is no retained earnings account in the trial balance but there is one on the balance sheet. The reason for this is that all the income statement accounts such as Revenue, Cost of Goods Sold, and expenses are eventually accumulated into Retained Earnings. That is, earnings are re-

---

exhibit 3-10   Income Statement and Balance Sheet

Double K Corporation
Income Statement
For the Year Ended December 31, 2003

Sales revenue..		$3,200
Expenses:		
Cost of goods sold	$2,000	
Selling expenses.....................................	200	
Miscellaneous expenses	100	2,300
Net income...		$ 900
EPS ($900 ÷ 1,000 shares)		$ 0.90

Double K Corporation
Balance Sheet
December 31, 2003

Assets		Liabilities and Owners' Equity	
Cash................	$ 7,900	Notes payable..................	$20,000
Inventory	8,000	Capital stock (1,000 shares).......	20,000
Land................	25,000	Retained earnings	900*
		Total liabilities and	
Total assets.........	$40,900	owners' equity...............	$40,900

*Beginning retained earnings + net income − dividends.

exhibit 3-11   Statement of Cash Flows

Double K Corporation Statement of Cash Flows For the Year Ended December 31, 2003		
Operating activities:		
Collections from customers	$ 3,200	
Purchase of inventory	(10,000)	
Paid expenses	(300)	$ (7,100)
Investing activities:		
Purchased land		(25,000)
Financing activities:		
Issued stock	$20,000	
Borrowed from bank	20,000	40,000
Net increase in cash		$ 7,900
Beginning cash balance		0
Ending cash balance		$ 7,900

flected on the income statement. The business then decides the amount of those earnings to be retained. Those earnings that are to be retained are then disclosed on the balance sheet.

Also, the statement of cash flows can be prepared by categorizing the items in the cash account as operating, investing, or financing, as shown in Exhibit 3-11.

Two final notes: First, the preparation of financial statements is rarely so simple. In reality, the procedure also involves the adjustment of some ledger accounts, which need to be brought current before they can be included in the balance sheet or the income statement. In Chapter 4, we will explain how accounts are adjusted (step 4, part 1) so that the financial statements will accurately reflect the current financial position and operating results of an enterprise.

Second, net income does not usually equal the ending retained earnings balance. Only in the first year of a company's operations would this be the case. Double K Corporation began operations in 2003 and paid no dividends during the year; so, its $900 net income on the income statement equals the retained earnings figure on the balance sheet. In future years, the figures would be different, since retained earnings is an accumulation of earnings from past years adjusted for dividends and other special items.

to summarize

Once journal entries have been made and posted to the related accounts, account balances are computed by summing the debit and credit entries in each account. A trial balance is prepared by listing each account along with its balance. An income statement and a balance sheet can be prepared from this trial balance. A statement of cash flows is prepared by analyzing the inflows and outflows of cash as detailed in the cash account.

5

Describe how technology has affected the first three steps of the accounting cycle.

WHERE DO COMPUTERS FIT IN ALL THIS?

Students often ask, "Do I really need to know the difference between a debit and a credit? Haven't computers taken care of that?" Computers have greatly facilitated a business's ability to quickly process huge amounts of information without making mathematical errors. Most computers can make millions of calculations per second and produce more documents in ten minutes than a person could in an entire week. The time spent posting journal entries and summarizing accounts into a trial balance has been greatly reduced as a result of computers.

But computers still can't think. That's your job. Walk up to a computer terminal and show it a sales invoice and the computer will just sit there and wait. Wait for what? For the answers to three questions: (1) What accounts are involved? (2) Did those accounts increase or decrease? (3) By how much did each account change?

Let's consider how the best-selling money management software package, Quicken®, has changed the accounting process. Quicken works a lot like a check register. For each check, you indicate the date, the check number, the payee, and the amount. Quicken then prompts you to indicate the nature of the expenditure by selecting from a list of accounts. For example, if the expenditure relates to your purchase of groceries, you would select the account "Food." Thus, all your transactions relating to "Food" will be grouped together, allowing you to quickly determine all food expenditures.

Now let's review what Quicken has done. First of all, since you indicated the transaction involved a check, Quicken knows that cash decreased. Quicken is programmed to know that when cash decreases, it involves a credit to the cash account. Quicken also has been programmed to know that debits have to equal credits, and since Cash was credited, the program knows that something was debited. Since you indicated "Food" (an expense) was the other account, Quicken debits that account, causing your expense account to increase (we now know that expenses increase with debits). Instead of telling Quicken which accounts to debit and credit, you are required to identify the accounts (question 1) and indicate if they increased or decreased (question 2). Quicken is able to determine, based on the answer to these two questions, which accounts were debited and which accounts were credited.

So has Quicken fundamentally changed the accounting process? No. It has increased the accuracy and speed with which the posting process is done, as well as the speed with which a variety of reports can be prepared. Quicken has also eliminated the need for the user to specify debit or credit. Because computers are so fast, the two-step process of identifying accounts and the direction of their change can be done as quickly as you can say "credit Cash." So why don't accountants get rid of these 500-year-old terms, debit and credit? The reason is that all accountants are familiar with and comfortable using these terms. When someone says "credit Cash," accountants everywhere know exactly what that means. Thus, debit and credit provide a useful shorthand method of communication.

It should be noted that computers also bring with them several disadvantages. The acronym "GIGO" (garbage in, garbage out) refers to the problems that result when data are entered incorrectly. If you tell the computer the wrong account or wrong amount, all the related accounts and reports will be wrong. If bookkeepers or accountants had been doing the posting, they might have caught an unrealistic figure or account and corrected the mistake at its source; computers accept data without question.

A related problem has to do with fixing an error once it has been identified. Unlike someone familiar with the accounting process, a computer cannot grasp the double-entry nature of accounting and realize that, for example, an incorrect amount may be posted to two accounts, not just one. As an example, suppose a customer calls and notifies you of an error in her account—a sale to her was incorrectly recorded as $100 instead of $10. You can correct the customer's account by making a $90 adjustment to Accounts Receivable, but Sales would need to be adjusted by $90 as well. A computer couldn't extrapolate this and would end up overlooking this Sales adjustment.

The computer has enhanced step 3 of the accounting cycle—summarizing. In fact, only in the smallest of businesses will you find the posting of journal entries and the preparation of a trial balance being done by hand. But in every business, from the largest to the smallest, you will find accountants still actively involved in analyzing transactions and turning those transactions into journal entries and eventually into useful accounting reports.

to summarize

The computer has changed certain aspects of the accounting cycle. The posting process has been substantially improved through the use of computers. In addition, computers have made the preparation of reports and statements easier. But computers have not replaced the need to analyze transactions and determine their effect on the accounting equation.

review of learning objectives

1 **Understand the process of transforming transaction data into useful accounting information.** The objective of the accounting process is to gather and transform transaction data into useful information that measures and communicates the results of business activity. The accounting system used to keep track of the many financial activities of a business should be tailor-made for that business and may be a manual or an automated system, depending on the organization's needs.

2 **Analyze transactions and determine how those transactions affect the accounting equation (step one of the accounting cycle).** The procedures for processing accounting data are based on double-entry accounting and the fundamental accounting equation: Assets = Liabilities + Owners' Equity. Revenues increase retained earnings, whereas expenses and dividends decrease retained earnings. Thus, these accounts have a direct impact on the amount of owners' equity. In terms of the increase/decrease relationship of accounts, assets, expenses, and dividends are increased by debits; liabilities, owners' equity, and revenues are increased by credits. The double-entry system of accounting ensures that the accounting equation will always balance because debit entries require equal credit entries; that is, total debits must always equal total credits when transactions are properly recorded.

3 **Record the effects of transactions using journal entries (step two of the accounting cycle).** The effects of

business events are recorded in the accounting system using journal entries. Journal entries detail the accounts involved in a transaction, whether the accounts increased or decreased, and the amount by which each account is affected. Each journal entry requires an equal amount of debits and credits. This equality ensures that the accounting equation will always be in balance.

4 **Summarize the resulting journal entries through posting and prepare a trial balance (step three of the accounting cycle).** Once journal entries are made, they are posted to individual accounts. The posting process involves simply copying each debit and credit from a journal entry into the associated account. A trial balance can be prepared to ensure that debits equal credits and that the accounting equation is in balance. From the trial balance, the primary financial statements can be prepared.

5 **Describe how technology has affected the first three steps of the accounting cycle.** Computers have changed the speed at which journal entries are processed through the accounting system. In most accounting systems, the posting process is done using computers. Computers ensure that no errors are made in transferring amounts from the journal entries to the accounts. Computers are also able to determine account balances and prepare reports quickly. Accountants are still required for the analysis and input of information into the accounting system.

key terms and concepts

account 84
accounting cycle 79
business documents 80
chart of accounts 102
compound journal entry 96

credit 86
debit 86
dividends 88
journal 90
journal entry 90

journalizing 90
ledger 102
posting 102
T-account 86
trial balance 105

review problem

The First Three Steps in the Accounting Cycle

Journal entries are given below for January 2003, the first month of operation for the Svendsen Service Company.

Jan. 2	Cash	40,000	
	Capital Stock		40,000
	Issued capital stock for cash.		
2	Insurance Expense	500	
	Cash		500
	Purchased a one-month insurance policy.		
2	Rent Expense	750	
	Cash		750
	Paid rent for the month of January.		
3	Shop Equipment	8,000	
	Cash		8,000
	Purchased shop equipment for cash.		
4	Supplies	3,000	
	Accounts Payable		3,000
	Purchased shop supplies on account.		
5	Automotive Equipment	11,500	
	Cash		3,500
	Notes Payable		8,000
	Purchased a truck. Paid $3,500 cash and issued a 30-day note for the balance.		
8	Cash	1,750	
	Service and Repair Revenue		1,750
	Received cash for repairs.		
9	Advertising Expense	300	
	Cash		300
	Paid cash for radio spot announcements.		
12	Automotive Expense	200	
	Cash		200
	Paid gas, oil, and service costs on the truck.		
14	Accounts Payable	3,000	
	Cash		3,000
	Paid $3,000 on account.		
16	Accounts Receivable	1,200	
	Service and Repair Revenue		1,200
	Repaired truck for Acme Drilling Company on account.		
18	Telephone Expense	75	
	Cash		75
	Paid for installation and telephone service for one month.		
19	Automotive Expense	180	
	Cash		180
	Paid for minor repairs on the truck.		
20	Cash	1,000	
	Notes Receivable	1,450	
	Service and Repair Revenue		2,450
	Collected $1,000 cash from Jones for truck repairs; accepted a 60-day note for the balance.		

(continued)

Jan. 24	Repairs and Maintenance Expense	150	
	Cash		150
	Paid cleaning and painting expenses on the building.		
25	Cash	1,500	
	Service and Repair Revenue		1,500
	Received cash for repairs and services from Hamilton, Inc.		
27	Supplies	2,500	
	Cash		2,500
	Purchased shop supplies.		
29	Office Equipment	1,250	
	Cash		1,250
	Purchased a computer.		
30	Cash	1,200	
	Accounts Receivable		1,200
	Collected receivables from Acme Drilling Company.		
31	Utilities Expense	900	
	Cash		900
	Paid the monthly utility bill.		
31	Automotive Expense	350	
	Cash		350
	Paid for gas, oil, and servicing of the truck.		

Required: Set up T-accounts, post all journal entries to the accounts, balance the accounts, and prepare a trial balance.

Solution The first step in solving this problem is to set up T-accounts for each item; then post all journal entries to the appropriate ledger accounts, as shown. Once the amounts are properly posted, account balances can be determined.

	Cash					Notes Receivable				Accounts Receivable					Supplies	
1/2	40,000	1/2	500		1/20	1,450			1/16	1,200	1/30	1,200		1/4	3,000	
1/8	1,750	1/2	750						Bal.	0				1/27	2,500	
1/20	1,000	1/3	8,000											Bal.	5,500	
1/25	1,500	1/5	3,500													
1/30	1,200	1/9	300													
		1/12	200													
		1/14	3,000													
		1/18	75			Shop Equipment				Automotive Equipment					Office Equipment	
		1/19	180													
		1/24	150		1/3	8,000			1/5	11,500				1/29	1,250	
		1/27	2,500													
		1/29	1,250													
		1/31	900													
		1/31	350													
Bal.	23,795															

	Notes Payable				Accounts Payable					Capital Stock				Service and Repair Revenue	
		1/5	8,000	1/14	3,000	1/4	3,000			1/2	40,000		1/8	1,750
						Bal.	0						1/16	1,200
													1/20	2,450
													1/25	1,500
													Bal.	6,900

(continued)

Insurance Expense		Rent Expense		Advertising Expense		Automotive Expense	
1/2 500		1/2 750		1/9 300		1/12 200	
						1/19 180	
						1/31 350	
						Bal. 730	

Telephone Expense		Repairs and Maintenance Expense		Utilities Expense	
1/18 75		1/24 150		1/31 900	

The final step is to prepare a trial balance to see whether total debits equal total credits for all accounts. List all the accounts with balances; then enter the balance in each account.

Svendsen Service Company
Trial Balance
January 31, 2003

	Debits	Credits
Cash	$23,795	
Accounts Receivable	0	
Notes Receivable	1,450	
Supplies	5,500	
Shop Equipment	8,000	
Automotive Equipment	11,500	
Office Equipment	1,250	
Accounts Payable		$ 0
Notes Payable		8,000
Capital Stock		40,000
Service and Repair Revenue		6,900
Insurance Expense	500	
Rent Expense	750	
Advertising Expense	300	
Automotive Expense	730	
Telephone Expense	75	
Repairs and Maintenance Expense	150	
Utilities Expense	900	
Totals	$54,900	$54,900

discussion questions

1. What is the basic objective of the accounting cycle?
2. Explain the first three steps in the accounting cycle.
3. What are the advantages of a computer-based accounting system? Does such a system eliminate the need for human judgment? Explain.
4. In a double-entry system of accounting, why must total debits always equal total credits?
5. Explain the increase/decrease, debit/credit relationship of asset, liability, and owners' equity accounts.

6. How are revenues, expenses, and dividends related to the basic accounting equation?

7. In what ways are dividend and expense accounts similar, and in what ways are they different?

8. How does understanding the mechanics of accounting help a businessperson who has no intention of practicing accounting?

9. Distinguish between a journal and a ledger.

10. Assume that Company A buys $1,500 of merchandise from Company B for cash. The merchandise originally cost Company B $1,000. What entries should the buyer and seller make, and what is the relationship of the accounts for this transaction?

11. Indicate how each of the following transactions affects the accounting equation.
    a. Purchase of supplies on account.
    b. Payment of wages.
    c. Cash sales of goods for more than their cost.
    d. Payment of monthly utility bills.
    e. Purchase of a building with a down payment of cash plus a mortgage.
    f. Cash investment by a stockholder.
    g. Payment of a cash dividend.
    h. Sale of goods on account for more than their cost.
    i. Sale of land at less than its cost.

12. What is a chart of accounts? What is its purpose?

13. If a trial balance appears to be correct (debits equal credits), does that guarantee complete accuracy in the accounting records? Explain.

14. What is the difference between a trial balance and a balance sheet?

15. Have computers eliminated the need to analyze transactions? Explain.

discussion cases

CASE 3-1

HOW DOES MICROSOFT (AND OTHER COMPANIES) DO IT?

MICROSOFT's revenues exceeded $19 billion in 1999. These revenues were generated by millions of transactions all over the world—in the United States, Canada, Europe, South America, and Asia. What is the process used by Microsoft to transform this tremendous amount of transaction data into summarized information reported to the general public in the form of financial statements?

CASE 3-2

ADVANTAGES AND DISADVANTAGES OF A COMPUTERIZED ACCOUNTING SYSTEM

Your soon-to-be father-in-law owns a small retail store. He has manually kept his business accounting records for over 20 years, but he is currently thinking about switching to a computerized accounting system. What advice would you give him about the advantages and the disadvantages of using a computerized accounting system?

CASE 3-3

WHEN IS A DEBIT A DEBIT?

Your new roommate, Susan, is confused. She has just received a notice from her bank indicating that her account has been debited for the cost of new checks. This has reduced her cash account. Susan just learned in her introductory accounting class that debiting Cash increases the account. She wonders why the bank has reduced her account by debiting it. How can you help Susan understand this situation?

CASE 3-4

UNDERSTANDING THE MECHANICS OF ACCOUNTING

As the CFO (Chief Financial Officer) of Rollins Engineering Company, you are looking for someone to fill the position of office manager. Part of the job description is to maintain the company's accounting records. This means that the office manager must be able to journalize transactions, post them to the ledger accounts, and prepare monthly trial balances. You have just interviewed the first applicant, Jay McMahon, who claims that he has studied accounting. As an initial check on his understanding of the basic mechanics of accounting, you give Jay a list of accounts randomly ordered and with assumed balances and ask him to prepare a trial balance. Jay prepares the following.

Trial Balance	Debits	Credits
Accounts Payable		$ 4,500
Salaries Expense		175,000
Consulting Revenues	$269,000	
Cash	82,100	
Utilities Expense	12,000	
Accounts Receivable		44,000
Supplies	11,000	
Rent Expense	30,000	
Capital Stock		77,000
Supplies Expense	33,000	
Office Equipment	15,000	
Retained Earnings		24,000
Other Expenses	6,400	
Salaries Payable	34,000	
Totals	$492,500	$324,500

Based solely on your assessment of Jay McMahon's understanding of accounting, would you hire him as office manager? Explain. Prepare a corrected trial balance that you can use as a basis for your discussion with Jay and future applicants. Explain how the basic accounting equation and the system of double-entry accounting provide a check on the accounting records.

CASE 3-5

EXERCISING ACCOUNTING JUDGMENT

You have recently started business as an accounting consultant. Companies come to you when they face difficult decisions about how to make certain journal entries. You are currently working on the following two problems, which are independent of one another.

a. Baggins Company sells hamburgers for $1.00 each. The cost of the materials used to make each hamburger is 30 cents. Baggins has a compensation plan in which its employees are paid in the form of cash and hamburgers. During 2003, Baggins paid cash salaries of $500,000 and also issued certificates to employees entitling them to 200,000 free hamburgers. The certificates are not redeemable until 2004. What journal entry or entries should Baggins make in 2003 to record this employee compensation information?

b. Radagast Company purchased a building for $100,000 cash on January 1, 2003. Because of poor business decisions, as of December 31, 2003, the building is worthless. Make all journal entries necessary in 2003 in connection with this building.

 **ex ercises**

EXERCISE 3-1

BASIC ACCOUNTING EQUATION

The fundamental accounting equation can be applied to your personal finances. For each of the following transactions, show how the accounting equation would be kept in balance. Example: Paid for semester's tuition (decrease assets: cash account; decrease owners' equity: expense account increases).

1. Took out a school loan for college.
2. Paid this month's rent.
3. Sold your old computer for cash at what it cost to buy it.
4. Received week's paycheck from part-time job.

5. Received interest on savings account.
6. Paid monthly payment on car loan (part of the payment is principal; the remainder is interest).

EXERCISE 3-2

ACCOUNTING ELEMENTS: INCREASE/DECREASE, DEBIT/CREDIT RELATIONSHIPS

The text describes the following accounting elements: assets, liabilities, owners' equity, capital stock, retained earnings, revenues, expenses, and dividends. Which of these elements are increased by a debit entry, and which are increased by a credit entry? Give a transaction for each item that would result in a net increase in its balance.

EXERCISE 3-3

EXPANDED ACCOUNTING EQUATION

Payless Department Store had the following transactions during the year:

1. Purchased inventory on account.
2. Sold merchandise for cash, assuming a profit on the sale.
3. Borrowed money from a bank.
4. Purchased land, making cash down payment and issuing a note for the balance.
5. Issued stock for cash.
6. Paid salaries for the year.
7. Paid a vendor for inventory purchased on account.
8. Sold a building for cash and notes receivable at no gain or loss.
9. Paid cash dividends to stockholders.
10. Paid utilities.

Using the following column headings, identify the accounts involved and indicate the net effect of each transaction on the accounting equation (+ increase; − decrease; 0 no effect). Transaction 1 has been completed as an example.

Transaction	Assets	=	Liabilities	+	Owners' Equity
1	+		+		0
	(Inventory)		(Accounts Payable)		

EXERCISE 3-4

CLASSIFICATION OF ACCOUNTS

For each of the accounts listed, indicate whether it is an asset (A), a liability (L), or an owners' equity (OE) account. If it is an account that affects owners' equity, indicate whether it is a revenue (R) or expense (E) account.

1. Cash
2. Sales
3. Accounts Receivable
4. Cost of Goods Sold
5. Insurance Expense
6. Capital Stock
7. Mortgage Payable
8. Salaries and Wages Expense
9. Retained Earnings
10. Salaries Payable
11. Accounts Payable
12. Interest Revenue
13. Inventory
14. Interest Receivable
15. Notes Payable
16. Equipment
17. Office Supplies
18. Utilities Expense
19. Interest Payable
20. Rent Expense

EXERCISE 3-5

NORMAL ACCOUNT BALANCES

For each account listed in Exercise 3-4, indicate whether it would normally have a debit (DR) balance or a credit (CR) balance.

EXERCISE 3-6

JOURNALIZING TRANSACTIONS

Record each of the following transactions in Chico's General Journal. (Omit explanations.)

1. Issued capital stock for $50,000 cash.
2. Borrowed $10,000 from a bank. Signed a note to secure the debt.
3. Purchased inventory from a supplier on credit for $8,000.

4. Paid the supplier for the inventory purchased in (3) above.
5. Sold inventory that cost $1,200 for $1,500 on credit.
6. Collected $1,500 from customers on transaction (5) above.
7. Paid salaries and rent of $25,000 and $1,200, respectively.

EXERCISE 3-7

JOURNALIZING TRANSACTIONS

Silva Company had the following transactions:

1. Purchased a new building, paying $20,000 cash and issuing a note for $50,000.
2. Purchased $15,000 of inventory on account.
3. Sold inventory costing $5,000 for $6,000 on account.
4. Paid for inventory purchased on account (item 2).
5. Issued capital stock for $25,000.
6. Collected $4,500 of accounts receivable.
7. Paid utility bills totaling $360.
8. Sold old building for $27,000, receiving $10,000 cash and a $17,000 note (no gain or loss on the sale).
9. Paid $2,000 cash dividends to stockholders.

Record the above transactions in general journal format. (Omit explanations.)

EXERCISE 3-8

JOURNAL ENTRIES

During June 2003, Husky, Inc., completed the following transactions. Prepare the journal entry for each transaction.

June 1   Received $200,000 for 2,000 shares of capital stock.
       2   Purchased $50,000 of equipment, with 25% down and 75% on a note payable.
       5   Paid utilities of $1,500 in cash.
       9   Sold equipment for $25,000 cash (no gain or loss).
    13   Purchased $100,000 of inventory, paying 50% down and 50% for credit.
    14   Paid $5,000 cash insurance premium for June.
    15   Sold inventory costing $30,000 for $45,000 to customers on account to be paid at a later date.
    20   Collected $3,000 from accounts receivable.
    24   Sold inventory costing $50,000 for $69,500 to customers for cash.
    25   Paid property taxes of $2,000.
    30   Paid $50,000 of accounts payable for inventory purchased on June 13.

EXERCISE 3-9

POSTING JOURNAL ENTRIES

Post the journal entries prepared in Exercise 3-8 to T-accounts, and determine the final balance for each account. (Assume all beginning account balances are zero.)

EXERCISE 3-10

CHALLENGING JOURNAL ENTRIES

The accountant for Han Company is considering how to journalize the following transactions:

a. The employees of Han Company earned $105,000. The employees received $90,000 in cash and were promised that they will receive the remaining $15,000 as a pension payment on the date that they retire.
b. On August 1, 2003, Han Company paid $1,800 cash for one year of rent on a building it is using. This one year of rent is scheduled to be in effect for the 12 months starting on August 1, 2003.

1. What journal entry should be made on the books of Han Company to record the employee compensation information in (a)?
2. Describe any assumptions necessary in making the employee compensation journal entry in (1).

3. Make the necessary journal entry on Han Company's books on August 1 to record the payment for the building rent described in (b).
4. Consider the journal entry made in (3). Is any adjustment to Han's books necessary as of December 31, 2003, as a consequence of the rent journal entry made on August 1?

EXERCISE 3-11

JOURNAL ENTRIES

The following transactions are for the Main Construction Corporation:

a. The firm purchased land for $300,000, $90,000 of which was paid in cash and a note payable signed for the balance.
b. The firm bought equipment for $75,000 on credit.
c. The firm paid $15,000 it owed to its suppliers.
d. The firm arranged for a $100,000 line of credit (the right to borrow funds as needed) from the bank. No funds have yet been borrowed.
e. One of the primary investors borrowed $50,000 from a bank. The loan is a personal loan.
f. The firm borrowed $65,000 on its line of credit.
g. The firm issued a $5,000 cash dividend to its stockholders.
h. An investor invested an additional $80,000 in the company in exchange for additional capital stock.
i. The firm repaid $7,500 of its line of credit.
j. The firm sold some of its products for $15,000—$5,000 for cash, the remainder on account.
k. Cost of sales in (j) are $8,000.
l. The firm received a $1,000 deposit from a customer for a product to be sold and delivered to that customer next month.

Analyze and record the transactions as journal entries. (Omit explanations.)

EXERCISE 3-12

ANALYSIS OF JOURNAL ENTRIES

The following journal entries are from the books of Kara Rachel Company:

a.	Cash	10,000	
	Capital Stock		10,000
b.	Cash	25,000	
	Loan Payable		25,000
c.	Buildings	50,000	
	Cash		5,000
	Mortgage Payable		45,000
d.	Inventory	25,000	
	Accounts Payable		25,000
e.	Accounts Receivable	42,000	
	Sales		42,000
	Cost of Goods Sold	21,000	
	Inventory		21,000
f.	Salary Expense	6,000	
	Cash		6,000
g.	Cash	37,000	
	Accounts Receivable		37,000
h.	Accounts Payable	20,000	
	Cash		20,000

For each of the journal entries, prepare an explanation of the business event that is being represented.

EXERCISE 3-13

JOURNALIZING AND POSTING TRANSACTIONS

Given the following T-accounts, describe the transaction that took place on each specified date during July:

Cash

7/5	9,500	7/1	3,420
7/28	8,000	7/23	2,000
		7/25	5,000
		7/30	5,500
Bal.	1,580		

Accounts Receivable

7/14	18,000	7/5	9,500
		7/28	8,000
Bal.	500		

Inventory

7/10	20,000	7/14	15,000
Bal.	5,000		

Equipment

7/30	1,500

Land

7/30	4,000

Accounts Payable

7/25	5,000	7/10	20,000
		Bal.	15,000

Sales Revenue

		7/14	18,000

Cost of Goods Sold

7/14	15,000

Rent Expense

7/23	2,000

Advertising Expense

7/1	3,420

EXERCISE 3-14

TRIAL BALANCE

The account balances from the ledger of Yakamoto, Inc., as of July 31, 2003, are listed here in alphabetical order. The balance for Retained Earnings has been omitted. Prepare a trial balance, and insert the missing amount for Retained Earnings.

Accounts Payable	$ 8,600	Land	$19,000
Accounts Receivable	2,000	Miscellaneous Expenses	1,400
Buildings	20,000	Mortgage Payable (due 2006)	24,000
Capital Stock	10,000	Rent Expense	3,000
Cash	19,600	Retained Earnings	?
Equipment	16,000	Salary Expense	10,000
Fees Earned	26,000	Supplies	600
Insurance Expense	3,600	Utilities Expense	400

EXERCISE 3-15

TRIAL BALANCE

Assume you work in the accounting department at Marshall, Inc. Your boss has asked you to prepare a trial balance as of November 30, 2003, using the following account balances from the company's ledger. Prepare the trial balance and insert the missing amount for Cost of Goods Sold.

Accounts Payable	$ 55,000	Notes Payable	$250,000
Accounts Receivable	25,000	Notes Receivable	20,000
Advertising Expense	5,000	Other Expenses	1,000
Buildings	150,000	Property Tax Expense	1,500
Capital Stock	173,000	Rent Expense	7,500
Cash	35,000	Retained Earnings	40,000
Cost of Goods Sold	?	Salaries Expense	155,000
Equipment	55,000	Salaries Payable	2,000
Inventory	200,000	Sales Revenue	375,000
Land	125,000	Short-Term Investments	15,000
Mortgage Payable	95,000	Utilities Expense	7,000

EXERCISE 3-16

RELATIONSHIPS OF THE EXPANDED ACCOUNTING EQUATION

Domino, Inc., had the following information reported. From these data, determine the amount of:

1. Capital stock at December 31, 2002.
2. Retained earnings at December 31, 2003.
3. Revenues for the year 2003.

	December 31, 2002	December 31, 2003
Total assets	$250,000	$300,000
Total liabilities	60,000	70,000
Capital stock	?	50,000
Retained earnings	150,000	?
Revenues for 2003		?
Expenses for 2003		205,000
Dividends paid during 2003		5,000

EXERCISE 3-17

JOURNAL ENTRY TO CORRECT AN ERROR

Legolas Company paid $5,000 cash for executive salaries. When the journal entry to record this $5,000 payment was made, the payment was mistakenly added to the cost of land purchased by Legolas. The $5,000 should have been recorded as salary expense. Make the journal entry necessary to correct this error.

problems

PROBLEM 3-1

JOURNAL ENTRIES AND TRIAL BALANCE

As of January 1, 2003, Kendrick Corporation had the following balances in its general ledger:

	Debits	Credits
Cash	$ 31,500	
Accounts Receivable	23,500	
Inventory	92,000	
Office Building	208,000	
Accounts Payable		$ 16,500
Mortgage Payable		180,000
Notes Payable		68,500
Capital Stock		57,500
Retained Earnings		32,500
Totals	$355,000	$355,000

Kendrick had the following transactions during 2003. All expenses were paid in cash, unless otherwise stated.

a. Accounts Payable as of January 1, 2003, were paid off.
b. Purchased inventory for $35,000 cash.
c. Collected $21,000 of receivables.
d. Sold $185,000 of merchandise, 85% for cash and 15% for credit. The Cost of Goods Sold was $98,500.
e. Paid $25,000 mortgage payment, of which $15,000 represents interest expense.

f. Paid salaries expense of $60,000.
g. Paid utilities of $6,300.
h. Paid installment of $5,000 on note.

Required:
1. Prepare journal entries to record each listed transaction. (Omit explanations.)
2. Set up T-accounts with the proper account balances at January 1, 2003, post the journal entries to the T-accounts, and prepare a trial balance for Kendrick Corporation at December 31, 2003.
3. **Interpretive Question:** If the debit and credit columns of the trial balance are in balance, does this mean that no errors have been made in journalizing the transactions? Explain.

PROBLEM 3-2

JOURNALIZING AND POSTING

Assume you are interviewing for a part-time accounting job at Spilker & Associates, Inc., and the interviewer gives you the following list of company transactions in September 2003.

Sept.
1 Received $150,000 for capital stock issued.
2 Paid $20,000 cash to employees for wages earned in September 2003.
4 Purchased $75,000 of running shoes and clothing on account for resale.
5 Paid utilities of $1,800 for September 2003.
9 Paid $1,500 cash for September's insurance premium.
11 Sold inventory of running shoes and clothing costing $35,000 for $70,000, with $20,000 received in cash and the remaining balance on credit.
15 Purchased $2,500 of supplies on account.
21 Received $25,000 from customers as payments on their accounts.
25 Paid $75,000 of accounts payable.

Using this list, you have been asked to do the following in the interview:

Required:
1. Journalize each of the transactions for September. (Omit explanations.)
2. Set up T-accounts, and post each of the journal entries made in (1).
3. **Interpretive Question:** If the business owners wanted to know at any given time how much cash the company had, where would you tell the owners to look? Why?

PROBLEM 3-3

JOURNAL ENTRIES FROM LEDGER ANALYSIS

T-accounts for RAM Technology, Inc., are shown below.

	Cash				Accounts Receivable				Inventory		
(a)	100,000	(b)	45,000	(e)	30,000	(i)	15,000	(d)	35,000	(e)	30,000
(c)	50,000	(d)	5,000								
(e)	25,000	(f)	20,000								
(i)	15,000	(g)	53,500								
		(h)	30,000								

	Building			Accounts Payable				Mortgage Payable		
(b)	150,000		(h)	30,000	(d)	30,000			(b)	105,000

	Notes Payable				Capital Stock				Sales Revenue	
(g)	50,000	(c)	50,000			(a)	100,000			(e)	55,000

	Cost of Goods Sold			Interest Expense			Wages Expense	
(e)	30,000		(g)	3,500		(f)	20,000	

Required:

1. Analyze these accounts and detail the appropriate journal entries that must have been made by RAM Technology, Inc. (Omit explanations.)
2. Determine the amount of net income/loss from the account information.

PROBLEM 3-4

JOURNALIZING AND POSTING TRANSACTIONS

Pat Bjornson, owner of Pat's Beauty Supply, completed the following business transactions during March 2003.

Mar. 1 Purchased $53,000 of inventory on credit.
    4 Collected $5,000 from customers as payments on their accounts.
    5 Purchased equipment for $3,000 cash.
    6 Sold inventory that cost $30,000 to customers on account for $40,000.
   10 Paid rent for March, $1,050.
   15 Paid utilities for March, $100.
   17 Paid a $300 monthly salary to the part-time helper.
   20 Collected $33,000 from customers as payments on their accounts.
   22 Paid $53,000 cash on account payable. (See March 1 entry.)
   25 Paid property taxes for March of $1,200.
   28 Sold inventory that cost $20,000 to customers for $30,000 cash.

Required:

1. For each transaction, give the entry to record it in the company's general journal. (Omit explanations.)
2. Set up T-accounts, and post the journal entries to their appropriate accounts.

PROBLEM 3-5

UNIFYING CONCEPTS: COMPOUND JOURNAL ENTRIES, POSTING, TRIAL BALANCE

J&W Merchandise Company had the following transactions during 2003.

a. Sam Jeakins began business by investing the following assets, receiving capital stock in exchange:

Cash	$ 20,000
Inventory	37,000
Land	25,500
Building	160,000
Equipment	12,500*
Totals	$255,000

*A note of $5,000 on the equipment was assumed by the company.

b. Sold merchandise that cost $30,000 for $45,000; $15,000 cash was received immediately, and the other $30,000 will be collected in 30 days.
c. Paid off the note of $5,000 plus $300 interest.
d. Purchased merchandise costing $12,000, paying $2,000 cash and issuing a note for $10,000.
e. Exchanged $2,000 cash and $8,000 in capital stock for office equipment costing $10,000.
f. Purchased a truck for $15,000 with $3,000 down and a one-year note for the balance.

Required:

1. Journalize the transactions. (Omit explanations.)
2. Post the journal entries using T-accounts for each account.
3. Prepare a trial balance at December 31, 2003.

PROBLEM 3-6

UNIFYING CONCEPTS: T-ACCOUNTS, TRIAL BALANCE, AND INCOME STATEMENT

The following list is a selection of transactions from Trafalga, Inc.'s business activities during 2003, the first year of operations.

General Ledger Software

a. Received $50,000 cash for capital stock.
b. Paid $5,000 cash for equipment.
c. Purchased inventory costing $18,000 on account.
d. Sold $25,000 of merchandise to customers on account. Cost of goods sold was $15,000.
e. Signed a note with a bank for a $10,000 loan.
f. Collected $9,500 cash from customers who had purchased merchandise on account.
g. Purchased land, $10,000, and a building, $60,000, for $15,000 cash and a 30-year mortgage of $55,000.
h. Made a first payment of $2,750 on the mortgage principal plus $2,750 in interest.
i. Paid $12,000 of accounts payable.
j. Purchased $1,500 of supplies on account.
k. Paid $2,500 of accounts payable.
l. Paid $7,500 in wages earned during the year.
m. Received $10,000 cash and $3,000 of notes in settlement of customers' accounts.
n. Received $3,250 in payment of a note receivable of $3,000 plus interest of $250.
o. Paid $600 cash for a utility bill.
p. Sold excess land for its cost of $3,000.
q. Received $1,500 in rent for an unused part of a building.
r. Paid off $10,000 note, plus interest of $1,200.

Required:
1. Set up T-accounts, and appropriately record the debits and credits for each transaction directly in the T-accounts. Leave room for a number of entries in the cash account.
2. Prepare a trial balance.
3. Prepare an income statement for the period. (Ignore income taxes and the EPS computation.)

PROBLEM 3-7

TRANSACTION ANALYSIS AND JOURNAL ENTRIES

Pacific Motors, Inc., entered into the following transactions during the month of August:

a. Purchased $1,500 of supplies on account from Major Supply Company. The cost of the supplies to Major Supply Company was $1,200.
b. Paid $600 to Valley Electric for the monthly utility bill.
c. Sold a truck to Fast Delivery, Inc. A $5,000 down payment was received with the balance of $12,000 due within 30 days. The cost of the delivery truck to Pacific Motors was $11,000.
d. Purchased a total of eight new cars and trucks from Japanese Motors, Inc., for a total of $96,000, one-half of which was paid in cash. The balance is due within 45 days. The total cost of the vehicles to Japanese Motors was $80,000.
e. Paid $1,875 to Silva's Automotive for repair work on cars for the current month.
f. Sold one of the new cars purchased from Japanese Motors to the town mayor, Ana Mecham. The sales price was $17,500, and was paid by Mecham upon delivery of the car. The cost of the particular car sold to Mecham was $12,100.
g. Borrowed $10,000 from a local bank to be repaid in one year with 12% interest.

Required:
1. For each of the transactions, make the proper journal entry on the books of Pacific Motors. (Omit explanations.)
2. For each of the transactions, make the proper journal entry on the books of the other party to the transaction, for example, (a) Major Supply Company, (b) Valley Electric. (Omit explanations.)
3. **Interpretive Question:** Why do some of the journal entries for Pacific Motors and other companies involved appear to be "mirror images" of each other?

PROBLEM 3-8

CORRECTING A TRIAL BALANCE

The following trial balance was prepared by a new employee.

Trial Balance Alden Company, Inc. For Year Ended November 30, 2003		
	Credits	**Debits**
Cash	$ 18,250	
Mortgage Payable		$ 78,900
Advertising Expense	9,600	
Capital Stock		102,000
Equipment	36,900	
Notes Payable		187,350
Inventory	148,000	
Wages Expense	87,150	
Notes Receivable	5,000	
Accounts Payable		19,750
Accounts Receivable		5,300
Rent Expense		8,750
Wages Payable	9,000	
Furniture		15,000
Other Expenses	2,950	
Sales Revenue		235,600
Buildings	104,700	
Cost of Goods Sold	113,050	
Property Tax Expense		1,300
Land		87,850
Retained Earnings		14,400
Utilties Expense	3,200	
Totals	$537,800	$756,200

Required: Prepare the corrected company trial balance. (Assume all accounts have "normal" balances and the recorded amounts are correct.)

PROBLEM 3-9

UNIFYING CONCEPTS: JOURNAL ENTRIES, T-ACCOUNTS, TRIAL BALANCE

Downtown Company, a retailer, had the following account balances as of April 30, 2003:

Cash	$10,100	
Accounts Receivable	4,900	
Inventory	16,000	
Land	26,000	
Building	24,000	
Furniture	4,000	
Notes Payable		$25,000
Accounts Payable		12,000
Capital Stock		30,000
Retained Earnings		18,000
Totals	$85,000	$85,000

During May, the company completed the following transactions.

May 3 Paid one-half of 4/30/03 accounts payable.
 6 Collected all of 4/30/03 accounts receivable.
 7 Sold inventory costing $7,700 for $6,000 cash and $4,000 on account.

(continued)

May 8 Sold one-half of the land for $13,000, receiving $8,000 cash plus a note for $5,000.
  10 Purchased inventory on account, $10,000.
  15 Paid installment of $5,000 on notes payable (entire amount reduces the liability account).
  21 Issued additional capital stock for $2,000 cash.
  23 Sold inventory costing $4,000 for $7,500 cash.
  25 Paid salaries of $2,000.
  26 Paid rent of $500.
  29 Purchased desk for $500 cash.

Required:
1. Prepare the journal entry for each transaction.
2. Set up T-accounts with the proper account balances at April 30, 2003, and post the entries to the T-accounts.
3. Prepare a trial balance as of May 31, 2003.

PROBLEM 3-10

UNIFYING CONCEPTS: FIRST STEPS IN THE ACCOUNTING CYCLE

The following balances were taken from the general ledger of Benson Company on January 1, 2003:

	Debits	Credits
Cash	$13,500	
Short-Term Investments	10,000	
Accounts Receivable	12,500	
Inventory	15,000	
Land	25,000	
Buildings	75,000	
Equipment	20,000	
Notes Payable		$17,500
Accounts Payable		12,500
Salaries and Wages Payable		2,500
Mortgage Payable		37,500
Capital Stock (7,000 shares outstanding)		70,000
Retained Earnings		31,000

During 2003, the company completed the following transactions:

a. Purchased inventory for $110,000 on credit.
b. Issued an additional $25,000 of capital stock (2,500 shares) for cash.
c. Paid property taxes of $4,500 for the year 2003.
d. Paid advertising and other selling expenses of $8,000.
e. Paid utilities expense of $6,500 for 2003.
f. Paid the salaries and wages owed for 2002. Paid additional salaries and wages of $18,000 during 2003.
g. Sold merchandise costing $105,000 for $175,000. Of total sales, $45,000 were cash sales and $130,000 were credit sales.
h. Paid off notes of $17,500 plus interest of $1,600.
i. On November 1, 2003, received a loan of $10,000 from the bank.
j. On December 30, 2003, made annual mortgage payment of $2,500 and paid interest of $3,700.
k. Collected receivables for the year of $140,000.
l. Paid off accounts payable of $112,500.
m. Received dividends and interest of $1,400 on short-term investments during 2003. (Record as Miscellaneous Revenue.)

n. Purchased additional short-term investments of $15,000 during 2003. (Note: Short-term investments are current assets.)

o. Paid 2003 corporate income taxes of $11,600.

p. Paid cash dividends of $7,600.

Required:

1. Journalize the 2003 transactions. (Omit explanations.)
2. Set up T-accounts with the proper account balances at January 1, 2003, and post the journal entries to the T-accounts.
3. Determine the account balances, and prepare a trial balance at December 31, 2003.
4. Prepare an income statement and a balance sheet. (Remember that the dividends account and all revenue and expense accounts are temporary retained earnings accounts.)
5. **Interpretive Question:** Why are revenue and expense accounts used at all?

competency enhancement opportunities

▷ Analyzing Real Company Information
▷ International Case
▷ Ethics Case
▷ Writing Assignment

▷ The Debate
▷ Cumulative Spreadsheet Project
▷ Internet Search

The following additional assignments provide opportunities for students to develop critical thinking, ethical perspectives, oral and written communication skills, experience with electronic research, and teamwork through group and business activities.

▷ **ANALYZING REAL COMPANY INFORMATION**

• Analyzing 3-1 (Microsoft)
The 1999 annual report for MICROSOFT is included in Appendix A. Locate that annual report and consider the following questions:

1. Find Microsoft's 1999 income statement. Assume that research and development expenditures were paid in cash. What journal entry did Microsoft make in 1999 to record research and development?
2. Find Microsoft's 1999 cash flow statement. What journal entry did Microsoft make in 1999 to record the issuance of common stock?
3. Again, looking at the cash flow statement—what journal entry did Microsoft make in 1999 to record the purchase of property and equipment?
4. Using information from the cash flow statement, re-create the journal entry Microsoft made in 1999 to record the purchase of investments. Using the beginning and ending balances from the balance sheet, comment on the change in the balance of the equity and other investments account between the beginning of 1999 and the end of 1999.

• Analyzing 3-2 (McDonald's)
A brief history of the origin of the McDONALD'S CORPORATION is given at the start of this chapter. The following questions are adapted from information appearing in McDonald's 1999 annual report.

1. In 1999, total sales at all McDonald's stores worldwide were $38.5 billion. There were 26,806 McDonald's stores operating in 1999. *Estimate* how many customers per day visit an average McDonald's store.
2. For the stores owned by the McDonald's Corporation (as opposed to those owned by franchisees), total sales in 1999 were $9.512 billion, and total cost of food and packaging was $3.205 billion. What journal entries would McDonald's make to record a $10 sale and to record the cost of food and packaging associated with the $10 sale?
3. McDonald's reported payment of cash dividends of $264.7 million in 1999. What journal entry was required?
4. McDonald's reported that the total income tax it owed for 1999 was $936.2 million. However, only $642.2 million in cash was paid for taxes during the year. What compound journal entry did McDonald's make to record its income tax expense for the year?

▶ INTERNATIONAL CASE

• Shanghai Petrochemical Company Limited

In July 1993, SHANGHAI PETROCHEMICAL COMPANY LIMITED became the first company organized under the laws of the People's Republic of China to publicly issue its shares on the worldwide market. Shanghai Petrochemical's shares now trade on the stock exchanges in Shanghai, Hong Kong, and New York. The following questions are adapted from information appearing in Shanghai Petrochemical's 1995 annual report.

1. In 1995, Shanghai Petrochemical reported sales of 11.835 billion renminbi (US$ 1 = 8.33 RMB) and cost of sales of RMB 9.016 billion. Make the necessary journal entries, using renminbi as the currency.
2. In 1995, Shanghai Petrochemical declared cash dividends of RMB 851.5 million. However, cash paid for dividends during the year was only RMB 818.8 million. Make the necessary compound journal entry to record the declaration and payment of cash dividends for the year.
3. In China, a 17% value added tax (VAT) is added to the invoiced value of all sales. This VAT is collected by the seller from the buyer and then held to be forwarded to the government. What journal entry would Shanghai Petrochemical make to record the sale, on account, of crude oil with an invoice sales value of $100 and a cost of $70?

▶ ETHICS CASE

• Should You Go the Extra Mile?

You work in a small convenience store. The store is very low-tech; you ring up the sales on an old-style cash register that merely records the amount of the sale. The store owner uses this cash register tape at the end of each day to verify that the correct amount of cash is in the cash register drawer. On a day-to-day basis, no other financial information is collected about store operations.

Since you started studying accounting, you have become a bit uneasy about your job because you see many ways that store operations could be improved through the gathering and use of financial information. Even though you are not an expert, you are quite certain that you could help the store owner set up an improved information system. However, you also know that this will take extra effort on your part, with no real possibility of receiving an increase in pay.

Should you say anything to the store owner, or should you just keep quiet and save yourself the trouble?

▷ **WRITING ASSIGNMENT**

• Accounting Is Everywhere!
Financial accounting information is frequently used in newspaper and magazine articles to provide background data on companies. Prepare a one-page report on the use of financial accounting data by the press. Proceed as follows:

1. Scan the articles in a recent copy of one of the popular business periodicals (such as *The Wall Street Journal*, *Forbes*, *Fortune*, or *Business Week*) for examples of the use of financial accounting data.
2. Identify and describe three interesting examples:

   • Detail the nature of the accounting data used.
   • Outline the point that the writer is trying to make by using the particular accounting data.

▷ **THE DEBATE**

• Are Computers the Hero or the Villain?
As explained in the body of the chapter, computers have revolutionized the accounting process. In addition to taking over the mundane jobs of posting and report formatting, computers have also changed the way we think about information. When accounting was done by hand, it was not possible to match individual sales with specific products, specific customers, the exact time of day of the sale, the income level of the customer, the customer's favorite TV shows and magazines, and the like. In short, computers have made it possible to use the raw financial data to track much more than just revenues and expenses. How far should the use of computers go?
    Divide your group into two teams.

• One team represents the computer technology group, "To Infinity, and Beyond!" Prepare a two-minute oral presentation supporting the notion that firms have a right to use their computer database systems to gather as much information about customers as possible, and even to sell that information to other firms. Now is the Information Age, and computers have made it possible to easily buy and sell information just like any other commodity.
• The other team represents "Right to Privacy." Prepare a two-minute oral presentation arguing that firms have no right to maintain databases containing individual customer information. A company's information system should relate to that company's products and processes, and customers have the right to interact with the firm anonymously.

▷ **CUMULATIVE SPREADSHEET PROJECT**
This spreadsheet assignment is a continuation of the spreadsheet assignment given in Chapter 2. If you completed that spreadsheet, you have a head start on this one.

1. Refer back to the financial statement numbers for Handyman Company for 2003 [given in part (1) of the Cumulative Spreadsheet Project assignment in Chapter 2]. Using the balance sheet and income statement created with those numbers, create spreadsheet cell formulas to compute and display values for the following ratios:
   a. Current ratio
   b. Debt ratio

    c. Asset turnover

    d. Return on equity

2. Determine the impact of each of the following transactions on the ratio values computed in (1). Treat each transaction independently, meaning that before determining the impact of each new transaction, you should reset the financial statement values to their original amounts. Each of the hypothetical transactions is assumed to occur on the last day of the year.

    a. Collected $20 cash from customer receivables.

    b. Purchased $30 in inventory on account.

    c. Purchased $100 in property, plant, and equipment. The entire amount of the purchase was financed with a mortgage. Principal repayment for the mortgage is due in 10 years.

    d. Purchased $100 in property, plant, and equipment. The entire amount of the purchase was financed with new stockholder investment.

    e. Borrowed $20 with a short-term loan payable. The $20 was paid out as a dividend to stockholders.

    f. Received $20 as an investment from stockholders. The $20 was paid out as a dividend to stockholders.

▶ **INTERNET SEARCH**

• *McDonald's*

Access McDONALD'S Web site at http://www.mcdonalds.com. Sometimes Web addresses change, so if this McDonald's address doesn't work, access the Web site for this textbook (http://albrecht.swcollege.com) for an updated link to McDonald's.

Once you've gained access to McDonald's Web site, answer the following questions:

1. Which has more calories—two hamburgers or one Big Mac?

2. How much money do you need to purchase a McDonald's franchise in the United States? What else is required to purchase a franchise?

3. Sometimes it isn't easy to find a company's financial statements in its Web site. Describe what you had to do to find a copy of McDonald's most recent annual report.

4. What information is contained in McDonald's most recent financial press release?

Completing the Accounting Cycle

chapter **f4**

learning objectives After studying this chapter, you should be able to:

1 Describe how accrual accounting allows for timely reporting and a better measure of a company's economic performance.

2 Explain the need for adjusting entries and make adjusting entries for unrecorded receivables, unrecorded liabilities, prepaid expenses, and unearned revenues.

3 Explain the preparation of the financial statements, the explanatory notes, and the audit report.

4 Perform a systematic analysis of financial statements.

5 Complete the closing process in the accounting cycle.

6 Understand how all the steps in the accounting cycle fit together.

expanded material

7 Make adjusting entries for prepaid expenses and unearned revenues when the original cash amounts are recorded as expenses and revenues.

GENERAL MOTORS, the brainchild of William Durant, was formed through the acquisition of a number of preexisting car makers. BUICK and OLDSMOBILE were acquired in 1908; CADILLAC and PONTIAC (originally called OAKLAND) were added in 1909. With so many acquisitions in those early years, General Motors' financing was quickly depleted, and Durant lost control of his company. With Durant fighting to regain the reins of General Motors, the company was in such turmoil that, at one point, CHEVROLET MOTOR COMPANY (another Durant creation) owned a majority of GM stock. After many deals, Durant found himself back in charge in 1916, and Chevrolet became a subsidiary of GM in 1918.

Following the end of World War I, an economic slowdown stretched Durant's financial resources past the breaking point, and in 1920 he lost control of General Motors for good. Pierre S. du Pont, a GM investor since 1914, became the company's new president. Du Pont brought to General Motors the financial resources and business connections associated with his own family's chemical empire. He was also instrumental in instituting the du Pont style of management and control. Implemented at General Motors by Alfred P. Sloan (who later went on to head GM until 1956), this system emphasized decentralized decision making; evaluations of managers of autonomous divisions were based on reaching specific financial goals. This "DuPont" system of evaluation is discussed later in the chapter.

Under Sloan's leadership, General Motors became the dominant car maker in the world, a position it still holds. In addition to implementing the DuPont system of evaluation and control, Sloan also formalized the caste system among GM's different automobile lines. For example, Chevrolets were targeted at the lower-income end of the market, while Cadillacs were aimed at the higher end. Sloan was also instrumental in creating the annual ritual of the "car model year" to encourage owners of older models to trade them in on new cars with the latest innovations.

Although General Motors' global market share has declined with stiff competition from Japanese, European (including DAIMLERCHRYSLER), and domestic (FORD) competitors, General Motors still sells more cars and trucks than any other company in the world. In 1999, GM sold 8.7 million vehicles, 15.8% of the worldwide total. GM also remains one of the largest private employers in the United States, ranking second behind WAL-MART in the 2000 Fortune 500 listing (see Exhibit 4-1).

In addition to being the most prolific car maker in the world, General Motors has the unenviable distinction of having posted the world record largest annual net loss. In 1992, GM reported a loss for the year of $23.5 billion. This record loss followed losses of $2.0 billion in 1990 and $4.5 billion in 1991.

How was General Motors able to stay in business while reporting these huge losses? During the same period it was reporting large losses on its income statement, GM was reporting healthy cash from operations on its cash flow statement. In fact, in 1992 (the year of the record loss), GM's positive cash from operations was $9.8 billion. This strong cash flow enabled GM to continue normal operations, pay its

setting the stage

---

exhibit 4-1   U.S. Companies with the Most Employees, 1999

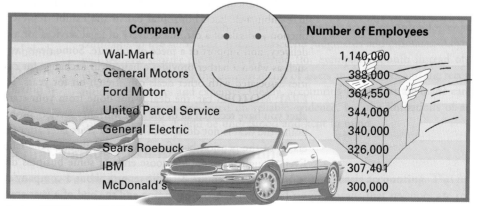

Company	Number of Employees
Wal-Mart	1,140,000
General Motors	388,000
Ford Motor	364,550
United Parcel Service	344,000
General Electric	340,000
Sears Roebuck	326,000
IBM	307,401
McDonald's	300,000

Source: 2000 Fortune 500 listing available at http://www.fortune.com

cash-basis accounting A system of accounting in which transactions are recorded and revenues and expenses are recognized only when cash is received or paid.

Karas Brothers Reported Income for 2003			
Cash-Basis Accounting		**Accrual-Basis Accounting**	
Cash receipts	$22,000	Revenues earned	$50,500
Cash disbursements	21,900	Expenses incurred	33,100
Income	$ 100	Income	$17,400

caution

Although accrual-basis net income is the measure of Karas Brothers' economic performance for the year, the cash flow information is useful in evaluating the need to obtain short-term loans, the ability to repay existing loans, and the like. The statement of cash flows is an essential companion to the accrual-basis income statement.

How do we explain this $17,300 difference? Under **cash-basis accounting**, Karas Brothers would report only $22,000 in revenue, the total amount of cash received during 2003. Similarly, the company would report only $21,900 of expenses (the amount actually paid) during 2003. The additional $11,200 of expenses incurred but not yet paid would not be reported. Using accrual-basis accounting, however, Karas earned $50,500 in revenues, which is the total increase in resources for the period (an increase of $22,000 in cash plus $28,500 in receivables). Similarly, Karas incurred a total of $33,100 in expenses, which should be matched with revenues earned to produce a realistic income measurement. The combined result of increasing revenues by $28,500 while increasing expenses by only $11,200 creates the $17,300 difference in net income ($28,500 − $11,200 = $17,300).

As this example shows, accrual-basis accounting provides a more accurate picture of a company's profitability. It matches earned revenues with the expenses incurred to generate those revenues. This helps investors, creditors, and others to better assess the operating results of a company and make more informed judgments concerning its profitability and earnings potential. Accrual-basis accounting is required by generally accepted accounting principles (GAAP).

to summarize

Users of accounting information need timely, periodic financial reports to make decisions. The revenue recognition and matching principles provide guidelines for assigning the appropriate amounts of revenues and expenses to each period under accrual accounting. Accrual-basis accounting provides a better measure of net income than does cash-basis accounting; it is therefore required by GAAP in reporting the results of company operations.

2

Explain the need for adjusting entries and make adjusting entries for unrecorded receivables, unrecorded liabilities, prepaid expenses, and unearned revenues.

adjusting entries Entries required at the end of each accounting period to recognize, on an accrual basis, revenues and expenses for the period and to report proper amounts for asset, liability, and owners' equity accounts.

ADJUSTING ENTRIES

As discussed in Chapter 3, transactions generally are recorded in a journal in chronological order and then posted to the ledger accounts. The entries are based on the best information available at the time. Although the majority of accounts are up-to-date at the end of an accounting period and their balances can be included in the financial statements, some accounts require adjustment to reflect current circumstances. In general, these accounts are not updated throughout the period because it is impractical or inconvenient to make such entries on a daily or weekly basis. At the end of each accounting period, in order to report all asset, liability, and owners' equity amounts properly and to recognize all revenues and expenses for the period on an accrual basis, accountants are required to make any necessary adjustments prior to preparing the financial statements. The entries that reflect these adjustments are called **adjusting entries**.

One difficulty with adjusting entries is that the need for an adjustment is not signaled by a specific event such as the receipt of a bill or the receipt of cash from a customer. Rather, adjusting entries are recorded on the basis of an analysis of the circumstances at the close of each accounting period. This analysis involves just two steps:

1. Determine whether the amounts recorded for all assets and liabilities are correct. If not, debit or credit the appropriate asset or liability account. In short, fix the balance sheet.
2. Determine what revenue or expense adjustments are required as a result of the changes in recorded amounts of assets and liabilities indicated in step 1. Debit or credit the appropriate revenue or expense account. In short, fix the income statement.

It should be noted that these two steps are interrelated and may be reversed. That is, revenue and expense adjustments may be considered first to fix the income statement, indicating which asset and liability accounts need adjustment to fix the balance sheet. As you will see, each adjusting entry involves at least one income statement account and one balance sheet account. T-accounts are helpful in analyzing adjusting entries and will be used in the illustrations that follow.

The areas most commonly requiring analysis to see whether adjusting entries are needed are:

1. Unrecorded receivables
2. Unrecorded liabilities
3. Prepaid expenses
4. Unearned revenues

As we illustrate and discuss adjusting entries, remember that the basic purpose of adjustments is to make account balances current in order to report all asset, liability, and owners' equity amounts properly and to recognize all revenues and expenses for the period on an accrual basis. This is done so that the income statement and the balance sheet will reflect the proper operating results and financial position, respectively, at the end of the accounting period.

Unrecorded Receivables

unrecorded receivables
Revenues earned during a period that have not been recorded by the end of that period.

In accordance with the revenue recognition principle of accrual accounting, revenues should be recorded when earned, regardless of when the cash is received. If revenue is earned but not yet collected in cash, a receivable exists. To ensure that all receivables are properly reported on the balance sheet in the correct amounts, an analysis should be made at the end of each accounting period to see whether there are any revenues that have been earned but have not yet been collected or recorded. These **unrecorded receivables** are earned and represent amounts that are receivable in the future; therefore, they should be recognized as assets.

To illustrate, we will pick up with the landscaping business we started in Chapter 3. Recall that we mow lawns, pull weeds, plant shrubs, and perform other related services. We are able to provide these services year round because we live in a region with a very mild climate. Our company reports on a calendar-year basis and has determined the following on December 31, 2003:

> On November 1, we entered into a year-long contract with an apartment complex to provide general landscaping services each week and bill the customer every three months. The terms of the contract state that we will earn $400 per month. As of December 31, Lawn Care Revenue of $800 ($400 for November and $400 for December) has not been recorded and will not be received until the end of January 2004. No entry has been made with regard to the contract.

As of year-end, no asset has been recorded, but an $800 receivable exists ($400 × 2), because two months' worth of revenue has been earned. To record this receivable, we must debit (increase) the asset Accounts Receivable for $800. With the debit, we have accomplished step 1 by fixing the balance sheet with regard to this transaction. Step 2 requires that we use the other half of the adjusting entry, the credit of $800, to fix the income statement. We know that the credit must be to a revenue or an expense account, and the nature of the transaction suggests that we should credit Lawn Care Revenue for $800. The adjusting entry is:

Dec. 31	Accounts Receivable	800	
	Lawn Care Revenue		800
	To record earned revenue not yet received.		

Adjusting entries are recorded in the general journal and are posted to the accounts in the general ledger in the same manner as other journal entries. Again note that each adjusting entry must involve at least one balance sheet account and at least one income statement account.

After this adjusting entry has been journalized and posted, the receivable will appear as an asset on the balance sheet, and the lawn care revenue is reported on the income statement. Through the adjusting entry, the asset (receivable) accounts are properly stated and revenues are appropriately reported.

Unrecorded Liabilities

unrecorded liabilities Expenses incurred during a period that have not been recorded by the end of that period.

Just as assets are created from revenues being earned before they are collected or recorded, liabilities can be created by expenses being incurred prior to being paid or recorded. These expenses, along with their corresponding liabilities, should be recorded when incurred, no matter when they are paid. Thus, adjusting entries are required at the end of an accounting period to recognize any **unrecorded liabilities** in the proper period and to record the corresponding expenses. As the expense is recorded (increased by a debit), the offsetting liability is also recorded (increased by a credit), showing the entity's obligation to pay for the expense. If such adjustments are not made, the net income measurement for the period will not reflect all appropriate expenses and the corresponding liabilities will be understated on the balance sheet.

To illustrate, we will assume that on December 31, 2003, our landscaping company has determined the following:

1. Your brother has worked for the company since its inception. He is paid every two weeks. The next payday is on Friday, January 5, 2004. On that day, your brother will be paid $700, the amount he earns every two weeks. Since December 31 falls halfway through the pay period, one-half of his wages should be allocated to 2003.
2. Recall from Chapter 3 that one of our options for financing our company was to borrow money from a bank. We borrowed $2,000 with the promise that on the first of every month we would make a $178 payment—a portion of that payment being attributed to interest[1] and a portion to principal. Our next payment is due on January 1, 2004, but the interest expense associated with that payment should be attributed to the period in which the money was actually used—December 2003. Assume that interest of $20 must be recognized on December 31, 2003.

To represent its current financial position and earnings, our landscaping company must record the impact of these events in the accounts, even though cash transactions have not yet occurred. The wages will not be paid until 2004. Under accrual-basis accounting, however, these costs are expenses of 2003 and should be recognized on this year's income statement, with the corresponding liability shown on the balance sheet as of the end of the year. To fix the balance sheet, Wages Payable must be credited (increased) for $350; recognition of this liability ensures that the balance sheet properly reports this liability, which was created during 2003 and exists as of the end of the year. The debit of this adjusting entry is to Wages Expense, resulting in the proper inclusion of this expense in the 2003 income statement. The adjusting journal entry is as follows:

Dec. 31	Wages Expense	350	
	Wages Payable		350
	To record obligation for wages.		

The liability for the interest for the month of December is recorded by a credit (increase) to Interest Payable; this fixes the balance sheet. The debit of the adjusting entry is to Interest

---

1 As noted in Chapter 3, *interest* is the cost of using money. The amount borrowed or lent is the *principal*. The *interest rate* is an annual rate stated as a percentage. The *period of time* involved may be stated in terms of a year. For example, if interest is to be paid for 3 months, time is 3/12, or 1/4 of a year. If interest is to be paid for 90 days, time is 90/365 of a year. Thus, the formula for computing interest is Interest = Principal × Interest Rate × Time (fraction of a year).

caution

A liability is not recorded for the total amount of interest that will have to be paid over the entire life of the loan. If we repay the loan on December 31, the future interest will not have to be paid, but the interest for the month of December that has passed will still be due.

Expense, which properly includes this expense on the 2003 income statement. The adjusting entry is:

Dec. 31	Interest Expense...............................	20	
	Interest Payable.............................		20
	To record interest incurred.		

The wages expense and interest expense would be shown on the income statement for the year ended December 31, and the liabilities (wages payable and interest payable) would be shown on the balance sheet as of December 31. Because of the adjusting entries, both the income statement and the balance sheet will more accurately reflect the financial situation of our landscaping company.

Prepaid Expenses

prepaid expenses Payments made in advance for items normally charged to expense.

Payments that a company makes in advance for items normally charged to expense are known as **prepaid expenses**. An example would be the payment of an insurance premium for three years. Theoretically, every resource acquisition is an asset, at least temporarily. Thus, the entry to record an advance payment should be a debit to an asset account (Prepaid Expenses) and a credit to Cash, showing the exchange of cash for another asset.

caution

Prepaid Expenses is a tricky name for an asset. Assets are reported in the balance sheet. Don't make the mistake of including Prepaid Expenses with the expenses on the income statement.

An expense is the using up of an asset. For example, when supplies are purchased, they are recorded as assets; when they are used, their cost is transferred to an expense account. The purpose of making adjusting entries for prepaid expenses is to show the complete or partial consumption of an asset. If the original entry is to an asset account, the adjusting entry reduces the asset to an amount that reflects its remaining future benefit and at the same time recognizes the actual expense incurred for the period.

For the unrecorded assets and liabilities discussed earlier, there was no original entry; the adjusting entry was the first time these items were recorded in the accounting records. For prepaid expenses, this is not the case. Because cash has already been paid (in the case of prepaid expenses), an original entry has been made to record the cash transaction. Therefore, the amount of the adjusting entry is the difference between what the updated balance should be and the amount of the original entry already recorded.

To illustrate adjustments for Prepaid Expenses, we will assume the following about our landscaping company:

1. On November 1, 2003, we purchased a six-month insurance policy on our old truck, paying a $600 premium.
2. On December 15, 2003, we purchased several months' worth of supplies (fertilizer, weed killer, etc.) at a total cost of $350. At year-end, $225 worth of supplies were still on hand.

For the prepaid insurance, we record the payment of $600 on November 1 as follows:

Nov. 1	Prepaid Insurance...............................	600	
	Cash...		600
	Paid a six-month insurance premium in advance.		

This entry shows that one asset (Cash) has been exchanged for another asset (Prepaid Insurance). Over the next six months we will use the auto insurance and the asset, Prepaid Insurance, will slowly be used up. As the asset is used, its cost is recorded as an expense.

At year-end, only those assets that still offer future benefits to the company should be reported on the balance sheet. Thus, an adjustment is required to reduce the prepaid insurance account to reflect the fact that only four months of prepaid insurance remain. See the following time line.

The adjusting journal entry to bring the original amounts to their updated balances at year-end is:

Dec. 31	Insurance Expense	200	
	Prepaid Insurance		200
	To record insurance expense for two months:		
	2 × $100 = $200.		

When the adjusting entry is journalized and posted, the proper amount of insurance expense ($200) will be shown as an expense on the income statement and the proper amount of prepaid insurance ($400) will be carried forward to the next period as an asset on the balance sheet. This is illustrated in the following T-accounts:

	Prepaid Insurance		Cash		Insurance Expense	
Original entry (11/1/03)	600			600		
Adjusting entry (12/31/03)		200			200	
Updated balances (12/31/03)	400				200	
	To balance sheet				To income statement	

When supplies are consumed in the normal course of business, the asset account (Supplies on Hand) must be adjusted and the used up portion charged as an operating expense (Supplies Expense) on the income statement. Thus, the adjustment for supplies is handled the same way as for any other prepaid asset.

We initially recorded $350 of supplies as an asset:

Dec. 15	Supplies on Hand	350	
	Cash		350
	Purchased supplies.		

At year-end, an adjustment must be made to recognize that only $225 worth of supplies remains. This also implies that $125 ($350 − $225) of the supplies have been used and should be charged to expense. The entries are summarized in the following T-accounts:

	Supplies on Hand		Cash		Supplies Expense	
Original entry (12/15/03)	350			350		
Adjusting entry (12/31/03)		125			125	
Updated balances (12/31/03)	225				125	
	To balance sheet				To income statement	

The adjusting entry is:

Dec. 31	Supplies Expense...................................	125	
	Supplies on Hand		125
	To record the use of supplies.		

Unearned Revenues

unearned revenues Cash amounts received before they have been earned.

Amounts received before the actual earning of revenues are known as **unearned revenues**. They arise when customers pay in advance of the receipt of goods or services. Because the company has received cash but has not yet given the customer the purchased goods or services, the unearned revenues are in fact liabilities. That is, the company must provide something in return for the amounts received. For example, a building contractor may require a deposit before proceeding on construction of a house. Upon receipt of the deposit, the contractor has unearned revenue, a liability. The contractor must construct the house to earn the revenue. If the house is not built, the contractor will be obligated to repay the deposit.

To illustrate the adjustments for unearned revenues, we will assume the following about our landscaping company:

> On December 1, a client pays you $225 for three months of landscaping services to be provided for the period beginning December 1, 2003, and ending February 29, 2004. This client is going to Hawaii for an extended vacation and would like you to take care of the grounds in her absence.

Typically, the original entry to record unearned revenue involves a debit to Cash and a credit to a liability account. In our example of landscaping revenue received three months in advance, the liability account would be Unearned Revenue, as shown on the next page.

caution

Unearned Revenue is a tricky name for a liability. Liabilities are reported in the balance sheet. Don't make the mistake of including Unearned Revenue with the revenues on the income statement.

The deposit received by a building contractor prior to the construction of a house is classified as unearned revenue.

Dec. 1	Cash.	225	
	Unearned Revenue		225
	Received three months' revenue in advance:		
	$75 × 3 = $225.		

The credit to the liability account, Unearned Revenue, is logically correct; until we provide the landscaping service, the revenue received in advance is unearned and is thus an obligation (liability).

The next step is to compute the updated balances at year-end. As illustrated with the following time line, on December 31, two months' services (2 × $75 = $150) are still unearned and should be shown as a liability, Unearned Revenue, on the balance sheet. At the same time, $75, or one month's services, has been earned (1 × $75 = $75) and should be reported as Landscaping Revenue on the income statement.

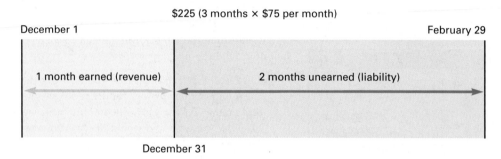

$225 (3 months × $75 per month)

Step 1 of the adjusting entry is to fix the balance sheet. The reported liability of $225 is too much since some of the unearned revenue has been earned. The remaining obligation is $150 (2 × $75), so the liability must be reduced (debited) by $75 ($225 − $150). The second half of the adjusting entry is used to correct the income statement. The $75 credit is made to Landscaping Revenue, reflecting the fact that one month's revenue has now been earned. The appropriate adjusting entry is:

Dec. 31	Unearned Revenue.	75	
	Landscaping Revenue		75
	To record landscaping revenue for one month:		
	$75 × 1 month = $75.		

These results are illustrated in the following T-accounts:

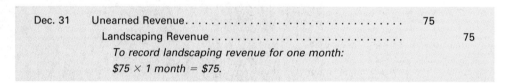

	Unearned Revenue	Cash	Landscaping Revenue
Original entry (12/1/03)	225	225	
Adjusting entry (12/31/03)	75		75
Updated balances (12/31/03)	150		75
	To balance sheet		To income statement

After the adjusting entry has been made on December 31, our accounts show $225 of cash received. Of this amount, $75 has been earned (1 month's service × $75) and would be reported as Landscaping Revenue on the income statement; $150 will not be earned until the next reporting period and would be shown as a liability on the balance sheet.

We should emphasize two characteristics of adjusting entries. First, adjusting entries made at the end of an accounting period *do not involve cash.* Cash has either changed hands prior to the end of the period (as is the case with prepaid expenses or unearned revenues), or cash will

net work

Airlines have a large amount of unearned revenue because customers pay for their tickets before the airlines provide the travel service. Visit the Web site of UNITED AIRLINES: http://www.ual.com

What title is given to Unearned Revenue for an airline? What liability was reported for Unearned Revenue in the most recent annual report?

change hands in a future period (as is the case with many unrecorded receivables and unrecorded liabilities). It is precisely because cash is *not* changing hands on the last day of the accounting period that most adjusting entries must be made.

Second, each adjusting entry involves a balance sheet account and an income statement account. In each case requiring adjustment, we are either generating an asset, using up an asset, recording an incurred but unrecorded expense, or recording revenue that has yet to be earned. Knowing that each adjusting entry has at least one balance sheet and one income statement account makes the adjustment process a little easier. Once you have determined that an adjusting entry involves a certain balance sheet account, you can then focus on identifying the corresponding income statement account that requires adjustment.

The 1999 financial statements for GENERAL MOTORS offer several illustrations of the potential impact of failing to make adjusting entries. GM reports that, as of December 31, 1999, it had unearned revenue totaling $9.504 billion. If GM had failed to make the adjustment necessary to record this unearned revenue, total revenue for 1999 would have been overstated by $9.504 billion, or 5.4%. In addition, GM reported that its total warranty liability as of December 31, 1999, was $15.284 billion. This warranty liability falls in the category of unrecorded liabilities that are not reported in the financial statements unless an appropriate adjusting entry is made. Finally, GM also reported a $35.521 billion asset related to future tax deductions; this asset would remain unrecorded unless a special adjusting entry were made at the end of the year to reflect the future tax benefits of events that had occurred in 1999 and preceding years.

to summarize

To present financial statements that accurately report the financial position and the results of operations on an accrual basis for specific periods of time, adjusting entries must be made. The four main categories of adjustments are unrecorded receivables, unrecorded liabilities, prepaid expenses, and unearned revenues. In analyzing accounts at the end of an accounting cycle, adjusting entries are made in order to recognize all earned revenues and all incurred expenses and to report the proper balances in the asset, liability, and owners' equity accounts. This requires a two-step analysis: (1) determine what adjustments are necessary to ensure that all asset and liability amounts have been properly recorded, and (2) determine which revenues or expenses must be adjusted to correspond with the changes in assets and liabilities recorded in step 1. With unrecorded receivables and unrecorded liabilities, there is no original entry. With prepaid expenses, the original entry includes a credit to Cash and a debit to an asset account. With unearned revenues, the original entry includes a debit to Cash and a credit to a liability account.

3

Explain the preparation of the financial statements, the explanatory notes, and the audit report.

PREPARING FINANCIAL STATEMENTS

Once all transactions have been analyzed, journalized, and posted and all adjusting entries have been made, the accounts can be summarized and presented in the form of financial statements. Financial statements can be prepared directly from the data in the adjusted ledger accounts. The data must only be organized into appropriate sections and categories so as to present them as simply and clearly as possible. Once the financial statements are prepared, explanatory notes are written. These notes clarify the methods and assumptions used in preparing the statements. In addition, the auditor must review the financial statements to make sure they are accurate, reasonable, and in accordance with generally accepted accounting principles. Finally, the financial statements are distributed to external users who analyze them in order to learn more about the financial condition of the company.

Financial Statement Preparation

To illustrate the preparation of financial statements from adjusted ledger accounts, a simplified adjusted trial balance for GENERAL MOTORS as of December 31, 1999, is provided in Exhibit 4-4.

From these data, an income statement and a balance sheet may be prepared for General Motors, as shown in Exhibits 4-5 and 4-6 on pages 145 and 146.

The ending retained earnings balance for General Motors for 1999 ($6,961), as reported on the balance sheet, is computed as follows:

Beginning retained earnings balance (from the adjusted trial balance)	$2,326
Add: Net income for the period (from the income statement)	6,002
Subtract: Dividends for the period (from the adjusted trial balance)	(1,367)
Ending retained earnings balance	$6,961

---

exhibit 4-4   Simplified Adjusted Trial Balance

General Motors Corporation
Simplified Adjusted Trial Balance
December 31, 1999
(in millions)

	Debits	Credits
Cash	$ 10,442	
Investments	12,519	
Receivables	86,721	
Inventories	10,638	
Property and Equipment	38,523	
Intangible Assets	8,527	
Deferred Taxes	15,277	
Other Assets	55,676	
Investment in Leases	36,407	
Accounts Payable		$ 21,516
Accrued Expenses		32,854
Current Debt		70,934
Long-Term Debt		62,745
Pensions and Other Retirement Benefits		37,505
Other Liabilities		28,532
Capital Stock and Other		13,683
Retained Earnings		2,326
Dividends	1,367	
Revenue from Sales		152,635
Financing Revenues		14,734
Other Income		9,189
Cost of Sales	126,809	
Selling, General and Administrative Expenses	18,845	
Depreciation and Amortization	12,318	
Interest Expense	7,750	
Income Tax Expense	3,118	
Other Expenses	1,716	
Totals	$446,653	$446,653

exhibit 4-5   Income Statement

General Motors Corporation
Statement of Income
For the Year Ended December 31, 1999
(in millions)

Revenue from sales		$152,635
Financing revenues		14,734
Total revenues		$167,369
Cost of sales	$126,809	
Selling, general and administrative expenses	18,845	
Depreciation and amortization	12,318	
Total operating expenses		157,972
Operating income		$ 9,397
Other income	$ 9,189	
Interest expense	(7,750)	
Income tax expense	(3,118)	
Other expenses	(1,716)	
Total other revenues and expenses		(3,395)
Net income		$ 6,002

This follows the computation of retained earnings discussed in Chapter 2.

A statement of cash flows is not shown here. To prepare a statement of cash flows, we need more detailed information about the nature of the cash receipts and cash disbursements during the year. The preparation of a statement of cash flows will be illustrated in Chapter 13.

The Notes

As discussed in Chapter 2, the notes to the financial statements tell about the assumptions and methods used in preparing the financial statements and also give more detail about specific items. A sample of the kind of information that appears in the notes for General Motors' financial statements is illustrated in Exhibit 4-7 on page 147. The first two notes, on revenue recognition and credit losses, illustrate how financial statement notes can summarize the accounting policies and assumptions that underlie the financial statements. The third note, on the debt associated with GM's financing subsidiary (GMAC), provides detailed information about a summary number that was reported in the financial statements. The fourth note, on GM's labor force, provides information that is deemed to be important to financial statement users, such as future labor costs, but that does not directly affect any of the reported historical financial statement numbers.

The financial statement notes serve to augment the summarized, numerical information contained in the financial statements. To highlight the importance of the notes, many financial statements have the following message printed at the bottom: "The notes are an integral part of these financial statements."

The Audit

As mentioned in Chapter 2, an independent audit, by CPAs from outside the company, is often conducted to ensure that the financial statements have been prepared in conformity with generally accepted accounting principles. With respect to the financial statements of General Motors, the audit procedures conducted by the external auditor, DELOITTE & TOUCHE, would probably include the following checks.

REVIEW OF ADJUSTMENTS   As you learned in the first part of this chapter, adjusting entries usually require more analysis, and more judgment, than do the regular journal entries recorded throughout the year. As part of the audit, the auditor will review these adjusting en-

exhibit 4-6   Balance Sheet

General Motors Corporation
Balance Sheet
December 31, 1999
(in millions)

Assets

Current assets:

Cash	$10,442	
Investments	12,519	
Receivables	86,721	
Inventories	10,638	
Total current assets		$120,320

Long-term assets:

Property and equipment	$38,523	
Intangible assets	8,527	
Deferred taxes	15,277	
Other assets	55,676	
Investment in leases	36,407	
Total long-term assets		154,410
Total assets		$274,730

Liabilities and Owners' Equity

Current liabilities:

Accounts payable	$21,516	
Accrued expenses	32,854	
Current debt	70,934	
Total current liabilities		$125,304
Long-term debt		62,745
Pensions and other retirement benefits		37,505
Other liabilities		28,532
Total liabilities		$254,086

Owners' equity

Capital stock and other	$13,683	
Retained earnings	6,961	
Total owners' equity		20,644
Total liabilities and owners' equity		$274,730

Note: This balance sheet is not an exact replica of General Motors' actual balance sheet due to simplifying modifications for this exhibit.

tries. Auditors pay particular attention to the adjustments involving unrecorded expenses. As mentioned in the text, companies don't like making these adjusting entries, because they increase reported liabilities and reduce reported net income. Accordingly, the auditor should review the business events of the year to make sure that no expenses have been left unrecorded.

SAMPLE OF SELECTED ACCOUNTS   For a number of accounts, the auditor undertakes a sampling process to see whether the items reported in the balance sheet actually exist. For example, General Motors reports an ending cash and equivalents balance of $10,442,000,000. The auditor will ask to see bank statements and will probably call the bank(s) to verify the existence of the cash. For inventory, the auditor will ask to physically see the inventory and will conduct a spot check to see whether the company inventory records match what is actually in the warehouse.

REVIEW OF ACCOUNTING SYSTEMS   The auditor will also evaluate General Motors' accounting systems. If a company has a good accounting system, with all transactions being recorded

exhibit 4-7   General Motors: Notes to the Financial Statements

General Motors Corporation
Notes to the Financial Statements (partial list)
For the Year Ended December 31, 1999

Revenue Recognition: Sales are generally recorded when products are shipped . . . to independent dealers.

Allowance for Credit Losses: Receivables are charged off [i.e., removed from the books] as soon as it is determined that the collateral cannot be repossessed, generally not more than 150 days after default.

Debt: Debt was as follows (in millions):

	Weighted-Average Interest Rate	December 31, 1999	December 31, 1998
Payable within one year:			
Current portion of debt	6.6%	$ 14,996	$ 12,701
Commercial paper	5.8%	33,229	34,487
All other	4.6%	18,727	15,208
Payable beyond one year:			
2000	—	—	13,154
2001	6.0%	16,854	10,322
2002	5.7%	15,100	8,561
2003	6.1%	8,786	7,919
2004	6.6%	5,550	1,208
2005 and after	7.4%	9,662	4,864
Unamortized discount		(622)	(671)
Total debt		$122,282	$107,753

Labor Force: The 1999 United Auto Workers (UAW) labor contract was ratified on October 13, 1999, covering a four-year term from 1999–2003. The contract included an annual salary increase of 3% per year, an up-front signing bonus of $1,350 per UAW employee. . . . The 1999 contract includes job security and sourcing provisions containing an employment floor set at 95% of 1996 employment levels in the event of net outsourcing.

in an efficient, orderly way, then the auditor has greater reason to be confident that the financial statements are reliable. On the other hand, if the company's accounting system is haphazard, with many missing documents and unexplained discrepancies, then the auditor must do more detailed work to verify the financial statements.

If the auditor finds that the financial statements have been prepared in conformance with generally accepted accounting principles, then the auditor provides a report to that effect. This report is attached and distributed as part of the financial statements. The audit report is discussed in more detail in Chapter 5.

to summarize

The adjusted trial balance provides the raw material for the preparation of the balance sheet and the income statement. The notes to the financial statements provide further information about the methods and assumptions used in preparing the financial statements as well as further detail about certain financial statement items. The audit is conducted by a CPA from outside the company who reviews the adjusting entries, performs tests to check the balances of selected accounts, and reviews the condition of the accounting systems.

4

Perform a systematic analysis of financial statements.

ANALYZING FINANCIAL STATEMENTS

Financial statements are prepared in order to be used. Once the balance sheet, income statement, statement of cash flows, notes, and audit report of a company are completed, the whole package is distributed to bankers, suppliers, and investors to be used in evaluating the company's financial health. Financial statement analysis was introduced in Chapter 2 with illustrations of the computation and interpretation of selected financial ratios. That discussion is extended here with the introduction of two general tools of financial statement analysis: the DuPont framework and common-size financial statements.

DuPont Framework

return on equity A measure of the amount of profit earned per dollar of investment, computed by dividing net income by equity.

As discussed in Chapter 2, **return on equity** (Net Income/Equity) is the single measure that summarizes the financial health of a company. Return on equity can be interpreted as the number of cents of net income an investor earns in one year by investing one dollar in the company. Return on equity (ROE) for **GENERAL MOTORS** for the year 1999 is computed below ($ in millions):

Net Income	$6,002
Equity	$20,644
Return on Equity	29.1%

DuPont framework A systematic approach for breaking down return on equity into three ratios: profit margin, asset turnover, and assets-to-equity ratio.

The **DuPont framework** (named after a system of ratio analysis developed internally at DuPont in the early part of the twentieth century) provides a systematic approach to identifying general factors contributing to return on equity. The insight behind the DuPont framework is that ROE can be decomposed into three components, as shown below.

$$\text{Return on Equity} = \text{Profitability} \times \text{Efficiency} \times \text{Leverage}$$
$$= \text{Profit Margin} \times \text{Asset Turnover} \times \text{Assets-to-Equity Ratio}$$
$$\frac{\text{Net Income}}{\text{Equity}} = \frac{\text{Net Income}}{\text{Revenue}} \times \frac{\text{Revenue}}{\text{Assets}} \times \frac{\text{Assets}}{\text{Equity}}$$

For each of the three ROE components—profitability, efficiency, and leverage—there is a correlating ratio that summarizes a company's performance in that area. These ratios are as follows:

profit margin A measure of the number of pennies in profit generated from each dollar of revenue; calculated by dividing net income by revenue.

asset turnover A measure of company efficiency, computed by dividing revenue by total assets.

assets-to-equity ratio A measure of the number of dollars of assets a company is able to acquire using each dollar of equity; calculated by dividing assets by equity.

- **Profit margin** is computed as (Net Income/Revenue) and is interpreted as the number of pennies in profit generated from each dollar of revenue.
- **Asset turnover** is computed as (Revenue/Assets) and is interpreted as the number of dollars in revenue generated by each dollar of assets.
- **Assets-to-equity ratio** is computed as (Assets/Equity) and is interpreted as the number of dollars of assets a company is able to acquire using each dollar invested by stockholders.

The DuPont analysis of General Motors' ROE for 1999 is as follows:

$$\text{Return on Equity} = \frac{\text{Net Income}}{\text{Revenue}} \times \frac{\text{Revenue}}{\text{Assets}} \times \frac{\text{Assets}}{\text{Equity}}$$

$$\frac{\$6,002}{\$20,644} = \frac{\$6,002}{\$176,558} \times \frac{\$176,558}{\$274,730} \times \frac{\$274,730}{\$20,644}$$

$$29.1\% = 3.4\% \times 0.64 \times 13.31$$

These three ratio values can be interpreted as follows:

- GM earned 3.4 cents in profit for each dollar in revenue.
- GM generated $0.64 in revenue for every dollar of assets.
- For every dollar invested by GM shareholders, GM was able to acquire $13.31 in assets; additional assets were acquired with borrowed funds.

STOP & THINK Is it good for a company to have a high assets-to-equity ratio?

Evaluation of whether these ratio values are too high or too low involves comparing the computed values to the ratio values of other companies in the same industry as General Motors. In addition, this year's ratio values can be compared to GM's own ratio values in past years. For example, if other companies in the auto industry have profit margins of 7.0%, it appears that GM's profitability (3.4%) is lower than that of its competitors. If the asset turnover value for GM's competitors is 1.00, the 0.64 value for GM suggests that GM is less efficient at using its assets to generate sales.

common-size financial statements Financial statements achieved by dividing all financial statement numbers by total revenues for the year.

Common-Size Financial Statements

A quick and easy way to get more information out of the financial statements is to divide all financial statement numbers for a given year by the total revenues for the year. The resulting financial statements, called **common-size financial statements**, show all amounts for a given year as a percentage of revenues for that year. A common-size income statement for General Motors, based on the income statement in Exhibit 4-5, is shown in Exhibit 4-8.

If General Motors' overall profitability is lower than its industry competitors, the common-size income statement can be used to pinpoint exactly where the problem lies. For example, if General Motors' competitors have cost of sales that is just 65.0% of total revenue, then the 71.8% for GM suggests that this expense may be too high.

A common-size balance sheet also expresses each amount as a percentage of total revenue for the year. A common-size balance sheet for General Motors, based on the balance sheet in Exhibit 4-6, is shown in Exhibit 4-9.

The most informative section of the common-size balance sheet is the asset section, which can be used to determine how efficiently a company is using its assets. For example, assume that GM's competitors have inventory levels equal to 5.0% of total revenues. This suggests that GM is maintaining higher inventory levels (6.0% of revenues) and is thus using its inventory less efficiently.

fyi

The amount of cash held by General Motors is quite low— 5.9% of revenues. For comparison, look at MICROSOFT's financial statements at the end of the text and you'll see that Microsoft has a very high 1999 cash balance equal to 87.3% of total revenues.

to summarize

Financial statements are used by various interested parties to examine a company's financial health. Two general techniques for financial statement

exhibit 4-8   Common-Size Income Statement

General Motors Corporation
Common-Size Income Statement
For the Year Ended December 31, 1999
(in millions)

		Amounts	% of Revenue
Revenue from sales		$152,635	
Financing revenues.		14,734	
Other income		9,189	
Total revenues		$176,558	100.0%
Cost of sales.	$126,809		71.8%
Selling, general and administrative expenses . . .	18,845		10.7%
Depreciation and amortization.	12,318		7.0%
Interest expense	7,750		4.4%
Income tax expense	3,118		1.8%
Other expenses.	1,716	170,556	1.0%
Net income.		$ 6,002	3.4%

exhibit 4-9   Common-Size Balance Sheet

General Motors Corporation
Common-Size Balance Sheet
December 31, 1999
(in millions)

	Amounts	% of Revenue
Assets		
Cash	$ 10,442	5.9%
Investments	12,519	7.1%
Receivables	86,721	49.1%
Inventories	10,638	6.0%
Property and equipment	38,523	21.8%
Intangible assets	8,527	4.8%
Deferred taxes	15,277	8.7%
Other assets	55,676	31.5%
Investment in leases	36,407	20.6%
Total assets	$274,730	155.6%*
Liabilities and Owners' Equity		
Accounts payable	$ 21,516	12.2%
Accrued expenses	32,854	18.6%
Current debt	70,934	40.2%
Long-term debt	62,745	35.5%
Pensions and other retirement benefits	37,505	21.2%
Other liabilities	28,532	16.2%
Capital stock and other	13,683	7.7%
Retained earnings	6,961	3.9%
Total liabilities and equities	$274,730	155.6%*

*Difference due to rounding.

business environment essay

Market Efficiency: Can Financial Statement Analysis Help You Win in the Stock Market? An efficient market is one in which information is reflected rapidly in prices. For example, if the real estate market in a city is efficient, then news of an impending layoff at a major employer in the city should quickly result in lower housing prices because of an anticipated decrease in demand. The major stock exchanges in the United States are often considered to be efficient markets in the sense that information about specific companies or about the economy in general is reflected almost immediately in stock prices. One implication of market efficiency is that, since current stock prices reflect all available information, future movements in stock prices should be unpredictable.

It seems clear that stock markets in the United States are efficient in a general sense, but accumulated evidence suggests the existence of a number of puzzling "anomalies" in the form of predictable patterns of stock returns. For example, prices tend to continue to drift upward for weeks or months after favorable earnings news is released. In addition, prices continue to climb for at least a year after a stock split is announced.

From an accounting standpoint, market efficiency relates to the usefulness of so-called fundamental analysis. Fundamental analysis is the practice of using financial data to calculate the underlying value of a firm and using this underlying value to identify over-

analysis are the DuPont framework and common-size financial statements. The DuPont framework is based on the insight that return on equity can be separated into three components, each with a correlating ratio: profitability (profit margin), efficiency (asset turnover), and leverage (assets-to-equity). Preparing common-size financial statements involves dividing all financial statement numbers by total revenue for the year.

CLOSING THE BOOKS

5
Complete the closing process in the accounting cycle.

We have almost reached the end of the accounting cycle. Thus far, the accounting cycle has included analyzing documents, journalizing transactions, posting to the ledger accounts, determining account balances, preparing a trial balance, making adjusting entries, and preparing the financial statements. Just two additional steps are needed: (1) journalizing and posting closing entries and (2) preparing a post-closing trial balance.

Real and Nominal Accounts

real accounts Accounts that are not closed to a zero balance at the end of each accounting period; permanent accounts appearing on the balance sheet.

To explain the closing process, we must first define two new terms. Certain accounts are referred to as **real accounts**. These accounts report the cumulative increases and decreases in certain account balances from the date the company was organized. Real accounts (assets, liabilities, and owners' equity) appear on the balance sheet and are permanent; they are not closed to a zero balance at the end of each accounting period. Balances existing in real accounts at the end of a period are carried forward to the next period.

nominal accounts Accounts that are closed to a zero balance at the end of each accounting period; temporary accounts generally appearing on the income statement.

Other accounts are known as **nominal accounts**. These accounts (revenues, expenses, and dividends) are temporary; they are really just subcategories of Retained Earnings and are reduced to a zero balance through the closing process at the end of each accounting period. Thus, nominal accounts begin with a zero balance at the start of each accounting cycle. Transactions throughout the period (generally a year) are journalized and posted to the nominal accounts. These are used to accumulate and classify all revenue and expense items, and also dividends, for that

and underpriced stocks. The notion of fundamental analysis is in conflict with market efficiency, because the analysis works only if current stock prices do not fully reflect all available accounting information. For this reason, fundamental analysis has frequently been regarded with skepticism by academics. A growing body of academic research, however, suggests that accounting data may be useful in predicting future stock returns. Ou and Penman (1989) and Holthausen and Larcker (1992) were the first to demonstrate that financial ratios derived from publicly available financial statements can be used to successfully forecast stock returns for the coming year. More recently, Abarbanell and Bushee (1998) showed that, using financial ratios to predict future earnings performance,

one can selectively invest in companies and earn an abnormal return of 13.2% per year. An abnormal return is the return over and above what one would earn with a diversified portfolio of stocks. So, contrary to what is expected of an efficient stock market, it looks like you *can* use publicly available accounting data to make money in the U.S. stock market.

Sources: Jane A. Ou and Stephen H. Penman, "Financial Statement Analysis and the Prediction of Stock Returns," *Journal of Accounting and Economics*, November 1989, p. 295; Robert W. Holthausen and David F. Larcker, "The Prediction of Stock Returns Using Financial Statement Information," *Journal of Accounting and Economics*, June 1992, p. 373; Jeffery S. Abarbanell and Brian J. Bushee, "Abnormal Returns to a Fundamental Analysis Strategy," *The Accounting Review*, January 1998, p. 19.

period. At the end of the accounting period, adjustments are made, the income statement is prepared, and the balances in the temporary accounts are then closed to Retained Earnings, a permanent account. These closing entries bring the income statement accounts back to a zero balance, which makes the accounts ready for a new accounting period. In addition, the closing entries transfer the net income or loss for the accounting period to Retained Earnings and reduce Retained Earnings for any dividends. Without closing entries, revenue and expense balances would extend from period to period, making it difficult to isolate the operating results of each accounting period.

Closing Entries

The actual mechanics of the closing process are not complicated. Revenue accounts normally have credit balances and are closed by being debited; expense accounts generally have debit balances and are closed by being credited. The difference between total revenues and total expenses represents the net income (or net loss) of the entity. For a corporation, net income is credited to Retained Earnings because income increases owners' equity. A net loss would be debited to Retained Earnings because a loss decreases owners' equity.

To illustrate the closing process, we will again refer to GENERAL MOTORS' financial information as discussed earlier on pages 144–146. The closing journal entry is:

closing entries Entries that reduce all nominal, or temporary, accounts to a zero balance at the end of each accounting period, transferring their preclosing balances to a permanent balance sheet account.

Dec. 31	Revenue from Sales	152,635	
	Financing Revenues	14,734	
	Other Income	9,189	
	Cost of Sales		126,809
	Selling, General and Administrative Expenses		18,845
	Depreciation and Amortization		12,318
	Interest Expense		7,750
	Income Tax Expense		3,118
	Other Expenses		1,716
	Retained Earnings		6,002
	To close revenues and expenses to Retained Earnings.		

Closing entries must be posted to the appropriate ledger accounts. Once posted, all nominal accounts will have a zero balance; that is, they will be "closed."

The dividends account is also a nominal (temporary) account that must be closed at the end of the accounting period. However, dividends are not expenses and will not be reported on an income statement; they are distributions to stockholders of part of a corporation's earnings. Thus, dividends reduce retained earnings. When dividends are declared by the board of directors of a corporation, the amount that will be paid is debited to Dividends and credited to a liability account, Dividends Payable, or to Cash if paid immediately. Because Dividends is a temporary account, it must be closed to Retained Earnings at the end of the accounting period. The dividends account is closed by crediting it and by debiting Retained Earnings, thereby reducing owners' equity, as illustrated below for General Motors.

Dec. 31	Retained Earnings	1,367	
	Dividends		1,367
	To close Dividends to Retained Earnings.		

post-closing trial balance A listing of all real account balances after the closing process has been completed; provides a means of testing whether total debits equal total credits for all real accounts prior to beginning a new accounting cycle.

The books are now ready for a new accounting cycle. The closing process for the revenues, expenses, and dividends of a corporation is shown schematically in Exhibit 4-10.

Preparing a Post-Closing Trial Balance

An optional last step in the accounting cycle is to balance the accounts and to prepare a **post-closing trial balance**. The accounts are to be balanced—debits and credits added and a balance

exhibit 4-10   The Closing Process

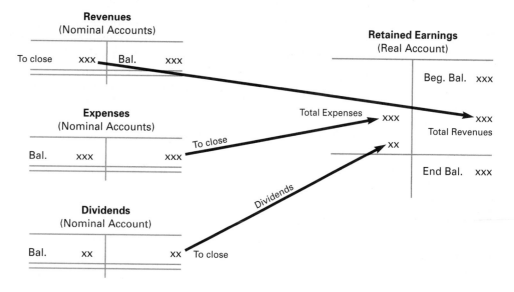

determined—only after the closing entries have been recorded and posted in the general ledger. The information for the post-closing trial balance is then taken from the ledger. The nominal accounts will not be shown since they have been closed and thus have zero balances. Only the real accounts will have current balances. This step is designed to provide some assurance that the previous steps in the cycle have been performed properly, prior to the start of a new accounting period. Exhibit 4-11 illustrates a post-closing trial balance for General Motors Corporation.

exhibit 4-11   Post-Closing Trial Balance

General Motors Corporation
Post-Closing Trial Balance
December 31, 1999
(in millions)

	Debits	Credits
Cash	$ 10,442	
Investments	12,519	
Receivables	86,721	
Inventories	10,638	
Property and Equipment	38,523	
Intangible Assets	8,527	
Deferred Taxes	15,277	
Other Assets	55,676	
Investment in Leases	36,407	
Accounts Payable		$ 21,516
Accrued Expenses		32,854
Current Debt		70,934
Long-Term Debt		62,745
Pensions and Other Retirement Benefits		37,505
Other Liabilities		28,532
Capital Stock and Other		13,683
Retained Earnings		6,961
Totals	$274,730	$274,730

to summarize

As part of the closing process, all nominal (temporary) accounts are closed to a zero balance. All real (permanent) accounts (balance sheet accounts for assets, liabilities, and owners' equity) are carried forward to the new reporting period. All nominal accounts (revenues, expenses, and dividends) are closed to Retained Earnings. Revenue accounts are closed by being debited; expense accounts are closed by being credited. Dividends also must be closed to Retained Earnings by being credited. A post-closing trial balance may be prepared to provide some assurance that the previous steps in the cycle have been performed properly.

6

Understand how all the steps in the accounting cycle fit together.

A SUMMARY OF THE ACCOUNTING CYCLE

We have now completed our discussion of the steps in the accounting cycle. By way of review, Exhibit 4-12 lists the sequence of the accounting cycle (presented earlier in Chapter 3). Many of the steps, such as analyzing transactions, occur continuously. Other steps, such as preparing the financial statements, generally occur only once during the cycle.

The financial statements that result from the accounting cycle provide useful information to investors, creditors, and other external users. These statements are included in the annual re-

exhibit 4-12   Sequence of the Accounting Cycle

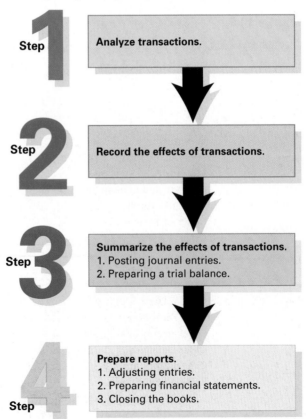

Exchange Transactions
(Businesses enter into exchange transactions
signaling the beginning of the accounting cycle)

Step **1**   Analyze transactions.

Step **2**   Record the effects of transactions.

Step **3**   Summarize the effects of transactions.
1. Posting journal entries.
2. Preparing a trial balance.

Step **4**   Prepare reports.
1. Adjusting entries.
2. Preparing financial statements.
3. Closing the books.

ports provided to stockholders. As illustrated earlier in the chapter, once the financial statements are made available to users, they can then be analyzed and compared to the financial statements of similar firms to detect strengths and weaknesses.

Origi
Adju
Upda

expanded material

Earlier in the chapter, the adjusting entries for prepaid expenses were made assuming that the prepayments were initially recorded as assets. Alternatively, the prepayments can be initially recorded as expenses; the correct amounts of assets and expenses can still be achieved through an appropriate year-end adjusting entry. Similarly, cash receipts in advance are sometimes initially recorded as revenues instead of as liabilities. Again, although not conceptually correct, it is done in the normal course of bookkeeping; any necessary adjustments can be made at year-end.

Origi
Adju
Upda

7

Make adjusting entries for prepaid expenses and unearned revenues when the original cash amounts are recorded as expenses and revenues.

ADJUSTING ENTRIES: ORIGINAL ENTRIES TO EXPENSE OR REVENUE

To illustrate the necessary adjusting process when expense prepayments are debited to an expense account, we will use the prepaid insurance example for the landscaping company that was illustrated earlier:

> On November 1, 2003, the landscaping company purchased a six-month insurance policy on its old truck, paying a $600 premium.

Assume that the $600 insurance prepayment was initially recorded as follows:

Nov. 1	Insurance Expense	600	
	Cash		600
	Paid six months' insurance in advance:		
	6 × $100 = $600.		

Notice that the debit is to Insurance Expense instead of Prepaid Insurance (as illustrated earlier). In order to fix the balance sheet at December 31, the asset Prepaid Insurance must be debited (increased) for $400 (4 × $100) to reflect the fact that four months of prepaid insurance still remain. The entire $400 is debited to Prepaid Insurance because, with the original debit to Insurance Expense, the existing balance in Prepaid Insurance is $0. The credit half of the adjusting entry is used to fix the income statement. The $400 credit is to Insurance Expense, representing the fact that too much insurance expense was initially recorded and some is being removed. The appropriate adjusting entry is as follows:

work
schec
rize a

Dec. 31	Prepaid Insurance.	400	
	Insurance Expense		400
	To record prepaid insurance for four months:		
	4 × $100 = $400.		

Taxes Payable for the appropriate amount. When the taxes are actually paid, Income Taxes Payable is debited, and Cash is credited.

The adjustment for income taxes presents a minor problem on the work sheet because the amount of income taxes to be paid cannot be determined until net income (net loss) has been computed. One way to solve this problem is to subtotal the work sheet columns, determine the balancing figure for pretax income, multiply that figure by the tax rate to determine the amount of the tax, and then make the adjusting entry for Income Tax Expense and Income Taxes Payable the same way as other adjustments are made.

With this approach, both income tax accounts—Income Tax Expense and Income Taxes Payable—are added on the work sheet following the column subtotals. To illustrate, we assume that ITEC, Inc., is subject to a tax rate of 25%. The work sheet shown in Exhibit 4-13 would be completed as follows:

	Adjustments		Income Statement		Balance Sheet	
	Debits	**Credits**	**Debits**	**Credits**	**Debits**	**Credits**
Subtotals	5,380	5,380	23,780	34,800	35,220	24,200
Income Tax Expense	2,755		2,755			
Income Taxes Payable		2,755				2,755
Totals	8,135	8,135	26,535	34,800	35,220	26,955
Net Income (to balance)			8,265*			8,265
Totals			34,800	34,800	35,220	35,220

*[$34,800 − $23,780 = $11,020 to balance the income statement columns: $11,020 × 0.25 = $2,755 Income Tax Expense and Income Taxes Payable; the balance ($11,020 − $2,755 = $8,265) is net income.]

REPORTING THE ENDING RETAINED EARNINGS BALANCE   We have explained and illustrated how the financial statements can be prepared from the income statement and balance sheet columns on the work sheet. To simplify the illustration (Exhibit 4-13), we assumed that ITEC, Inc., was organized on January 1, 2003, and therefore had no previous retained earnings balance. Normally, a work sheet will show the beginning retained earnings on the trial balance, which will be extended as a credit to the balance sheet columns. In addition, if a corporation has paid its stockholders dividends during the period, the dividends account will be shown on the trial balance and extended as a debit to the balance sheet columns. When preparing the balance sheet, these amounts must be considered in determining the ending retained earnings balance. The net income balancing figure on the work sheet is added to the beginning retained earnings amount; any amount shown for dividends is subtracted. The resulting figure is the amount of ending retained earnings to be reported on the balance sheet; thus:

> Beginning Retained Earnings
> + Net Income
> − Dividends
> ─────────────────────
> Ending Retained Earnings

For the ITEC illustration, the beginning Retained Earnings balance was zero since the company had just been established. There also were no dividends paid. Therefore, the ending balance for retained earnings ($8,265) was simply the amount of net income for the period. For the next accounting period, ITEC would start with a balance of $8,265 in its retained earnings account, add the net income balancing figure for that period, and subtract any dividends to determine the ending retained earnings balance to report on the balance sheet.

The income statement and balance sheet for ITEC, Inc., as prepared from the work sheet, are shown in Exhibits 4-14 and 4-15, respectively.

exhibit 4-14   Income Statement for ITEC, Inc.

ITEC, Inc.
Income Statement
For the Year Ended December 31, 2003

Sales revenue	$34,700	
Rent revenue	100	
Total revenues		$34,800
Less cost of goods sold		21,000
Gross profit		$13,800
Less operating expenses:		
Salaries expense	$ 2,200	
Truck rental expense	400	
Insurance expense	40	
Supplies expense	140	2,780
Income before income taxes		$11,020
Income tax expense		2,755
Net income		$ 8,265

exhibit 4-15   Balance Sheet for ITEC, Inc.

ITEC, Inc.
Balance Sheet
December 31, 2003

Assets

Cash	$24,270	
Accounts receivable	3,000	
Inventory	3,000	
Supplies on hand	110	
Prepaid insurance	440	
Prepaid truck rental	4,400	
Total assets		$35,220

Liabilities and Owners' Equity

Liabilities:		
Accounts payable	$ 3,000	
Unearned rent revenue	500	
Salaries payable	700	
Income taxes payable	2,755	$ 6,955
Owners' equity:		
Capital stock	$20,000	
Retained earnings	8,265*	28,265
Total liabilities and owners' equity		$35,220

*Beginning Retained Earnings + Net Income − Dividends = Ending Retained Earnings.

APPENDIX B: SPECIAL JOURNALS

So far we have shown all journal entries in general journal format, as explained in Chapter 3. With many businesses having hundreds or even thousands of transactions every day, it is impractical and inefficient to use only one journal. Instead, they group transactions into similar classes and use a **special journal** for each. These special journals can be maintained on paper or in a computerized system; the basic principles are the same. In this appendix, we refer to a manual system.

special journal A book of original entry for recording similar transactions that occur frequently.

The Sales Journal

One of the most frequently occurring business transactions involves the sale of goods or services, either for cash or on credit. Cash sales are generally recorded in a cash receipts journal. When merchandise is sold on credit, a prenumbered sales invoice is prepared. This invoice specifies the date of the sale, the amount and kinds of merchandise sold, and the price. One copy of the invoice is sent to the accounting department to be used as the basis for an entry in the **sales journal**. This journal is a chronological listing of all credit sales, as shown in Exhibit 4-16.

sales journal A special journal in which credit sales are recorded.

This sales journal page has no columns for sales discounts (reductions in price offered to customers who pay within a specified period), sales returns, or sales taxes. Antler Corporation records all credit sales at their gross amounts and notes sales discounts at the time of collection (in the Cash Receipts Journal). Sales returns, which involve a debit to Sales Returns and Allowances and a credit to Accounts Receivable, are recorded by Antler in the general journal. Many companies include sales discounts and returns in the sales journal, but we have omitted them here for the sake of simplicity. (The concepts of sales discounts and returns are covered more fully in Chapter 6.) If Antler were operating in a state with sales taxes, the taxes would be entered in a Sales Taxes Payable (credit) column, with the total posted to the sales taxes payable account at the same time Accounts Receivable and Sales Revenue are posted. (The concept of sales taxes is covered more fully in Chapter 8.)

e x h i b i t   4 - 1 6   A Sample Page in a Sales Journal for Antler Corporation

					SALES JOURNAL			

Date	Customer	Invoice No.	Post. Ref.	Amount
2003 Jan. 2	Lee Smith	125	105.7	600
5	Roger Jameson	126	105.5	250
6	Ralph Smith	127	105.8	315
8	John Anderson	128	105.1	216
9	Carl Hartford	129	105.4	822
12	Mike Taylor	130	105.9	610
16	Marvin Brinkerhoff	131	105.3	507
23	Roy Avondet	132	105.2	125
27	Jay Rasmussen	133	105.6	350
28	Jerry Woolsey	134	105.11	816
				4,611
				(105) (400)

The sales journal differs from the general journal in several respects. First, because all transactions are similar, the entries do not require separate explanations. Second, there are no debit and credit columns because the total is always posted as a debit to Accounts Receivable (account 105) and a credit to Sales Revenue (account 400). Third, the sales journal includes a column for the sales invoice number for easy reference to a source of additional information.

Having a single total posted to Accounts Receivable saves time and keeps the general ledger in manageable form. However, it does make it difficult, if not impossible, for a company to monitor the activity of individual accounts. Maintaining a separate account for each customer within the general ledger creates a different sort of problem—a voluminous general ledger with many accounts receivable accounts, plus Cash, Inventory, and so forth. The same problem exists for Accounts Payable.

subsidiary ledger A grouping of individual accounts that in total equal the balance of a control account in the general ledger.

control account A summary account in the general ledger that is supported by detailed individual accounts in a subsidiary ledger.

To handle this problem, companies generally keep at least three ledgers: the general ledger, which contains all the balance sheet and income statement accounts; the accounts receivable subsidiary ledger; and the accounts payable subsidiary ledger. The **subsidiary ledgers** contain separate accounts (in alphabetical order) for each customer and creditor, showing all debits, credits, and a balance. They are called subsidiary ledgers because they back up, or support, the account balances in the general ledger. The total of all accounts in the accounts receivable subsidiary ledger, for example, equals the balance in Accounts Receivable in the general ledger. Accounts Receivable is called a **control account** because it summarizes the individual accounts in the accounts receivable subsidiary ledger. Exhibit 4-17 illustrates the relationship between the general and subsidiary ledgers.

As the sales journal entries are posted to the accounts receivable subsidiary ledger accounts, the individual account numbers are entered in the sales journal posting reference column. The number of the sales journal page and the date of the transaction are similarly entered as a posting reference in the subsidiary accounts. These cross-references quickly direct accountants to the source of additional information, while serving as a means of checking their work. Exhibit 4-18 shows the posting of the sales transactions to the general ledger. Note that the total posted to Accounts Receivable in the general ledger equals the total of all postings to the accounts receivable subsidiary ledger.

The Purchases Journal

A second frequently occurring transaction involves the purchase of merchandise for resale, either for cash or on credit. Cash purchases are recorded in a cash disbursements journal and will be discussed later. Credit purchases are chronologically recorded in a **purchases journal**. The individual entries are posted to accounts in the accounts payable subsidiary ledger throughout the accounting period. At the end of the period, the total is posted to both Accounts Payable and Purchases.

purchases journal A special journal in which credit purchases are recorded.

The purchases and sales journals are similar, except that the sales journal includes invoice numbers and the purchases journal includes invoice dates. The date is useful for identifying the beginning of a discount period. A sample page from a purchases journal is shown in Exhibit 4-19 on page 166. As with the sales journal, Antler Corporation handles discounts at the time of payment. (The concept of purchase discounts is covered more fully in Chapter 7.)

This purchases journal is used for recording credit purchases of inventory only. Credit purchases of equipment, supplies, other such items, and purchase returns would be recorded in the general journal. Exhibit 4-20 on page 167 illustrates the posting of the purchases journal to the accounts payable subsidiary ledger and to the general ledger.

Each purchase is posted to the individual creditor's account in the accounts payable subsidiary ledger; the total of $4,851 is posted to Accounts Payable (202) and Purchases (450) in the general ledger. Like the sales journal, the purchases journal is cross-referenced to the general and subsidiary ledgers. The cumulative total of all balances in the accounts payable subsidiary ledger equals the balance in the accounts payable account.

exhibit 4-17   The General and Subsidiary Ledgers

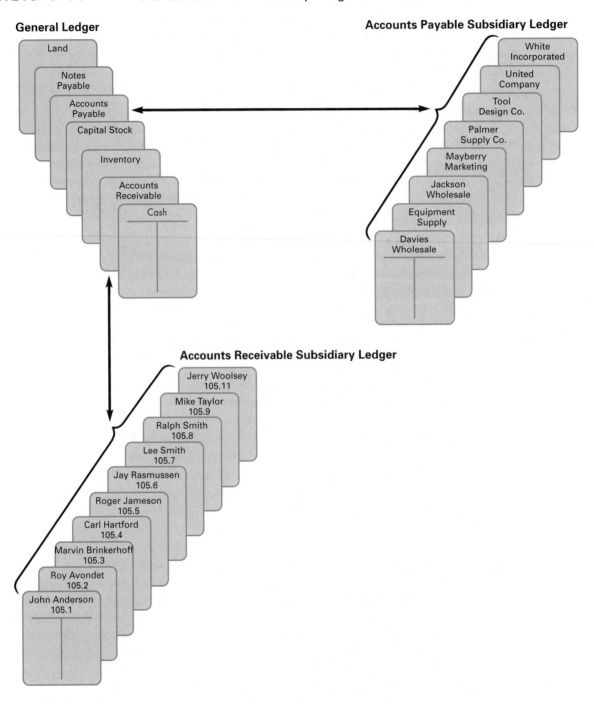

The Cash Receipts Journal

cash receipts journal A special journal in which all cash received, from sales, interest, rent, or other sources, is recorded.

Another special journal is the **cash receipts journal**, which includes all cash received from sales, interest, rent, or other sources. Exhibit 4-21 on page 168 shows a typical page from a cash receipts journal and the posting of its entries.

The cash receipts journal usually includes columns for Cash (DR), Sales Discounts (DR), Accounts Receivable (CR), and Sales Revenue (CR). In addition, an Other Accounts (CR) column is used to record all "irregular" cash transactions, that is, all items that do not fall naturally into a labeled column such as Cash or Accounts Receivable. Examples are collections of in-

exhibit 4-18   Posting from the Sales Journal

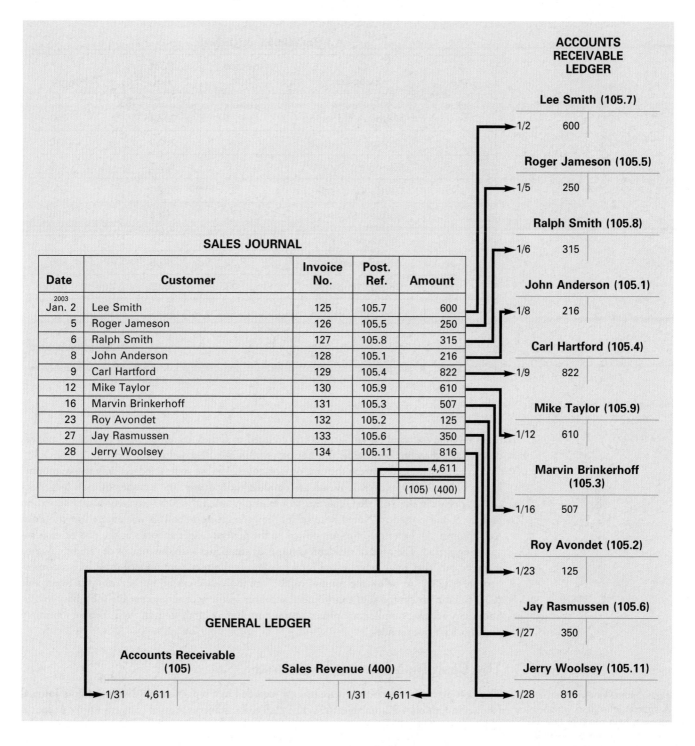

terest, rents, or notes receivable. The Other Accounts column is added for cross-checking purposes. A check mark (√) is placed below the total to indicate that the individual items have been posted.

Exhibit 4-21 shows that on January 7, $588 was received from Lee Smith in payment of a $600 bill (debit Cash, credit Accounts Receivable). The $12 difference is a 2% discount ($600 × 0.02 = $12) offered by Antler to customers who pay within 10 days (debit Sales Discounts). The $125 cash sale on January 12 was debited to Cash and credited to Sales Revenue. The in-

exhibit 4-19   A Sample Page in a Purchases Journal for Antler Corporation

PURCHASES JOURNAL

Date	Supplier	Invoice Date	Post. Ref.	Amount
2003 Jan. 2	Mayberry Marketing	2003 Jan. 1	202.4	300
5	Jackson Wholesale	4	202.3	616
6	Equipment Supply	5	202.2	485
12	Davies Wholesale	11	202.1	690
14	Jackson Wholesale	12	202.3	150
15	Palmer Supply Co.	14	202.5	810
22	White Incorporated	22	202.8	800
29	United Company	28	202.7	600
30	Tool Design Co.	29	202.6	400
				4,851
				(202) (450)

terest revenue collected on January 18 was credited to Other Accounts. Mike Taylor did not receive a sales discount because he did not pay within the 10-day discount period.

In posting the entries from the cash receipts journal to the general ledger, only those amounts in the Other Accounts (CR) column are handled individually; the number of each ledger account appears in the Post. Ref. column. For example, when the $150 payment was collected on January 9 and posted to Notes Receivable, the account number 103 was entered in the Post. Ref. column. All other columns are posted to the general ledger as totals at the end of each accounting period. The total of the debit columns is compared with the total of the credit columns to make sure that total debits equal total credits. As the totals are posted, their account numbers are entered just below the column totals. The individual entries in the Accounts Receivable (CR) column are posted to the customers' accounts in the accounts receivable subsidiary ledger. Subsidiary account numbers are placed in the Post. Ref. column to indicate that these subsidiary postings have been made.

The Cash Disbursements Journal

cash disbursements journal A special journal in which all cash paid out for supplies, merchandise, salaries, and other items is recorded.

The cash payments of a business are usually recorded in a separate **cash disbursements journal** (shown in Exhibit 4-22 on page 169). The cash disbursements journal contains Other Accounts (CR), Cash (CR), Purchase Discounts (CR), Accounts Payable (DR), Sales Salaries Expense (DR), General and Administrative Salaries Expense (DR), and Other Accounts (DR) columns. The Purchase Discounts and Accounts Payable columns are used to account for payments for merchandise previously purchased. The Sales and the General and Administrative Salaries Expense columns are used to record the payment of salaries (if a separate payroll journal is not kept). The Other Accounts (DR) column is used to record cash purchases of merchandise and other payments for which there are no special columns. As with the other journals, the parenthetical numbers at the bottoms of the columns mean those column totals have been posted to their respective general ledger accounts.

e x h i b i t 4 - 2 0   Posting from the Purchases Journal

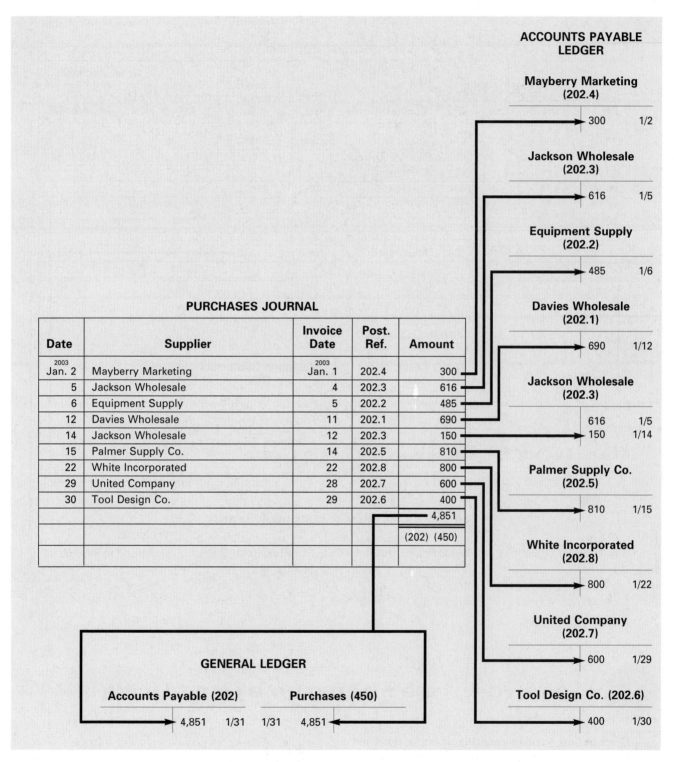

In reading Exhibit 4-22, notice that on February 1 the company made a $588 payment to satisfy the $600 payable to United Company. The 2% discount of $12 was taken because payment was made within 10 days of purchase. The payments to Equipment Supply and Mayberry Marketing were for the full amounts because they were not made within the 10-day discount period (see the purchases journal in Exhibit 4-20).

exhibit 4-21   The Cash Receipts Journal

CASH RECEIPTS JOURNAL

Cash DR	Sales Discounts DR	Date	Receipt No.	Account Name	Post. Ref.	Accounts Receivable CR	Sales Revenue CR	Other Accounts	
								Post. Ref.	Amount CR
588.00	12.00	2003 Jan. 7	621	Lee Smith	105.7	600.00			
150.00		9	622	Notes Receivable				103	150.00
125.00		12	623	Cash Sales			125.00		
805.56	16.44	15	624	Carl Hartford	105.4	822.00			
50.00		18	625	Interest Revenue				513	50.00
30.00		22	626	Cash Sales			30.00		
122.50	2.50	29	627	Roy Avondet	105.2	125.00			
610.00		29	628	Mike Taylor	105.9	610.00			
2,481.06	30.94					2,157.00	155.00		200.00
(101)	(404)					(105)	(400)		(✔)

GENERAL LEDGER

Cash (101)

1/31 2,481.06

Notes Receivable (103)

1/31 150.00

Accounts Receivable (105)

1/31 2,157.00

Sales Revenue (400)

1/31 155.00

Sales Discounts (404)

1/31 30.94

Interest Revenue (513)

1/31 50.00

ACCOUNTS RECEIVABLE SUBSIDIARY LEDGER

Roy Avondet (105.2)

1/29 125.00

Carl Hartford (105.4)

1/15 822.00

Lee Smith (105.7)

1/7 600.00

Mike Taylor (105.9)

1/29 610.00

review of learning objectives

1 **Describe how accrual accounting allows for timely reporting and a better measure of a company's economic performance.** Accounting information is needed on a timely basis for decision-making purposes. This requires that the total life of a business be divided into accounting periods, generally a year or less, for which reports are prepared. Some of the data presented in the periodic reports must be tentative because dividing a company's life into relatively short reporting periods requires that allocations and estimates be made.

The necessity for periodic reporting further requires that accrual accounting be used to provide accurate statements of financial position and results of operations for an accounting period. Accrual-basis accounting means that revenues are recognized as they are earned, not necessarily when cash is received; expenses are recognized as they are incurred, not necessarily when cash is paid. Accrual-basis accounting provides a more accurate picture of a company's financial position and operating results than does cash-basis accounting. The cash

e x h i b i t   4 - 2 2   The Cash Disbursements Journal

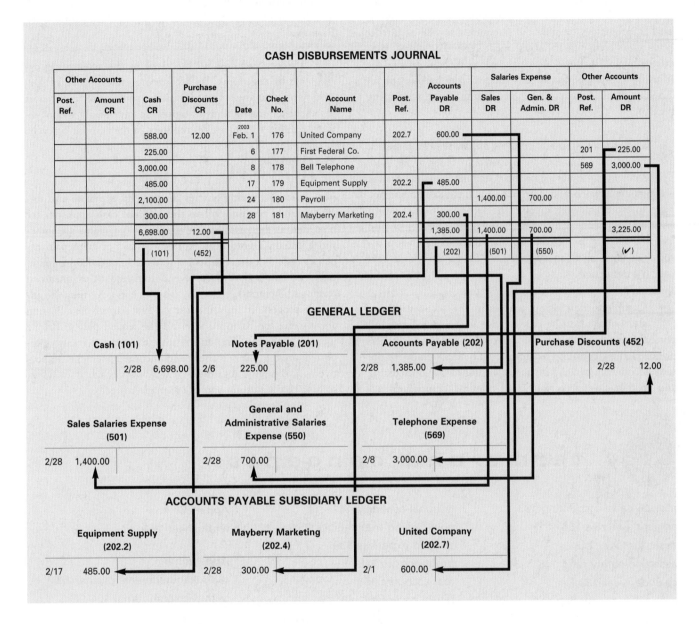

flow statement is also very important in the financial position analysis.

2 **Explain the need for adjusting entries and make adjusting entries for unrecorded receivables, unrecorded liabilities, prepaid expenses, and unearned revenues.** At the end of an accounting period, there are potentially many important events that have as yet not been recorded. Some important events occur outside the normal accounting process, while other events occur slowly over time. An important part of the accounting process is to review the financial condition and operating activities of the company for the period to make sure that all assets, liabilities, revenues, and expenses have been recorded. These year-end adjustments are called adjusting entries and may be classified under four headings: unrecorded

receivables, unrecorded liabilities, prepaid expenses, and unearned revenues. The analysis process involved in making an adjusting entry involves two steps. First, determine whether an asset or liability has been recorded for the proper amount and, if not, correct it (fix the balance sheet). Second, determine what revenue or expense adjustment is needed because of the asset or liability adjustment just made (fix the income statement).

3 **Explain the preparation of the financial statements, the explanatory notes, and the audit report.** After the adjusting entries have been posted to the accounts, an adjusted trial balance is prepared. This adjusted trial balance provides the raw data for the preparation of the balance sheet and the income statement; preparation of the statement of cash flows requires more detailed information about cash receipts and cash disbursements. The notes to the financial statements provide further information about the methods and assumptions used in preparing the financial statements as well as further detail about certain financial statement items. The audit is conducted by a CPA from outside the company who reviews the adjusting entries, performs tests to check the balances of selected accounts, and reviews the condition of the accounting systems.

4 **Perform a systematic analysis of financial statements.** Financial statements are prepared in order to be used. Two general techniques for financial statement analysis are the DuPont framework and common-size financial statements. The DuPont framework involves the decomposition of return on equity into three components: profitability, efficiency, and leverage. Preparation of common-size financial statements involves dividing all financial statement amounts by total revenue for the period.

5 **Complete the closing process in the accounting cycle.** Once adjusting entries have been journalized and posted to the accounts and the financia l statements have been prepared, the accounting records should be made ready for the next accounting cycle. This is accomplished by journalizing and posting closing entries for all nominal (temporary) ac-

counts. Revenue accounts are closed by being debited; expense accounts and the dividends account are closed by being credited. Revenues, expenses, and dividends are closed to Retained Earnings.

6 **Understand how all the steps in the accounting cycle fit together.** The accounting cycle consists of specific steps to analyze, record, classify, summarize, and report the exchange transactions of economic entities. By way of review, Exhibit 4-12 identifies the steps in the accounting cycle.

expanded material

7 **Make adjusting entries for prepaid expenses and unearned revenues when the original cash amounts are recorded as expenses and revenues.** Prepayments are sometimes initially recorded as expenses instead of as prepaid expenses (assets); cash receipts for revenue in advance are sometimes initially recorded as revenues instead of as unearned revenues (liabilities). However, the concepts governing the adjusting process are the same: use the first part of the adjusting entry to fix the balance sheet and the second part to fix the income statement. The end result (the updated balances reported on the balance sheet and income statement, respectively) is the same regardless of which approach is used, assuming that adjusting entries are made correctly.

key terms and concepts

accrual-basis accounting 133

adjusting entries 136

asset turnover 148

assets-to-equity ratio 148

calendar year 133

cash-basis accounting 136

closing entries 152

common-size financial statements 149

DuPont framework 148

fiscal year 133

matching principle 134

nominal accounts 151

post-closing trial balance 152

prepaid expenses 139

profit margin 148

real accounts 151

return on equity 148

revenue recognition principle 134

time-period concept 133

unearned revenues 141

unrecorded liabilities 138

unrecorded receivables 137

Appendix A:

work sheet 157

Appendix B:

cash disbursements journal 166

cash receipts journal 164

control account 163

purchases journal 163

sales journal 162

special journal 162

subsidiary ledger 163

review problem

The Accounting Cycle   This review problem provides a useful summary of the entire accounting cycle. The following post-closing trial balance is for Sports Haven Company as of December 31, 2002.

Sports Haven Company
Post-Closing Trial Balance
December 31, 2002

	Debits	Credits
Cash.	$17,500	
Accounts Receivable.	17,000	
Inventory	28,800	
Supplies on Hand.	1,200	
Prepaid Building Rental	24,000	
Accounts Payable.		$18,000
Capital Stock (3,600 shares outstanding).		54,000
Retained Earnings.		16,500
Totals.	$88,500	$88,500

Following is a summary of the company's transactions for 2003.

a. At the beginning of 2003, the company issued 1,500 new shares of stock at $20 per share.
b. Total inventory purchases were $49,500; all purchases were made on credit and are recorded in the inventory account.
c. Total sales were $125,000; $102,900 were on credit, the rest were for cash. The cost of goods sold was $47,500; the inventory account is reduced at the time of each sale.
d. In December, a customer paid $3,500 cash in advance for merchandise that was temporarily out of stock. The advance payments received from customers are initially recorded as liabilities. The $3,500 is not included in the sales figures in (c) above.
e. The company paid $66,500 on accounts payable during the year.
f. The company collected $102,000 of accounts receivable during the year.
g. The company purchased $600 of supplies for cash during 2003, debiting Supplies on Hand.
h. The company paid $850 for advertising during the year, debiting Prepaid Advertising.
i. Total salaries paid during the year were $45,000.
j. The company paid $650 during the year for utilities.
k. Dividends of $7,500 were paid to stockholders in December.

On December 31, 2003, the company's accountant gathers the following information to adjust the accounts:

l. As of December 31, salaries of $750 had been earned by employees but will not be paid until January 3, 2004.
m. A count at December 31 shows $800 of supplies still on hand.
n. The prepaid advertising paid during 2003 includes $400 paid on December 1, 2003, for a series of radio advertisements to be broadcast throughout December 2003 and January 2004. The balance in the account, $450, represents advertisements that were broadcast during 2003.
o. On December 31, 2002, the company rented an office building for two years and paid $24,000 in cash (the full rental fee for 2003 and 2004). The payment was recorded with a debit to Prepaid Building Rental. No entries have been made for building rent in 2003.
p. On December 20, 2003, a bill for $150 was received for utilities. No entry was made to record the receipt of the bill, which is to be paid on January 4, 2004.
q. As of December 31, 2003, the merchandise paid for in advance [transaction (d)] was still out of stock. The company expects to receive the merchandise and fill the order by January 15, 2004.
r. The company's income is taxed at a rate of 15%.

Required:
1. Make entries in the general journal to record each of the transactions [items (a) through (k)].
2. Using T-accounts to represent the general ledger accounts, post the transactions recorded in the general journal. Enter the beginning balances in the accounts that appear in the De-

cember 31, 2002, post-closing trial balance before posting 2003 transactions. When all trans-actions have been posted to the T-accounts, determine the balance for each account.

3. Prepare a trial balance as of December 31, 2003.
4. Record adjusting entries [items (l) through (r)] in the general journal; post these entries to the general ledger (T-accounts).
5. Prepare an income statement and balance sheet for 2003.
6. Record closing entries [label (s) and (t)] in the general journal; post these entries to the general ledger (T-accounts).
7. Prepare a post-closing trial balance.

Solution

1. Following are the journal entries to record the transactions for the year. Several of these are summary entries representing numerous individual transactions.

(a)   Cash   30,000
            Capital Stock   30,000

The company issued additional shares of stock, so Capital Stock must be credited to reflect the increase in owners' equity. Since the company received cash of $30,000 (1,500 shares at $20 per share), Cash is also increased.

(b)   Inventory.   49,500
            Accounts Payable   49,500

The company purchased $49,500 of goods on credit. Inventory is increased (debited) for this amount. Accounts Payable is credited to show the increase in liabilities.

(c)   Accounts Receivable   102,900
        Cash   22,100
            Sales Revenue   125,000

Total sales were $125,000, so Sales Revenue must be increased (credited) by that amount. Of this amount, $102,900 were on credit, and $22,100 were cash sales. We increase the asset accounts, Accounts Receivable and Cash, by debiting them.

(c)   Cost of Goods Sold   47,500
            Inventory   47,500

The cost of the merchandise sold during the year was $47,500. Cost of Goods Sold (expense) must be increased (debited) by this amount. Since the goods were sold, Inventory (asset) must be reduced by a credit of $47,500.

(d)   Cash   3,500
            Unearned Sales Revenue   3,500

Cash is debited (increased) by the amount received from the customer. The company recorded the advance payments for merchandise by crediting a liability account, Unearned Sales Revenue.

(e)   Accounts Payable   66,500
            Cash.   66,500

The company's payments on its accounts reduce the amount of its obligation to creditors, so Accounts Payable (liability) is debited to decrease it by the amount paid. Cash must also be decreased (credited).

(f)   Cash.   102,000
            Accounts Receivable   102,000

Since the company has collected some of its receivables from customers, Accounts Receivable is credited to show a decrease. Cash is increased (debited).

(g)   Supplies on Hand   600
            Cash.   600

The company purchased $600 of supplies. By debiting Supplies on Hand, an increase is shown in that asset account. Cash must be credited to show a decrease.

(h)	Prepaid Advertising	850	
	Cash		850

The company purchased $850 of advertising and chose to initially debit an asset account, Prepaid Advertising. Since cash was paid, it must be reduced by a credit.

(i)	Salaries Expense	45,000	
	Cash		45,000

(j)	Utilities Expense	650	
	Cash		650

For transactions (i) and (j), an expense account must be debited to show that expenses have been incurred. Cash must be credited (reduced).

(k)	Dividends	7,500	
	Cash		7,500

Dividends must be debited to show a decrease in owners' equity resulting from a distribution of earnings. Cash must be reduced by a credit.

2. T-accounts with the beginning balances and journal entries posted are shown here. (Note that accounts with more than one entry must be "balanced" by drawing a rule and entering the debit or credit balance below it.)

Cash

Beg.		(e)	66,500
bal.	17,500	(g)	600
(a)	30,000	(h)	850
(c)	22,100	(i)	45,000
(d)	3,500	(j)	650
(f)	102,000	(k)	7,500
Updated			
bal.	54,000		

Accounts Receivable

Beg.		(f)	102,000
bal.	17,000		
(c)	102,900		
Updated			
bal.	17,900		

Inventory

Beg.		(c)	47,500
bal.	28,800		
(b)	49,500		
Updated			
bal.	30,800		

Supplies on Hand

Beg.		
bal.	1,200	
(g)	600	
Updated		
bal.	1,800	

Prepaid Building Rental

Beg.		
bal.	24,000	

Prepaid Advertising

(h)	850	

Accounts Payable

(e)	66,500	Beg.	
		bal.	18,000
		(b)	49,500
		Updated	
		bal.	1,000

Unearned Sales Revenue

		(d)	3,500

Capital Stock

		Beg.	
		bal.	54,000
		(a)	30,000
		Updated	
		bal.	84,000

Retained Earnings

		Beg.	
		bal.	16,500

Dividends

(k)	7,500	

Sales Revenue

		(c)	125,000

Cost of Goods Sold

(c)	47,500	

Salaries Expense

(i)	45,000	

Utilities Expense

(j)	650	

3.   The balance of each account is entered in a trial balance. Each column in the trial balance is totaled to determine that total debits equal total credits.

Sports Haven Company
Trial Balance
December 31, 2003

	Debits	Credits
Cash.	$ 54,000	
Accounts Receivable.	17,900	
Inventory .	30,800	
Supplies on Hand.	1,800	
Prepaid Building Rental	24,000	
Prepaid Advertising	850	
Accounts Payable.		$ 1,000
Unearned Sales Revenue .		3,500
Capital Stock .		84,000
Retained Earnings.		16,500
Dividends.	7,500	
Sales Revenue .		125,000
Cost of Goods Sold .	47,500	
Salaries Expense	45,000	
Utilities Expense.	650	
Totals .	$230,000	$230,000

---

4.   The adjusting entries for Sports Haven Company are presented in journal form and explained. Updated T-accounts are provided showing the posting of the adjusting entries.

(l)   Salaries Expense 750
          Salaries Payable 750

As of December 31, there is an unrecorded liability and expense of $750 for salaries owed to employees. Because the salaries were earned in 2003, the liability and related expense must be recorded in 2003.

(m)   Supplies Expense. 1,000
          Supplies on Hand 1,000

Supplies on Hand (asset) has a debit balance before adjustment of $1,800 [beginning balance of $1,200 plus $600 of supplies purchased during the year, transaction (g)]. Since $800 of supplies are on hand at the end of the year, Supplies on Hand should be reduced (credited) by $1,000. Supplies Expense must be debited to show that $1,000 of supplies were used during the period.

(n)   Advertising Expense. 650
          Prepaid Advertising. 650

Prepaid Advertising has a debit balance before adjustment of $850, the total amount paid for advertising during the year [transaction (h)]. This amount includes $400 that was paid for radio advertising throughout December 2003 and January 2004. Only that portion that applies to 2004 should be shown as Prepaid Advertising, $200 ($400 ÷ 2 months), since it is not an expense of the current year. The remainder, $650, is advertising expense for the period. Thus, the asset account, Prepaid Advertising, must be credited for $650, and Advertising Expense must be increased by a debit of $650.

(o) Building Rent Expense   12,000
        Prepaid Building Rental   12,000

The original entry at the end of 2002 was a debit to the asset account, Prepaid Building Rental, and a credit to Cash. An adjusting entry is needed to record rent expense of $12,000 for 2003 ($24,000 ÷ 2 years). The expense account must be debited and the asset account must be reduced by a credit. The remaining $12,000 in Prepaid Building Rental reflects the portion of the total payment for building rent expense in 2004.

(p) Utilities Expense   150
        Utilities Payable   150

As of December 31, 2003, there is an unrecorded liability and expense of $150 for utilities. Because the expense was incurred in 2003, an adjusting entry is needed to record the liability and related expense.

(q) No entry required.

The original entry to record the advance payment from a customer was made by crediting a liability [transaction (d)]. As of December 31, no revenue has been earned. The company still has an obligation to deliver goods or refund the advanced payment. Therefore, no adjustment is required, since the liability is already properly recorded.

(r) Income Tax Expense   2,595
        Income Taxes Payable   2,595

The remaining adjustment is for income taxes. The difference between total revenues and total expenses is the amount of income before taxes, $17,300. This amount is multiplied by the applicable tax rate of 15% to determine income taxes for the period. The expense account is debited to show the income taxes incurred for the year and the liability account is credited to show the obligation to the government.

Cash			
Beg.		(e)	66,500
bal.	17,500	(g)	600
(a)	30,000	(h)	850
(c)	22,100	(i)	45,000
(d)	3,500	(j)	650
(f)	102,000	(k)	7,500
Updated			
bal.	54,000		

Accounts Receivable			
Beg.		(f)	102,000
bal.	17,000		
(c)	102,900		
Updated			
bal.	17,900		

Inventory			
Beg.		(c)	47,500
bal.	28,800		
(b)	49,500		
Updated			
bal.	30,800		

Supplies on Hand			
Beg.		(m)	1,000
bal.	1,200		
(g)	600		
Updated			
bal.	800		

Prepaid Building Rental			
Beg.		(o)	12,000
bal.	24,000		
Updated			
bal.	12,000		

Prepaid Advertising			
(h)	850	(n)	650
Updated			
bal.	200		

Accounts Payable			
(e)	66,500	Beg.	
		bal.	18,000
		(b)	49,500
		Updated	
		bal.	1,000

Salaries Payable		
	(l)	750

Utilities Payable		
	(p)	150

Income Taxes Payable	
	(r) 2,595

Unearned Sales Revenue	
	(d) 3,500

Capital Stock	
	Beg. bal. 54,000
	(a) 30,000
	Updated bal. 84,000

Retained Earnings	
	Beg. bal. 16,500

Dividends	
(k) 7,500	

Sales Revenue	
	(c) 125,000

Cost of Goods Sold	
(c) 47,500	

Salaries Expense	
(i) 45,000	
(l) 750	
Updated bal. 45,750	

Utilities Expense	
(j) 650	
(p) 150	
Updated bal. 800	

Advertising Expense	
(n) 650	

Supplies Expense	
(m) 1,000	

Building Rent Expense	
(o) 12,000	

Income Tax Expense	
(r) 2,595	

5. Data for the financial statements may be taken from the adjusted ledger accounts and reported as follows:

Sports Haven Company
Income Statement
For the Year Ended December 31, 2003

Sales revenue	$125,000	
Less cost of goods sold	47,500	
Gross profit		$77,500
Less operating expenses:		
Salaries expense	$ 45,750	
Utilities expense	800	
Advertising expense	650	
Supplies expense	1,000	
Building rent expense	12,000	60,200
Income before income taxes		$17,300
Income tax expense		2,595
Net income		$14,705

Earnings per share:
$14,705 ÷ 5,100 shares = $2.88 (rounded)

Sports Haven Company
Balance Sheet
December 31, 2003

Assets

Cash	$54,000	
Accounts receivable	17,900	
Inventory	30,800	
Supplies on hand	800	
Prepaid building rental	12,000	
Prepaid advertising	200	
Total assets		$115,700

Liabilities and Owners' Equity

Liabilities:		
Accounts payable	$ 1,000	
Salaries payable	750	
Utilities payable	150	
Income taxes payable	2,595	
Unearned sales revenue	3,500	
Total liabilities		$ 7,995
Owners' equity:		
Capital stock (5,100 shares outstanding)	$84,000	
Retained earnings	23,705*	
Total owners' equity		107,705
Total liabilities and owners' equity		$115,700

*Note that in preparing the balance sheet, net income must be added to the beginning balance in Retained Earnings and dividends must be subtracted ($16,500 + $14,705 − $7,500 = $23,705).

---

6. The next step is to record the closing entries in the general journal and then post those entries to the general ledger (T-accounts). T-accounts are shown with all previous entries and the closing entries [items (s) and (t)] posted.

   The first entry is to close the revenue account and each of the expense accounts. Sales Revenue has a credit balance; it is debited to reduce the balance to zero. The expense accounts are closed by crediting them. The difference in total revenues and total expenses is $14,705 (net income for the period). Net income represents an increase in retained earnings. All of this is captured in the single, compound closing entry (s), as follows:

(s)	Sales Revenue	125,000	
	Cost of Goods Sold		47,500
	Salaries Expense		45,750
	Utilities Expense		800
	Advertising Expense		650
	Supplies Expense		1,000
	Building Rent Expense		12,000
	Income Tax Expense		2,595
	Retained Earnings		14,705

Second, Dividends, a nominal account, must also be closed to Retained Earnings.

(t)	Retained Earnings	7,500	
	Dividends		7,500

Cash

Beg.		(e)	66,500
bal.	17,500	(g)	600
(a)	30,000	(h)	850
(c)	22,100	(i)	45,000
(d)	3,500	(j)	650
(f)	102,000	(k)	7,500
Updated			
bal.	54,000		

Accounts Receivable

Beg.		(f)	102,000
bal.	17,000		
(c)	102,900		
Updated			
bal.	17,900		

Inventory

Beg.		(c)	47,500
bal.	28,800		
(b)	49,500		
Updated			
bal.	30,800		

Supplies on Hand

Beg.		(m)	1,000
bal.	1,200		
(g)	600		
Updated			
bal.	800		

Prepaid Building Rental

Beg.		(o)	12,000
bal.	24,000		
Updated			
bal.	12,000		

Prepaid Advertising

(h)	850	(n)	650
Updated			
bal.	200		

Accounts Payable

(e)	66,500	Beg.	
		bal.	18,000
		(b)	49,500
		Updated	
		bal.	1,000

Salaries Payable

		(l)	750

Utilities Payable

		(p)	150

Income Taxes Payable

		(r)	2,595

Unearned Sales Revenue

		(d)	3,500

Capital Stock

		Beg.	
		bal.	54,000
		(a)	30,000
		Updated	
		bal.	84,000

Retained Earnings

(t)	7,500	Beg.	
		bal.	16,500
		(s)	14,705
		Updated	
		bal.	23,705

Dividends

(k)	7,500	(t)	7,500

Sales Revenue

(s)	125,000	(c)	125,000

Cost of Goods Sold

(c)	47,500	(s)	47,500

Salaries Expense

(i)	45,000	(s)	45,750
(l)	750		

Utilities Expense

(j)	650	(s)	800
(p)	150		

Advertising Expense

(n)	650	(s)	650

Supplies Expense

(m)	1,000	(s)	1,000

Building Rent Expense

(o)	12,000	(s)	12,000

Income Tax Expense

(r)	2,595	(s)	2,595

7. The final (optional) step in the accounting cycle is to prepare a post-closing trial balance. This procedure is a check on the accuracy of the closing process. It is a listing of all ledger account balances at year-end. Note that only real accounts appear because all nominal accounts have been closed to a zero balance in preparation for the next accounting cycle.

Sports Haven Company
Post-Closing Trial Balance
December 31, 2003

	Debits	Credits
Cash	$ 54,000	
Accounts Receivable	17,900	
Inventory	30,800	
Supplies on Hand	800	
Prepaid Building Rental	12,000	
Prepaid Advertising	200	
Accounts Payable		$ 1,000
Salaries Payable		750
Utilities Payable		150
Income Taxes Payable		2,595
Unearned Sales Revenue		3,500
Capital Stock		84,000
Retained Earnings		23,705
Totals	$115,700	$115,700

discussion questions

1. Why are financial reports prepared on a periodic basis?
2. Distinguish between reporting on a calendar-year and on a fiscal-year basis.
3. When are revenues generally recognized (recorded)?
4. What is the matching principle?
5. Explain why accrual-basis accounting is more appropriate than cash-basis accounting for most businesses.
6. Why are accrual-based financial statements considered somewhat tentative?
7. Why are adjusting entries necessary?
8. Since there are usually no source documents for adjusting entries, how does the accountant know when to make adjusting entries and for what amounts?
9. The analysis process for preparing adjusting entries involves two basic steps. Identify the two steps and explain why both are necessary.
10. Why are supplies not considered inventory? What type of account is Supplies on Hand?
11. Cash is not one of the accounts increased or decreased in an adjusting entry. Why?
12. Which are prepared first: the year-end financial statements or the general journal adjusting entries? Explain.
13. Of what value are the notes to the financial statements and the audit report, both of which are usually included in the annual report to shareholders?
14. Describe the DuPont framework for analysis of financial statements.
15. What is a common-size financial statement? What are its advantages?
16. What is the most informative section of the common-size balance sheet? Explain.
17. Distinguish between real and nominal accounts.
18. What is the purpose of closing entries?
19. What is the purpose of the post-closing trial balance? Explain where the information for the post-closing trial balance comes from.

expanded material

20. Explain why there are alternative ways of recording certain transactions, either as assets or expenses, or as liabilities or revenues.

discussion cases

CASE 4-1

USING FINANCIAL STATEMENTS FOR INVESTMENT DECISIONS

Several doctors are considering the purchase of a small real estate business as an investment. Because you have some training in the mechanics of the accounting cycle, they have hired you to review the real estate company's accounting records and to prepare a balance sheet and an income statement for their use. In analyzing various business documents, you verify the following data.

The account balances at the beginning of the current year were as follows:

Cash in Bank	$ 7,800
Notes Receivable (from Current Owner)	10,000
Supplies on Hand	750
Prepaid Office Rent	4,500
Accounts Payable	450
Owners' Equity	22,600

During the current year, the following summarized transactions took place:

a. The owner paid $1,200 to the business to cover the interest on the note receivable ($10,000 $\times$ 0.12 $\times$ 1 year). Nothing was paid on the principal.

b. Real estate commissions earned during the year totaled $45,500. Of this amount, $1,000 has not been received by year-end.

c. The company purchased $500 of supplies during the year. A count at year-end shows $300 worth still on hand.

d. The $4,500 paid for office rental was for 18 months, beginning in January of this year.

e. Utilities paid during the year amounted to $1,500.

f. During the year, $400 of accounts payable were paid; the balance in Accounts Payable at year-end is $300, with the adjustment being debited to Miscellaneous Office Expense.

g. The owner paid himself $1,500 a month as a salary and paid a part-time secretary $2,400 for the year. (Ignore payroll taxes.)

On the basis of the above data, prepare a balance sheet and an income statement for the real estate business. Does the business appear profitable? Does the balance sheet raise any questions or concerns? What other information might the doctors want to consider in making this investment decision?

CASE 4-2

ACCOUNTING AND ETHICAL ISSUES INVOLVING THE CLOSING PROCESS

Silva and Wanita Rodriques are the owners of Year-Round Landscape, Inc., a small landscape and yard service business in southern California. The business is three years old and has grown significantly, especially during the past year. To sustain this growth, Year-Round Landscape must expand operations.

In the past, the Rodriques have been able to secure funds for the business from personal resources. Now those resources are exhausted, and the Rodriques are seeking a loan from a local bank.

To satisfy bank requirements, Year-Round Landscape, Inc., must provide a set of financial statements, including comparative income statements showing the growth in earnings over the past three years. In analyzing the records, Silva notices that the nominal accounts have not yet been closed for this year. Furthermore, Silva is aware of a major contract that is to be signed on January 3, only three days after the December 31 year-end for the business. Silva suggests that the closing process be delayed one week so that this major contract can be included in this year's operating results. Silva estimates that this contract will increase current year earnings by 20%.

What accounting issues are involved in this case? What are the ethical issues?

CASE 4-3

WRESTLING WITH YOUR CONSCIENCE AND GAAP

You are the controller for South Valley Industries. Your assistant has just completed the financial statements for the current year and has given them to you for review. A copy of the statements also has been given to the president of the company. The income statement reports a net income for the year of $50,000 and earnings per share of $2.50.

In reviewing the statements, you realize the assistant neglected to record adjusting entries. After making the necessary adjustments, the company shows a net loss of $10,000. The difference is due to an unusually large amount of unrecorded expenses at year-end. You realize that these expenses are not likely to be found by the independent auditors.

You wonder if it would be better to delay the recording of the expenses until the first part of the subsequent year in order to avoid reporting a net loss on the income statement for the current year. A significant increase in revenues is expected in the coming year, and the expenses in question could be "absorbed" by the higher revenues.

What issues are involved in this case? What course of action would you take?

CASE 4-4

expanded material

MAKING SURE OPERATING RESULTS ARE ACCURATE

Dian Karen and Kathy Gillen are considering forming a company to purchase a small business that specializes in interior decoration services. The business records show a modest profit over each of the past five years (approximately $5,000 net income per year). However, the past year's operating results appear to be much better, as shown by the unaudited income statement.

Fashion Design, Inc.
Income Statement
For the Year Ended December 31, 2003

Revenues:		
Consulting revenues	$51,000	
Commissions on furnishings sold	18,000	
Total revenues		$69,000
Expenses:		
Advertising expense	$ 1,200	
Rent expense	4,800	
Salaries expense	36,000	
Supplies expense	500	
Utilities expense	1,800	
Other expenses	1,500	45,800
Income before taxes		$23,200
Income taxes (estimated at 25%)		5,800
Net income		$17,400
EPS: $17,400 ÷ 1,000 shares = $17.40 per share		

In an attempt to verify what appears to be unusually high net income for 2003, Karen and Gillen hire a CPA to audit the records. The CPA discovers the following:

a. The company pays salaries on the 1st and 15th of each month. Salaries amounting to $2,500 have been earned by employees by December 31 but will not be paid until January 1. No adjusting entry has been made.

b. Of the $18,000 in commissions received by December 31, 30% will not be earned until completion of a job in mid-February of 2004. All commissions received have been recorded as revenues.

c. A $10,000 payment was received on November 1 for a consulting assignment that is only one-half earned at December 31. The total amount was credited to Consulting Revenues when received.

d. The rent is $400 per month and must be paid in advance on a one-year lease. A check for $4,800 was given to the landlord on March 1, 2003, and recorded as rent expense on that date.

According to the CPA, except for these data, the income statement appears to accurately reflect the operating results of Fashion Design, Inc.

Answer the following questions:

1. Do the 2003 operating results offer encouragement to Karen and Gillen as potential investors? Explain.
2. What adjustments (if any) are required to make the income statement more accurately reflect the results of operations for the year?
3. What is the impact on the balance sheet (if any) of the data discovered by the CPA?

exercises

EXERCISE 4-1

REPORTING INCOME: CASH VERSUS ACCRUAL ACCOUNTING

On December 31, 2003, Matt Morgan completed the first year of operations for his new computer retail store. The following data were obtained from the company's accounting records:

Sales to customers	$197,000
Collections from customers	145,000
Interest earned and received on savings accounts	2,500
Cost of goods sold	98,500
Amounts paid to suppliers for inventory	103,000
Wages owed to employees at year-end	3,500
Wages paid to employees	40,000
Utility bill owed: to be paid next month	1,100
Interest due at 12/31 on loan to be paid in March of next year	1,200
Amount paid for one and one-half years' rent, beginning Jan. 1, 2003	17,500
Income taxes owed at year-end	4,000

1. How much net income (loss) should Matt report for the year ended December 31, 2003, according to (a) cash-basis accounting and (b) accrual-basis accounting?
2. Which basis of accounting provides the better measure of operating results for Matt?

EXERCISE 4-2

REPORTING INCOME: CASH VERSUS ACCRUAL ACCOUNTING

On December 31, Brian Silvaggi completed the first year of operations for his new business. The following data are available from the company's accounting records:

Sales to customers	$145,000
Collections from customers	125,000
Interest earned and received on savings accounts	1,500
Amount paid for one and one-half years' rent	3,600
Utility bill owed: to be paid next month	960
Cost of goods sold	80,000
Amount paid to suppliers for materials	83,000
Wages paid to employees	47,500
Wages owed to employees at year-end	1,200
Interest due at 12/31 on a loan to be paid the middle of next year	800

1. How much net income (loss) should Brian report for the year ended December 31 according to (a) cash-basis accounting and (b) accrual-basis accounting?
2. Which basis of accounting provides the better measure of operating results for Brian?

EXERCISE 4-3

CLASSIFYING ACCOUNT BALANCES

For each of the following accounts, indicate whether it would be found in the income statement or in the balance sheet.

1. Cash	10. Interest Receivable	19. Sales Revenue
2. Inventory	11. Capital Stock	20. Insurance Expense
3. Salaries Expense	12. Accounts Payable	21. Machinery
4. Prepaid Salaries	13. Buildings	22. Land
5. Retained Earnings	14. Mortgage Payable	23. Salaries Payable
6. Office Supplies Expense	15. Interest Expense	24. Prepaid Insurance
7. Accounts Receivable	16. Accounts Payable	25. Notes Payable
8. Cost of Goods Sold	17. Notes Receivable	26. Dividends
9. Maintenance Expense	18. Office Supplies	

EXERCISE 4-4

CLASSIFICATIONS OF ACCOUNTS REQUIRING ADJUSTING ENTRIES

For each type of adjustment listed, indicate whether it is an unrecorded receivable, an unrecorded liability, an unearned revenue, or a prepaid expense at December 31, 2003.

1. Property taxes that are for the year 2003, but are not to be paid until 2004.
2. Rent revenue earned during 2003, but not collected until 2004.
3. Salaries earned by employees in December 2003, but not to be paid until January 5, 2004.
4. A payment received from a customer in December 2003 for services that will not be performed until February 2004.
5. An insurance premium paid on December 29, 2003, for the period January 1, 2004, to December 31, 2004.
6. Gasoline charged on a credit card during December 2003. The bill will not be received until January 15, 2004.
7. Interest on a certificate of deposit held during 2003. The interest will not be received until January 7, 2004.
8. A deposit received on December 15, 2003, for rental of storage space. The rental period is from January 1, 2004, to December 31, 2004.

EXERCISE 4-5

ADJUSTING ENTRIES: PREPAID EXPENSES AND UNEARNED REVENUES

Boswell Group is a professional corporation providing management consulting services. The company initially debits assets in recording prepaid expenses and credits liabilities in recording unearned revenues. Give the entry that Boswell would use to record each of the following transactions on the date it occurred. Prepare the adjusting entries needed on December 31, 2003.

1. On July 1, 2003, the company paid a three-year premium of $7,200 on an insurance policy that is effective July 1, 2003, and expires June 30, 2006.
2. On February 1, 2003, Boswell paid its property taxes for the year February 1, 2003, to January 31, 2004. The tax bill was $1,800.
3. On May 1, 2003, the company paid $180 for a three-year subscription to an advertising journal. The subscription starts May 1, 2003, and expires April 30, 2006.
4. Boswell received $1,800 on September 15, 2003, in return for which the company agreed to provide consulting services for 18 months beginning immediately.
5. Boswell rented part of its office space to Bristle Brush Company. Bristle paid $1,200 on November 1, 2003, for the next six months' rent.

6. Boswell loaned $100,000 to a client. On November 1 the client paid $24,000, which represents two years' interest in advance (November 1, 2003, through October 31, 2005).

EXERCISE 4-6

Spread-Sheet Software

ADJUSTING ENTRIES: PREPAID EXPENSES AND UNEARNED REVENUES

Cannon Group provides computer network consulting services. The company initially debits assets in recording prepaid expenses and credits liabilities in recording unearned revenues. Give the appropriate entry that Cannon would use to record each of the following transactions on the date it occurred. Prepare the adjusting entries needed on December 31, 2003. (Round all numbers to the nearest dollar.)

1. On April 1, 2003, the company paid $250 for a two-year subscription to a computer networking journal. The subscription starts April 1, 2003, and expires March 31, 2005.
2. On May 1, 2003, Cannon paid $2,300 in property taxes for the year May 1, 2003, to April 30, 2004.
3. On June 15, 2003, Cannon received $25,000 for a contract to provide consulting services for 18 months beginning immediately.
4. On July 1, 2003, the company paid a two-year premium of $15,000 on an insurance policy that is effective July 1, 2003, and expires June 30, 2005.
5. Cannon rented part of its office building to Ross Graphics, LLC. Ross paid $1,500 on September 1, 2003, for the next six months' rent.
6. Cannon loaned $150,000 to a client. On October 1, 2003, the client paid $18,000 for interest in advance (October 1, 2003, to September 30, 2004).

EXERCISE 4-7

ADJUSTING ENTRIES

Shop Rite Services is ready to prepare its financial statements for the year ended December 31, 2003. The following information can be determined by analyzing the accounts:

1. On August 1, 2003, Shop Rite received a $4,800 payment in advance for rental of office space. The rental period is for one year beginning on the date payment was received. Shop Rite recorded the receipt as unearned rent.
2. On March 1, 2003, Shop Rite paid its insurance agent $3,000 for the premium due on a 24-month corporate policy. Shop Rite recorded the payment as prepaid insurance.
3. Shop Rite pays its employee wages the middle of each month. The monthly payroll (ignoring payroll taxes) is $22,000.
4. Shop Rite received a note from a customer on June 1, 2003, as payment for services. The amount of the note is $1,000 with interest at 12%. The note and interest will be paid on June 1, 2005.
5. On December 20, 2003, Shop Rite received a $2,500 check for services. The transaction was recorded as unearned revenue. By year-end, Shop Rite had completed three-fourths of the contracted services. The rest of the services won't be completed until at least the middle of January 2004.
6. On September 1, Shop Rite purchased $500 worth of supplies. At December 31, 2003, one-fourth of the supplies had been used. Shop Rite initially recorded the purchase of supplies as an asset.

Where appropriate, prepare adjusting journal entries at December 31, 2003, for each of these items.

EXERCISE 4-8

ADJUSTING ENTRIES

Consider the following two independent situations:

1. On June 1, Brown Company received $4,800 cash for a two-year subscription to its monthly magazine. The term of the subscription begins on June 1. Make the entry to record the receipt of the subscription on June 1. Also make the necessary adjusting entry at December 31. The company uses an account called Unearned Subscription Revenue.

2. Clark Company pays its employees every Friday for a five-day workweek. Salaries of $200,000 are earned equally throughout the week. December 31 of the current year is a Tuesday.

    a. Make the adjusting entry at December 31.

    b. Make the entry to pay the week's salaries on Friday, January 3, of the next year. Assume that all employees are paid for New Year's Day.

EXERCISE 4-9

ADJUSTING ENTRIES

Consider the following items for Burton Company:

1. On November 1 of the current year, Burton Company borrowed $150,000 at 8% interest. As of December 31, no interest expense has been recognized.

2. On September 1 of the current year, Burton Company rented to another company some excess space in one of its buildings. Burton Company received $18,000 cash on September 1. The rental period extends for six months, starting on September 1. Burton Company credited the account Unearned Rent Revenue upon receipt of the rent paid in advance.

3. At the beginning of the year, Burton Company had $900 of supplies on hand. During the year, another $5,400 of supplies were purchased for cash and recorded in the asset account Office Supplies. At the end of the year, Burton Company determined that $1,400 of supplies remained on hand.

4. On February 1 of the current year, Burton Company loaned Dridge Company $100,000 at 9% interest. The loan amount, plus accrued interest, will be repaid in one year.

For each of the items, make the appropriate adjusting journal entry, if any, necessary in Burton Company's books as of December 31.

EXERCISE 4-10

Spread-Sheet Software

ADJUSTING ENTRIES

Davis Company opened a Web page design business on January 1 of the current year. The following information relates to Davis Company's operations during the current year:

1. On February 1, Davis Company rented a new office. Before moving in, it prepaid a year's rent of $24,000 cash.

2. On March 31, Davis Company borrowed $50,000 from a local bank at 15%. The loan is to be repaid, with interest, after one year. As of December 31, no interest payments had yet been made.

3. Davis Company bills some of its customers in advance for its design services. During the year Davis received $60,000 cash in advance from its customers. As of December 31, Davis's accountant determined that 40% of that amount had not yet been earned.

4. On June 15, Davis Company purchased $1,400 of supplies for cash. On September 14, Davis made another cash purchase of $1,100. As of December 31, Davis's accountant determined that $1,700 of supplies had been used during the year.

5. Before closing its books, Davis Company found a bill for $800 from a free-lance programmer who had done work for the company in November. Davis had not yet recorded anything in its books with respect to this bill. Davis plans to pay the bill in January of next year.

For each of the items, make the initial entry, where appropriate, to record the transaction and, if necessary, the adjusting entry at December 31.

EXERCISE 4-11

ANALYSIS OF ACCOUNTS

Answer the following questions:

1. If office supplies on hand amounted to $4,000 at the beginning of the period and total purchases of office supplies during the period amounted to $22,000, determine the ending balance of office supplies on hand if office supplies expense for the period amounted to $20,000.

2. If beginning and ending accounts receivable were $10,000 and $12,000, respectively, and total sales made on account for the period amounted to $52,000, determine the amount of cash collections from customers on account for the period.

3. Assume all rent revenues are received in advance and accounted for as unearned rent, and beginning and ending balances of unearned rent are $3,000 and $2,500, respectively. If total rent revenue for the period amounts to $15,000, determine the amount of rent collections in advance for the period.

EXERCISE 4-12

DUPONT FRAMEWORK

The following information is for Ina Company:

	2003	2002	2001
Total assets	$200,000	$160,000	$180,000
Total liabilities	90,000	80,000	100,000
Stockholders' equity	110,000	80,000	80,000
Sales	800,000	600,000	600,000
Net income	40,000	20,000	10,000

For the years 2001, 2002, and 2003, compute:

1. Return on equity
2. Profit margin
3. Asset turnover
4. Assets-to-equity ratio

EXERCISE 4-13

DUPONT FRAMEWORK

The numbers below are for Iffy Company and Model Company for the year 2003:

	Iffy	Model
Cash	$ 120	$ 900
Accounts receivable.	600	4,500
Inventory.	480	6,000
Property, plant, and equipment	3,440	15,000
Total liabilities.	3,190	18,150
Stockholders' equity	1,450	8,250
Sales	10,000	75,000
Cost of goods sold.	9,200	66,750
Wages expense	700	5,250
Net income	100	3,000

1. Compute return on equity, profit margin, asset turnover, and the assets-to-equity ratio for both Iffy and Model.
2. Briefly explain why Iffy's return on equity is lower than Model's.

EXERCISE 4-14

DUPONT FRAMEWORK

The numbers below are for Question Company and Standard Company for the year 2003:

	Question	Standard
Cash	$ 60	$ 300
Accounts receivable.	600	4,000
Inventory.	1,400	3,650
Plant and equipment	1,000	8,650

(continued)

	Question	Standard
Total liabilities	$ 2,448	$13,280
Stockholders' equity	612	3,320
Sales	10,000	50,000
Cost of goods sold.	7,350	36,750
Wages expense	700	3,500
Other expenses	1,900	8,500
Net income	50	1,250

1. Compute return on equity, profit margin, asset turnover, and the assets-to-equity ratio for both Question and Standard.
2. Briefly explain why Question's return on equity is lower than Standard's.

EXERCISE 4-15

DUPONT FRAMEWORK FOR ANALYZING FINANCIAL STATEMENTS

The income statement and balance sheet for the Rollins Company are provided below. Using the DuPont framework, compute the profit margin, asset turnover, assets-to-equity ratio, and resulting return on equity for the year 2003.

Rollins Company
Income Statement
For the Year Ended December 31, 2003

Revenue from services		$151,920
Operating expenses:		
Insurance expense	$ 5,480	
Rent expense	500	
Office supplies expense	2,960	
Salaries expense	55,000	63,940
Net income		$ 87,980

Rollins Company
Balance Sheet
December 31, 2003

Assets		Liabilities and Owners' Equity	
Cash.	$ 22,000	Accounts payable	$ 54,800
Accounts receivable	40,000	Capital stock.	50,000
Notes receivable.	12,800	Retained earnings	150,000
Machinery	180,000		
		Total liabilities	
Total assets.	$254,800	and owners' equity	$254,800

EXERCISE 4-16

DUPONT FRAMEWORK FOR ANALYZING FINANCIAL STATEMENTS

Using the income statement and balance sheet for the Jacobson and Sons Company, compute the three components of return on equity—profitability, efficiency, and leverage—based on the DuPont framework, for the year 2003.

Jacobson and Sons Co.
Income Statement
For the Year Ended December 31, 2003

Revenues		$265,000
Expenses:		
Supplies expense	$138,600	
Salaries expense	26,700	
Utilities expense	6,500	
Rent expense	17,100	
Other expenses	8,700	197,600
Net income		$ 67,400

Jacobson and Sons Co.
Balance Sheet
December 31, 2003

Assets		Liabilities and Owners' Equity	
Cash	$ 38,900	Accounts payable	$ 17,100
Accounts receivable	31,000	Notes payable	17,200
Supplies	46,300	Capital stock	30,000
Land	25,000	Retained earnings	173,600
Buildings	96,700		
		Total liabilities	
Total assets	$237,900	and owners' equity	$237,900

EXERCISE 4-17

COMMON-SIZE BALANCE SHEET

The following data are taken from the comparative balance sheet prepared for Elison Company:

	2003	2002
Cash	$ 68,000	$ 50,000
Accounts receivable	86,000	80,000
Inventory	136,000	60,000
Property, plant, and equipment	182,000	110,000
Total assets	$472,000	$300,000

Sales for 2003 were $2,000,000. Sales for 2002 were $1,600,000.

1. Prepare the asset section of a common-size balance sheet for Elison Company for 2003 and 2002.
2. Overall, Elison is less efficient at using its assets to generate sales in 2003 than in 2002. What asset or assets are responsible for this decreased efficiency?

EXERCISE 4-18

COMMON-SIZE INCOME STATEMENT

Comparative income statements for Callister Company for 2003 and 2002 are given on the following page.

1. Prepare common-size income statements for Callister Company for 2003 and 2002.
2. The profit margin for Callister is lower in 2003 than in 2002. What expense or expenses are causing this lower profitability?

	2003	2002
Sales	$1,600,000	$900,000
Cost of goods sold	1,020,000	480,000
Gross profit	$ 580,000	$420,000
Selling and administrative expenses	200,000	160,000
Operating income	$ 380,000	$260,000
Interest expense	80,000	60,000
Income before taxes	$ 300,000	$200,000
Income tax expense	90,000	60,000
Net income	$ 210,000	$140,000

EXERCISE 4-19

REAL AND NOMINAL ACCOUNTS

Classify each of the following accounts as either a real account (R) or a nominal account (N):

1. Cash
2. Sales Revenue
3. Accounts Receivable
4. Cost of Goods Sold
5. Prepaid Insurance
6. Capital Stock
7. Retained Earnings
8. Insurance Expense
9. Salaries Payable
10. Interest Expense
11. Insurance Premiums Payable
12. Salaries Expense
13. Accounts Payable
14. Prepaid Salaries
15. Utilities Expense
16. Notes Payable
17. Inventory
18. Property Tax Expense
19. Rent Expense
20. Interest Payable
21. Income Taxes Payable
22. Dividends
23. Buildings
24. Office Supplies
25. Income Tax Expense

EXERCISE 4-20

CLOSING ENTRY

The income statement for Eriksen Enterprises for the year ended June 30, 2003, is provided.

Eriksen Enterprises
Income Statement
For the Year Ended June 30, 2003

Sales revenue	$187,000
Cost of goods sold	(122,000)
Selling and general expenses	(20,500)
Income before income taxes	$ 44,500
Income tax expense	(17,800)
Net income	$ 26,700

1. Prepare a journal entry to close the accounts to Retained Earnings.
2. What problem may arise in closing the accounts if the information from the income statement is used?

EXERCISE 4-21

CLOSING ENTRY

Revenue and expense accounts of Rushford Publishing Company for November 30, 2003, are given as follows. Prepare a compound journal entry that will close the revenue and expense accounts to the retained earnings account.

	Debits	Credits
Sales Revenue		$250,500
Cost of Goods Sold	$124,500	
Salaries Expense	35,000	
Interest Expense	1,000	

(continued)

	Debits	Credits
Rent Expense	$ 9,300	
Insurance Expense	1,700	
Property Tax Expense	800	
Supplies Expense	1,000	
Advertising Expense	10,000	

EXERCISE 4-22

CLOSING DIVIDENDS AND PREPARING A POST-CLOSING TRIAL BALANCE

A listing of account balances taken from the adjusted ledger account balances of Farmers' Co-Op shows the following:

Cash	$ 22,580
Accounts Receivable	56,480
Inventory	78,360
Prepaid Insurance	6,520
Land	136,000
Accounts Payable	28,640
Notes Payable	40,000
Salaries Payable	9,000
Taxes Payable	24,400
Unearned Rent	15,200
Mortgage Payable	90,000
Capital Stock	44,000
Dividends	20,000
Retained Earnings	68,700

All revenue and expense accounts have been closed to Retained Earnings. Dividends has not yet been closed.

Prepare (1) the closing entry for Dividends and (2) a post-closing trial balance for December 31, 2003.

EXERCISE 4-23

CLOSING DIVIDENDS AND PREPARING A POST-CLOSING TRIAL BALANCE

Below is a listing of account balances taken from the adjusted ledger account balances of Goldsmith Corporation.

Cash	$25,500
Accounts Receivable	24,000
Inventory	60,000
Prepaid Advertising	5,500
Building	95,000
Land	35,000
Accounts Payable	20,000
Wages Payable	5,000
Income Taxes Payable	4,000
Mortgage Payable	55,000
Notes Payable	27,500
Unearned Rent	2,500
Capital Stock	95,500
Dividends	15,500
Retained Earnings	51,000

All revenues and expense accounts have been closed to Retained Earnings. Dividends has not yet been closed.

Prepare (1) the closing entry for Dividends and (2) a post-closing trial balance for December 31, 2003.

EXERCISE 4-24

ADJUSTING ENTRIES

The trial balance of Dallas Company shows the following balances, among others, on December 31, 2003, the end of its first fiscal year:

Rent Revenue	$ 36,800
Office Supplies Expense	2,700
Mortgage Payable	130,000

Inspection of the company's records reveals that:

1. Rent revenue of $2,800 is unearned at December 31, 2003.
2. Interest of $7,800 on the mortgage is payable semiannually on March 1 and September 1.
3. Office supplies of $500 are on hand on December 31. When purchases of office supplies were made during the year, they were charged to the office supplies expense account.

Given this information, prepare journal entries to adjust the books as of December 31, 2003.

pr**o**blems

PROBLEM 4-1

CASH- AND ACCRUAL-BASIS ACCOUNTING

In the course of your examination of the books and records of Hickory Company, you find the following data:

Salaries earned by employees in 2003	$ 53,000
Salaries paid in 2003	55,000
Total sales revenue in 2003	838,000
Cash collected from sales in 2003	900,000
Utilities expense incurred in 2003	5,000
Utility bills paid in 2003	4,800
Cost of goods sold in 2003	532,000
Cash paid on purchases in 2003	411,000
Inventory at December 31, 2003	320,000
Tax assessment for 2003	5,000
Taxes paid in 2003	4,900
Rent expense for 2003	30,000
Rent paid in 2003	25,000

Required:

1. Compute Hickory's net income for 2003 using cash-basis accounting.
2. Compute Hickory's net income for 2003 using accrual-basis accounting.
3. **Interpretive Question:** Why is accrual-basis accounting normally used? Can you see any opportunities for improperly reporting income under cash-basis accounting? Explain.

PROBLEM 4-2

ADJUSTING ENTRIES

The information presented below is for Sun Marketing, Inc.

a. Salaries for the period December 26, 2003, through December 31, 2003, amounted to $14,240 and have not been recorded or paid. (Ignore payroll taxes.)
b. Interest of $6,000 is payable for three months on a 15%, $160,000 loan and has not been recorded.
c. Rent of $24,000 was paid for six months in advance on December 1 and debited to Prepaid Rent.
d. Rent of $82,000 was credited to an unearned revenue account when received. Of this amount, $33,400 is still unearned at year-end.
e. The expired portion of an insurance policy is $1,000. Prepaid Insurance was originally debited.

f.   Interest revenue of $300 from a $2,000 note has been earned but not collected or recorded.

Required: Prepare the adjusting entries that should be made on December 31, 2003. (Omit explanations.)

PROBLEM 4-3

ADJUSTING ENTRIES

The information presented below is for Averrett Marketing, Inc.

a.   Rent of $56,500 was credited to an unearned revenue account when received. Of this amount, $24,750 is still unearned at year-end.

b.   Interest revenue of $4,500 from a $65,000 note has been earned but not collected or recorded.

c.   Salaries for the period December 26, 2003, to December 31, 2003, amounted to $11,500 and have not been recorded or paid. (Ignore payroll taxes.)

d.   Interest of $8,000 is payable for September 2003 through December 2003 on a 12%, $200,000 loan and has not been recorded.

e.   The expired portion of an insurance policy is $2,150. Prepaid Insurance was originally debited.

f.   Rent of $18,000 was paid for six months in advance on November 15, 2003, and debited to Prepaid Rent.

Required: Prepare the adjusting entries that should be made on December 31, 2003. (Omit explanations.)

PROBLEM 4-4

YEAR-END ANALYSIS OF ACCOUNTS

An analysis of cash records and account balances of Wells, Inc., for 2003 is as follows:

	Account Balances Jan. 1, 2003	Account Balances Dec. 31, 2003	Cash Received or Paid in 2003
Wages Payable	$2,600	$3,000	
Unearned Rent	4,500	5,000	
Prepaid Insurance	100	120	
Paid for wages			$29,600
Received for rent			12,000
Paid for insurance			720

Required: Determine the amounts that should be included on the 2003 income statement for (1) wages expense, (2) rent revenue, and (3) insurance expense.

PROBLEM 4-5

YEAR-END ANALYSIS OF ACCOUNTS

An analysis of cash records and account balances of Computer Networking, Inc., for 2003 is as follows:

	Account Balances Jan. 1, 2003	Account Balances Dec. 31, 2003	Cash Received or Paid in 2003
Salaries Payable	$10,750	$12,750	
Unearned Rent	23,250	26,500	
Prepaid Insurance	2,000	3,100	
Paid for salaries			$125,000
Received for rent			64,250
Paid for insurance			12,600

Required: Determine the amounts that should be included on the 2003 income statement for (1) salaries expense, (2) rent revenue, and (3) insurance expense.

PROBLEM 4-6

ACCOUNT CLASSIFICATIONS AND DEBIT-CREDIT RELATIONSHIPS

Using the format provided, for each account identify (1) whether the account is a balance sheet (B/S) or an income statement (I/S) account; (2) whether it is an asset (A), a liability (L), an owners' equity (OE), a revenue (R), or an expense (E) account; (3) whether the account is a real or a nominal account; (4) whether the account will be "closed" or left "open" at year-end; and (5) whether the account normally has a debit or a credit balance. The following example is provided:

Account Title	(1) B/S or I/S	(2) A, L, OE, R, E	(3) Real or Nominal	(4) Closed or Open	(5) Debit/ Credit
Cash	B/S	A	Real	Open	Debit

1. Accounts Receivable
2. Accounts Payable
3. Prepaid Insurance
4. Mortgage Payable
5. Rent Expense
6. Sales Revenue
7. Cost of Goods Sold
8. Dividends
9. Capital Stock
10. Inventory
11. Retained Earnings
12. Prepaid Rent
13. Supplies on Hand
14. Utilities Expense
15. Income Taxes Payable
16. Interest Revenue
17. Notes Payable
18. Income Tax Expense
19. Wages Payable
20. Unearned Rent Revenue
21. Land
22. Unearned Consulting Fees
23. Interest Receivable
24. Consulting Fees

PROBLEM 4-7

ANALYZING FINANCIAL STATEMENTS

Refer to the financial statements for Sports Haven Company for the year-ended December 31, 2003 (shown in the review problem for this chapter, pp. 176–177).

Required:

1. Using the DuPont framework, compute:
   a. The profit margin
   b. The asset turnover
   c. The assets-to-equity ratio
   d. The overall return on equity
2. Prepare a common-size income statement.
3. **Interpretive Question:** What is the value of common-size financial statements?

PROBLEM 4-8

ANALYZING FINANCIAL STATEMENTS

The income statement and the balance sheet for the Hamblin Company for the year ended December 31, 2003, are provided below.

Hamblin Company
Income Statement
For the Year Ended December 31, 2003

Sales revenue		$270,000
Expenses:		
Cost of goods sold	$150,000	
Salaries expense	45,000	
Interest expense	10,500	205,500
Net income		$ 64,500

Hamblin Company
Balance Sheet
December 31, 2003

Assets

Cash	$ 49,500	
Accounts receivable	22,500	
Inventory	15,000	
Land	225,000	
Total assets		$312,000

Liabilities and Owners' Equity

Liabilities:		
Accounts payable		$ 15,000
Owners' equity:		
Capital stock	$202,500	
Retained earnings	94,500	
Total owners' equity		297,000
Total liabilities and owners' equity		$312,000

Required:

1. Using the DuPont framework, compute Hamblin's return on equity (ROE).
2. Prepare a common-size balance sheet, using total revenue as the basis for comparison.
3. **Interpretive Question:** Based on your analysis in (1) and (2), does Hamblin Company appear to be in good shape?

PROBLEM 4-9

General Ledger Software

CLOSING ENTRIES

The income statement for Home Light, Inc., for the year ended December 31, 2003, is as follows:

Home Light, Inc.
Income Statement
For the Year Ended December 31, 2003

Sales revenue		$452,000
Less expenses:		
Cost of goods sold	$363,000	
Salaries expense	72,000	
Interest expense	5,250	
Office supplies expense	3,820	
Insurance expense	4,930	
Property tax expense	11,200	
Total expenses		460,200
Net loss		$ (8,200)

Required: Dividends of $20,000 were paid on December 30, 2003.

1. Give the entry required on December 31, 2003, to properly close the income statement accounts.
2. Give the entry required to close the dividends account at December 31, 2003.

PROBLEM 4-10

CLOSING ENTRIES

The income statement for Quality Plumbing, Inc., for the year ended December 31, 2003, is as follows:

General Ledger Software

Quality Plumbing, Inc.
Income Statement
For the Year Ended December 31, 2003

Sales revenue		$623,400
Less expenses:		
Cost of goods sold	$447,000	
Wages expense	98,350	
Utilities expense	1,720	
Insurance expense	2,790	
Property tax expense	2,110	
Rent expense	26,000	
Advertising expense	9,830	
Interest expense	4,300	
Total expenses		592,100
Net income		$ 31,300

Dividends of $23,200 were paid on December 30, 2003.

Required:

1. Give the entry required on December 31, 2003, to properly close the income statement accounts.
2. Give the entry required to close the dividends account at December 31, 2003.

PROBLEM 4-11

General Ledger Software

Spread-Sheet Software

UNIFYING CONCEPTS: ADJUSTING AND CLOSING ENTRIES

The unadjusted and adjusted trial balances of White Company as of December 31, 2003, are presented below.

White Company
Trial Balance
December 31, 2003

	Unadjusted		Adjusted	
	Debits	**Credits**	**Debits**	**Credits**
Cash	$ 21,250		$ 21,250	
Accounts Receivable	11,250		11,250	
Supplies on Hand	5,195		3,895	
Prepaid Rent	17,545		7,545	
Prepaid Insurance	1,985		1,100	
Buildings (net)	95,000		95,000	
Land	45,720		45,720	
Accounts Payable		$ 9,350		$ 9,350
Wages Payable				5,700
Income Taxes Payable				580
Interest Payable		450		1,050
Notes Payable		65,000		65,000
Capital Stock		84,320		84,320
Consulting Fees Earned		142,380		142,380
Wages Expense	92,335		98,035	
Rent Expense			10,000	
Interest Expense	3,500		4,100	
Insurance Expense	585		1,470	
Supplies Expenses	4,365		5,665	
Income Tax Expense	2,770		3,350	
Totals	$301,500	$301,500	$308,380	$308,380

Required:
1. Prepare the journal entries that are required to adjust the accounts at December 31, 2003.
2. Prepare the journal entry that is required to close the accounts at December 31, 2003.

PROBLEM 4-12

UNIFYING CONCEPTS: ANALYSIS OF ACCOUNTS

The bookkeeper for Careless Company accidentally pressed the wrong computer key and erased the amount of Retained Earnings. You have been asked to analyze the following data and provide some key numbers for the board of directors meeting, which is to take place in 30 minutes. With the exception of Retained Earnings, the following account balances are available at December 31, 2003.

Cash	$122,000	Accounts Receivable	$ 98,000
Furniture (net)	80,000	Inventory	320,000
Accounts Payable	240,000	Notes Payable	500,000
Land	520,000	Supplies on Hand	20,000
Buildings (net)	480,000	Capital Stock	600,000
Sales Revenue	830,000	Dividends	40,000
Salaries Expense	100,000	Retained Earnings	?
Cost of Goods Sold	440,000		

Required:
1. Compute the amount of total assets at December 31, 2003.
2. Compute the amount of net income for the year ended December 31, 2003.
3. After all closing entries are made, what is the amount of Retained Earnings at December 31, 2003?
4. What was the beginning Retained Earnings balance at January 1, 2003?

PROBLEM 4-13

UNIFYING CONCEPTS: ANALYSIS AND CORRECTION OF ERRORS

At the end of November 2003, the general ledger of Porridge Milling Company showed the following amounts:

Assets	$64,250
Liabilities	28,800
Owners' Equity	62,000

The company's bookkeeper is new on the job and does not have much accounting experience. Because the bookkeeper has made numerous errors, total assets do not equal liabilities plus owners' equity. The following is a list of errors made.

a. Inventory that cost $42,000 was sold, but the entry to record cost of goods sold was not made.
b. Credit sales of $12,100 were posted to the general ledger as $21,100. The accounts receivable were posted correctly.
c. Inventory of $12,500 was purchased on account and received before the end of November, but no entry to record the purchase was made until December.
d. November salaries payable of $5,000 were not recorded until paid in December.
e. Common stock was issued for $18,500 and credited to Accounts Payable.
f. Inventory purchased for $31,050 was incorrectly posted to the asset account as $13,500. No error was made in the liability account.

Required: Determine the correct balances of assets, liabilities, and owners' equity at the end of November.

PROBLEM 4-14

UNIFYING CONCEPTS: THE ACCOUNTING CYCLE

The post-closing trial balance of Anderson Company at December 31, 2002, is shown here.

Anderson Company
Post-Closing Trial Balance
December 31, 2002

	Debits	Credits
Cash.	$ 15,000	
Accounts Receivable.	20,000	
Inventory	30,000	
Land.	150,000	
Accounts Payable.		$ 25,000
Notes Payable		35,000
Capital Stock		125,000
Retained Earnings		30,000
Totals	$215,000	$215,000

During 2003, Anderson Company had the following transactions:

a. Inventory purchases were $80,000, all on credit (debit Inventory).
b. An additional $10,000 of capital stock was issued for cash.
c. Merchandise that cost $100,000 was sold for $180,000; $100,000 were credit sales and the balance were cash sales. (Debit Cost of Goods Sold and credit Inventory for sale of merchandise.)
d. The notes were paid, including $7,000 interest.
e. $105,000 was collected from customers.
f. $95,000 was paid to reduce accounts payable.
g. Salaries expense was $30,000, all paid in cash.
h. A $10,000 cash dividend was declared and paid.

Required:
1. Prepare journal entries to record each of the 2003 transactions.
2. Set up T-accounts with the proper balances at January 1, 2003, and post the journal entries to the T-accounts.
3. Prepare an income statement for the year ended December 31, 2003, and a balance sheet as of that date. Also prepare a statement of retained earnings.
4. Prepare the entries necessary to close the nominal accounts, including Dividends.
5. Post the closing entries to the ledger accounts [label (i) and (j)] and prepare a post-closing trial balance at December 31, 2003.

competency enhancement opportunities

▶ Analyzing Real Company Information
▶ International Case
▶ Ethics Case
▶ Writing Assignment

▶ The Debate
▶ Cumulative Spreadsheet Project
▶ Internet Search

The following additional assignments provide opportunities for students to develop critical thinking, ethical perspectives, oral and written communication skills, experience with electronic research, and teamwork through group and business activities.

▶ **ANALYZING REAL COMPANY INFORMATION**

• *Analyzing 4-1 (Microsoft)*
Using MICROSOFT's 1999 annual report contained in Appendix A, answer the following questions:

1. Microsoft discloses that as of June 30, 1999, the company had received cash of $4.239 billion that had not been earned as of that date. Accordingly, the company made an adjusting entry to recognize the unearned revenue. Provide the adjusting entry that was made by Microsoft.
2. Read the note related to Microsoft's unearned revenue and determine what this amount relates to—operating systems, applications, and so forth.
3. Using the DuPont framework, determine Microsoft's return on equity.

• *Analyzing 4-2 (Hewlett-Packard and Compaq)*
Selected financial statement information for HEWLETT-PACKARD and COMPAQ is given in the table below. Using this information, answer the following questions.

(in millions)	Hewlett-Packard	Compaq
Assets	$35,297	$27,277
Equity	18,295	14,834
Net income	3,491	569
Sales	42,370	38,525

1. Compute each firm's return on equity using the DuPont framework.
2. Identify the primary reason for the significant difference between the two return on equity ratios.
3. Based on the ratios used in the DuPont framework, can you determine which firm has more debt? Which ratio provided this insight?

• *Analyzing 4-3 (Campbell Soup)*
Information from the 1999 income statement for CAMPBELL SOUP COMPANY is shown below.

(in millions)	1999 52 weeks	1998 52 weeks	1997 52 weeks
Net Sales	**$6,424**	**$6,696**	**$6,614**
Costs and expenses			
Cost of products sold	3,050	3,233	3,412
Marketing and selling expenses	1,634	1,518	1,370
Administrative expenses	304	300	271
Research and development expenses	66	71	68
Other expenses (Note 7)	64	64	140
Restructuring charges (Note 6)	36	262	204
Total costs and expenses	5,154	5,448	5,465

(continued)

Earnings Before Interest and Taxes	$1,270	$1,248	$1,149
Interest expense (Note 8)	184	189	166
Interest income	11	14	8
Earnings before taxes	1,097	1,073	991
Taxes on earnings (Note 11)	373	384	357
Earnings from Continuing Operations	724	689	634
Earnings (Loss) from Discontinued Operations (Note 3)		(18)	79
Cumulative Effect of Change in Accounting Principle (Note 4)		(11)	
Net Earnings	$ 724	$ 660	$ 713

Using the information from the income statement, perform the following:

1. Prepare common-size income statements for 1999 and 1998. Can you identify any significant changes in expenses and revenues as a percentage of total revenue over the two-year period?
2. Using the information from the 1999 income statement, prepare the journal entry that would be required to close the nominal accounts to Retained Earnings.

INTERNATIONAL CASE

• Exchange Rate Adjustments

Given the international economy in which many firms operate, it is not unusual for companies to have transactions with companies in foreign countries. Relatedly, it is becoming common for some of those transactions to be denominated in a foreign currency. That is, if a company in the United States makes a purchase from a company in Japan, it is possible that the U.S. company will have to pay Japanese yen when the invoice comes due.

For example, suppose American, Inc., purchased inventory from Japan, Inc., on December 15, 2002. Japan, Inc., expects to receive 1,000,000 Japanese yen in 30 days. To record a journal entry for this purchase, you would need to know what 1,000,000 yen are worth today. Suppose that on December 15, 2002, one yen is worth $0.07 (this is called an exchange rate). What journal entry would be made on American, Inc.'s books?

Since exchange rates change every day, the amount of U.S. dollars to be paid on January 15, 2003, will likely be different than the originally recorded $70,000. In addition, to correctly state the liability on December 31, 2002, an adjustment will be required. Suppose that at year-end, one Japanese yen is worth $0.08. What adjusting entry would be made to reflect this change in exchange rates as of December 31, 2002? (HINT: The accounts being adjusted with this journal entry will be the accounts payable account and an exchange gain or loss.)

When the invoice is paid on January 15, 2003, it is likely that the number of U.S. dollars required to purchase 1,000,000 Japanese yen will again have changed. Suppose exchange rates have increased to $0.09. Provide the journal entry to pay the invoice.

ETHICS CASE

• Do Two Wrongs Make a Right?

Jex Varner, chief financial officer of Wyndam, Inc., is involved in a meeting with the firm's newly hired external auditors, Ernst & Price. The external auditors have noted several adjusting entries that they believe should be reflected in the current period's financial statements. Specifically, there are questions

l. Interest expense depends on how much interest-bearing debt a company has. In 2003, Handyman reported interest expense of $9 on long-term debt of $207. [Note: To simplify this exercise, we will ignore interest expense on the short-term loan payable.] Because Handyman is expected to have the same amount of long-term debt in 2004, our best guess is that interest expense will remain the same.

m. Income tax expense is determined by how much pretax income a company has. And, the most reasonable assumption to make is that a company's tax rate, equal to income tax expense divided by pretax income, will stay constant from year to year. Handyman's income tax rate in 2003 was 33% ($4/$12).

2. Repeat (1) assuming that forecasted sales growth in 2004 is 20% instead of 40%. Clearly state any assumptions that you make.

▶ **INTERNET SEARCH**

• General Motors

We began this chapter with an introduction to GENERAL MOTORS; we will end this chapter with a look at its Web site. Access GM's Web site at http://www.gm.com. Sometimes Web addresses change, so if this address doesn't work, access the Web site for this textbook (http://albrecht.swcollege.com) for an updated link to GM.

Once you have located the company's Web site, answer the following questions:

1. Locate GM's financial statements. Write down the path you took to get to the statements. In your opinion, is GM's Web site easy to navigate relative to others you have accessed?

2. In the chapter, we computed GM's return on equity for 1999. Using the information contained in GM's most recent annual report, compute the company's return on equity using the DuPont framework. Provide these computations for the two most recent periods. Using the DuPont framework, identify the ratio(s) that highlight the reasons for any changes in return on equity over the two-year period and compare the results with those obtained from 1999.

3. Access the company's note information relating to accounting estimates. Since these estimates result in most adjusting entries, identify who makes these estimates and, as a result, who is responsible for making the adjusting entries.

4. As pointed out in the chapter, revenue is recognized when it is earned and a promise of payment has been received. Using the note relating to revenue recognition, identify when GM recognizes revenue for its various segments within the firm.

Ensuring the
Integrity of
Financial
Information

chapter

f5

learning objectives After studying this chapter, you should be able to:

1 Identify the types of problems that can appear in financial statements.

2 Describe the safeguards employed within a firm to ensure that financial statements are free from problems.

3 Understand the need for monitoring by independent parties.

4 Describe the role of auditors and how their presence affects the integrity of financial statements.

5 Explain the role of the Securities and Exchange Commission in adding credibility to financial statements.

PHAR-MOR,[1] a dry goods retailer based in Youngstown, Ohio, was founded in 1982 by Mickey Monus. Within 10 years, Phar-Mor, with over 300 stores, was operating in nearly every state in the United States. Phar-Mor's strategy was to sell household products and prescription drugs at prices lower than those of other discount stores. Phar-Mor's prices were so low and its expansion was conducted so quickly that even WAL-MART, the king of discount prices, was nervous. Sam Walton once said that the only company he feared at all in the expansion of Wal-Mart was Phar-Mor.[2]

Today, with fewer than 140 stores, Phar-Mor is struggling to build a profitable business from the rubble of a financial statement fraud that exceeded $1 billion. Apparently, certain Phar-Mor executives used financial statements showing healthy profits to obtain more than $1 billion in credit and capital for the company. Investors in Phar-Mor included SEARS, ROEBUCK & CO., WESTINGHOUSE ELECTRIC CORPORATION, and mall developer Edward DeBartolo Sr. (the former owner of the San Francisco 49ers).

Phar-Mor's financial statements appeared to present an extremely profitable company. In reality, the company never made a legitimate profit. Phar-Mor actually had $238 million in pretax losses in 1992 alone. Schemers at the company kept two sets of accounting records: an official ledger that they sometimes manipulated with false entries, called "raisins," and another, nicknamed the "cookies," where they kept track of the false entries. They would refer to their fraud as "putting raisins in the cookies."

For six years, some company officials seemingly used the company as their personal plaything, falsifying financial ledgers and allegedly raiding company coffers. Officers diverted more than $10 million from Phar-Mor to prop up the WORLD BASKETBALL LEAGUE (the defunct minor-league basketball venture) and stole more than $500,000 for personal use. How could a company appear in its financial statements to be so profitable and yet in reality be losing money? How could a company with a reputation as good as Phar-Mor's deceive the public by misrepresenting its profitability, and what was the price of this deception?

Phar-Mor emerged from bankruptcy in September 1995 with 102 stores. In July 1999, the company had 139 stores in 24 states and reported a profit from its operations of $15 million. However, the debt incurred by the company to finance its recovery wiped out all that profit. For the fiscal year ended July 3, 1999, Phar-Mor reported a net loss of $1.6 million.

setting the stage

In Chapters 1 and 2, you were introduced to financial accounting and shown the outputs (financial statements) of the financial reporting process. You learned that the balance sheet, income statement, and statement of cash flows are reports used by organizations to summarize their financial results for various users. In Chapters 3 and 4, the accounting cycle, the method of entering and processing financial transaction information in the accounting records, was described. You learned that transaction data are captured by journal entries, journal entry data are summarized in accounts and ledgers, ledger information is summarized on trial balances, and trial balance information provides the basis for the balance sheet, income statement, and statement of cash flows.

In Chapters 1 through 4, the assumption was made that the financial reporting process always works the way it should and that the resulting financial statements are accurate. In reality, however, because of unintentional errors, as well as intentional deception or fraud (such as in the Phar-Mor case), the resulting financial statements sometimes contain errors or omissions that can mislead investors, creditors, and other users.

In this chapter, we show how financial statements might be manipulated, and we discuss the safeguards built into the financial reporting system to prevent these abuses. We also examine the role that auditors play in ensuring that the financial statements fairly represent the financial performance of the firm.

1 Most of these facts relating to Phar-Mor appeared in Gabriella Stern, "Chicanery at Phar-Mor Ran Deep, Close Look at Discounter Shows," *The Wall Street Journal*, January 20, 1994, p. 1.

2 Mark F. Murray, "When a Client Is a Liability," *Journal of Accountancy*, September 1992, pp. 54–58.

1. *Validity.* Only valid transactions are recorded. If fictitious sales are recorded, for example, reported revenues will be too high, and the integrity of the financial statements will be lost.
2. *Authorization.* All transactions are properly authorized. If, for example, any employee could authorize purchases, a company might make duplicate purchases of the same items or purchase unneeded items.
3. *Completeness.* All legitimate transactions are recorded and the records are complete. If, for example, all liabilities are not recorded, a company will report a more favorable financial condition than actually exists.
4. *Classification.* All transactions are properly classified. For example, the current portion of long-term debt should be classified as a current liability. Incorrect classification would result in incorrect liability subtotals that would affect such ratios as the current ratio.
5. *Timeliness.* All transactions are recorded in the proper time period. A company might try to make its revenues and income look better than they are, for example, by recording early January sales in December.
6. *Valuation.* All transactions are properly valued. For example, if a receivable is uncollectible, it should not be classified as a current asset.
7. *Posting and summarization.* All transactions are properly included in subsidiary records and correctly summarized. Errors could occur, for example, if an accounts receivable entry was posted to the accounts payable account.

Control Activities (Procedures)

Control activities or **control procedures** are those policies and procedures, in addition to the control environment and accounting system, that management has adopted to provide reasonable assurance that the company's established objectives will be met and that financial reports are accurate. Generally, control activities fall into five categories: adequate segregation of duties, proper procedures for authorization, adequate documents and records, physical control over assets and records, and independent checks on performance.

ADEQUATE SEGREGATION OF DUTIES
A good internal control system should provide for the appropriate **segregation of duties**. This means that no one department or individual should be responsible for handling all phases of a transaction. In some small businesses, this segregation is not possible because the limited number of employees prevents division of all the different functions. Nevertheless, there are three functions that should be performed by separate departments or by different people.

1. *Authorization.* Authorizing and approving the execution of transactions; for example, approving the sale of a building or land.
2. *Record keeping.* Recording the transactions in the accounting journals.
3. *Custody.* Having physical possession of or control over the assets involved in transactions, including operational responsibility; for example, having the key to the safe in which cash or investment securities are kept or, more generally, having control over the production function.

By separating the responsibilities for these duties, a company realizes the efficiency derived from specialization and also reduces the errors, both intentional and unintentional, that might otherwise occur.

An example of a problem resulting from the nonsegregation of the custody and record-keeping functions occurred when a young employee of a wholesale candy distributor both opened incoming mail and kept the accounts receivable file. Needing money for a family emergency, she stole $300 and did not show the receivable as collected. After realizing how easy it was, over time she took $76,000 by delaying the recording of receivables collected. She was eventually caught, but her theft affected the financial statements because receivables were misstated, as was the financial health of the company.

PROPER PROCEDURES FOR AUTHORIZATION
A strong system of internal control requires proper authorization for every transaction. In the typical corporate organization, this authorization originates with the stockholders who elect a board of directors. It is then delegated

---

control activities (procedures) Policies and procedures used by management to meet their objectives; generally divided into adequate segregation of duties, proper procedures for authorization of transactions and activities, adequate documents and records, physical control over assets and records, and independent checks on performance.

segregation of duties A strategy to provide an internal check on performance through separation of authorization of transactions from custody of related assets, separation of operational responsibilities from record-keeping responsibilities, and separation of custody of assets from accounting personnel.

from the board of directors to upper-level management and eventually throughout the organization. While the board of directors and upper-level management possess a fairly general power of authorization, a clerk usually has limited authority. Thus, the board would authorize dividends, a general change in policies, or a merger; a clerk would be restricted to authorizing credit or a specific cash transaction. Only certain people should be authorized to enter data into accounting records and prepare accounting reports.

ADEQUATE DOCUMENTS AND RECORDS   A key to good controls is an adequate system of documentation and records. As explained in Chapter 3, documents are the physical, objective evidence of accounting transactions. Their existence allows management to review any transaction for appropriate authorization. Documents are also the means by which information is communicated throughout an organization. In short, adequate documentation provides evidence that the recording and summarizing functions that lead to financial reports are being performed properly. A well-designed document has several characteristics: (1) it is easily interpreted and understood, (2) it has been designed with all possible uses in mind, (3) it has been prenumbered for easy identification and tracking, and (4) it is formatted so that it can be handled quickly and efficiently. Documents can be actual pieces of paper or information in a computer database.

PHYSICAL CONTROL OVER ASSETS AND RECORDS   Some of the most crucial policies and procedures involve the use of adequate **physical safeguards** to protect resources. For example, a bank would not allow significant amounts of money to be transported in an ordinary car. Similarly, a company should not leave its valuable assets unprotected. Examples of physical safeguards are fireproof vaults for the storage of classified information, currency, and marketable securities; and guards, fences, and remote control cameras for the protection of equipment, materials, and merchandise. Records and documents are also important resources and must be protected. Re-creating lost or destroyed records can be costly and time-consuming, so companies make backup copies of records. The high cost of backup records (often on microfilm) is usually more than justified in protecting such valuable resources.

Providing proper safeguards reduces opportunities for employees to misappropriate assets. Each firm needs a comprehensive security program specifically engineered to protect its corporate assets. An example of a fraud committed in a setting of poor physical safeguards was the

physical safeguards Physical precautions used to protect assets and records, such as locks on doors, fireproof vaults, password verification, and security guards.

Many companies use physical safeguards, such as surveillance cameras, to protect their resources.

An Example of Poor Controls Earlier in this chapter (pages 210–211), the $3.01 million theft by Jane W., proof operator in a bank, was discussed. Her fraud was possible because of poor internal controls in her bank. Here are some of the major control weaknesses that existed.

1. All documents were to be accessible to external auditors. Yet Jane kept a locked cabinet next to her desk and only she had a key. A customer whose statement had been altered by Jane complained, but was told that he would have to wait until Jane returned from vacation; the documentation relating to his account was in Jane's locked cabinet.

2. The bank required every employee and every officer to take a consecutive two-week vacation. At Jane's request, management allowed this control to be broken. Based on her memos that "proof would get behind if she took a two-week vacation," Jane was allowed to take her vacation one day at a time. In addition, no one was allowed to perform Jane's most sensitive duties while she was away.

3. General ledger entries were supposed to be approved by an individual other than the person who completed the entries. In order to override this control, Jane had her employees presign 10 or 12 general ledger approvals, so she wouldn't have to "bother" them when they were busy.

4. Opening and closing procedures were supposed to be in place to protect the bank, but many employees had all the keys necessary and could enter the bank at will.

crime against the PERINI CORPORATION. Approximately $1,150,000 of checks were written on the company's accounts by an employee. Access to the checks was easy because Perini kept its supply of unused checks in the same unlocked storeroom where the styrofoam coffee cups were stored. Every clerk and secretary had access to the storeroom. The checks had been written on a check-writing machine, which automatically signed the president's name. Despite inherent control procedures in the machine, and its CPA firm's warning to implement specific control procedures, the company found it inconvenient to use most of the control procedures. For example, the machine deposited signed checks into a box that was supposed to be locked; the key was supposed to be kept by an employee in a different department. No such employee was assigned, however, and the box was left unlocked. Furthermore, no one paid attention to the machine's counter, which kept track of the number of checks written for comparison with vouchers authorized for payment.

independent checks Procedures for continual internal verification of other controls.

INDEPENDENT CHECKS ON PERFORMANCE   Having **independent checks** on performance is a valuable control technique. Independent checks incorporate reviews of functions, as well as the internal checks created from a proper segregation of duties.

There are many ways to independently check performance. Using independent reviewers, such as auditors, is one of the most common. In addition, mandatory vacations, where another employee performs the vacationing person's duties, periodic rotations or transfers, or merely having someone independent of the accounting records reconcile the bank statement are all types of independent checks.

Reporting on Internal Controls

Public companies are required to include in their annual report a statement signed by management that acknowledges their responsibility for maintaining a good system of internal controls. The statement shown in Exhibit 5-1 on page 216 was included in the 1999 annual report of SARA LEE CORPORATION.

5. An effective internal audit function was supposed to be in place. For a period of two years, however, no internal audit reports were issued. Even when the reports were issued, internal auditors did not check employees' bank accounts or perform a critical control test, such as surprise openings of the bank's incoming and outgoing mail to and from the Federal Reserve.

6. Employees' bank accounts were not regularly reviewed by internal audit or by management. On the rare occasions when they were reviewed, numerous deposits to and checks drawn on Jane's account that exceeded her annual salary were not questioned.

7. Loans were supposed to be made to employees only if the employees met all lending standards required of normal customers. At one point, the bank made a $170,000 mortgage loan to Jane, without requiring any explanation as to how the loan would be repaid or how she could afford such a house.

8. Managers were supposed to be reviewing key documents and reports daily. Either managers didn't review these reports, or they didn't pay close attention to the reports when they did perform the reviews. There were daily fluctuations in the reports of over $3 million. The reports revealed huge deposits to and checks drawn on Jane's account. In addition, Jane appeared on the overdraft report 97 times during the first four years she was employed.

Source: W. S. Albrecht, G. Wernz, and T. Williams, *Fraud: Bringing Light to the Dark Side of Business,* Irwin, 1995, p. 265.

to summarize

Most organizations have an internal control system that, among other things, helps ensure integrity in financial reports. The various elements of control that relate to financial reporting are summarized as follows:

Control Environment	Accounting System	Control Procedures
1. Management philosophy and operating style.	1. Valid transactions.	1. Segregation of duties.
2. Organizational structure.	2. Properly authorized transactions.	2. Proper procedures for authorization.
3. Audit committee.	3. Completeness.	3. Adequate documents and records.
	4. Proper classification.	4. Physical control over assets and records.
	5. Proper timing.	5. Independent checks on performance.
	6. Proper valuation.	
	7. Correct summarization.	

Public companies are required to include in their annual report a statement signed by management that describes and accepts responsibility for the internal controls of the company.

3

Understand the need for monitoring by independent parties.

THE NEED FOR MONITORING

A firm's internal control structure is designed to minimize the occurrence of intentional and unintentional problems in a firm's financial statements. But a system of internal controls provides

exhibit 5-1   Sara Lee's 1999 Management Letter

Management's Report on Financial Information

Management of Sara Lee Corporation is responsible for the preparation and integrity of the financial information included in this annual report. The financial statements have been prepared in accordance with generally accepted accounting principles and, where required, reflect our best estimates and judgments.

It is the corporation's policy to maintain a control-conscious environment through an effective system of internal accounting controls supported by formal policies and procedures communicated throughout the corporation. These controls are adequate to provide reasonable assurance that assets are safeguarded against loss or unauthorized use and to produce the records necessary for the preparation of financial information. There are limits inherent in all systems of internal control based on the recognition that the costs of such systems should be related to the benefits to be derived. We believe the corporation's systems provide this appropriate balance.

The control environment is complemented by the corporation's internal auditors, who perform extensive audits and evaluate the adequacy of and the adherence to these controls, policies and procedures. In addition, the corporation's independent public accountants have developed an understanding of our accounting and financial controls, and have conducted such tests as they consider necessary to support their report below.

The Board of Directors pursues its oversight role for the financial statements through the Audit Committee, which is composed solely of outside directors. The Audit Committee meets regularly with management, the corporate internal auditors and Arthur Andersen LLP, jointly and separately, to receive reports on management's process of implementation and administration of internal accounting controls, as well as auditing and financial reporting matters. Both Arthur Andersen LLP and the internal auditors have unrestricted access to the Audit Committee.

The corporation maintains high standards in selecting, training and developing personnel to help ensure that management's objectives of maintaining strong, effective internal controls and unbiased, uniform reporting standards are attained. We believe it is essential for the corporation to conduct its business affairs in accordance with the highest ethical practices as expressed in Sara Lee Corporation's Global Business Standards.

John H. Bryan

John H. Bryan
Chairman of the Board
and Chief Executive Officer

Judith A. Sprieser

Judith A. Sprieser
Senior Vice President
and Chief Financial Officer

assurance as to the quality of the resulting financial information only if the system is functioning properly. What, or who, makes sure the system is functioning properly? What happens when disagreements in judgment arise? Who referees to ensure that the estimates and judgments that are reflected in the financial statements are reasonable? In this section, we discuss a mechanism, developed over time, that attempts to ensure that the financial statements provide an accurate and fair presentation of a company's financial status.

Let's return to our landscaping example. You have determined that your annual salary is a fixed monthly amount plus an annual bonus based on the net income of the business. The better the business performs, the higher your pay. Many companies actually reward their top executives using similar incentive plans (though many of these incentive plans can become quite complex). Now, what is your incentive? Well, it seems pretty clear that your incentive is to report as high a net income figure as possible. The higher your company's net income, the higher your annual bonus.

How can you increase net income given your current level of operations? Since you are a person of integrity and honor, falsifying transactions (e.g., fraudulent financial reporting) is out of the question. One possibility is to review your estimates regarding the percentage of revenues to be recognized and the percentage of accounts receivable that may be uncollectible.

Recall from a previous section that we had two of our landscaping friends provide us with independent estimates of the percentage of completion on our condominium landscaping project. Suppose that one estimate was that the project was 50% complete. The other was that the project was 60% complete. Which would you select as being more accurate? Well, the 60% estimate would result in a higher net income, which would mean a higher year-end bonus this year. Also, using the 60% estimate would be reasonable because it was provided by an independent source.

You also examine your accounts receivable to determine what percentage of those receivables might be uncollectible in the future.[4] Since you are dealing with estimates about future events, there is no right answer. You estimate that uncollectible receivables could be anywhere from 2 to 4% of the existing Accounts Receivable balance. Should you split the difference and say 3%? You could, but why not say 2%? After all, 2% is a possible outcome, and if you use the estimate of 2%, net income will be higher, again resulting in a higher year-end bonus for you.

Financial statements are full of estimates and judgments. Here we have illustrated just two areas involving estimates—revenues and uncollectible accounts. The financial statements of large companies involve many estimates relating to the future life of equipment and buildings, the amount to be paid in the future for warranties on products and services, and the amount of future benefits to be paid to retirees, to name a few. You might expect all these estimates to average out. That is, sometimes those that have a favorable effect on net income are used, and sometimes those that have an unfavorable effect are used. If estimates were randomly chosen, this would probably happen. But remember that these estimates aren't randomly chosen. In the case of your landscaping business, you are choosing the estimates.

Suppose that in every case involving an estimate, you elected to present the estimate that was most favorable to the firm's net income. Your annual bonus would certainly look nice, but would the resulting financial statements provide a fair assessment of your company's financial performance? Maybe, maybe not.

As part owner[5] of the landscaping company, and with your compensation based on net income, you might have a tough time being objective when it comes to making estimates; you have an economic incentive to influence net income in a certain direction. But you also recognize the need to provide relevant and reliable financial information relating to the performance of the company.

As you wrestle with this issue of estimates in the financial statements, there is another issue to consider as well. We stated that an internal control system is designed to minimize the occurrence of errors and irregularities in the financial reporting process. While the system should not allow errors in posting or transactions to be fabricated, how do we know that the internal control system is running as designed? How can you obtain some assurance that errors, biased disagreements in judgment, and fraudulent financial reporting are not a part of your accounting system? In the next section, we discuss another major factor that ensures that financial information is presented with reliability and integrity.

to summarize

Because accounting involves estimates and judgment, management has an opportunity to influence the outputs of the accounting process. Managers of a business often have an incentive to provide financial statement information that appears as favorable as possible. While the vast majority of managers would not intentionally bias the financial statements, their incentives may cause them to influence the process.

---

4 As you will learn in Chapter 6, the estimate of uncollectible accounts receivable will affect the expense for the period, thereby affecting net income.

5 Recall that you own only part of the company. Your parents and the bank (we illustrated both of these possibilities) own the other part.

4

Describe the role of auditors and how their presence affects the integrity of financial statements.

THE ROLE OF AUDITORS IN THE ACCOUNTING PROCESS

Someone needs to check and make sure that the accounting system is running as designed and that the resulting financial statements fairly present the financial performance of the company. Auditors are that "someone." Auditors provide management (and stockholders) with some assurance that the internal control system is functioning properly and that the financial statements fairly represent the financial performance of the firm. Two types of auditors are typically employed by management—internal and external auditors.

Internal Auditors

internal auditors An independent group of experts (in controls, accounting, and operations) who monitor operating results and financial records, evaluate internal controls, assist with increasing the efficiency and effectiveness of operations, and detect fraud.

Most large organizations have a staff of **internal auditors**, an independent group of experts in controls, accounting, and operations. This group's major purpose is to monitor operating results and financial records, evaluate internal controls, assist with increasing the efficiency and effectiveness of operations, and even detect fraud. The internal audit staffs in some large organizations include over 100 individuals. The audit manager reports directly to the president (or other high-level executive officer) and to the audit committee of the board of directors. By performing independent evaluations of an organization's internal controls, the internal auditors are helping preserve integrity in the reporting process. Employees who know that internal auditors are reviewing operations and reports are less likely to manipulate records. Even if they do, their actions may be revealed by the work of the internal auditors.

Internal auditors' responsibilities vary considerably, depending upon the organization. Some internal audit staffs consist of only one or two employees who spend most of their time performing reviews of financial records or internal controls. Other organizations may have a large number of auditors who search for and investigate fraud, work to improve operational efficiency and effectiveness, and make sure their organization is complying with various laws and regulations.

Organizations that have a competent group of internal auditors generally have fewer financial reporting problems than do organizations that don't have internal auditors. An example of an industry that generally did not have effective internal audit staffs is the savings and loan industry, where many companies went bankrupt during the late 1980s. In many of those companies, managers who were committing fraud did not want internal auditors, who would have made it more difficult for management to manipulate financial statements.

External Auditors

external auditors Independent CPAs who are retained by organizations to perform audits of financial statements.

generally accepted auditing standards (GAAS) Auditing standards developed by the AICPA.

Probably the greatest safeguard in the financial reporting system in the United States is the requirement that firms have external audits. **External auditors** examine an organization's financial statements to determine if they are prepared and presented in accordance with generally accepted accounting principles and are free from material (significant) misstatement. External audits are performed by certified public accounting (CPA) firms. CPA audits are required by the Securities and Exchange Commission and the major stock exchanges for all companies whose stock is publicly traded. Even companies that are not public, however, often employ CPAs to perform audits of their financial statements. Banks and other lenders usually require audits, and audits can instill confidence in users of financial reports. In conducting audits, CPAs are required by **generally accepted auditing standards (GAAS)** to provide reasonable assurance that significant fraud or misstatement is not present in financial statements. Because CPAs cannot audit every transaction of an organization, and because detecting collusive management deception is sometimes impossible, it is not possible for auditors to guarantee that financial statements are "correct." Instead, they can only provide reasonable assurance that financial statements are "presented fairly." Even with audits, there are still a few occasions when major financial statement fraud is not detected.

CPA audits of financial statements have become very important in the United States because of the enormous size of many corporations. Because the stockholders, who own corporations, are usually different individuals from a company's management, audits provide comfort to these owners/investors that management is carrying out its stewardship function appropriately.

STOP & THINK What could auditors do to ensure that the financial reporting system is working properly? Be specific.

What Do Auditors Do?

While management has the primary responsibility of ensuring that the internal control system is functioning properly, internal auditors provide an independent assessment of how well the controls are working. External auditors usually study the internal control system to see if they can rely on it as they perform their audits. After all, if the internal control system is functioning correctly, it increases the likelihood that the resulting financial information is reliable. Often the external auditors will rely on the assessment of the internal controls made by the internal auditors.

Auditors gain confidence in the quality of the reporting process using several different processes: interviews, observation, sampling, confirmation, and analytical procedures. Several of these processes are used by both internal and external auditors, while some are used primarily by external auditors. Exhibit 5-2 provides a summary of these procedures and indicates who uses them most often. A brief discussion of each process then follows.

net work

Access the AICPA's Web site at http://www.aicpa.org and locate the section on Assurance Services. In addition to auditing, with what other assurance services are CPAs involved?

INTERVIEWS   Auditors *interview* employees to ensure that procedures are understood, proper documentation is being made, and proper authorization is being obtained. Through interviews, auditors identify potential weaknesses in the control system that will be examined using testing procedures.

OBSERVATION   *Observation* is done to verify compliance with procedures and to ensure that accounting records agree with physical records. For example, auditors in a bank will count the cash in a vault to ensure that recorded amounts agree with the actual cash on hand. Auditors will also verify the existence of inventory by doing a physical count of product. In addition to using observation to verify the existence of assets, auditors will also use observation to ensure that employees are complying with proper procedures.

SAMPLING   As mentioned previously, auditors cannot examine every transaction. Typically, they will select a *sample of transactions* for analysis. Based on the results of their analysis of the sample, they may conclude that the internal control procedures are being complied with, resulting in reliable financial information. Auditors may also conclude from the results that the internal control system is not reliable, resulting in further testing being required.

CONFIRMATION   Used primarily by external auditors, *confirmations* are used to verify the balances in accounts that result from transactions with outsiders. For example, customers are often contacted and asked to verify account balances. Banks are contacted to verify loan amounts, lines of credit, and other account balances. This procedure ensures that the balances listed on the financial statements do, in fact, exist.

ANALYTICAL PROCEDURES   *Analytical procedures* are used to provide guidance to external auditors as they attempt to identify areas that may deserve attention. Analytical procedures involve the use of such techniques as comparative ratio analysis (the same ratio analysis we have been doing in Chapters 2, 3, and 4). By comparing the results of ratio analysis from one period to the next, auditors may be able to identify areas where additional investigation may be appropriate.

exhibit 5-2   Audit Processes Used by Auditors

	Internal Auditors	External Auditors
Interviews	X	X
Observation	X	X
Sampling	X	X
Confirmation	—	X
Analytical procedures	—	X

THE SECURITIES AND EXCHANGE COMMISSION

5

Explain the role of the Securities and Exchange Commission in adding credibility to financial statements.

Securities and Exchange Commission (SEC) The government body responsible for regulating the financial reporting practices of most publicly owned corporations in connection with the buying and selling of stocks and bonds.

In addition to the role of independent internal and external auditors, the U.S. government plays a role in ensuring the integrity of financial information. The **Securities and Exchange Commission (SEC)** is responsible for ensuring that investors, creditors, and other financial statement users are provided with reliable information upon which to make investment decisions.

The SEC is an agency of the federal government.[6] The SEC was organized in the 1930s because of financial reporting and stock market abuses. One such abuse was price manipulation. It was not uncommon in the 1920s for stockbrokers or dealers to indulge in "wash sales" or "matched orders," in which successive buy and sell orders created a false impression of stock activity and forced prices up. This maneuver allowed those involved to reap huge profits before the price fell back to its true market level. Outright deceit by issuing false and misleading financial statements was another improper practice. The objective of these manipulative procedures was to make profits at the expense of unwary investors.

One classic example of a major fraud that may have contributed to the formation of the SEC is the Ivar Kreugar case. During the 1920s, the most widely held securities in the United States, and perhaps the world, were the stocks and bonds of KREUGAR & TOLL, INC., a Swedish match company. These securities were popular because they paid high dividends (over 20% annually) and were sold in small denominations, making them attractive to both large and small investors. Ivar Kreugar, known as the "Match King," became wealthy and famous as a financial genius, building his business into a multibillion-dollar international enterprise. In fact, Kreugar defrauded millions of investors by personally creating false and misleading financial statements. Instead of being paid out of profits, the dividends were paid out of capital that was raised by selling securities to unsuspecting investors. Eventually, the giant pyramid collapsed, Kreugar committed suicide, and Kreugar & Toll, Inc., went bankrupt. On the day Kreugar died, his company's stock was selling for $5 a share. Within weeks, it was selling for five cents a share. The American public was outraged, and some have speculated that this major fraud was instrumental in causing Congress to enact securities legislation to prevent such deception from happening again.

The Securities Act of 1933 requires most companies planning to issue new debt or stock securities to the public to submit a registration statement to the SEC for approval. The SEC examines these statements for completeness and adequacy before permitting companies to sell securities through securities exchanges. The Securities Exchange Act of 1934 requires all public companies to file detailed periodic reports with the SEC.

The SEC requires a considerable amount of information to be included in these filings. Among other things, a company must submit financial statements that have been audited by CPAs and that contain an opinion issued by those CPAs.

Of the many reports required by the SEC, the following have the most direct impact on financial reporting:

- *Registration statements.* These include various forms that must be filed and approved before a company can sell securities through the securities exchanges.
- *Form 10-K.* This report must be filed annually within 90 days after the close of each fiscal year. The report contains extensive financial information, including audited financial statements by independent CPAs. The 10-K also requires additional disclosure beyond that typically provided in the audited financial statements. Examples of additional information include the executive compensation of top management and the details of property, plant, and equipment transactions.
- *Form 10-Q.* This report must be filed quarterly for all publicly held companies. It contains certain financial information and requires a CPA's involvement.

Because the SEC has statutory power to mandate any reporting requirement it feels is needed, it has considerable influence in setting generally accepted accounting principles and disclosure

---

6 Most of the information on the SEC was taken from K. Fred Skousen, *An Introduction to the SEC*, 5th ed., South-Western Publishing Co., 1991, pp. 3–6.

requirements for financial statements. Generally, the SEC accepts the accounting pronouncements of the Financial Accounting Standards Board and other bodies such as the AICPA. In addition, the SEC has the power to establish rules for any CPA associated with audited financial statements submitted to the commission.

The SEC is given broad enforcement powers under the 1934 Act. If the rules of operation for stock exchanges prove to be ineffectual in implementing the requirements of the SEC, the SEC can alter or supplement them. The SEC can suspend trading of a company's stock for not more than 10 days (a series of orders has enabled the SEC to suspend trading for extended periods, however) and can suspend all trading on any exchange for up to 90 days. If substantive hearings show that the issuer failed to comply with the requirements of the securities laws, the SEC can "de-list" any security. Brokers and dealers can be prevented, either temporarily or permanently, from working in the securities market, and investigations can be initiated, if deemed necessary, to determine violations of any of the Acts or rules administered by the SEC.

The Effect of the 1934 Act on Independent Accountants

Accountants are involved in the preparation and review of a major portion of the reports and statements required by the 1934 Act. Accountants also can be censured, and their work is subject to approval by the SEC. The financial statements in the annual report to stockholders and in the 10-K report must be audited. In addition, accountants consult and assist in the preparation of the quarterly 10-Q reports and the other periodic reports.

More recently, the SEC under Chairman Arthur Levitt has initiated a major push to reduce the manipulation of reported earnings by a company's management. In a speech given on September 28, 1998, Mr. Levitt identified several techniques of what he called "Accounting Hocus Pocus." The SEC's objective is to prevent the manipulation of earnings and reduce fraudulent financial reporting by limiting the flexibility with which management is currently interpreting certain auditing and accounting standards.

---

to summarize

The Securities and Exchange Commission is an agency of the federal government whose purpose is to assist investors in public companies by regulating stock and bond markets and by requiring certain disclosures. Although the SEC has statutory authority to establish accounting principles, it basically accepts pronouncements of the FASB and AICPA as authoritative. Common reports required by the SEC are registration statements and Forms 10-K and 10-Q. Because the SEC can suspend trading and even de-list securities, it is a powerful organization that significantly influences financial reporting in the United States.

---

review of learning objectives

1 **Identify the types of problems that can appear in financial statements.** Three types of problems can affect financial statements: (1) Errors involve unintentional mistakes that can enter the accounting system at the transaction and journal entry stage or when journal entries are posted to accounts. These errors, when detected, are immediately fixed.

(2) Disagreements in judgment occur because of the differing incentives of those associated with the financial statements. While management may have an incentive to present an optimistic view of the company's performance, auditors have an incentive to ensure full disclosure of all relevant issues. These differing incentives typically result in financial statements that

fairly reflect the financial performance of the company. (3) Fraudulent financial reporting involves intentional misrepresentations in the financial statements. Safeguards are built into the accounting and reporting system to minimize the possibility that these problems will be reflected in the financial statements.

2 **Describe the safeguards employed within a firm to ensure that financial statements are free from problems.** Internal controls are safeguards built into an organization that help to protect assets and increase reliability of the accounting records. The three basic internal control structure categories are (1) the control environment, (2) the accounting systems, and (3) the control procedures. The five types of control procedures are (1) segregation of duties, (2) procedures for authorizations, (3) documents and records, (4) physical safeguards, and (5) independent checks. The control environment is comprised of such things as management's philosophy and operating style, the organizational structure, and the audit committee.

3 **Understand the need for monitoring by independent parties.** Because management has an incentive to portray the performance of the firm as positively as possible, there may be a tendency to be overly optimistic when it comes to making estimates and assessments regarding future events. As a result, there is a need for someone to independently evaluate the projections made by management to ensure that those projections, taken as a whole, result in financial statements that fairly reflect the financial performance of the business.

4 **Describe the role of auditors and how their presence affects the integrity of financial statements.** Most large organizations have internal auditors who are "independent" internal control experts. They examine the various functions and divisions of the business to evaluate internal controls, operating efficiency and effectiveness, and compliance with laws and company policy. Internal auditors usually report to top management or the board of directors and increase the reliability of financial statements by ensuring that internal controls function as they should.

External audits are required of most public companies by the Securities and Exchange Commission. By conducting audits of financial statements according to generally accepted auditing standards put into effect by the AICPA, external audits provide "reasonable assurance" that financial statements are presented fairly and are not materially misstated. External audits must be performed by CPAs who are licensed by the individual states in which they practice.

5 **Explain the role of the Securities and Exchange Commission in adding credibility to financial statements.** The SEC is the agency of the federal government charged with the responsibility of assisting investors by making sure they are provided with reliable information upon which to make investment decisions. The SEC was organized in the 1930s and requires certain periodic reports such as the Forms 10-Q and 10-K of companies that sell stock publicly in the United States. It adds credibility to financial statements by requiring independent audits, reviewing financial statements itself, and sanctioning firms that violate its standards.

key terms and concepts

accounting system 211

audit committee 211

control activities (procedures) 212

control environment 210

external auditors 218

Foreign Corrupt Practices Act (FCPA) 209

generally accepted auditing standards (GAAS) 218

independent checks 214

internal auditors 218

internal control structure 209

organizational structure 210

physical safeguards 213

Securities and Exchange Commission (SEC) 222

segregation of duties 212

discussion questions

1. How can a person tell whether an entry to an expense account is payment for a legitimate expenditure or a means of concealing a theft of cash?

2. How would it be possible to overstate revenues? What effect would an overstatement of revenues have on total assets?

3. What is the Foreign Corrupt Practices Act, and how is it important to financial reporting?
4. What are the major elements of a system of internal controls?
5. Identify five different types of control procedures.
6. How do internal auditors add to the credibility of financial statements?
7. What is the purpose of a financial statement audit by CPAs?
8. Do you believe that outside auditors (CPAs) who examine the financial statements of a company, while being paid by that company, can be truly independent?
9. The SEC requires companies to register with it when they sell stocks or bonds and also requires periodic reporting thereafter. Which of these reports, the initial registration statements or the subsequent periodic reports, do you believe would be scrutinized more closely by the SEC?
10. What do you suspect is the relationship between the FASB and the SEC?

discussion cases

CASE 5-1

AUDITING A COMPANY

Jerry Stillwell, the owner of a small company, asked Jones, a CPA, to conduct an audit of the company's financial statements. Stillwell told Jones that the audit needed to be completed in time to submit audited financial statements to a bank as part of a loan application. Jones immediately accepted the assignment and agreed to provide an auditor's report within two weeks.

Because Jones was busy, he hired two accounting students to perform the audit. After two hours of instruction, he sent them off to conduct the audit. Jones told the students not to spend time reviewing the internal controls, but instead to concentrate on proving the mathematical accuracy of the ledgers and other financial records.

The students followed Jones's instructions, and after 10 days, they provided the financial statements, which did not include notes. Jones reviewed the statements and prepared an auditor's report. The report did not refer to generally accepted accounting principles and contained no mention of any qualifications or disclosures. Briefly describe the problems with this audit.

CASE 5-2

AUDITING PRACTICE

A few years ago, the owners of an electronics wholesale company committed massive fraud by overstating revenues on the financial statements. They recorded three large fictitious sales near the end of the year to the retailers SILO, CIRCUIT CITY, and WAL-MART. The three transactions overstated revenues, receivables, and income by nearly $20 million. As part of the audit procedures, the external auditors sent requests for confirmation to the three stores to ensure that they did, in fact, owe the electronics company $20 million. In the meantime, the owners of the electronics company rented mailboxes in the cities where the three "customers" were headquartered, using names very similar to those of the three "customers." The requests for confirmation were sent to the mailboxes. The owners completed the confirmations and sent them back to the auditors, confirming the $20 million in receivables. With respect to the fraud, answer the following two questions:

1. What journal entries would the fraud perpetrators have entered into the financial records to overstate revenues?
2. Should the external auditors be held liable for not catching the fraud?

EXERCISE 5-1

ACCOUNTING ERRORS—TRANSACTION ERRORS

How would the following errors affect the account balances and the basic accounting equation, *Assets = Liabilities + Owners' Equity*? How do the misstatements affect income?

a. The purchase of a truck is recorded as an expense instead of an asset.
b. A cash payment on accounts receivable is received but not recorded.
c. Fictitious sales on account are recorded.
d. A clerk misreads a handwritten invoice for repairs and records it as $1,500 instead of $1,800.
e. Payment is received on December 31 for the next three months' rent and is recorded as revenue.

EXERCISE 5-2

ERRORS IN FINANCIAL STATEMENTS

The following financial statements are available for SHERWOOD REAL ESTATE COMPANY:

Balance Sheet

Assets			Liabilities		
Cash	$	1,300	Accounts payable	$ 100,000	
Receivable from sale			Mortgage payable	6,000,000	
of real estate		5,000,000	Total liabilities		$ 6,100,000
Interest receivable*		180,000			
Real estate properties		6,000,000	**Stockholders' Equity**		
			Capital stock	$ 10,000	
			Retained earnings	5,071,300	
			Total stockholders' equity		5,081,300
			Total liabilities and stock-		
Total assets		$11,181,300	holders' equity		$11,181,300

*Interest Receivable applies to Receivable from sale of real estate.

Income Statement

Gain on sale of real estate	$3,200,000
Interest income*	180,000
Total revenues	$3,380,000
Expenses	1,200,000
Net income	$2,180,000

*Interest Income applies to Receivable from sale of real estate.

Sherwood Company is using these financial statements to entice investors to buy stock in the company. However, a recent FBI investigation revealed that the sale of real estate was a fabricated transaction with a fictitious company that was recorded to make the financial statements look better. The sales price was $5,000,000 with a zero cash down payment and a $5,000,000 receivable. Prepare financial statements for Sherwood Company showing what its total assets, liabilities, stockholders' equity, and income really are with the sale of real estate removed.

EXERCISE 5-3

APPROPRIATENESS OF ACCOUNTING RULES

In the early 1990s, the top executive of a large oil refining company (based in New York) was convicted of financial statement fraud. One of the issues in the case involved the way the company accounted for its oil inventories. In particular, the company would purchase crude oil from exploration companies and then process the oil into finished oil products, such as jet fuel, diesel fuel, and so forth. Because there was a ready market for these finished products, as soon as the company purchased the crude oil, it would value its oil inventory at the selling prices of the finished products less the cost to refine the oil. Although the case involved fraud, the type of accounting used was also questioned because it allowed the company to recognize profit before the actual sale (and even refining) of the oil. Nevertheless, one of the large CPA firms attested to the use of this method. If you were the judge in this case, would you be critical of this accounting practice?

EXERCISE 5-4

INTERNAL CONTROL PROCEDURES

As an auditor, you have discovered the following problems with the accounting system control procedures of Jefferson Retailers. For each of the following occurrences, tell which of the five internal control procedures was lacking. Also, recommend how the company should change its procedures to avoid the problem in the future.

a. Jefferson Retailers' losses due to bad debts have increased dramatically over the past year. In an effort to increase sales, the managers of certain stores have allowed large credit sales to occur without review or approval.

b. An accountant hid his theft of $200 from the company's bank account by changing the monthly reconciliation. He knew the manipulation would not be discovered.

c. Steve Meyer works in the storeroom. He maintains the inventory records, counts the inventory, and has unlimited access to the storeroom. He occasionally steals items of inventory and hides the theft by including the value of the stolen goods in his inventory count.

d. Receiving reports are sometimes filled out days after shipments have arrived.

EXERCISE 5-5

INTERNAL AUDITING—STAFFING INTERNAL AUDITS

A manufacturing corporation recently reassigned one of its accounting managers to the internal audit department. He had successfully directed the western-area accounting office, and the corporation thought his skills would be valuable to the internal audit department. The director of the internal audit division knew of this individual's experience in the western-area accounting office and assigned him to audit that same office.

Should the internal auditor be assigned to audit the same office in which he recently worked? What problems could arise in this situation?

EXERCISE 5-6

INTERNAL AUDITING

Which of the following is not applicable to the internal audit function?

a. Deter or catch employee fraud.

b. Issue an opinion for investors regarding the reliability of the financial statements.

c. Be guided by its own set of professional standards.

d. Help to ensure that the accounting function is performed correctly and that the financial statements are prepared accurately.

EXERCISE 5-7

INTERNAL AUDITING—EXTERNAL AUDITOR'S RELIANCE ON INTERNAL AUDITORS

North, CPA, is planning an audit of the financial statements of General Company. In determining the nature, timing, and extent of the auditing procedures, North is considering General's internal audit function, which is staffed by Tyler.

1. In what ways may Tyler's work be relevant to North?

2. What factors should North consider and what inquiries should North make in deciding whether to rely on Tyler's work?

EXERCISE 5-8

ENSURING THE INTEGRITY OF FINANCIAL REPORTING

Three college seniors with majors in accounting are discussing alternative career plans. All three want to enter careers that will help to ensure the integrity of financial reporting. The first wants to become an internal auditor. She believes that by ensuring appropriate internal controls within a company, the financial statements will be reliable. The second wants to go to work in public accounting and perform external audits of companies. He believes that external auditors are independent and can make sure that financial statements are correct. The third student believes that neither choice will be adding much value to the integrity of financial statements because, in both cases, the auditors will be receiving their pay (either directly or indirectly) from the companies they audit. He believes the only way to make a real difference is to work for the Securities and Exchange Commission, using the "arm of government regulation" to force companies to issue appropriate financial statements and then punishing them (through jail sentences and large fines) when their financial statements are misleading. In your opinion, which of these three students will make the largest contribution toward ensuring integrity in the financial statements?

EXERCISE 5-9

EXTERNAL AUDITORS—PURPOSE OF AN AUDIT
What is the purpose of external auditors providing an opinion on a company's financial statements?

EXERCISE 5-10

AUDITING FINANCIAL STATEMENTS
The Utah Lakers professional basketball team has recently decided to sell stock and become a public company. In determining what it must do to file a registration statement with the SEC, the company realizes that it needs to have an audit opinion to accompany its financial statements. The company has recently approached two accounting students at a major university and asked them to "audit" its financial statements to be submitted to the SEC. Should the two accounting students accept the work and perform the audit?

EXERCISE 5-11

SECURITIES AND EXCHANGE COMMISSION—AUTHORITY TO SET ACCOUNTING STANDARDS
Which organization—the Securities and Exchange Commission, the American Institute of Certified Public Accountants, or the Financial Accounting Standards Board—has federal government authority to set accounting standards and reporting requirements? Some people have argued that all accounting rule making should be done by the federal government. Do you agree? Why or why not?

EXERCISE 5-12

SECURITIES AND EXCHANGE COMMISSION—ROLE OF THE SEC
Describe the role of the Securities and Exchange Commission and its influence on the practice of auditing.

EXERCISE 5-13

SECURITIES AND EXCHANGE COMMISSION—INFORMATION NEEDED FOR INVESTING
As an investor you are considering buying stock in a relatively new company. American Shipping, Ltd., has been in existence for 10 years and is now about to go public. The first stock offering will be listed on the New York Stock Exchange next week.

1. What kind of information would you like to know before investing in the company? Where can you find this information?
2. How does the SEC protect the securities market from companies that are fraudulent or in poor financial condition?
3. Besides stock market investors, what other parties might be interested in knowing financial data about companies?

EXERCISE 5-14

AUDITING NEGLIGENCE
A few years ago, the officers of PHAR-MOR, a discount retail chain, were convicted of issuing fraudulent financial statements. It was learned at the trial that the company overstated its inventory by moving inventory from store to store and counting the same inventory several times. For example, a case of Coca-Cola would be counted at one store and then moved to another store and counted again. In a separate civil trial, Phar-Mor's auditors were accused of performing negligent audits because they didn't catch these inventory movements. Do you believe that the external auditors were negligent in this case?

EXERCISE 5-15

SECURITIES AND EXCHANGE COMMISSION
Many people have argued that the purpose of the SEC is to protect investors. Some believe that the best way to do this is by preventing weak companies from issuing stock. Others say that the SEC should require full disclosure and then let the buyer beware. Which do you think is more appropriate: a preventive role or a disclosure role?

competency enhancement opportunities

▶ Analyzing Real Company Information
▶ International Case
▶ Ethics Case
▶ Writing Assignment

▶ The Debate
▶ Cumulative Spreadsheet Project
▶ Internet Search

The following additional assignments provide opportunities for students to develop critical thinking, ethical perspectives, oral and written communication skills, experience with electronic research, and teamwork through group and business activities.

▶ **ANALYZING REAL COMPANY INFORMATION**

• Analyzing 5-1 (Microsoft)
The 1999 annual report for MICROSOFT is included in Appendix A. Locate that annual report and consider the following questions:

1. With respect to the report of the external auditors to "the Board of Directors and Stockholders of Microsoft Corporation":
    a. Who is Microsoft's external auditor?
    b. How long after the end of Microsoft's fiscal year did the external auditor complete the audit?
2. With respect to the report of management concerning the financial statements:
    a. Who is responsible for the financial statements?
    b. After reading the paragraph on internal control, indicate whether you agree or disagree with the following statement: "The purpose of an internal control system is to ensure that all transactions are always recorded and that all assets are always completely safeguarded."
    c. After looking at the description of the members of the audit committee, do you think that Bill Gates is a member of that committee?

• Analyzing 5-2 (Circle K)
At one time, CIRCLE K was the second-largest convenience store chain in the United States (behind 7-ELEVEN). At its peak, Circle K, based in Phoenix, Arizona, operated 4,685 stores in 32 states. Circle K's rapid expansion was financed through long-term borrowing. Interest on this large debt, combined with increased price competition from convenience stores operated by oil companies, squeezed the profits of Circle K. For the fiscal year ended April 30, 1990, Circle K reported a loss of $773 million. In May 1990, Circle K filed for Chapter 11 bankruptcy protection. Subsequently, Circle K was taken over by TOSCO, a large independent oil company.

1. In the fiscal year ended April 30, 1989, Circle K experienced significant financial difficulty. Reported profits were down 74.5% from the year before. In the president's letter to the shareholders, Circle K explained that 1989 was a "disappointing" year and that management was seeking some outside company to come in and buy out the Circle K shareholders. How do you think all this bad news was reflected in the auditor's report accompanying the financial statements dated April 30, 1989?

2. As mentioned, Circle K reported a loss of $773 million for the year ended April 30, 1990. Just a week after the end of the fiscal year, the CEO was fired. One week after that, Circle K declared bankruptcy. The audit report was completed approximately two months later. How do you think the news of the bankruptcy was reflected in the auditor's report accompanying the financial statements dated April 30, 1990?

▷ INTERNATIONAL CASE

• *Do the Financial Statements Give a True and Fair View?*

SWIRE PACIFIC, LTD., based in Hong Kong, is one of the largest companies in the world. The primary operations of the company are in the region of Hong Kong, China, and Taiwan where it has operated for over 125 years. Swire operates CATHAY PACIFIC AIRWAYS and has extensive real estate holdings in Hong Kong. The 1996 auditor's report (prepared by PRICE WATERHOUSE) for Swire Pacific, dated March 14, 1997, read as follows (in part):

> An audit includes examination, on a test basis, of evidence relevant to the amounts and disclosures in the accounts. It also includes an assessment of the significant estimates and judgments made by the directors in the preparation of the accounts, and of whether the accounting policies are appropriate to the Company's and the Group's circumstances, consistently applied and adequately disclosed. . . .
>
> In our opinion the accounts give a true and fair view, in all material respects, of the state of affairs of the Company and the Group as at 31st December 1996. . . .

Although the concept of a "true and fair view" is not part of the auditor's terminology in the United States, it is used by auditors all over the world and is also discussed as part of International Accounting Standards (IAS). The "true and fair view" concept states that an auditor must make sure that the financial statements give an honest representation of the economic status of the company, even if the company violates generally accepted accounting principles in order to do so.

1. Review the opinion language in the auditor's report for MICROSOFT (see Appendix A). Does the audit report state unconditionally that Microsoft's financial statements are a fair representation of the economic status of the company?
2. Auditors in the United States concentrate on performing audits to ensure that financial statements are prepared in accordance with generally accepted accounting principles. What economic and legal realities in the United States would make it difficult for U.S. auditors to apply the "true and fair view" concept?

▷ ETHICS CASE

• *Blowing the Whistle on Former Partners*

On St. Patrick's Day in 1992, CHAMBERS DEVELOPMENT COMPANY, one of the largest landfill and waste management firms in the United States, announced that it had been engaging in improper accounting for years. Wall Street fear (over what this announcement implied about the company's track record of steady earnings growth) sent Chambers' stock price plunging by 62% in one day.

The improper accounting by Chambers had been discovered in the course of the external audit. The auditors found that $362 million in expenses had not been reported since Chambers first became a public company in 1985. If this amount of additional expense had been reported, it would have completely wiped out all the profit reported by Chambers since it first went public. The difficult part of this situation was that a large number of the financial staff working for Chambers were former partners in the audit firm performing the audit. These accountants had first worked as independent external auditors at Chambers, then were hired by Chambers, and subsequently were audited by their old partners.

What ethical and economic issues did the auditors of Chambers Development Company face as they considered whether to blow the whistle on their former partners?

WRITING ASSIGNMENT

• External Auditors

Visit or call a local CPA firm (or the local office of a multi-office CPA firm). Ask about career opportunities, the size of the firm's staff, who some of its major clients are, and other facts about the firm. Then, write a one-page summary of your visit.

THE DEBATE

• Who Needs Internal Control?

An internal control system is intended to ensure that all transactions are properly approved and recorded, that assets and records are safeguarded, and that operations run efficiently. As with any other system in a business, an internal control system costs money to operate.

Divide your group into two teams.

- One team represents the "Hire Honest and Smart" group. Prepare a two-minute oral presentation supporting the notion that if a company would focus on hiring only honest and smart employees, it would not need to spend money designing and operating an internal control system. Most of the functions of internal control are to prevent employees from stealing and to make it difficult for inept employees to commit costly mistakes.
- The other team represents the "No Trust" group. Prepare a two-minute oral presentation arguing that a company must set up a careful internal control system because, given the right opportunity and motive, any employee can turn into a thief. In addition, a company cannot rely on the good intentions of employees to keep the business running smoothly. Instead, top management must design systems that will keep things running smoothly in spite of the mistakes of employees.

CUMULATIVE SPREADSHEET PROJECT

This spreadsheet assignment is a continuation of the spreadsheet assignment given in Chapter 2. If you completed that spreadsheet, you have a head start on this one.

1. Refer back to the financial statement numbers for Handyman Company for 2003 [given in part (1) of the Cumulative Spreadsheet Project assignment in Chapter 2]. Using the balance sheet and income statement created with those numbers, create spreadsheet cell formulas to compute and display values for the following ratios:

  a. Current ratio
  b. Debt ratio
  c. Asset turnover
  d. Return on equity

2. To observe the impact that errors and fraudulent transactions can have on the financial statements, determine what the ratios computed in (1) would have been if (1) each of the following transactions was recorded as described and (2) the transaction was recorded correctly. Treat each transaction independently, meaning that before determining the impact of each new transaction you should reset the financial statement values to their original amounts. Each of the hypothetical transactions is assumed to occur on the last day of the year.

  a. Created receivables by creating fictitious sales of $140 all on account.
  b. Purchased $80 of inventory on account but incorrectly increased the property, plant, and equipment account instead of increasing Inventory.
  c. Borrowed $60 with a short-term payable. The liability was incorrectly recorded as Long-Term Debt.
  d. An inventory purchase on account in the amount of $90 was not recorded until the next year.

▶ **INTERNET SEARCH**

• Phar-Mor

Access the Web site of PHAR-MOR at http://www.pharmor.com. Sometimes Web addresses change, so if this address doesn't work, access the Web site for this textbook (http://albrecht.swcollege.com) for an updated link.

Once you've gained access to the site, answer the following questions:

1. When was Phar-Mor founded? How many stores does the company have today? In how many states is the company doing business?
2. Locate Phar-Mor's most recent press release. What is the topic of the press release?
3. Review Phar-Mor's annual report to determine any lingering effects of the fraud that was revealed by the company in 1992.
4. Evaluate Phar-Mor's current financial position as compared to 1999.

comprehensive problem 1-5

As a recently hired accountant for a small business, SMC, Inc., you are provided with last year's balance sheet, income statement, and post-closing trial balance to familiarize yourself with the business.

SMC, Inc.
Balance Sheet
December 31, 2002

Assets

Cash	$34,500	
Accounts receivable	25,000	
Inventory	10,000	
Supplies	200	
Total assets		$69,700

Liabilities and Stockholders' Equity

Liabilities:

Accounts payable	$12,000	
Salaries payable	1,000	
Income taxes payable	3,675	
Total liabilities		$16,675

Stockholders' equity:

Capital stock (10,000 shares outstanding)	$25,000	
Retained earnings	28,025	
Total stockholders' equity		53,025
Total liabilities and stockholders' equity		$69,700

SMC, Inc.
Income Statement
For the Year Ended December 31, 2002

Sales revenue	$110,000	
Rent revenue	1,000	
Total revenues		$111,000
Less cost of goods sold		60,000
Gross margin		$ 51,000
Less operating expenses:		
Supplies expense	$ 400	
Salaries expense	22,000	
Miscellaneous expense	4,100	26,500
Income before taxes		$ 24,500
Less income taxes		3,675
Net income		$ 20,825
Earnings per share ($20,825 ÷ 10,000 shares)		$ 2.08

SMC, Inc.
Post-Closing Trial Balance
December 31, 2002

	Debits	Credits
Cash	$34,500	
Accounts Receivable	25,000	
Inventory	10,000	
Supplies	200	
Accounts Payable		$12,000
Salaries Payable		1,000
Income Taxes Payable		3,675
Capital Stock		25,000
Retained Earnings		28,025
Totals	$69,700	$69,700

You are also given the following information that summarizes the business activity for the current year, 2003.

a. Issued 5,000 additional shares of capital stock for $10,000 cash.
b. Borrowed $5,000 on January 2, 2003, from Downtown Bank as a long-term loan. Interest for the year is $500, payable on January 2, 2004.
c. Paid $3,600 cash on November 1 to lease a truck for one year.
d. Received $1,200 on November 1 from a tenant for six months' rent.
e. Paid $600 on October 1 for a one-year insurance policy.
f. Purchased $500 of supplies for cash.
g. Purchased inventory for $100,000 on account.
h. Sold inventory for $150,000 on account; cost of the merchandise sold was $80,000.
i. Collected $120,000 cash from customers' accounts receivable.
j. Paid $70,000 cash for inventories purchased during the year.
k. Paid $25,000 for sales reps' salaries, including $1,000 owed at the beginning of 2003.
l. No dividends were paid during the year.
m. The income taxes payable for the year were paid. Income taxes are based on a 15% corporate tax rate.
n. For adjusting entries, all prepaid expenses are initially recorded as assets, and all unearned revenues are initially recorded as liabilities.
o. At year-end, $150 worth of supplies are on hand.
p. At year-end, an additional $5,000 of sales salaries are owed, but have not yet been paid.

You are asked to do the following:

1. Journalize the transactions for the current year, 2003, using the accounts listed on the financial statements and other appropriate accounts (you may omit explanations).
2. Set up T-accounts and enter the beginning balances from the December 31, 2002, post-closing trial balance for SMC. Post all current year journal entries to the T-accounts.
3. Journalize and post any necessary adjusting entries at the end of 2003. (Hint: Items b, c, d, e, m, o, and p require adjustment.)
4. After the adjusting entries are posted, prepare a trial balance, a balance sheet, and an income statement for 2003. (Hint: Income before income taxes should equal $39,600.)
5. Journalize and post closing entries for 2003 and prepare a post-closing trial balance.
6. Using the DuPont framework, compute the return on equity for SMC for 2002 and 2003.
7. **Interpretive Question:** What is your overall assessment of the financial health of SMC, Inc.?

part **f2**

Operating Activities

Selling a Product or a Service

chapter

f6

learning objectives After studying this chapter, you should be able to:

1 Understand the three basic types of business activities: operating, investing, and financing.

2 Use the two revenue recognition criteria to decide when the revenue from a sale or service should be recorded in the accounting records.

3 Properly account for the collection of cash and describe the business controls necessary to safeguard cash.

4 Record the losses resulting from credit customers who do not pay their bills.

5 Evaluate a company's management of its receivables by computing and analyzing appropriate financial ratios.

6 Match revenues and expenses by estimating and recording future warranty and service costs associated with a sale.

expanded material

7 Reconcile a checking account.

8 Understand how receivables can be used by a company to get cash immediately.

9 Account for the impact of changing exchange rates on the value of accounts receivable denominated in foreign currencies.

Jerry Yang was born in Taiwan in 1968. His father died when he was just two, so Jerry and his brother were raised by their mother, an English professor at a university in Taipei. Jerry's mother moved the family to San Jose, California, in 1978. In spite of what he calls a "very short attention span," Jerry was an excellent student—he was valedictorian of his high school class, and he completed his bachelor's and master's degrees in electrical engineering at Stanford University in a total of just four years.[1]

David Filo was born in Wisconsin in 1966. He describes his parents as "hippie wannabes," who moved their family to Moss Bluff, Louisiana, to join a commune. David eventually left the commune to attend Tulane University where he studied computer engineering. David then went to Stanford as a graduate student, working part-time as a teaching assistant. As luck would have it, one of his students was Jerry Yang. Jerry and David's friendship was strengthened when they both went on a six-month academic exchange program to Japan in 1992.

In 1993, Jerry and David were supposed to be working on their Ph.D. theses in computer-aided design at Stanford. Instead, they found themselves spending more and more research time surfing through the incredible amount of information available on the newly created "World Wide Web." Their first project was to write software that scanned the Web for NBA player statistics. The first Web site that Jerry designed was dedicated to another of his sports passions—sumo wrestling.

Jerry and David quickly learned that the key to surfing the vast quantities of information on the Web was to be able to organize the information. They compiled a list of their favorite Web sites, which they e-mailed to friends and posted on the Web under the title "Jerry's Guide to the World Wide Web." This title was a bit unwieldy, so they came up with the shorthand title "YAHOO!" Jerry and David liked the irreverent, lively tone of the name; they then went back and developed a "formal" title to fit the Yahoo! acronym: Yet Another Hierarchical Officious Oracle.

By 1994, thousands were using Yahoo! to access information on the Web. In fact, the demand was so great that Jerry and David were spending 20-plus hours a day on their "hobby." In addition, the resources of the Stanford computer network were being taxed by Yahoo! users, and university officials asked Jerry and David to find another computer to host their service. Interest in hosting the Yahoo! service was high, and representatives from MCI WORLDCOM, AOL, and NETSCAPE visited Jerry and David in their disheveled 10-by-10-foot work space in a trailer on the Stanford campus. Jerry and David accepted Netscape's offer of help, and the Yahoo! service moved over to the Netscape computer network in 1995.

In March 1995, Jerry and David were finally convinced that their Web search hobby could actually be turned into a business. They accepted a $4 million investment from SEQUOIA, a venture capital firm. Realizing that they lacked business expertise, they chose Tim Koogle, another Stanford graduate who was running a $400 million high-tech equipment company, to join them in running their company. In essence, Jerry and David hired Koogle to be their boss. In Yahoo!'s organizational hierarchy, Koogle bears the title of chief executive officer (CEO), and Jerry and David are officially titled the "Chief Yahoos." This team has turned Yahoo! into the most recognized name among Internet companies. As of June 2000, Yahoo! had a total market value of $76 billion.

So, how does Yahoo! make money? Throughout its history, Yahoo! has generated almost all of its revenue through the sale of advertising space on its Web pages. For example, in 1999, 90.4% of Yahoo!'s $588.6 million in revenue was generated through advertising. Yahoo!'s advertising fees are described as follows in the company's 1998 annual report:

The Company's standard rates for banner advertising currently range from approximately $6.00 per thousand impressions for run of network [general advertising] to approxi-

> **fyi**
>
> Jonathan Swift coined the word *yahoo* in his book *Gulliver's Travels*. The "yahoos" were savage humans who lived in a land where horses were the dominant species. Swift, a noted satirist, used the term *yahoo* to illustrate how easy it is to justify committing atrocities against people once they are categorized with an unfavorable label.

setting the stage

1 The Yahoo! background material was obtained from the following sources: Beverly Schuch, "Yang and Filo: Chief Yahoos!" *CNN Pinnacle*, November 14, 1999, Transcript #99111400V39; and Brent Schlender, "How a Virtuoso Plays the Web," *Fortune*, March 6, 2000, p. F-79.

mately $90.00 per thousand impressions for highly targeted audiences and properties.

The key factor in generating this advertising revenue is maintaining high traffic through its Web sites. In March 2000, Yahoo!'s traffic averaged 625 million page views per day, originating from a pool of 145 million different Yahoo! users worldwide. Yahoo!'s growth in annual revenues from 1995 through 1999 averaged 353% per year, as illustrated in Exhibit 6-1. The challenge facing Yahoo! is to expand its revenue base from advertising into the exploding realm of e-commerce. For example, Yahoo! plans to significantly increase the amount of revenue it generates through commissions on e-commerce transactions facilitated through services such as Yahoo! Shopping and Yahoo! Auctions.

For Internet companies such as Yahoo!, investors are extremely interested in the amount of revenue reported in the income statement. In fact, in the gold rush of e-commerce, investors are more concerned about how much e-business a company is doing than about whether the company is able to generate immediate profits. The amount of revenue reported by an Internet company is a key indicator of how large the company is in the Internet economy. For example, as of 1999, AMAZON.COM had never reported a profit (revenue minus expenses) in its history; the company lost $720 million in 1999 alone. Yet, because of the $1.6 billion in revenue it reported in 1999, Amazon.com is viewed as a major player in the burgeoning Internet economy. As a result, Amazon.com had a market value of $16.4 billion in May 2000.

The amount of revenue reported by traditional companies, such as GENERAL MOTORS, WAL-MART, and GENERAL ELECTRIC, is also of interest to investors because increased revenues almost always lead to increased profits. Consequently, there is sometimes great pressure on companies to report as much revenue as possible. To balance this pressure, accounting rules have been established to govern exactly when it is appropriate for a company to report the revenue from a transaction in the income statement. These accounting rules are not just conceptual toys for accountants; investor

---

exhibit 6 - 1   Growth in Yahoo! Revenue: 1995–1999

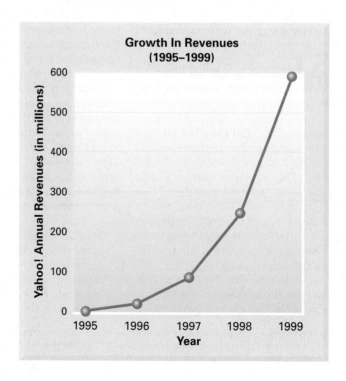

concern about whether MICROSTRATEGY, *a software company, was correctly applying the accounting rules associated with revenue caused the company's stock price to drop from $333 per share on March 10, 2000, to $22.25 per share just 10 weeks later.*[2]

In this chapter, you will study the accounting rules governing the proper recognition of revenue. You will also learn how to account for cash collections and how to handle customer accounts that are uncollectible. Selling goods and services, collecting the cash, and handling customer accounts are fundamental to the operation of any business. Accordingly, properly recording these activities is fundamental to the practice of accounting.

MAJOR ACTIVITIES OF A BUSINESS

1

Understand the three basic types of business activities: operating, investing, and financing.

In the first five chapters, you were introduced to the accounting environment, the basic financial statements, and the accounting cycle (the way business transactions are entered into the accounting records). That material was necessary for you to understand some basic terminology and procedures used in accounting. Accounting has often been called the language of business. By studying the first five chapters, you should now be somewhat familiar with this new business language.

With the basics behind us, it is now time to use accounting to understand how businesses work, how the various activities of business are accounted for, and how businesses report their operating results to investors. The activities of most businesses can be divided into three groups:

- Operating activities
- Investing activities
- Financing activities

operating activities Transactions and events that involve selling products or services and incurring the necessary expenses associated with the primary activities of the business.

Operating activities involve selling products or services, buying inventory for resale, and incurring and paying for necessary expenses associated with the primary activities of the business. The operating activities of a motel, for example, would include renting rooms (the selling activity); buying soap, shampoo, and other supplies to operate the motel; and incurring and paying for electricity, heat, water, cleaning, television and telephone service, and salaries and taxes of workers. The operating activities of a grocery store would include buying produce, meats, canned goods, and other items for resale; selling products to customers; and incurring and paying for expenses associated with the store's operations such as utilities, salaries, and taxes. The operating activities of YAHOO! include selling advertising space on the company's Web pages, paying employees to maintain the Yahoo! system and to develop new software, and paying to advertise the Yahoo! brand name on TV and in magazines. It is easy to identify operating activities because they are always associated with the primary purpose of a business.

A motel deals with operating activities on a daily basis when renting rooms, buying supplies, and paying utility expenses.

In this chapter we cover the operating activities for selling products and services, the recognition of revenues from those sales, accounting for cash, and problems associated with collecting receivables arising from sales. In Chapter 7 we examine the purchase of inventory for resale to customers and the necessary accounting procedures. In Chapter 8 we conclude our discussion of operating activities by considering other operating expenses and how revenues and expenses are combined to compute the net income of a business. Incurring and paying for operating expenses such

2 Michael Schroeder, "SEC Widens MicroStrategy Investigation," *The Wall Street Journal*, May 24, 2000, p. C1.

as employee compensation, insurance, advertising, research and development, and income taxes are also covered in Chapter 8.

Investing activities involve the purchase of assets for use in the business. The assets purchased as part of investing activities include property, plant, and equipment, as well as financial assets such as investments in stocks and bonds of other companies. Investing activities are distinguishable from operating activities because they occur less frequently and the amounts involved in each transaction are usually quite large. For example, while most businesses buy and sell inventory or services to customers on a daily basis (operating activities), only rarely do they buy and sell buildings, equipment, and stocks and bonds of other companies. It is important to note that buying inventory for resale is an operating activity, not an investing activity. Investing activities are covered in Chapters 9 and 12.

Financing activities involve raising money to finance a business by means other than operations. In addition to earning money through profitable operations, there are two other ways to fund a business: (1) money can be borrowed from creditors (debt financing), or (2) money can be raised by selling stock or ownership interests in the business to investors (equity financing). Debt financing is the subject of Chapter 10, while equity financing will be discussed in Chapter 11.

Once you have studied Chapters 6 through 12, you will have a good understanding of how businesses operate, invest, and are financed. That knowledge should be helpful in the future if you own your own business, invest in companies as a stockholder, work for a financial institution (or other lender of funds), or work in any position where a knowledge of business is essential.

After studying the operating, investing, and financing activities of a business, you will be ready to combine your knowledge of how businesses operate with the basic accounting knowledge you gained from Chapters 1 through 5. To do this, we will study in detail the statement of cash flows, which is structured around the three activities of a business (Chapter 13). You will discover that preparation of a statement of cash flows requires a sound understanding of the balance sheet and the income statement, as well as a good grasp of how the activities of a business tie together. Exhibit 6-2 provides a graphical road map of the business and reporting activities that will be discussed in the subsequent eight chapters.

Although Chapters 6 through 12 are organized around business activities, it is important to understand how these activities relate to the basic financial statements. To help you understand these relationships, at the beginning of each of the next seven chapters, we present basic financial statements that highlight the accounts that will be covered in that chapter. As you can

investing activities Transactions and events that involve the purchase and sale of property, plant, equipment, and other assets not generally held for resale.

financing activities Transactions and events whereby resources are obtained from, or repaid to, owners (equity financing) and creditors (debt financing).

e x h i b i t   6 - 2   Major Activities of a Business

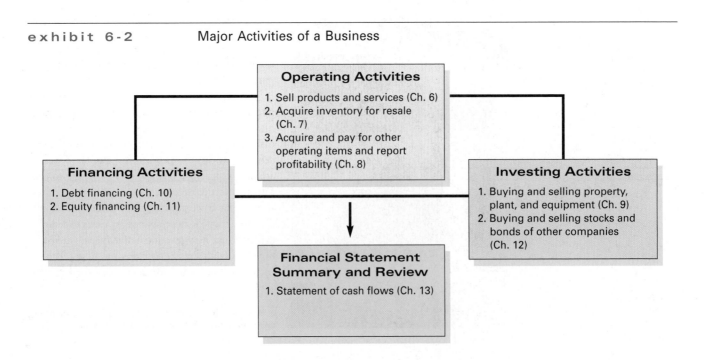

exhibit 6-3   Financial Statement Items Covered in This Chapter

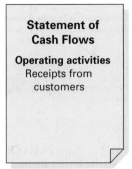

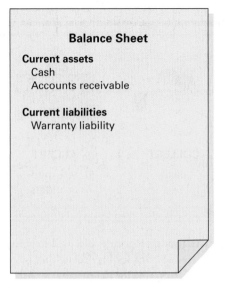

see in Exhibit 6-3, Cash, Accounts Receivable, and Warranty Liability on the balance sheet; Sales, Bad Debt Expense, and Warranty Expense on the income statement; and Receipts from Customers on the statement of cash flows are covered in Chapter 6.

to summarize

Activities of a business can be divided into (1) operating activities, (2) investing activities, and (3) financing activities. Operating activities involve selling products or services, buying inventory for resale, and incurring and paying for necessary expenses associated with the primary activities of a business. Investing activities include purchasing assets for use in the business and making investments in such items as stocks and bonds. Financing activities include raising money to finance a business by means other than operations.

2

Use the two revenue recognition criteria to decide when the revenue from a sale or service should be recorded in the accounting records.

RECOGNIZING REVENUE

The operations of a business revolve around the sale of a product or a service. MCDONALD'S sells fast food; MICROSOFT sells software and continuing customer support; BANK OF AMERICA loans money and sells financial services; YAHOO! sells advertising space on its Web pages. Just as the sale of a product or service is at the heart of any business, proper recording of the revenue from sales and services is fundamental to the practice of accounting. A simple time line illustrating the business issues involved with a sale is given in Exhibit 6-4.

Consideration of this time line raises a number of very interesting accounting questions:

- When should revenue be recognized—when the initial order is placed, when the good or service is provided, when the cash is collected, or later, when there is no longer any chance that the customer will return the product or demand a refund because of faulty service?

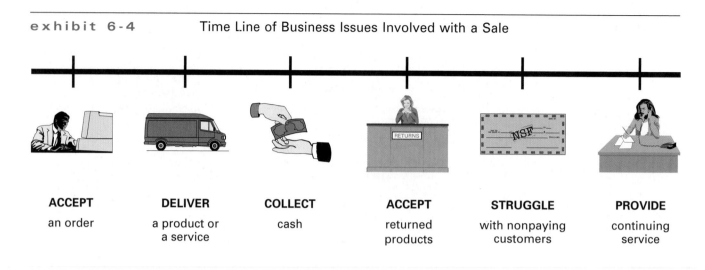

ACCEPT	DELIVER	COLLECT	ACCEPT	STRUGGLE	PROVIDE
an order	a product or a service	cash	returned products	with nonpaying customers	continuing service

- What accounting procedures are used to manage and safeguard cash as it is collected?
- How do you account for bad debts, that is, customers who don't pay their bills?
- How do you account for the possibility that sales this year may obligate you to make warranty repairs and provide continuing customer service for many years to come?

The following sections will address these accounting issues, beginning with the important question of when to recognize revenue.

When Should Revenue Be Recognized?

revenue recognition The process of recording revenue in the accounting records; occurs after (1) the work has been substantially completed and (2) cash collection is reasonably assured.

Revenue recognition is the phrase that accountants use to refer to the recording of a sale through a journal entry in the formal accounting records. Revenue is usually recognized when two important criteria have been met:

1. The work has been substantially completed (the company has done something), and
2. Cash, or a valid promise of future payment, has been received (the company has received something in return).

As a practical matter, most companies record sales when goods are shipped to customers. Credit sales are recognized as revenues before cash is collected, and revenue from services is usually recognized when the service is performed, not necessarily when cash is received.

To illustrate, we will assume that on a typical business day Farm Land Products sells 30 sacks of fertilizer for cash and 20 sacks on credit, all at $10 per sack. Given these data, the $500 of revenue is recorded as follows:

Cash	300	
Accounts Receivable	200	
Sales Revenue		500

Sold 30 sacks of fertilizer for cash and 20 sacks on credit.

Although the debit entries are made to different accounts, the credit entry for the full amount is to a revenue account. Thus, accrual-basis accounting requires the recognition of $500 in revenue instead of the $300 that would be recognized if the focus were merely on cash collection.

This example is a simple illustration of how sales are recorded and revenue is recognized. In reality, sales transactions are usually more complex, involving such things as uncertainty about exactly when the transaction is actually completed and whether a valid promise of payment has actually been received from the customer. These difficulties are compounded by the fact that companies often have an understandable desire to report revenue as soon as possible in order to enhance their reported performance and make it easier to get loans or attract investors. The discussion below will further examine the two revenue recognition criteria (work done and cash collectible) to see how accountants apply these rules to ensure that reported revenue fairly reflects the economic performance of a business.

Application of the Revenue Recognition Criteria

The Farm Land example was used to illustrate a straightforward case of revenue recognition at the time a sale is made. The Farm Land customers bought $500 worth of fertilizer, paying $300 cash and promising to pay $200 later; the $500 of revenue was recognized immediately. But what if the terms of the sale had also required Farm Land to deliver the fertilizer to the customers at no extra charge? In this case, proper application of the "work done" revenue recognition criterion would require that the revenue not be recorded until actual delivery had taken place. Alternatively, assume that the fertilizer sale was accompanied by a guarantee that, within 30 days, customers could return the unused portion of fertilizer for a full refund. If very few customers ever seek a refund, revenue should still be recognized at the time of sale. But, for example, if over 70% of fertilizer customers later seek refunds, the "cash collectible" revenue recognition criterion suggests that no revenue should be recognized until the completion of the 30-day return period; Farm Land then becomes reasonably assured of the amount of cash it will collect from the $500 in sales. This situation illustrates the need for accountants to exercise professional judgment and account for the economic reality of a transaction instead of blindly relying on technical legal rules about whether a sale has taken place. Other examples of the application of the revenue recognition criteria are given below.

YAHOO! As mentioned in the opening scenario of this chapter, Yahoo! derives most of its revenue from the sale of banner advertising space on its Web pages. In 1998, Yahoo!'s standard rates ranged from 0.6 cents per "impression" (the appearance of an advertisement on a page viewed by a user) for general markets to 9 cents per impression for more focused markets. In general, Yahoo! recognizes advertising revenue as the impressions occur. This revenue recognition practice makes sense if Yahoo! is reasonably certain of collecting payment for these impressions because Yahoo! has completed its work of providing the impressions. Yahoo! often guarantees an advertiser a minimum number of impressions. To the extent that the minimum guaranteed impressions are not met as of the date the financial statements are prepared, Yahoo! delays recognizing the advertising revenue until the guaranteed number of impressions is reached.

STOP & THINK As you might expect, not all software companies support this revenue recognition practice; they would prefer to recognize all of the revenue from a software sale immediately at the time of the sale. Microsoft, on the other hand, has been very supportive of the rule. Why do you think Microsoft supports the accounting rule that many other software firms oppose?

MICROSOFT The nature of the computer software industry presents several sticky revenue recognition issues. The installation of software and the promise of software upgrades require software companies to consider when the earnings process is substantially complete. Are the revenue recognition criteria satisfied at the point of sale, when the software is installed, or after promised upgrades are delivered? Microsoft recognizes a portion (80% for the Office 97 software) of the software price as revenue immediately upon delivery of the software to you. The rest of the software price is recognized as revenue gradually over time as the technical support service is provided.

BOEING BOEING recognizes revenue from commercial aircraft sales at the time the aircraft is delivered to the airline. For example, in 1999 Boeing recognized revenue from the delivery of 620 commercial aircraft, including 320 737s. In contrast, many of Boeing's government contracts require years of work before any product is delivered. If Boeing did not recognize any revenue during this extended production period, its economic activity for that period would be understated. Thus, the accounting rules allow Boeing to recognize revenue piecemeal as it reaches "scheduled performance milestones." This type of "pro-

Worried about Revenues! Today the to-bacco industry faces an unprecedented antismoking onslaught. An increasing number of lawsuits are alleging that smoking, and even secondhand smoke, causes cancer and other diseases and that the tobacco companies are at fault because their sales practices get people hooked on addictive drugs. (By the way, if you wish to read a careful assessment of the health risks associated with cigarettes, read the financial reports of the tobacco companies. By federal law, these reports must be provided to all interested investors, and, to ensure that investors are not mis-led, the Securities and Exchange Commission monitors these disclosures to make sure that they are not overly optimistic. Accordingly, these financial statement disclosures contain a much more evenhanded view than do most public statements on this controversial issue.) Although they are very large and extremely profitable, the tobacco companies are worried about future revenues. They are concerned that antismoking activity will result in fewer smokers and fewer sales. As a result, the big tobacco companies have been diversifying into other businesses, so that now a significant amount of their revenues comes from nontobacco sales. For example, two large tobacco companies now own the following:

portional performance" technique is commonly used to recognize revenue from transactions that extend over a long time period, such as for highway construction projects or season tickets for a professional sports team.

RENT-A-CENTER   RENT-A-CENTER operates 2,440 rent-to-own stores in the United States under both its own name and the name "ColorTyme." Customers rent furniture, VCRs, and other consumer goods under an agreement giving them ownership of the item if they continue to make their payments for the entire rental period. Rent-to-own stores attract customers who cannot afford the outright purchase of consumer goods and who anticipate difficulty in receiving credit through normal channels. Thus, a big concern for Rent-A-Center is collecting the full amount of cash due under a rental contract. In fact, Rent-A-Center states that only about 25% of its customers complete the full term of their agreement. With such a high likelihood of customers stopping payments on their rental agreements, Rent-A-Center recognizes revenue from a specific contract only gradually as the cash is actually collected.

f y i

According to generally accepted auditing standards, auditors are often required to confirm Accounts Receivable balances directly with the company that supposedly owes the money. This can provide an independent check on the existence of the receivables.

CENDANT   Discount-club retailers, such as SAM'S CLUB, are an increasing presence in the market. In 1999, for example, Sam's Club locations had total sales of $24.8 billion. The revenue recognition issue with these clubs is when to recognize the revenue from the up-front membership fees. In 1998, a dispute about the accounting for membership fees exploded in the face of CENDANT, which markets consumer goods and travel services to its members. Cendant had been recognizing its membership fees evenly over the 12-month membership period. However, the Securities and Exchange Commission ruled that, because members can cancel at any time and get their money back, Cendant should not recognize any revenue until the end of the membership period. The change caused Cendant to revise its reported 1997 results from a net income of $55.4 million to a net loss of $217.2 million. The uproar over this change caused the company's market value to plummet by $20 billion.

	Philip Morris	**Loews**
Major Cigarette Brands	Marlboro	Newport
	Benson & Hedges	Maverick
	Merit	Kent
	Virginia Slims	True
	Basic	Old Gold
Other Major Businesses	Post Cereals	14 hotels
and Products	Jell-O	Diamond Offshore Drilling
	Kool-Aid	CNA Financial
	Oscar Mayer	Bulova
	Miller Beer	
	Kraft	
1999 Revenues (billions)	$78.6	$21.5
% of Revenue from Tobacco Sales	60%	18.9%

Sources: 1999 Form 10-K filings by Philip Morris and Loews. In addition to these two tobacco companies, R.J. Reynolds Tobacco was, until 1999, part of the same company as Nabisco. Those two have now been split.

STOP & THINK Many colleges and universities prepare financial statements that are released to the public. When do you think a college or university should recognize revenue from student tuition?

As mentioned initially, the accounting for most sales transactions is straightforward—the revenue is recognized when the sale is made. However, as illustrated by the examples in this section, when the "work" associated with a sale extends over a significant period of time, or when cash collectibility is in doubt, the accountant must use professional judgment in applying the revenue recognition criteria to determine the proper time to record the sale.

Properly recognizing revenue is made more difficult by the fact that companies often have an understandable desire to report revenue as soon as possible. For example, for a company that is applying for a large loan or making an initial public offering of stock, it is critical that reported revenue, and thus reported net income, be as high as possible. In addition, company managers are often scrambling to make revenue or profit targets. In many cases, the managers' bonuses depend on whether these targets are met. Accordingly, managers often have great interest in making sure that revenue is recognized this year rather than waiting until next year. Receivables and revenue continue to be ripe areas for abuse or outright fraud because the associated accounting journal entry is so temptingly easy to make: debit Accounts Receivable and credit Revenue.

to summarize

Revenue is recognized when the work is done and when cash collectibility is reasonably assured. The entries to record revenue from the sale of merchandise or from the performance of a service involve debits to Cash or Accounts Receivable and credits to Sales Revenue or Service Revenue.

3

Properly account for the collection of cash and describe the business controls necessary to safeguard cash.

CASH COLLECTION

Recall the Farm Land Products example in which fertilizer was sold, partially for cash and partially on credit. Farm Land recorded the sales as follows:

Cash.	300	
Accounts Receivable	200	
Sales Revenue		500
Sold 30 sacks of fertilizer for cash and 20 sacks on credit.		

Subsequent collection of the $200 accounts receivable is recorded as follows:

Cash.	200	
Accounts Receivable		200
Collected cash for $200 credit sale.		

Note that Sales Revenue is not credited again when the cash is collected; the revenue was already recognized when the sale was made.

The following T-accounts show that the net result of these two transactions is an increase in Cash and Sales Revenue of $500.

	Cash		**Accounts Receivable**		**Sales Revenue**	
Original sale	300		200			500
Collection of account	200			200		
Final balances	500					500
	To balance sheet				To income statement	

These two entries illustrate simple sales and collection transactions. Many companies, however, offer sales discounts and must deal with merchandise returns. The accounting for discounts and returns is explained below.

Sales Discounts

sales discount A reduction in the selling price that is allowed if payment is received within a specified period.

In many sales transactions, the buyer is given a discount if the bill is paid promptly. Such incentives to pay quickly are called **sales discounts**, or cash discounts, and the discount terms are typically expressed in abbreviated form. For example, 2/10, n/30 means that a buyer will receive a 2% discount from the selling price if payment is made within 10 days of the date of purchase, but that the full amount must be paid within 30 days or it will be considered past due. (Other common terms are 1/10, n/30 and 2/10, EOM. The latter means that a 2% discount is granted if payment is made within 10 days after the date of sale; otherwise the balance is due at the end of the month.) A 2% discount is a strong incentive for a customer to pay within 10 days because it is equivalent to paying an annual interest rate of about 36% to wait and pay after the discount period.[3] In fact, if the amount owed is substantial, most firms will borrow money, if necessary, to take advantage of a sales discount. The interest rate they will have to pay a lending institution to borrow the money is considerably less than the effective interest rate of missing the sales discount.

If an account receivable is paid within a specified discount period, the entry to record the receipt of cash is different from the cash receipt entry shown earlier. Thus, if the $200 in Farm

---

3 This is calculated by computing an annual interest rate for the period that the money is "sacrificed." With terms 2/10, n/30, a buyer who pays on the 10th day instead of the 30th "sacrifices" the money for 20 days. Since 2% is earned in 20 days, and there are just over 18 periods of 20 days in a year, earnings would be 18 × 2%, or approximately 36% annual interest.

Land credit sales were made with discount terms of 2/10, n/30, and if the customers paid within the discount period, the entry to record the receipt of cash is:

Cash.	196	
Sales Discounts ($200 $\times$ 0.02)	4	
Accounts Receivable.		200
Collected cash within the discount period for $200 credit sale.		

contra account An account that is offset or deducted from another account.

Sales Discounts is a **contra account** (specifically, a contra-revenue account), which means that it is deducted from sales revenue on the income statement. This account is included with other revenue accounts in the general ledger, but unlike other revenue accounts, it has a debit balance rather than a credit balance.

Sales Returns and Allowances

Customers often return merchandise, either because the item is defective or for a variety of other reasons. Most companies generally accept merchandise returns in order to maintain good customer relations. When merchandise is returned, the company must make an entry to reduce revenues and to reduce either Cash (a cash refund) or Accounts Receivable (an adjustment to the customer's account). A similar entry is required when the sales price is reduced because the merchandise was defective or damaged during shipment to the customer.

To illustrate the type of entry needed, we will assume that before any payments on account are made, Farm Land customers return goods costing $150; $100 in returns were made by cash customers, and $50 in returns were made by credit customers. The entry to record the return of merchandise is:

Sales Returns and Allowances	150	
Cash		100
Accounts Receivable		50
Received $150 of returned merchandise; $100 from cash customers and $50 from credit customers.		

sales returns and allowances A contra-revenue account in which the return of, or allowance for reduction in the price of, merchandise previously sold is recorded.

The credit customers will be sent a credit memorandum for the return, stating that credit has been granted and that the balance of their accounts (in total) is now $150 ($200 original credit purchase − $50 returns). Like Sales Discounts, **Sales Returns and Allowances** is a contra account that is deducted from sales revenue on the income statement. The income statement presentation for the revenue accounts, assuming payment within the discount period on the $150 balance in Accounts Receivable, is as follows:

Income Statement		
Sales revenue	$500	
Less: Sales discounts*	(3)	
Less: Sales returns and allowances	(150)	
Net sales revenue		$347

*($200 − $50) $\times$ 0.02 = $3
Note that when merchandise is returned, sales discounts for the subsequent payment are granted only on the selling price of the merchandise not returned.

It might seem that the use of contra accounts (Sales Discounts and Sales Returns and Allowances) involves extra steps that would not be necessary if discounts and returns of merchandise were deducted directly from Sales Revenue. Although such direct deductions would have the same final effect on net income, the contra accounts separate initial sales from all returns,

gross sales Total recorded sales before deducting any sales discounts or sales returns and allowances.

net sales Gross sales less sales discounts and sales returns and allowances.

cash Coins, currency, money orders, checks, and funds on deposit with financial institutions; the most liquid of assets.

f y i

In its balance sheet (see Appendix A), MICROSOFT follows the common practice of combining cash and short-term investments (bonds and U.S. Treasury securities) for the total Cash amount.

f y i

Consider the case of an employee who both receives payments and keeps the books. He or she could pocket a cash payment from one customer and not record the receipt until payment is received from a second customer. The second customer's payment could be recorded when a third customer pays, and so on. This type of delayed recording of payments is called *lapping*; it allows an employee to use company money for extended periods of time.

allowances, and discounts. This permits a company's management to analyze the extent to which customers are returning merchandise, receiving allowances, and taking advantage of discounts. If management find that excessive amounts of merchandise are being returned, they may decide that the company's sales returns policy is too liberal or that the quality of its merchandise needs improvement.

A company's total recorded sales, before any discounts or returns and allowances, are referred to as **gross sales**. When sales discounts or sales returns and allowances are deducted from gross sales, the resulting amount is referred to as **net sales**.

Control of Cash

Cash includes coins, currency, money orders and checks (made payable or endorsed to the company), and money on deposit with banks or savings institutions that are available for use to satisfy the company's obligations. All the various transactions involving these forms of cash are usually summarized and reported under a single balance sheet account, Cash.

Because it is the easiest asset to spend if it is stolen, cash is a tempting target and must be carefully safeguarded. Several control procedures have been developed to help management monitor and protect cash. In Chapter 5, internal controls for cash and other assets were discussed. Because cash is particularly vulnerable to loss or misuse, however, we will discuss three important controls that are an integral part of accounting for cash.

One of the most important controls is that the handling of cash be separated from the recording of cash. The purpose of this separation of duties is that it becomes more difficult for theft or errors to occur when two or more people are involved. If the cash records are maintained by an employee who also has access to the cash itself, cash can be stolen or "borrowed," and the employee can cover up the shortage by falsifying the accounting records.

A second cash control practice is to require that all cash receipts be deposited daily in bank accounts. This disciplined, rigid process ensures that personal responsibility for the handling of cash is focused on the individual assigned to make the regular deposit. In addition, this process prevents the accumulation of a large amount of cash—even the most trusted employee can be tempted by a large cash hoard.

A third cash control practice is to require that all cash expenditures (except those paid out of a miscellaneous petty cash fund) be made with prenumbered checks. As we all know from managing our personal finances, payments made with pocket cash are quickly forgotten and easily concealed. In contrast, payments made by check are well documented, both in our personal check registers and by our bank.

In addition to safeguarding cash, a business must ensure that cash is wisely managed. In fact, many businesses establish elaborate control and budgeting procedures for monitoring cash balances and estimating future cash needs. Companies also try to keep only minimum balances in no-interest or low-interest checking accounts; other cash is kept in more high-yielding investments such as certificates of deposit.

to summarize

The amount of cash collected from customers can be reduced because of sales discounts and sales returns and allowances. On the income statement, sales discounts and sales returns and allowances are subtracted from gross sales to arrive at net sales. Cash is a tempting target for fraud or theft, so companies must carefully monitor and control the way cash is handled and accounted for. Common controls include (1) separation of duties in handling and accounting for cash, (2) daily deposits of all cash receipts, and (3) payment of all expenditures by prenumbered checks.

4

Record the losses resulting from credit customers who do not pay their bills.

receivables Claims for money, goods, or services.

accounts receivable A current asset representing money due for services performed or merchandise sold on credit.

---

f y i

Credit card sales can be viewed as a way for a business to reap the benefit of increased credit sales without having to set up a bookkeeping and collection service for accounts receivable. The credit card company screens customers based on their creditworthiness, sends out the bills, collects the cash, and bears the cost of any uncollectible accounts. A business that accepts credit card sales pays a fee ranging from 1 to 5 percent of credit card sales.

---

bad debt An uncollectible account receivable.

direct write-off method The recording of actual losses from uncollectible accounts as expenses during the period in which accounts receivable are determined to be uncollectible.

ACCOUNTING FOR CREDIT CUSTOMERS WHO DON'T PAY

The term **receivables** refers to a company's claims for money, goods, or services. Receivables are created through various types of transactions, the two most common being the sale of merchandise or services on credit and the lending of money. On a personal level, we are all familiar with credit. Because credit is so readily available, we can buy such items as cars, refrigerators, and big-screen TVs, even when we cannot afford to pay cash for them. Major retail companies such as SEARS, oil companies such as SHELL, and credit card companies such as VISA, MASTERCARD, and AMERICAN EXPRESS have made credit available to almost every person in the United States. We live in a credit world—not only on the individual level, but also at the wholesale and manufacturing business levels.

In business, credit sales give rise to the most common type of receivables: accounts receivable. **Accounts receivable** are the amounts owed to a business by its credit customers and are usually collected in cash within 10 to 60 days. Accounts receivable result from informal agreements between a company and its credit customers; a more formal contract, including interest on the unpaid balance, is called a note receivable. Other receivables may result from loans to officers or employees of a company, for example. To identify and maintain the distinction between these receivables, businesses establish a separate general ledger account for each classification. If the amount of a receivable is material, it is separately identified on the balance sheet. Receivables that are to be converted to cash within a year (or the normal operating cycle) are classified as current assets and listed on the balance sheet below Cash. In this section of the chapter, we discuss the accounting issues associated with credit customers who don't pay.

When companies sell goods and services on credit (as most do), there are usually some customers who do not pay for the merchandise they purchase; these are referred to as **bad debts**. In fact, most businesses expect a small percentage of their receivables to be uncollectible. If a firm tries too hard to eliminate the possibility of losses from nonpaying customers, it usually makes its credit policy so restrictive that valuable sales are lost. On the other hand, if a firm extends credit too easily, the total cost of maintaining the accounts receivable system may exceed the benefit gained from attracting customers by allowing them to buy on credit (due to the number of accounts to track and uncollectible receivables to try to collect). Because of this dilemma, most firms carefully monitor their credit sales and accounts receivable to ensure that their policies are neither too restrictive nor too liberal.

When an account receivable becomes uncollectible, a firm incurs a bad debt loss. This loss is recognized as a cost of doing business, so it is classified as a selling expense. There are two ways to account for losses from uncollectible accounts: the direct write-off method and the allowance method.

Direct Write-Off Method

With the **direct write-off method**, an uncollectible account is recognized as an expense at the time it is determined to be uncollectible. For example, assume that during the year 2003, Farm Land Products had total credit sales of $300,000. Of this amount, $250,000 was subsequently collected in cash during the year, leaving a year-end balance in Accounts Receivable of $50,000 ($300,000 − $250,000). The summary journal entries to record this information are:

Accounts Receivable	300,000	
Sales Revenue		300,000
To record total credit sales for the year.		
Cash	250,000	
Accounts Receivable		250,000
To record total cash collections for the year.		

Overstating Receivables One of the easiest ways to overstate income is to overstate receivables. For example, Michael Weinstein, former chairman and CEO of COATED SALES, INC., orchestrated a financial fraud scheme that ultimately cost investors close to $100 million. Coated Sales, Inc., was a New Jersey company that manufactured textiles coated with special chemicals, used for making such products as yacht sails, bullet-proof vests, conveyor belts, and parachutes. The company was best known for supplying the fabric used in the sails of the America's Cup–winning yacht *Stars and Stripes*.

Coated Sales was started as the second career of millionaire entrepreneur Michael Weinstein, who had "retired" in his 30s and sold the discount drug store chain he had built. Looking for a new business, he became interested in textiles through a friend. The proposition was simple: take unfinished textiles, known as gray goods, and finish them with specialized coatings or treatments. The company's earnings, though minuscule at first, began to double and even triple every year—sometimes every six months.

The fraud was instigated by inflating Coated's sales and earnings through the creation of phony invoices purporting to show sales of goods. Coated officials "prebilled" invoices to customers so they could obtain payment for goods before they were shipped.

Assume that one credit customer, Jake Palmer, has an account balance of $1,500 that remains unpaid for several months in 2004. If, after receiving several past-due notices, Palmer still does not pay, Farm Land will probably turn the account over to an attorney or a collection agency. Then, if collection attempts fail, the company may decide that the Palmer account will not be collected and write it off as a loss. The entry to record the expense under the direct write-off method is:

Bad Debt Expense	1,500	
Accounts Receivable.		1,500
To write off the uncollectible account of Jake Palmer.		

bad debt expense An account that represents the portion of the current period's credit sales that are estimated to be uncollectible.

Bad Debt Expense is usually considered a selling expense on the income statement. Although the direct write-off method is objective (the account is written off at the time it proves to be uncollectible), it most likely would violate the matching principle, which requires that all costs and expenses incurred in generating revenues be identified with those revenues period by period. With the direct write-off method, sales made near the end of one accounting period may not be recognized as uncollectible until the next period. In this example, the revenue from the sale to Jake Palmer is recognized in 2003, but the expense from the bad debt is not recognized until 2004. As a result, expenses are understated in 2003 and overstated in 2004. This makes the direct write-off method unacceptable from a theoretical point of view. The direct write-off method is allowable only if bad debts involve small, insignificant amounts.

The Allowance Method

allowance method The recording of estimated losses due to uncollectible accounts as expenses during the period in which the sales occurred.

The **allowance method** satisfies the matching principle because it accounts for uncollectibles during the same period in which the sales occurred. With this method, a firm uses its experience (or industry averages) to estimate the amount of receivables arising from this year's credit sales that will ultimately become uncollectible. That estimate is recorded as bad debt expense in the period of sale. Although the use of estimates may result in a somewhat imprecise expense figure, this is generally thought to be a less serious problem than the direct write-off method's failure to match bad debt expenses with the sales that caused them. In addition, with experience, these estimates tend to be quite accurate.

Coated then began sending out false invoices to customers, recording receivables, and obtaining funds for sales that never occurred. To prevent the customers from denying the sales, the company involved the customers in the racket. For example, Robert Solomon of GLOBE SPORTS PRODUCTS paid the fictitious bills and would then receive the money back from Weinstein. Due to the inflated sales and receivables, the value of Coated's stock rose from $1.50 per share in its initial public offering to over $12 per share in 1987. From 1984 to 1987, sales allegedly rose from $9.9 million to over $90 million.

In addition, Weinstein inflated accounts receivable by billing fictitious customers. He used the inflated accounts receivable account to secure large bank loans. For example, BANCBOSTON FINANCIAL COMPANY loaned Coated $45 million, based on the supposed existence of $51 million in accounts receivable that served as collateral for the loan.

Coated's auditor, KPMG PEAT MARWICK, withdrew because of its suspicions. Within days, Coated Sales' stock value tumbled from $8 to $2 a share. Shortly thereafter, the corporation's credit dried up, forcing it to declare bankruptcy.

Source: Graham Button, "Homeless Jailbird," *Forbes*, August 17, 1992, p. 13.

To illustrate the allowance method, assume that Farm Land Products estimates that the bad debts created by its $300,000 in credit sales in 2003 will ultimately total $4,500. Note that this is a statistical estimate—on average, bad debts will be $4,500, but Farm Land does not yet know exactly which customers will be the ones who will fail to pay. The entry to record this estimated bad debt expense for 2003 is:

Bad Debt Expense	4,500	
Allowance for Bad Debts		4,500
To record the estimated bad debt expense for the current year.		

allowance for bad debts A contra account, deducted from Accounts Receivable, that shows the estimated losses from uncollectible accounts.

Bad Debt Expense is a selling expense on the income statement, and **Allowance for Bad Debts** is a contra account to Accounts Receivable on the balance sheet. An allowance account is used because the company does not yet know which receivables will not be collected. Later on, for example, in 2004, as actual losses are recognized, the balance in Allowance for Bad Debts is reduced. For example, if in 2004 Jake Palmer's receivable for $1,500 is specifically identified as being uncollectible, the entry is:

Allowance for Bad Debts	1,500	
Accounts Receivable		1,500
To write off the uncollectible account of Jake Palmer.		

Note that the write-off entry in 2004 does not affect net income in 2004. Instead, the net income in 2003, when the credit sale to Jake Palmer was originally made, already reflects the estimated bad debt expense. Think of this entry as follows: The $1,500 Jake Palmer account has been shown to be bad, so it is "thrown away" via a credit to Accounts Receivable. In addition, Allowance for Bad Debts, which is a general estimate of the amount of bad accounts, is reduced by $1,500 because the bad Palmer account has been specifically identified and eliminated. In one entry, the amounts in Accounts Receivable and Allowance for Bad Debts have been reduced. Assume that the balance in Accounts Receivable was $50,000 and the balance in Allowance for Bad Debts was $4,500 before the Palmer account was written off. The net amount in Accounts

Receivable after the $1,500 write-off is exactly the same as it was before the entry, as shown here.

Before Write-Off Entry		After Write-Off Entry	
Accounts receivable	$50,000	Accounts receivable	
		($50,000 − $1,500)	$48,500
Less allowance for		Less allowance for bad	
bad debts	4,500	debts ($4,500 − $1,500)	3,000
Net balance	$45,500	Net balance	$45,500

net realizable value of accounts receivable The net amount that would be received if all receivables considered collectible were collected; equal to total accounts receivable less the allowance for bad debts.

The net balance of $45,500 reflects the estimated **net realizable value of accounts receivable**, that is, the amount of receivables the company actually expects to collect.

The following T-account shows the kinds of entries that are made to Allowance for Bad Debts:

Allowance for Bad Debts	
Actual write-offs of uncollectible accounts	Estimates of uncollectible accounts

Occasionally, a customer whose account has been written off as uncollectible later pays the outstanding balance. When this happens, the company reverses the entry that was used to write off the account and then recognizes the payment. For example, if Jake Palmer pays the $1,500 after his account has already been written off, the entries to correct the accounting records are:

Accounts Receivable	1,500	
Allowance for Bad Debts		1,500
To reinstate the balance previously written off as uncollectible.		
Cash	1,500	
Accounts Receivable		1,500
Received payment in full of previously written-off accounts receivable.		

Because customers sometimes pay their balances after their accounts are written off, it is important for a company to have good control over both the cash collection procedures and the accounting for accounts receivable. Otherwise, such payments as the previously written-off $1,500 could be pocketed by the employee who receives the cash, and it would never be missed. This is one reason that most companies separate the handling of cash from the recording of cash transactions in the accounts.

Because the amount recorded in Bad Debt Expense affects both the reported net realizable value of the receivables and net income, companies must be careful to use good estimation procedures. These estimates can focus on an examination of either the total number of credit sales during the period or the outstanding receivables at year-end to determine their collectibility.

ESTIMATING UNCOLLECTIBLE ACCOUNTS RECEIVABLE AS A PERCENTAGE OF CREDIT SALES One method of estimating bad debt expense is to estimate uncollectible receivables as a percentage of credit sales for the period. If a company uses this method, the amount of uncollectibles will be a straight percentage of the current year's credit sales. That percentage will be a projection based on experience in prior years, modified for any changes expected for the current period. For example, in the Farm Land example, credit sales for the year of $300,000 are expected to generate bad debts of $4,500, indicating that 1.5% of all credit sales are expected to be uncollectible ($4,500 ÷ $300,000 = 1.5%). Farm Land would evaluate the percentage each year, in light of its continued experience, to see whether the same percentage still seems reasonable. In addition, if economic conditions have changed for Farm Land's customers (such as the onset of a recession making it more likely that debts will remain uncollected), the percentage would be adjusted.

When this percentage of sales method is used, the existing balance (if there is one) in Allowance for Bad Debts does not affect the amount computed and is not included in the adjusting entry to record bad debt expense. The 1.5% of the current year's sales that is estimated to be uncollectible is calculated and entered separately, and then added to the existing balance. For example, if the existing credit balance is $2,000, the $4,500 will be added, making the new credit balance $6,500. The rationale for not considering the existing $2,000 balance in Allowance for Bad Debts is that it relates to previous periods' sales and reflects the company's estimate (as of the beginning of the year) of prior years' accounts receivable that are expected to be uncollectible.

STOP & THINK Should a company work to reduce its bad debt expense to zero? Explain.

In determining the percentage of credit sales that will be uncollectible, a company must estimate the total amount of loss on the basis of experience or industry averages. Obviously, a company that has been in business for several years should be able to make more accurate estimates than a new company. Many established companies use a three- or five-year average as the basis for estimating losses from uncollectible accounts.

ESTIMATING UNCOLLECTIBLE ACCOUNTS RECEIVABLE AS A PERCENTAGE OF TOTAL RECEIVABLES

Another way to estimate uncollectible receivables is to use a percentage of total receivables. Using this method, the amount of uncollectibles is a percentage of the total receivables balance at the end of the period. Assume that Farm Land decides to use this method and determines that 12% of the $50,000 in the year-end Accounts Receivable will ultimately be uncollectible. Accordingly, the credit balance in Allowance for Bad Debts should be $6,000 ($50,000 × 0.12). If there is no existing balance in Allowance for Bad Debts representing the estimate of bad accounts left over from prior years, then an entry for $6,000 is made. If the account has an existing balance, however, only the net amount needed to bring the credit balance to $6,000 is added. For example, an existing credit balance of $2,000 in Allowance for Bad Debts results in the following adjusting entry:

Bad Debt Expense...	4,000	
Allowance for Bad Debts		4,000
To adjust the allowance account to the desired balance		
($6,000 − $2,000 = $4,000).		

In all cases, the ending balance in Allowance for Bad Debts should be the amount of total receivables estimated to be uncollectible.

In estimating bad debt expense, the percentage of sales method focuses on an estimation based directly on the level of the current year's credit sales. With the percentage of total receivables method, the focus is on estimating total bad debts existing at the end of the period; this number is compared to the leftover bad debts from prior years, and the difference is bad debt expense, the new bad debts created in the current period. These two techniques are merely alternative estimation approaches. In practice, as a check, a company would probably use both procedures to ensure that they yield roughly consistent results.

Aging Accounts Receivable In the example just given, the correct amount of the ending Allowance for Bad Debts balance was computed by applying the estimated uncollectible percentage (12%) to the entire Accounts Receivable balance ($50,000). In a more refined method of estimating the appropriate ending balance in Allowance for Bad Debts, a company bases its calculations on how long its receivables have been outstanding. With this procedure, called **aging accounts receivable**, each receivable is categorized according to age, such as current, 1–30 days past due, 31–60 days past due, 61–90 days past due, 91–120 days past due, and over 120 days past due. Once the receivables in each age classification are totaled, each total is multiplied by

aging accounts receivable
The process of categorizing each account receivable by the number of days it has been outstanding.

exhibit 6-5   Aging Accounts Receivable

| | | | | Days Past Due | | | |
Customer	Balance	Current	1–30	31–60	61–90	91–120	Over 120
A. Adams	$10,000	$10,000					
R. Bartholomew	6,500			$ 5,000			$1,500
F. Christiansen	6,250	5,000	$1,250				
G. Dover	7,260			7,260			
M. Ellis	4,000	4,000					
G. Erkland	2,250				$2,250		
R. Fisher	1,500		500			$1,000	
J. Palmer	1,500		1,500				
E. Zeigler	10,740	4,000	6,740				
Totals	$50,000	$23,000	$9,990	$12,260	$2,250	$1,000	$1,500

Estimate of Losses from Uncollectible Accounts

Age	Balance	Percentage Estimated to Be Uncollectible	Amount
Current	$23,000	1.5	$ 345
1–30 days past due	9,990	4.0	400
31–60 days past due	12,260	20.0	2,452
61–90 days past due	2,250	40.0	900
91–120 days past due	1,000	60.0	600
Over 120 days past due	1,500	80.0	1,200
Totals	$50,000		$5,897*

*Receivables that are likely to be uncollectible.

an appropriate uncollectible percentage (as determined by experience), recognizing that the older the receivable, the less likely the company is to collect. Exhibit 6-5 shows how Farm Land could use an aging accounts receivable analysis to estimate the amount of its $50,000 ending balance in Accounts Receivable that will ultimately be uncollectible.

The allowance for bad debts estimate obtained using the aging method is $5,897. If the existing credit balance in Allowance for Bad Debts is $2,000, the required adjusting entry is:

Bad Debt Expense	3,897	
Allowance for Bad Debts.		3,897

To adjust the allowance account to the desired ending balance ($5,897 − $2,000 = $3,897).

caution

The aging method is merely a more refined technique for estimating the desired balance in Allowance for Bad Debts.

The aging of accounts receivable is probably the most accurate method of estimating uncollectible accounts. It also enables a company to identify its problem customers. Companies that base their estimates of uncollectible accounts on credit sales or total outstanding receivables also often age their receivables as a way of monitoring the individual accounts receivable balances.

Real-World Illustration of Accounting for Bad Debts

The application of bad debt accounting is illustrated using the financial statements of YAHOO! for 1997–1999. As shown in Exhibit 6-6, Yahoo! reported accounts receivable at the end of 1999

exhibit 6-6   Bad Debt Expense for Yahoo!

Year	Ending Accounts Receivable	Ending Bad Debt Allowance	Bad Debt Allowance as a Percentage of Accounts Receivable
1999	$65,748*	$11,322	17.2%
1998	40,036	5,947	14.9%
1997	14,683	2,772	18.9%

*Dollar amounts are in millions.

of $65.7 million and a bad debt allowance for bad debts of $11.3 million. In other words, credit customers owed Yahoo! $65.7 million as of the end of 1999; however, Yahoo!'s best estimate was that $11.3 million of this amount would never be collected. This bad debt allowance amounted to 17.2% of the Accounts Receivable balance, down from 18.9% in 1997 but up from 14.9% in 1998. For a company operating in a stable economic environment with little change in the nature of its credit customers, this percentage would be expected to be about the same from year to year. In the case of Yahoo!, operating in the volatile Internet economy, it appears that there has been some variation in the collectibility of accounts receivable from one year to the next.

to summarize

Accounts receivable arise from credit sales to customers. Even though companies monitor their customers carefully, there are usually some who do not pay for the merchandise they purchase. There are two ways of accounting for losses from uncollectible receivables: the direct write-off method and the allowance method. The allowance method is generally accepted in practice because it is consistent with the matching principle. Two ways of estimating losses from uncollectible receivables are (1) as a percentage of credit sales and (2) as some fraction of total outstanding receivables. A common method for applying the latter technique uses an aging accounts receivable analysis.

5

Evaluate a company's management of its receivables by computing and analyzing appropriate financial ratios.

ASSESSING HOW WELL COMPANIES MANAGE THEIR RECEIVABLES

As you recall from the DuPont framework explained in Chapter 4, an important element of overall company performance is the efficient use of assets. With regard to accounts receivable, inefficient use means that too much cash is tied up in the form of receivables. A company that collects its receivables on a timely basis has cash to pay its bills. Companies that do not do a good job of collecting receivables are often cash poor, paying interest on short-term loans to cover their cash shortage or losing interest that could be earned by investing cash.

There are several methods of evaluating how well an organization is managing its accounts receivable. The most common method involves computing two ratios, accounts receivable turnover and average collection period. The **accounts receivable turnover** ratio is an attempt to determine how many times during the year a company is "turning over" or collecting its receivables. It is a measure of how many times old receivables are collected and replaced by new receivables. Accounts receivable turnover is calculated as follows:

accounts receivable turnover A measure used to indicate how fast a company collects its receivables; computed by dividing sales by average accounts receivable.

$$\text{Accounts Receivable Turnover} = \frac{\text{Sales Revenue}}{\text{Average Accounts Receivable}}$$

Notice that the numerator of this ratio is sales revenue, not credit sales. Conceptually, one might consider comparing the level of accounts receivable to the amount of credit sales instead of total sales. However, companies rarely, if ever, disclose how much of their sales are credit sales. For this ratio, you can think of cash sales as credit sales with a very short collection time (0 days). Also note that the denominator uses average accounts receivable instead of the ending balance. This recognizes that sales are generated throughout the year; the average Accounts Receivable balance is an approximation of the amount that prevailed during the year. If the Accounts Receivable balance is relatively unchanged during the year, then using the ending balance is acceptable and common. The following are the accounts receivable turnover ratios for two well-known companies for 1999:

$$\text{Wal-Mart} \quad \frac{\$165.013 \text{ billion}}{\$1.230 \text{ billion}} = 134.2 \text{ times}$$

$$\text{Boeing} \quad \frac{\$57.993 \text{ billion}}{\$3.371 \text{ billion}} = 17.2 \text{ times}$$

From this analysis, you can see that WAL-MART turns its receivables over much more often than does BOEING. This is not surprising given the different nature of the two businesses. Wal-Mart sells primarily to retail customers for cash. Remember, from Wal-Mart's standpoint, a credit card sale is the same as a cash sale since Wal-Mart receives its money instantly; it is the credit card company that must worry about collecting the receivable. Boeing, on the other hand, sells to airlines and governments that have established business credit relationships with Boeing. Thus, the nature of its business dictates that Boeing has a much larger fraction of its sales tied up in the form of accounts receivable than does Wal-Mart.

Accounts receivable turnover can then be converted into the number of days it takes to collect receivables by computing a ratio called **average collection period**. This ratio is computed by dividing 365 (or the number of days in a year) by the accounts receivable turnover as follows:

average collection period A measure of the average number of days it takes to collect a credit sale; computed by dividing 365 days by the accounts receivable turnover.

$$\text{Average Collection Period} = \frac{365}{\text{Accounts Receivable Turnover}}$$

Computing this ratio for both Wal-Mart and Boeing shows that it takes Wal-Mart only 2.7 days (365 ÷ 134.2) on average to collect its receivables, while Boeing takes an average of 21.2 days (365 ÷ 17.2).

Consider what might happen to Boeing's average collection period during an economic recession. During a recession, purchasers are often strapped for cash and try to delay paying on their accounts for as long as possible. Boeing might be faced with airlines that still want to buy airplanes but wish to stretch out the payment period. The result would be a rise in Boeing's average collection period; more of Boeing's resources would be tied up in the form of accounts receivable. In turn, Boeing would have to increase its borrowing in order to pay its own bills since it would be collecting less cash from its slow-paying customers. Proper receivables management involves balancing the desire to extend credit in order to increase sales with the need to collect the cash quickly in order to pay off your own bills.

to summarize

Careful management of accounts receivable is a balance between extending credit to increase your sales and collecting cash quickly to reduce your need to borrow. Two ratios commonly used in monitoring the level of receivables are accounts receivable turnover and average collection period. The level of these ratios is determined by how well a company manages its receivables, as well as by what kind of business the company is in.

6

Match revenues and expenses by estimating and recording future warranty and service costs associated with a sale.

RECORDING WARRANTY AND SERVICE COSTS ASSOCIATED WITH A SALE

Let's return to the Farm Land example in which 50 sacks of fertilizer were sold for $500. Assume that as part of each sale, Farm Land offers to send a customer service representative to the home or place of business of any purchaser who wants more detailed instructions on how to apply the fertilizer. Historical experience suggests that the buyer of one fertilizer sack in ten will request a visit from a Farm Land representative, and the material and labor cost of each visit averages $35. So, with 50 sacks of fertilizer sold, Farm Land has obligated itself to provide, on average, $175 in future customer service [(50 ÷ 10) × $35]. Proper matching requires that this $175 expense be estimated and recognized in the same period in which the associated sale is recognized. Otherwise, if the company waited to record customer service expense until the actual visits are requested, this period's sales revenue would be reported in the same income statement with customer service expense arising from last period's sales. The accountant is giving up some precision because the service expense must be estimated in advance. This sacrifice in precision is worth the benefit of being able to better match revenues and expenses.

The entry to recognize Farm Land's estimated service expense from the sale of 50 sacks of fertilizer is as follows:

Customer Service Expense...	175	
Estimated Liability for Service.................................		175
Estimated customer service costs on sales [(50 ÷ 10) × $35].		

The credit entry, Estimated Liability for Service, is a liability. When actual expenses are incurred in providing the customer service, the liability is eliminated with the following type of entry:

Estimated Liability for Service	145	
Wages Payable (to service employees)		100
Supplies		45
Actual customer service costs incurred.		

This entry shows that supplies and labor were required to honor the service agreements. This procedure results in the service expense being recognized at the time of sale, not necessarily when the actual service occurs.

After these two journal entries are made, the remaining balance in Estimated Liability for Service will be $30, shown as follows:

Estimated Liability for Service

Estimate at time of sale		175
Actual service costs incurred	145	
Remaining balance		30

The $30 balance represents the estimated amount of service that still must be provided in the future resulting from the sale of the 50 sacks of fertilizer. If actual experience suggests that the estimated service cost is too high, a lower estimate would be made in connection with subsequent fertilizer sales. If estimated liability for service is too low, a higher estimate is made for subsequent sales. The important point is that the accountant would not try to go back and "fix" an estimate that later proves to be inexact; the accountant merely monitors the relationship between the estimated and actual service costs in order to adjust future estimates accordingly.

The accounting just shown for estimated service costs is the same procedure used for estimated warranty costs. For example, GENERAL MOTORS promises automobile buyers that it will fix, at no charge to the buyer, certain mechanical problems for a certain period of time. GM estimates and records this warranty expense at the time the automobile sales are made. At the end of 1999, GM reported an existing liability for warranty costs of $15.3 billion. This amount is what GM estimates it will have to spend on warranty repairs in 2000 (and later years) on cars sold in 1999 (and earlier).

to summarize

In addition to bad debt expense, there are other costs that must be estimated and recognized at the time a sale is made in order to ensure the proper matching of revenues and expenses. If a company makes promises about future warranty repairs or continued customer service as part of the sale, the value of these promises should be estimated and recorded as an expense at the time of the sale.

expanded material

Thus far the chapter has covered the main topics associated with selling goods or services, collecting the proceeds from those sales, and estimating and recording bad debt expense and service expense. The expanded material will cover three additional topics. First, an important tool of cash control, the bank reconciliation, will be explained. Second, the use of receivables to get cash immediately will be illustrated. Finally, the financial statement implications of making sales denominated in foreign currencies will be illustrated.

7

Reconcile a checking account.

RECONCILING THE BANK ACCOUNT

With the exception of small amounts of petty cash kept for miscellaneous purposes, most cash is kept in various bank accounts. Generally, only a few employees are authorized to sign checks, and they must have their signatures on file with the bank.

Each month the business receives a bank statement that shows the cash balance at the beginning of the period, the deposits, the amounts of the checks processed, and the cash balance at the end of the period. With the statement, the bank includes all of that month's canceled checks (or at least a listing of the checks), as well as debit and credit memos (for example, an explanation of charges for **NSF [not sufficient funds] checks** and service fees). From a bank's perspective, customers' deposits are liabilities; hence, debit memos reduce the company's cash balance, and credit memos increase the balance.

The July bank statement for one of Hunt Company's accounts is presented in Exhibit 6-7. This statement shows all activity in the cash account as recorded by the bank and includes four bank adjustments to Hunt's balance—a bank service charge of $7 (the bank's monthly fee), $60 of interest paid by First Security Bank on Hunt's average balance, a $425 transfer into another account, and a $3,200 direct deposit made by a customer who regularly deposits payments directly to Hunt's bank account. Other adjustments that are commonly made by a bank to a company's account include:

NSF (not sufficient funds) check A check that is not honored by a bank because of insufficient cash in the check writer's account.

exhibit 6-7   July Bank Statement for Hunt Company

First Security Bank
Helena, Montana 59601   Statement of Account

HUNT COMPANY   Account Number 325-78126
1900 S. PARK LANE
HELENA, MT 59601   Date of Statement JULY 31, 2003

Check Number	Checks and Withdrawals	Deposits and Additions	Date	Balance
			6/30	13,000
620	140		7/01	12,860
621	250	1,500	7/03	14,110
622	860		7/05	13,250
623	210		7/08	13,040
		2,140	7/09	15,180
624	205		7/10	14,975
626	310		7/14	14,665
	425 T		7/15	14,240
		3,200 D	7/18	17,440
628	765		7/19	16,675
629	4,825		7/22	11,850
630	420		7/24	11,430
632	326	1,600	7/25	12,704
		2,100	7/26	14,804
633	210		7/29	14,594
635	225		7/31	14,369
	7 SC	60 I	7/31	14,422
	9,178	**10,600**		**14,422**
	TOTAL CHECKS AND WITHDRAWALS	TOTAL DEPOSITS AND ADDITIONS		BALANCE

NSF = Not Sufficient Funds   D = Direct Deposit   I = Interest   T = Transfer Out of Account
SC = Service Charge   MS = Miscellaneous   ATM = Automated Teller Machine Transaction

1. *NSF (not sufficient funds).* This is the cancellation of a prior deposit that could not be collected because of insufficient funds in the check writer's (payer's) account. When a check is received and deposited in the payee's account, the check is assumed to represent funds that will be collected from the payer's bank. When a bank refuses to honor a check because of insufficient funds in the account on which it was written, the check is returned to the payee's bank and is marked "NSF." The amount of the check, which was originally recorded as a deposit (addition) to the payee's account, is deducted from the account when the check is returned unpaid.

2. *MS (miscellaneous).* Other adjustments made by a bank.

3. *ATM (automated teller machine) transactions.* These are deposits and withdrawals made by the depositor at automated teller machines.

4. *Withdrawals for credit card transactions paid directly from accounts.* These types of cards, called debit cards, are like using plastic checks. Instead of the card holder getting a bill or statement, the amount charged is deducted from the card holder's bank balance.

It is unusual for the ending balance on the bank statement to equal the amount of cash recorded in a company's cash account. The most common reasons for differences are:

1. *Time period differences.* The time period of the bank statement does not coincide with the timing of the company's postings to the cash account.
2. *Deposits in transit.* These are deposits that have not been processed by the bank as of the bank statement date, usually because they were made at or near the end of the month.
3. *Outstanding checks.* These are checks that have been written and deducted from a company's cash account but have not cleared or been deducted by the bank as of the bank statement date.
4. *Bank debits.* These are deductions made by the bank that have not yet been recorded by the company. The most common are monthly service charges, NSF checks, and bank transfers out of the account.
5. *Bank credits.* These are additions made by the bank to a company's account before they are recorded by the company. The most common source is interest paid by the bank on the account balance.
6. *Accounting errors.* These are numerical errors made by either the company or the bank. The most common is transposition of numbers.

bank reconciliation The process of systematically comparing the cash balance as reported by the bank with the cash balance on the company's books and explaining any differences.

The process of determining the reasons for the differences between the bank balance and the company's cash account balance is called a **bank reconciliation**. This usually results in adjusting both the bank statement and the book (cash account) balances. If the balances were not reconciled (if the cash balance were left as is), the figure used on the financial statements would probably be incorrect, and external users would not have accurate information for decision making. More importantly, the bank reconciliation can serve as an independent check to ensure that the cash is being accounted for correctly within the company.

We will use Hunt Company's bank account to illustrate a bank reconciliation. The statement shown in Exhibit 6-7 indicates an ending balance of $14,422 for the month of July. After arranging the month's canceled checks in numerical order and examining the bank statement, Hunt's accountant notes the following:

1. A deposit of $3,100 on July 31 was not shown on the bank statement. (It was in transit at the end of the month.)
2. Checks No. 625 for $326, No. 631 for $426, and No. 634 for $185 are outstanding. Check No. 627 was voided at the time it was written.
3. The bank's service charge for the month is $7.
4. A direct deposit of $3,200 was made by Joy Company, a regular customer.
5. A transfer of $425 was made out of Hunt's account into the account of Martin Custodial Service for payment owed.
6. The bank paid interest of $60 on Hunt's average balance.
7. Check No. 630 for Thelma Jones's wages was recorded in the accounting records as $240 instead of the correct amount, $420.
8. The cash account in the general ledger shows a balance on July 31 of $13,937.

The bank reconciliation is shown in Exhibit 6-8. Since the bank and book balances now agree, the $16,585 adjusted cash balance is the amount that will be reported on the financial statements. If the adjusted book and bank balances had not agreed, the accountant would have had to search for errors in bookkeeping or in the bank's figures. When the balances finally agree, any necessary adjustments are made to the cash account to bring it to the correct balance. The entries to correct the balance include debits to Cash for all reconciling additions to the book balance and credits to Cash for all reconciling deductions from the book balance. Additions and deductions from the bank balance do not require adjustments to the company's books; the deposits in transit and the outstanding checks have already been recorded by the company, and, of course, bank errors are corrected by notifying the bank and having the bank make corrections. The adjustments required to correct Hunt's cash account are:

Cash	3,260	
Accounts Receivable		3,200
Interest Revenue		60

*To record the additions due to the July bank reconciliation
(a $3,200 deposit made by Joy Company and $60 interest).*

Custodial Expense	425	
Miscellaneous Expense	7	
Wages Expense	180	
Cash		612

*To record the deductions due to the July bank reconciliation
(service charge, $7; a $180 recording error, check No.
630; bank transfer of $425 to Martin Custodial Service).*

to summarize

Because most payments are made by check, companies need to reconcile
monthly bank statements with the cash balance reported on the company's
books. This reconciliation process involves determining reasons for the differences and bringing the book and bank balances into agreement. Adjusting entries are then made for additions to and deductions from the book balance.

8

Understand how
receivables can be used by
a company to get cash
immediately.

USING RECEIVABLES TO GET CASH IMMEDIATELY

Sometimes companies need cash prior to the due dates of their receivables. Often, in these circumstances, such companies will sell or "factor" their accounts receivables to financing or factoring companies. Factoring companies charge a percentage of the receivable, usually ranging

exhibit 6-8   July Bank Reconciliation for Hunt Company

**Hunt Company
Bank Reconciliation
July 31, 2003**

Balance per bank statement		$14,422	Balance per books		$13,937
Additions to bank balance:			*Additions to book balance:*		
Deposit in transit		3,100	Direct deposit	$ 3,200	
Total		$17,522	Interest	60	3,260
			Total		$17,197
Deductions from bank balance:			*Deductions from book balance:*		
Outstanding checks: 625	$326		Service charge	$ 7	
631	426		Bank transfer	425	
634	185	(937)	Error in recording check No. 630		
			(for Jones's wages)	180	(612)
Adjusted bank balance		**$16,585**	**Adjusted book balance**		**$16,585**

from 2 to 15%, to buy receivables. If a company has notes receivable, these notes can be sold to a bank or finance company; selling a note is called "discounting" the note.

Selling or "Factoring" Accounts Receivable

To illustrate, assume that Reno Trucking Company has a $1,000 receivable from Bunker Metals that has terms n/30. Rather than wait the 30 days to collect the receivable, Reno Trucking could sell or "factor" the receivable at the Easy-Money Factoring Company for a 5% discount fee. If Reno Trucking needs the money to pay drivers' salaries and other expenses and factors the receivable, it would receive 95% of the $1,000, or $950, from Easy-Money Factoring. Sometimes accounts receivable are factored with "recourse," meaning that Reno Trucking must pay the receivable if Bunker Metals defaults. At times, usually for a larger discount fee, receivables are sold "without recourse," meaning that Reno Trucking has no obligation to pay, even if Bunker Metals defaults.

As an actual example, there is a small trucking company in Salt Lake City that owns five trucks and has another seven owner-operated trucks leased to it. The company primarily hauls steel from a large manufacturing plant in Utah to Chicago and hauls reclining chairs back to Utah from Chicago. Because the company is always pressed for cash, every receivable it has is factored at a rate of 6%. This means that the company receives only $94 on every $100 of receivables. Since the trucking company generally collects the receivables in 60 days, and there are approximately six 60-day periods in a year, the company is effectively paying 36% interest (6% × 6). Better cash management could make the company much more profitable.

Discounting Notes Receivable

An account receivable is an informal agreement between the seller and the credit buyer. No formal contract is drawn up, and no interest rate is specified on the account (unless the customer fails to pay within the specified time). Sometimes customers sign formal contracts, called notes, when they buy merchandise or services on credit. Even more often, customers from whom accounts receivable are past due sign interest-bearing notes to receive additional time to make payment. A **note receivable** is a claim against someone, evidenced by an unconditional written promise to pay a sum of money on or before a specified future date. Depending on the length of time until the due date, the note may be classified as a current asset or a long-term asset. In addition, it may be either a trade note receivable or a nontrade note receivable. A trade note receivable represents an amount due from a customer who purchased merchandise. Businesses often accept notes receivable from customers because they are contractual obligations that usually earn interest. A nontrade note receivable arises from the lending of money to an individual or company other than a customer (for example, an employee). Exhibit 6-9 shows a typical note receivable.

There are several key terms associated with a note receivable. The **maker** of a note is the person or entity who signs the note and who must make payment on or before the due date. The **payee** is the person or entity to whom payment will be made. The **principal** is the face amount of the note. The **maturity date** is the date the note becomes due. The **interest rate** is the percentage of the principal that the payee annually charges the maker for the loan; the interest is the dollar amount paid by the maker in accordance with this rate. Interest can also be thought of as the service charge, or rent, for the use of money. The formula for computing the interest on a note is:

$$\text{Principal} \times \text{Interest Rate} \times \text{Time (in terms of a year)} = \text{Interest}$$

For example, if Komatsu Company accepts from Solomon Company a 12%, three-month, $2,000 note receivable, the interest is calculated as:

$$\$2,000 \times 0.12 \times 3/12 = \$60$$

Note that the 12% stated interest rate is based on a one-year period, even though the note is only for three months. Interest rates are traditionally stated in annual terms no matter what

note receivable A claim against a debtor, evidenced by an unconditional written promise to pay a certain sum of money on or before a specified future date.

maker A person (entity) who signs a note to borrow money and who assumes responsibility to pay the note at maturity.

payee The person (entity) to whom payment on a note is to be made.

principal The amount that will be paid on a note or other obligation at the maturity date.

maturity date The date on which a note or other obligation becomes due.

interest rate The cost of using money, expressed as an annual percentage.

exhibit 6-9   Note Receivable

$2,000	Helena, Montana	July 15, 2003
PRINCIPAL	LOCATION	DATE

Ninety (90) days **AFTER DATE**   Solomon Company   **PROMISES**

TO PAY TO THE ORDER OF   Komatsu Company
                                                PAYEE

Two thousand and no/100   **DOLLARS**

PAYABLE AT   First Security Bank

FOR VALUE RECEIVED, WITH INTEREST AT   12 percent per annum

John Doe
SIGNATURE OF MAKER

the term length of the credit agreement. If the $2,000 note is accepted in settlement of Solomon's unpaid account with Komatsu Company, the journal entry to record the note in Komatsu's books is:

Notes Receivable	2,000	
Accounts Receivable		2,000
Accepted 3-month, 12% note from Solomon Company in lieu of		
payment of its account receivable.		

When the note matures and payment is made (three months later), Komatsu's entry to record the receipt of cash would be:

Cash	2,060	
Notes Receivable		2,000
Interest Revenue		60
Received payment from Solomon Company for $2,000 note plus		
interest.		

maturity value The amount of an obligation to be collected or paid at maturity; equal to principal plus any interest.

Principal plus interest ($2,060 in this example) is known as the **maturity value** of the note. If the note is not paid by the maturity date, negotiations with the maker usually result in the company extending the period for payment, issuing a new note, or retaining an attorney or collection agency to collect the money. If the note eventually proves to be worthless, it is written off as a loss against Allowance for Bad Debts. Often, when an agency or attorney is attempting to collect notes receivable, they are classified on the balance sheet as special receivables.

discounting a note receivable The process of the payee's selling notes to a financial institution for less than the maturity value.

Because notes receivable are contractual promises to pay money in the future, they are negotiable. They can be sold to banks and other financial institutions. The selling of a note to a financial institution is referred to as **discounting a note receivable**. This means that the holder of a note who needs cash before a note matures can sell the note (simply by endorsing it) to a financial institution. The maker of the note, therefore, owes the money to the financial institution or other endorsee. To a financial institution, purchasing a note for cash is just like making a loan; cash is given out now in return for repayment of principal with interest in the future. To a company selling a note, discounting is a way of receiving cash earlier than would otherwise be possible.

to summarize

Companies that need cash prior to the time their accounts receivable are due often "factor" or sell those receivables to factoring companies that charge a factoring fee. Notes receivable are formal, interest-bearing credit agreements between a company and credit customers. Notes receivable are negotiable and can be discounted, or sold.

9

Account for the impact of changing exchange rates on the value of accounts receivable denominated in foreign currencies.

FOREIGN CURRENCY TRANSACTIONS

All of the sales illustrated to this point in the text have been denominated in U.S. dollars. However, many U.S. companies do a large portion of their business in foreign countries. For example, 29% of **MICROSOFT**'s sales in 1999 were denominated in currencies other than the U.S. dollar. So, what would Microsoft have to do to record a software sale denominated in Japanese yen or British pounds? This section answers that question.

When a U.S. company sells a good or provides a service to a party in a foreign country, the transaction amount is frequently denominated in U.S. dollars. The U.S. dollar is a relatively stable currency, and buyers from Azerbaijan to Zimbabwe are often eager to avoid the uncertainty associated with payments denominated in their local currencies. For example, no matter where they are located, buyers and sellers of crude oil almost always write the contract price in terms of U.S. dollars. A U.S. company accounts for a sales contract with a foreign buyer with the sales price denominated in U.S. dollars in the way illustrated previously in this chapter; no new accounting issues are raised. However, if a U.S. company enters into a transaction in which the price is denominated in a foreign currency, the U.S. company must use special accounting procedures to recognize the change in the value of the transaction as foreign currency exchange rates fluctuate. For example, if Microsoft makes a sale with a price of 100,000 Indonesian rupiah, Microsoft knows that it will eventually collect 100,000 rupiah, but Microsoft does not know what those rupiah will be worth, in U.S. dollar terms, until the actual rupiah payment is received. Such a transaction is called a **foreign currency transaction**; the accounting for these transactions is demonstrated in the following section.

foreign currency transaction A sale in which the price is denominated in a currency other than the currency of the seller's home country.

Foreign Currency Transaction Example

To illustrate the accounting for a sale denominated in a foreign currency, assume that American Company sold goods with a price of 20,000,000 Korean won on April 23 to one of its Korean customers. Payment in Korean won is due July 12. American Company prepares quarterly financial statements on June 30. The following exchange rates apply:

	U.S. Dollar Value of One Korean Won	Event
April 23	$0.0010	Sale
June 30	0.0007	Financial statements prepared
July 12	0.0008	Payment received on account

On April 23, each Korean won is worth one-tenth of one U.S. cent. In other words, it takes 1,000 Korean won (1/0.0010) to buy one U.S. dollar. At this exchange rate, the 20,000,000-Korean-won contract is worth $20,000 (20,000,000 $\times$ $0.0010).

On April 23, American Company records the sale and the account receivable in its books as follows:

Accounts Receivable (fc).	20,000	
Sales Revenue.		20,000

Note that this journal entry is exactly the same as those illustrated earlier in the chapter. The (fc) indicates that the Accounts Receivable asset is denominated in a foreign currency and, thus, subject to exchange rate fluctuations. Because the financial statements of American Company are reported in U.S. dollars, all transaction amounts must be converted into their U.S. dollar equivalents when they are entered into the formal accounting system.

On June 30, American Company prepares its quarterly financial statements. Because the 20,000,000-Korean-won contract price has not yet been collected in cash, American Company still has a receivable denominated in Korean won and must reflect the effect of the change in the exchange rate on the U.S. dollar value of that receivable. In this case the Korean won has decreased in value and is worth only $0.0007 on June 30. If American Company had to settle the contract on June 30, it would receive only $14,000 (20,000,000 × $0.0007). Thus, American Company must recognize an exchange loss of $6,000, or 20,000,000 × ($0.0010 − $0.0007). On July 12, American Company receives payment from its Korean customer. In the interim the value of the Korean won has increased slightly to $0.0008. When the receivable is collected, the 20,000,000 Korean won are worth $16,000 (20,000,000 × $0.0008), so now American Company has experienced a gain relative to its position on June 30. The effects of the fluctuation in the value of the Korean won can be summarized as follows:

f y i

The wide fluctuations in exchange rates in this illustration are unusual, but not unprecedented. For example, as part of the Asian financial crisis of 1997, the number of Korean won needed to purchase one U.S. dollar increased from 917.77 on October 23, 1997, to 1,952.68 on December 23, 1997.

	U.S. Dollar Value of the Receivable	Gain or Loss
April 23	$20,000	Not applicable
June 30	14,000	$6,000 loss
July 12	16,000	$2,000 gain

This information would be reported in American Company's three primary financial statements in the second quarter (ending June 30) and the third quarter (beginning July 1) as follows:

Second Quarter:

Income Statement		Balance Sheet		Statement of Cash Flows	
Sales revenue	$20,000	Accounts receivable	$14,000	Cash collected from customers	$ 0
Foreign exchange loss	(6,000)				

Third Quarter:

Income Statement		Balance Sheet		Statement of Cash Flows	
Sales revenue	$ 0	Cash	$16,000	Cash collected from customers	$16,000
Foreign exchange gain	2,000	Accounts receivable	0		

The net result of the sale in the second quarter, the collection of cash in the third quarter, and the changing exchange rates in between is to record a sale of $20,000, the collection of cash of $16,000, and a net exchange loss of $4,000 (a $6,000 loss in the second quarter and a $2,000 gain in the third quarter). The important point to note is that the sale is measured at the exchange rate on the date of sale and that any fluctuations between the sale date and the settlement date are recognized as exchange gains or losses.

What could American Company have done in the previous example to reduce its exposure to the risk associated with changing exchange rates? The easiest thing would have been to denominate the transaction in U.S. dollars. Then the risk of exchange rate changes would have fallen on the Korean company. Secondly, American Company could have locked in the price of Korean won by entering into a forward contract with a foreign currency broker. A forward contract is an example of a derivative contract. Derivatives are becoming more and more commonplace in today's business environment, and in Chapter 12 we examine derivatives and their uses and risks.

to summarize

When a U.S. company makes a sale that is denominated in a foreign currency, the sale is called a foreign currency transaction. The sale is measured at the exchange rate on the date of sale, and any fluctuations between the sale date and the settlement date are recognized as exchange gains or losses.

review of learning objectives

1 **Understand the three basic types of business activities: operating, investing, and financing.** The three major types of business activities are: (1) operating activities, (2) investing activities, and (3) financing activities. Operating activities include selling products or services, buying inventory for resale, and incurring and paying for necessary expenses associated with the primary activities of a business. Investing activities include purchasing property, plant, and equipment for use in the business or purchasing investments, such as stocks and bonds of other companies. Financing activities include raising money by means other than operations to finance a business. The two common financing activities are borrowing (debt financing) and selling ownership or equity interests (equity financing) in the company.

2 **Use the two revenue recognition criteria to decide when the revenue from a sale or service should be recorded in the accounting records.** Revenue is recognized when the work is done and when cash collectibility is reasonably assured. The entries to record revenue from the sale of merchandise or from the performance of a service involve debits to Cash or Accounts Receivable and credits to Sales Revenue or Service Revenue. In general, revenues are recognized at the time of a sale. If cash is collected before a service is provided or a product is delivered, however, then revenue should not be recognized until the promised action has been completed. Revenue for long-term contracts is recognized in proportion to the amount of the contract completed.

3 **Properly account for the collection of cash and describe the business controls necessary to safeguard cash.** The amount of cash collected from customers can be reduced because of sales discounts and sales returns and allowances. Sales discounts are reductions in the payments required of customers who pay their accounts quickly. Sales returns and allowances are payment reductions granted to dissatisfied customers. On an income statement, sales discounts and sales returns and allowances are subtracted from gross sales to arrive at net sales. Cash is a tempting target for fraud or theft, so companies must carefully monitor and control the way cash is handled and accounted for. Common controls include (1) separation of duties in the handling of and accounting for cash, (2) daily deposits of all cash receipts, and (3) payment of all expenditures by prenumbered checks.

4 **Record the losses resulting from credit customers who do not pay their bills.** Accounts receivable balances are generally collected from 10 to 60 days after the date of sale. There are two ways to account for losses from uncollectible receivables: the direct write-off method and the allowance method. Only the allowance method is generally acceptable because it matches expenses with revenues. Losses from uncollectible receivables can be estimated (1) as a percentage of total credit sales for the period or (2) as a percentage of total outstanding receivables. One technique for estimating uncollectible receivables as a percentage of total receivables is to perform an aging of accounts receivable.

5 **Evaluate a company's management of its receivables by computing and analyzing appropriate financial ratios.** Careful management of accounts receivable is a balance between extending credit to increase sales and collecting cash quickly to reduce the need to borrow. Two ratios commonly used in monitoring the level of receivables are accounts receivable turnover and average collection period. The level of these ratios is determined by how well a company manages its receivables, as well as by what kind of business the company is in.

6 **Match revenues and expenses by estimating and recording future warranty and service costs associated with a sale.** If a company makes promises about future warranty repairs or continued customer service as part of a sale, the value of these promises is estimated and recorded as an expense at the time of the sale. If experience suggests that the original estimate was in error, adjustments are made to the estimates made in relation to subsequent sales; however, no attempt is made to go back and "fix" the original estimates.

expanded material

7 **Reconcile a checking account.** Most cash is kept in bank accounts, which are reconciled each month. Bank reconciliations adjust the bank and book balances so that they are the same correct amount. Differences arise between the book and bank balances because the company knows about some cash transactions before the bank does (such as deposits in transit and outstanding checks) and because the bank knows about some cash transactions before the company does (such as bank service charges).

8 **Understand how receivables can be used by a company to get cash immediately.** Sometimes companies that need cash in a hurry sell or "factor" their receivables. Companies buying receivables, known as factoring or financing companies, usually charge a discount of 2 to 15% of the receivable. Receivables can be factored with or without recourse. A note receivable is a claim against a debtor, evidenced by an unconditional written promise to pay a sum of money on or before a specified future date. The amount of interest to be earned annually is equal to: principal $\times$ interest rate $\times$ time period (in terms of one year) of the note. Notes can be discounted at a bank or other financial institution. Discounting allows the original payee of a note to receive money prior to the maturity date.

9 **Account for the impact of changing exchange rates on the value of accounts receivable denominated in foreign currencies.** U.S. companies transact large amounts of business with foreign parties. When the transaction is denominated in U.S. dollars, no new accounting issues are introduced. However, when a U.S. company enters into a transaction in which the price is denominated in a foreign currency, the U.S. company must use special accounting procedures to recognize the change in the value of the transaction as foreign currency exchange rates fluctuate. The sale is measured at the exchange rate on the date of sale, and any fluctuations between the sale date and the settlement date are recognized as exchange gains or losses.

key terms and concepts

accounts receivable 249

accounts receivable turnover 255

aging accounts receivable 253

allowance for bad debts 251

allowance method 250

average collection period 256

bad debt expense 250

bad debts 249

cash 248

contra account 247

direct write-off method 249

financing activities 240

gross sales 248

investing activities 240

net realizable value of accounts receivable 252

net sales 248

operating activities 239

receivables 249

revenue recognition 242

sales discounts 246

sales returns and allowances 247

expanded material

bank reconciliation 260

discounting a note receivable 263

foreign currency transaction 264

interest rate 262

maker 262

maturity date 262

maturity value 263

note receivable 262

NSF (not sufficient funds) checks 258

payee 262

principal 262

was touted as one of the hottest stocks on Wall Street. In 1987, after only six years in business, the company had a market valuation exceeding $211 million, giving its "genius" president a paper fortune of $109 million. Lawsuits, however, alleged that the company was nothing more than a massive fraud scheme that fooled major banks, two CPA firms, an investment banker, and a prestigious law firm.

ZZZZ Best was started as a carpet-cleaning business by Barry Minkow, a 15-year-old high school student, in 1981. Although ZZZZ Best had impressive growth as a carpet-cleaning business, the growth was not nearly fast enough for the impatient Minkow. In 1985, ZZZZ Best announced that it was expanding into the insurance restoration business, restoring buildings that had been damaged by fire, floods, and other disasters. During 1985 and 1986, ZZZZ Best reported undertaking several large insurance restoration projects. The company reported high profits from these restoration jobs. A public stock offering in 1986 stated that 86% of ZZZZ Best Corporation's business was in the insurance restoration area.

Based on the company's high growth and reported income in 1987, a spokesperson for a large brokerage house was quoted in *Business Week* as saying that "Barry Minkow is a great manager and ZZZZ Best is a great company." He recommended that his clients buy ZZZZ Best stock. That same year, the Association of Collegiate Entrepreneurs and the Young Entrepreneurs' Organization placed Minkow on their list of the top 100 young entrepreneurs in America; and the mayor of Los Angeles honored Minkow with a commendation that said that he had "set a fine entrepreneurial example of obtaining the status of a millionaire at the age of 18."

Unfortunately, ZZZZ Best's insurance business, its impressive growth, and its high reported income were totally fictitious. In fact, the company never once made a legitimate profit. Barry Minkow himself later said that he was a "fraudster" who convincingly deceived almost everyone involved with the company. Through the use of widespread collusion among company officials, Minkow was even able to hide the fraud from ZZZZ Best's external auditor. For example, when ZZZZ Best reported an $8.2 million contract to restore a building in San Diego, the external auditor demanded to see the building; this was difficult since neither the building nor the job existed. However, officials of ZZZZ Best gained access to a construction site and led the auditor through a tour of an unfinished building in San Diego to show that the "restoration" work was ongoing. The situation became very complicated for ZZZZ Best when the auditor later asked to see the finished job. ZZZZ Best had to spend $1 million to lease the building and hire contractors to finish six of the eight floors in ten days. The auditor was led on another tour and wrote a memo saying, "Job looks very good." The auditor was subsequently faulted for looking only at what ZZZZ Best officials chose to show, without making independent inquiries.

Minkow's house of cards finally came crashing down as it became apparent to banks, suppliers, investors, and the auditors that the increasing difficulty ZZZZ Best was having with paying its bills was entirely inconsistent with a company reporting so much revenue and profit. In January 1988, a federal grand jury in Los Angeles returned a 57-count indictment, charging 11 individuals—including ZZZZ Best founder and president, Barry Minkow—with engaging in a massive fraud scheme. Minkow was later convicted and sentenced to 25 years in a federal penitentiary in Colorado.

ZZZZ Best grossly inflated its operating results by reporting bogus revenue and receivables. What factors prevent a company from continuing to report fraudulent results indefinitely? What could the auditor have done to uncover the ZZZZ Best fraud?

Source: This description is based on articles in *The Wall Street Journal, Forbes,* and investigative proceedings of the U.S. House of Representatives, Subcommittee on Energy and Commerce hearings: *The Wall Street Journal,* July 7, 1987, p. 1; July 9, 1987, p. 1; August 23, 1988, p. 1; U.S. House of Representatives, Subcommittee on Oversight and Investigation of the Committee on Energy and Commerce, January 27, 1988; U.S. House of Representatives, Subcommittee on Oversight and Investigation of the Committee on Energy and Commerce, February 1, 1988; Daniel Akst, "How Barry Minkow Fooled the Auditors," *Forbes,* October 2, 1989, p. 126.

CASE 6-2

RECOGNIZING REVENUE

HealthCare, Inc.,* operates a number of medical testing facilities around the United States. Drug manufacturers, such as **MERCK** and **BRISTOL-MYERS SQUIBB**, contract with HealthCare

*The name of the actual company has been changed.

for testing of their newly developed drugs and other medical treatments. HealthCare advertises, gets patients, and then administers the drugs or other experimental treatments, under a doctor's care, to determine their effectiveness. The Food and Drug Administration requires such human testing before allowing drugs to be prescribed by doctors and sold by pharmacists. A typical contract might read as follows:

> HealthCare, Inc., will administer the new drug, "Lexitol," to 50 patients, once a week for 10 weeks, to determine its effectiveness in treating male baldness. Merck will pay HealthCare, Inc., $100 per patient visit, to be billed at the conclusion of the test period. The total amount of the contract is $50,000 (50 patients × 10 visits × $100 per visit).

Given these kinds of contracts, when should HealthCare recognize revenue—when contracts are signed, when patient visits take place, when drug manufacturers are billed, or when cash is collected?

CASE 6-3

CREDIT POLICY REVIEW

The president, vice president, and sales manager of Moorer Corporation were discussing the company's present credit policy. The sales manager suggested that potential sales were being lost to competitors because of Moorer Corporation's tight restrictions on granting credit to consumers. He stated that if credit policies were loosened, the current year's estimated credit sales of $3,000,000 could be increased by at least 20% next year with an increase in uncollectible accounts receivable of only $10,000 over this year's amount of $37,500. He argued that because the company's cost of sales is only 25% of revenues, the company would certainly come out ahead.

The vice president, however, suggested that a better alternative to easier credit terms would be to accept consumer credit cards such as VISA or MASTERCARD. She argued that this alternative could increase sales by 40%. The credit card finance charges to Moorer Corporation would be 4% of the additional sales.

At this point, the president interrupted by saying that he wasn't at all sure that increasing credit sales of any kind was a good thing. In fact, he suggested that the $37,500 of uncollectible accounts receivable was altogether too high. He wondered whether the company should discontinue offering sales on account.

With the information given, determine whether Moorer Corporation would be better off under the sales manager's proposal or the vice president's proposal. Also, address the president's suggestion that credit sales of all types be abolished.

# **ex**ercises

EXERCISE 6-1

RECOGNIZING REVENUE

Supposedly, there is an over 200-year wait to buy GREEN BAY PACKERS season football tickets. The fiscal year-end (when they close their books) for the Green Bay Packers is March 30 of each year. If the Packers sell their season football tickets in February for the coming football season, when should the revenue from those ticket sales be recognized?

EXERCISE 6-2

RECOGNIZING REVENUE

James Dee Company cleans the outside walls of buildings. The average job generates revenue of $800,000 and takes about two weeks to complete. Customers are required to pay for a job within 30 days after its completion. James Dee Company guarantees its work for five years—

if the building walls get dirty within five years, James Dee will clean them again at no charge. James Dee is considering recognizing revenue using one of the following methods:

a. Recognize revenue when James Dee signs the contract to do the job.
b. Recognize revenue when James Dee begins the work.
c. Recognize revenue immediately after the completion of the job.
d. Recognize revenue 30 days after the completion of the job when the cash is collected.
e. Wait until the five-year guarantee period is over before recognizing any revenue.

Which revenue recognition option would you recommend to James Dee? Explain your answer.

EXERCISE 6-3

RECOGNIZING REVENUE—LONG-TERM CONSTRUCTION PROJECTS

In the year 2002, Salt Lake City, Utah, will host the Winter Olympics. To get ready for the Olympics, most of the major roads and highways in and around Salt Lake City are being renovated. It will take over three years to complete the highway projects, and WASATCH CONSTRUCTORS, the construction company performing the work, probably doesn't want to wait until the work is completed to recognize revenue. How would you suggest that the revenue on these highway construction projects be recognized?

EXERCISE 6-4

REVENUE RECOGNITION

Yummy, Inc., is a franchiser that offers for sale an exclusive franchise agreement for $30,000. Under the terms of the agreement, the purchaser of a franchise receives a variety of services associated with the construction of a Yummy Submarine and Yogurt Shop, access to various product supply services, and continuing management advice and assistance once the retail unit is up and running. The contract calls for the franchise purchaser to make cash payments of $10,000 per year for three years to Yummy, Inc.

How should Yummy, Inc., account for the sale of a franchise contract? Specifically, when should the revenue and receivable be recognized?

EXERCISE 6-5

CONTROL OF CASH

Molly Maloney is an employee of Marshall Company, a small manufacturing concern. Her responsibilities include opening the daily mail, depositing the cash and checks received into the bank, and making the accounting entries to record the receipt of cash and the reduction of receivables. Explain how Maloney might be able to misuse some of Marshall's cash receipts. As a consultant, what control procedures would you recommend?

EXERCISE 6-6

RECORDING SALES TRANSACTIONS

On June 24, 2003, Hansen Company sold merchandise to Jill Selby for $80,000 with terms 2/10, n/30. On June 30, Selby paid $39,200 on her account and was allowed a discount for the timely payment. On July 20, Selby paid $24,000 on her account and returned $16,000 of merchandise, claiming that it did not meet contract terms.

Record the necessary journal entries on June 24, June 30, and July 20.

EXERCISE 6-7

RECORDING SALES TRANSACTIONS

Lopez Company sold merchandise on account to Atlantic Company for $4,000 on June 3, 2003, with terms 2/10, n/30. On June 7, 2003, Lopez Company received $200 of returned merchandise from Atlantic Company and issued a credit memorandum for the appropriate amount. Lopez Company received payment for the balance of the bill on June 21, 2003.

Record the necessary journal entries on June 3, June 7, and June 21.

EXERCISE 6-8

ESTIMATING BAD DEBTS

The trial balance of Stardust Company at the end of its 2003 fiscal year included the following account balances:

Account	
Accounts receivable	$48,900
Allowance for bad debts	2,500 (debit balance)

The company has *not yet* recorded any bad debt expense for 2003.

Determine the amount of bad debt expense to be recognized by Stardust Company for 2003, assuming the following independent situations:

1. An aging accounts receivable analysis indicates that probable uncollectible accounts receivable at year-end amount to $4,500.
2. Company policy is to maintain a provision for uncollectible accounts receivable equal to 3% of outstanding accounts receivable.
3. Company policy is to estimate uncollectible accounts receivable as equal to 0.5% of the previous year's annual sales, which were $200,000.

EXERCISE 6-9

ACCOUNTING FOR BAD DEBTS

The following data were associated with the accounts receivable and uncollectible accounts of Hilton, Inc., during 2003:

a. The opening credit balance in Allowance for Bad Debts was $900,000 at January 1, 2003.
b. During 2003, the company realized that specific accounts receivable totaling $920,000 had gone bad and had been written off.
c. An account receivable of $50,000 was collected during 2003. This account had previously been written off as a bad debt in 2002.
d. The company decided that Allowance for Bad Debts would be $920,000 at the end of 2003.

1. Prepare journal entries to show how these events would be recognized in the accounting system using:
   a. The direct write-off method.
   b. The allowance method.
2. Discuss the advantages and disadvantages of each method with respect to the matching principle.

EXERCISE 6-10

ACCOUNTING FOR UNCOLLECTIBLE ACCOUNTS RECEIVABLE

Dodge Company had the following information relating to its accounts receivable at December 31, 2002, and for the year ended December 31, 2003:

Accounts receivable balance at 12/31/02	$ 900,000
Allowance for bad debts at 12/31/02 (credit balance)	50,000
Gross sales during 2003 (all credit)	5,000,000
Collections from customers during 2003	4,500,000
Accounts written off as uncollectible during 2003	60,000
Estimated uncollectible receivables at 12/31/03	110,000

Dodge Company uses the percentage of receivables method to estimate bad debt expense.

1. At December 31, 2003, what is the balance of Dodge Company's Allowance for Bad Debts? What is the bad debt expense for 2003?
2. At December 31, 2003, what is the balance of Dodge Company's gross accounts receivable?

EXERCISE 6-11

AGING OF ACCOUNTS RECEIVABLE

Cicero Company's accounts receivable reveal the following balances:

Age of Accounts	Receivable Balance
Current	$600,000
1–30 days past due	320,000
31–60 days past due	80,000
61–90 days past due	50,000
91–120 days past due	9,000

The credit balance in Allowance for Bad Debts is now $26,000. After a thorough analysis of its collection history, the company estimates that the following percentages of receivables will eventually prove uncollectible:

Current	0.4%
1–30 days past due	3.0
31–60 days past due	12.0
61–90 days past due	60.0
91–120 days past due	90.0

Prepare an aging schedule for the accounts receivable, and give the journal entry for recording the necessary change in the allowance for bad debts account.

EXERCISE 6-12

Spread-Sheet Software

AGING OF ACCOUNTS RECEIVABLE

The following aging of accounts receivable is for Harry Company at the end of its first year of business:

Aging of Accounts Receivable December 31, 2003					
	Overall	Less Than 30 Days	31 to 60 Days	61 to 90 Days	Over 90 Days
Ken Nelson	$ 10,000	$ 8,000		$1,000	$1,000
Elaine Anderson	40,000	31,000	$ 4,000		5,000
Bryan Crist	12,000	3,000	4,000	2,000	3,000
Renee Warner	60,000	50,000	10,000		
Nelson Hsia	16,000	10,000	6,000		
Stella Valerio	25,000	20,000		5,000	
Totals	$163,000	$122,000	$24,000	$8,000	$9,000

Harry Company has collected the following bad debt information from a consultant familiar with Harry's industry:

Age of Account	Percentage Ultimately Uncollectible
Less than 30 days	2%
31–60 days	10
61–90 days	30
Over 90 days	75

1. Compute the appropriate Allowance for Bad Debts as of December 31, 2003.
2. Make the journal entry required to record this allowance. Remember that, since this is Harry's first year of operations, the allowance account at the beginning of the year was $0.
3. What is Harry's net accounts receivable balance as of December 31, 2003?

EXERCISE 6-13

DIRECT WRITE-OFF VERSUS ALLOWANCE METHOD

The vice president for Tres Corporation provides you with the following list of accounts receivable written off in the current year. (These accounts were recognized as bad debt expense at the time they were written off; i.e., the company was using the direct write-off method.)

Date	Customer	Amount
March 30	Rasmussen Company	$12,000
July 31	Dodge Company	7,500
September 30	Larsen Company	10,000
December 31	Peterson Company	12,000

Tres Corporation's sales are all on an n/30 credit basis. Sales for the current year total $3,600,000, and analysis has indicated that uncollectible receivable losses historically approximate 1.5% of sales.

1. Do you agree or disagree with Tres Corporation's policy concerning recognition of bad debt expense? Why or why not?
2. If Tres were to use the percentage of sales method for recording bad debt expense, by how much would income before income taxes change for the current year?

EXERCISE 6-14

ACCOUNTING FOR UNCOLLECTIBLE RECEIVABLES— PERCENTAGE OF SALES METHOD

The trial balance of Sporting House, Inc., shows a $100,000 outstanding balance in Accounts Receivable at the end of 2002. During 2003, 75% of the total credit sales of $4,000,000 was collected, and no receivables were written off as uncollectible. The company estimated that 1.5% of the credit sales would be uncollectible. During 2004, the account of Larry Johnson, who owed $1,200, was judged to be uncollectible and was written off. At the end of 2004, the amount previously written off was collected in full from Mr. Johnson.

Prepare the necessary journal entries for recording all the preceding transactions relating to uncollectibles on the books of Sporting House, Inc.

EXERCISE 6-15

COMPARING THE PERCENTAGE OF SALES AND THE PERCENTAGE OF RECEIVABLES METHODS

Keefer Company uses the percentage of sales method for computing bad debt expense. As of January 1, 2003, the balance of Allowance for Bad Debts was $200,000. Write-offs of uncollectible accounts during 2003 totaled $240,000. Reported bad debt expense for 2003 was $320,000, computed using the percentage of sales method.

Keith & Harding, the auditors of Keefer's financial statements, compiled an aging accounts receivable analysis of Keefer's accounts at the end of 2003. This analysis has led Keith & Harding to estimate that, of the accounts receivable Keefer has as of the end of 2003, $700,000 will ultimately prove to be uncollectible.

Given their analysis, Keith & Harding, the auditors, think that Keefer should make an adjustment to its 2003 financial statements. What adjusting journal entry should Keith & Harding suggest?

EXERCISE 6-16

RATIO ANALYSIS

The following are summary financial data for Parker Enterprises, Inc., and Boulder, Inc., for three recent years:

	Year 3	Year 2	Year 1
Net sales (in millions):			
Parker Enterprises, Inc.	$ 3,700	$ 3,875	$ 3,882
Boulder, Inc.	17,825	16,549	15,242
Net accounts receivable (in millions):			
Parker Enterprises, Inc.	1,400	1,800	1,725
Boulder, Inc.	5,525	5,800	6,205

1. Using the above data, compute the accounts receivable turnover and average collection period for each company for years 2 and 3.
2. Which company appears to have the better credit management policy?

EXERCISE 6-17

ASSESSING HOW WELL COMPANIES MANAGE THEIR RECEIVABLES

Assume that Hickory Company has the following data related to its accounts receivable:

	2002	2003
Net sales	$1,425,000	$1,650,000
Net receivables:		
Beginning of year	375,000	333,500
End of year	420,000	375,000

Use these data to compute accounts receivable turnover ratios and average collection periods for 2002 and 2003. Based on your analysis, is Hickory Company managing its receivables better or worse in 2003 than it did in 2002?

EXERCISE 6-18

MEASURING ACCOUNTS RECEIVABLE QUALITY

The following accounts receivable information is for Happy Tiny Company:

	2003	2002	2001
Accounts receivable	$300,000	$260,000	$220,000
Allowance for bad debts	18,000	17,000	16,000

Did the creditworthiness of Happy Tiny's customers increase or decrease between 2001 and 2003? Explain.

EXERCISE 6-19

ACCOUNTING FOR WARRANTIES

Rick Procter, president of Sharp Television Stores, has been concerned recently about declining sales due to increased competition in the area. Rick has noticed that many of the national stores selling television sets and appliances have been placing heavy emphasis on warranties in their marketing programs. In an effort to revitalize sales, Rick has decided to offer free service and repairs for one year as a warranty on his television sets. Based on experience, Rick believes that first-year service and repair costs on the television sets will be approximately 5% of sales. The first month of operations following the initiation of Rick's new marketing plan showed significant increases in sales of TV sets. Total sales of TV sets for the first three months under the warranty plan were $10,000, $8,000, and $12,000, respectively.

1. Assuming that Rick prepares adjusting entries and financial statements for his own use at the end of each month, prepare the appropriate entry to recognize customer service (warranty) expense for each of these first three months.
2. Prepare the appropriate entry to record services provided to repair sets under warranty in the second month, assuming that the following costs were incurred: labor (paid in cash), $550; supplies, $330.

EXERCISE 6-20

ACCOUNTING FOR WARRANTIES

Johnson Auto sells used cars and trucks. During 2003, it sold 51 cars and trucks for a total of $1,350,000. Johnson provides a 12-month, 12,000-mile warranty on the used cars and trucks sold. Johnson estimates that it will cost $25,000 in labor and $13,000 in parts to service (during the following year) the cars and trucks sold in 2003.

In January 2004, Steve Martin brought his truck in for warranty repairs. Johnson Auto fixed the truck under its warranty agreement. It cost Johnson $400 in labor and $275 in parts to fix Steve Martin's truck. Prepare the journal entries to record (1) Johnson Auto's estimated customer service liability as of December 31, 2003, and (2) the costs incurred in repairing the truck in January 2004.

expanded material

EXERCISE 6-21

PREPARING A BANK RECONCILIATION

Prepare a bank reconciliation for Oldroyd Company at January 31, 2003, using the information shown.

1. Cash per the accounting records at January 31 amounted to $72,802; the bank statement on this same date showed a balance of $64,502.
2. The canceled checks returned by the bank included a check written by the Oldham Company for $1,764 that had been deducted from Oldroyd's account in error.
3. Deposits in transit as of January 31, 2003, amounted to $10,928.
4. The following amounts were adjustments to Oldroyd Company's account on the bank statement:
    a. Service charges of $26.
    b. An NSF check of $1,400.
    c. Interest earned on the account, $40.
5. Checks written by Oldroyd Company that have not yet cleared the bank include four checks totaling $5,778.

EXERCISE 6-22

PREPARING A BANK RECONCILIATION

The records of Denna Corporation show the following bank statement information for December:

a. Bank balance, December 31, 2003, $87,450
b. Service charges for December, $50
c. Rent collected by bank, $1,000
d. Note receivable collected by bank (including $300 interest), $2,300
e. December check returned marked NSF (check was a payment of an account receivable), $200
f. Bank erroneously reduced Denna's account for a check written by Dunna Company, $1,000
g. Cash account balance, December 31, 2003, $81,200
h. Outstanding checks, $9,200
i. Deposits in transit, $5,000

1. Prepare a bank reconciliation for December.
2. Prepare the entry to correct the cash account as of December 31, 2003.

EXERCISE 6-23

RECONCILING BOOK AND BANK BALANCES

Jensen Company has just received the September 30, 2003, bank statement summarized in the following schedule:

	Charges	Deposits	Balance
Balance, September 1			$ 5,100
Deposits recorded during September		$27,000	32,100
Checks cleared during September	$27,300		4,800
NSF check, J. J. Jones	50		4,750
Bank service charges	10		4,740
Balance, September 30			4,740

Cash on hand (recorded on Jensen's books but not deposited) on September 1 and September 30 amounted to $200. There were no deposits in transit or checks outstanding at September 1, 2003. The cash account for September reflected the following:

Cash

Sept. 1 Balance	5,300	Sept. Checks	28,000
Sept. Deposits	29,500		

Answer the following questions. (Hint: It may be helpful to prepare a complete bank reconciliation.)

1. What is the ending balance per the cash account before adjustments?
2. What adjustments should be added to the depositor's books?
3. What is the total amount of the deductions from the depositor's books?
4. What is the total amount to be added to the bank's balance?
5. What is the total amount to be deducted from the bank's balance?

EXERCISE 6-24

JOURNAL ENTRIES FOR NOTES RECEIVABLE

Prepare journal entries for the following transactions for Stansworth Plumbing for 2003:

July   1   Installed a sprinkling system for Chuck's Engineering and billed $12,600 for the job.
Sept.   1   Chuck's had not yet paid for the sprinkling system. Stansworth agreed to accept a three-month note for the full amount with interest at an annual rate of 14%.
Dec.   1   Chuck's Engineering paid the note in full.

EXERCISE 6-25

FACTORING RECEIVABLES AND BORROWING MONEY

Nixon Enterprises is experiencing a temporary shortage of cash. To cover the shortage, the financial vice president of the company proposed that some of the company's accounts receivable be sold (factored). A factoring company has offered to buy up to $2 million of the company's receivables on a without recourse basis at a fee of 16% of the amount factored.

As an alternative, another vice president of the company has proposed borrowing an equivalent amount from South Willow Bank, pledging the outstanding receivables as collateral for the loan. Under the terms of the borrowing agreement, Nixon Enterprises would receive 80% of the value of all receivables assigned to the bank and would be charged a 1% loan origination (service) fee based on the actual dollar amount of cash received and 12% annual interest on the outstanding loan. The company estimates that the loan will be repaid in two months.

Evaluate the two alternatives. Which one is better from the company's perspective?

EXERCISE 6-26

General Ledger Software

ACCOUNTING FOR NOTES RECEIVABLE

Escondido Company frequently sells merchandise on promissory notes. The following transactions relate to one such note:

Feb.   1   Sold merchandise for $9,000 to Marta Tabor; accepted a 6-month, 11% note.
Aug.   1   On this date (due date of the note), Marta Tabor did not make payment.
Oct.   1   Collected the maturity value (principal plus interest as of August 1) of the note from Marta Tabor, together with 15% interest on the maturity value from August 1.

Prepare the journal entries to record the above transactions.

EXERCISE 6-27

International

FOREIGN CURRENCY TRANSACTION

Rabona Slice, a U.S. company, sold 100,000 cases of tropical fruit to Ben Thanh Market, a Vietnamese firm, for 2.5 billion Vietnamese dong. The sale was made on November 17, 2003, when one U.S. dollar equaled 14,000 dong. Payment of 2.5 billion Vietnamese dong was due to Rabona Slice on January 16, 2004. At December 31, 2003, one U.S. dollar equaled 15,000 dong, and on January 16, 2004, one U.S. dollar equaled 15,600 dong.

1. What will be the value of the accounts receivable on December 31, 2003, in Vietnamese dong?

2. What will be the value of the accounts receivable on December 31, 2003, in U.S. dollars?
3. Will Rabona Slice recognize an exchange gain or loss at December 31, 2003? Explain.
4. Will Rabona Slice recognize an exchange gain or loss on January 16, 2004? Explain.
5. In connection with this sale, what amount will Rabona Slice report as Sales Revenue in its income statement for 2003?
6. In connection with this sale, what amount will Rabona Slice report as Cash Collected from Customers in its statement of cash flows for 2004?

EXERCISE 6-28

FOREIGN CURRENCY TRANSACTION

American, Inc., sells one widget to Japanese Company at an agreed-upon price of 1,000,000 yen. On the day of the sale, one yen is equal to $0.01. American, Inc., maintains its accounting records in U.S. dollars. Therefore, the amount in yen must be converted to U.S. dollars.

1. Provide the journal entry that would be made by American, Inc., on the day of the sale, assuming Japanese Company pays for the widget on the day of the sale.
2. Most sales are on account, meaning that payment will not be received for 30 days or even longer. What issues will arise for American, Inc., if the sale is made with payment due in 30 days? (Hint: What might happen to the value of the yen in relation to the dollar during the 30-day period?)
3. Suppose that 30 days from the date of the sale the value of one yen is equal to $0.008. What journal entry would be made when the 1,000,000 yen are received by American, Inc.?

PROBLEM 6-1

RECOGNIZING REVENUE

Brad Company sells ships. Each ship sells for over $25 million. Brad never starts building a ship until it receives a specific order from a customer. Brad usually takes about four years to build a ship. After construction is completed and during the first three years the customer uses the ship, Brad agrees to repair anything on the ship free of charge. The customers pay for the ships over a period of ten years after the date of delivery.

Brad Company is considering the following alternatives for recognizing revenue from its sale of ships:

a. Recognize revenue when Brad receives the order to do the job.
b. Recognize revenue when Brad begins the work.
c. Recognize revenue proportionately during the four-year construction period.
d. Recognize revenue immediately after the customer takes possession of the ship.
e. Wait until the three-year guarantee period is over before recognizing any revenue.
f. Wait until the ten-year payment period is over before recognizing any revenue.

Required:

1. Which of the methods, (a) through (f), should Brad use to recognize revenue? Support your answer.
2. **Interpretive Question:** A member of Congress has introduced a bill that would require the SEC to crack down on lenient revenue recognition practices by shipbuilding companies. This bill would require Brad Company to use method (f) above. The "logic" behind the congressperson's bill is that no revenue should ever be recognized until the complete amount of cash is in hand. You have been hired as a lobbyist by Brad Company to speak against this bill. What arguments would you use on Capitol Hill to sway representatives to vote against this bill?

PROBLEM 6-2

RECOGNIZING REVENUE

The Ho Man Tin Tennis Club sells lifetime memberships for $20,000 each. A lifetime membership entitles a person to unlimited access to the club's tennis courts, weight room, exercise equipment, and swimming pool. Once a lifetime membership fee is paid, it is not refundable for any reason.

Judy Chan and her partners are the owners of Ho Man Tin Tennis Club. In order to overcome a cash shortage, they intend to seek investment funds from new partners. Judy and her partners are meeting with their accountant to provide information for preparation of financial statements. They are considering when they should recognize revenue from the sale of lifetime memberships.

Required: Answer the following questions:

1. When should the lifetime membership fees be recognized as revenue? Remember, they are nonrefundable.
2. **Interpretive Question:** What incentives would Judy and her partners have for recognizing the entire amount of the lifetime membership fee as revenue at the time it is collected? Since the entire amount will ultimately be recognized anyway, what difference does the timing make?

PROBLEM 6-3

General Ledger Software

SALES TRANSACTIONS

Company R and Company S entered into the following transactions:

a. Company R sold merchandise to Company S for $40,000, terms 2/10, n/30.
b. Prior to payment, Company S returned $3,000 of the merchandise for credit.
c. Company S paid Company R in full within the discount period.
d. Company S paid Company R in full after the discount period. [Assume that transaction (c) did not occur.]

Required: Prepare journal entries to record the transactions for Company R (the seller).

PROBLEM 6-4

CASH FRAUD

Mac Faber was the controller of the Lewiston National Bank. In his position of controller, he was in charge of all accounting functions. He wrote cashier's checks for the bank and reconciled the bank statement. He alone could approve exceptions to credit limits for bank customers, and even the internal auditors reported to him. Unknown to the bank, Mac had recently divorced and was supporting two households. In addition, many of his personal investments had soured, including a major farm implement dealership that had lost $40,000 in the last year. Several months after Mac had left the bank for another job, it was discovered that a vendor had paid twice and that the second payment had been deposited in Mac's personal account. Because Mac was not there to cover his tracks (as he had been on previous occasions), an investigation ensued. It was determined that Mac had used his position in the bank to steal $117,000 over a period of two years. Mac was prosecuted and sentenced to 30 months in a federal penitentiary.

Required:
1. What internal control weaknesses allowed Mac to perpetrate the fraud?
2. What motivated Mac to perpetrate the fraud?

PROBLEM 6-5

ANALYSIS OF ALLOWANCE FOR BAD DEBTS

Boulder View Corporation accounts for uncollectible accounts receivable using the allowance method.

As of December 31, 2002, the credit balance in Allowance for Bad Debts was $130,000. During 2003, credit sales totaled $10,000,000, $90,000 of accounts receivable were written off as uncollectible, and recoveries of accounts previously written off amounted to $15,000. An aging of accounts receivable at December 31, 2003, showed the following:

Classification of Receivable	Accounts Receivable Balance as of December 31, 2003	Percentage Estimated Uncollectible
Current	$1,140,000	2%
1–30 days past due	600,000	10
31–60 days past due	400,000	23
Over 60 days past due	120,000	75
	$2,260,000	

Required:

1. Prepare the journal entry to record bad debt expense for 2003, assuming bad debts are estimated using the aging of receivables method.
2. Record journal entries to account for the actual write-off of $90,000 uncollectible accounts receivable and the collection of $15,000 in receivables that had previously been written off.

PROBLEM 6-6

ACCOUNTING FOR ACCOUNTS RECEIVABLE

Assume that Dome Company had the following balances in its receivable accounts on December 31, 2002:

Accounts receivable $400,000
Allowance for bad debts .... 10,200 (credit balance)

Transactions during 2003 were as follows:

Gross credit sales $1,600,000
Collections of accounts receivable ($1,560,000 less cash discounts
   of $20,000) 1,540,000
Sales returns and allowances (from credit sales) 10,000
Accounts receivable written off as uncollectible 6,000
Balance in Allowance for Bad Debts on December 31, 2003
   (based on percent of total accounts receivable) 12,000

Required:

1. Prepare entries for the 2003 transactions.
2. What amount will Dome Company report for:
   a. Net sales in its 2003 income statement?
   b. Total accounts receivable on its balance sheet of December 31, 2003?

PROBLEM 6-7

ANALYSIS OF RECEIVABLES

Juniper Company was formed in 1993. Sales have increased on the average of 5% per year during its first ten years of existence, with total sales for 2002 amounting to $400,000. Since incorporation, Juniper Company has used the allowance method to account for uncollectible accounts receivable.

On January 1, 2003, the company's Allowance for Bad Debts had a credit balance of $5,000. During 2003, accounts totaling $3,500 were written off as uncollectible.

Required:

1. What does the January 1, 2003, credit balance of $5,000 in Allowance for Bad Debts represent?
2. Since Juniper Company wrote off $3,500 in uncollectible accounts receivable during 2003, was the prior year's estimate of uncollectible accounts receivable overstated?
3. Prepare journal entries to record:
   a. The $3,500 write-off of receivables during 2003.
   b. Juniper Company's 2003 bad debt expense, assuming an aging of the December 31, 2003, accounts receivable indicates that potential uncollectible accounts at year-end total $9,000.

PROBLEM 6-8

COMPUTING AND RECORDING BAD DEBT EXPENSE

During 2003, Wishbone Corporation had a total of $5,000,000 in sales, of which 80% were on credit. At year-end, the Accounts Receivable balance showed a total of $2,300,000, which had been aged as follows:

Age	Amount
Current	$1,900,000
1–30 days past due	200,000
31–60 days past due	100,000
61–90 days past due	70,000
Over 90 days past due	30,000
	$2,300,000

Prepare the journal entry required at year-end to record the bad debt expense under each of the following independent conditions. Assume, where applicable, that Allowance for Bad Debts had a credit balance of $5,500 immediately before these adjustments.

Required:
1. Use the direct write-off method. (Assume that $60,000 of accounts are determined to be uncollectible and are written off in a single year-end entry.)
2. Based on experience, uncollectible accounts existing at year-end are estimated to be 3% of total accounts receivable.
3. Based on experience, uncollectible accounts are estimated to be the sum of:

   1% of current accounts receivable
   6% of accounts 1–30 days past due
   10% of accounts 31–60 days past due
   20% of accounts 61–90 days past due
   30% of accounts over 90 days past due

PROBLEM 6-9

General Ledger Software

UNIFYING CONCEPTS: AGING OF ACCOUNTS RECEIVABLE AND UNCOLLECTIBLE ACCOUNTS

Delta Company has found that, historically, 0.5% of its current accounts receivable, 1% of accounts 1 to 30 days past due, 1.5% of accounts 31 to 60 days past due, 3% of accounts 61 to 90 days past due, and 10% of accounts over 90 days past due are uncollectible. The following schedule shows an aging of the accounts receivable as of December 31, 2003:

		Days Past Due			
	Current	1–30	31–60	61–90	Over 90
Balance	$45,600	$9,850	$4,100	$850	$195

The balances at December 31, 2003, in selected accounts are as follows. (Assume that the allowance method is used.)

Sales revenue	$120,096
Sales returns	1,209
Allowance for bad debts	113 (credit balance)

Required:
1. Given these data, make the necessary adjusting entry (or entries) for uncollectible accounts receivable on December 31, 2003.
2. On February 14, 2004, Lori Jacobs, a customer, informed Delta Company that she was going bankrupt and would not be able to pay her account of $46. Make the appropriate entry (or entries).
3. On June 29, 2004, Lori Jacobs was able to pay the amount she owed in full. Make the appropriate entry (or entries).

4. Assume that Allowance for Bad Debts at December 31, 2003, had a debit balance of $113 instead of a credit balance of $113. Make the necessary adjusting journal entry that would be needed on December 31, 2003.

PROBLEM 6-10

ESTIMATING UNCOLLECTIBLE ACCOUNTS

Ulysis Corporation makes and sells clothing to fashion stores throughout the country. On December 31, 2003, before adjusting entries were made, it had the following account balances on its books:

Accounts receivable.	$ 2,320,000
Sales revenue, 2003 (60% were credit sales)	16,000,000
Allowance for bad debts (credit balance).	4,000

Required:

1. Make the appropriate adjusting entry on December 31, 2003, to record the allowance for bad debts if uncollectible accounts receivable are estimated to be 3% of accounts receivable.

2. Make the appropriate adjusting entry on December 31, 2003, to record the allowance for bad debts if uncollectible accounts receivable are estimated on the basis of an aging of accounts receivable; the aging schedule reveals the following:

	Balance of Accounts Receivable	Percent Estimated to Become Uncollectible
Current	$1,200,000	0.5%
1–30 days past due	800,000	1
31–60 days past due	200,000	4
61–90 days past due	80,000	20
Over 90 days past due.	40,000	30

3. Now assume that on March 3, 2004, it was determined that a $64,000 account receivable from Petite Corners is uncollectible. Record the bad debt, assuming:
   a. The direct write-off method is used.
   b. The allowance method is used.

4. Further assume that on June 4, 2004, Petite Corners paid this previously written-off debt of $64,000. Record the payment, assuming:
   a. The direct write-off method had been used on March 3 to record the bad debt.
   b. The allowance method had been used on March 3 to record the bad debt.

5. **Interpretive Question:** Which method of accounting for bad debts, direct write-off or allowance, is generally used? Why?

PROBLEM 6-11

THE AGING METHOD

The following aging of accounts receivable is for Coby Company at the end of 2003:

Aging of Accounts Receivable December 31, 2003					
	Overall	**Less Than 30 Days**	**31 to 60 Days**	**61 to 90 Days**	**Over 90 Days**
Travis Campbell	$ 50,000	$ 40,000	$ 5,000	$ 2,000	$ 3,000
Linda Reed	35,000	31,000	4,000		
Jack Riding	110,000	100,000	10,000		
Joy Riddle	20,000	3,000	10,000	4,000	3,000
Afzal Shah	90,000	60,000	21,000	4,000	5,000
Edna Ramos	80,000	60,000	16,000		4,000
Totals	$385,000	$294,000	$66,000	$10,000	$15,000

Briton Company
Bank Reconciliation for August 2003
Prepared by Kim Lee

Balance per bank statement	$192,056	Balance per books	$169,598
Additions to bank balance:		*Additions to book balance:*	
Deposits in transit	8,000	Note collected by bank	250
		Interest earned	600
Deductions from bank balance:		*Deductions from book balance:*	
Outstanding checks:		NSF check	(1,800)
#201	(19,200)	Bank service charges	(48)
#204	(5,000)		
#205	(4,058)		
#295	(195)		
#565	(1,920)		
#567	(615)		
#568	(468)		
Adjusted bank balance	**$168,600**	**Adjusted book balance**	**$168,600**

In examining the bank reconciliation, you decide to review canceled checks returned by the bank. You find that check stubs for check nos. 201, 204, 205, and 295 indicate that these checks were supposedly voided when written. All other bank reconciliation data have been verified as correct.

Required:
1. Compute the amount suspected stolen by Kim.
2. **Interpretive Question:** Describe how Kim accounted for the stolen money. What would have prevented the theft?

PROBLEM 6-15

ACCOUNTING FOR A NOTE RECEIVABLE

The following information is for Lyman Irrigation Company:

Mar. 1 Sold sprinkling pipe to Federated Farms for $16,000, terms 2/10, n/30 (omit entries for cost of goods sold or inventory).

Mar. 12 Accepted a $16,000, three-month, 10% note from Federated Farms in payment of its account.

June 12 Collected the note plus interest.

Required:
1. Prepare journal entries for the transactions.
2. **Interpretive Question:** What would be the purpose of Lyman "discounting" the note at a bank on April 30?

PROBLEM 6-16

ACCOUNTING FOR A NOTE RECEIVABLE

On May 1, your company accepted a $24,000, three-month, 12% note from a customer in exchange for services rendered.

Required:
1. As the accountant for the company, prepare an appropriate journal entry to record the acceptance of the note.
2. On August 1, the customer notified you that the note amount could not be repaid until October 1. You agreed on a new, two-month note with an interest rate of 18%. The face amount of this note includes the principal and accrued interest on the original note. Prepare the appropriate journal entry on August 1.
3. Prepare the appropriate entry to record the collection in full of the note plus interest on October 1.

PROBLEM 6-17

ACCOUNTING FOR A FOREIGN CURRENCY TRANSACTION

On December 19, 2003, Mr. Kitty Company performed services for Cartour Company. The contracted price for the services was 20,000 euros, to be paid on March 23, 2004. On Decem-

ber 19, 2003, one euro equaled $0.94. On December 31, 2003, one euro equaled $0.98, and on March 23, 2004, one euro equaled $0.91. Mr. Kitty is a U.S. company.

Required:

1. Make the journal entry on Mr. Kitty's books to record the provision of services on December 19, 2003.
2. Make the necessary adjusting entry on Mr. Kitty's books on December 31 to adjust the account receivable to its appropriate U.S. dollar value.
3. Make the journal entry on Mr. Kitty's books to record the collection of the 20,000 euros on March 23.
4. **Interpretive Question:** Why would Mr. Kitty, a U.S. company, agree to denominate the contract in euros instead of in U.S. dollars?

competency enhancement opportunities

▶ Analyzing Real Company Information
▶ International Case
▶ Ethics Case
▶ Writing Assignment

▶ The Debate
▶ Cumulative Spreadsheet Project
▶ Internet Search

The following additional assignments provide opportunities for students to develop critical thinking, ethical perspectives, oral and written communication skills, experience with electronic research, and teamwork through group and business activities.

▶ **ANALYZING REAL COMPANY INFORMATION**

• *Analyzing 6-1 (Microsoft)*
The 1999 annual report for MICROSOFT is included in Appendix A. Locate that annual report and consider the following questions:

1. Provide the summary journal entry that Microsoft would have made to record its revenue for the fiscal year ended June 30, 1999 (assume all sales were on account).
2. Given Microsoft's beginning and ending balances in accounts receivable, along with your journal entry from Part 1, estimate the amount of cash collected from customers during the year.
3. Notice that Microsoft has an unearned revenue account. The balance in that account increased from 1998 to 1999. Provide the summary journal entry that was made to record that increase.
4. Locate Microsoft's note on revenue recognition. What is Microsoft's revenue recognition policy?

• *Analyzing 6-2 (Bank of America)*
BANK OF AMERICA is one of the oldest banks in America, as well as one of the largest. Founded in the late 1800s, Bank of America has grown from a strictly California-based bank to one with operations in over 20 states. Information from Bank of America's annual report follows. (Amounts are in millions.)

nounce that it had exceeded analysts' expectations. Without these changes, BioMedic will report EPS of $1.21 per share.

What issues should John consider before he makes the changes to the income statement? Would John be doing something wrong by making these changes? Would John be breaking the law?

▶ WRITING ASSIGNMENT

• *Revenue Recognition for Health Clubs*

The health fitness business has become increasingly popular as the sedentary lifestyle of most Americans has caused a large percentage of the population to feel, and be, out of shape. Health clubs have popped up all over, and with these clubs come some interesting accounting issues. Members typically sign up for one year and pay an up-front fee, followed by a monthly payment. The up-front fee covers, among other things, a health assessment by a club expert as well as a customized training program. For the monthly fee, members get the use of the facilities. The big accounting question is: How should the up-front fee be accounted for? Can the entire amount of the up-front fee be recognized at the beginning of the contract, or should it be recognized over the course of the year? Prepare a one-page paper explaining your point of view.

▶ THE DEBATE

• *Bad Debt Expense: Relevance Versus Reliability*

When it comes to recognizing bad debt expense, the allowance method is used because it complies with the matching principle (e.g., expenses are matched with revenues in the period in which those revenues are earned). However, the allowance method requires estimation, and the estimates may not be reliable. An alternative is to use the direct write-off method. Under the direct write-off method, when a receivable is deemed worthless it is written off, and the bad debt expense is recognized at that time. This method requires no estimates and is thus more reliable.

Divide your group into two teams.

- One team represents "The Direct Write-Off Method." Prepare a two-minute oral argument supporting the use of this method.
- The other team represents "The Allowance Method." Prepare a two-minute presentation supporting your position.

▶ CUMULATIVE SPREADSHEET PROJECT

This spreadsheet assignment is a continuation of the spreadsheet assignments given in earlier chapters. If you completed those spreadsheets, you have a head start on this one. If needed, review the spreadsheet assignment for Chapter 4 to refresh your memory on how to construct forecasted financial statements.

1. Handyman wishes to prepare a forecasted balance sheet and income statement for 2004. Use the original financial statement numbers for 2003 [given in part (1) of the Cumulative Spreadsheet Project assignment in Chapter 2] as the basis for the forecast, along with the following additional information:
    a. Sales in 2004 are expected to increase by 40% over 2003 sales of $700.
    b. In 2004, Handyman expects to acquire new property, plant, and equipment costing $80.

  c. The $160 in other operating expenses reported in 2003 includes $5 of depreciation expense.

  d. No new long-term debt will be acquired in 2004.

  e. No cash dividends will be paid in 2004.

  f. New short-term loans payable will be acquired in an amount sufficient to make Handyman's current ratio in 2004 exactly equal to 2.0.

Note: These statements were constructed as part of the spreadsheet assignment in Chapter 4; you can use that spreadsheet as a starting point if you have completed that assignment.

  For this exercise, the current assets are expected to behave as follows:

  i. Cash and inventory will increase at the same rate as sales.

  ii. The forecasted amount of accounts receivable in 2004 is determined using the forecasted value for the average collection period. For simplicity, do the computations using the end-of-period accounts receivable balance instead of the average balance. The average collection period for 2004 is expected to be 14.08 days.

Clearly state any additional assumptions that you make.

2. Repeat (1), with the following change in assumptions:

  a. Average collection period is expected to be 9.06 days.

  b. Average collection period is expected to be 20.00 days.

3. Comment on the differences in the forecasted values of accounts receivable in 2004 under each of the following assumptions about the average collection period: 14.08 days, 9.06 days, and 20.00 days. Under which assumption will Handyman's forecasted cash flow from operating activities be higher? Explain.

▶ INTERNET SEARCH

• *Yahoo!*

YAHOO! is one of the best-known Internet brand names in the world. Access Yahoo!'s Web site at http://www.yahoo.com and answer the following questions. Sometimes Web addresses change, so if this address doesn't work, access the Web site for this textbook (http://albrecht.swcollege.com) for an updated link.

1. On its home page, Yahoo! has a link to information about job openings at the company. Use that link to find out what kind of benefits Yahoo! offers its employees.

2. Look at the current job openings at Yahoo! and identify one opening in the general field of finance.

3. Yahoo! is proud of the proliferation of "local Yahoos!" based in foreign countries. List the Asian countries in which a local Yahoo! is currently in operation.

4. Search the Yahoo! press release archive to find the most recent announcement about quarterly financial results. What was Yahoo!'s reported total revenue in the most recent quarter?

Inventory

f7

learning objectives After studying this chapter, you should be able to:

1 Identify what items and costs should be included in inventory and cost of goods sold.

2 Account for inventory purchases and sales using both a perpetual and a periodic inventory system.

3 Calculate cost of goods sold using the results of an inventory count and

understand the impact of errors in ending inventory on reported cost of goods sold.

4 Apply the four inventory cost flow alternatives: specific identification, FIFO, LIFO, and average cost.

5 Use financial ratios to evaluate a company's inventory level.

expanded material

6 Analyze the impact of inventory errors on reported cost of goods sold.

7 Describe the complications that arise when LIFO or average cost is used with a perpetual inventory system.

8 Apply the lower-of-cost-or-market method of accounting for inventory.

9 Explain the gross margin method of estimating inventories.

SEARS, ROEBUCK & COMPANY began as the result of an inventory mistake. In 1886, a shipment of gold watches was mistakenly sent to a jeweler in Redwood Falls, Minnesota. When the jeweler refused to accept delivery of the unwanted watches, they were purchased by an enterprising railroad agent who saw an opportunity to make some money. Richard Sears sold all of those watches, ordered more, and started the R. W. SEARS WATCH COMPANY. The next year, Sears moved his operation to Chicago, where he found a partner in watchmaker Alvah Roebuck, and in 1893 they incorporated under the name "Sears, Roebuck & Co."

The company's initial growth was fueled by mail-order sales to farmers. Sears bought goods in volume from manufacturers. Then, taking advantage of cheap parcel post and rural free delivery (RFD) rates, Sears shipped the goods directly to the customers, thereby bypassing the profit markups of the chain of middlemen usually standing between manufacturers and farmers. Sales growth was partially driven by the persuasive advertising copy written by Richard Sears for the famous Sears catalog. In fact, his product descriptions have been politely called "fanciful." But the company compensated by backing its products with an unconditional money-back guarantee for dissatisfied customers.

The next wave of growth at Sears began in 1925 when the first Sears retail store was opened in Chicago. The shift from mail-order catalog sales to retail outlet sales paralleled the rise in popularity of the automobile in the United States. The automobile made it practical for rural customers to shop in the city. Reflecting the importance of the automobile, Sears pioneered the provision of free parking lots next to its stores. In the post–World War II boom, Sears' sales skyrocketed, leaving chief rival MONTGOMERY WARD far behind.

The 1980s was a decade of diversification at Sears. Actually, the diversification had begun in 1931 when Sears started selling ALLSTATE auto insurance, first by mail and then from its retail locations. In the 1980s, Sears acquired DEAN WITTER, a financial services firm, and COLDWELL BANKER, a real estate firm. In addition, Sears launched the Discover® credit card and backed Prodigy®, the first widespread online service (a joint project with IBM and CBS).

In the early 1990s, the diversified Sears empire began to show increasing weakness, culminating in a reported loss of almost $2.3 billion in 1992. The company's management responded by going back to the basics of retail marketing. The financial services operations (including the Discover card) and the real estate operations (along with the famous Sears Tower in Chicago) were sold. Sears focused on clothing sales in its mall-based stores and appliance and automotive product sales in its off-the-mall stores. In addition, Sears returned to emphasizing its in-house Sears credit card. In 1999, almost half of all Sears' sales were financed with the Sears credit card. During 1999, over 39 million people used the Sears card, and over 21 million owed Sears money as of the end of the year.

Sears is continuing to leverage one of its biggest assets—its in-house brand names such as Kenmore and Craftsman. In fact, sales of Sears appliances and tools make up two-thirds of the company's annual revenue. Currently, Sears is the leader in appliance sales and outsells the next 12 competitors combined. Sears has also streamlined its purchasing, cut 30% of its dealer network, and is keeping more popular fashions in stock in its clothing department. This streamlining has resulted in higher inventory turnover. As a result of these changes and others, Sears' stock price has risen from $15 per share in 1992 to as high as $50 per share in 1999.[1]

setting the stage

Like Sears, every business has products or services that it sells. Some companies, usually referred to as diversified companies or conglomerates, sell many unrelated products and services, just as Sears did in the 1980s. Other companies focus on a core set of products or services, as Sears did in the 1990s.

In Chapter 6, the focus was on revenues and receivables arising from the sale of products and services. In this chapter, the focus is on accounting for the products and services that are sold.

---

1 This description is based on the Sears Company History at http://www.sears.com; "Sears, Roebuck and Co.," *International Directory of Company Histories*, Vol. 18 (Detroit: St. James Press, 1997), pp. 475–479.

Exhibit 7-1 shows how the financial statements are affected by the material covered in this chapter. The inventory and accounts payable accounts on the balance sheet, cost of goods sold on the income statement, and payments for inventory on the statement of cash flows are discussed in this chapter.

Traditionally, companies have been divided into two groups: service companies and product companies. Companies such as hotels, cable TV networks, banks, carpet cleaners, and firms of lawyers, accountants, or engineers sell services. In contrast, supermarkets, steel mills, and book stores sell products. Because the practice of accounting evolved in a business environment dominated by manufacturing and merchandising firms, the accounting for service companies is significantly less developed than the accounting for companies that sell products. In this chapter we discuss traditional accounting for product companies, emphasizing cost of goods sold and inventory. In Chapter 8 we will discuss operating expenses that are common to both service and product firms. Further discussion of the developing area of accounting for service companies is included in Chapter 3 in the management accounting part of this text.

STOP & THINK The clear separation between product and service companies is disappearing. For example, does MICROSOFT sell a product or a service? What about MCDONALD'S—product or service?

Inventory accounting is considerably more complex for manufacturing firms than for merchandising firms. In a retail or wholesale business, the cost of goods sold is simply the costs incurred in purchasing the merchandise sold during the period; inventory is simply the cost of products purchased and not yet sold. Manufacturing firms, however, produce the goods they sell, so inventory and cost of goods sold must include all manufacturing costs of the products produced and sold. Because it is much easier to understand the concept of inventory and cost of goods sold in the context of retail and wholesale firms, manufacturing firms will not be considered in detail in this chapter. The details of inventory accounting for manufacturing firms will be covered in Chapter 2 in the management accounting part of this text.

Fifty years ago, inventory was arguably the most important asset on the balance sheet. However, changes in the economy have led to a decrease in the relative importance of inventory. For example, as illustrated in Exhibit 7-2, inventory for the 50 largest companies in the United States declined steadily from 15.4% of total assets in 1987 to 7.4% of total assets in 1998. This trend is a

---

e x h i b i t   7 - 1   Financial Statement Items Covered in This Chapter

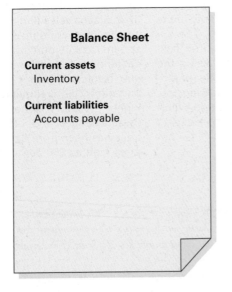

Balance Sheet

Current assets
Inventory

Current liabilities
Accounts payable

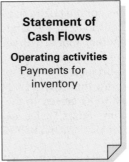

Statement of Cash Flows

Operating activities
Payments for
inventory

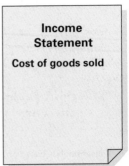

Income Statement

Cost of goods sold

FOE
nati
mea
me
ship
tain
me
the

FOE
pin
me
me
shi
ow
shi

con
me
ow
con
oth
usu
bas

e

exhibit 7-2   How Much Inventory Do Companies Have?

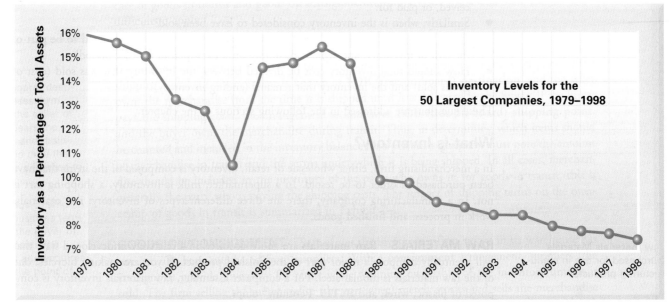

**Inventory Levels for the
50 Largest Companies, 1979–1998**

Source: Standard and Poor's *COMPUSTAT.*

result of two factors: more efficient management of inventory because of improved information technology and a decrease in the prominence of old-style, smokestack industries that carried large inventories. Companies in the growth industries of services, technology, and information often have little or no inventory.

1

Identify what items and costs should be included in inventory and cost of goods sold.

inventory Goods held for resale.

cost of goods sold The expenses incurred to purchase or manufacture the merchandise sold during a period.

INVENTORY AND COST OF GOODS SOLD

Inventory is the name given to goods that are either manufactured or purchased for resale in the normal course of business. A car dealer's inventory is comprised of automobiles; a grocery store's inventory consists of vegetables, meats, dairy products, canned goods, and bakery items; SEARS' inventory is composed of shirts, appliances, DieHard® batteries, and more. Like other items of value, such as cash or equipment, inventory is classified as an asset and reported on the balance sheet. When products are sold, they are no longer assets. The costs to purchase or manufacture the products must be removed from the asset classification (inventory) on the balance sheet and reported on the income statement as an expense—**cost of goods sold**.

The time line in Exhibit 7-3 illustrates the business issues involved with inventory.

exhibit 7-3   Time Line of Business Issues Involved with Inventory

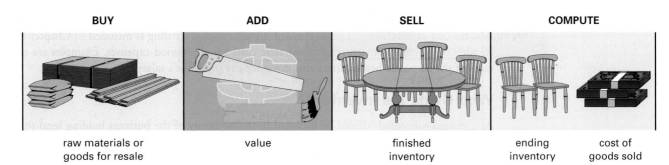

BUY	ADD	SELL	COMPUTE
raw materials or goods for resale	value	finished inventory	ending inventory cost of goods sold

Technology Is Changing the Way Companies View Inventory In the good old days, a company would buy inventory, hold it for a while, and then sell it to a customer. Businesses now realize that inventory sitting on a shelf costs money—money that is tied up in inventory cannot be used for other purposes. Technology now allows companies to shorten the time that money is tied up in inventory. An entire discipline, supply-chain management, has developed to determine the most cost-efficient method for procuring and moving raw materials, work in process, finished goods, and items that have been sold from the supplier to the producer to the eventual end user.

The relationship between PROCTER & GAMBLE (P&G) and WAL-MART provides an example of how technology is being used to manage inventory. In 1999, Wal-Mart was easily P&G's largest customer, accounting for 12% of its sales. Using electronic data interchange (EDI), P&G has access to certain portions of Wal-Mart's inventory data. When Wal-Mart's inventory reaches a certain level, P&G automatically processes and ships an order to the appropriate Wal-Mart warehouse to ensure that Wal-Mart never is out of stock of P&G products. Companies are able to establish such mutually beneficial relationships because technology now allows the sharing of information at a very low cost.

Ending Inventory and Cost of Goods Sold

cost of goods available for sale The cost of all merchandise available for sale during the period; equal to the sum of beginning inventory and net purchases.

Inventory purchased or manufactured during the period is added to beginning inventory, and the total cost of this inventory is called the **cost of goods available for sale**. At the end of an accounting period, total cost of goods available for sale must be allocated between inventory still remaining (to be reported in the balance sheet as an asset) and inventory sold during the period (to be reported in the income statement as an expense, Cost of Goods Sold).

This cost allocation process is extremely important because the more cost that is said to remain in ending inventory, the less cost is reported as cost of goods sold in the income statement. This is why accurately determining who owns the inventory is such a big issue. Making a mistake with inventory ownership will result in misstating both the income statement and the balance sheet. For this reason, accountants must be careful of inventory errors because they directly affect reported net income. The impact of inventory errors is illustrated later in the chapter.

The cost allocation process also involves a significant amount of accounting judgment. Identical inventory items are usually purchased at varying prices throughout the year, so to calculate the amount of ending inventory and cost of goods sold, the accountant must determine which items (the low cost or high cost) remain and which were sold. Again, this decision can directly affect the amount of reported cost of goods sold and net income. The use of inventory cost flow assumptions is discussed later in the chapter.

to summarize

Inventory is composed of goods held for sale in the normal course of business. Cost of goods sold is the cost of inventory sold during the period. For a manufacturing firm, the three types of inventory are raw materials, work in process, and finished goods. All costs incurred in producing and getting inventory ready to sell should be added to inventory cost. The costs associated with the selling effort itself are operating expenses of the period. Inventory should be recorded on the books of the company holding legal title.

At the end of an accounting period, the total cost of goods available for sale during the period must be allocated between ending inventory and cost of goods sold.

2

Account for inventory purchases and sales using both a perpetual and a periodic inventory system.

ACCOUNTING FOR INVENTORY PURCHASES AND SALES

To begin a more detailed study of inventory accounting, we must first establish a solid understanding of the journal entries used to record inventory transactions. The accounting procedures for recording purchases and sales using both a periodic and a perpetual inventory system are detailed in this section.

Overview of Perpetual and Periodic Systems

Some businesses track changes in inventory levels on a continuous basis, recording each individual purchase and sale to maintain a running total of the inventory balance. This is called a perpetual inventory system. Other businesses rely on quarterly or yearly inventory counts to reveal which inventory items have been sold. This is called a periodic inventory system.

perpetual inventory system
A system of accounting for inventory in which detailed records of the number of units and the cost of each purchase and sales transaction are prepared throughout the accounting period.

PERPETUAL You own a discount appliance superstore. Your biggest-selling items are washers, dryers, refrigerators, microwaves, and dishwashers. You advertise your weekly sale items on local TV stations, and your sales volume is quite heavy. You have 50 salespeople who work independently of one another. You have found that customers get very upset if they come to buy an advertised item and you have run out. In this business environment, would it make sense to keep a running total of the quantity remaining of each inventory item and update it each time a sale is made? Yes, the benefit of having current information on each inventory item would make it worthwhile to spend a little extra time to update the inventory records when a sale is made.

This appliance store would probably use a **perpetual inventory system**. With a perpetual system, inventory records are updated whenever a purchase or a sale is made. In this way, the inventory records at any given time reflect how many of each inventory item should be in the warehouse or out on the store shelves. A perpetual system is most often used when each individual inventory item has a relatively high value or when there are large costs to running out of or overstocking specific items.

periodic inventory system
A system of accounting for inventory in which cost of goods sold is determined and inventory is adjusted at the end of the accounting period, not when merchandise is purchased or sold.

PERIODIC You operate a newsstand in a busy metropolitan subway station. Almost all of your sales occur during the morning and the evening rush hours. You sell a diverse array of items— newspapers, magazines, pens, snacks, and other odds and ends. During rush hour, your business is a fast-paced pressure cooker; the longer you take with one customer, the more chance that the busy commuters waiting in line for service will tire of waiting and you will lose sales. In this business environment, would it make sense to make each customer wait while you meticulously check off on an inventory sheet exactly which items were sold? No, the delay caused by this detailed bookkeeping would cause you to lose customers. It makes more sense to wait until the end of the day, count up what inventory you still have left, compare that to what you started with, and use those numbers to deduce how many of each inventory item you sold during the day.

This subway newsstand scenario is an example of a situation where a **periodic inventory system** is appropriate. With a periodic system, inventory records are not updated when a sale is made; only the dollar amount of the sale is recorded. Periodic systems are most often used when inventory is composed of a large number of diverse items, each with a relatively low value.

IMPACT OF INFORMATION TECHNOLOGY Over the past 25 years, advances in information technology have lowered the cost of maintaining a perpetual inventory system. As a result, more businesses have adopted perpetual systems so that they can more closely track inven-

A newsstand will wait until the end of the day to count inventory by comparing what items it started with to what is left. This is an example of a periodic inventory system.

STOP & THINK If you buy your groceries with a credit card or a bank debit card, what kind of information can the supermarket accumulate about you?

tory levels. The most visible manifestation of this trend is in supermarkets. Twenty years ago, the checkout clerk rang up the price of each item on a cash register. After the customers walked out of the store with their groceries, the store knew the total amount of the purchase but did not know which individual items had been sold. This was a periodic inventory system. Now, with laser scanning equipment tied into the supermarket's computer system, most supermarkets operate under a perpetual system. The store manager knows exactly what you bought and exactly how many of each item should still be left on the store shelves.

Perpetual and Periodic Journal Entries

The following transactions for Grantsville Clothing Store will be used to illustrate the differences in bookkeeping procedures between a business using a perpetual inventory system and one using a periodic inventory system:

a. Purchased on account: 1,000 shirts at a cost of $10 each for a total of $10,000.
b. Purchased on account: 300 pairs of pants at a cost of $18 each for a total of $5,400.
c. Paid cash for separate shipping costs on the shirts purchased in (a), $970. The supplier of the pants purchased in (b) included the shipping costs in the $18 purchase price.
d. Returned 30 of the shirts (costing $300) to the supplier because they were stained.
e. Paid for the shirt purchase. A 2% discount was given on the $9,700 bill [(1,000 purchased − 30 returned) × $10] because of payment within the ten-day discount period (payment terms were 2/10, n/30).
f. Paid $5,400 for the pants purchase. No discount was allowed because payment was made after the discount period.
g. Sold on account: 600 shirts at a price of $25 each for a total of $15,000.
h. Sold on account: 200 pairs of pants at a price of $40 each for a total of $8,000.
i. Accepted return of 50 shirts by dissatisfied customers.

The journal entries for the perpetual inventory system should seem familiar to you—a perpetual system has been assumed in all earlier chapters of the text. A perpetual system was assumed because it is logical and is the system all companies would choose if there were no cost to updating the inventory records each time a sale or purchase is made. As mentioned, a periodic inventory system is sometimes a practical necessity.

PURCHASES   With a perpetual system, all purchases are added (debited) directly to Inventory. With a periodic system, the inventory balance is only updated using an inventory count at the end of the period; inventory purchases during the period are recorded in a temporary holding account called Purchases. As will be illustrated later, at the end of the period, the balance in Purchases is closed to Inventory in connection with the computation of cost of goods sold.

Entries (a) and (b) to record the shirt and pants purchases are given below:

		Perpetual			**Periodic**	
a.	Inventory	10,000		Purchases	10,000	
	Accounts Payable		10,000	Accounts Payable		10,000
b.	Inventory	5,400		Purchases	5,400	
	Accounts Payable		5,400	Accounts Payable		5,400

TRANSPORTATION COSTS   The cost of transporting the inventory is an additional inventory cost. Sometimes, as with the pants in the Grantsville Clothing example, the shipping cost is already included in the purchase price, so a separate entry to record the transportation costs is not needed. When a separate payment is made for transportation costs, it is recorded as follows:

		Perpetual			**Periodic**	
c.	Inventory	970		Freight In	970	
	Cash		970	Cash		970

With a perpetual inventory system, transportation costs are added directly to the inventory balance. With a periodic inventory system, another temporary holding account, Freight In, is created, and transportation costs are accumulated in this account during the period. Like the purchases account, Freight In is closed to Inventory at the end of the period in connection with the computation of cost of goods sold.

PURCHASE RETURNS   With a perpetual system, the return of unsatisfactory merchandise to the supplier results in a decrease in Inventory. In addition, since no payment will have to be made for the returned merchandise, Accounts Payable is reduced by the same amount. With a periodic system, the amount of the returned merchandise is recorded in yet another temporary holding account called Purchase Returns. Purchase Returns is a contra account to Purchases and is also closed to Inventory as part of the computation of cost of goods sold.

		Perpetual			**Periodic**	
d.	Accounts Payable	300		Accounts Payable	300	
	Inventory		300	Purchase Returns		300

If the returned merchandise had already been paid for, the supplier would most likely return the purchase price. In this case, the debit would be to Cash instead of to Accounts Payable.

Inventory Fraud: The Great Salad Oil Case One of the most common ways of committing major financial statement fraud and reporting income that is higher than it should be is to overstate a company's inventory. If ending inventory is overstated, cost of goods sold is understated and net income is overstated. The overstatement of inventory and income can attract investors and boost the stock price. In addition, since inventory can often be pledged as collateral to borrow money from banks, its overstatement increases a company's borrowing power. Consider the famous case of ALLIED CRUDE VEGETABLE OIL, one of the best-known inventory frauds of all time.

Founded in 1957 by Tino De Angelis, Allied Crude Vegetable Oil was set up on an old petroleum tank farm in Bayonne, New Jersey. De Angelis used the soybean oil that was supposedly in the tanks as collateral to borrow money from financial institutions. He then hired AMERICAN EXPRESS WAREHOUSING, LTD. (a subsidiary of AMERICAN EXPRESS) to take charge of storing, inspecting, and documenting the oil. The warehousing receipts issued by the warehouse workers were used as evidence of the oil.

De Angelis handpicked 22 men to work at the tank farm, and they fooled the American Express inspectors with considerable ease. For example, one of them would climb to the top of a tank, drop in a weighted tape measure, and then shout down to the inspector that the tank was full. In most cases the tanks were

usually high. For external reporting purposes, the shrinkage amount would probably be combined with normal cost of goods sold, and the title "Cost of Goods Sold" would be given to the total. Notice that if this practice is followed, reported cost of goods sold would be the same under both a perpetual and a periodic inventory system. The difference is that, with a perpetual system, company management knows how much of the goods was actually sold and how much represents inventory shrinkage.

With a periodic inventory system, no journal entry for inventory shrinkage is made because the amount of shrinkage is unknown. Instead, the ending inventory amount derived from the physical count is used to make the second periodic inventory closing entry (refer back to the previous section). Using the $5,950 ending inventory amount, the appropriate periodic inventory closing entry is:

Cost of Goods Sold	9,926	
Inventory ($15,876 − $5,950)		9,926
Adjustment of inventory account to appropriate ending balance.		

The Income Effect of an Error in Ending Inventory

As shown in the previous section, the results of the physical inventory count directly affect the computation of cost of goods sold with a periodic system and inventory shrinkage with a perpetual system. Errors in the inventory count will cause the amount of cost of goods sold or inventory shrinkage to be misstated. To illustrate, assume that the correct inventory count for Grantsville Clothing is $5,950 but that the ending inventory value is mistakenly computed to be $6,450. The impact of this $500 ($6,450 − $5,950) inventory overstatement is as follows:

empty, although some were filled with seawater and topped with a thin slick of oil. Moreover, the tanks were connected by a jungle of pipes that allowed the workers to pump whatever oil there was from one tank to another.

The maneuvers gave De Angelis an "endless" supply of oil and borrowing power. If anyone had checked a statistical report issued by the U.S. Census Bureau, he or she would have found that the oil supposedly stored at the tank farm totaled twice as much as all the oil in the country. By the close of 1963, the warehouse receipts represented 937 million pounds of oil when actually only 100 million pounds existed.

The salad oil scandal was revealed when De Angelis was unable to make payments on an investment. The ensuing investigation revealed a fraud that was conservatively estimated at $200 million. Most of the losses were borne by 51 major banking and brokerage houses in the United States and Europe, 20 of which collapsed.

De Angelis pleaded guilty to four federal counts of fraud and conspiracy and was given a 20-year sentence. The millions of dollars loaned to De Angelis were never found, and it is generally believed that the missing oil never existed. In fact, when one oil tank that supposedly contained $3,575,000 worth of oil was opened, seawater ran out for 12 consecutive days.

Source: Marshall B. Romney and W. Steve Albrecht, "The Use of Investigative Agencies by Auditors," *The Journal of Accountancy,* October 1979, p. 61.

	Periodic System	Perpetual System
Beginning inventory	$ 0	$ 0
Plus: Net purchases	15,876	15,876
Cost of goods available for sale	$15,876	$15,876
Less: Ending inventory	6,450	6,776 (from inventory system)
Cost of goods sold	$ 9,426	$ 9,100 (from inventory system)
Goods lost or stolen	unknown	326 ($6,776 − $6,450)
Total cost of goods sold, lost, or stolen	$ 9,426	$ 9,426

The $500 inventory overstatement reduces the reported cost of goods sold, lost, or stolen by $500, from $9,926 (computed earlier) to $9,426. This is because if we mistakenly think that we have more inventory remaining, then we will also mistakenly think that we must have sold less. Conversely, if the physical count understates ending inventory, total cost of goods sold will be overstated.

Since an inventory overstatement decreases reported cost of goods sold, it will also increase reported gross margin and net income. For this reason, the managers of a firm that is having difficulty meeting profit targets are sometimes tempted to "mistakenly" overstate ending inventory. Because of this temptation, auditors must take care to review a company's inventory counting process and also to physically observe a sample of the actual inventory. Many new accounting graduates who are hired by public accounting firms spend a portion of their first year on the job checking the inventory counts done by clients. The benefits of this exposure are twofold: (1) these new auditors get an opportunity to see what a business actually does, and (2) the inventory count provides assurance that the inventory amount stated on the financial statements is accurate.

to summarize

A physical inventory count is necessary to ensure that inventory records match the actual existing inventory. If a perpetual system is used, an inventory count can be used to compute the amount of inventory shrinkage during the period. An error in the reported ending inventory amount can have a significant effect on reported cost of goods sold, gross margin, and net income. For example, overstatement of ending inventory results in understatement of cost of goods sold and overstatement of net income.

4

Apply the four inventory cost flow alternatives: specific identification, FIFO, LIFO, and average cost.

INVENTORY COST FLOW ASSUMPTIONS

Consider the following transactions for the Ramona Rice Company for the year 2003.

Mar. 23   Purchased 10 kilos of rice, $4 per kilo.
Nov. 17   Purchased 10 kilos of rice, $9 per kilo.
Dec. 31   Sold 10 kilos of rice, $10 per kilo.

The surprisingly difficult question to answer with this simple example is "How much money did Ramona make in 2003?" As you can see, it depends on which rice was sold on December 31. There are three possibilities:

	Case #1 Sold Old Rice	Case #2 Sold New Rice	Case #3 Sold Mixed Rice
Sales ($10 × 10 kilos)	$100	$100	$100
Cost of goods sold (10 kilos)	40	90	65
Gross margin	$ 60	$ 10	$ 35

FIFO (first in, first out) An inventory cost flow assumption whereby the first goods purchased are assumed to be the first goods sold so that the ending inventory consists of the most recently purchased goods.

LIFO (last in, first out) An inventory cost flow assumption whereby the last goods purchased are assumed to be the first goods sold so that the ending inventory consists of the first goods purchased.

average cost An inventory cost flow assumption whereby cost of goods sold and the cost of ending inventory are determined by using an average cost of all merchandise available for sale during the period.

In Case #1, it is assumed that the 10 kilos of rice sold on December 31 were the old ones, purchased on March 23 for $4 per kilo. Accountants call this a **FIFO (first in, first out)** assumption. In Case #2, it is assumed that the company sold the new rice, purchased on November 17 for $9 per kilo. Accountants call this a **LIFO (last in, first out)** assumption. In Case #3, it is assumed that all the rice is mixed together, so the cost per kilo is the average cost of all the rice available for sale, or $6.50 per kilo [($40 + $90) ÷ 20 kilos]. Accountants call this an **average cost** assumption.

The point of the Ramona Rice example is this: in most cases, there is no feasible way to track exactly which units were sold. Accordingly, in order to compute cost of goods sold, the accountant must make an assumption. Note that this is not a case of tricky accountants trying to manipulate the reported numbers; instead, this is a case in which income simply cannot be computed unless the accountant uses his or her judgment and makes an assumption.

All three of the assumptions described in the example—FIFO, LIFO, and average cost—are acceptable under U.S. accounting rules. An interesting question is whether a company would randomly choose one of the three acceptable methods, or whether the choice would be made more strategically. For example, if Ramona Rice were preparing financial statements to be used to support a bank loan application, which assumption would you suggest that the company make? On the other hand, if Ramona were completing its income tax return, which assumption would be the best? This topic of strategic accounting choice will be discussed later in this chapter.

In the following sections, we will examine in more detail the different cost flow assumptions used by companies to determine inventories and cost of goods sold.

Specific Identification Inventory Cost Flow

specific identification A method of valuing inventory and determining cost of goods sold whereby the actual costs of specific inventory items are assigned to them.

An alternative to the assumptions just described is to specifically identify the cost of each particular unit that is sold. This approach, called **specific identification**, is often used by automobile dealers and other businesses that sell a limited number of units at a high price. To illustrate the specific identification inventory costing method, we will consider the September 2003 records of Nephi Company, which sells one type of bicycle.

Sept. 1   Beginning inventory consisted of 10 bicycles costing $200 each.
    3   Purchased 8 bicycles costing $250 each.
  18   Purchased 16 bicycles costing $300 each.
  20   Purchased 10 bicycles costing $320 each.
  25   Sold 28 bicycles, $400 each.

These inventory records show that during September the company had 44 bicycles (10 from beginning inventory and 34 that were purchased during the month) that it could have sold. However, only 28 bicycles were sold, leaving 16 on hand at the end of September. Using the specific identification method of inventory costing requires that the individual costs of the actual units sold be charged against revenue as cost of goods sold. To compute cost of goods sold and ending inventory amounts with this alternative, a company must know which units were actually sold and what the unit cost of each was.

Suppose that of the 28 bicycles sold by Nephi on September 25, 8 came from the beginning inventory, 4 came from the September 3 purchase, and 16 came from the September 18 purchase. With this information, cost of goods sold and ending inventory are computed as follows:

	Bicycles	Costs
Beginning inventory	10	$ 2,000
Net purchases	34	10,000
Goods available for sale	44	$12,000
Ending inventory	16	4,600
Cost of goods sold	28	$ 7,400

The cost of ending inventory is the total of the individual costs of the bicycles still on hand at the end of the month, or:

2 bicycles from beginning inventory, $200 each	$ 400
4 bicycles purchased on September 3, $250 each	1,000
0 bicycles purchased on September 18, $300 each	0
10 bicycles purchased on September 20, $320 each	3,200
Total ending inventory (16 units)	$4,600

Similarly, the cost of goods sold is the total of the costs of the specific bicycles sold, or:

8 bicycles from beginning inventory, $200 each	$1,600
4 bicycles purchased on September 3, $250 each	1,000
16 bicycles purchased on September 18, $300 each	4,800
0 bicycles purchased on September 20, $320 each	0
Total cost of goods sold (28 units)	$7,400

For many companies, it is impractical, if not impossible, to keep track of specific units. In that case, an assumption must be made as to which units were sold during the period and which are still in inventory, as illustrated earlier in the Ramona Rice example.

It is very important to remember that the accounting rules do not require that the assumed flow of goods for costing purposes match the actual physical movement of goods purchased and sold. In some cases, the assumed cost flow may be similar to the physical flow, but firms are not required to match the assumed accounting cost flow to the physical flow. A grocery store, for example, usually tries to sell the oldest units first to minimize spoilage. Thus, the physical flow of goods would reflect a FIFO pattern, but the grocery store could use a FIFO, LIFO, or average cost assumption in determining the ending inventory and cost of goods sold numbers to be reported in the financial statements. On the other hand, a company that stockpiles coal must first sell the coal purchased last since it is on top of the pile. That company might use the LIFO cost assumption, which reflects physical flow, or it might use one of the other alternatives.

In the next few sections, we will illustrate the FIFO, LIFO, and average inventory costing methods. The bicycle inventory data for Nephi Company will again be used in illustrating the different inventory cost flows.

FIFO Cost Flow Assumption

With FIFO, it is assumed that the oldest units are sold and the newest units remain in inventory. Using the FIFO inventory cost flow assumption, the ending inventory and cost of goods sold for Nephi Company are:

	Bicycles	**Costs**
Beginning inventory	10	$ 2,000
Net purchases	34	10,000
Goods available for sale	44	$12,000
Ending inventory	16	5,000
Cost of goods sold	28	$ 7,000

The $7,000 cost of goods sold and $5,000 cost of ending inventory are determined as follows:

FIFO cost of goods sold (oldest 28 units):

10 bicycles from beginning inventory, $200 each	$2,000
8 bicycles purchased on September 3, $250 each	2,000
10 bicycles purchased on September 18, $300 each	3,000
Total FIFO cost of goods sold	$7,000

FIFO ending inventory (newest 16 units):

6 bicycles purchased on September 18, $300 each	$1,800
10 bicycles purchased on September 20, $320 each	3,200
Total FIFO ending inventory	$5,000

LIFO Cost Flow Assumption

LIFO is the opposite of FIFO. With LIFO, the cost of the most recent units purchased is transferred to cost of goods sold. When prices are rising, as they are in the Nephi Company example, LIFO provides higher cost of goods sold, and hence lower net income, than FIFO. This is because the newest (high-priced) goods are assumed to have been sold. Using the LIFO inventory cost flow assumption, the ending inventory and cost of goods sold for Nephi Company are:

	Bicycles	**Costs**
Beginning inventory	10	$ 2,000
Net purchases	34	10,000
Goods available for sale	44	$12,000
Ending inventory	16	3,500
Cost of goods sold	28	$ 8,500

The $8,500 cost of goods sold and $3,500 cost of ending inventory are determined as follows:

LIFO cost of goods sold (newest 28 units):

10 bicycles purchased on September 20, $320 each...............................	$3,200
16 bicycles purchased on September 18, $300 each.............................	4,800
2 bicycles purchased on September 3, $250 each	500
Total LIFO cost of goods sold	$8,500

LIFO ending inventory (oldest 16 units):

10 bicycles from beginning inventory, $200 each..............................	$2,000
6 bicycles purchased on September 3, $250 each	1,500
Total LIFO ending inventory	$3,500

Average Cost Flow Assumption

With average costing, an average cost must be computed for all the inventory available for sale during the period. The average unit cost for Nephi Company during September is computed as follows:

	Bicycles	Costs
Beginning inventory	10	$ 2,000
Net purchases	34	10,000
Goods available for sale	44	$12,000
$12,000 ÷ 44 units = $272.73 per unit		

With the average cost assumption, cost of goods sold is computed by multiplying the number of units sold by the average cost per unit. Similarly, the cost of ending inventory is computed by multiplying the number of units in ending inventory by the average cost per unit. These calculations are as follows:

Average Cost of Goods Sold: 28 Units × $272.73 per Unit = $7,636 (rounded)

Average Ending Inventory: 16 Units × $272.73 per Unit = $4,364 (rounded)

This information can be shown as follows:

	Bicycles	Costs
Beginning inventory	10	$ 2,000
Net purchases	34	10,000
Goods available for sale	44	$12,000
Ending inventory.......................................	16	4,364
Cost of goods sold	28	$ 7,636

A Comparison of All Inventory Costing Methods

The cost of goods sold and ending inventory amounts we have calculated using the three cost flow assumptions are summarized along with the resultant gross margins as follows:

	FIFO	LIFO	Average
Sales revenue (28 × $400)....................	$11,200	$11,200	$11,200
Cost of goods sold	7,000	8,500	7,636
Gross margin	$ 4,200	$ 2,700	$ 3,564
Ending inventory...........................	$ 5,000	$ 3,500	$ 4,364

Note that the net result of each of the inventory cost flow assumptions is to allocate the total cost of goods available for sale of $12,000 between cost of goods sold and ending inventory.

CONCEPTUAL COMPARISON From a conceptual standpoint, LIFO gives a better reflection of cost of goods sold in the income statement than does FIFO because the most recent goods ("last in"), with the most recent costs, are assumed to have been sold. Thus, LIFO cost of goods sold matches current revenues with current costs. Average cost is somewhere between LIFO and FIFO. On the balance sheet, however, FIFO gives a better measure of inventory value because, with the FIFO assumption, the "first in" units are sold and the remaining units are the newest ones with the most recent costs. In summary, LIFO gives a conceptually better measure of income, but FIFO gives a conceptually better measure of inventory value on the balance sheet.

FINANCIAL STATEMENT IMPACT COMPARISON As illustrated in the Nephi Company example, in times of rising inventory prices (the most common situation in the majority of industries today), cost of goods sold is highest with LIFO and lowest with FIFO. As a result, gross margin, net income, and ending inventory are lowest with LIFO and highest with FIFO. With the impact on the reported financial statement numbers being so uniformly bad, you may be wondering why any company would ever voluntarily choose to use LIFO (during times of inflation). It might further surprise you to learn that, since 1974, hundreds of U.S. companies have voluntarily switched from FIFO to LIFO and that over half of the large companies in the United States currently use LIFO in accounting for at least some of their inventories.

STOP & THINK Over the entire life of a company—from its beginning with zero inventory until its final closeout when the last inventory item is sold—is aggregate cost of goods sold more, less, or the same as aggregate purchases? How is this relationship affected by the inventory cost flow assumption used?

The attractiveness of LIFO can be explained with one word—TAXES. If a company uses LIFO in a time of rising prices, reported cost of goods sold is higher, reported taxable income is lower, and cash paid for income taxes is lower. In fact, LIFO was invented in the 1930s in the United States for the sole purpose of allowing companies to lower their income tax payments. In most instances where accounting alternatives exist, firms are allowed to use one accounting method for tax purposes and another for financial reporting. In 1939, however, when the Internal Revenue Service (IRS) approved the use of LIFO, it ruled that firms may use LIFO for tax purposes only if they also use LIFO for financial reporting purposes. Therefore, companies must choose between reporting higher profits and paying higher taxes with FIFO or reporting lower profits and paying lower taxes with LIFO.

---

to summarize

Some companies can use specific identification as a method of valuing inventory and determining cost of goods sold. In most cases, however, an accountant must make an inventory cost flow assumption in order to compute cost of goods sold and ending inventory. With FIFO (first in, first out), it is assumed that the oldest inventory units are sold first. With LIFO (last in, first out), it is assumed that the newest units are sold first. With the average cost assumption, the total goods available for sale are used to compute an average cost per unit for the period; this average cost is then used in calculating cost of goods sold and ending inventory. LIFO produces a better matching of current revenues and current expenses in the income statement; FIFO yields a balance sheet inventory value that is closer to the current value of the inventory. The primary practical attraction of LIFO is that it lowers income tax payments.

5

Use financial ratios to evaluate a company's inventory level.

ASSESSING HOW WELL COMPANIES MANAGE THEIR INVENTORIES

Money tied up in the form of inventories cannot be used for other purposes. Therefore, companies try hard to minimize the necessary investment in inventories while at the same time assuring that they have enough inventory on hand to meet customer demand. In recent years a method of inventory management called just-in-time (JIT) inventory has become popular. JIT, which will be described in Chapter 7 in the management accounting section of this text, is an inventory management method that attempts to have exactly enough inventory arrive just in time for sale. Its purpose is to minimize the amount of money needed to purchase and hold inventory.

Evaluating the Level of Inventory

inventory turnover A measure of the efficiency with which inventory is managed; computed by dividing cost of goods sold by average inventory for a period.

Two widely used measurements of how effectively a company is managing its inventory are the inventory turnover ratio and number of days' sales in inventory. **Inventory turnover** provides a measure of how many times a company turns over, or replenishes, its inventory during a year. The calculation is similar to the accounts receivable turnover discussed in Chapter 6. It is calculated by dividing cost of goods sold by average inventory as follows:

$$\text{Inventory Turnover} = \frac{\text{Cost of Goods Sold}}{\text{Average Inventory}}$$

The average inventory amount is the average of the beginning and ending inventory balances. The inventory turnover ratios for SEARS, SAFEWAY, and CATERPILLAR for 1999 are as follows (dollar amounts are in billions):

	Sears	Safeway	Caterpillar
Cost of goods sold	$27.212	$20.349	$14.481
Beginning inventory	5.322	1.856	2.842
Ending inventory	5.648	2.445	2.594
Average inventory	5.485	2.151	2.718
Inventory turnover	4.96	9.46	5.33

From this analysis, you can see that Safeway, the supermarket, turns its inventory over more frequently than Sears, the department store, and Caterpillar, the equipment dealer. This result is what we would have predicted given that the companies are in different businesses and have different types of inventory.

number of days' sales in inventory An alternative measure of how well inventory is being managed; computed by dividing 365 days by the inventory turnover ratio.

Inventory turnover can also be converted into the **number of days' sales in inventory**. This ratio is computed by dividing 365, or the number of days in a year, by the inventory turnover, as follows:

$$\frac{\text{Number of Days'}}{\text{Sales in Inventory}} = \frac{365}{\text{Inventory Turnover}}$$

Computing this ratio for Sears, Safeway, and Caterpillar yields the following:

	Number of Days' Sales in Inventory
Sears	73.6 days
Safeway	38.6 days
Caterpillar	68.5 days

> **caution**
>
> Sometimes these two inventory ratios are computed using ending inventory rather than average inventory. This is appropriate if the inventory balance does not change much from the beginning to the end of the year.

business environment essay

Phar-Mor Cooks Up Inventory Fraud
Recall the introductory scenario from Chapter 5 that detailed the rise and fall of PHAR-MOR. That case resulted from an elaborate inventory fraud perpetrated by top management over several years. Phar-Mor's inventory ostensibly grew from $11 million in 1989 to $153 million in 1991, but much of this inventory had been "created" by fabricating financial data and misleading the external auditors.

Because Phar-Mor did not keep a perpetual inventory system, the company estimated the value of its inventory by using a ratio involving the cost of the items purchased and their retail value. Inventory was counted, valued at its retail price, and then multiplied by this ratio to obtain an approximation of its cost. Phar-Mor officials manipulated the ratio to ensure that inventory was inflated and that cost of goods sold was understated. In addition, when Phar-Mor's accountants made journal entries reducing Inventory (with a credit), the corresponding debit (which should have

net work

In addition to Safeway, another large supermarket chain is KROGER, based in Cincinnati. Access Kroger's Web site at http://kroger.com.

Is Kroger's inventory turnover higher or lower than Safeway's? Does Kroger use LIFO or FIFO?

Individuals analyzing how effective a company's inventory management is would compare these ratios with those of other firms in the same industry and with comparable ratios for the same firm in previous years.

Impact of the Inventory Cost Flow Assumption

As mentioned previously, in times of rising prices, the use of LIFO results in higher cost of goods sold and lower inventory values. All three of the companies in the ratio illustration on the previous page use LIFO. Each company includes supplemental disclosures in the financial statement notes that allow users to compute what reported inventory and cost of goods sold would have been if the company had used FIFO. To illustrate the impact that the choice of inventory cost flow assumption can have on the reported numbers, consider the following comparison for Caterpillar for 1999:

	Reported LIFO Numbers	Numbers if Using FIFO
Cost of goods sold	$14.481	$12.481
Average inventory	2.718	4.718
Inventory turnover	5.33	2.65
Number of days' sales in inventory	68.5 days	137.7 days

The difference in cost of goods sold for 1999 is not great because inflation was relatively low in that year. However, the difference in the reported average inventory balance reflects the cumulative effect of inflation for the many years since Caterpillar first started using LIFO. The impact on the ratio values is dramatic. Of course, the difference between LIFO and FIFO is not as great for most companies as shown here for Caterpillar, but the general point is that the choice of inventory cost flow assumption can affect the conclusions drawn about the financial statements—if the financial statement user is not careful.

Number of Days' Purchases in Accounts Payable

In Chapter 6, we introduced the average collection period ratio. In this chapter we have discussed the computation of the number of days' sales in inventory. Taken together, these two ratios indicate the length of a firm's operating cycle. The two ratios measure the amount of time it takes, on average, from the point when inventory is purchased to the point when cash is col-

been made to Cost of Goods Sold) was made to an asset account (with the clever name of "Cookies"). This "cookies" account would then be broken into smaller pieces and reallocated to individual stores. Because the "Cookies" were broken into pieces, the smaller numbers avoided attracting the external auditors' attention. Another tactic used by Phar-Mor was to artificially inflate the inventory numbers at the company's fiscal year-end (June 30) and attribute the inflated numbers to a buildup of inventory in preparation for the 4th of July.

These falsifications and more resulted in financial statement fraud amounting to over $1 billion in losses. The external auditors in the case were found guilty of fraud—not because the audit firm was an active participant in the scheme, but because the auditors were reckless with regard to the conduct of the audit.

Sources: Most of these facts relating to Phar-Mor appeared in Gabriella Stern, "Chicanery at Phar-Mor Ran Deep, Close Look at Discounter Shows," *The Wall Street Journal*, January 20, 1994, p. 1; Mark F. Murray, "When a Client is a Liability," *Journal of Accountancy*, September 1992, pp. 54–58.

lected from the customer who purchased the inventory. For example, Sears' 253-day operating cycle for 1999 is depicted below:

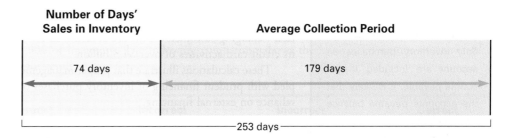

Is Sears' operating cycle too long, too short, or just right? That is difficult to tell without information from prior years and from competitors. But by including one additional ratio in the analysis, we can learn more about how Sears is managing its operating cash flow. The **number of days' purchases in accounts payable** reveals the average length of time that elapses between the purchase of inventory on account and the cash payment for that inventory. The number of days' purchases in accounts payable is computed by dividing total inventory purchases by average accounts payable and then dividing the result into 365 days:

number of days' purchases in accounts payable A measure of how well operating cash flow is being managed; computed by dividing total inventory purchases by average accounts payable and then dividing 365 days by the result.

$$\text{Number of Days' Purchases in Accounts Payable} = \frac{365 \text{ Days}}{\text{Purchases/Average Accounts Payable}}$$

The amount of inventory purchased during a year is computed by combining cost of goods sold with the change in the inventory balance for the year. If inventory increased during the year, then inventory purchases are equal to cost of goods sold plus the increase in the inventory balance. Similarly, if inventory decreased during the year, inventory purchases are equal to cost of goods sold minus the decrease in the inventory balance.

The number of days' purchases in accounts payable indicates how long a company takes to pay its suppliers. For example, Sears' number of days' purchases in accounts payable for 1999 is computed as follows (dollar figures are in millions):

Cost of goods sold for 1999	$27,212
Add increase in inventory during 1999	326
Inventory purchases during 1999	$27,538
Average accounts payable during 1999	$ 6,862

These perpetual system complications are illustrated below using the same Nephi Company example used earlier, but now assuming that sales occurred at different times during the month.

Sept. 1 Beginning inventory consisted of 10 bicycles costing $200 each.
     3 Purchased 8 bicycles costing $250 each.
     5 Sold 12 bicycles, $400 each.
   18 Purchased 16 bicycles costing $300 each.
   20 Purchased 10 bicycles costing $320 each.
   25 Sold 16 bicycles, $400 each.

When a perpetual system is used and sales occur during the period, the identification of the "last in" units must be evaluated at the time of each individual sale, as follows:

September 5 sale of 12 bicycles, identification of "last in" units:

8 bicycles purchased on September 3, $250 each	$2,000	
4 bicycles in beginning inventory, $200 each	800	
		$2,800

September 25 sale of 16 bicycles, identification of "last in" units:

10 bicycles purchased on September 20, $320 each	$3,200	
6 bicycles purchased on September 18, $300 each	1,800	
		5,000
Total perpetual LIFO cost of goods sold		$7,800

This $7,800 amount for LIFO cost of goods sold under a perpetual inventory system compares to the $8,500 LIFO cost of goods sold computed earlier in the chapter assuming a periodic inventory system. Again, the difference arises because the "last in" units are identified at the end of the period with a periodic system; with a perpetual system, the "last in" units are identified at the time of each individual sale.

A similar difference arises with the average cost method because, with a perpetual system, a new average cost per unit must be determined at the time each individual sale is made. This process is illustrated as follows:

September 5 sale of 12 bicycles, determination of average cost:

10 bicycles in beginning inventory, $200 each	$2,000	
8 bicycles purchased on September 3, $250 each	2,000	
Total cost of goods available for sale on September 5		$4,000

Average cost on September 5: $4,000 ÷ 18 bicycles = $222.22 per bicycle
September 5 cost of goods sold:
  12 bicycles × $222.22 per bicycle = $2,667 (rounded)

September 25 sale of 16 bicycles, determination of average cost:

6 (18 − 12) bicycles; remaining cost ($4,000 − $2,667)	$1,333	
16 bicycles purchased on September 18, $300 each	4,800	
10 bicycles purchased on September 20, $320 each	3,200	
Total cost of goods available for sale on September 25		$9,333

Average cost on September 25: $9,333 ÷ 32 bicycles = $291.66 per bicycle
September 25 cost of goods sold:
  16 bicycles × $291.66 per bicycle = $4,667 (rounded)
Total cost of goods sold: $2,667 + $4,667 = $7,334

This $7,334 cost of goods sold under the perpetual average method compares with $7,636 cost of goods sold under the periodic average method. Again, the difference is that one overall average cost for all goods available for sale during the period is used with a periodic system; with a perpetual system, a new average cost is computed at the time of each sale.

By the way, no complications arise in using FIFO with a perpetual system. This is because, no matter when sales occur, the "first in" units are always the same ones. So, FIFO periodic and FIFO perpetual yield the same numbers for cost of goods sold and ending inventory.

Because of the complications associated with computing perpetual LIFO and perpetual average cost, many businesses that use average cost or LIFO for financial reporting purposes use a simple FIFO assumption in maintaining their day-to-day perpetual inventory records. The perpetual FIFO records are then converted to periodic average cost or LIFO for the financial reports.

to summarize

Using the average cost and LIFO inventory cost flow assumptions with a perpetual inventory system leads to some complications. These complications arise because the identity of the "last in" units changes with each new inventory purchase, as does the average cost of units purchased up to that point.

8

Apply the lower-of-cost-or-market method of accounting for inventory.

REPORTING INVENTORY AT AMOUNTS BELOW COST

All the inventory costing alternatives we have discussed in this chapter have one thing in common: they report inventory at cost. Occasionally, however, it becomes necessary to report inventory at an amount that is less than cost. This happens when the future value of the inventory is in doubt—when it is damaged, used, or obsolete, or when it can be replaced new at a price that is less than its original cost.

Inventory Valued at Net Realizable Value

net realizable value The selling price of an item less reasonable selling costs.

When inventory is damaged, used, or obsolete, it should be reported at no more than its **net realizable value**. This is the amount the inventory can be sold for, minus any selling costs. Suppose, for example, that an automobile dealer has a demonstrator car that originally cost $18,000 and now can be sold for only $16,000. The car should be reported at its net realizable value. If a commission of $500 must be paid to sell the car, the net realizable value is $15,500, or $2,500 less than cost. This loss is calculated as follows:

Cost		$18,000
Estimated selling price	$16,000	
Less selling commission	500	15,500
Loss		$ 2,500

To achieve a good matching of revenues and expenses, a company must recognize this estimated loss as soon as it is determined that an economic loss has occurred (even before the car is sold). The journal entry required to recognize the loss and reduce the inventory amount of the car is:

Loss on Write-Down of Inventory (Expense)	2,500	
Inventory		2,500
To write down inventory to its net realizable value.		

By writing down inventory to its net realizable value, a company recognizes a loss when it happens and shows no profit or loss when the inventory is finally sold. Using net realizable values means that assets are not being reported at amounts that exceed their future economic benefits.

Inventory Valued at Lower of Cost or Market

Inventory must also be written down to an amount below cost if it can be replaced new at a price that is less than its original cost. In the electronics industry, for instance, the costs of computers and compact disc players have fallen dramatically in recent years. When goods remaining in ending inventory can be replaced with identical goods at a lower cost, the lower unit cost must be used in valuing the inventory (provided that the replacement cost is not higher than net realizable value or lower than net realizable value minus a normal profit). This is known as the **lower-of-cost-or-market (LCM) rule.** (In a sense, a more precise name would be the lower-of-actual-or-replacement-cost rule.)

The **ceiling,** or maximum market amount at which inventory can be carried on the books, is equivalent to net realizable value, which is the selling price less estimated selling costs. The ceiling is imposed because it makes no sense to value an inventory item above the amount that can be realized upon sale. For example, assume that a company purchased an inventory item for $10 and expected to sell it for $14. If the selling costs of the item amounted to $3, the ceiling or net realizable value would be $11 ($14 − $3).

The **floor** is defined as the net realizable value minus a normal profit. Thus, if the inventory item costing $10 had a normal profit margin of 20%, or $2, the floor would be $9 (net realizable value of $11 less normal profit of $2). This is the lowest amount at which inventory should be carried in order to prevent showing losses in one period and large profits in subsequent periods.

In applying this LCM rule, you can follow certain basic guidelines:

1. Define market value as:
   a. replacement cost, if it falls between the ceiling and the floor.
   b. the floor, if the replacement cost is less than the floor.
   c. the ceiling, if the replacement cost is higher than the ceiling.
   (As a practical matter, when replacement cost, ceiling, and floor are compared, market is always the middle value.)
2. Compare the defined market value with the original cost and choose the lower amount.

The following chart gives four separate examples of the application of the LCM rule; the resulting LCM amount is highlighted in each case.

| Item | Number of Items in Inventory | Original Cost (LIFO, FIFO, etc.) | Market | | |
			Replacement Cost	Net Realizable Value (Ceiling)	Net Realizable Value Minus Normal Profit (Floor)
A	10	$17	$16	$15	$10
B	8	21	18	23	16
C	30	26	21	31	22
D	20	19	16	34	25

The LCM rule can be applied in one of three ways: (1) by computing cost and market figures for each item in inventory and using the lower of the two amounts in each case, (2) by computing cost and market figures for the total inventory and then applying the LCM rule to that total, or (3) by applying the LCM rule to categories of inventory. For a clothing store, categories of inventory might be all shirts, all pants, all suits, or all dresses.

To illustrate, we will use the above data to show how the LCM rule would be applied to each inventory item separately and to total inventory. (The third method is similar to the second, except that it may involve several totals, one for each category of inventory.)

---

lower-of-cost-or-market (LCM) rule A basis for valuing inventory at the lower of original cost or current market value.

ceiling The maximum market amount at which inventory can be carried on the books; equal to net realizable value.

floor The minimum market amount at which inventory can be carried on the books; equal to net realizable value minus a normal profit.

Item	Number of Items in Inventory	Original Cost	Market Value	LCM for Individual Items
A	10	$17 × 10 units = $ 170	$15 × 10 units = $ 150	$ 150
B	8	$21 × 8 units = 168	$18 × 8 units = 144	144
C	30	$26 × 30 units = 780	$22 × 30 units = 660	660
D	20	$19 × 20 units = 380	$25 × 20 units = 500	380
		$1,498	$1,454	$1,334

$44

$164

Using the first method, applying the LCM rule to individual items, inventory is valued at $1,334, a write-down of $164 from the original cost. With the second method, using total inventory, the lower of total cost ($1,498) or total market value ($1,454) is used for a write-down of $44. The write-down is smaller when total inventory is used because the increase in market value of $120 in item D offsets decreases in items A, B, and C. In practice, each of the three methods is acceptable, but once a method has been selected, it should be followed consistently.

The journal entry to write down the inventory to the lower of cost or market applying the LCM rule to individual items is:

Loss on Write-Down of Inventory (Expense)...................... 164
   Inventory 164
   To write down inventory to lower of cost or market.

The amount of this entry would have been $44 if the LCM rule had been applied to total inventory.

The LCM rule has gained wide acceptance because it reports inventory on the balance sheet at amounts that are consistent with future economic benefits. With this method, losses are recognized when they occur, not necessarily when a sale is made.

to summarize

The recorded amount of inventory should be written down (1) when it is damaged, used, or obsolete and (2) when it can be replaced (purchased new) at an amount that is less than its original cost. In the first case, inventory is reported at its net realizable value, an amount that allows a company to break even when the inventory is sold. In the second case, inventory is written down to the lower of cost or market. When using the lower-of-cost-or-market rule, market is defined as falling between the ceiling and floor. Ceiling is defined as the net realizable value; floor is net realizable value minus a normal profit margin. In no case should inventory be reported at an amount that exceeds the ceiling or is less than the floor. These reporting alternatives are attempts to show assets at amounts that reflect realistic future economic benefits.

9

Explain the gross margin method of estimating inventories.

METHOD OF ESTIMATING INVENTORIES

We have assumed that the number of inventory units on hand is known by a physical count that takes place at the end of each accounting period. For the periodic inventory method, this physical count is the only way to determine how much inventory is on hand at the end of a period. For the perpetual inventory method, the physical count verifies the quantity on hand or indicates the amount of inventory shrinkage or theft. There are times, however, when a company needs to know the dollar amount of ending inventory, but a physical count is either impossible or impractical. For example, many firms prepare quarterly, or even monthly, financial statements, but it is too expensive and time-consuming to count the inventory at the end of each period. In such cases, if the perpetual inventory method is being used, the balance in the inventory account is usually assumed to be correct. With the periodic inventory method, however, some estimate of the inventory balance must be made. A common method of estimating the dollar amount of ending inventory is the gross margin method.

The Gross Margin Method

gross margin method A procedure for estimating the amount of ending inventory; the historical relationship of cost of goods sold to sales revenue is used in computing ending inventory.

With the **gross margin method**, a firm uses available information about the dollar amounts of beginning inventory and purchases, and the historical gross margin percentage to estimate the dollar amounts of cost of goods sold and ending inventory.

To illustrate, we will assume the following data for Payson Brick Company:

Net sales revenue, January 1 to March 31	$100,000
Inventory balance, January 1.	15,000
Net purchases, January 1 to March 31	65,000
Gross margin percentage	
(historically determined percentage of net sales)	40%

With this information, the dollar amount of inventory on hand on March 31 is estimated as follows:

	Dollars	Percentage of Sales
Net sales revenue	$100,000	100%
Cost of goods sold:		
Beginning inventory. $15,000		
Net purchases 65,000		
Total cost of goods available for sale. $80,000		
Ending inventory ($80,000 − $60,000) . . . . . . 20,000 (3)*		
Cost of goods sold ($100,000 − $40,000).	60,000 (2)*	60%
Gross margin ($100,000 × 0.40)	$ 40,000 (1)*	40%

*The numbers indicate the order of calculation.

In this example, gross margin is first determined by calculating 40% of sales (step 1). Next, cost of goods sold is found by subtracting gross margin from sales (step 2). Finally, the dollar amount of ending inventory is obtained by subtracting cost of goods sold from total cost of goods available for sale (step 3). Obviously, the gross margin method of estimating cost of goods sold and ending inventory assumes that the historical gross margin percentage is appropriate for the current period. This assumption is a realistic one in many fields of business. In cases where the gross margin percentage has changed, this method should be used with caution.

The gross margin method of estimating ending inventories is also useful when a fire or other calamity destroys a company's inventory. In these cases, the dollar amount of inventory lost must be determined before insurance claims can be made. The dollar amounts of sales, purchases, and beginning inventory can be obtained from prior years' financial statements and from customers, suppliers, and other sources. Then the gross margin method can be used to estimate the dollar amount of inventory lost.

to summarize

The gross margin method is a common technique for estimating the dollar amount of inventory. The historical gross margin percentage is used in conjunction with sales to estimate cost of goods sold. This estimated cost of goods sold amount is subtracted from cost of goods available for sale to yield an estimate of ending inventory.

review of learning objectives

1 **Identify what items and costs should be included in inventory and cost of goods sold.** Inventory is composed of goods held for sale in the normal course of business. Cost of goods sold is the cost of inventory sold during the period. For a manufacturing firm, the three types of inventory are raw materials, work in process, and finished goods. All costs incurred in producing and getting inventory ready to sell should be added to inventory cost. The costs associated with the selling effort itself are operating expenses of the period. Inventory should be recorded on the books of the company holding legal title. Goods in transit belong to the company paying for the shipping. Goods on consignment belong to the supplier/owner, not to the business holding the inventory for possible sale. At the end of an accounting period, the total cost of goods available for sale during the period must be allocated between ending inventory and cost of goods sold.

2 **Account for inventory purchases and sales using both a perpetual and a periodic inventory system.** With a perpetual inventory system, the inventory account is adjusted for every sale or purchase transaction. Discounts on purchases, returns of merchandise, and the cost of transporting goods intended for resale into the firm are also adjustments made directly to the inventory account. With a periodic inventory system, inventory-related items are recorded in temporary holding accounts that are closed to Inventory at the end of the period. The closing entries for a periodic system involve closing Purchases, Freight In, Purchase Returns, and Purchase Discounts to Inventory, and then adjusting the inventory account balance to reflect the appropriate amount given the results of the ending inventory physical count.

3 **Calculate cost of goods sold using the results of an inventory count and understand the impact of errors** in ending inventory on reported cost of goods sold. Obtaining an accurate inventory amount involves counting the physical units and then properly computing the cost of those units. Special care must be taken in dealing with goods in transit and consigned goods. When a perpetual inventory system is used, the ending inventory count provides an opportunity to compute inventory shrinkage. When ending inventory is not correctly counted, both cost of goods sold and net income will be reported incorrectly. For example, an overstatement in ending inventory leads to an overstatement in reported net income.

4 **Apply the four inventory cost flow alternatives: specific identification, FIFO, LIFO, and average cost.** The four major costing methods used in accounting for inventories are specific identification, FIFO, LIFO, and average cost. Each of these may result in different dollar amounts of ending inventory, cost of goods sold, gross margin, and net income. A firm may choose any costing alternative without regard to the way goods physically flow through that firm. With FIFO, the oldest units are assumed to be sold first; with LIFO, the newest units are assumed to be sold first. LIFO matches current revenues and current expenses in the income statement; FIFO results in current values being reported in the balance sheet. During an inflationary period, LIFO provides the lowest reported income and, therefore, lower taxes.

5 **Use financial ratios to evaluate a company's inventory level.** Companies assess how well their inventory is being managed by using two ratios: (1) inventory turnover and (2) number of days' sales in inventory. Inventory turnover is computed as cost of goods sold divided by average inventory; it tells how many times during the period the company turned over, or replenished, its inventory. The number of days' sales in inventory is computed by dividing 365 by the inventory turnover value. A company's choice of inventory cost flow assumption can significantly affect the values of these inventory ratios. The sum of the average collection period and the number of days' sales in inventory is the length of time between the purchase of inventory and the collection of cash from the sale of that inventory. Comparing this sum to the number of days' purchases in accounts payable reveals how much of a company's operating cycle it must finance through external financing.

expanded material

6 **Analyze the impact of inventory errors on reported cost of goods sold.** Inventory errors can have a significant effect on reported cost of goods sold, gross margin, and net income. In addition, a misstatement of an ending inventory balance affects net income, both in the current year and in the next year. Errors in beginning and ending inventory have the opposite effect on cost of goods sold, gross margin, and net income. Errors in inventory correct themselves after two years if the physical count at the end of the second year shows the correct amount of ending inventory for that period.

7 **Describe the complications that arise when LIFO or average cost is used with a perpetual inventory system.** Using the average cost and LIFO inventory cost flow assumptions with a perpetual inventory system leads to some complications. These complications arise because the identity of the "last in" units changes with each new inventory purchase, as does the average cost of units purchased up to that point.

8 **Apply the lower-of-cost-or-market method of accounting for inventory.** Sometimes inventory must be reported at amounts below cost. This occurs (1) when inventory is damaged, used, or obsolete, or (2) when the replacement cost drops below the original inventory cost. In the first case, inventory is valued at a net realizable value; in the second, it is valued at the lower of cost or market. When lower-of-cost-or-market valuation is used, market is defined as the replacement cost of the inventory; in no case can the value be greater than the item's net realizable value (the ceiling) or less than net realizable value minus a normal profit (the floor).

9 **Explain the gross margin method of estimating inventories.** Although most firms take a physical count of inventory at the end of each year, they sometimes need to estimate the value of inventory prior to year-end. The gross margin method is a common technique for estimating the dollar amount of inventory. The historical gross margin percentage is used in conjunction with sales to estimate cost of goods sold. This estimated cost of goods sold amount is subtracted from cost of goods available for sale to yield an estimate of ending inventory.

key terms and concepts

average cost 308

consignment 297

cost of goods available for sale 298

cost of goods sold 295

FIFO (first in, first out) 308

finished goods 296

FOB (free-on-board) destination 297

FOB (free-on-board) shipping point 297

inventory 295

inventory shrinkage 305

inventory turnover 313

LIFO (last in, first out) 308

net purchases 304

number of days' purchases in accounts payable 315

number of days' sales in inventory 313

periodic inventory system 299

perpetual inventory system 299

raw materials 296

specific identification 309

work in process 296

expanded material

ceiling 322

floor 322

gross margin method 324

lower-of-cost-or-market (LCM) rule 322

net realizable value 321

review problem

Inventory Cost Flow Alternatives

Lehi Wholesale Distributors buys printers from manufacturers and sells them to office supply stores. During January 2003, its periodic inventory records showed the following:

Jan. 1 Beginning inventory consisted of 26 printers at $200 each.
10 Purchased 10 printers at $220 each.
15 Purchased 20 printers at $250 each.
28 Purchased 9 printers at $270 each.
31 Sold 37 printers.

Required:

Calculate ending inventory and cost of goods sold, using:

1. FIFO inventory.
2. LIFO inventory.
3. Average cost.

Solution

When computing ending inventory and cost of goods sold, it is usually easiest to get an overview first. The following calculations are helpful:

Beginning inventory, 26 units at $200 each	$ 5,200
Purchases: 10 units at $220	$ 2,200
20 units at $250	5,000
9 units at $270	2,430
Total purchases (39 units)	$ 9,630
Cost of goods available for sale (65 units)	$14,830
Less ending inventory (28 units)	?
Cost of goods sold (37 units)	?

Given a beginning inventory, only ending inventory and cost of goods sold will vary with the different inventory costing alternatives. Because ending inventory and cost of goods sold are complementary numbers whose sum must equal total goods available for sale, you can calculate only one of the two missing numbers in each case and then compute the other by subtracting the first number from goods available for sale. Thus, in the calculations that follow, we will always calculate ending inventory first.

1. FIFO Inventory
Since we know that 28 units are left in ending inventory, we look for the last 28 units purchased because the first units purchased would all be sold. The last 28 units purchased were:

9 units at $270 each on January 28 =	$2,430
19 units at $250 each on January 15 =	4,750
Ending inventory	$7,180

Ending inventory is $7,180, and cost of goods sold is $7,650 ($14,830 − $7,180).

2. LIFO Inventory
The first 28 units available would be considered the ending inventory (since the last ones purchased are the first ones sold). The first 28 units available were:

Beginning inventory: 26 units at $200 =	$5,200
January 10 purchase: 2 units at $220 =	440
Ending inventory	$5,640

Thus,

Cost of goods available for sale	$14,830
Ending inventory	5,640
Cost of goods sold	$ 9,190

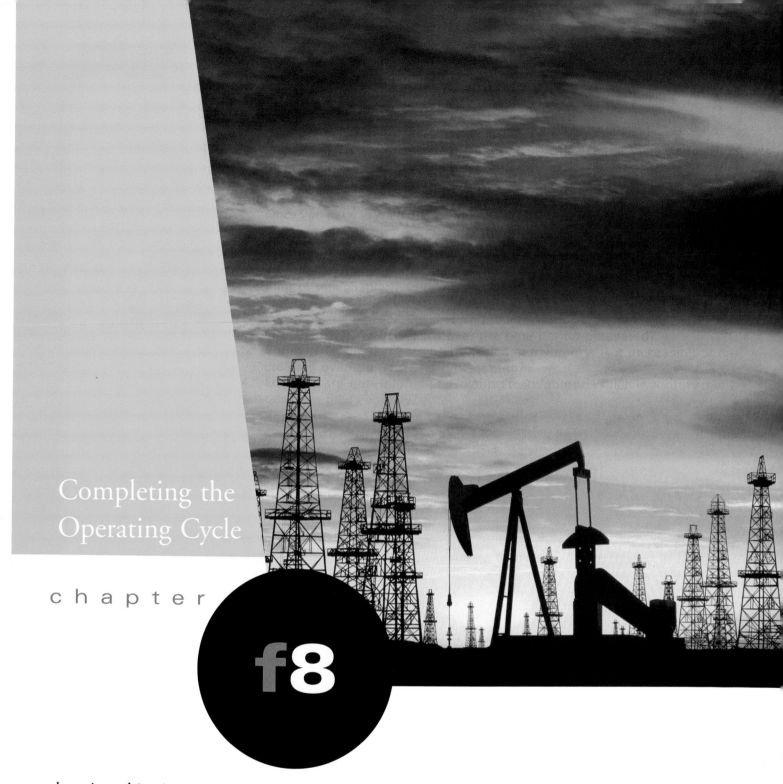

Completing the Operating Cycle

chapter f8

learning objectives
After studying this chapter, you should be able to:

1 Account for the various components of employee compensation expense.

2 Compute income tax expense, including appropriate consideration of deferred tax items.

3 Distinguish between contingent items that should be recognized in the financial statements and those that should be merely disclosed in the financial statement notes.

4 Understand when an expenditure should be recorded as an asset and when it should be recorded as an expense.

5 Prepare an income statement summarizing operating activities as well as other revenues and expenses, extraordinary items, and earnings per share.

Before 1850, the primary use for petroleum was as a medicine. Known variously as Seneca oil, American oil, and rock oil, a mixture of water and petroleum was reportedly good for rheumatism, chronic cough, ague, toothache, corns, neuralgia, urinary disorders, indigestion, and liver ailments. The oil was collected by wringing out woolen blankets that had been thrown onto the surfaces of ponds that had been fouled by seeping oil. Oil was also a nuisance by-product of drilling wells in search of underground salt brine deposits.

Gradually, additional properties of oil were discovered. It was found that oil could serve as a lubricant for the machinery that was becoming more common as the Industrial Revolution progressed. In addition, distilled oil was found to burn well in the household lamps that had traditionally burned vegetable oil or sperm whale oil. As the demand for petroleum increased, the search for oil began in earnest. A group of investors hired Edwin L. Drake to drill for oil in northwestern Pennsylvania, where oil had long been found in springs and wells. In late August 1859, Drake struck oil at a depth of 69½ feet, creating an oil well that yielded 25 barrels per day. This discovery touched off an oil rush in western Pennsylvania, and the opportunities to get rich were soon fanned by the increased demand for lubricating oil associated with the North's war production during the Civil War.

In those early days, Cleveland, Ohio, was the center of oil refining, and one of the earliest players in the refining business was John D. Rockefeller. Rockefeller had started his business career in Cleveland as a bookkeeper(!) in 1855. By saving his earnings, he acquired some investment capital, and, with a partner, he put up $4,000 to begin a refinery in Cleveland in 1862. Rockefeller's aggressive business tactics aroused controversy almost from the beginning. In particular, Rockefeller was accused of negotiating favorable freight rates with the railroads hauling his oil whereas his competitors were required to pay the stated rates. In 1872, Rockefeller was able to persuade a large number of his Cleveland refining competitors to sell out to him by convincing them that he had arranged such a favorable deal with the railroads that competing head-to-head with him would be impossible.

Rockefeller was eager to expand the business interests of his STANDARD OIL COMPANY OF OHIO into other areas, but the incorporation laws in existence at the time made it difficult for corporations to merge. Therefore, Rockefeller created a "trust," which was basically a corporation of corporations. The stockholders of each corporation transferred their shares to the care of the nine trustees of the STANDARD OIL TRUST; in exchange, the stockholders received trust certificates. Thereafter, the nine trustees ran the businesses and the stockholders received the dividends. When the Ohio Supreme Court ruled this trust illegal in 1892, lawyers for Standard Oil sought another business structure that would preserve the essence of the trust. They found the answer in the incorporation laws of the state of New Jersey, which allowed the formation of a holding company that would own shares of various corporations, duplicating the function of the central trust. In 1899, legal ownership of the companies controlled by Rockefeller was transferred to a holding company called the STANDARD OIL COMPANY OF NEW JERSEY.

In the early 1890s, the spirit of reform spread over the United States. Many people felt that Big Business was too powerful and must be reined in by the federal government. President Theodore Roosevelt set the tone by proclaiming himself a "trustbuster," and his administration vigorously pursued an antitrust case against Standard Oil. In 1911, the U.S. Supreme Court mandated the breakup of the Standard Oil Company into 34 smaller companies. Many of those companies are still very well known, as evidenced by the partial list contained in Exhibit 8-1.

The largest piece of the dismembered Standard Oil Trust was the Standard Oil Company of New Jersey, which changed its named to EXXON in 1972. Exxon now operates in over 100 countries, exploring for oil, producing petrochemical products, and transporting oil and natural gas. In

fyi

The oil boom did not hit Texas until 1901 when a well on Spindletop Hill, south of Beaumont, Texas, began to gush 100,000 barrels of oil a day.

fyi

John D. Rockefeller used some of his Standard Oil profits to found the University of Chicago in 1891.

setting the stage

fyi

The federal antitrust case against MICROSOFT has been compared to the Standard Oil case of 1911, with Bill Gates playing the role of a modern-day Rockefeller.

exhibit 8-1   Companies Descended from the Original Standard Oil

	Total Revenue for 1999 (in millions)
Amoco (subsidiary of BP Amoco)	$ 33,000*
Ashland	20,293
Atlantic Richfield (merger with BP Amoco pending)	13,055
Chevron	36,586
Conoco	27,309
ExxonMobil	185,527
Pennzoil–Quaker State	2,989
Total	$318,759

By contrast, the #1 company in the Fortune 500 revenue listing in 1999 was General Motors with revenues of $189,058 million.

*Estimated

Source: *The Wall Street Journal*, December 2, 1998, p. B1, updated.

many places, the company is known as ESSO, representing the initials "SO" for Standard Oil. To illustrate the size of Exxon's operations, the company had worldwide proved oil reserves of 11.3 billion barrels and proved natural gas reserves of 56.8 trillion cubic feet as of December 31, 1999. On December 1, 1998, Exxon (the former Standard Oil Company of New Jersey) announced an agreement to merge with MOBIL (the former STANDARD OIL COMPANY OF NEW YORK), thus reuniting these two pieces of the vast empire built by John D. Rockefeller. The formal joining of the two companies was completed on November 30, 1999, creating EXXONMOBIL.[1]

In Chapters 6 and 7, we discussed the accounting for sales and the cost of inventory sold. For firms that sell a product, the cost of the inventory sold typically represents the largest expense. For example, cost of goods sold was the largest expense category for EXXONMOBIL in 1999, totaling 42% of sales. For WAL-MART, cost of goods sold was 79% of sales in 1999. Although cost of goods sold represents a significant expense for those companies such as ExxonMobil and Wal-Mart that manufacture and/or sell a product, it is certainly not the only expense. And for those companies that sell a service, other expenses such as employee compensation or advertising can be far more significant than cost of goods sold.

In this chapter, we discuss a number of these other significant operating issues. We will begin with a discussion of two significant operating expenses that are incurred by almost every firm: employee compensation and income taxes. We also discuss the accounting for the costs associated with contingencies, which are items that are not fully resolved at the time the financial statements are prepared. Two common examples of contingencies are lawsuits and environmental cleanup obligations. Also in this chapter we discuss how one determines whether a cost should be recorded as an asset (capitalized) or recorded as an expense. The expense versus capitalize issue has arisen many

1 Information for this description was obtained from Daniel J. Boorstin, *The Americans: The Democratic Experience* (New York: Random House, 1973) and Ida M. Tarbell, *The History of the Standard Oil Company* (New York: MacMillan Company, 1904).

times over the years as accountants have wrestled with how to account for advertising costs, research costs, and others.

The financial statement items covered in this chapter are illustrated in Exhibit 8-2. Various operating items affecting the income statement are covered in the chapter. The two most significant are employee compensation and income taxes. The balance sheet items discussed are pension liabilities, deferred income tax liabilities, and contingent liabilities. The accounting aspects of these balance sheet items are intriguing in that both the pension and deferred tax items are sometimes reported as assets rather than liabilities. In addition, contingent liabilities are frequently not reported on the balance sheet at all. The details of all these topics, and more, are discussed in this chapter.

1

Account for the various components of employee compensation expense.

EMPLOYEE COMPENSATION

Often, one of the largest operating expenses of a business is the salaries and wages of its employees. But the cost of employees is not simply the expense associated with the current period's wages. As the following time line illustrates, issues associated with employee compensation can extend long after the employee has retired.

Employee Compensation Event Line

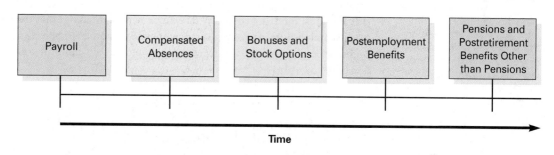

---

exhibit 8-2   Financial Statement Items Covered in This Chapter

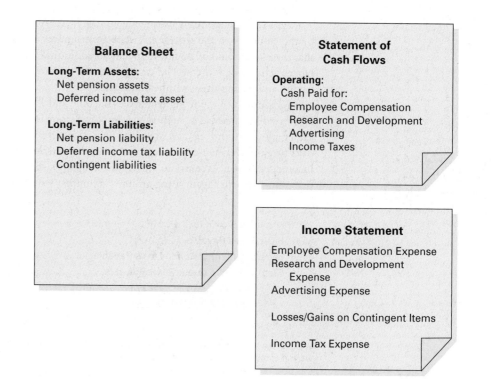

Payroll relates to the salaries and wages earned by employees for work done in the current period. Wages are paid anywhere from weekly to monthly, depending on the company. Compensated absences exist when an employer agrees to pay workers for sick days or vacation days. These obligations must be estimated and accrued in the period that the employee earns those days off. Many employees are paid bonuses based on some measure of performance (such as income or sales volume). Those bonuses are often paid quarterly or annually. One way to provide bonuses to employees is through the granting of stock options. In some cases, employees may earn what are termed "postemployment benefits," which kick in if an employee is laid off or terminated. Finally, firms offer benefits to their employees upon retirement. We will discuss each of these items in further detail in the sections that follow.

Payroll

In its simplest form, accounting for payroll involves debiting Salaries Expense and crediting Salaries Payable when employees work and then debiting Salaries Payable and crediting Cash when wages are paid. However, accounting for salaries and related payroll taxes is never quite that simple and can, in fact, be quite complex. This is primarily because every business is legally required to withhold certain taxes from employees' salaries and wages.

Very few people receive their full salary as take-home pay. For example, an employee who earns $30,000 a year probably takes home between $20,000 and $25,000. The remainder is withheld by the employer to pay the employee's federal and state income taxes, **Social Security (FICA) taxes**,[2] and any voluntary or contractual withholdings that the employee has authorized (such as union dues, medical insurance premiums, and charitable contributions). Thus, the accounting entry to record the expense for an employee's monthly salary (computed as 1/12 of $30,000) might be:

Social Security (FICA) taxes Federal Insurance Distributions Act taxes imposed on the employee and the employer; used mainly to provide retirement benefits.

Salaries Expense	2,500	
FICA Taxes Payable, Employees		191
Federal Withholding Taxes Payable		400
State Withholding Taxes Payable		200
Salaries Payable		1,709
To record Mary Perrico's salary for July.		

All the credit amounts (which are arbitrary in this example) are liabilities that must be paid by the employer to the federal and state governments and to the employee. It should be noted that these withholdings do not represent an additional expense to the employer because the employee actually pays them. The employer merely serves as an agent for the governments for collecting and paying these withheld amounts.

In addition to remitting employees' income and FICA taxes, companies must also pay certain payroll-related taxes, such as the employer's portion of the FICA tax (an amount equal to the employee's portion) and state and federal unemployment taxes. The payroll-related taxes paid by employers are expenses to the company and are included in operating expenses on the income statement. An entry to record the company's share of payroll taxes relating to Mary Perrico's employment (again using arbitrary amounts) would be:

Payroll Tax Expense	279	
FICA Taxes Payable, Employer		191
Federal Unemployment Taxes Payable		18
State Unemployment Taxes Payable		70
To record employer payroll tax liabilities associated with Mary Perrico's salary for July.		

2 Congress has split FICA taxes into two parts—Social Security and Medicare. For the purposes of this chapter, we will combine the two.

The different liabilities recorded in the preceding two entries for payroll would be eliminated as payments are made. The entries to account for the payments are:

FICA Taxes Payable	382	
Federal Withholding Taxes Payable	400	
Federal Unemployment Taxes Payable	18	
Cash		800
Paid July withholdings and payroll taxes to federal government.		
State Withholding Taxes Payable	200	
State Unemployment Taxes Payable	70	
Cash		270
Paid July withholdings and payroll taxes to state government.		
Salaries Payable	1,709	
Cash		1,709
Paid July salary to Mary Perrico.		

As these entries show, three checks are written for payroll-related expenses: one to the federal government, one to the state, and one to the employee.

One further point about salaries and wages needs to be made. The period of time covered by the payroll may not coincide with the last day of the year for financial reporting. Thus, if the reporting year ends on Wednesday, December 31, and the salaries and wages for that week will be paid Monday, January 5 of the following year, then the company must show the salaries and wages earned from Monday through Wednesday (December 29, 30, and 31) as a liability on the December 31 balance sheet. To accomplish this, the company would record an end-of-year adjusting entry to record the salaries and wages earned for those three days.

Compensated Absences

Suppose that you work for a business that provides each employee one day of sick leave for each full month of employment. When should that sick day (or compensated absence) be accounted for? When it is taken by the employee? When it is earned by the employee? And how much of an accrual should be associated with the compensated absences?

The matching principle requires that the expense associated with the compensated absence be accounted for in the period in which it is earned by the employee. Some of the conceptual issues associated with accounting for compensated absences are similar to those addressed in accounting for bad debts. In the case of bad debts, if we waited until we were sure a customer wasn't going to pay, then we could be certain about our bad debt expense. But we may not find out that we are not going to be paid until several periods later, and as a result, the bad debt expense would be reflected in the wrong accounting period. So instead of waiting until accounts are dishonored, we estimate the expense for each period. The same is true with compensated absences. Although we could wait until those sick days are taken and then know exactly what they will cost, it may be years before we know. Rather than wait, we estimate instead. For example, if you earn both $100 a day and one sick day per month, then it makes sense for your employer to recognize an expense (and accrue a liability) of $100 per month related to your sick pay. This would be done with the following journal entry:

Salaries Expense	100	
Sick Days Payable		100
To recognize accrued sick pay.		

When you take that sick day (and let's not forget that the government will take its share of your sick pay also), the journal entry would be:

Sick Days Payable	100	
Various Taxes Payable		20
Cash.		80
To record payment of sick day net of FICA, federal, and state taxes.		

Now suppose that you don't take your sick day until next year. Assume also that you received a $10 raise per day. This makes our estimate of $100 incorrect, so we will fix that estimate in the period in which you take the sick day. The journal entry in this instance would be:

Sick Days Payable	100	
Salaries Expense	10	
Various Taxes Payable		22
Cash.		88
To record payment of sick day net of FICA, federal, and state taxes.		

The same procedures would apply when accounting for accrued vacation pay or other types of compensated absences.

Bonuses

bonus Additional compensation, beyond the regular compensation, that is paid to employees if certain objectives are achieved.

Many companies offer employee **bonus** plans that allow employees to receive additional compensation should certain objectives be achieved. These bonus plans sometimes apply to all employees although more often they are restricted to members of top management. In many instances, the terms of the bonus plan are defined using financial statement numbers. For example, in its 1999 proxy statement filed with the Securities and Exchange Commission (SEC), **EXXON-MOBIL** disclosed that it has a management bonus plan targeted at 1,000 of its managers. The plan grants a certain number of award units to the managers; a manager is entitled to receive cash equal to the company's reported earnings per share for each award unit held. For example, ExxonMobil's chief executive officer (CEO), Lee R. Raymond, received 301,140 of these award units in 1999. With ExxonMobil's earnings per share in 1999 being $2.25, these award units added $677,565 (301,140 award units $\times$ $2.25) to Raymond's base salary of $2,110,417.

The purpose of an earnings-based bonus plan is to encourage managers to work harder and smarter to improve the performance of the company. However, such a plan also increases the incentive of managers to manipulate reported earnings. In fact, one of the factors looked at by auditors in evaluating the risk of financial statement fraud in a company is whether the company has an earnings-based management bonus plan.

Stock Options

employee stock options Rights given to employees to purchase shares of stock of a company at a predetermined price.

Employee stock options have become an increasingly popular way to compensate top executives. Under a stock option plan, managers are given the option of purchasing shares of the company's stock in the future at a price that is specified today. For example, in 1999, Lee Raymond, CEO of ExxonMobil, was granted 425,000 options, each allowing him to buy one share of ExxonMobil stock in the future for $83.56, which was the market value of ExxonMobil shares on the date the options were granted. Raymond will make money from these options if he is able to improve the performance of ExxonMobil and increase its stock price. If, for example, the company's stock price were to increase to $100.00 per share, these 425,000 options, allowing Raymond to buy ExxonMobil shares at the fixed price of $83.56, would be worth $6,987,000 [425,000 $\times$ ($100.00 - $83.56)]. Stock options are an attractive way to compensate top management because the options pay off only if the managers are able to increase the value of the company, which is exactly what the owners of the company (the stockholders) desire.

There has been significant debate in the United States about how to compute the compensation expense associated with employee stock options. The debate centers around the issue of what the value of an option is. Two methods for valuing employee options for accounting purposes are described below.

INTRINSIC VALUE METHOD　The "intrinsic value" of an option is the value it has if it must be exercised immediately. For example, if a company's stock price is $50 and it issues an option allowing an employee to buy a share of stock for $50, the option has no "intrinsic value" because the employee would be just as well off purchasing the company's stock in the market for $50, just as anyone not holding an option could do.

FAIR VALUE METHOD　The "fair value" of an option stems from the possibility that the employee may want to exercise the option in the future if the company's stock price goes up. For example, even if an option exercise price of $50 is equal to the stock price on the date the option is granted to an employee, there is a chance that the stock price may increase during the life of the option. This means that an option with no "intrinsic value" can still have substantial economic value because the employee holding the option may be able to buy the stock at less than its market value some time in the future. Exact computation of the fair value of options involves complex formulas derived using stochastic calculus, but commercially available software packages make option valuation no more difficult than using a spreadsheet.

The fair value method, with its theoretically correct emphasis on estimating the actual value of the options granted to employees, is backed by the FASB. Nevertheless, the vast majority of U.S. corporations opposed the FASB's attempt in 1994 to require recognition of a stock option compensation expense. The reason for this opposition was simple: recognition of a stock option compensation expense would reduce reported earnings. The surprising vigor of the opposition to the fair value method caused the FASB to reluctantly approve the following accounting treatment:

- Companies are allowed to use the intrinsic value method. For most stock option plans, this means that no expense is recognized.
- Companies are encouraged, but not required, to adopt the fair value method for employee stock options. The fair value method results in compensation expense being recognized for almost all stock option plans.
- Those companies choosing to use the intrinsic value method must disclose what their net income would have been if they had used the fair value method.

Like most U.S. companies, ExxonMobil uses the intrinsic value method. In 1999, ExxonMobil granted over 22 million employee stock options, all with intrinsic values of $0 as of the grant date. Thus, ExxonMobil reported no compensation expense in relation to these 22 million options. In the notes to its financial statements, ExxonMobil discloses that these 22 million options had a total fair value of $149 million. This amount would have been recognized as compensation expense (spread over the number of years employees are required to stay with the company to earn the options) if ExxonMobil had used the fair value method.

> **f y i**
>
> MICROSOFT reports that if it had used the fair value method instead of the intrinsic value method in 1999, its reported compensation expense would have been increased by $1.1 billion.

postemployment benefits
Benefits paid to employees who have been laid off or terminated.

Postemployment Benefits

Postemployment benefits are perhaps the least common of the topics covered in this section on employee compensation. **Postemployment benefits** are those benefits that are incurred after an employee has ceased to work for an employer but before that employee retires. A common example is a company-provided severance package for employees who have been laid off. This severance package might include salary for a certain time period, retraining costs, education costs, and the like. Although the company may not know the exact postemployment cost, accounting standards require that the amount be estimated and accrued in the period in which the decision is made to cut back the labor force. For example, suppose a company decides to close a segment of its operations, thereby laying off a certain percentage of its labor force. The company must estimate the costs associated with the benefits offered to those laid-off employees and would record the following journal entry:

What Goes into Pensions? A pension is an agreement between an employer and the employees that the employees will receive a certain sum of money upon retirement. That money may be paid in a single sum or over several years. In addition, employers often offer other postretirement benefits such as medical and life insurance. Consider how difficult it can be to account for these items.

Let's assume that you are 25 years old when you start working for your current employer. Your employer's pension plan states that upon retirement you will receive medical and life insurance benefits in addition to a monthly pension check. The pension will

be a percentage, commonly 2%, of your average annual salary over the last five years of your employment multiplied by the number of years of employment. What factors need to be considered in determining the employer's future liability?

As you can imagine, estimating these various factors involves some enormous assumptions. Plus, once the estimates have been made, the fact that those expenditures will not be made for 40 years (assuming you retire when you turn 65) must be factored in.

As if that isn't enough, the employer must do this computation for every employee. In the case of large companies, such as EXXONMOBIL with 106,000 employees, the computations are staggering. Fortunately, businesses have help in the form of actuaries. Actuaries make their living predicting the future. They

---

pension An agreement between an employer and employees that provides for benefits upon retirement.

defined contribution plan A pension plan under which the employer contributes a defined amount to the pension fund; after retirement, the employees receive the amount contributed plus whatever it has earned.

defined benefit plan A pension plan under which the employer defines the amount that retiring employees will receive and contributes enough to the pension fund to pay that amount.

Salaries Expense	xxx
Benefits Payable	xxx
To record postemployment benefits for laid-off employees.	

When the benefits are paid, a journal entry would be made to reduce the payable and to record the cash outflow.

Pensions

A **pension** is cash compensation received by an employee after that employee has retired. Two primary types of pension plans exist. A **defined contribution plan** requires the company to place a certain amount of money into a pension fund each year on behalf of the employees. Then, after the employees retire, they receive the money contributed to the pension fund plus the earnings on those contributions. With a **defined benefit plan**, on the other hand, the company promises the employees a certain monthly cash amount after they retire, based on factors such as number of years worked by the employee, employee's highest salary, and so forth.

The accounting for a defined contribution plan is quite simple—a company merely reports pension expense equal to the amount of cash it is required to contribute to its employees' pension fund during the year. Normally, no balance sheet liability is reported in connection with a defined contribution plan because, once the company has made the required contribution to the pension fund, it has no remaining obligation to the employees.

STOP & THINK Who bears the risks associated with a defined contribution plan—the employer or the employee? Which party bears the risks associated with a defined benefit plan?

The accounting issues associated with defined benefit plans are much more complex because the ultimate amount that a company will have to pay into its employees' pension fund depends on how long the employees work before retiring, what their highest salaries are, how long the employees live after they retire, and how well the investments in the pension fund perform. The accounting concept underlying this complexity, however, is still the same basic idea of matching: the income statement this year should contain all expenses related to generating revenue this year, whether those expenses are paid in cash this year (like cash wages) or are not expected to be paid for many years (like pension benefits).

estimate birth and death rates, trends in inflation, health-care costs, salaries, and other relevant information. There are about 14,000 actuaries in the United States, compared to over 1 million accountants.

So, if you start thinking that accounting is difficult and you become uncomfortable with all the assumptions and estimates, remember that it could be worse: you could be studying to be an actuary!

Postretirement Benefit	Factors to Consider
Medical insurance	What will health-care costs be in the future?
	How long will you live to enjoy those health insurance benefits?
	(The longer you live, the greater the cost.)
Life insurance	What will insurance premiums be for the remainder of your employment?
Pension check	How long will you work?
	What will your average annual salary be in your last five years of employment?
	How long will you or your spouse live after you retire?

PENSION-RELATED ITEMS IN THE FINANCIAL STATEMENTS   Each of the major balance sheet and income statement items related to pension accounting is briefly introduced below.

- *Pension fund.* When a company has a defined benefit pension plan, it is required by U.S. federal law to establish a separate pension fund to ensure that employees receive the defined benefits promised under the plan. The pension fund is basically a large investment fund of stocks and bonds. The company still owns these pension fund assets, but it cannot use them for any purpose except to pay pension benefits to employees.

- *Pension obligation.* The promise to make defined benefit pension payments to employees represents a liability to the company making the promise. The amount of this liability is quite difficult to estimate because it depends on future salary increases, employee turnover, employee life span, and so forth. The estimation of the liability is done by professionals called actuaries. These are the same individuals who provide the computations that life insurance companies use in setting premiums.

- *Net pension asset or liability.* One possible way to present the pension information on a balance sheet is to list the pension plan assets among the long-term assets and the pension liability as a long-term liability. However, the accounting standards stipulate that these two items be offset against one another and a single net amount be shown as either a net pension asset or a net pension liability.

- *Pension-related interest cost.* The estimated pension obligation represents an amount owed by a company to its employees. Accordingly, a pension-related interest cost is recognized each year; the amount of this interest cost is the increase in the pension obligation resulting from interest on the unpaid pension obligation.

- *Service cost.* The amount of a company's pension obligation increases each year as employees work and earn more pension benefits. This increase in the pension obligation is an expense associated with work done during the year and is called the pension service cost.

- *Return on pension fund assets.* The cost of a company's pension plan is partially offset by the return that the company earns on the assets in its pension fund.

- *Pension expense.* Just as pension liabilities and assets are offset against one another to arrive at a single net liability or asset to be reported on the balance sheet, the three components of pension expense (interest cost, service cost, and return on pension fund assets) are netted against one another to yield a single number that is reported on the income statement.

ILLUSTRATION FROM EXXONMOBIL'S FINANCIAL STATEMENTS   In the notes to its 1999 financial statements, ExxonMobil discloses the following about its pension benefit obligation and its pension fund. All numbers are in millions of dollars.

	U.S. Plans	Non-U.S. Plans	Total
Pension benefit obligation	$8,032	$11,628	$19,660
Pension fund assets	7,965	8,689	16,654
Net pension liability	$ 67	$ 2,939	$ 3,006

Note that ExxonMobil has separated its pension plans into those covering employees in the United States and those covering employees located outside the United States. This is a useful separation because the laws governing the maintenance of pension plans vary from country to country; U.S. laws are generally viewed as giving more protection to the rights of the employees covered by pension plans than foreign laws do. Also note that ExxonMobil's pension plans are "underfunded," meaning that the market value of the assets in the pension funds is less than the estimated pension liability. ExxonMobil also provides the following information about its pension expense in 1999. Again, all of the numbers are in millions.

	U.S. Plans	Non-U.S. Plans	Total
Service cost	$ 249	$ 312	$ 561
Interest cost	555	608	1,163
Less: Expected return on fund assets	(601)	(599)	(1,200)
Other miscellaneous items	(35)	217	182
Net pension expense	$ 168	$ 538	$ 706

Note the significant reduction in reported pension expense caused by the expected return on pension fund assets; without the return on the pension fund, ExxonMobil's pension expense would be more than twice as high.

Postretirement Benefits Other Than Pensions

In addition to pension benefits, employers often offer employees other benefits after their retirement. For example, ExxonMobil promises its employees that it will continue to cover them with health-care and life insurance plans after retirement. These types of plans are typically less formal than pension plans and often are not backed by assets accumulated in a separate fund. For example, ExxonMobil has only a $600 million separate fund set up to cover its estimated $2.6 billion obligation to cover the health-care needs of employees.

The accounting rules require companies to currently recognize the expense and long-term liability associated with the postretirement benefits that are earned in the current year, in keeping with the normal practice of matching expenses to the period in which they are initially incurred. The actual accounting is complex but similar to that required for pensions. The potential liabilities for these future payments can be quite significant for many firms. GENERAL MOTORS has the largest postretirement benefit plan in the United States, with a nonpension postretirement obligation totaling $44.683 billion as of December 31, 1999. Interestingly, General Motors clearly indicates that although it is reporting a liability for these postretirement benefits, it does not recognize these benefits as a legal obligation. In the notes to the 1999 financial statements, GM's management states:

> GM has disclosed in the consolidated financial statements certain amounts associated with estimated future postretirement benefits other than pensions and characterized such amounts as "accumulated postretirement benefit obligations," "liabilities," or "obligations." Notwithstanding the recording of such amounts and the use of these terms, GM

caution

The *expected*, not the actual, return on the pension fund assets is subtracted in computing pension expense. The accounting for the difference between expected and actual return involves deferring gains and losses, corridor amounts, and other complexities best left for an intermediate accounting course.

does not admit or otherwise acknowledge that such amounts or existing postretirement benefit plans of GM (other than pensions) represent legally enforceable liabilities of GM.

As illustrated in this section, compensation expense includes much more than just wages and salaries. Companies presumably have calculated that the value of the services provided by employees justifies the additional compensation cost beyond salaries and wages. The fact that employees earn benefits in one year that they do not receive until later, sometimes many years later, necessitates careful accounting to ensure that compensation expense is reported in the year in which it is earned.

to summarize

Employee compensation is not limited to just the current period's payroll. The cost of employees also includes compensated absences, bonuses, stock options, postemployment benefits, pensions, and other postretirement benefits. Most companies account for employee stock options using the intrinsic value method, meaning that, typically, no compensation expense is recognized. A pension obligation is reported on the balance sheet as the difference between the obligation and the amount in an associated pension fund. Pension expense is the sum of interest cost and service cost, less the expected return on the pension fund assets.

2

Compute income tax
expense, including
appropriate consideration
of deferred tax items.

TAXES

In addition to the payroll taxes described in the previous section, companies are responsible for paying several other taxes to federal, state, and/or local governments, including sales taxes, property taxes, and income taxes. The accounting for these taxes is described next.

Sales Taxes

Most states and some cities charge a sales tax on retail transactions. These taxes are paid by customers to the seller, who in turn forwards them to the state or city. Sales taxes collected from customers represent a current liability until remitted to the appropriate governmental agency. For example, assume that a sporting goods store in Denver prices a pair of skis at $200 and that the combination of state and city sales tax is 6.5%. When the store sells the skis, it collects $213 and records the transaction as follows:

Cash.	213	
Sales Revenue		200
Sales Tax Payable.		13

Sold a pair of skis for $200. Collected $213, including 6.5% sales tax.

sales tax payable Money
collected from customers
for sales taxes that must be
remitted to local govern-
ments and other taxing authorities.

The sales revenue is properly recorded at $200, and the $13 is recorded as **Sales Tax Payable**, a liability. Then, on a regular basis, a sales tax return is completed and filed with the state or city tax commission, and sales taxes collected are paid to those agencies. Note that the collection of the sales tax from customers creates a liability to the state but does not result in the recognition of revenue when collected or an expense when paid to the state. The company acts as an agent of the state in collecting the sales tax and recognizes a liability only until the collected amount is remitted to the state.

Property Taxes

Property taxes are usually assessed by county or city governments on land, buildings, and other company assets. The period covered by the assessment of property taxes is often from July 1 of one year to June 30 of the next year. If a property taxpayer is on a calendar-year financial reporting basis (or on a fiscal-year basis ending on a day other than June 30), the property tax assessment year and the company's financial reporting year will not coincide. Therefore, when the company prepares its financial statements at calendar-year end, it must report a prepaid tax asset (if taxes are paid at the beginning of the tax year) or a property tax liability (if taxes are paid at the end of the tax year) for the taxes associated with the first portion of the assessment year. To illustrate, assume that Yokum Company pays its property taxes of $3,600 on June 30, 2002, for the period July 1, 2002, to June 30, 2003. If the company is on a calender-year basis and records the prepayment as an asset, then the adjusting entry at December 31, 2002, would be:

Property Tax Expense...	1,800	
Prepaid Property Taxes....................................		1,800
To record property tax expense for 6 months.		

The prepaid property taxes account balance of $1,800 would be shown on Yokum's balance sheet at December 31, 2002, as a current asset. On June 30, 2003, property tax expense would be recognized for the period January 1, 2003, through June 30, 2003, with the following entry:

Property Tax Expense...	1,800	
Prepaid Property Taxes....................................		1,800
To record property tax expense for the property assessment period		
January 1–June 30, 2003.		

Income Taxes

Corporations pay income taxes just as individuals do. This corporate income tax is usually reported as the final expense on the income statement. For example, in 1999, the final three lines in **EXXONMOBIL**'s income statement were as follows, with all numbers in millions:

	1999	1998	1997
Income before income taxes	$11,150	$12,083	$19,337
Income taxes	3,240	3,939	7,605
Net income	$ 7,910	$ 8,144	$11,732

The $3.240 billion in income tax expense reported by ExxonMobil in 1999 is not necessarily equal to the amount of cash paid for income taxes during the year. In fact, ExxonMobil paid $3.805 billion for income taxes in 1999. Reported income tax expense may differ from the actual amount of cash paid for taxes for two reasons. First, like many other expenses, income taxes are not necessarily paid in cash in the year in which they are incurred. The important point to remember is that reported income tax expense reflects the amount of income taxes attributable to income earned during the year, whether the tax was actually paid in cash during the year or not.

The second reason reported income tax expense may differ from the actual amount of cash paid for taxes is that income tax expense is based on reported financial accounting income, whereas the amount of cash paid for income taxes is dictated by the applicable government tax law. The $3.240 billion income tax expense reported by ExxonMobil in 1999 reflects the total estimated amount of income tax the company expects will eventually be paid based on the income reported in the current year's income statement. However, because the income computed using the tax rules is almost always different from the income computed using financial accounting standards, some of this tax may not have to be paid for several years. In addition, tax rules may require income tax to be paid on income before the financial accounting standards consider that income to be "earned." These differences in tax law income and financial accounting income give rise to deferred income tax items, which are discussed in this section.

Corporations in the United States compute two different income numbers—financial income for reporting to stockholders and taxable income for reporting to the Internal Revenue Service (IRS). The existence of these two "sets of books" seems unethical to some, illegal to others. However, the difference between the stockholders' need for information and the government's need for efficient revenue collection makes the computation of the two different income numbers essential. The different purposes of these reporting systems were summarized by the U.S. Supreme Court in the *Thor Power Tool* case (1979):

> The primary goal of financial accounting is to provide useful information to management, shareholders, creditors, and others properly interested; the major responsibility of the accountant is to protect these parties from being misled. The primary goal of the income tax system, in contrast, is the equitable collection of revenue.

In summary, U.S. corporations compute income in two different ways, and rightly so. Nevertheless, the existence of these two different numbers that can each be called "income before taxes" makes it surprisingly difficult to define what is meant by "income tax expense."

Deferred Tax Example

Assume that you invest $1,000 by buying shares in a mutual fund on January 1. Also assume that the income tax rate is 40%. According to the tax law, any economic gain you experience through an increase in the value of your mutual fund shares is not taxed until you actually sell your shares. The rationale behind this tax rule is that until you sell your shares, you don't have the cash to pay any tax. Now, assume further that the economy does well and that the value of your mutual fund shares increases to $1,600 by December 31. You decide to prepare partial financial statements to summarize your holdings and the performance of your shares during the year. These financial statements are as follows:

Balance Sheet		Income Statement	
Assets:		Revenues:	
Mutual Fund Shares	$1,600	Gain on Mutual Fund Investment	$600

A moment's consideration reveals that this balance sheet and income statement are misleading. Yes, it is true that your shares are now worth $1,600, but if and when you liquidate the shares, you will have to pay income tax of $240 [($1,600 − $1,000) × .40]. Thus, you are overstating your economic position by only reporting the $1,600 in mutual fund shares; you should also report that a liability of $240 exists in relation to these shares. Similarly, it is misleading to report the $600 gain on your income statement without also reporting that, at some future time, you will have to pay $240 in income tax on that gain. A more accurate set of financial statements would appear as follows:

Balance Sheet		Income Statement	
Assets:		Revenues:	
Mutual Fund Shares	$1,600	Gain on Mutual Fund Investment	$600
Liabilities:		Expenses:	
Deferred Income Tax Liability	$ 240	Income Tax Expense	$240

The appropriate journal entry to recognize income tax expense in this case is as follows:

Income Tax Expense	240	
Deferred Income Tax Liability		240

Note that the deferred income tax liability is not a legal liability because, as far as the IRS is concerned, you do not currently owe any tax on the increase in the value of your mutual fund. Nevertheless, the deferred tax liability is an economic liability that should be reported now because it reflects an obligation that will have to be paid in the future as a result of an event (the increase in the value of the mutual fund shares) that occurred this year.

Now, what if the mutual fund shares had decreased in value from $1,000 to $400? Consider whether the following set of financial statements would accurately reflect your economic position and performance:

Balance Sheet		**Income Statement**	
Assets:		Expenses:	
Mutual Fund Shares	$400	Loss on Mutual Fund Investment	$600

Again, these financial statements are somewhat misleading because they ignore the future tax implications of the change in the value of the mutual fund shares. In this case, when the shares are sold, you will realize a taxable loss of $600. If you have other investment income, that loss can be used to reduce your total taxable income by $600, which will save you $240 ($600 × .40 in income taxes. Thus, in a real sense, this loss on the mutual funds is not all bad because it will provide you with a $240 reduction in income taxes in the year in which you sell the shares. This reduction in taxes is an asset, a deferred income tax asset, because it represents a probable future economic benefit that has arisen from an event (the drop in the value of the mutual fund shares) that occurred this year. Similarly, the income statement effect of this future savings in taxes is to soften the blow of the reported $600 loss. The loss that occurred this year will result in an income tax benefit in the future, so the benefit is reported on this year's income statement, as follows:

Balance Sheet		**Income Statement**	
Assets:		Expenses:	
Mutual Fund Shares	$400	Loss on Mutual Fund Investment	$ 600
		Less: Income Tax Benefit	(240)
Deferred Income Tax Asset	$240		
		Net Loss	$ 360

The journal entry to recognize the income tax "expense" is as follows:

Deferred Income Tax Asset	240	
Income Tax Expense.		240

Notice that Income Tax Expense is credited, or reduced, in this entry. If there are other income taxes for the year, this credit will result in a reduction in reported income tax expense. If there are no other income taxes, then the credit amount will be reported on the income statement as an addition to income under the title "income tax benefit."

As this simple mutual fund example illustrates, the amount of income tax expense reported on a company's income statement is not necessarily the same as the amount of income tax the company must pay on taxable income generated during the year. There are literally hundreds

f y i

The value of the deferred tax asset depends on your having other investment income in the future against which the loss on the mutual fund shares can be offset. Thus, accounting for deferred tax assets is complicated by the fact that one must make an assumption about the likelihood that a company will have enough taxable income in the future to be able to take advantage of the deferred tax benefit.

of accounting areas in which income is taxed by the taxing authorities in a different year than the year in which the income is reported to the financial statement users in the income statement. The details of deferred income tax accounting are among the most complicated issues covered in intermediate accounting courses.

to summarize

The amount of sales tax collected is reported as a liability until the funds are forwarded to the appropriate government agency. When property taxes are paid in advance, the amount is reported as a prepaid asset until the time period covered by the property tax has expired. Reported income tax expense is not merely the amount of income tax that a company legally owes for a given year. Because of differences between financial accounting rules and income tax rules, revenues and expense can enter into the computation of income in different years for financial accounting purposes and for income tax purposes. Proper accounting for deferred income taxes ensures that reported income tax expense for a year represents all of the income tax consequences arising from transactions undertaken during the year.

3

Distinguish between contingent items that should be recognized in the financial statements and those that should be merely disclosed in the financial statement notes.

contingency Circumstances involving potential losses or gains that will not be resolved until some future event occurs.

CONTINGENCIES

By its very nature, business is full of uncertainty. As discussed in relation to employee compensation and taxes, proper recording of an expense in the current period frequently requires making estimates about what will occur in future periods. Sometimes the very existence of an asset or liability depends on the occurrence, or nonoccurrence, of a future event. For example, whether a company will have to make a payment as a result of a lawsuit arising from events occurring this year depends on a judge or jury ruling that may not be known for several years. In accounting terms, a **contingency** is an uncertain circumstance involving a potential gain or loss that will not be resolved until some future event occurs. In this section, we discuss the conceptual issues associated with contingencies and the accounting for events for which the outcome is uncertain.

If you were a financial statement user, would you want to be informed of events known to management that might have an adverse effect on the company's future? Consider as an example a lawsuit filed against a company. Because litigation can take years, how should that company account for the possibility of a loss? Would you want the company to wait until the lawsuit is resolved before informing financial statement users of the litigation? Of course not. You would want to know about the lawsuit if the outcome could potentially materially affect the operations of the company. But would you want to know about every lawsuit filed against the company? Probably not.

Accounting standard-setters have addressed this issue and determined that the proper disclosure for a contingency depends upon the assessed outcome. The first thing to note is that accounting standard-setters determined that accounting for contingent gains is, in most cases, inappropriate. Contingent gains are typically not accounted for until the future event relating to the contingent gain resolves itself. Contingent liabilities are to be accounted for differently depending on an assessment of the likely outcome of the contingency. Exhibit 8-3 contains the relevant terms, definitions, and proper accounting for contingent liabilities.

If you think about it, this probability spectrum makes a great deal of sense. For example, if it is likely that your company will lose a lawsuit in which it is the defendant, then it would be appropriate to account for that outcome now by recognizing a loss and establishing a payable. If the likelihood of your company losing the case is slight, then it makes sense to do nothing. And if you are unsure of the outcome, then disclosure in the notes seems appropriate.

exhibit 8-3   Accounting for Contingent Liabilities

Term	Definition	Accounting
Probable	The future event is likely to occur.	Estimate the amount of the contingency and make the appropriate journal entry; provide detailed disclosure in the notes.
Reasonably possible	The chance of the future event occurring is more than remote but less than likely.	Provide detailed disclosure of the possible liability in the notes.
Remote	The chance of the future event occurring is slight.	No disclosure required.

STOP & THINK Why might a company hesitate to assess the likelihood of losing an ongoing lawsuit as being probable? If you were the attorney for the plaintiff, how could you use the resulting information from the financial statements?

The problem in implementing these terms relates to assessing the likelihood of an outcome. Who is to say if your company will lose a lawsuit? The company must obtain objective assessments as to the possible outcome of future events. In the case of litigation, the company would ask its attorneys about the possible outcome. The firm auditing the company might use its own attorneys to assess the possible outcome. In any case, companies are required to make objective assessments as to the likely outcome of contingent events and then account for those events based on that assessment.

MICROSOFT's 1999 annual report (see Appendix A) contains the company's disclosure relating to contingencies. At the time, the company was being investigated by the Justice Department for potential monopolistic practices. Note that the disclosure relating to the antitrust contingency is minimal, consisting of just two paragraphs. Contrast Microsoft's disclosure with the 1999 disclosure provided by PHILIP MORRIS, the tobacco company, relating to its involvement in ongoing tobacco litigation. The company provides over seven pages of disclosure relating to its potential liability.

Environmental Liabilities

environmental liabilities Obligations incurred because of damage done to the environment.

Environmental liabilities have gained increasing attention of late because of their potential magnitude. **Environmental liabilities** are obligations incurred because of damage done by companies to the environment. Common environmental liabilities include cleanup costs associated with oil spills, toxic waste dumps, or air pollution. These liabilities are usually brought to the company's attention as a result of fines or penalties imposed by the federal government or when damage that is caused by the company is recognized. Although the accounting and disclosures associated with environmental liabilities fall under the guidelines for contingencies discussed in the previous section, environmental liabilities present a unique problem.

In the case of a lawsuit, one can typically make a reasonable estimate as to the upper bound of the potential settlement. For example, if your company is being sued for $4 million, it is unlikely that any potential settlement will be higher than that amount. In the case of environmental liabilities, it is often very difficult to estimate the cost of environmental cleanup. Thus, while the company may deem it probable that a liability exists, estimating that liability can be difficult. Recall that the contingency standard requires a liability to be recorded on the company's books if it is probable and estimable. If a potential liability is possible and estimable, the standards require note disclosure.

What about the situation where a potential liability is probable but cannot be estimated with much accuracy, as is often the case with environmental liabilities? Obviously, if a company cannot estimate a probable obligation, it makes sense to provide extensive note disclosure. Most companies will estimate a least a minimum amount and provide note disclosure as to the possibility of additional costs. As an illustration, EXXONMOBIL disclosed the information in Exhibit 8-4 in its 1991 and 1999 annual reports in connection with lawsuits filed as a result of the *Exxon Valdez* oil spill. Note that in 1991, the company sounds quite optimistic that it has set-

exhibit 8-4   ExxonMobil—1991 and 1999 Disclosures Concerning *Exxon Valdez* Oil Spill

Disclosure in 1991

On March 24, 1989, the Exxon Valdez, a tanker owned by Exxon Shipping Company, a subsidiary of Exxon Corporation, ran aground on Bligh Reef in Prince William Sound off the port of Valdez, Alaska, and released approximately 260,000 barrels of crude oil. More than 315 lawsuits, including class actions, have been brought in various courts against Exxon Corporation and certain of its subsidiaries.

On October 8, 1991, the United States District Court for the District of Alaska approved a civil agreement and consent decree.... These agreements provided for guilty pleas to certain misdemeanors, the dismissal of all felony charges and the remaining misdemeanor charges by the United States, and the release of all civil claims against Exxon ... by the United States and the state of Alaska. The agreements also released all claims related to or arising from the oil spill by Exxon....

Payments under the plea agreement totaled $125 million—$25 million in fines and $100 million in payments to the United States and Alaska for restoration projects in Alaska. Payments under the civil agreement and consent decree will total $900 million over a ten-year period. The civil agreement also provides for the possible payment, between September 1, 2002, and September 1, 2006, of up to $100 million for substantial loss or decline in populations, habitats, or species in areas affected by the oil spill which could not have been reasonably anticipated on September 25, 1991.

The remaining cost to the corporation from the Valdez accident is difficult to predict and cannot be determined at this time. It is believed the final outcome, net of reserves already provided, will not have a materially adverse effect upon the corporation's operations or financial condition.

Disclosure in 1999

On September 24, 1996, the United States District Court for the District of Alaska entered a judgment in the amount of $5.058 billion in the Exxon Valdez civil trial that began in May 1994. The District Court awarded approximately $19.6 million in compensatory damages to fisher plaintiffs, $38 million in prejudgment interest on the compensatory damages and $5 billion in punitive damages to a class composed of all persons and entities who asserted claims for punitive damages from the corporation as a result of the Exxon Valdez grounding. The District Court also ordered that these awards shall bear interest from and after entry of the judgment. The District Court stayed execution on the judgment pending appeal based on a $6.75 billion letter of credit posted by the corporation. The corporation has appealed the judgment. The corporation has also appealed the District Court's denial of its renewed motion for a new trial. The United States Court of Appeals for the Ninth Circuit heard oral arguments on the appeals on May 3, 1999. The corporation continues to believe that the punitive damages in this case are unwarranted and that the judgment should be set aside or substantially reduced by the appellate courts.

The ultimate cost to ExxonMobil from the lawsuits arising from the Exxon Valdez grounding is not possible to predict and may not be resolved for a number of years.

tled the bulk of the claims related to the oil spill and that any further claims "will not have a materially adverse effect" upon the company. This optimistic disclosure is particularly interesting in light of the $5 billion adverse judgment discussed in the 1999 disclosure.

to summarize

Contingent liabilities depend on some future event to determine if a liability actually exists. Companies are required to assess the likelihood of certain future events occurring and then, based on that assessment, provide appropriate disclosure. If the company deems the future event to be likely, the journal entries are made and the liability is accrued. If the future event is deemed reasonably possible, note disclosure is required. For those events considered remote, no disclosure is required. Environmental liabilities represent a case where a liability exists but measurement is difficult. A minimum liability is typically established along with extensive note disclosure.

CAPITALIZE VERSUS EXPENSE

4

Understand when an expenditure should be recorded as an asset and when it should be recorded as an expense.

To this point in the text, we have assumed that the decision of expensing a cost to the income statement or capitalizing an expenditure and placing it on the balance sheet as an asset is an easy one. In reality, that decision is often difficult and one that makes accounting judgment critical. For example, should a building that cost $1 million and is expected to benefit 20 future periods be capitalized and placed on the balance sheet? The answer is pretty clear—of course. What about office supplies that are used this period? Will they benefit future periods? No, and as a result, the costs of those supplies should be expensed. What about research and development costs? Should they be capitalized as an asset or expensed to the income statement? Now you see the problem. Sometimes it is difficult to determine whether an expenditure will benefit the future. Exhibit 8-5 provides an expense/asset continuum that demonstrates the difficulty of the decision to capitalize or expense a cost.

The endpoints of the continuum are easy. The decision starts to get fuzzy, though, once you leave the endpoints. Do repairs and maintenance benefit future periods (and therefore need to be capitalized), or are they necessary expenditures just to keep a machine running (and should be expensed)? To illustrate the issues involved in deciding whether an expenditure should be capitalized or expensed, two specific areas will be discussed—research and development (R&D) and advertising.

Research and Development

Research is an activity undertaken to discover new knowledge that will be useful in developing new products, services, or processes. Development involves the application of research findings to develop a plan or design for new or improved products and processes. **EXXONMOBIL** reports that, from 1997 through 1999, it spent an average of $715 million per year on R&D activities.

Because of the uncertainty surrounding the future economic benefit of R&D activities, the FASB decided in 1974 that research and development expenditures should be expensed in the period incurred. Among the arguments for expensing R&D costs is the frequent inability to find a definite causal re-

STOP & THINK Would you expect that a rule requiring all firms to expense R&D outlays would cause R&D expenditures to decrease? Why or why not?

---

exhibit 8-5   Expense/Asset Continuum

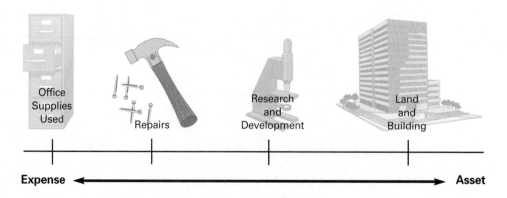

f y i

The International Accounting Standards Board (IASB) has established an R&D accounting rule that many think is superior to the FASB rule. The IASB rule requires research costs to be expensed and development costs to be capitalized. Research costs are defined as those R&D costs incurred before technological feasibility has been established.

lationship between the expenditures and future revenues. Sometimes very large expenditures do not generate any future revenue, while relatively small expenditures lead to significant discoveries that generate large revenues. The FASB found it difficult to establish criteria that would distinguish between those R&D expenditures that would most likely benefit future periods and those that would not.

In summary, the FASB concluded that R&D expenditures are undertaken to benefit future periods, but that it is impractical to identify which R&D expenditures actually do provide future economic benefit. Accordingly, all R&D costs are to be recorded as expenses in the year they are incurred. This rule leads to a systematic overstatement of R&D expenses and a systematic understatement of R&D assets. The rule was roundly criticized in 1974 as the FASB prepared to release it. The FASB received many comments predicting that if firms were required to expense all R&D costs, they would be forced to significantly cut back on research expenditures to avoid hurting reported earnings. This, according to these comment letters, would cripple the U.S. economy. And the U.S. economy did indeed suffer in the mid-1970s, and R&D expenditures did decrease, but these occurrences may have had more to do with skyrocketing oil prices and double-digit inflation than with the R&D accounting rule passed by the FASB.

Advertising

Every year in the two weeks of hype preceding the Super Bowl, we hear about the incredible number of media people covering the event and about how much money advertisers are paying for a 30-second spot during the broadcast. We also hear a little bit about the football teams. With advertising costs running in excess of $2 million for 30 seconds, one has to believe that the advertisers expect some future economic benefit from the advertising. So, should advertising costs be capitalized or expensed?

For accounting purposes, the general presumption is that advertising costs should be expensed because of the uncertainty of the future benefits. However, in selected cases in which the future benefits are more certain, advertising costs should be capitalized. This type of advertising involves targeted advertising to customers who have purchased products in the past. Such advertising is also characterized by the ability to estimate how many customers will respond favorably. For example, SEARS discloses in the notes to its 1999 financial statements that it expenses newspaper, television, and radio advertising costs but capitalizes the cost of specialty catalogs and other direct response advertising. As of December 31, 1999, Sears reported an "advertising asset" of $180 million in its balance sheet. Of course, this is a rather small amount compared to the $1.63 billion in advertising that Sears expensed during 1999.

As these discussions of R&D and advertising illustrate, capitalize-or-expense decisions can be quite difficult from a conceptual standpoint. The general rule of thumb is that, when there is significant uncertainty about whether an expenditure should be capitalized or expensed, expense it. This approach is in line with the traditional conservatism of accounting, but be aware that it can result in a significant understatement of the economic assets of a company.

t o   s u m m a r i z e

Conceptually, a cost should be recorded as an asset whenever it has a probable future economic benefit. In practice, it is frequently quite difficult to tell when a cost should be recorded as an asset (capitalized) and when it should be recorded as an expense. In some areas, such as research and development (R&D) and advertising, specific accounting rules have been developed to create more uniformity about which costs should be expensed and which should be capitalized.

review problem

The Income Statement

From the following information prepare an income statement for Southern Corporation for the year ended December 31, 2003. Assume that there are 200,000 shares of stock outstanding.

Sales Returns	$ 50,000
Sales Discounts	70,000
Gross Sales Revenue	9,000,000
Flood Loss	80,000
Income Taxes on Operations	500,000
Administrative Salaries Expense	360,000
Sales Salaries Expense	800,000
Rent Expense (General and Administrative)	32,000
Utilities Expense (General and Administrative)	4,000
Supplies Expense (General and Administrative)	16,000
Delivery Expense (Selling)	6,300
Payroll Tax Expense (Selling)	6,000
Automobile Expense (General and Administrative)	3,800
Insurance Expense (General and Administrative)	34,000
Advertising Expense (Selling)	398,000
Interest Revenue	6,000
Interest Expense	92,000
Insurance Expense (Selling)	7,000
Entertainment Expense (Selling)	7,200
Miscellaneous Selling Expenses	15,000
Miscellaneous General and Administrative Expenses	10,800
Tax rate applicable to flood loss	30%
Cost of Goods Sold	5,950,000

Solution

The first step in preparing an income statement is classifying items, as follows:

Revenue Accounts

Sales Returns	$ 50,000
Sales Discounts	70,000
Gross Sales Revenue	9,000,000

Cost of Goods Sold Accounts

Cost of Goods Sold	$5,950,000

Selling Expense Accounts

Sales Salaries Expense	$800,000
Delivery Expense	6,300
Payroll Tax Expense	6,000
Advertising Expense	398,000
Insurance Expense	7,000
Entertainment Expense	7,200
Miscellaneous Selling Expenses	15,000

General and Administrative Expense Accounts

Administrative Salaries Expense	$360,000
Rent Expense	32,000
Utilities Expense	4,000
Supplies Expense	16,000
Automobile Expense	3,800
Insurance Expense	34,000
Miscellaneous General and Administrative Expenses	10,800

Other Revenue and Expense Accounts

Interest Revenue	$ 6,000
Interest Expense	92,000

Miscellaneous Accounts

Income Taxes on Operations	$500,000

Extraordinary Item Accounts

Flood Loss	$80,000
Tax rate	30%

Once the accounts are classified, the income statement is prepared by including the accounts in the following format:

Net Sales Revenue (Gross Sales Revenue − Sales Returns − Sales Discounts)
−   Cost of Goods Sold
=   Gross Margin
−   Selling Expenses
−   General and Administrative Expenses
=   Operating Income
+/− Other Revenues and Expenses (add Net Revenues, subtract Net Expenses)
=   Income before Income Taxes
−   Income Taxes on Operations
=   Income before Extraordinary Items
+/− Extraordinary Items (add Extraordinary Gains, subtract Extraordinary Losses, net of applicable taxes)
=   Net Income

After net income has been computed, earnings per share is calculated and added to the bottom of the statement. It is important that the proper heading be included.

Southern Corporation
Income Statement
For the Year Ended December 31, 2003

Revenues:		
Gross sales revenue	$9,000,000	
Less: Sales returns	(50,000)	
Less: Sales discounts	(70,000)	
Net sales revenue		$8,880,000

(continued)

both U.S. and international income. The effective tax rate is computed by dividing current taxes by income before income taxes.

b. As of June 30, 1999, Microsoft had $1,709 million in deferred income tax liabilities. What was the source of most of this deferred tax liability?

2. Find Microsoft's financial statement note concerning "employee stock and savings plans."

a. Briefly describe Microsoft's employee stock purchase plan.

b. Microsoft also has an employee stock option plan whereby certain key employees are granted incentive stock options that allow them to buy Microsoft stock at a fixed price in the future. If Microsoft's stock price continues to rise, these options could be very valuable. Microsoft is not required to report any expense associated with the granting of these options. However, Microsoft is required to estimate the value of these options and disclose what net income would have been if this value had been recognized as an expense. How much would Microsoft's 1999 net income have decreased if the value of the incentive stock options had been recognized as an expense?

International

• Analyzing 8-2 (General Motors)

GENERAL MOTORS has the largest set of private pension plans in the world. The company has many different pension plans covering different groups of employees. The following information was extracted from the notes to GM's 1999 financial statements. All numbers are in millions of U.S. dollars. As you can see, for reporting purposes these plans are separated into U.S. plans and non-U.S. plans.

	U.S. Plans Pension Benefits		Non-U.S. Plans Pension Benefits	
	1999	1998	1999	1998
Projected benefit obligation at end of year	$73,269	$76,963	$ 9,728	$10,283
Fair value of plan assets at end of year	80,462	75,007	7,062	5,976
Funded status	$ 7,193	$ (1,956)	$(2,666)	$ (4,307)

1. The projected benefit obligation is the measure of the value of the pension benefits earned by GM's employees that has not yet been paid. What is GM's total projected benefit obligation?

2. To ensure that employees will be able to collect their pension benefits, GM is required by law to set aside funds in a pension plan. What is the total value of assets in all of these pension funds?

3. Why do you think GM is required to separate its disclosure of pension plans into U.S. and non-U.S. plans?

• Analyzing 8-3 (IBM)

Note P to IBM's 1999 financial statements describes how taxes affect IBM's operations. Among the information given is the following (all amounts are in millions of U.S. dollars):

	1999	1998	1997
Earnings before income taxes:			
U.S. operations	$ 5,892	$2,960	$3,193
Non-U.S. operations	5,865	6,080	5,834
Total earnings before income taxes	$11,757	$9,040	$9,027
Provision for income taxes:			
U.S. operations	$ 2,005	$ 991	$ 974
Non-U.S. operations	2,040	1,721	1,960
Total income taxes	$ 4,045	$2,712	$2,934
Total other taxes			
(Social Security, real estate,			
personal property, and other taxes)	$ 2,831	$2,859	$2,774

1. a. Compute the effective tax rate (income taxes/earnings before income taxes) for both U.S. and non-U.S. operations for 1997, 1998, and 1999.
   b. For each year 1997–1999, compute the percentage of the total tax burden that was made up of income taxes.
2. A deferred tax asset is a tax deduction that has already occurred and has been reported as a financial accounting expense but cannot be used to reduce income taxes until a future year. As of December 31, 1999, IBM reports that it has a deferred tax asset of $3.737 billion related to employee benefits. How would such a deferred tax asset arise?

INTERNATIONAL CASE

• Hutchison Whampoa

In Hong Kong, Li Ka-shing is known as "Superman." Li's personal wealth is estimated to be in excess of $1 billion, and there is a saying in Hong Kong that for every dollar spent, five cents goes into Li's pocket. Li and his family fled from China in 1940 in order to escape the advancing Japanese army. Li dropped out of school at age 13 to support his family by selling plastic trinkets on the streets of Hong Kong. Later, he scraped together enough money to buy a company that produced plastic flowers. His big success came when he bought the real estate surrounding his factory and watched the land skyrocket in value. Today, Li continues his simple lifestyle even though the companies he controls comprise over 10% of the value of the Hong Kong stock market. When asked why his sons have much nicer houses and cars than he does, Li responded, "My sons have a rich father; I did not."

Li is chairman of HUTCHISON WHAMPOA LIMITED. Hutchison has five major business segments: property development, container port operations, retailing, telecommunications, and energy. In 1999, Hutchison Whampoa reported net income of HK$118.735 billion (equivalent to approximately US$15.3 billion).

1. Assume that one of Hutchison Whampoa's overseas subsidiaries earns income of $1,000. The income tax rate in Hong Kong is 15%. When this income of $1,000 is transferred to the parent company in Hong Kong, it will be taxed, but no income tax is owed until then. What journal entry should Hutchison Whampoa make to record the income tax consequences of this $1,000 in income?

The following transactions occurred for Zepplin during January of 2003:

Jan. 1   Paid rent on the computer equipment, $1,800.

5   Recorded sales for the week, 125 units at $220 per unit. (The company uses a periodic inventory system.)

5   Paid wages payable and taxes payable from the prior period.

5   Collected $15,000 from customers on account during the week.

8   Purchased office supplies for cash, $350.

10   Received 50 YO-660s from the manufacturer at a cost of $160 per unit.

11   Paid accounts payable, $17,500.

12   Collected $27,000 from customers on account during the week.

12   Recorded sales for the week, 140 units at $220 per unit.

15   Paid monthly rent for the office and warehouse, $3,000.

15   Received 140 YO-660s from the manufacturer at a cost of $162 per unit.

18   A customer returned a YO-660 and requested a refund. A check was immediately mailed to the customer in the amount of $220.

19   Collected $38,000 from customers on account during the week.

19   Recorded sales for the week, 115 units at $220 per unit.

20   Paid the semimonthly payroll for the pay period ending on January 15. Salaries and wages total $5,300 and payroll taxes were as follows: FICA taxes payable, employee, $405; FICA taxes payable, employer, $405; state withholding taxes payable, $280; federal withholding taxes payable, $810; federal unemployment taxes payable, $50; state unemployment taxes payable, $150.

22   Received notice that a customer owing Zepplin $440 had filed bankruptcy and would be unable to pay.

23   Paid the taxes payable from the payroll on January 20.

24   Received 190 YO-660s from the manufacturer at a cost of $160 per unit.

25   Purchased office supplies for cash, $730.

25   Paid accounts payable, $39,000.

26   Collected $44,500 from customers on account during the week.

26   Recorded sales for the week, 135 units at $225 per unit.

29   Customers returned 5 YO-660s and requested refunds. Checks were immediately mailed to each customer in the amount of $220 each.

30   Received 130 YO-660s from the manufacturer at a cost of $160 per unit.

31   Collected $21,800 from customers on account.

31   Recorded sales for the partial week, 65 units at $225 per unit.

31   Accrued the semimonthly payroll for the pay period ending on January 31. Salaries and wages total $5,400 and payroll taxes were as follows: FICA taxes payable, employee, $410; FICA taxes payable, employer, $410; state withholding taxes payable, $285; federal withholding taxes payable, $820; federal unemployment taxes payable, $55; state unemployment taxes payable, $160.

Required:

1. Provide the required journal entries to record each of the above events.
2. Make the adjusting entries necessary to (1) record bad debt expense for the period and (2) to adjust inventory and office supplies. A count of inventory and office supplies revealed 160 YO-660s on hand and supplies valued at $800.
3. Prepare a trial balance as of January 31, 2003.
4. Prepare an income statement and a balance sheet for Zepplin Enterprises.
5. Prepare a common-size income statement for Zepplin Enterprises.
6. Compute Zepplin's number of days' sales in inventory, number of days' sales in accounts receivable, and number of days' sales in accounts payable ratios. What can you conclude about the company's liquidity position based on this analysis?

f3
p a r t

Investing and Financing Activities

Investments in Property, Plant, and Equipment and in Intangible Assets

chapter

f9

learning objectives   After studying this chapter, you should be able to:

1 Identify the two major categories of long-term operating assets: property, plant, and equipment and intangible assets.

2 Understand the factors important in deciding whether to acquire a long-term operating asset.

3 Record the acquisition of property, plant, and equipment through a simple purchase as well as through a lease, by self-construction, and as part of the purchase of several assets at once.

4 Compute straight-line and units-of-production depreciation expense for plant and equipment.

5 Account for repairs and improvements of property, plant, and equipment.

6 Identify whether a long-term operating asset has suffered

a decline in value and record the decline.

7 Record the discarding and selling of property, plant, and equipment.

8 Account for the acquisition and amortization of intangible assets and understand the special difficulties associated with accounting for intangibles.

9 Use the fixed asset turnover ratio as a measure of how

efficiently a company is using its property, plant, and equipment.

expanded material

10 Compute declining-balance and sum-of-the-years'-digits depreciation expense for plant and equipment.

11 Account for changes in depreciation estimates.

Thomas Edison received $300,000 in investment funds in 1878 in order to start his EDISON ELECTRIC LIGHT COMPANY. Today, GENERAL ELECTRIC is the direct descendant of Edison's company and, with a market value of $583 billion (as of October 2000), is the most valuable company in the world. General Electric has been a fixture in corporate America since the late 1800s and is the only one of the 12 companies in the original Dow Jones Industrial Average that is still included among the 30 companies making up the Dow today.[1]

The stated purpose of the creation of the Edison Electric Light Company was the development of an economically practical electric light bulb. After a year of experimentation, Thomas Edison discovered that carbonized bamboo would provide a long-lasting light filament that was also easy to produce. Edison quickly found that delivering electric light to people's homes required more than a light bulb, however. So, he developed an entire electricity generation and distribution system, inventing new pieces of equipment when he couldn't find what he needed. The first public electric light system was built in London, followed soon after by the Pearl Street Station system in New York City in 1882. In 1892, Edison's company merged with the THOMSON-HOUSTON ELECTRIC COMPANY (developer of alternating-current [AC] equipment that could transmit over longer distances than Edison's direct-current [DC] system), and the General Electric Company (GE) was born.

From the beginning, General Electric's strength has been research. In addition to improving the design of the light bulb (including the development in the early 1900s of gas-filled, tungsten-filament bulbs that are the model for bulbs still used today), GE was also instrumental in developing almost every familiar household appliance—the iron, washing machine, refrigerator, range, air conditioner, dishwasher, and more. In addition, GE research scientists helped create FM radio, aircraft jet engines, and nuclear-power reactors.

Today, General Electric operates in a diverse array of businesses, ranging from train locomotives to medical CT scanners to consumer financing to the NBC television network. When Jack Welch became CEO of GE in 1981, his goal was to make GE number one or number two in each market segment in which it operates, or else get out of that particular line of business. This strategy has enabled GE's success to continue—its market value has grown by an average of 25% per year over the past 19 years.

To support its broad array of businesses, General Electric maintains a vast quantity of long-term assets that cost over $101 billion to acquire. In 1999 alone, GE spent an additional $15.5 billion in acquiring long-term operating assets and received $6.3 billion for disposing of old assets. Its long-term assets include $3.3 billion in rail cars, $6.7 billion in buildings, $20.8 billion in machinery, and $26.0 billion in "intangible" assets.

setting the stage

In Chapters 6 through 8, operating activities of a business and the assets and liabilities arising from those operations were discussed. In this and the next three chapters, investing and financing activities are covered. In this chapter, investments in long-term assets that are used in the business, such as buildings, property, land, and equipment, are discussed. In Chapter 10, long-term debt financing is covered. In Chapter 11, equity financing is discussed. Once you understand debt and equity securities, as discussed in Chapters 10 and 11, you will understand how these same securities can be purchased as investments. Therefore, in Chapter 12, investments in stocks and bonds (securities) of other companies are discussed. Exhibit 9-1 shows the balance sheet and income statement accounts as well as the cash flow items that will be covered in this chapter.

The two primary categories of long-term assets discussed in this chapter are (1) property, plant, and equipment and (2) intangible assets. Because property, plant, and equipment and intangible assets are essential to a business in carrying out its operating activities, they are sometimes called

---

1 This description is based on General Electric Company History at http://ge.com/ibhis0.htm; General Electric Company, *International Directory of Company Histories*, vol. 12 (Detroit: St. James Press, 1996), pp. 193–197; 1999 Annual Report of the General Electric Company.

Lease or Buy? Leasing is an integral part of American business. From its beginning, a major aspect of IBM's business has been the leasing, rather than the outright sale, of its equipment. Over the years, Ray Kroc's MCDONALD'S empire has made more money leasing land and buildings to franchisees than it has made selling hamburgers. In short, leasing has long been a popular method of acquiring and financing operating assets. For example, airlines such as AMERICAN, DELTA, SOUTH-WEST, and UNITED often lease many of their airplanes. Retail chains such as WAL-MART and SAFEWAY often lease their stores.

Virtually any type of operating asset can be acquired by leasing. Companies often lease such assets as rail cars, automobiles and trucks, airplanes, and various other types of equipment, as well as real estate. There are several reasons why a company might choose to lease rather than purchase an asset. A purchase transaction often requires a significant cash outlay in the form of a down payment at the date of purchase; leasing, therefore, can be used to minimize the amount of

ment, and more. In 1999, the total original cost of assets leased by GE Capital Services to other companies was $31.0 billion.

Assets Acquired by Self-Construction

Sometimes buildings or equipment are constructed by a company for its own use. This may be done to save on construction costs, to utilize idle facilities or idle workers, or to meet a special set of technical specifications. Self-constructed assets, like purchased assets, are recorded at cost, including all expenditures incurred to build the asset and make it ready for its intended use. These costs include the materials used to build the asset, the construction labor, and some reasonable share of the general company overhead (electricity, insurance, supervisors' salaries, etc.) during the time of construction.

Another cost that is included in the cost of a self-constructed asset is the interest cost associated with money borrowed to finance the construction project. Just as the cost to rent a crane to be used to construct a building would be included in the cost of the building, the cost to "rent" money to finance the construction project should also be included in the building cost. Interest that is recorded as part of the cost of a self-constructed asset is called **capitalized interest**. The amount of interest that should be capitalized is that amount that could have been saved if the money used on the construction project had instead been used to repay loans.

The following illustration demonstrates the computation of the cost of a self-constructed asset. Wheeler Resorts decided to construct a new hotel using its own workers. The construction project lasted from January 1 to December 31, 2000. Building materials costs for the project were $4,500,000. Total labor costs attributable to the project were $2,500,000. Total company overhead (costs other than materials and labor) for the year was $10,000,000; of this amount, it is determined that 15% can be reasonably assigned as part of the cost of the construction project. A construction loan was negotiated with Wheeler's bank; during the year, Wheeler was able to borrow from the bank to pay for materials, labor, etc. The total amount of interest paid on this construction loan during the year was $500,000. The total cost of the self-constructed hotel is computed as follows:

> **capitalized interest** Interest that is recorded as part of the cost of a self-constructed asset.

Materials	$4,500,000
Labor	2,500,000
Overhead allocation ($10,000,000 × 0.15)	1,500,000
Capitalized interest	500,000
Total hotel cost	$9,000,000

cash paid initially to acquire the asset. For some types of assets, such as computers, leasing enables the lessee to avoid risks of obsolescence if the appropriate terms are written into the lease agreement.

Another potential advantage of leasing is that if the agreement can be recorded as an operating lease, the lessee does not have to report any related liability. This is an important consideration if a company is concerned about the effect of reporting additional debt on the balance sheet. Before criteria were established for classifying leases as operating or capital, almost all leases were treated as operating leases. Often the

primary purpose of a leasing arrangement was to acquire an asset without reporting any related liability. Some companies are still using leasing for this purpose. They do so by writing the terms of a lease agreement in a manner that circumvents the generally accepted accounting capitalization criteria. The result is that some leasing transactions are reported as simple rental agreements (operating leases) when in fact they have many characteristics of a purchase transaction. Leasing and other forms of "off-balance-sheet financing" are of major concern to the accounting profession and financial statement users.

The new hotel would be reported in Wheeler's balance sheet at a total cost of $9,000,000. As with other long-term operating assets, self-constructed assets are reported at the total cost necessary to get them ready for their intended use.

STOP & THINK What is the difference between capitalized interest and regular interest?

The amount of capitalized interest reported by several large U.S. companies, relative to their total interest expense, is displayed in Exhibit 9-4. As you can see, General Electric capitalized only an insignificant amount of its $10.013 billion in interest during 1999. On the other hand, EXXONMOBIL capitalized more than one-third of its interest during 1999.

Acquisition of Several Assets at Once

basket purchase The purchase of two or more assets acquired together at a single price.

A **basket purchase** occurs when two or more assets are acquired together at a single price. A typical basket purchase is the purchase of a building along with the land on which the building sits. Because there are differences in the accounting for land and buildings, the purchase price

---

exhibit 9-4   Magnitude of Capitalized Interest for Several Large U.S. Companies

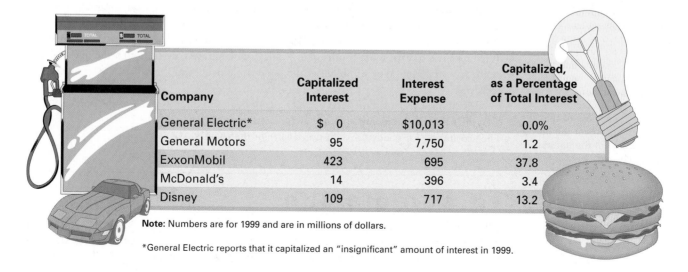

Company	Capitalized Interest	Interest Expense	Capitalized, as a Percentage of Total Interest
General Electric*	$ 0	$10,013	0.0%
General Motors	95	7,750	1.2
ExxonMobil	423	695	37.8
McDonald's	14	396	3.4
Disney	109	717	13.2

Note: Numbers are for 1999 and are in millions of dollars.

*General Electric reports that it capitalized an "insignificant" amount of interest in 1999.

must be allocated between the two assets on some reasonable basis. The relative fair market values of the assets are usually used to determine the respective costs to be assigned to the land and the building.

To illustrate, we will assume that Wheeler Resorts purchases a 40,000-square-foot building on 2.6 acres of land for $3,600,000. How much of the total cost should be assigned to the land and how much to the building? If an appraisal indicates that the fair market values of the land and the building are $1,000,000 and $3,000,000, respectively, the resulting allocated costs would be $900,000 and $2,700,000, calculated as follows:

Asset	Fair Market Value	Percentage of Total Value	Apportionment of Lump-Sum Cost
Land	$1,000,000	25%	0.25 × $3,600,000 = $ 900,000
Building	3,000,000	75	0.75 × $3,600,000 = 2,700,000
Total	$4,000,000	100%	$3,600,000

In this case, the fair market value of the land is $1,000,000, or 25% of the total market value of the land and building. Therefore, 25% of the actual cost, or $900,000, is allocated to the land, and 75% of the actual cost, or $2,700,000, is allocated to the building. The journal entry to record this basket purchase is:

Land	900,000	
Building..	2,700,000	
Cash...		3,600,000
Purchased 2.6 acres of land and a 40,000-square-foot building.		

If part of the purchase price is financed by a bank, an additional credit to Notes Payable or Mortgage Payable would be included in the entry.

Sometimes one company will buy all the assets of another company. For example, in its 1999 annual report, General Electric discloses that its financing subsidiary, GE Capital Services, acquired **JAPAN LEASING**, which leases fleets of automobiles to Japanese corporations. Similarly, in its 1999 annual report (included in Appendix A), **MICROSOFT** discloses that, in November 1998, it purchased **LINKEXCHANGE** for $265 million. The purchase of an entire company raises a number of accounting issues. The first, already discussed above, is how to allocate the purchase price to the various assets acquired. In general, all acquired assets are recorded on the books of the acquiring company at their fair values as of the acquisition date.

The second major accounting issue associated with the purchase of an entire company is the recording of goodwill. **Goodwill** represents all the special competitive advantages enjoyed by a company, such as a trained staff, good credit rating, reputation for superior products and services, and an established network of suppliers and customers. These factors allow an established business to earn more profits than would a new business, even though the new business might have the same type of building, the same equipment, and the same type of production processes.

When one company purchases another established business, the excess of the purchase price over the value of the identifiable net assets is assumed to represent the purchase of goodwill. The accounting for goodwill is illustrated later in the chapter.

goodwill An intangible asset that exists when a business is valued at more than the fair market value of its net assets, usually due to strategic location, reputation, good customer relations, or similar factors; equal to the excess of the purchase price over the fair market value of the net assets purchased.

to summarize

When property, plant, and equipment assets are purchased, they are recorded at cost, which includes all expenditures associated with acquiring and getting them ready for their intended use, such as sales tax, shipping, and installation.

Sometimes assets are acquired by lease rather than purchase. A lease may be a simple short-term rental agreement, called an operating lease, or it may be substantially the same as a purchase transaction. In the latter case, called a capital lease, the party acquiring the asset (the lessee) records the asset and related liability as if the property had been purchased and financed with long-term debt. When a company constructs an asset for its own use, the recorded cost includes materials, labor, a reasonable allocation of overhead, and the cost of interest used to finance the construction. When two or more assets are acquired for a single price in a basket purchase, the relative fair market values are used to determine the respective costs.

CALCULATING AND RECORDING DEPRECIATION EXPENSE

4

Compute straight-line and units-of-production depreciation expense for plant and equipment.

depreciation The process of cost allocation that assigns the original cost of plant and equipment to the periods benefited.

The second element in accounting for plant and equipment is the allocation of an asset's cost over its useful life. The matching principle requires that this cost be assigned to expense in the periods benefited from the use of the asset. The allocation procedure is called **depreciation**, and the allocated amount, recorded in a period-ending adjusting entry, is an expense that is deducted from revenues in order to determine income. It should be noted that the asset "plant" normally refers to buildings only; land is recorded as a separate asset and is not depreciated because it is usually assumed to have an unlimited useful life.

Accounting for depreciation is often confusing because students tend to think that depreciation expense reflects the decline in an asset's value. The concept of depreciation is nothing more than a systematic write-off of the original cost of an asset. The undepreciated cost is referred to as **book value**, which represents that portion of the original cost not yet assigned to the income statement as an expense. A company never claims that an asset's recorded book value is equal to its market value. In fact, market values of assets could increase at the same time that depreciation expense is being recorded.

book value For a long-term operating asset, the asset's original cost less any accumulated depreciation.

salvage value The amount expected to be received when an asset is sold at the end of its useful life.

To calculate depreciation expense for an asset, you need to know (1) its original cost, (2) its estimated useful life, and (3) its estimated salvage, or residual, value. **Salvage value** is the amount expected to be received when the asset is sold at the end of its useful life. When an asset is purchased, its actual life and salvage value are obviously unknown. They must be estimated as realistically as is feasible, usually on the basis of experience with similar assets. In some cases, an asset will have little or no salvage value. If the salvage value is not significant, it is usually ignored in computing depreciation.

Several methods can be used for depreciating the costs of assets for financial reporting. In the main part of this chapter, we describe two: straight-line and units-of-production. In the expanded material section of this chapter, we describe two more depreciation methods: sum-of-the-years'-digits and declining-balance.

straight-line depreciation method The depreciation method in which the cost of an asset is allocated equally over the periods of an asset's estimated useful life.

The **straight-line depreciation method** assumes that an asset will benefit all periods equally and that the cost of the asset should be assigned on a uniform basis for all accounting periods. If an asset's benefits are thought to be related to its productive output (miles driven in an automobile, for example), the **units-of-production method** is usually appropriate.

units-of-production method The depreciation method in which the cost of an asset is allocated to each period on the basis of the productive output or use of the asset during the period.

To illustrate straight-line and units-of-production depreciation methods, we assume that Wheeler Resorts purchased a van on January 1 for transporting hotel guests to and from the airport. The following facts apply:

Acquisition cost	$24,000
Estimated salvage value	$2,000
Estimated life:	
In years	4 years
In miles driven	60,000 miles

To illustrate, we again consider Wheeler Resorts' van, which has an expected life of 60,000 miles. With the units-of-production method, if the van is driven 12,000 miles during the first year, the depreciation expense for that year is calculated as follows:

$$\frac{\$24{,}000 - \$2{,}000}{60{,}000 \text{ miles}} \times 12{,}000 \text{ miles} = \$4{,}400 \text{ depreciation expense}$$

The entry to record units-of-production depreciation at the end of the first year of the van's life is:

Depreciation Expense	4,400	
Accumulated Depreciation, Hotel Van		4,400
To record depreciation for the first year of the hotel van's life.		

The depreciation schedule for the four years is shown in Exhibit 9-6. This exhibit assumes that 18,000 miles were driven the second year, 21,000 the third year, and 9,000 the fourth year.

exhibit 9-6 Depreciation Schedule with Units-of-Production Depreciation

	Miles Driven	Depreciation Expense	Accumulated Depreciation	Book Value
Acquisition date	—	—	—	$24,000
End of year 1	12,000	$ 4,400	$ 4,400	19,600
End of year 2	18,000	6,600	11,000	13,000
End of year 3	21,000	7,700	18,700	5,300
End of year 4	9,000	3,300	22,000	2,000
		$22,000		

Note that part of the formulas for straight-line and units-of-production depreciation is the same. In both cases, cost − salvage value is divided by the asset's useful life. With straight-line, life is measured in years; with units-of-production, life is in miles or hours. With units-of-production, the depreciation per mile or hour must then be multiplied by the usage for the year to determine depreciation expense.

What if the van lasts longer than four years or is driven for more than 60,000 miles? Once the $22,000 difference between cost and salvage value has been recorded as depreciation expense, there is no further expense to record. Thus, any additional years or miles are "free" in the sense that no depreciation expense will be recognized in connection with them. However, as other vans are purchased in the future, the initial estimates of their useful lives will be adjusted to reflect the experience with previous vans.

What if the van lasts less than four years or is driven fewer than 60,000 miles? This topic is covered later in the chapter in connection with the accounting for the disposal of property, plant, and equipment.

A Comparison of Depreciation Methods

The amount of depreciation expense will vary according to the depreciation method used by a company. Exhibit 9-7 compares the annual depreciation expense for Wheeler Resorts' van under the straight-line and units-of-production depreciation methods. As this schedule makes clear, the total amount of depreciation is the same regardless of which method is used.

Straight-line is by far the most commonly used depreciation method because it is the simplest to apply and makes intuitive sense. For example, in the notes to its 1999 financial statements (see Appendix A), MICROSOFT discloses that it depreciates its property, plant, and equipment using the straight-line method over useful lives ranging from 1 to 15 years.

exhibit 9-7   Comparison of Depreciation Expense Using Different Depreciation Methods

	Straight-Line Depreciation	Units-of-Production Depreciation
End of year 1	$ 5,500	$ 4,400
End of year 2	5,500	6,600
End of year 3	5,500	7,700
End of year 4	5,500	3,300
Totals	$22,000	$22,000

Partial-Year Depreciation Calculations

Thus far, depreciation expense has been calculated on the basis of a full year. Businesses purchase assets at all times during the year, however, so partial-year depreciation calculations are often required. To compute depreciation expense for less than a full year, first calculate the depreciation expense for the year and then distribute it evenly over the number of months the asset is held during the year.

To illustrate, assume that Wheeler Resorts purchased its $24,000 van on July 1 instead of January 1. The depreciation calculations for the first one and one-half years, using straight-line depreciation, are shown in Exhibit 9-8. The units-of-production method has been omitted from the exhibit; midyear purchases do not complicate the calculations with this method because it involves number of miles driven, hours flown, and so on, rather than time periods.

exhibit 9-8   Partial-Year Depreciation

Method	Full-Year Depreciation	Depreciation 1st Year (6 months)	Depreciation 2nd Year (12 months)
Straight-line	$5,500	$2,750 ($5,500 × ½)	$5,500

In practice, many companies simplify their depreciation computations by taking a full year of depreciation in the year an asset is purchased and none in the year the asset is sold, or vice versa. This is allowed because depreciation is based on estimates, and in the long run, the difference in the amounts is usually immaterial.

Units-of-Production Method with Natural Resources

natural resources Assets that are physically consumed or waste away, such as oil, minerals, gravel, and timber.

depletion The process of cost allocation that assigns the original cost of a natural resource to the periods benefited.

Another common use for the units-of-production method is with natural resources. **Natural resources** include such assets as oil wells, timber tracts, coal mines, and gravel deposits. Like all other assets, newly purchased or developed natural resources are recorded at cost. This cost must be written off as the assets are extracted or otherwise depleted. This process of writing off the cost of natural resources is called **depletion** and involves the calculation of a depletion rate for each unit of the natural resource. Conceptually, depletion is exactly the same as depreciation; with plant and equipment, the accounting process is called depreciation, whereas with natural resources it is called depletion.

To illustrate, assume that Power-T Company purchases a coal mine for $1,200,000 cash. The entry to record the purchase is:

Coal Mine	1,200,000	
Cash.		1,200,000
Purchased a coal mine for $1,200,000.		

If the mine contains an estimated 200,000 tons of coal deposits (based on a geologist's estimate), the depletion expense for each ton of coal extracted and sold will be $6 ($1,200,000/200,000 tons). Here, the unit of production is the extraction of one ton of coal. If 12,000 tons of coal are mined and sold in the current year, the depletion entry is:

Depletion Expense	72,000	
Accumulated Depletion, Coal Mine		72,000
To record depletion for the year: 12,000 tons at $6 per ton.		

After the first year's depletion expense has been recorded, the coal mine is shown on the balance sheet as follows:

Coal mine	$1,200,000
Less: Accumulated depletion	72,000
Book value	$1,128,000

But how do you determine the number of tons of coal in a mine? Because most natural resources cannot be counted, the amount of the resource owned is an estimate. The depletion calculation is therefore likely to be revised as new information becomes available. When an estimate is changed, a new depletion rate per unit is calculated and used to compute depletion during the remaining life of the natural resource or until another new estimate is made. Coverage of accounting for changes in estimates is included in the expanded material section of this chapter.

to summarize

Depreciation is the process whereby the cost of an asset is allocated over its useful life. Two common and simple methods of depreciation are straight-line and units-of-production. The straight-line and units-of-production methods allocate cost proportionately over an asset's life on the bases of time and use, respectively. Regardless of which method is used, depreciation is only an allocation of an asset's cost over the periods benefited and is not a method of valuation. Natural resources are assets, such as gravel deposits or coal mines, that are consumed or that waste away. The accounting process of depreciation for natural resources is called depletion.

5

Account for repairs and improvements of property, plant, and equipment.

REPAIRING AND IMPROVING PROPERTY, PLANT, AND EQUIPMENT

Sometime during its useful life, an asset will probably need to be repaired or improved. The accounting issue associated with these postacquisition expenditures is whether they should be immediately recognized as an expense or be added to the cost of the asset (capitalized). Remember from the discussion in Chapter 8 that an expenditure should be capitalized if it is expected to have an identifiable benefit in future periods.

Two types of expenditures can be made on existing assets. The first is ordinary expenditures for repairs, maintenance, and minor improvements. For example, a truck requires oil changes and periodic maintenance. Because these types of expenditures typically benefit only the period in which they are made, they are expenses of the current period.

The second type is an expenditure that lengthens an asset's useful life, increases its capacity, or changes its use. These expenditures are capitalized; that is, they are added to the asset's cost instead of being expensed in the current period. For example, overhauling the engine of a delivery truck involves a major expenditure to extend the useful life of the truck. To qualify for capitalization, an expenditure should meet three criteria: (1) it must be significant in amount; (2) it should benefit the company over several periods, not just during the current one; and (3) it should increase the productive life or capacity of the asset.

To illustrate the differences in accounting for capital and ordinary expenditures, assume that Wheeler Resorts also purchases a delivery truck for $42,000. This truck has an estimated useful life of eight years and a salvage value of $2,000. The straight-line depreciation is $5,000 per year [($42,000 − $2,000)/8 years]. If the company spends $1,500 each year for normal maintenance, its annual recording of these expenditures is:

Repairs and Maintenance Expense	1,500	
Cash		1,500
Spent $1,500 for maintenance of delivery truck.		

This entry has no effect on either the recorded cost or the depreciation expense of the truck. Now suppose that at the end of the sixth year of the truck's useful life, Wheeler spends $8,000 to overhaul the engine. This expenditure will increase the truck's remaining life from two to four years, but will not change its estimated salvage value. The depreciation for the last four years will be $4,500 per year, calculated as shown below.

	Depreciation before Overhaul		Depreciation after Overhaul
Original cost	$42,000	Original cost	$42,000
Less salvage value	2,000	Accumulated depreciation	
Cost to be allocated (depreciable amount)	$40,000	(prior to overhaul)	30,000
Original life of asset	8 years	Remaining book value	$12,000
Original depreciation per year ($40,000/8)	$5,000	Capital expenditure (overhaul)	8,000
Usage before overhaul	× 6 years	New book value	$20,000
Accumulated depreciation prior to overhaul	$30,000	Less salvage value	2,000
		New depreciable amount	$18,000
		Remaining life	4 years
		New annual depreciation ($18,000/4)	$4,500

The journal entry to record the $8,000 capitalized expenditure is:

Delivery Truck	8,000	
Cash		8,000
Spent $8,000 to overhaul the engine of the $42,000 truck.		

Another example of a capital expenditure is the cost of land improvements. Certain improvements are considered permanent, such as moving earth to change the land contour. Such an expenditure would be capitalized as part of the land account. Other expenditures may have a limited life, such as those incurred in building a road, a sidewalk, or a fence. These expenditures would be capitalized in a separate land improvements account and be depreciated over their useful lives.

It is often difficult to determine whether a given expenditure should be capitalized or expensed. The two procedures produce a different net income, however, so it is extremely important that such expenditures be properly classified. When in doubt, accepted practice is to record an expenditure as an expense to ensure that the asset is not reported at an amount that exceeds its future benefit.

to summarize

There are two types of expenditures for existing long-term operating assets: capital and ordinary. In general, for an expenditure to be capitalized, it must (1) be significant in amount, (2) provide benefits for more than one period, and (3) increase the productive life or capacity of an asset. Ordinary expenditures merely maintain an asset's productive capacity at the level originally projected. Capital expenditures are added to the cost of an asset and thus affect future depreciation, whereas ordinary expenditures are expenses of the current period.

6

Identify whether a long-term operating asset has suffered a decline in value and record the decline.

impairment A decline in the value of a long-term operating asset.

RECORDING IMPAIRMENTS OF ASSET VALUE

As mentioned earlier, the value of a long-term asset depends on the future cash flows expected to be generated by that asset. Occasionally, events occur after the purchase of an asset that significantly reduce its value. For example, a decline in the consumer demand for high-priced athletic shoes can cause the value of a shoe-manufacturing plant to plummet. Accountants call this **impairment**. When an asset is impaired, the event should be recognized in the financial statements, both as a reduction in the reported value of the asset in the balance sheet and as a loss in the income statement. Of course, the value of long-term assets can also increase after the purchase date. In the United States, these increases are not recorded, as explained more fully later in this section.

Recording Decreases in the Value of Property, Plant, and Equipment

According to U.S. accounting rules, the value of an asset is impaired when the sum of estimated future cash flows from that asset is less than the book value of the asset. This computation ignores the time value of money. As illustrated in the example below, this is a strange impairment threshold—a more reasonable test would be to compare the book value to the fair value of the asset.

Once it has been determined that an asset is impaired, the amount of the impairment is measured as the difference between the book value of the asset and the fair value. To summarize, the existence of an impairment loss is determined using the sum of the estimated future cash flows from the asset, ignoring the time value of money. The amount of the impairment loss is measured using the fair value of the asset, which does incorporate the time value of money. The practical result of this two-step process is that an impairment loss is not recorded unless it is quite certain that the asset has suffered a permanent decline in value.

To illustrate, assume that Wheeler Resorts purchased a fitness center building five years ago for $600,000. The building has been depreciated using the straight-line method with a 20-year useful life and no residual value. Wheeler estimates that the building has a remaining useful life of 15 years, that net cash inflow from the building will be $25,000 per year, and that the fair value of the building is $230,000.

Annual depreciation for the building has been $30,000 ($600,000 ÷ 20 years). The current book value of the building is computed as follows:

Original cost	$600,000
Accumulated depreciation ($30,000 × 5 years)	150,000
Book value	$450,000

The book value of $450,000 is compared with the $375,000 ($25,000 × 15 years) sum of future cash flows (ignoring the time value of money) to determine whether the building is impaired. The sum of future cash flows is only $375,000, which is less than the $450,000 book value, so an impairment loss should be recognized. The loss is equal to the $220,000 ($450,000 − $230,000) difference between the book value of the building and its fair value. The impairment loss would be recorded as follows:

Accumulated Depreciation, Building	150,000	
Loss on Impairment of Building	220,000	
Building ($600,000 − $230,000)		370,000
Recognized $220,000 impairment loss on building.		

This journal entry basically records the asset as if it were being acquired brand new at its fair value of $230,000. The existing accumulated depreciation balance is wiped clean, and the new recorded value of the asset is its fair value of $230,000 ($600,000 − $370,000). After an impairment loss is recognized, no restoration of the loss is allowed even if the fair value of the asset later recovers.

The odd nature of the impairment test can be seen if the facts in the Wheeler example are changed slightly. Assume that net cash inflow from the building will be $35,000 per year and that the fair value of the building is $330,000. With these numbers, no impairment loss is recognized, even though the fair value of $330,000 is less than the book value of $450,000, because the sum of future cash flows of $525,000 ($35,000 × 15 years) exceeds the book value. Thus, in this case the asset would still be recorded at its book value of $450,000, even though its fair value is actually less. As mentioned above, the practical impact of the two-step impairment test is that no impairment losses are recorded unless the future cash flow calculations offer very strong evidence of a permanent decline in asset value. The impairment test is summarized in Exhibit 9-9.

STOP & THINK Do you think businesses would prefer an impairment test involving only the comparison of the book value of an asset to its fair value? Explain.

RITE AID, one of the largest retail drugstore chains in the United States, provides an example of the reporting of an impairment loss. As of February 27, 1999, Rite Aid operated 3,821 drugstores. During 1998 and 1999, Rite Aid experienced significant financial difficulties and initiated a plan to vacate some markets and to close or consolidate some stores in other markets. In connection with this plan, Rite Aid recorded a $94 million loss "for impairment losses associated with land, buildings, fixtures, leasehold improvements, prescription files, lease acquisition costs and goodwill."

---

exhibit 9-9   Impairment Test

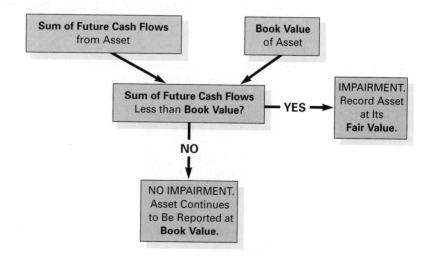

Recording Increases in the Value of Property, Plant, and Equipment

Under U.S. accounting standards, increases in the value of property, plant, and equipment are not recognized. Gains from increases in asset value are recorded only if and when the asset is sold. Thus, in the Wheeler example discussed above, if the fair value of the building rises to $800,000, the building would still be reported in the financial statements at its depreciated book value of $450,000. This is an example of the conservative bias that often exists in the accounting rules: losses are recognized when they occur, but the recognition of gains is deferred until the asset is sold.

Although increases in the value of property, plant, and equipment are not recognized in the United States, accounting rules in other countries do allow for their recognition. For example, companies in Great Britain often report their long-term operating assets at their fair values. Because this upward revaluation of property, plant, and equipment is allowable under international accounting standards, it will be interesting to watch over the next decade or so to see whether sentiment grows to allow this practice in the United States as well.

---

to summarize

When an asset's value declines after it is purchased, it is said to be impaired. Recording an impairment loss is a two-step process. First, the recorded book value of the asset is compared with the sum of future cash flows expected to be generated by the asset. Second, if the sum of future cash flows is lower, then a loss is recognized in an amount equal to the difference between the book value of the asset and its fair value. According to U.S. accounting rules, increases in the value of property, plant, and equipment are not recognized.

7

Record the discarding and selling of property, plant, and equipment.

DISPOSAL OF PROPERTY, PLANT, AND EQUIPMENT

Plant and equipment eventually become worthless or are sold. When a company removes one of these assets from service, it has to eliminate the asset's cost and accumulated depreciation from the accounting records. There are basically three ways to dispose of an asset: (1) discard or scrap it, (2) sell it, or (3) exchange it for another asset.

Discarding Property, Plant, and Equipment

When an asset becomes worthless and must be scrapped, its cost and its accumulated depreciation balance should be removed from the accounting records. If the asset's total cost has been depreciated, there is no loss on the disposal. If, on the other hand, the cost is not completely depreciated, the undepreciated cost represents a loss on disposal.

To illustrate, we assume that Wheeler Resorts, Inc., purchases a computer for $15,000. The computer has a five-year life and no estimated salvage value and is depreciated on a straight-line basis. If the computer is scrapped after five full years, the entry to record the disposal is as follows:

Accumulated Depreciation, Computer	15,000	
Computer		15,000
Scrapped $15,000 computer.		

If Wheeler must pay $300 to have the computer dismantled and removed, the entry to record the disposal is:

Accumulated Depreciation, Computer	15,000	
Loss on Disposal of Computer.............................	300	
Computer...		15,000
Cash		300
Scrapped $15,000 computer and paid disposal costs of $300.		

If the computer had been scrapped after only four years of service (and after $12,000 of the original cost has been depreciated), there would have been a loss on disposal of $3,300 (including the disposal cost), and the entry would have been:

Accumulated Depreciation, Computer	12,000	
Loss on Disposal of Computer	3,300	
Computer...		15,000
Cash		300
Scrapped $15,000 computer and recognized loss of $3,300		
(including $300 disposal costs).		

Don't think of the losses recognized above as "bad" or the gains as "good." A loss on disposal simply means that, given the information we now have, it appears that we didn't record enough depreciation expense in previous years. As a result, the book value of the asset is higher than the amount we can get on disposal. Similarly, a gain means that too much depreciation expense was recognized in prior years, making the book value of the asset lower than its actual disposal value.

Selling Property, Plant, and Equipment

A second way of disposing of property, plant, and equipment is to sell it. If the sales price of the asset exceeds its book value (the original cost less accumulated depreciation), there is a gain on the sale. Conversely, if the sales price is less than the book value, there is a loss.

To illustrate, we refer again to Wheeler's $15,000 computer. If the computer is sold for $600 after five full years of service, assuming no disposal costs, the entry to record the sale is:

Cash	600	
Accumulated Depreciation, Computer	15,000	
Computer...		15,000
Gain on Sale of Computer		600
Sold $15,000 computer at a gain of $600.		

Because the asset was fully depreciated, its book value was zero and the $600 cash received represents a gain. If the computer had been sold for $600 after only four years of service, there would have been a loss of $2,400 on the sale, and the entry to record the sale would have been:

Cash	600	
Accumulated Depreciation, Computer	12,000	
Loss on Sale of Computer..................................	2,400	
Computer...		15,000
Sold $15,000 computer at a loss of $2,400.		

The $2,400 loss is the difference between the sales price of $600 and the book value of $3,000 ($15,000 − $12,000). The amount of a gain or loss is thus a function of two factors: (1) the amount of cash received from the sale, and (2) the book value of the asset at the date of sale. The book value can vary from the market price of the asset for two reasons: (1) the accounting for the asset is not intended to show market value in the financial statements, and (2) it is difficult to estimate salvage value and useful life at the outset of an asset's life.

Exchanging Property, Plant, and Equipment

A third way of disposing of property, plant, and equipment is to exchange it for another asset. Such exchanges occur regularly with cars, trucks, machines, and other types of large equipment. When dissimilar assets are exchanged, such as a truck for a computer, the transaction is accounted for exactly as outlined previously: the acquired asset is recorded in the books at its fair market value, and a gain or loss may be recognized depending on the difference between this market value and the book value of the asset that was disposed of. Accounting for exchanges of similar assets can be more complicated and therefore is not discussed in this text. For a full treatment of the accounting for the exchange of similar assets, see an intermediate accounting text.

to summarize

There are three ways of disposing of assets: (1) discarding (scrapping), (2) selling, and (3) exchanging. If a scrapped asset has not been fully depreciated, a loss equal to the undepreciated cost or book value is recognized. When an asset is sold, there is a gain if the sales price exceeds the book value and a loss if the sales price is less than the book value.

8

Account for the acquisition and amortization of intangible assets and understand the special difficulties associated with accounting for intangibles.

amortization The process of cost allocation that assigns the original cost of an intangible asset to the periods benefited.

Fortune magazine posts its Fortune 500 list on its Web site, http://fortune.com. The information posted includes the reported equity and market values for the 500 largest companies in the United States. What are the differences between reported equity and the market value of equity for THE COCA-COLA COMPANY and for GENERAL MOTORS CORPORATION?

ACCOUNTING FOR INTANGIBLE ASSETS

Intangible assets are rights and privileges that are long-lived, are not held for resale, have no physical substance, and usually provide their owner with competitive advantages over other firms. Familiar examples are patents, franchises, licenses, and goodwill. Although intangible assets have no physical substance, they are accounted for in the same way as other long-term operating assets. That is, they are originally recorded at cost, and the cost is allocated over the useful or legal life, whichever is shorter. The periodic allocation to expense of an intangible asset's cost is called **amortization**. Conceptually, depreciation (with plant and equipment), depletion (with natural resources), and amortization (with intangible assets) are exactly the same thing. Straight-line amortization is generally used for intangible assets.

The traditional accounting model is designed for manufacturing and merchandising companies. Accordingly, accountants have developed intricate and sophisticated accounting methods for use with buildings, equipment, inventory, and receivables. The accounting procedures for gathering and reporting useful information about intangible assets are not as well developed. As the business environment is increasingly dominated by information, service, and reputation, the accounting profession is facing the challenge of improving the accounting for intangible assets.

The importance of intangible assets can be illustrated by considering **GENERAL ELECTRIC**. As mentioned in Chapter 2, if the balance sheet were perfect, the amount of owners' equity would be equal to the market value of the company. On December 31, 1999, GE's reported equity was equal to $42.557 billion. The actual market value of GE on December 31, 1999, was $511 billion. The reason for the large difference between the recorded value and the actual value is that a traditional balance sheet excludes many important intangible economic assets. Examples of GE's important intangible economic assets are its track record of successful products and its entrenched market position in the many industries in which it operates. These intangible factors are by far the most valuable assets owned by GE, but they fall outside the traditional accounting process.

As with many accounting issues, accounting for intangibles involves a trade-off between relevance and reliability. Information concerning intangible assets is relevant, but to meet the standard for recognition in the financial statements, the recorded amount for the intangible must also be reliable. As a result, accounting for intangibles focuses on identifying the costs associated with securing or developing the intangible assets.

Because intangible assets are characterized by a lack of physical qualities, it is difficult to determine the value and life of any future benefits those assets might produce. As a result, it is difficult to separate expenditures that are essentially operating expenses from those that give rise to intangible assets. For example, advertising and promotion campaigns and training programs provide future benefits to the firm. If this were not the case, firms would not spend the millions of dollars on these programs that they do. From an accounting perspective, however, it is extremely difficult to measure the amount and life of the benefits generated by such programs. Therefore, as discussed in Chapter 8, expenditures for these and similar items are typically written off as an expenses in the period incurred.

The accounting for intangible assets is illustrated below with a discussion of the accounting for patents, franchises, and licenses.

Patents

patent An exclusive right granted for 17 years by the federal government to manufacture and sell an invention.

A **patent** is an exclusive right to produce and sell a commodity that has one or more unique features. In the United States, patents are issued to inventors by the federal government and have a legal life of 17 years. Patents may be obtained on new products developed in a company's own research laboratories, or they may be purchased from others. If a patent is purchased from others, its cost is simply the purchase price, and it is recorded as an asset (patent). The cost of the patent is amortized over the useful life of the patent, which may or may not coincide with the patent's legal life.

The cost of a patent for a product developed within a firm is difficult to determine. Should it include research and development costs as well as legal fees to obtain the patent? Should other company expenses such as administrative costs be included? Because of the high degree of uncertainty about their future benefits, U.S. accounting rules dictate that research and development costs must be expensed in the period in which they are incurred. Therefore, all research and development costs of internally developed patents are expensed as they are incurred.

To illustrate the accounting for patents, assume that Wheeler Resorts, Inc., acquires, for $200,000, a patent granted seven years earlier to another firm. The entry to record the purchase of the patent is:

Patent	200,000	
Cash		200,000
Purchased patent for $200,000.		

Because 7 years of its 17-year legal life have already elapsed, the patent now has a legal life of only 10 years, although it may have a shorter useful life. If its useful life is assumed to be eight years, one-eighth of the $200,000 cost should be amortized each year for the next eight years. The entry each year to record the patent amortization expense is:

Amortization Expense, Patent	25,000	
Patent		25,000
To amortize one-eighth of the cost of the patent.		

Notice that in the above entry, the patent account was credited. Alternatively, a contra-asset account, such as Accumulated Amortization, could have been credited. In practice, however, crediting the intangible asset account directly is more common. This is different from the normal practice of crediting Accumulated Depreciation for buildings or equipment.

fyi

The U.S. rule for accounting for research and development differs from the international rule. According to international accounting rules, research and development costs that are incurred after the technological feasibility of a project has been demonstrated should be capitalized as an asset.

units-of-production depreciation, each mile driven, hour used, or other measurement of useful life is assigned an equal amount of depreciation. Sometimes, a depreciation method that does not assign costs equally over the life of the asset is preferred. For example, if most of an asset's benefits will be realized in the earlier periods of the asset's life, the method used should assign more depreciation to the earlier years and less to the later years. Examples of these "accelerated" depreciation methods are the declining-balance and the sum-of-the-years'-digits methods. These methods are merely ways of assigning more of an asset's depreciation to earlier periods and less to later periods.

To illustrate these depreciation methods, we will again use the Wheeler Resorts example from earlier in the chapter. Assume again that Wheeler Resorts purchased a van for transporting hotel guests to and from the airport. The following facts apply:

Acquisition cost	$24,000
Estimated salvage value	$2,000
Estimated life:	
In years	4 years
In miles driven	60,000 miles

Declining-Balance Method of Depreciation

declining-balance depreciation method An accelerated depreciation method in which an asset's book value is multiplied by a constant depreciation rate (such as double the straight-line percentage, in the case of double-declining-balance).

The **declining-balance depreciation method** provides for higher depreciation charges in the earlier years of an asset's life than does the straight-line method. The declining-balance method involves multiplying a fixed rate, or percentage, by a decreasing book value. This rate is a multiple of the straight-line rate. Typically, it is twice the straight-line rate, but it also can be 175, 150, or 125% of the straight-line rate. Our depreciation of Wheeler's hotel van will illustrate the declining-balance method using a fixed rate equal to twice the straight-line rate. This method is often referred to as the double-declining-balance depreciation method.

Declining-balance depreciation differs from the other depreciation methods in two respects: (1) the initial computation ignores the asset's salvage value, and (2) a constant depreciation rate is multiplied by a decreasing book value. The salvage value is not ignored completely because the depreciation taken during the asset's life cannot reduce the asset's book value below the estimated salvage value.

The double-declining-balance (DDB) rate is twice the straight-line rate, computed as follows:

$$\frac{1}{\text{Estimated life (years)}} \times 2 = \text{DDB rate}$$

This rate is multiplied times the book value at the beginning of each year (cost − accumulated depreciation) to compute the annual depreciation expense for the year. If the 150% declining

business environment essay

"**Pay Me Now or Pay Me Later?**" Given the choice of paying income taxes now or later, an overwhelming majority of U.S. taxpayers would choose to pay later. Although it is illegal to evade income taxes, the postponement or "deferral" of tax payments is not only legal but is also a fundamental principle of good tax planning.

One way that businesses can defer income taxes is through the selection of accounting methods. The LIFO (last-in, first-out) method of inventory valuation, for example, is used primarily for the purpose of postponing tax payments. In some cases, companies use one accounting method for their financial statements and another for their tax returns.

Depreciation is the most common cause of differences between net income on the income statement

balance were being used instead, the 2 in the rate formula would be replaced by 1.5 and so on for any other percentages.

To illustrate, the depreciation calculation for the van using the 200% (or double) declining-balance method is:

Straight-line rate   4 years = ¼ = 25%
Double the straight-line rate   25% × 2 = 50%
Annual depreciation   50% × undepreciated cost (book value)

caution

With declining-balance depreciation, the asset is not depreciated below its salvage value, though this figure is ignored in the initial computations.

Based on this information, the formula for double-declining-balance depreciation can be expressed as (straight-line rate × 2) × (cost − accumulated depreciation) = current year's depreciation expense. The double-declining-balance depreciation for the four years is shown in Exhibit 9-11. As you review this exhibit, note that the book value of the van at the end of year 4 is $2,000, its salvage value.

If Wheeler had applied the declining-balance method to depreciate the hotel van on the basis of 150% of the straight-line rate, the fixed rate would have been 37.5%, computed as follows: 25% × 1.50 = 37.5%. Using the 37.5% fixed rate, the annual depreciation of the hotel van would have been as follows:

First year: $24,000 × 37.5% = $9,000
Second year: $24,000 − $9,000 = $15,000 × 37.5% = $5,625
Third year: $15,000 − $5,625 = $9,375 × 37.5% = $3,516
Fourth year: $9,375 − $3,516 = $5,859 − $2,000 salvage value = $3,859

---

exhibit 9-11   Depreciation Schedule with Double-Declining-Balance Depreciation

	Computation	Annual Depreciation Expense	Accumulated Depreciation	Book Value
Acquisition date	—	—	—	$24,000
End of year 1	$24,000 × 0.50	$12,000	$12,000	12,000
End of year 2	12,000 × 0.50	6,000	18,000	6,000
End of year 3	6,000 × 0.50	3,000	21,000	3,000
End of year 4	*	1,000	22,000	2,000
		$22,000		

*In year 4, depreciation expense cannot exceed $1,000 because the book value cannot be reduced below salvage value.

and taxable income on the tax return. Most companies use straight-line depreciation for financial statements to maximize income reported to stockholders while using the accelerated methods permitted by the tax rules to minimize taxable income in the early years of asset life. This allows companies to save cash by reducing the amount of taxes paid currently. Although the total amount of asset cost to be deducted will ultimately be the same for tax and financial reporting, the deferral of income taxes enables a business to earn additional income by investing cash that is retained as a result of delaying tax payments to future years.

The amount of income taxes that companies can defer is by no means insignificant. For example, GENERAL ELECTRIC was able to delay the payment of $1.499 billion in taxes in 1999 because of differences between financial accounting rules and income tax regulations.

Since a total book value of $5,859 remains at the end of year 3, the remaining book value less the estimated salvage value is expensed in year 4.

DEPRECIATION FOR INCOME TAX PURPOSES Net income reported on the financial statements prepared for stockholders, creditors, and other external users often differs from taxable income reported on income tax returns. The most common cause of differences between financial reporting and tax returns is the computation of depreciation. Depreciation for income tax purposes must be computed in accordance with federal income tax law, which specifies rules to be applied in computing tax depreciation for various categories of assets. Income tax rules are designed to achieve economic objectives, such as stimulating investment in productive assets.

The income tax depreciation system in the United States is called the Modified Accelerated Cost Recovery System (MACRS). MACRS is based on declining-balance depreciation and is designed to allow taxpayers to quickly deduct the cost of assets acquired. Allowing this accelerated depreciation deduction for income tax purposes gives companies tax benefits for investing in new productive assets. Presumably, this will spur investment, create jobs, and make voters more likely to reelect their representatives.

Sum-of-the-Years'-Digits Method of Depreciation

sum-of-the-years'-digits (SYD) depreciation method The accelerated depreciation method in which a constant balance (cost minus salvage value) is multiplied by a declining depreciation rate.

Like the declining-balance method, the **sum-of-the-years'-digits (SYD) depreciation method** provides for a proportionately higher depreciation expense in the early years of an asset's life. It is therefore appropriate for assets that provide greater benefits in their earlier years (such as trucks, machinery, and equipment) as opposed to assets that benefit all years equally (as buildings do). The formula for calculating SYD is:

$$\frac{\text{Number of years of life remaining at beginning of year}}{\text{Sum-of-the-years'-digits}} \times (\text{Cost} - \text{Salvage value}) = \text{Depreciation expense}$$

The numerator is the number of years of estimated life remaining at the beginning of the current year. The van, with a four-year life, would have four years remaining at the beginning of the first year, three at the beginning of the second, and so on. The denominator is the sum of the years of the asset's life. The sum of the years' digits for the van is 10 (4 + 3 + 2 + 1). In other words, the numerator decreases by one year each year, whereas the denominator remains the same for each year's calculation of depreciation. Also note that the asset's cost is reduced by the salvage value in computing the annual depreciation expense as is done for the straight-line method but not for the declining-balance method.

The depreciation on the van for the first two years is:

First year: $\frac{4}{10} \times (\$24,000 - \$2,000) = \$8,800$
Second year: $\frac{3}{10} \times (\$24,000 - \$2,000) = \$6,600$

The depreciation schedule for four years is shown in Exhibit 9-12.

---

exhibit 9-12   Depreciation Schedule with Sum-of-the-Years'-Digits Depreciation

	Annual Depreciation Expense	Accumulated Depreciation	Book Value
Acquisition date	—	—	$24,000
End of year 1	$ 8,800	$ 8,800	15,200
End of year 2	6,600	15,400	8,600
End of year 3	4,400	19,800	4,200
End of year 4	2,200	22,000	2,000
Total	$22,000		

The entry to record the sum-of-the-years'-digits depreciation for the first year is:

Depreciation Expense	8,800	
Accumulated Depreciation, Hotel Van.		8,800
To record the first year's depreciation for the hotel van.		

Subsequent years' depreciation entries would show depreciation expense of $6,600, $4,400, and $2,200.

When an asset has a long life, the computation of the denominator (the sum-of-the-years'-digits) can become quite involved. There is, however, a simple formula for determining the denominator. It is:

$$\frac{n(n + 1)}{2} \quad \text{where n is the life (in years) of the asset}$$

Given that the van has a useful life of four years, the formula works as follows:

$$\frac{4(5)}{2} = 10$$

As you can see, the answer is the same as if you had added the years' digits (4 + 3 + 2 + 1). If an asset has a 10-year life, the sum of the years' digits is:

$$\frac{10(11)}{2} = 55$$

The depreciation fraction in year 1 would be 10/55, in year 2, 9/55, and so on.

A Comparison of Depreciation Methods

Now that you have been introduced to the four most common depreciation methods, we can compare them both graphically and by using the Wheeler Resorts van example. Exhibit 9-13 compares the straight-line, sum-of-the-years'-digits, and declining-balance depreciation methods with regard to the relative amount of depreciation expense incurred in each year for an asset that has a five-year life. The units-of-production method is not illustrated because there would not be a standard pattern of cost allocation. Exhibit 9-14 shows the results for the Wheeler Resorts' van for all four depreciation methods.

e x h i b i t   9 - 1 3   Comparison of Depreciation Methods

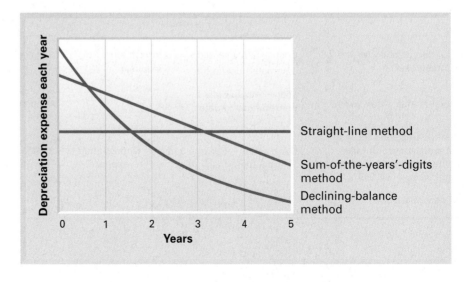

Comparison of Depreciation Expense Using Different Depreciation Methods

	Straight-Line Depreciation	Units-of-Production Depreciation	DDB Depreciation	SYD Depreciation
Year 1	$ 5,500	$ 4,400	$12,000	$ 8,800
Year 2	5,500	6,600	6,000	6,600
Year 3	5,500	7,700	3,000	4,400
Year 4	5,500	3,300	1,000	2,200
Totals	$22,000	$22,000	$22,000	$22,000

to summarize

Two depreciation methods that allow for more depreciation expense in the early years of an asset's life are the declining-balance and the sum-of-the-years'-digits methods. The declining-balance method involves multiplying the asset's declining book value by a fixed rate that is a multiple of the straight-line rate. Sum-of-the-years'-digits depreciation is computed by multiplying (cost − salvage value) by a declining ratio based on the number of years in the asset's estimated life.

11

Account for changes in depreciation estimates.

CHANGES IN DEPRECIATION ESTIMATES

As mentioned earlier in the chapter, useful lives and salvage values are only estimates. Wheeler Resorts' van, for example, was assumed to have a useful life of four years and a salvage value of $2,000. In reality, the van's life and salvage value may be different from the original estimates. If, after three years, Wheeler realizes that the van will last another three years and that the salvage value will be $3,000 instead of $2,000, the accountant would need to calculate a new depreciation expense for the remaining three years. Using straight-line depreciation, the calculations would be as follows:

	Formula	Calculation	Total Depreciation
Annual depreciation for the first three years	$\dfrac{\text{Cost} - \text{Salvage value}}{\text{Estimated useful life}} = \dfrac{\text{Depreciation}}{\text{expense}}$	$\dfrac{\$24,000 - \$2,000}{4 \text{ years}} = \$5,500$	$16,500
Book value after three years	$\dfrac{\text{Cost} - \text{Accumulated}}{\text{depreciation to date}} = \text{Book value}$	$24,000 − $16,500 = $7,500	
Annual depreciation for last three years (based on new total life of six years and new salvage value of $3,000)	$\dfrac{\text{Book value} - \text{Salvage value}}{\text{Remaining useful life}} = \dfrac{\text{Depreciation}}{\text{expense}}$	$\dfrac{\$7,500 - \$3,000}{3 \text{ years}} = \$1,500$	4,500
Total depreciation			$21,000

exhibit 9-15   Depreciation Schedule When There Is a Change in Estimate

	Annual Depreciation Expense	Accumulated Depreciation	Book Value
Acquisition date	—	—	$24,000
Year 1	$ 5,500	$ 5,500	18,500
Year 2	5,500	11,000	13,000
Year 3	5,500	16,500	7,500
Change			
Year 4	1,500	18,000	6,000
Year 5	1,500	19,500	4,500
Year 6	1,500	21,000	3,000
Total	$21,000		

The example shows that a change in the estimate of useful life or salvage value does not require a modification of the depreciation expense already taken. New information affects depreciation only in future years. Exhibit 9-15 shows the revised depreciation expense. Similar calculations, although more complex, would apply if either the sum-of-the-years'-digits or the declining-balance depreciation method had been used.

to summarize

Because depreciation is only an estimate, changes in estimates of useful life or salvage value may be required as new information becomes available. When there is a change in estimate, past periods' depreciation amounts remain the same. The only change is in future years' depreciation where the remaining book value is allocated over the new life (in the case of a change in useful life), or the difference between the book value and the new salvage value is allocated over the remaining life (in the case of a change in salvage value).

review of learning objectives

1 Identify the two major categories of long-term operating assets: property, plant, and equipment and intangible assets. There are two major types of operating assets. Property, plant, and equipment are long-lived, tangible assets acquired for use in a business. This category includes land, buildings, machinery, equipment, and furniture. Intangible assets are long-lived assets used in a business, but they have no physical substance. Common intangible assets are patents, licenses, franchises, and goodwill.

2 Understand the factors important in deciding whether to acquire a long-term operating asset. The value of long-term operating assets stems from the fact that they help companies generate future cash flows. Capital budgeting is the name given to the process whereby decisions are made about acquiring long-term operating assets. Capital budgeting involves comparing the cost of the asset to the value of the expected cash inflows, after adjusting for the time value of money. The value of a long-term operating asset can disappear instantly if events lower the expectations about the future cash flows generated by the asset.

3 Record the acquisition of property, plant, and equipment through a simple purchase as well as through a lease, by self-construction, and as part of the purchase of several assets at once. Property, plant, and equipment may be acquired by purchase, lease, or self-construction. When purchased, the assets are recorded at cost, which includes all expenditures associated with acquiring them and getting them ready for their intended use. When these types of assets are leased, the lease agreement may be classified as an operating lease or as a capital lease. An operating lease results in a short-term use of the asset without recording the asset on the books of the user, the lessee. Instead, the lessee records only the rental expense paid each period. If the lease is for a longer term and meets the conditions of a capital lease, the lessee records the leased property as an asset and the related liability as if the property had been purchased and financed with long-term debt. The asset is recorded at the present value of the lease rental payments, which usually is equivalent to the current market value or the cash equivalent price. When a company constructs an asset for its own use, the recorded cost includes building materials, labor, a reasonable allocation of general administrative costs, and capitalized interest equal to the amount of interest that could have been avoided if the construction expenditures had been used to repay loans.

If two or more assets are acquired in a "basket" purchase, the relative fair market value method is used to assign costs to individual assets. If one company buys all the assets of another company, the excess of the purchase price over the aggregate fair value of the acquired net assets is recorded as goodwill, an intangible asset.

4 Compute straight-line and units-of-production depreciation expense for plant and equipment. Depreciation is the process of allocating the cost of plant and equipment to expense in the periods that are benefited from the use of the asset. The two most common and simple methods of depreciation are straight-line and units-of-production.

The straight-line method is the only method that results in the same amount of depreciation for each full year. The units-of-production method allocates cost over the useful life measured in units of output or usage. Both methods require salvage value to be subtracted from the original cost in computing depreciation expense.

The units-of-production method is also used with natural resources such as coal, gravel, and timber. Depletion expense for a year is computed by first computing a depletion rate by dividing the cost assigned to the natural resource by the estimated number of remaining units to be extracted. This depletion rate is multiplied by the number of units extracted for the year to arrive at the dollar amount of depletion for the year.

5 Account for repairs and improvements of property, plant, and equipment. Expenditures incurred for property, plant, and equipment after acquisition may be classified as either ordinary expenditures or capital expenditures. Since ordinary expenditures merely maintain an asset's productive capacity at the level originally projected, they are reported as repairs and maintenance expense and do not affect the asset's reported cost. For an expenditure to be classified as a capital expenditure, it must (1) increase the productive life or annual capacity of the asset, (2) be significant in amount, and (3) benefit the company over several periods. Because capital expenditures are added to the cost of an asset, they affect future depreciation, whereas ordinary expenditures are expenses of the current period.

6 Identify whether a long-term operating asset has suffered a decline in value and record the decline. Impairment is the decline in a long-term operating asset's value after it is purchased. In recording an impairment loss, the recorded book value of the asset is first compared with the sum of future cash flows to be generated by the asset. Next, if the book value is lower, a loss is recognized. The amount of the loss is the difference between the book value of the asset and its fair value. According to U.S. accounting rules, increases in the value of property, plant, and equipment are not recognized.

7 Record the discarding and selling of property, plant, and equipment. Property, plant, and equipment may be disposed of by discarding, selling, or exchanging. When an asset is sold, a gain is reported if the sales price exceeds the book value, or a loss is reported if the book value exceeds the sales price.

8 Account for the acquisition and amortization of intangible assets and understand the special difficulties associated with accounting for intangibles. Intangible assets are rights and privileges that are long-lived, are not held for resale, have no physical substance, and usually provide competitive advantages for the owner. Common examples are patents, franchises, licenses, and goodwill. Patents acquired by purchase are recorded at cost and amortized over the shorter of their economic life or their 17-year legal life. Research and development costs incurred internally in a firm are expensed as incurred even if they may result in the development of a legal patent. Franchises and licenses are exclusive rights to perform services or sell a product in certain geographic areas. The cost of acquiring a franchise or license is recorded as an asset, which is then amortized over its useful or legal life, whichever is shorter. Goodwill occurs when a business is purchased and the purchase price exceeds the total value of the identifiable assets less outstanding liabilities assumed. The excess purchase price that cannot be allocated to specific assets is called goodwill and is recorded as an intangible asset. Goodwill is amortized as an expense over its expected life, not to exceed 40 years. Because it is often difficult to trace the development of specific intangible assets to specific costs, it is difficult to reliably recognize the assets in the financial statements.

9 **Use the fixed asset turnover ratio as a measure of how efficiently a company is using its property, plant, and equipment.** Fixed asset turnover is computed as sales divided by average property, plant, and equipment (fixed assets) and is interpreted as the number of dollars in sales generated by each dollar of fixed assets. Fixed asset turnover ratios can be meaningfully compared only between firms in similar industries.

expanded material

10 **Compute declining-balance and sum-of-the-years'-digits depreciation expense for plant and equipment.** The two most common accelerated depreciation methods are declining-balance and sum-of-the-years'-digits. The declining- balance method is different from straight-line, units-of-production, and sum-of-the-years'-digits depreciation. The salvage value is ignored in the declining-balance method in the annual computation, but the book value of the

asset cannot be less than the salvage value at the end of any reporting year. With declining-balance, the depreciation rate is calculated by multiplying a desired factor (such as 1.5 or 2.0) by the straight-line depreciation rate. This rate is then multiplied times the book value to determine annual depreciation expense. The declining-balance method is the basis for the MACRS income tax depreciation calculations in the United States. With sum-of-the-years'-digits depreciation, a ratio, computed by dividing the number of years of estimated life remaining at the beginning of the year by the sum of the years of the asset's life, is multiplied by the book value (cost − salvage value) of the asset to determine annual depreciation expense.

11 **Account for changes in depreciation estimates.** Useful lives and salvage values of plant and equipment are only estimates and may need adjustment during an asset's life. Changes in estimates of useful life or salvage value do not require modification of depreciation expense already taken. Rather, only future depreciation amounts are affected by changes in estimates.

k(e)y terms and concepts

amortization 416

basket purchase 403

book value 405

capital budgeting 397

capital lease 400

capitalized interest 402

depletion 409

depreciation 405

fixed asset turnover 420

franchise 418

goodwill 404

impairment 412

intangible assets 396

lease 399

lessee 399

lessor 399

license 418

long-term operating assets 396

natural resources 409

operating lease 399

patent 417

property, plant, and equipment 396

salvage value 405

straight-line depreciation method 405

time value of money 397

units-of-production method 405

expanded material

declining-balance depreciation method 422

sum-of-the-years'-digits (SYD) depreciation method 424

r(e)view problems

Property, Plant, and Equipment

Swift Motor Lines is a trucking company that hauls crude oil in the Rocky Mountain states. It currently has 20 trucks. The following information relates to a single truck:

a. Date truck was purchased, July 1, 2000.
b. Cost of truck:

Truck	$125,000
Paint job	3,000
Sales tax	7,000

c. Estimated useful life of truck, 120,000 miles.
d. Estimated salvage value of truck, $27,000.
e. 2002 expenditures on truck:
   (1) $6,000 on new tires and regular maintenance.
   (2) On January 1, spent $44,000 to completely rework the truck's engine; increased the total life to 200,000 miles but left expected salvage value unchanged.
f. Miles driven:

```
2000. . . . . . . . . . . . . . . . . . . . . .   11,000
2001. . . . . . . . . . . . . . . . . . . . .     24,000
2002 (after reworking of engine) .  20,000
2003. . . . . . . . . . . . . . . . . . . . . .   14,000
```

Required: Record journal entries to account for the following. (Use the units-of-production depreciation method.)

1. The purchase of the truck.
2. The expenditures on the truck during 2002.
3. Depreciation expense for:
   a. 2000
   b. 2001
   c. 2002
   d. 2003

Solution

1. Truck Purchase

The cost of the truck includes both the amount paid for it and all costs incurred to get it in working condition. In this case, the cost includes both the paint job and the sales tax. Thus, the entry to record the purchase is:

```
Truck . . . . . . . . . . . . . . . . . . . . . . . . . . . . . . . . . . . . . . . . . . . . . . . . . 135,000
    Cash . . . . . . . . . . . . . . . . . . . . . . . . . . . . . . . . . . . . . . . . . . . .            135,000
        Purchased truck for cash.
```

2. Expenditures

The expenditure of $6,000 is an ordinary expenditure and is expensed in the current year. The engine overhaul is capitalized. The entries are:

```
Repairs and Maintenance Expense. . . . . . . . . . . . . . . . . . . . . . . . . . . . .  6,000
    Cash . . . . . . . . . . . . . . . . . . . . . . . . . . . . . . . . . . . . . . . . . . . . .            6,000
        Recorded purchase of new tires and regular maintenance
        on truck.
Truck . . . . . . . . . . . . . . . . . . . . . . . . . . . . . . . . . . . . . . . . . . . . . . . . . . 44,000
    Cash . . . . . . . . . . . . . . . . . . . . . . . . . . . . . . . . . . . . . . . . . . . . .           44,000
        Recorded major overhaul to truck's engine.
```

3. Depreciation Expense

The formula for units-of-production depreciation on the truck is:

$$\frac{\text{Cost} - \text{Salvage value}}{\text{Total miles expected to be driven}} \times \frac{\text{Number of miles}}{\text{driven in any year}} = \text{Depreciation expense}$$

Journal entries and calculations are as follows:

a. 2000:

```
Depreciation Expense . . . . . . . . . . . . . . . . . . . . . . . . . . . . . . . . . . . . .  9,900
    Accumulated Depreciation, Truck. . . . . . . . . . . . . . . . . . . . . . . . . .            9,900
        Recorded depreciation expense for 2000.
```

$$\frac{\$135,000 - \$27,000}{120,000 \text{ miles}} \times 11,000 \text{ miles} = \$9,900 \text{ or } \$0.90 \text{ per mile} \times 11,000 \text{ miles}$$

b. 2001:

Depreciation Expense.	21,600	
Accumulated Depreciation, Truck		21,600
Recorded depreciation expense for 2001.		

$0.90 × 24,000 miles = $21,600

c. 2002:

Depreciation Expense.	14,600	
Accumulated Depreciation, Truck		14,600
Recorded depreciation expense for 2002.		

$$\frac{\$135,000 - \$9,900 - \$21,600 + \$44,000 - \$27,000}{\underset{(200,000 - 11,000 - 24,000)}{165,000 \text{ miles}}} \times 20,000 \text{ miles} = \$14,600 \text{ or } \$0.73^* \text{ per mile} \times 20,000 \text{ miles}$$

*Rounded to the nearest cent.

d. 2003:

Depreciation Expense.	10,220	
Accumulated Depreciation, Truck		10,220
Recorded depreciation expense for 2003.		

$0.73 × 14,000 miles = $10,220

expanded material

Property, Plant, and Equipment

Swift Motor Lines is a trucking company that hauls crude oil in the Rocky Mountain states. It currently has 20 trucks. The following information relates to a single truck:

a. Date truck was purchased, July 1, 2000.
b. Cost of truck:

Truck	$125,000
Paint job	3,000
Sales tax	7,000

c. Estimated useful life of truck, eight years.
d. Estimated salvage value of truck, $27,000
e. 2002 expenditures on truck:
   (1) $6,000 on new tires and regular maintenance.
   (2) On January 1, spent $44,000 to completely rework the truck's engine. As a result of the engine work, the remaining life of the truck is increased to nine years, but the expected salvage value remains the same.

Required:

Record journal entries to account for the following. (Use the sum-of-the-years'-digits depreciation method.)

1. The purchase of the truck.
2. Depreciation expense for:
   a. 2000
   b. 2001
   c. 2002
3. The expenditures on the truck during 2002.

Assuming Landon Company amortizes franchises over a 10-year period, record the following:

1. The purchase of the franchise on January 1, 2002.
2. The amortization of the franchise and goodwill at December 31, 2002.
3. The amortization of the franchise and goodwill at December 31, 2003.

EXERCISE 9-17

COMPUTING GOODWILL

Stringtown Company purchased Stansbury Island Manufacturing for $1,800,000 cash. The book value and fair value of the assets of Stansbury Island as of the date of the acquisition are listed below:

	Book Value	Market Value
Cash	$ 30,000	$ 30,000
Accounts receivable	300,000	300,000
Inventory	350,000	600,000
Property, plant, and equipment	500,000	900,000
Totals	$1,180,000	$1,830,000

In addition, Stansbury Island had liabilities totaling $400,000 at the time of the acquisition.

1. At what amounts will the individual assets of Stansbury Island be recorded on the books of Stringtown, the acquiring company?
2. How will Stringtown account for the liabilities of Stansbury Island?
3. How much goodwill will be recorded as part of this acquisition?

EXERCISE 9-18

FIXED ASSET TURNOVER

Handy Corner Stores reported the following asset values in 2002 and 2003:

	2003	2002
Cash	$ 30,000	$ 20,000
Accounts receivable	400,000	300,000
Inventory	600,000	350,000
Land	200,000	150,000
Buildings	600,000	500,000
Equipment	300,000	200,000

In addition, Handy Corner had sales of $2,000,000 in 2003. Cost of goods sold for the year was $1,500,000.

Compute Handy Corner's fixed asset turnover ratio for 2003.

expanded material

EXERCISE 9-19

ACQUISITION AND DEPRECIATION OF ASSETS

Montana Oil Company, which prepares financial statements on a calendar-year basis, purchased new drilling equipment on July 1, 2003. A breakdown of the cost follows:

Cost of drilling equipment	$ 75,000
Cost of cement platform	25,000
Installation charges	13,000
Freight costs for drilling equipment	2,000
Total	$115,000

Assuming that the estimated life of the drilling equipment is 10 years and its salvage value is $5,000:

1. Record the purchase on July 1, 2003.
2. Assume that the drilling equipment was recorded at a total cost of $95,000. Calculate the depreciation expense for 2003 using the following methods:
   a. Sum-of-the-years'-digits.
   b. Double-declining-balance.
   c. 150% declining-balance.
3. Prepare the journal entry to record the depreciation for 2003 in accordance with 2(a).

EXERCISE 9-20

ACQUISITION AND DEPRECIATION

At the beginning of 2003, Lowham's Guest Ranch constructed a new walk-in freezer that had a useful life of 10 years. At the end of 10 years, the motor could be salvaged for $2,000. In addition to construction costs that totaled $10,000, the following costs were incurred:

Sales taxes on components	$1,250
Delivery costs	800
Installation of motor	200
Painting of both interior and exterior of freezer	100

1. What is the cost of the walk-in freezer to Lowham's Guest Ranch?
2. Compute the amount of depreciation to be taken in the first year assuming Lowham's Guest Ranch uses the
   a. Double-declining-balance method.
   b. Sum-of-the-years'-digits method.

EXERCISE 9-21

DEPRECIATION COMPUTATIONS

Techno Company purchases a $400,000 piece of equipment on January 2, 2001, for use in its manufacturing process. The equipment's estimated useful life is 10 years with no salvage value. Techno uses 150% declining-balance depreciation for all its equipment.

1. Compute the depreciation expense for 2001, 2002, and 2003.
2. Compute the book value of the equipment on December 31, 2003.

EXERCISE 9-22

DEPRECIATION CALCULATIONS

The University of Northern Utah purchased a new van on January 1, 2002, for $30,000. The estimated life of the van was five years or 95,000 miles, and its salvage value was estimated to be $2,000. Compute the amount of depreciation expense for 2002, 2003, and 2004 using the following methods:

1. Double-declining-balance.
2. 175% declining-balance.
3. Sum-of-the-years'-digits.

EXERCISE 9-23

DEPRECIATION CALCULATIONS

On January 1, 2002, MAC Corporation purchased a machine for $60,000. The machine cost $800 to deliver and $2,000 to install. At the end of 10 years, MAC expects to sell the machine for $2,000. Compute depreciation expense for 2002 and 2003 using the following methods:

1. Double-declining-balance.
2. 150% declining-balance.
3. Sum-of-the-years'-digits.

EXERCISE 9-24

ACCOUNTING FOR NATURAL RESOURCES

On January 1, 2002, Castle Investment Corporation purchased a coal mine for cash, having taken into consideration the favorable tax consequences and the inevitable energy crunch in

useful life in productive output of 75,000 units. Actual output for the first two years was: year 1, 20,000 units; year 2, 15,000 units.

Required:
1. Compute the amount of depreciation expense for the first year, using each of the following methods:
    a. Straight-line.
    b. Units-of-production.
2. What was the book value of the machine at the end of the first year, assuming that straight-line depreciation was used?
3. If the machine is sold at the end of the fourth year for $15,000, how much should the company report as a gain or loss (assuming straight-line depreciation)?

PROBLEM 9-8

PURCHASE OF MULTIPLE ASSETS FOR A SINGLE SUM

On April 1, 2003, Mission Company paid $360,000 in cash to purchase land, a building, and equipment. The appraised fair market values of the assets were as follows: land, $90,000; building, $260,000; and equipment, $50,000. The company incurred legal fees of $3,000 to determine that it would have a clear title to the land. Before the facilities could be used, Mission had to spend $2,500 to grade and landscape the land, $4,000 to put the equipment in working order, and $15,000 to renovate the building. The equipment was then estimated to have a useful life of six years with no salvage value, and the building would have a useful life of 20 years with a net salvage value of $15,000. Both the equipment and the building are to be depreciated on a straight-line basis. The company is on a calendar-year reporting basis.

Required:
1. Allocate the single purchase price to the individual assets acquired.
2. Prepare the journal entry to acquire the land, building, and equipment.
3. Prepare the journal entry to record the title search, landscape, put the equipment in working order, and renovate the building.
4. Prepare the journal entries on December 31, 2003, to record the depreciation on the building and the equipment.

PROBLEM 9-9

BASKET PURCHASE AND PARTIAL-YEAR DEPRECIATION

On April 1, 2003, Rosenberg Company purchased for $200,000 a tract of land on which was located a fully equipped factory. The following information was compiled regarding this purchase:

	Market Value	Seller's Book Value
Land	$ 75,000	$ 30,000
Building	100,000	75,000
Equipment	50,000	60,000
Totals	$225,000	$165,000

Required:
1. Prepare the journal entry to record the purchase of these assets.
2. Assume that the building is depreciated on a straight-line basis over a remaining life of 20 years and the equipment is depreciated on a straight-line basis over five years. Neither the building nor the equipment is expected to have any salvage value. Compute the depreciation expense for 2003 assuming the assets were placed in service immediately upon acquisition.

PROBLEM 9-10

ACQUISITION, DEPRECIATION, AND SALE OF AN ASSET

On January 2, 2001, Union Oil Company purchased a new airplane. The following costs are related to the purchase:

Airplane, base price	$112,000
Cash discount	3,000
Sales tax	4,000
Delivery charges	1,000

Required:
1. Prepare the journal entry to record the payment of these items on January 2, 2001.
2. Ignore your answer to part 1 and assume that the airplane cost $90,000 and has an expected useful life of five years or 1,500 hours. The estimated salvage value is $3,000. Using units-of-production depreciation and assuming that 300 hours are flown in 2002, calculate the amount of depreciation expense to be recorded for the second year.
3. Ignore the information in parts 1 and 2 and assume that the airplane costs $90,000, that its expected useful life is five years, and that its estimated salvage value is $5,000. The company now uses the straight-line depreciation method. On January 1, 2004, the following balances are in the related accounts:

Airplane	$90,000
Accumulated Depreciation, Airplane	51,000

Prepare the necessary journal entries to record the sale of this airplane on July 1, 2004, for $40,000.

PROBLEM 9-11

ACQUISITION, DEPRECIATION, AND SALE OF AN ASSET

On July 1, 2003, Philip Ward bought a used pickup truck at a cost of $5,300 for use in his business. On the same day, Ward had the truck painted blue and white (his company's colors) at a cost of $800. Mr. Ward estimates the life of the truck to be three years or 40,000 miles. He further estimates that the truck will have a $450 scrap value at the end of its life, but that it will also cost him $50 to transfer the truck to the junkyard.

Required:
1. Record the following journal entries:
   a. July 1, 2003: Paid all bills pertaining to the truck. (No previous entries have been recorded concerning these bills.)
   b. December 31, 2003: The depreciation expense for the year, using the straight-line method.
   c. December 31, 2004: The depreciation expense for 2004, again using the straight-line method.
   d. January 2, 2005: Sold the truck for $2,600 cash.
2. What would the depreciation expense for 2003 have been if the truck had been driven 8,000 miles and the units-of-production method of depreciation had been used?
3. **Interpretive Question:** In part 1(d), there is a loss of $650. Why did this loss occur?

PROBLEM 9-12

ACCOUNTING FOR NATURAL RESOURCES

On April 30, 2001, Lindon Oil Company purchased an oil well, with estimated reserves of 100,000 barrels of oil, for $1 million cash.

Required:

Prepare journal entries for the following:

1. Record the purchase of the oil well.
2. During 2001, 10,000 barrels of oil were extracted from the well. Record the depletion expense for 2001.
3. During 2002, 18,000 barrels of oil were extracted from the well. Record the depletion expense for 2002.

PROBLEM 9-13

ASSET IMPAIRMENT

Delta Company owns plant and equipment on the island of Lagos. The cost and book value of the building are $2,800,000 and $2,400,000, respectively. Until this year, the market value of the factory was $7 million. However, a new dictator just came to power and declared martial law. As a result of the changed political status, the future cash inflows from the use of the factory are expected to be greatly reduced. Delta now believes that the output from the factory will generate cash inflows of $100,000 per year for the next 20 years. In addition, the market value of the factory building is now just $1,300,000. Delta is not sure how to account for the sudden impairment in value.

Required:
1. Explain how to decide whether an impairment loss is to be recognized.
2. Prepare the necessary journal entry, if any, to account for an impairment in the value of the factory.

▶ Analyzing Real Company Information

▶ International Case

▶ Ethics Case

▶ Writing Assignment

▶ The Debate

▶ Cumulative Spreadsheet Project

▶ Internet Search

The following additional assignments provide opportunities for students to develop critical thinking, ethical perspectives, oral and written communication skills, experience with electronic research, and teamwork through group and business activities.

▶ ## ANALYZING REAL COMPANY INFORMATION

• *Analyzing 9-1 (Microsoft)*

Using MICROSOFT's 1999 annual report contained in Appendix A, answer the following questions:

1. As a percentage of total assets, is Microsoft's investment in property, plant, and equipment increasing or decreasing over time? Which of Microsoft's assets is increasing the fastest as a percentage of total assets? What does that indicate Microsoft is doing?

2. Reference the notes to the financial statements. Which depreciation method does Microsoft use? Estimate the average useful life of Microsoft's depreciable assets (i.e., not including land) by dividing the ending balance in the depreciable asset accounts by the depreciation expense for the year. Does the resulting estimated useful life seem reasonable?

3. Microsoft notes in its statement of cash flows that $583 million of property, plant, and equipment was purchased in 1999. Using that information along with the detailed information from the notes, compute (a) the original cost of the equipment disposed of during 1999 and (b) the accumulated depreciation associated with that equipment. (HINT: For property, plant, and equipment, beginning balance + purchases − disposals = ending balance; a similar calculation is used for accumulated depreciation.)

• *Analyzing 9-2 (FedEx)*

FEDEX delivers packages around the world. To accomplish this task, FedEx has made huge investments in long-term assets.

1. Identify what you consider to be the major long-term assets of FedEx. Review the information shown at the top of the next page from FedEx's balance sheet (numbers are in thousands) to see how well you did.

	2000	1999
Property and Equipment, at Cost (Notes 1, 3, 4 and 12):		
Flight equipment	$ 4,960,204	$ 4,556,747
Package handling and ground support equipment	3,430,316	3,193,620
Computer and electronic equipment	2,088,510	2,114,492
Other	2,479,540	2,332,227
	$12,958,570	$12,197,086
Less accumulated depreciation and amortization	6,846,647	6,454,579
Net property and equipment	$ 6,111,923	$ 5,742,507

2. FedEx uses the straight-line depreciation method in depreciating most of its assets. For each major category—flight equipment, package handling and ground support equipment (mainly trucks and buildings), and computer and electronic equipment—provide an estimate (or a range) as to what you would deem a reasonable useful life for each category.
3. Using the information above, compute the accumulated depreciation associated with the property and equipment sold during 2000 given that depreciation for the year was $997,735,000.
4. FedEx reports a balance of $328 million in its goodwill account at the end of 2000. In the notes to its annual report, the company reported amortization for the period of $11.7 million. Given that the company uses the straight-line method for amortizing its intangible assets, compute the approximate number of years left for amortizing goodwill.

• Analyzing 9-3 (U.S. Steel)

1. U.S. STEEL provides the following information in the notes to its financial statements relating to its use of the straight-line method of depreciation. Can you interpret the information contained in the note?

> *Long-lived assets*—Depreciation is generally computed using a modified straight-line method based upon estimated lives of assets and production levels. The modification factors range from a minimum of 85% at a production level below 81% of capability, to a maximum of 105% for a 100% production level. No modification is made at the 95% production level, considered the normal long-range level.

2. U.S. Steel also provides information relating to the balances in its individual property, plant and equipment accounts, as shown at the top of the next page. In very general terms, how old is the company's property, plant, and equipment? Provide support for your answer.

18. Property, Plant and Equipment

(In millions)	December 31	
	1999	**1998**
Land and depletable property	$ 152	$ 151
Buildings	484	469
Machinery and equipment	8,007	7,711
Leased assets	105	108
Total	$8,748	$8,439
Less accumulated depreciation,		
depletion and amortization	6,232	5,939
Net	$2,516	$2,500

INTERNATIONAL CASE

• Cadbury Schweppes

CADBURY SCHWEPPES is a company based in the United Kingdom. You can probably guess some of the company's products from its name. The company produces Cadbury chocolates and Schweppes tonic water, among other things. But the company also owns the brands Dr. Pepper, A&W, 7 Up, and Crush. The company licenses these brands to distributors around the world.

Although most accounting rules in the United Kingdom are similar to those used in the United States, there are some differences. For example, companies in the United Kingdom are allowed to revalue their property, plant, and equipment upward based on the appraisals of experts. Cadbury Schweppes notes in its 1996 annual report that assets are revalued every five years and that, "The Group properties were professionally revalued at 30 September 1995." Information contained in the company's notes indicates that the company's land and buildings had an appraised value of 392 million British pounds and a book value of 314 million British pounds.

1. Can you compose the journal entry made by Cadbury Schweppes accountants to write the assets up in value? What would be the credit portion of the journal entry? (HINT: Although you may not know the exact answer, think about it and make an educated guess. Would the credit be to another asset account? Would it be to a liability account?)
2. Suppose that in the next year, the assets were again revalued and it was determined that a difference existed between market value and book value of only 70 million British pounds. How would this year's journal entry differ from the previous year's?

ETHICS CASE

• Strategic Accounting Method Choices

You saw in Chapter 6 that a company's management selects the percentage to be used when computing bad debt expense. You noted in Chapter 7 that management is allowed to choose the method for valuing inventory. In this chapter you found that management gets to choose the method used for depreciating assets, the estimated salvage value, and the estimated useful life.

Suppose that you are involved in negotiations with the local labor union regarding wages for your company's employees. Labor leaders are asking that their members be given an average annual raise of 12%. The company president has asked you to prepare a set of financial statements that portrays the company's performance as being mediocre at best. The president also makes it clear that she does not want you to prepare fraudulent financial statements. All estimates must be within the bounds of reason.

So you come up with the following:

- Change the percentage used for estimating bad debts from 1.5% to 2%.
- Elect to use the LIFO method for valuing inventory because the prices associated with inventory have been rising.
- Change the average estimated salvage value of long-term assets from 15% to 10% of historical cost.
- Change the depreciation method from straight-line to an accelerated method.
- Change the average estimated useful life of long-term assets from 10 years to 7 years.

As you know, each of these changes will result in net income being lower. Each of these changes is also still within the bounds of reason required by the company president.

1. Would it be appropriate to make the changes described above in order to obtain favorable terms from the labor union negotiators?
2. If the above changes are made, what sort of disclosure do you think should be required?

▶ WRITING ASSIGNMENT

• Gains Are Good, Losses Are Bad—Right?

When a long-term asset is sold for more than its book value, we record a gain. When a long-term asset is sold for less than its book value, we record a loss.

Your assignment is to write a two-page memo addressing the following questions:

1. What factors affect a long-term asset's book value?
2. What factors affect a long-term asset's fair value?
3. Should financial statement users expect an asset's book value to equal its fair value?
4. In the case of an asset sold for a loss, if we knew when we purchased the asset what we know at the point of sale, how would depreciation expense have differed if our objective was to ensure that book value equaled fair value when the asset was sold?
5. Is recognizing a loss on the sale of a long-term asset a bad thing? Is a gain good?

▶ THE DEBATE

• Depreciating an Asset with an Increasing Value

Paul Didericksen owns and operates a limousine service. He purchases luxury cars and hires drivers to transport people from place to place. Last year, Paul expanded his operations by renting out luxury vehicles on a daily basis for such events as weddings, proms, etc. One car Paul purchased for rental is a 1957 FORD Thunderbird. He paid $45,000 for the car and rents it for $250 per day.

Paul's accountant recently provided financial information indicating that the Thunderbird has a book value of $36,000. Paul questions this figure because he recently received an offer of $53,000 for the Thunderbird. Paul thinks that the car should not be depreciated because its value is increasing. In fact, Paul argues that the asset should be written up in value rather than down.

Divide your group into two teams and prepare to represent the following positions:

- The first team supports the position that the Thunderbird should be depreciated because it is used in generating revenues. You are also to provide support against writing the asset up to its fair market value.
- The second team argues that the Thunderbird should not be depreciated because its value is increasing rather than decreasing. Also, your group is to argue that the car should be written up to its fair value on the company's books.

▷ **CUMULATIVE SPREADSHEET PROJECT**

This spreadsheet project is a continuation of the spreadsheet projects in earlier chapters. If you completed those spreadsheets, you have a head start on this one.

1. Handyman wishes to prepare a forecasted balance sheet and income statement for 2004. Use the original financial statement numbers for 2003 [given in part (1) of the Cumulative Spreadsheet Project assignment in Chapter 2] as the basis for the forecast, along with the following additional information:

   a. Sales in 2004 are expected to increase by 40% over 2003 sales of $700.
   b. Cash will increase at the same rate as sales.
   c. The forecasted amount of accounts receivable in 2004 is determined using the forecasted value for the average collection period. For simplicity, do the computations using the end-of-period accounts receivable balance instead of the average balance. The average collection period for 2004 is expected to be 14.08 days.
   d. The forecasted amount of inventory in 2004 is determined using the forecasted value for the number of days' sales in inventory (computed using the end-of-period inventory balance). The number of days' sales in inventory for 2004 is expected to be 107.6 days.
   e. The forecasted amount of accounts payable in 2004 is determined using the forecasted value for the number of days' purchases in accounts payable (computed using the end-of-period accounts payable balance). The number of days' purchases in accounts payable for 2004 is expected to be 48.34 days.
   f. The $160 in operating expenses reported in 2003 breaks down as follows: $5 depreciation expense, $155 other operating expenses.
   g. No new long-term debt will be acquired in 2004.
   h. No cash dividends will be paid in 2004.
   i. New short-term loans payable will be acquired in an amount sufficient to make Handyman's current ratio in 2004 exactly equal to 2.0.

   Note: These statements were constructed as part of the spreadsheet assignment in Chapter 7; you can use that spreadsheet as a starting point if you have completed that assignment. *Clearly state any additional assumptions that you make.*

   For this exercise, add the following additional assumptions:

   j. The forecasted amount of property, plant, and equipment (PP&E) in 2004 is determined using the forecasted value for the fixed asset turnover ratio. For simplicity, compute the fixed asset turnover ratio using the end-of-period *gross* PP&E balance. The fixed asset turnover ratio for 2004 is expected to be 3.518 times.

    k. In computing depreciation expense for 2004, use straight-line depreciation and assume a 30-year useful life with no residual value. Gross PP&E acquired during the year is only depreciated for half the year. In other words, depreciation expense for 2004 is the sum of two parts: (1) a full year of depreciation on the beginning balance in PP&E, assuming a 30-year life and no residual value, and (2) a half-year of depreciation on any new PP&E acquired during the year, based on the change in the Gross PP&E balance.

Clearly state any additional assumptions that you make.

2. Repeat (1), with the following changes in assumptions:
    a. Fixed asset turnover ratio is expected to be 6.000 times.
    b. Fixed asset turnover ratio is expected to be 2.000 times.

3. Comment on the differences in the forecasted values of the following items in 2004 under each of the following assumptions about the fixed asset turnover ratio: 3.518 times, 6.000 times, and 2.000 times:
    a. Property, plant, and equipment.
    b. Depreciation expense.
    c. Income tax expense.
    d. Paid-in capital.

4. Return the fixed asset turnover ratio to 3.518 times. Now, repeat (1), with the following changes in assumptions:
    a. Estimated useful life is expected to be 15 years.
    b. Estimated useful life is expected to be 60 years.

5. Comment on the differences in the forecasted values of the following items in 2004 under each of the following assumptions about the estimated useful life of property, plant, and equipment: 30 years, 15 years, and 60 years.
    a. Depreciation expense.
    b. Income tax expense.

▷ **INTERNET SEARCH**

• General Electric

We began this chapter with a review of the history of GENERAL ELECTRIC. Let's go to GE's Web site at http://www.ge.com and learn a little more about the company and its financial position. Sometimes Web addresses change, so if this address doesn't work, access the Web site for this textbook (http://albrecht.swcollege.com) for an updated link to GE.

    Once you have gained access to General Electric's Web site, answer the following questions:

1. General Electric was formed in 1892 and constructed the nation's first industrial research laboratory In 1900. Can you identify where this laboratory was located?

2. Locate the company's most recent balance sheet. What percentage of total assets does property, plant, and equipment represent for General Electric? Is that percentage increasing, decreasing, or remaining constant?

3. Access the notes to the financial statements. What depreciation method does General Electric use for most of its manufacturing plant and equipment?

4. Find the note relating specifically to property, plant, and equipment. What types of property, plant, and equipment does General Electric own? Is GE involved strictly in producing light bulbs?

Long-Term Debt Financing

c h a p t e r

f10

learning objectives After studying this chapter, you should be able to:

1 Use present value concepts to measure long-term liabilities.

2 Account for long-term liabilities, including notes payable and mortgages payable.

3 Account for capital lease obligations and understand the significance of operating leases being excluded from the balance sheet.

4 Account for bonds, including the original issuance, the payment of interest, and the retirement of bonds.

5 Use debt-related financial ratios to determine the degree of a company's financial leverage and its ability to repay loans.

expanded material

6 Amortize bond discounts and bond premiums using either the straight-line method or the effective-interest method.

In 1923, two brothers, Walt and Roy Disney, founded the DISNEY BROTHERS STUDIO as a partnership to produce animated features for film. Five years later, the Disney Brothers Studio released its first animated film with sound effects and dialogue, *Steamboat Willie*, featuring a soon-to-become-famous mouse, Mickey. Pluto was introduced to American audiences in 1930, and Goofy was created just two years later. Walt Disney earned his first Academy Award in 1932 with the release of *Flowers and Trees*, the first full-color animated film. Donald Duck appeared on the scene in 1934, and in 1937 *Snow White and the Seven Dwarfs* was released, accompanied by the first comprehensive merchandising campaign.

But Walt Disney's vision encompassed more than animated films. In 1952, Disney began designing and creating Disneyland, which opened on July 17, 1955. Beginning in the late 1950s, the television shows *Disneyland* (which ran for 29 seasons under various names) and *The Mickey Mouse Club* were also successful Disney ventures. Though Walt Disney passed away in 1966, his influence is still felt around the world. We have Walt Disney World in Florida and Disneylands in Anaheim, California; Paris; and Tokyo. In November 2000, Disney was even scheduled to open an indoor theme park, DisneyQuest, in Chicago.

Disney's company has expanded far beyond what even he could have foreseen. THE WALT DISNEY COMPANY is now involved in television and radio stations; international film distribution; home video production; live theatrical entertainment; online computer programs; interactive computer games; telephone company partnerships; cruise lines; Disney Stores; newspaper, magazine, and book publishing; Internet marketing; and the convention business. In the past decade, The Walt Disney Company has grown over 600%. How has the company financed this growth? In part through very successful operations, but these have not been enough. The company has also borrowed to finance its expansion. As of September 30, 1999, The Walt Disney Company had long-term debt totaling over $9 billion. This long-term financing includes lines of credits with U.S. banks as well as loans denominated (or made) in Japanese yen and Italian lira. The effective interest rates on Disney's loans range from 2.7 to 6.4%.[1]

setting the stage

net work

Speaking of debt, let's take a look at our government's debt situation. To see what the national debt is to the penny, go to http://www.publicdebt.treas.gov/opd/opd.htm. What was the national debt 100 years ago? 200 years ago?

How does the market determine the appropriate rate of interest that Disney, or any company, must pay when it borrows money? What factors affect interest rates, and how do interest rate changes influence the value of a liability? What other types of liabilities are affected by interest rates? In this chapter, we will introduce various types of long-term liabilities. We will explain a concept used in measuring the present value of an obligation due in the future. This concept—the time value of money—is useful for computing the value of bonds and notes, as in the Disney example, as well as for computing mortgage payments and pension obligations. In the main part of this chapter, we discuss the measurement of long-term liabilities and introduce numerous types of long-term liabilities—notes, mortgages, leases, and bonds. The basic accounting procedures associated with several of these liabilities are also discussed. In the expanded material, the complexities associated with the amortization of a bond issued at a premium or discount are discussed. Exhibit 10-1 highlights the financial statement accounts discussed in this chapter.

MEASURING LONG-TERM LIABILITIES

1

Use present value concepts to measure long-term liabilities.

Conceptually, the value of a liability is the cash that would be required to pay the liability in full today. Because money has a time value, most people are willing to accept less money today than they would if a liability were paid in the future. Therefore, with the exception of Accounts Payable, liabilities to be paid in the future usually involve interest.

---

1 The information for this scenario was obtained from Disney's Web site at http://www.disney.com.

How Interest Rates Affect Mortgage Payments The interest rate on a mortgage is as important as the amount of the loan in determining whether a person can afford a mortgage. This is because the amount of interest paid over an extended period of time will be at least equal to, or even two or three times, the amount of the loan. The table on the next page shows the monthly payments on a $100,000, 25-year mortgage at interest rates from 7 to 14%, as well as the qualifying annual income.

The qualifying annual income is the minimum amount a person must earn to afford the payments at each interest rate. The FEDERAL HOME LOAN MORT-GAGE CORPORATION and most lending institutions recommend that the monthly payment not exceed 28% of a person's monthly gross income. If, for example, you earn $30,000 a year, you should pay no more than $700 a month on a mortgage, which would be a $100,000 mortgage at 7% or a $58,000 mortgage at 14%. For this reason, most people "shop around" for the lowest mortgage rates—and even then, many will not qualify for a loan.

To calculate the monthly payments on a smaller or larger mortgage, divide the amount by $100,000, then multiply that percentage by the figure in the table. For example, the monthly payment on a $60,000 mortgage at 9% is $503.40 [($60,000/$100,000) × $839].

mortgage are usually pledged as security or collateral on the loan. Individuals commonly obtain home mortgages, and companies frequently use plant mortgages. In either case, a mortgage generally requires periodic (usually monthly) payments of principal plus interest.

To illustrate the accounting for a mortgage, we will assume that McGiven Automobile Company borrows $100,000 on January 1 to purchase a new showroom and signs a mortgage agreement pledging the showroom as collateral on the loan. If the mortgage is at 8% for 30 years, and the monthly payment is $733.76, payable on January 31 with subsequent payments due at the end of each month thereafter, the entries to record the acquisition of the mortgage and the first monthly payment are:

Jan. 1	Cash	100,000	
	Mortgage Payable		100,000
	Borrowed $100,000 to purchase the automobile showroom.		
Jan. 31	Mortgage Payable	67.09	
	Interest Expense	666.67	
	Cash		733.76
	Made first month's mortgage payment.		

As this entry shows, only $67.09 of the $733.76 payment is applied to reduce the mortgage; the remainder is interest ($100,000 × 0.08 × $\frac{1}{12}$). In each successive month, the amount applied to reduce the mortgage will increase slightly until, toward the end of the 30-year mortgage, almost all of the payment will be for principal. A **mortgage amortization schedule** identifies how much of each mortgage payment is interest and how much is principal reduction, as shown in Exhibit 10-3. Note that during the first 20 years of McGiven's $100,000, 8%, 30-year mortgage, more of each mortgage payment is for interest than for principal.

At the end of each year, a mortgage is reported on the balance sheet in two places: (1) the principal to be paid during the next year is shown as a current liability, and (2) the balance of the mortgage payable is shown as a long-term liability. Further, any accrued interest on the mort-

mortgage amortization schedule A schedule that shows the breakdown between interest and principal for each payment over the life of a mortgage.

$100,000, 25-Year Mortgage			
Interest Rate	Monthly Payment	Total Amount Paid	Qualifying Annual Income
7%	$ 707	$212,100	$30,300
8%	772	231,600	33,086
9%	839	251,700	35,957
10%	909	272,700	38,957
11%	980	294,000	42,000
12%	1,053	315,900	45,129
13%	1,128	338,400	48,343
14%	1,204	361,200	51,600

exhibit 10-3　　　Mortgage Amortization Schedule ($100,000, 30-Year Mortgage at 8%)

	End-of-Year Totals			
Year	Monthly Payment	Principal Paid during Year	Interest Paid during Year	Outstanding Mortgage Balance
1	$733.76	$ 835	$7,970	$99,165
2	733.76	905	7,900	98,260
3	733.76	980	7,825	97,280
4	733.76	1,061	7,744	96,219
5	733.76	1,149	7,656	95,070
10	733.76	1,712	7,093	87,725
15	733.76	2,551	6,254	76,783
20	733.76	3,800	5,005	60,080
25	733.76	5,661	3,144	36,793
30	733.76	8,434	371	0

Total payments over life of mortgage: $264,154*
*$733.76 × 360 payments = $264,154.

gage is reported as a current liability, and the interest expense for the year is included with other expenses on the income statement.

to summarize

Long-term interest-bearing notes are obligations that will be repaid over several years. Interest on the note is computed by multiplying the outstanding balance of the note times the rate of interest. Mortgages payable are long-term liabilities that arise when companies borrow money to buy land, construct buildings, or purchase additional operating assets. Mortgages are tied to specific assets. They are amortized over a period of time and involve periodic, usually monthly, payments that include both principal and interest.

3

Account for capital lease obligations and understand the significance of operating leases being excluded from the balance sheet.

ACCOUNTING FOR LEASE OBLIGATIONS

As discussed in Chapter 9, a company may choose to lease rather than purchase an asset. If a lease is a simple, short-term rental agreement, called an operating lease, lease payments are recorded as Rent Expense by the lessee and as Rent Revenue by the lessor. However, if the terms of a lease agreement meet specific criteria (see Chapter 9, page 401), the transaction is classified as a capital lease and is accounted for as if the asset had been purchased with long-term debt. The lessee records the leased property as an asset and recognizes a liability to the lessor.

In Chapter 9, we focused on the recording of assets acquired under capital leases, using assumed amounts for the present value. Here we will explain how the present value of a capital lease is determined. To illustrate the measurement and recording of a capital lease, we will assume that Malone Corporation leases a mainframe computer from Macro Data, Inc., on December 31, 2002. The lease requires annual payments of $10,000 for 10 years, with the first payment due on December 31, 2003.[2] The rate of interest applicable to the lease is 14% compounded annually.

Assuming the lease meets the criteria for a capital lease, Malone Corporation will record the computer and the related liability at the present value of the future lease payments. From Table II, on page 484, the factor for the present value of an annuity for 10 payments at 14% is 5.2161.

A construction company may choose to lease large equipment rather than purchase such an asset.

2 Readers should be aware that the illustration of a capital lease presented here assumes that lease payments are made at the end of each year, with the present values based on an ordinary annuity. Usually, lease payments are made at the beginning of each lease period, which requires present value calculations using the concept of an annuity in advance or "annuity due." These calculations are explained in intermediate accounting texts.

This factor is multiplied by the annual lease payment to determine the present value. The entry to record the lease on Malone's books is:

2002			
Dec. 31	Leased Computer............................	52,161	
	Lease Liability		52,161
	Leased a computer from Macro Data, Inc., for		
	$10,000 a year for 10 years discounted at		
	14% ($10,000 × 5.2161 = $52,161).		

If Malone Corporation uses a calendar year for financial reporting, the December 31, 2003 balance sheet will report the leased asset in the property, plant, and equipment section and the lease liability in the liabilities section.

A schedule of the computer lease payments is presented in Exhibit 10-4. Each year the lease liability account balance is multiplied by 14% to determine the amount of interest included in each of the annual $10,000 lease payments.

exhibit 10-4   Schedule of Computer Lease Payments

Year	Annual Payment	Interest Expense (0.14 × Lease Liability)	Principal	Lease Liability
				$52,161
1	$10,000	(0.14 × $52,161) = $7,303	$2,697	49,464
2	10,000	(0.14 × 49,464) = 6,925	3,075	46,389
3	10,000	(0.14 × 46,389) = 6,494	3,506	42,883
4	10,000	(0.14 × 42,883) = 6,004	3,996	38,887
5	10,000	(0.14 × 38,887) = 5,444	4,556	34,331
6	10,000	(0.14 × 34,331) = 4,806	5,194	29,137
7	10,000	(0.14 × 29,137) = 4,079	5,921	23,216
8	10,000	(0.14 × 23,216) = 3,250	6,750	16,466
9	10,000	(0.14 × 16,466) = 2,305	7,695	8,771
10	10,000	(0.14 × 8,771) = 1,229*	8,771	0

*Rounded.

Note that this is the same procedure used with a mortgage when determining the amount of each payment that is applied to reduce the principal and the amount that is considered interest expense.

The remainder of the payment is a reduction in the liability. For example, the first lease payment is recorded as follows:

2003			
Dec. 31	Interest Expense	7,303	
	Lease Liability	2,697	
	Cash		10,000
	Paid annual lease payment for computer		
	($52,161 × 0.14 = $7,303; $10,000 − $7,303 = $2,697).		

Similar entries would be made in each of the remaining nine years of the lease, except that the principal payment (reduction in Lease Liability) would increase while the interest expense would decrease. Interest expense decreases over the lease term because a constant rate (14%) is applied to a decreasing principal balance.

Although the asset and liability accounts have the same balance at the beginning of the lease term, they seldom remain the same during the lease period. The asset and the liability are accounted for separately, with the asset being depreciated using one of the methods discussed in Chapter 9.

Operating Leases

When a lease is accounted for as a capital lease, the lease obligation (and an associated leased asset) will appear on the balance sheet of the company using the leased asset. If, on the other hand, a company is able to classify a lease as an operating lease according to the criteria outlined in Chapter 9, *nothing will appear on the balance sheet.* Neither the leased asset nor the lease liability will be recognized. For this reason, an operating lease is often referred to as a form of "off-balance-sheet financing"—the economic obligation associated with the financing arrangement entered into to secure the use of an asset is not reported on the balance sheet.

Because operating leases are not reported on the balance sheet, accounting rules require companies to disclose operating lease details in the financial statement notes so that financial statement users will be aware of these off-balance-sheet obligations. The information from the operating lease note from DISNEY's 1999 financial statements is reproduced below:

The company has various real estate operating leases, including retail outlets for the distribution of consumer products and office space for general and administrative purposes. Future minimum lease payments under these non-cancelable operating leases totaled $2.2 billion at September 30, 1999, payable as follows [in millions]:

2000	$ 297
2001	262
2002	239
2003	216
2004	185
Thereafter	1,019

Recall that the obligation to make this $2.2 billion in operating lease payments is *not* reported as a liability on Disney's balance sheet.

---

to summarize

A lease is a contract whereby the lessee makes periodic payments to the lessor for the use of an asset. A simple short-term rental agreement, or operating lease, involves only the recording of rent expense by the lessee and rent revenue by the lessor. A capital lease is accounted for as a debt-financed purchase of the leased asset. Both the asset and the liability are initially recorded by the lessee at the present value of the future lease payments discounted at the applicable interest rate. Subsequently, the asset is depreciated and the lease liability is written off as periodic payments are made. Part of each lease payment is interest expense, computed at a constant interest rate, and the remainder is a reduction of the principal amount of the liability. Operating leases are a form of off-balance-sheet financing because the obligation to make future operating lease payments is not recognized as a liability on the balance sheet. Companies are required to disclose the amount of their future operating lease payments in the notes to the financial statements.

4

Account for bonds, including the original issuance, the payment of interest, and the retirement of bonds.

bond A contract between a borrower and a lender in which the borrower promises to pay a specified rate of interest for each period the bond is outstanding and repay the principal at the maturity date.

debentures (unsecured bonds) Bonds for which no collateral has been pledged.

secured bonds Bonds for which assets have been pledged in order to guarantee repayment.

registered bonds Bonds for which the names and addresses of the bondholders are kept on file by the issuing company.

coupon bonds Unregistered bonds for which owners receive periodic interest payments by clipping a coupon from the bond and sending it to the issuer as evidence of ownership.

term bonds Bonds that mature in one single sum at a specified future date.

serial bonds Bonds that mature in a series of installments at specified future dates.

callable bonds Bonds for which the issuer reserves the right to pay the obligation before its maturity date.

convertible bonds Bonds that can be traded for, or converted to, other securities after a specified period of time.

zero-coupon bonds Bonds issued with no promise of interest payments; only a single payment will be made.

THE NATURE OF BONDS

A **bond** is a contract between the borrowing company (issuer) and the lender (investor) in which the borrower promises to pay a specified amount of interest at the end of each period the bond is outstanding and to repay the principal at the maturity date of the bond contract. Bonds generally have maturity dates exceeding 10 years and, as a result, are another example of a long-term liability.

Types of Bonds

Bonds can be categorized on the basis of various characteristics. The following classification system considers three characteristics:

1. The extent to which bondholders are protected.
   a. **Debentures** (or **unsecured bonds**). Bonds that have no underlying assets pledged as security, or collateral, to guarantee their repayment.
   b. **Secured bonds**. Bonds that have a pledge of company assets, such as land or buildings, as a protection for lenders. If the company fails to meet its bond obligations, the pledged assets can be sold and used to pay the bondholders. Bonds that are secured with the issuer's assets are often referred to as "mortgage bonds."
2. How the bond interest is paid.
   a. **Registered bonds**. Bonds for which the issuing company keeps a record of the names and addresses of all bondholders and pays interest only to those whose names are on file.
   b. **Coupon bonds**. Unregistered bonds for which the issuer has no record of current bondholders but instead pays interest to anyone who can show evidence of ownership. Usually, these bonds have a printed coupon for each interest payment. When a payment is due, the bondholder clips the coupon from the certificate and sends it to the issuer as evidence of bond ownership. The issuer then sends an interest payment to the bondholder.
3. How the bonds mature.
   a. **Term bonds**. Bonds that mature in one single sum on a specified future date.
   b. **Serial bonds**. Bonds that mature in a series of installments.
   c. **Callable bonds**. Term or serial bonds that the issuer can redeem at any time at a specified price.
   d. **Convertible bonds**. Term or serial bonds that can be converted to other securities, such as stocks, after a specified period, at the option of the bondholder. (The accounting for this type of bond is discussed in advanced accounting texts.)

Two other types of bonds that are often encountered are zero-coupon bonds and junk bonds. **Zero-coupon bonds** are issued with no promise of interest payments. The company issuing the bonds promises only to repay a fixed amount at the maturity date. While the idea of having to make no interest payments might be initially appealing to the issuer, remember that the present value of the bond is affected by both the single payment at the end of the bond's life and the annuity payment. If this annuity (interest) payment will not be part of the bond, potential buyers will pay much less for the bond. For this reason, zero-coupon bonds are often referred to as *deep-discount bonds*.

Junk bonds are high-risk bonds issued by companies in weak financial condition or with large amounts of debt already outstanding. These bonds typically yield returns of at least 12%, but some may return in excess of 20%. Of course, with these high returns comes greater risk.

Characteristics of Bonds

When an organization issues bonds, it usually sells them to underwriters (brokers and investment bankers), who in turn sell them to various institutions and to the public. At the time of the original sale, the company issuing the bonds chooses a trustee to represent the bondholders. In most cases, the trustee is a large bank or trust company to which the company issuing the bonds delivers a contract called a bond indenture, deed of trust, or trust indenture. The

junk bonds Bonds issued by companies in weak financial condition with large amounts of debt already outstanding; these bonds yield high rates of return because of high risk.

bond indenture A contract between a bond issuer and a bond purchaser that specifies the terms of a bond.

principal (face value or maturity value) The amount that will be paid on a bond at the maturity date.

bond maturity date The date at which a bond principal or face amount becomes payable.

bond indenture specifies that in return for an investment of cash by investors, the company promises to pay a specific amount of interest (based on a specified, or stated, rate of interest) each period the bonds are outstanding and to repay the **principal** (also called **face value** or **maturity value**) of the bonds at a specified future date (the **bond maturity date**). It is the duty of the trustee to protect investors and to make sure that the bond issuer fulfills its responsibilities.

The total value of a single "bond issue" often exceeds several million dollars. A bond issue is generally divided into a number of individual bonds, which may be of varying denominations. The principal, or face value, of each bond is usually $1,000 or a multiple thereof. Note that the price of bonds is quoted as a percentage of $1,000 face value. Thus, a bond quoted at 98 is selling for $980 (98% × $1,000), and a bond quoted at 103 is selling for $1,030 (103% × $1,000). By issuing bonds in small denominations, a company increases the chances that a broad range of investors will be able to compete for the purchase of the bonds. This increased demand usually results in the bonds selling for a higher price.

In most cases, the market price of bonds is influenced by (1) the riskiness of the bonds and (2) the interest rate at which the bonds are issued. The first factor, riskiness of the bonds, is determined by general economic conditions and the financial status of the company selling the bonds, as measured by organizations (MOODY'S or STANDARD AND POOR'S, for instance) that regularly assign a rating, or a grade, to all corporate bonds.

Companies strive to earn as high a bond rating as possible because the higher the rating, the lower the interest rate they will have to pay to attract buyers. For example, using the widely cited Moody's bond rating, an Aaa bond is a bond of the highest quality with the least risk of nonpayment. As of October 2000, bonds with this rating were paying interest of approximately 6.6%. A high-risk bond, on the other hand, will have a low rating, which means the company will have to offer a higher rate of interest to attract buyers. For example, as of October 2000, the bonds of financially troubled CHIQUITA BRANDS (the banana company) were rated B1 by Moody's, a rating indicating that the bonds were "highly speculative." Lenders were requiring an interest rate of more than 30% to induce them to purchase these bonds.

to summarize

Bonds are certificates of debt issued by companies or government agencies, guaranteeing a stated interest rate and repayment of the principal at a specified maturity date. Corporations issue bonds as a form of long-term borrowing to finance the acquisition of operating assets, such as land, buildings, and equipment. Bonds can be classified by their level of security (debentures versus secured bonds), by the way interest is paid (registered versus coupon bonds), and by the way they mature (term bonds, serial bonds, callable bonds, and convertible bonds).

Determining a Bond's Issuance Price

When a company issues bonds, it is generally promising to make two types of payments: (1) a payment of interest of a fixed amount at equal intervals (usually semiannually but sometimes quarterly or annually) over the life of the bond and (2) a single payment—the principal, or face value, of the bond—at the maturity date. For example, assume that Denver Company issues 10%, five-year bonds with a total face value of $800,000. Interest is to be paid semiannually. This information tells us that Denver Company agrees to pay $40,000 ($800,000 × 0.10 × ½ year) in interest every six months and also agrees to pay to the investors the principal amount of $800,000 at the end of five years. The following diagram reflects this agreement between Denver Company and the bond investors:

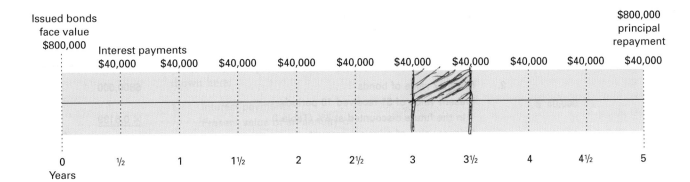

Issued bonds
face value
$800,000

Interest payments
$40,000 $40,000 $40,000 $40,000 $40,000 $40,000 $40,000 $40,000 $40,000 $40,000

$800,000
principal
repayment

0   ½   1   1½   2   2½   3   3½   4   4½   5

Years

In this example, we assumed that the bonds were issued at their face value of $800,000. However, bonds are frequently issued at a price that is more or less than their face value. The actual price at which bonds are issued is affected by the interest rate investors are seeking at the time the bonds are sold in relation to the interest rate specified by the borrower in the bond indenture. How, then, is the issuance price of bonds determined?

Essentially, present value concepts are used to measure the effect of time on the value of money. The price should equal the present value of the interest payments (an annuity) plus the present value of the bond's face value at maturity. These present values are computed using the **market rate of interest** (also called the **effective rate** or **yield rate**), which is the rate investors expect to earn on their investment. It is contrasted with the **stated rate of interest**, which is the rate printed on the bond (10% in the Denver Company example).

If the effective rate is equal to the stated rate, the bonds will sell at face value (that is, at $800,000). If the effective rate is higher than the stated rate, the bonds will sell at a **bond discount** (at less than the face value) because the investors desire a higher rate than the company is promising to pay. Likewise, if the effective rate is lower than the stated rate, the bonds will sell at a **bond premium** (at more than face value) because the company is promising to pay a higher rate than the market is paying at that time.

Consider the following scenario: If Company A is issuing bonds with a stated rate of 12% and the market rate for similar bonds is 10%, what will happen to the price of Company A's bonds? Investors, eager to receive a 12% return, will bid the price of the bonds up until the price at which the bonds sell yields a 10% return. The amount paid for the bonds over and above the maturity value is the bond premium. If Company A were issuing bonds with a stated rate of 8%, no one would buy the bonds until the price was lowered sufficiently to allow investors to earn a return of 10%. The difference between the selling price and the maturity value would be the amount of the bond discount.

We will use the Denver Company bonds example (from page 470) to explain how the price is computed in each situation.

STOP & THINK If the market rate of interest is higher than the rate of interest stated on the bonds, will the bonds sell at a price higher or lower than the face value? Think about the question this way: Is the higher rate more attractive to investors, and if it is, what would investors do as a result?

market rate (effective rate or yield rate) of interest The actual interest rate earned or paid on a bond investment.

stated rate of interest The rate of interest printed on the bond.

bond discount The difference between the face value and the sales price when bonds are sold below their face value.

bond premium The difference between the face value and the sales price when bonds are sold above their face value.

BONDS ISSUED AT FACE VALUE   Denver Company has agreed to issue $800,000 bonds and pay 10% interest, compounded semiannually. Assume that the effective interest rate demanded by investors for bonds of this level of risk is also 10%. Using the effective interest rate, which happens to be the same as the stated rate, the calculation to determine the price at which the bonds will be issued is shown at the top of the next page. (Note that because the interest is compounded semiannually, the interest rate is halved and the five-year bond life is treated as 10 six-month periods.)

The calculation shows why the bonds sell at face value. At the effective rate, the sum of the present value of the interest payments and the payment at maturity is $800,000, which is the issuance price at the stated rate. This equality of present values will occur only when the effective rate and the stated rate are the same.

In this computation, the $6,000 in column (1) is the actual cash paid each six months. Column (2) shows the interest expense for each six months, which is the amount that will be reported on the income statement. Column (3), which is the difference between columns (1) and (2), represents the amortization of the premium. Column (4) shows the carrying, or book, value of the bonds (that is, the total of the bonds payable and the unamortized bond premium), which is the amount that will be reported on the balance sheet each period. Using the effective-interest method, the bond carrying value is always equal to the present value of the bond obligation. As the carrying value decreases, while the effective rate of interest remains constant, the interest expense also decreases from one period to the next, as illustrated in column (2) of the amortization schedule.

To help you translate this table into the entries for the interest payments and premium amortization at the end of each six-month period, we have provided the semiannual journal entries for year 3.

Year 3, End of First Six Months

Bond Interest Expense	5,542	
Bond Premium	458	
Cash		6,000

To record effective-interest expense on Central Trucking Company bonds for the first six months of year 3.

Year 3, End of Second Six Months

Bond Interest Expense	5,519	
Bond Premium	481	
Bond Interest Payable		6,000

To record effective-interest expense on Central Trucking Company bonds for the second six months of year 3.

Because the straight-line method would show a constant amortization ($12,463/20 = $623.15 per six-month period) on a decreasing bond balance, the straight-line interest rate cannot be constant. When the straight-line results differ significantly from the effective-interest results, generally accepted accounting principles require use of the effective-interest method.

The effective-interest method of amortizing a bond discount is essentially the same as amortizing a bond premium. The main difference is that the bond carrying value is increasing instead of decreasing.

to summarize

When bonds are issued at a premium or a discount, the premium or discount must be amortized over the life of the bond. A discount or premium results when the market rate and the stated rate are different. Because of this difference, bond interest expense recognized on the income statement is not equal to the amount of cash paid for interest. The objective of amortization is to reflect the actual bond interest expense incurred over the life of the bond. Two methods of amortization are available—the straight-line method and the effective-interest method. The straight-line method amortizes an equal amount of premium or discount every period. When the effective-interest method is used, the amount of discount or premium amortized each period is equal to the market rate of interest multiplied by the bond's carrying value.

table I

The Present Value of $1 Due in *n* Periods*

Period	1%	2%	3%	4%	5%	6%	7%	8%	9%	10%	12%	14%	15%	16%	18%	20%
1	.9901	.9804	.9709	.9615	.9524	.9434	.9346	.9259	.9174	.9091	.8929	.8772	.8696	.8621	.8475	.8333
2	.9803	.9612	.9426	.9246	.9070	.8900	.8734	.8573	.8417	.8264	.7972	.7695	.7561	.7432	.7182	.6944
3	.9706	.9423	.9151	.8890	.8638	.8396	.8163	.7938	.7722	.7513	.7118	.6750	.6575	.6407	.6086	.5787
4	.9610	.9238	.8885	.8548	.8227	.7921	.7629	.7350	.7084	.6830	.6355	.5921	.5718	.5523	.5158	.4823
5	.9515	.9057	.8626	.8219	.7835	.7473	.7130	.6806	.6499	.6209	.5674	.5194	.4972	.4761	.4371	.4019
6	.9420	.8880	.8375	.7903	.7462	.7050	.6663	.6302	.5963	.5645	.5066	.4556	.4323	.4104	.3704	.3349
7	.9327	.8706	.8131	.7599	.7107	.6651	.6227	.5835	.5470	.5132	.4523	.3996	.3759	.3538	.3139	.2791
8	.9235	.8535	.7894	.7307	.6768	.6274	.5820	.5403	.5019	.4665	.4039	.3506	.3269	.3050	.2660	.2326
9	.9143	.8368	.7664	.7026	.6446	.5919	.5439	.5002	.4604	.4241	.3606	.3075	.2843	.2630	.2255	.1938
10	.9053	.8203	.7441	.6756	.6139	.5584	.5083	.4632	.4224	.3855	.3220	.2697	.2472	.2267	.1911	.1615
11	.8963	.8043	.7224	.6496	.5847	.5268	.4751	.4289	.3875	.3503	.2875	.2366	.2149	.1954	.1619	.1346
12	.8874	.7885	.7014	.6246	.5568	.4970	.4440	.3971	.3555	.3186	.2567	.2076	.1869	.1685	.1372	.1122
13	.8787	.7730	.6810	.6006	.5303	.4688	.4150	.3677	.3262	.2897	.2292	.1821	.1625	.1452	.1163	.0935
14	.8700	.7579	.6611	.5775	.5051	.4423	.3878	.3405	.2992	.2633	.2046	.1597	.1413	.1252	.0985	.0779
15	.8613	.7430	.6419	.5553	.4810	.4173	.3624	.3152	.2745	.2394	.1827	.1401	.1229	.1079	.0835	.0649
16	.8528	.7284	.6232	.5339	.4581	.3936	.3387	.2919	.2519	.2176	.1631	.1229	.1069	.0930	.0708	.0541
17	.8444	.7142	.6050	.5134	.4363	.3714	.3166	.2703	.2311	.1978	.1456	.1078	.0929	.0802	.0600	.0451
18	.8360	.7002	.5874	.4936	.4155	.3503	.2959	.2502	.2120	.1799	.1300	.0946	.0808	.0691	.0508	.0376
19	.8277	.6864	.5703	.4746	.3957	.3305	.2765	.2317	.1945	.1635	.1161	.0829	.0703	.0596	.0431	.0313
20	.8195	.6730	.5537	.4564	.3769	.3118	.2584	.2145	.1784	.1486	.1037	.0728	.0611	.0514	.0365	.0261
25	.7798	.6095	.4776	.3751	.2953	.2330	.1842	.1460	.1160	.0923	.0588	.0378	.0304	.0245	.0160	.0105
30	.7419	.5521	.4120	.3083	.2314	.1741	.1314	.0994	.0754	.0573	.0334	.0196	.0151	.0116	.0070	.0042
40	.6717	.4529	.3066	.2083	.1420	.0972	.0668	.0460	.0318	.0221	.0107	.0053	.0037	.0026	.0013	.0007
50	.6080	.3715	.2281	.1407	.0872	.0543	.0339	.0213	.0134	.0085	.0035	.0014	.0009	.0006	.0003	.0001
60	.5504	.3048	.1697	.0951	.0535	.0303	.0173	.0099	.0057	.0033	.0011	.0004	.0002	.0001	†	†

*The formula used to derive the values in this table was $PV = F \dfrac{1}{(1 + i)^n}$ where PV = present value, F = future amount to be discounted, i = interest rate, and n = number of periods.
†The value of 0 to four decimal places.

table II   The Present Value of an Annuity of $1 per Number of Payments*

Number of Payments	1%	2%	3%	4%	5%	6%	7%	8%	9%	10%	12%	14%	15%	16%	18%	20%
1	0.9901	0.9804	0.9709	0.9615	0.9524	0.9434	0.9346	0.9259	0.9174	0.9091	0.8929	0.8772	0.8596	0.8621	0.8475	0.8333
2	1.9704	1.9416	1.9135	1.8861	1.8594	1.8334	1.8080	1.7833	1.7591	1.7355	1.6901	1.6467	1.6257	1.6052	1.5656	1.5278
3	2.9410	2.8839	2.8286	2.7751	2.7232	2.6730	2.6243	2.5771	2.5313	2.4869	2.4018	2.3216	2.2832	2.2459	2.1743	2.1065
4	3.9820	3.8077	3.7171	3.6299	3.5460	3.4651	3.3872	3.3121	3.2397	3.1699	3.0373	2.9137	2.8850	2.7982	2.6901	2.5887
5	4.8884	4.7135	4.5797	4.4518	4.3295	4.2124	4.1002	3.9927	3.8897	3.7908	3.6048	3.4331	3.3522	3.2743	3.1272	2.9906
6	5.7985	5.6014	5.4172	5.2421	5.0757	4.9173	4.7665	4.6229	4.4859	4.3553	4.1114	3.8887	3.7845	3.6847	3.4976	3.3255
7	6.7282	6.4720	6.2303	6.0021	5.7864	5.5824	5.3893	5.2064	5.0330	4.8684	4.5638	4.2883	4.1604	4.0386	3.8115	3.6046
8	7.6517	7.3255	7.0197	6.7327	6.4632	6.2098	5.9713	5.7466	5.5348	5.3349	4.9676	4.6389	4.4873	4.3436	4.0776	3.8372
9	8.5660	8.1622	7.7861	7.4353	7.1078	6.8017	6.5152	6.2469	5.9952	5.7590	5.3282	4.9464	4.7716	4.6065	4.3030	4.0310
10	9.4713	8.9826	8.5302	8.1109	7.7217	7.3601	7.0236	6.7101	6.4177	6.1446	5.6502	5.2161	5.0188	4.8332	4.4941	4.1925
11	10.3676	9.7868	9.2526	8.7605	8.3064	7.8869	7.4987	7.1390	6.8052	6.4951	5.9377	5.4527	5.2337	5.0286	4.6560	4.3271
12	11.2551	10.5733	9.9540	9.3851	8.8633	8.3838	7.9427	7.5361	7.1607	6.8137	6.1944	5.6603	5.4206	5.1971	4.7932	4.4392
13	12.1337	11.3484	10.6350	9.9856	9.3936	8.8527	8.3577	7.9038	7.4869	7.1034	6.4235	5.8424	5.5831	5.3423	4.9095	4.5327
14	13.0037	12.1062	11.2961	10.5631	9.8986	9.2950	8.7455	8.2442	7.7862	7.3667	6.6282	6.0021	5.7245	5.4675	5.0081	4.6106
15	13.8651	12.8493	11.9379	11.1184	10.3797	9.7122	9.1079	8.5595	8.0607	7.6061	6.8109	6.1422	5.8474	5.5755	5.0916	4.6755
16	14.7179	13.5777	12.5611	11.6523	10.8378	10.1059	9.4466	8.8514	8.3126	7.8237	6.9740	6.2651	5.9542	5.6685	5.1624	4.7296
17	15.5623	14.2919	13.1661	12.1657	11.2741	10.4773	9.7632	9.1216	8.5436	8.0216	7.1196	6.3729	6.0472	5.7487	5.2223	4.7746
18	16.3983	14.9920	13.7535	12.6593	11.6896	10.8276	10.0591	9.3719	8.7556	8.2014	7.2497	6.4674	6.1280	5.8178	5.2732	4.8122
19	17.2260	15.6785	14.3238	13.1339	12.0853	11.1581	10.3356	9.6036	8.9501	8.3649	7.3658	6.5504	6.1982	5.8775	5.3162	4.8435
20	18.0456	16.3514	14.8775	13.5903	12.4622	11.4699	10.5940	9.8181	9.1285	8.5136	7.4694	6.6231	6.2593	5.9288	5.3527	4.8696
25	22.0232	19.5235	17.4131	15.6221	14.0939	12.7834	11.6536	10.6748	9.8226	9.0770	7.8431	6.8729	6.4641	6.0971	5.4669	4.9476
30	25.8077	22.3965	19.6004	17.2920	15.3725	13.7648	12.4090	11.2578	10.2737	9.4269	8.0552	7.0027	6.5660	6.1772	5.5168	4.9789
40	32.8347	27.3555	23.1148	19.7928	17.1591	15.0463	13.3317	11.9246	10.7574	9.7791	8.2438	7.1050	6.6418	6.2335	5.5482	4.9966
50	39.1961	31.4236	25.7298	21.4822	18.2559	15.7619	13.8007	12.2335	10.9617	9.9148	8.3045	7.1327	6.6605	6.2463	5.5641	4.9995
60	44.9550	34.7609	27.6756	22.6235	18.9293	16.1614	14.0392	12.3766	11.0480	9.9672	8.3240	7.1401	6.6651	6.2482	5.5553	4.9999

*The formula used to derive the values in this table was $PV = F\left(\dfrac{1 - \dfrac{1}{(1 + i)^n}}{i}\right)$ where PV = present value, F = periodic payment to be discounted, i = interest rate, and n = number of payments.

table III

(Future Value)

Amount of $1 Due in *n* Periods

Period	1%	2%	3%	4%	5%	6%	7%	8%	9%	10%	12%	14%	15%	16%	18%	20%
1	1.0100	1.0200	1.0300	1.0400	1.0500	1.0600	1.0700	1.0800	1.0900	1.1000	1.1200	1.1400	1.1500	1.1600	1.1800	1.2000
2	1.0201	1.0404	1.0609	1.0816	1.1025	1.1236	1.1449	1.1664	1.1881	1.2100	1.2544	1.2996	1.3225	1.3456	1.3924	1.4400
3	1.0303	1.0612	1.0927	1.1249	1.1576	1.1910	1.2250	1.2597	1.2950	1.3310	1.4049	1.4815	1.5209	1.5609	1.6430	1.7280
4	1.0406	1.0824	1.1255	1.1699	1.2155	1.2625	1.3108	1.3605	1.4116	1.4641	1.5735	1.6890	1.7490	1.8106	1.9388	2.0736
5	1.0510	1.1041	1.1593	1.2167	1.2763	1.3382	1.4026	1.4693	1.5386	1.6105	1.7623	1.9254	2.0114	2.1003	2.2878	2.4883
6	1.0615	1.1262	1.1941	1.2653	1.3401	1.4185	1.5007	1.5869	1.6771	1.7716	1.9738	2.1950	2.3131	2.4364	2.6996	2.9860
7	1.0721	1.1487	1.2299	1.3159	1.4071	1.5036	1.6058	1.7138	1.8280	1.9487	2.2107	2.5023	2.6600	2.8262	3.1855	3.5832
8	1.0829	1.1717	1.2668	1.3686	1.4775	1.5938	1.7182	1.8509	1.9926	2.1436	2.4760	2.8526	3.0590	3.2784	3.7589	4.2998
9	1.0937	1.1951	1.3048	1.4233	1.5513	1.6895	1.8385	1.9990	2.1719	2.3579	2.7731	3.2519	3.5179	3.8030	4.4355	5.1598
10	1.1046	1.2190	1.3439	1.4802	1.6289	1.7908	1.9672	2.1589	2.3674	2.5937	3.1058	3.7072	4.0456	4.4114	5.2338	6.1917
11	1.1157	1.2434	1.3842	1.5395	1.7103	1.8983	2.1049	2.3316	2.5804	2.8531	3.4785	4.2262	4.6524	5.1173	6.1759	7.4031
12	1.1268	1.2682	1.4258	1.6010	1.7959	2.0122	2.2522	2.5182	2.8127	3.1384	3.8960	4.8179	5.3502	5.9360	7.2876	8.9161
13	1.1381	1.2936	1.4685	1.6651	1.8856	2.1329	2.4098	2.7196	3.0658	3.4523	4.3635	5.4924	6.1528	6.8858	8.5994	10.699
14	1.1495	1.3195	1.5126	1.7317	1.9799	2.2609	2.5785	2.9372	3.3417	3.7975	4.8871	6.2613	7.0757	7.9875	10.147	12.839
15	1.1610	1.3459	1.5580	1.8009	2.0789	2.3966	2.7590	3.1722	3.6425	4.1772	5.4736	7.1379	8.1371	9.2655	11.973	15.407
16	1.1726	1.3728	1.6047	1.8730	2.1829	2.5404	2.9522	3.4259	3.9703	4.5950	6.1304	8.1372	9.3576	10.748	14.129	18.488
17	1.1843	1.4002	1.6528	1.9479	2.2920	2.6928	3.1588	3.7000	4.3276	5.0545	6.8660	9.2765	10.761	12.467	16.672	22.186
18	1.1961	1.4282	1.7024	2.0258	2.4066	2.8543	3.3799	3.9960	4.7171	5.5599	7.6900	10.575	12.375	14.462	19.673	26.623
19	1.2081	1.4568	1.7535	2.1068	2.5270	3.0256	3.6165	4.3157	5.1417	6.1159	8.6128	12.055	14.231	16.776	23.214	31.948
20	1.2202	1.4859	1.8061	2.1911	2.6533	3.2071	3.8697	4.6610	5.6044	6.7275	9.6463	13.743	16.366	19.460	27.393	38.337
30	1.3478	1.8114	2.4273	3.2434	4.3219	5.7435	7.6123	10.062	13.267	17.449	29.959	50.950	66.211	85.849	143.37	237.37
40	1.4889	2.2080	3.2620	4.8010	7.0400	10.285	14.974	21.724	31.409	45.259	93.050	188.88	267.86	378.72	750.37	1469.7
50	1.6446	2.6916	4.3839	7.1067	11.467	18.420	29.457	46.901	74.357	117.39	289.00	700.23	1083.6	1670.7	3927.3	9100.4
60	1.8167	3.2810	5.8916	10.519	18.679	32.987	57.946	101.25	176.03	304.48	897.59	2595.9	4383.9	7370.1	20555.	56347.

table IV   Amount of an Annuity of $1 per Number of Payments

Number of Payments	1%	2%	3%	4%	5%	6%	7%	8%	9%	10%	12%	14%	15%	16%	18%	20%
1	1.0000	1.0000	1.0000	1.0000	1.0000	1.0000	1.0000	1.0000	1.0000	1.0000	1.0000	1.0000	1.0000	1.0000	1.0000	1.0000
2	2.0100	2.0200	2.0300	2.0400	2.0500	2.0600	2.0700	2.0800	2.0900	2.1000	2.1200	2.1400	2.1500	2.1600	2.1800	2.2000
3	3.0301	3.0604	3.0909	3.1216	3.1525	3.1836	3.2149	3.2464	3.2781	3.3100	3.3744	3.4396	3.4725	3.5056	3.5724	3.6400
4	4.0604	4.1216	4.1836	4.2465	4.3101	4.3746	4.4399	4.5061	4.5731	4.6410	4.7793	4.9211	4.9934	5.0665	5.2154	5.3680
5	5.1010	5.2040	5.3091	5.4163	5.5256	5.6371	5.7507	5.8666	5.9847	6.1051	6.3528	6.6101	6.7424	6.8771	7.1542	7.4416
6	6.1520	6.3081	6.4684	6.6330	6.8019	6.9753	7.1533	7.3359	7.5233	7.7156	8.1152	8.5355	8.7537	8.9775	9.4420	9.9299
7	7.2135	7.4343	7.6625	7.8983	8.1420	8.3938	8.6540	8.9228	9.2004	9.4872	10.8090	10.7305	11.0668	11.4139	12.1415	12.9159
8	8.2857	8.5830	8.8923	9.2142	9.5491	9.8975	10.2598	10.6366	11.0285	11.4359	12.2997	13.2328	13.7268	14.2401	15.3270	16.4991
9	9.3685	9.7546	10.1591	10.5828	11.0266	11.4913	11.9780	12.4876	13.0210	13.5795	14.7757	16.0853	16.7858	17.5185	19.0859	20.7989
10	10.4622	10.9497	11.4639	12.0061	12.5779	13.1808	13.8164	14.4866	15.1929	15.9374	17.5487	19.3373	20.3037	21.3215	23.5213	25.9587
11	11.5668	12.1687	12.8078	13.4864	14.2068	14.9716	15.7836	16.6455	17.5603	18.5312	20.6546	23.0445	24.3493	25.7329	28.7551	32.1504
12	12.6825	13.4121	14.1920	15.0258	15.9171	16.8699	17.8885	18.9771	20.1407	21.3843	24.1331	27.2707	29.0017	30.8502	34.9311	39.5805
13	13.8093	14.6803	15.6178	16.6268	17.7130	18.8821	20.1406	21.4953	22.9534	24.5227	28.0291	32.0887	34.3519	36.7862	42.2187	48.4966
14	14.9474	15.9739	17.0863	18.2919	19.5986	21.0151	22.5505	24.2149	26.0192	27.9750	32.3926	37.5811	40.5047	43.6720	50.8180	59.1959
15	16.0969	17.2934	18.5989	20.0236	21.5786	23.2760	25.1290	27.1521	29.3609	31.7725	37.2797	43.8424	47.5804	51.6595	60.9653	72.0351
16	17.2579	18.6393	20.1569	21.8248	23.6575	25.6725	27.8881	30.3243	33.0034	35.9497	42.7535	50.9804	55.7178	60.9250	72.9390	87.4421
17	18.4304	20.0121	21.7616	23.6975	25.8404	28.2129	30.8402	33.7502	36.9737	40.5447	48.8837	59.1176	65.0751	71.6730	87.0680	105.9306
18	19.6147	21.4123	23.4144	25.6454	28.1324	30.9057	33.9990	37.4502	41.3013	45.5992	55.7497	68.3941	75.8364	84.1407	103.7403	128.1167
19	20.8190	22.8406	25.1169	27.6712	30.5390	33.7600	37.3790	41.4463	46.0185	51.1591	63.4397	78.9692	88.2118	98.6032	123.4135	154.7400
20	22.0190	24.2974	26.8704	29.7781	33.0660	36.7856	40.9955	45.7620	51.1601	57.2750	72.0524	91.0249	102.4436	115.3797	146.6280	186.6880
30	34.7849	40.5681	47.5754	56.0849	66.4388	79.0582	94.4608	113.2832	136.3075	164.4940	241.3327	356.7868	434.7451	530.3117	790.9480	1181.8816
40	48.8864	60.4020	75.4013	95.0255	120.7998	154.7620	199.6351	259.0565	337.8824	442.5926	767.0914	1342.0251	1779.0903	2360.7572	4163.2130	7343.8578
50	64.4632	84.5794	112.7969	152.6671	209.3480	290.3359	406.5289	573.7702	815.0836	1163.9085	2400.0182	4994.5213	7217.7163	10435.6488	21813.0937	45497.1908
60	81.6697	114.0515	163.0534	237.9907	353.5837	533.1282	813.5204	1253.2133	1944.7921	3034.8164	7471.6411	18535.1333	29219.9916	46057.5085	114189.6665	281732.5718

review of learning objectives

1 **Use present value concepts to measure long-term liabilities.** Obligations that will not be paid or otherwise satisfied within one year are classified on the balance sheet as long-term liabilities. Some common types of long-term liabilities are notes payable, mortgages payable, lease obligations, and pension obligations. The present value of a long-term liability is the current value, which is computed by discounting the known future amount using the current interest rate. If the present value amounts of assets or liabilities are known and a future amount is desired, then the present value must be compounded to arrive at a future amount that includes both principal and interest.

2 **Account for long-term liabilities, including notes payable and mortgages payable.** Interest-bearing notes are recorded on the books of the issuer at face value. Interest expense is incurred based on the rate of interest, the carrying value of the note, and the passage of time. Interest Expense is debited for the amount of interest incurred and Cash or Interest Payable is credited.

Mortgage liabilities are paid by a series of regular payments that include interest expense and a reduction of the principal of the mortgage note. The balance sheet liability at any given time is the present value of the remaining mortgage payments.

3 **Account for capital lease obligations and understand the significance of operating leases being excluded from the balance sheet.** A firm can acquire new assets by either purchasing or leasing them. Leasing involves periodic payments over the life of the lease. The lease is classified as an operating lease if it is short term and does not meet any of the criteria of a capital lease. If the lease meets one of the specified capital lease criteria, it is treated as a purchase and referred to as a capital lease. As such, it is recorded as both an asset and a long-term liability. The asset is depreciated and the liability is reduced as lease payments are made. Operating leases are a form of off-balance-sheet financing because the obligation to make the future operating lease payments is not recognized on the balance sheet. However, the amount of future operating lease payments is disclosed in the notes to the financial statements.

4 **Account for bonds, including the original issuance, the payment of interest, and the retirement of bonds.** Accounting for bonds by the borrowing company (the issuer)

includes three elements: accounting for their issuance, for interest payments, and for their retirement. If bonds are sold at face value, Cash is debited and Bonds Payable is credited. More often, however, bonds are sold at a premium or a discount. The bond liability is recorded at face value in the bonds payable account, and the premium or discount is recorded in a separate account and added to (in the case of a premium) or subtracted from (in the case of a discount) Bonds Payable on the balance sheet. When interest is paid, Bond Interest Expense is debited and Cash is credited. An adjustment is made to bond interest expense if the bond is sold at a premium or discount. At the date a bond matures, the borrowing company pays the face value to the investors, and the bonds are canceled. If the bonds are retired before maturity, a gain or loss will be recognized when the carrying value of the bonds differs from the amount paid to retire the bonds.

5 **Use debt-related financial ratios to determine the degree of a company's financial leverage and its ability to repay loans.** Higher leverage allows a company to expand without requiring additional stockholder investment. However, higher leverage also makes repayment of debt less certain. Both the debt ratio (total liabilities divided by total assets) and the debt-to-equity ratio (total liabilities divided by total stockholders' equity) measure the level of a company's leverage. These ratios are also sometimes computed using only interest-bearing debt instead of total liabilities. The times interest earned ratio (operating income divided by interest expense) measures how much cushion a company has in terms of being able to make its periodic interest payments.

expanded material

6 **Amortize bond discounts and bond premiums using either the straight-line method or the effective-interest method.** If bonds are issued at a discount, the bond interest expense for the year is the amount of interest paid plus the bond discount amortized during that year. If the bonds are sold at a premium, the bond interest expense for the year is the interest paid minus the bond premium amortized that year. Bond premiums and discounts generally should be amortized using the effective-interest method. The straight-line method is allowed provided that the two methods produce similar results.

Equity Financing

chapter

f11

learning objectives   After studying this chapter, you should be able to:

1 Distinguish between debt and equity financing, and describe the advantages and disadvantages of organizing a business as a proprietorship or a partnership.

2 Describe the basic characteristics of a corporation and the nature of common and preferred stock.

3 Account for the issuance and repurchase of common and preferred stock.

4 Understand the factors that affect retained earnings, describe the factors determining whether a company can and should pay cash dividends, and account for cash dividends.

5 Describe the purpose of reporting comprehensive income in the equity section of the balance sheet, and prepare a statement of stockholders' equity.

expanded material

6 Account for stock dividends and distinguish them from stock splits.

7 Explain prior-period adjustments and prepare a statement of retained earnings.

8 Understand basic proprietorship and partnership accounting.

In 1882, two young newspaper reporters, Charles Dow and Edward Jones, teamed up to provide the Wall Street financial community with handwritten news bulletins. In 1889, when the staff of DOW JONES & COMPANY had grown to 50, they decided to convert the bulletin service into a daily newspaper. The first issue of *The Wall Street Journal* appeared on July 8, 1889. Clarence Barron, who operated a financial news service in Boston, was the paper's first out-of-town reporter. Barron purchased Dow Jones & Company in 1902 for $130,000, and his heirs still hold majority control of the company today.

In the 1940s, *The Wall Street Journal* began publishing more than just business news, expanding its coverage to include economics, politics, and general news. Today, *The Wall Street Journal* has a paid circulation of 1.8 million and is read by an estimated 4.9 million people every day. Dow Jones also publishes *The Wall Street Journal Europe* and *The Asian Wall Street Journal*, and each day it contributes special business pages to 23 Spanish and Portuguese language newspapers in Latin American countries. *The Wall Street Journal* is also a leader in Web-based news, with more than 500,000 paid subscribers for http://wsj.com as of September 30, 2000. This is particularly impressive in that the public is accustomed to getting information for free on the Web.

The Wall Street Journal is the flagship of the company, but the name "Dow Jones" is best known because of the Dow Jones Industrial Average that is cited in the news every day. "The Dow" is widely used to reflect the general health of the U.S. economy. So, what is it? Simply put, the Dow Jones Industrial Average measures the average movement of the stock prices of selected U.S. companies. The very first value of the average was 40.94 on May 26, 1896. Charles Dow computed this value by adding the share prices of 12 important companies chosen by him (GENERAL ELECTRIC was one of them) and then dividing by 12. Thus, the average price per share for these 12 companies was $40.94. Since 1928, the average has included 30 companies selected by the editors of *The Wall Street Journal*. The average is no longer computed by simply averaging share prices, but the underlying concept remains the same. Changes in the companies included in the average are rare. Nevertheless, since 1990, 11 companies have been replaced to reflect the decreasing importance of manufacturing in the U.S. economy. For example, BETHLEHEM STEEL, which had been in "The Dow" since 1928, was replaced in March 1997 by WAL-MART. In 1999, the first two NASDAQ companies were added to "The Dow"—MICROSOFT and INTEL. The 30 companies included in the average as of October 16, 2000, are listed in Exhibit 11-1. The 30 companies in the average are listed every day in *The Wall Street Journal*, often on page C3.[1]

setting the stage

DOW JONES & COMPANY is an appropriate symbol of capitalism—a corporation that has done business in and around the spiritual heart of capitalistic finance, the New York Stock Exchange, for over one hundred years. With the disintegration of the former Soviet Union and the rapid conversion of China into a "socialist market" economy, it seems that the economic battle of capitalism and communism has been won by capitalism. As the history of many of the companies profiled in earlier chapters (MICROSOFT, SEARS, YAHOO!, GENERAL ELECTRIC) illustrates, the true story of capitalism is not the story of rich "capitalists" exploiting the masses, but rather the story of unknown individuals using a free market to find outside investor financing that will turn their ideas into reality. Accounting for investor financing is the topic of this chapter.

This is the second chapter on financing activities. In the previous chapter, financing through borrowing (debt) was discussed. Another way organizations raise money to finance operations is from investments by owners. In corporations, those investments take the form of stock purchases. In proprietorships and partnerships, they take the form of capital investments in the business. Exhibit 11-2 shows the financial statement items that will be covered in this chapter.

1 This description is based on information obtained from Dow Jones & Company History at http://dowjones.com; Dow Jones & Company, *International Directory of Company Histories*, vol. 19 (Detroit: St. James Press, 1998), pp. 128–131.

e x h i b i t   1 1 - 1   The 30 Firms Included in the Dow Jones Industrial Average (as of October 16, 2000)

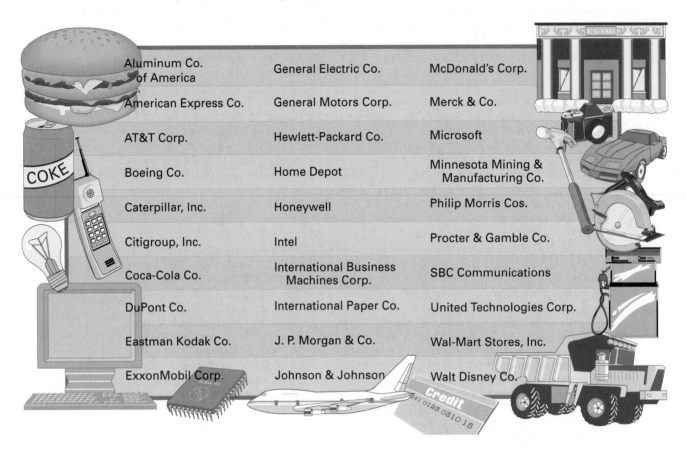

Aluminum Co. of America	General Electric Co.	McDonald's Corp.
American Express Co.	General Motors Corp.	Merck & Co.
AT&T Corp.	Hewlett-Packard Co.	Microsoft
Boeing Co.	Home Depot	Minnesota Mining & Manufacturing Co.
Caterpillar, Inc.	Honeywell	Philip Morris Cos.
Citigroup, Inc.	Intel	Procter & Gamble Co.
Coca-Cola Co.	International Business Machines Corp.	SBC Communications
DuPont Co.	International Paper Co.	United Technologies Corp.
Eastman Kodak Co.	J. P. Morgan & Co.	Wal-Mart Stores, Inc.
ExxonMobil Corp.	Johnson & Johnson	Walt Disney Co.

e x h i b i t   1 1 - 2   Financial Statement Items Covered in This Chapter

Balance Sheet

Stockholders' equity
 Contributed capital
 Retained earnings
 Treasury stock

Statement of Cash Flows

Financing activities
 Sale of stock
 Purchase of
  treasury stock
 Payments of
  dividends

Certain basic characteristics are common to all investor financing, no matter what the form of business. The first is that owner investments affect the equity accounts of the business. Second, together with the liabilities, these owners' equity accounts show the sources of the cash that was used to buy the assets. There are three primary ways to bring money into a business: borrowing (debt financing), selling owners' interests (equity financing), and earning profits (also reflected in the equity accounts through the retained earnings account).

In the first part of this chapter, we illustrate the accounting for equity financing in the context of corporations. In the expanded material section of the chapter, we show how equity financing is accounted for in proprietorships and partnerships.

1

Distinguish between debt and equity financing, and describe the advantages and disadvantages of organizing a business as a proprietorship or a partnership.

RAISING EQUITY FINANCING

Most business owners do not have enough excess personal cash to establish and expand their companies. Therefore, they eventually need to look for money from outsiders, either in the form of loans or as funds contributed by investors. The business issues associated with investor financing are summarized in the time line in Exhibit 11-3.

The factors affecting the choice between borrowing and seeking additional investment funds are described in this section of the chapter. This section also outlines the advantages and disadvantages of organizing a business as a proprietorship or a partnership. The decision to incorporate and the process that a corporation follows in soliciting investor funds are described in the next section. The bulk of the chapter is devoted to the accounting procedures used to give a proper reporting of stockholders' equity to the investors. Of course, proper financial reporting to current and potential investors is one of the primary reasons for the existence of financial accounting.

Difference between a Loan and an Investment

Imagine that you own a small business and need $40,000 for expansion. What is the difference between borrowing the $40,000 and finding a partner who will invest the $40,000? If you borrow the money, you must guarantee to repay the $40,000 with interest. If you fail to make these payments, the lender can haul you into court and use the power of the law to force repayment. On the other hand, if your company does very well and you generate more than enough cash to repay the $40,000 plus interest, the lender does not get to share in your success. You owe the lender $40,000 plus interest and not a penny more. So, a loan is characterized by a fixed, legal obligation to repay a specified amount, whether the borrowing company performs poorly or performs well.

If you receive $40,000 in investment funds from a new partner, the partner now shares in your company's failures and successes. If business is bad and the investor is never able to recover

---

exhibit 11-3   Time Line of Business Issues Involved with Investor Financing

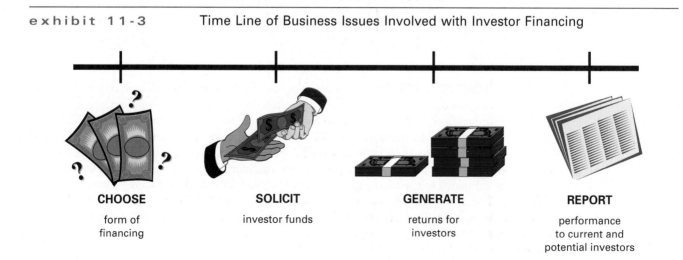

CHOOSE
form of
financing

SOLICIT
investor funds

GENERATE
returns for
investors

REPORT
performance
to current and
potential investors

his or her $40,000 investment—well, that's the way it goes. The law will not help the investor recover the investment because the very nature of an investment is that the investor accepts the risk of losing everything. However, in exchange for accepting this risk, the investor also gets to share in the success if the company does well. For example, if you had loaned $40,000 to Bill Gates for **MICROSOFT**'s expansion back in 1986, you would have been repaid the $40,000 plus a little interest. If you had invested that same $40,000 in Microsoft, however, your investment would have grown in value to $14.4 million by October 2000. Thus, an investment is characterized by a higher risk of losing your money, balanced by the chance of sharing in the wealth if the company does well.

Proprietorships and Partnerships

As explained in Chapter 2, a business can be organized as a proprietorship, a partnership, or a corporation. These three types of organization are merely different types of legal contracts that define the rights and responsibilities of the owner or owners of the business. The advantages and disadvantages of proprietorships and partnerships are discussed below. Corporations are discussed in the next section.

proprietorship A business owned by one person.

partnership An association of two or more individuals or organizations to carry on economic activity.

A **proprietorship** is a business owned by one person. A **partnership** is a business owned by two or more persons or entities. In most respects, proprietorships and partnerships are similar to each other but very different from corporations. Both a proprietorship and a partnership are characterized by ease of formation, limited life, and unlimited liability.

EASE OF FORMATION Proprietorships and partnerships can be formed with few legal formalities. When a person decides to establish a proprietorship, he or she merely acquires the necessary cash, inventory, equipment, and other assets; obtains a business license; and begins providing goods or services to customers. The same is true for a partnership, except that because two or more persons are involved, they must decide together which assets will be acquired and how business will be conducted.

LIMITED LIFE Because proprietorships and partnerships are not legal entities that are separate and distinct from their owners, they are easily terminated. In the case of a proprietorship, the owner can decide to dissolve the business at any time. For a partnership, anything that terminates or changes the contract between the partners legally dissolves the partnership. Among the events that dissolve a partnership are

1. the death or withdrawal of a partner,
2. the bankruptcy of a partner,
3. the admission of a new partner,
4. the retirement of a partner, or
5. the completion of the project for which the partnership was formed.

The occurrence of any of these events does not necessarily mean that a partnership must cease business; rather, the existing partnership is legally terminated, and another partnership must be formed.

UNLIMITED LIABILITY Proprietorships and partnerships have unlimited liability, which means that the proprietor or partners are personally responsible for all debts of the business. If a partnership is in poor financial condition, creditors first attempt to satisfy their claims from the assets of the partnership. After those assets are exhausted, creditors may seek payment from the personal assets of the partners. In addition, because partners are responsible for one another's actions (within the scope of the partnership), creditors may seek payment for liabilities created by a departed or bankrupt partner from the personal assets of the remaining partners. This unlimited liability feature is probably the single most significant disadvantage of a proprietorship or partnership. It can deter a wealthy person from joining a partnership for fear of losing personal assets.

to summarize

A loan is a fixed, legal obligation to repay a specified amount, whether the borrowing company performs poorly or performs well. With an investment, the investor risks losing the investment funds if the company performs poorly but shares in the wealth if the company does well. A proprietorship is a business owned by one person. A partnership is a business owned by two or more persons. Both types of businesses are easy to start and easy to terminate. A major disadvantage of proprietorships and partnerships is the unlimited liability of the owner or partners.

2

Describe the basic characteristics of a corporation and the nature of common and preferred stock.

corporation A legal entity chartered by a state; ownership is represented by transferable shares of stock.

CORPORATIONS AND CORPORATE STOCK

Corporations are the dominant form of business enterprise in the United States. Established as separate legal entities, **corporations** are legally distinct from the persons responsible for their creation. In many respects, they are accorded the same rights as individuals; they can conduct business, be sued, enter into contracts, and own property. Firms are incorporated by the state in which they are organized and are subject to that state's laws and requirements.

Characteristics of a Corporation

Corporations have several characteristics that distinguish them from proprietorships and partnerships. These characteristics are discussed below.

limited liability The legal protection given stockholders whereby they are responsible for the debts and obligations of a corporation only to the extent of their capital contributions.

LIMITED LIABILITY   **Limited liability** means that in the event of corporate bankruptcy, the maximum financial loss any stockholder can sustain is his or her investment in the corporation (unless fraud can be proved). Because a corporation is a separate legal entity and is responsible for its own acts and obligations, creditors usually cannot look beyond the corporation's assets for satisfaction of their claims. This limited liability feature is probably the main reason for the

Corporations are the dominant form of business in the United States. As a corporation, MICROSOFT is a legal entity, and its ownership is represented by transferable shares of stock.

Investing in the Stock Market "October," said Mark Twain, "is one of the peculiarly dangerous months to speculate in stocks. Others are July, January, September, April, November, May, March, June, December, August, and February." Despite Mark Twain's warning, stocks have always been one of the most prestigious and desired investments. These days, stock trading is easier than ever. There are scores of Internet stock trading firms that will allow you to buy and sell as many shares as you wish for less than $10 per trade. For some people, Internet stock trading has become the ultimate video game, with shooting lasers and fighting ninjas being replaced by stock price charts and the Federal Reserve Board.

This textbook won't make you an expert in picking promising stocks. In fact, you should be suspicious of any book or investment adviser claiming to have the secrets to deciphering the stock market. Here are some practical guidelines to help you avoid some of the pitfalls when deciding to buy stock:

of the corporation. In smaller companies, the board of directors is usually made up of members of that management team.

Several types of stock can be authorized by the charter and issued by the corporation. The most familiar types are common stock and preferred stock, and the major difference between them concerns the degree to which their holders are allowed to participate in the rights of ownership of the corporation.

Common Stock

> **common stock** The most frequently issued class of stock; usually, it provides a voting right but is secondary to preferred stock in dividend and liquidation rights.

Certain basic rights are inherent in the ownership of **common stock**. These rights are as follows:

1. The right to vote in corporate matters such as the election of the board of directors or the undertaking of major actions such as the purchase of another company.
2. The preemptive right, which permits existing stockholders to purchase additional shares whenever stock is issued by the corporation. This allows common stockholders to maintain the same percentage of ownership in the company if they choose to do so.
3. The right to receive cash dividends if they are paid. As explained later, corporations do not have to pay cash dividends, and the amount received by common stockholders is sometimes limited.
4. The right to ownership of all corporate assets once obligations to everyone else have been satisfied. This means that once all loans have been repaid and the claims of the preferred stockholders have been met (as discussed below), all the excess assets belong to the common stockholders.

> **fyi**
>
> Occasionally, a corporation will have more than one class of common stock. For example, Dow Jones & Company has common stock and Class B common stock. Each Class B share gets 10 votes in corporate matters, and most of the Class B shares are owned by the descendants of Clarence Barron.

In essence, the common stockholders of a corporation are the true owners of the business. They delegate their decision-making authority to the board of directors, who in turn delegate authority for day-to-day operations to managers hired for that purpose. Thus, a distinguishing characteristic of business ownership as a common stockholder of a corporation is a clear separation between owning the business and operating the business.

Preferred Stock

> **preferred stock** A class of stock that usually provides dividend and liquidation preferences over common stock.

The term "preferred stock" is somewhat misleading because it gives the impression that **preferred stock** is better than common stock. Preferred stock isn't better; it's different. A good way to think of preferred stock is that preferred stockholders give up some of the ownership rights of the common stockholders in exchange for some of the protection enjoyed by lenders.

In most cases, preferred stockholders are not allowed to vote for the corporate board of directors. In addition, preferred stockholders are usually allowed to receive only a fixed cash dividend, meaning that if the company does well, preferred stockholders do not get to share in the

1. Do not make hasty, emotional decisions about buying and selling stocks.
2. Do not "fall in love" with stocks so that you are no longer objective in appraising them.
3. Remember, you will seldom, if ever, buy stocks at their lowest price and sell them at their highest price.
4. There are stock market "fads," so when you buy at the height of a stock's popularity, you almost always pay too much.

5. Don't invest in stocks unless you can afford to lose the money you invest or at least have no access to it for a long time.
6. Plan to hold your stock investments for a long time. Most stock market millionaires were not speculators, and commissions on frequent sales and purchases will eat up your short-term gains.

Source: W. S. Albrecht, *Money Wise* (Salt Lake City, Utah: Deseret Book Company, 1983), pp. 134–139.

success. In exchange for these limitations, in the event that the corporation is liquidated, preferred stockholders are entitled to receive their cash dividends and have their claims fully paid before any cash is paid to common stockholders.

Preferred stock may also include other types of privileges, the most common of which is convertibility. **Convertible preferred stock** is preferred stock that can be converted to common stock at a specified conversion rate. For example, the notes to **MICROSOFT**'s 1999 financial statements (see Appendix A) reveal that the investors who purchased 12.5 million shares of Microsoft convertible preferred stock in December 1996 were able to exchange those preferred shares (if they wish) for Microsoft common stock beginning in December 1999. Convertible preferred stock can be very appealing to investors. They can enjoy the dividend privileges of the preferred stock while having the option to convert to common stock if the market value of the common stock increases significantly. By issuing shares of stock with varying rights and privileges, companies can appeal to a wider range of investors.

> **convertible preferred stock**
> Preferred stock that can be converted to common stock at a specified conversion rate.

to summarize

A corporation is a business entity that has a legal existence separate from that of its owners; it can conduct business, own property, and enter into contracts. The five major features of a corporation are (1) limited liability for stockholders, (2) easy transferability of ownership, (3) the ability to raise large amounts of capital, (4) separate taxation, and (5) for large corporations, closer regulation by government. Common stock confers four basic rights upon its owners: (1) the right to vote in corporate matters, (2) the right to maintain proportionate ownership, (3) the right to receive cash dividends, and (4) the ownership of all excess corporate assets upon liquidation of the corporation. Preferred stock typically carries preferential claims to dividend and liquidation privileges but has no voting rights.

3

Account for the issuance and repurchase of common and preferred stock.

ACCOUNTING FOR STOCK

In this section we focus on the accounting for the issuance of stock as well as the accounting for stock repurchases.

Issuance of Stock

par value A nominal value assigned to and printed on the face of each share of a corporation's stock.

Each share of common stock usually has a **par value** printed on the face of the stock certificate. For example, the common stock of DOW JONES & COMPANY has a $1 par value. This par value has little to do with the market value of the shares. In October 2000, each Dow Jones common share with a $1 par value was selling for about $55 per share. When par-value stock sells for a price above par, it is said to sell at a premium. In most states it is illegal to issue stock for a price below par value. If stock were issued at a discount (below par), stockholders could later be held liable to make up the difference between their investment and the par value of the shares they purchased. The par value multiplied by the total number of shares outstanding is usually equal to a company's "legal capital," and it represents the amount of the invested funds that cannot be returned to the investors as long as the corporation is in existence. This legal capital requirement was originally intended to protect a company's creditors; without it, excessive dividends could be paid, leaving nothing for creditors. The par value really was of more importance a hundred years ago and is something of a historical oddity today. These days, most states allow the sale of no-par stock.

When par-value stock is issued by a corporation, usually Cash is debited, and the appropriate stockholders' equity accounts are credited. For par-value common stock, the equity accounts credited are Common Stock, for an amount equal to the par value, and Paid-In Capital in Excess of Par, Common Stock, for the premium on the common stock.

To illustrate, we will assume that the Boston Lakers Basketball Team (a corporation) issued 1,000 shares of $1 par-value common stock for $50 per share. The entry to record the stock issuance is:

Cash (1,000 shares × $50)	50,000	
Common Stock (1,000 shares × $1 par value)		1,000
Paid-In Capital in Excess of Par,		
Common Stock (1,000 shares × $49)		49,000
Issued 1,000 shares of $1 par-value common stock at		
$50 per share.		

contributed capital The portion of owners' equity contributed by investors (the owners) in exchange for shares of stock.

A similar entry would be made if the stock being issued were preferred stock. The total par value of the common and preferred stock, along with the associated amounts of paid-in capital in excess of par, constitutes a corporation's **contributed capital**.

This illustration points out two important elements in accounting for the issuance of stock: (1) the equity accounts identify the type of stock being issued (common or preferred), and (2) the proceeds from the sale of the stock are divided into the portion attributable to its par value and the portion paid in excess of par value. These distinctions are important because the owners' equity section of the balance sheet should correctly identify the specific sources of capital so that the respective rights of the various stockholders can be known.

If the stock being issued has no par value, only one credit is included in the entry. To illustrate, assume that the Lakers' stock does not have a par value and that the corporation issued 1,000 shares for $50 per share. The entry to record this stock issuance would be:

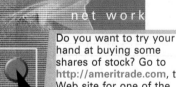

Cash	50,000	
Common Stock		50,000
Issued 1,000 shares of no-par stock at $50 per share.		

Although stock is usually issued for cash, other considerations may be involved. To illustrate the kinds of entries made when stock is issued for noncash considerations, we will assume that a prospective stockholder exchanged a piece of land for 5,000 shares of the Boston Lakers' $1 par-value common stock. Assuming the market value of the stock at the date of the exchange was $40 per share, the entry is:

Land (5,000 shares × $40)	200,000	
Common Stock (5,000 shares × $1)		5,000
Paid-In Capital in Excess of Par,		
Common Stock (5,000 shares × $39)		195,000
Issued 5,000 shares of $1 par-value common stock for land		
(5,000 shares × $40 per share = $200,000).		

When noncash considerations are received in payment for stock, the assets or services received should be recorded at the current market value of the stock issued. If the market value of the stock cannot be determined, the market value of the assets or services received should be used as the basis for recording the transaction.

Accounting for Stock Repurchases

Sometimes, when a company has excess cash or needs some of its shares of stock back from investors, it may purchase some of its own outstanding stock. This repurchased stock is called **treasury stock** by accountants. There are many reasons for a firm to buy its own stock. Five of the most common are that management:

treasury stock Issued stock that has subsequently been reacquired by the corporation.

1. wants the stock for a profit-sharing, bonus, or stock-option plan for employees,
2. feels that the stock is selling for an unusually low price and is a good buy,
3. wants to stimulate trading in the company's stock,
4. wants to remove some shares from the market in order to avoid a hostile takeover, or
5. wants to increase reported earnings per share by reducing the number of shares of stock outstanding.

Many successful U.S. companies have ongoing stock repurchase plans. For example, **MICROSOFT** disclosed in its 1999 annual report (Appendix A) that it spent $2.95 billion in 1999 to repurchase 44 million of its own shares. **COCA-COLA** spent $2.8 billion in the years 1997–1999 repurchasing its own shares. The most aggressive stock buyback program is **GENERAL ELECTRIC**'s—a number of years ago GE announced its intention to spend a total of $13 billion buying back its own shares. As of the end of 1999, GE had already exceeded this amount, spending a cumulative total of $22.6 billion on stock repurchases.

When a firm purchases stock of another company, the investment is included as an asset on the balance sheet. However, a corporation cannot own part of itself, so treasury stock is not considered an asset. Instead, it is a contra-equity account and is included on the balance sheet as a deduction from stockholders' equity. Think of it this way: when a corporation issues shares, its equity is increased; when the corporation buys those shares back, its equity is reduced. The reporting of treasury stock is illustrated in the stockholders' equity section of the balance sheet for General Electric in Exhibit 11-4.

 For General Electric, the total amount invested by stockholders is $11,384 million, which is the sum of common stock at par ($594 million) and paid-in capital in excess of par (other capital of $10,790 million). And yet GE has spent $22,567 million buying back shares from stockholders. How is this possible?

Notice that the $22.567 billion spent by General Electric to buy back its own shares as of December 31, 1999, is shown as a subtraction from total share owners' equity. By the way, the "other capital" included in GE's equity section is primarily composed of paid-in capital in excess of par. Also, the "unrealized gains" and "currency translation adjustment" items are quite interesting and controversial, as will be explained in a later section.

Treasury stock is usually accounted for on a cost basis; that is, the stock is debited at its cost (market value) on the date of repurchase. To illustrate, we assume that 100 shares of the $1 par-value common stock were reacquired by the Boston Lakers for $60 per share. The entry to record the repurchase is:

Treasury Stock, Common	6,000	
Cash (100 shares × $60)		6,000
Purchased 100 shares of treasury stock at $60 per share.		

exhibit 1 1 - 4   Share Owners' Equity for General Electric

	1999	1998
General Electric Company **December 31, 1999 and 1998** **Share Owners' Equity** **(in millions of U.S. dollars)**		
Common stock	$ 594	$ 594
Unrealized gains on investment securities—net	626	2,402
Accumulated currency translation adjustments	(1,370)	(738)
Other capital	10,790	6,808
Retained earnings	54,484	48,553
Less common stock held in treasury	(22,567)	(18,739)
Total share owners' equity	$42,557	$38,880

The effect of this entry is to reduce both total assets (Cash) and total stockholders' equity by $6,000.

When treasury stock is reissued, the treasury stock account must be credited for the original amount paid to reacquire the stock. If the treasury stock's reissuance price is greater than its cost, an additional credit must be made to an account called Paid-In Capital, Treasury Stock. Together, these credits show the net increase in total stockholders' equity. At the same time, the cash account is increased by the total amount received upon reissuance of the treasury stock.

To illustrate, we assume that 40 of the 100 shares of the treasury stock that were originally purchased for $60 per share are reissued at $80 per share. The entry to record that reissuance is:

Cash (40 shares × $80).................................	3,200	
Treasury Stock, Common (40 shares × $60 cost)...........		2,400
Paid-In Capital, Treasury Stock [40 × ($80 − $60)]...........		800
Reissued 40 shares of treasury stock at $80 per share.		

The company now has a balance of $3,600 in the treasury stock account (60 shares at $60 per share).

Sometimes the reissuance price of treasury stock is less than its cost. As before, the entry involves a debit to Cash for the amount received and a credit to Treasury Stock for the cost of the stock. However, because an amount less than the repurchase cost has been received, an additional debit is required. The debit is to Paid-In Capital, Treasury Stock if there is a balance in that account from previous transactions, or to Retained Earnings if there is no balance in the paid-in capital, treasury stock account.

To illustrate, we will consider two more treasury stock transactions. First, we assume that another 30 shares of treasury stock are reissued for $40 per share, $20 less than their cost. Because Paid-In Capital, Treasury Stock has a balance of $800, the entry to record this transaction is:

Cash (30 shares × $40)	1,200	
Paid-In Capital, Treasury Stock................................	600	
Treasury Stock, Common (30 shares × $60 cost)................		1,800
Reissued 30 shares of treasury stock at $40 per share; *original cost was $60 per share.*		

Equity Financing | **Chapter 11** | f523

Note that after this transaction is recorded, the balance in Paid-In Capital, Treasury Stock is $200 ($800 − $600).

Next, we assume that the company reissues 20 additional shares at $45 per share. The entry to record this transaction is:

Cash (20 shares × $45)	900	
Paid-In Capital, Treasury Stock	200	
Retained Earnings	100	
Treasury Stock (20 shares × $60 cost)		1,200
Reissued 20 shares of treasury stock at $45 per share; original cost was $60 per share.		

In this transaction, the selling price was $300 less than the cost of the treasury stock. Because the paid-in capital, treasury stock account had a balance of only $200, Retained Earnings was debited for the remaining $100.

Balance Sheet Presentation

We have discussed the ways in which stock transactions affect owners' equity accounts. We will now show how these accounts are summarized and presented on the balance sheet. The following data, with the addition of the preferred stock information in (1), summarize the stock transactions of the Boston Lakers shown earlier:

1. $40 par-value preferred stock: issued 1,000 shares at $45 per share.
2. $1 par-value common stock: issued 1,000 shares at $50 per share.
3. $1 par-value common stock: issued 5,000 shares for land with a fair market value of $200,000.
4. Treasury stock, common: purchased 100 shares at $60; reissued 40 shares at $80; reissued 30 shares at $40; reissued 20 shares at $45.

With these data, and assuming a Retained Earnings balance of $100,000, the stockholders' equity section would be as shown in Exhibit 11-5.

---

exhibit 11-5   Stockholders' Equity for Boston Lakers

Boston Lakers Basketball Team **Stockholders' Equity**	
Preferred stock ($40 par value, 1,000 shares issued and outstanding)	$ 40,000
Common stock ($1 par value, 6,000 shares issued, 5,990 shares outstanding)*	6,000
Paid-in capital in excess of par, preferred stock	5,000
Paid-in capital in excess of par, common stock	244,000
Total contributed capital	$295,000
Retained earnings (to be discussed)	100,000
Total contributed capital and retained earnings	$395,000
Less treasury stock (10 shares of $1 par common at cost of $60 per share)	(600)
Total stockholders' equity	$394,400

*Treasury shares are described as being issued but not outstanding. Thus, 6,000 common shares have been issued, but only 5,990 are outstanding because 10 are held by the Boston Lakers as treasury shares.

to summarize

When a company issues stock, it debits Cash or a noncash account (Property, for example) and credits various stockholders' equity accounts. Shares typically are assigned a par value, which is usually small in relation to the market value of the shares. Amounts received upon issuance of shares are divided into par value and paid-in capital in excess of par. A company's own stock that is repurchased is known as treasury stock and is included in the financial statements as a contra-stockholders' equity account. Treasury stock is usually accounted for on a cost basis. The stockholders' equity section of a balance sheet contains separate accounts for each type of stock issued, amounts paid in excess of par values, treasury stock, and retained earnings.

4

Understand the factors that affect retained earnings, describe the factors determining whether a company can and should pay cash dividends, and account for cash dividends.

retained earnings The portion of a corporation's owners' equity that has been earned from profitable operations and not distributed to stockholders.

dividends Distributions to the owners (stockholders) of a corporation.

cash dividend A cash distribution of earnings to stockholders.

fyi

Fortune magazine maintains a list of the top 50 e-companies, called the Fortune e-50. A random sample of 10 of these companies indicated that only one of the 10 paid cash dividends to common stockholders in 1999. Thus, we see that high-tech, high-growth companies are not likely to pay cash dividends. By the way, the only one of the sampled e-50 companies to pay cash dividends to common stockholders was IBM, not exactly a young start-up.

RETAINED EARNINGS

Common stockholders can invest money in a corporation in two ways. First, as described in the previous section, common stockholders can buy shares of stock. Second, when the corporation makes money, the common stockholders can allow the corporation to keep those earnings to be reinvested in the business. **Retained earnings** is the name given to the aggregate amount of corporate earnings that have been reinvested in the business. The retained earnings balance is increased each year by net income and decreased by losses, dividends, and some treasury stock transactions (as illustrated earlier).

Remember, retained earnings is not the same as cash. In fact, a company can have a large Retained Earnings balance and be without cash, or it can have a lot of cash and a very small Retained Earnings balance. For example, on December 31, 1999, DOW JONES & COMPANY had a Cash balance of $86 million but a Retained Earnings balance of $810 million. Although both Cash and Retained Earnings are usually increased when a company has earnings, they typically are increased by different amounts. This occurs for two reasons: (1) the company's net income, which increases Retained Earnings, is accrual-based, not cash-based; and (2) cash from earnings may be invested in productive assets such as inventories, used to pay off loans, or spent in any number of ways, many of which do not affect net income or retained earnings. In summary, cash is an asset; retained earnings is one source of financing (along with borrowing and direct stockholder investment) that a corporation can use to get funds to acquire assets.

Cash Dividends

If you had your own business and wanted to withdraw money for personal use, you would simply withdraw it from the company's checking account or cash register. In a corporation, a formal action by the board of directors is required before money can be distributed to the owners. In addition, such payments must be made on a pro rata basis. That is, each owner must receive a proportionate amount on the basis of ownership percentage. These pro rata distributions to owners are called **dividends**. When paid in the form of cash, they are called **cash dividends**. The amount of dividends an individual stockholder receives depends on the number of shares owned and on the per-share amount of the dividend.

SHOULD A COMPANY PAY CASH DIVIDENDS?   Note that a company does not have to pay cash dividends. Theoretically, a company that does not pay dividends should be able to reinvest its earnings in assets that will enable it to grow more rapidly than its dividend-paying competitors. This added growth will presumably be reflected in increases in the per-share price of the stock. In practice, most public companies pay regular cash dividends, but some well-known companies do not. For example, MICROSOFT has never paid cash dividends to its common stockholders.

So, should a corporation pay cash dividends or not? Well, the surprising answer is that no one knows the answer to that question. Ask your finance professor what he or she thinks. Although no one knows the theoretically best dividend policy, three general observations can be made:

- Stable companies pay out a large portion of their income as cash dividends.
- Growing companies (such as Microsoft) pay out a small portion of their income as cash dividends. They keep the funds inside the company for expansion.
- Companies are very cautious about raising dividends to a new level because once investors come to expect a certain level of dividends, they see it as very bad news if the company reduces the dividends back to the old level.

STOP & THINK If you were a Microsoft shareholder, would you want to receive a high level of cash dividends, or would you prefer that Bill Gates use your share of the profits for business expansion?

Although cash dividends are the most common type of dividend, corporations can distribute other types of dividends as well. A stock dividend is a distribution of additional shares of stock to stockholders. Stock dividends will be discussed in the expanded material section of this chapter. A property dividend is a distribution of corporate assets (for example, the stock of another firm) to stockholders. Property dividends are quite rare. In this section, only the accounting for cash dividends will be discussed.

ACCOUNTING FOR CASH DIVIDENDS   Three important dates are associated with dividends: (1) declaration date, (2) date of record, and (3) payment date. The first is when the board of directors formally declares its intent to pay a dividend. On this **declaration date**, the company becomes legally obligated to pay the dividend. Assuming that the board of directors votes on December 15, 2003, to declare an $8,000 dividend, this liability may be recorded as follows:

declaration date The date on which a corporation's board of directors formally decides to pay a dividend to stockholders.

Dividends	8,000	
Dividends Payable		8,000
Declared dividend on December 15, 2003.		

At the end of the year, the dividends account is closed to Retained Earnings by the following entry:

Retained Earnings	8,000	
Dividends		8,000
To close Dividends to Retained Earnings.		

From this entry, you can see that a declaration of dividends reduces Retained Earnings and, eventually, the amount of cash on hand. Thus, though not considered to be an expense, dividends do reduce the amount a company could otherwise invest in productive assets.

Alternatively, a declaration of dividends can be recorded by debiting Retained Earnings directly. However, using the dividends account instead of Retained Earnings allows a company to keep separate records of dividends paid to preferred and common stockholders. Whichever method is used, the end result is the same: a decrease in Retained Earnings.

date of record The date selected by a corporation's board of directors on which the stockholders of record are identified as those who will receive dividends.

The second important dividend date is the **date of record**. Falling somewhere between the declaration date and the payment date, this is the date selected by the board of directors on which the stockholders of record are identified as those who will receive dividends. Because many corporate stocks are in flux—being bought and sold daily—it is important that the stockholders who will receive the dividends be identified. No journal entry is required on the date of record; the date of record is simply noted in the minutes of the directors' meeting and in a letter to stockholders.

dividend payment date The date on which a corporation pays dividends to its stockholders.

As you might expect, the third important date is the **dividend payment date**. This is the date on which, by order of the board of directors, dividends will be paid. The entry to record a dividend payment would typically be:

Dividends Payable 8,000	
Cash	8,000
Paid dividends declared on December 15, 2003.	

The following press release, made by Dow Jones on January 19, 2000 (declaration date), identifies both the date of record and the dividend payment date:

> Dow Jones & Company announced that its Board of Directors voted today to increase the quarterly dividend on the common stock and Class B common stock to 25 cents a share from 24 cents a share. The 4.2% increase, the first for Dow Jones in four years, raises the indicated annual dividend rate to one dollar per share. The first new quarterly dividend is payable March 1 to shareholders of record as of February 1.

fyi

When Dow Jones announced its dividend increase on January 19, 2000, its stock price increased by just 1.9% over the following two days. This is a small price rise and may suggest that investors already were aware of the planned dividend increase.

As mentioned earlier, once a dividend-paying pattern has been established, the expectation of dividends is built into the per-share price of the stock. A reduction in the dividend usually produces a sharp drop in the price. Similarly, an increased dividend usually triggers an increase in the stock price. Dividend increases are usually considered to set a precedent, indicating that future dividends will be at this per-share amount or more. With this in mind, boards of directors are careful about increasing or decreasing dividends.

DIVIDEND PREFERENCES   When cash dividends are declared by a corporation that has both common and preferred stock outstanding, how the dividends are allocated to the two classes of investors depends on the rights of the preferred stockholders. These rights are identified when the stock is approved by the state. Two "dividend preferences," as they are called, are (1) current-dividend preference and (2) cumulative-dividend preference.

Current-Dividend Preference   Preferred stock has a dividend percentage associated with it and is typically described as follows: "5% preferred, $40 par-value stock, 1,000 shares outstanding." The first figure—"5%" in this example—is a percentage of the par value and can be any amount, depending on the particular stock. So, $2 per share (0.05 × $40 par) is the amount that will be paid in dividends to preferred stockholders each year that dividends are declared. The fact that preferred stock dividends are fixed at a specific percentage of their par value makes them somewhat similar to the interest paid to bondholders. The **current-dividend preference** requires that when dividends are paid, this percentage of the preferred stock's par value be paid to preferred stockholders before common stockholders receive any dividends.

current-dividend preference The right of preferred stockholders to receive current dividends before common stockholders receive dividends.

To illustrate the payment of different types of dividends, the following data from the Boston Lakers Basketball Team will be used throughout this section. (The various combinations of dividend preferences illustrated over the next few pages are summarized in Cases 1 to 4 in Exhibit 11-6.) As a reminder, the outstanding stock includes:

- Preferred stock: 5%, $40 par value, 1,000 shares issued and outstanding.
- Common stock: $1 par value, 6,000 shares issued, 5,990 shares outstanding.

e x h i b i t   1 1 - 6   Dividend Preferences: Summary of Cases 1 to 4

Case	Preferred Dividend Feature	Years in Arrears	Total Dividend	Preferred Dividend	Common Dividend
1	5%, Noncumulative	Not applicable	$ 1,500	$1,500	$ 0
2	5%, Noncumulative	Not applicable	3,000	2,000	1,000
3	5%, Cumulative	2	5,000	5,000	0
4	5%, Cumulative	2	11,000	6,000	5,000

To begin, note that, as with all preferred stock, the Lakers' 5% preferred stock has a current-dividend preference: Before any dividends can be paid to common stockholders, preferred stockholders must be paid a total of $2,000 ($40 × 0.05 × 1,000 shares). Thus, if only $1,500 of dividends are declared (Case 1), preferred stockholders will receive the entire dividend payment. If $3,000 are declared (Case 2), preferred stockholders will receive $2,000 and common stockholders, $1,000.

Cumulative-Dividend Preference   The **cumulative-dividend preference** can be quite costly for common stockholders because it requires that preferred stockholders be paid current dividends plus all unpaid dividends from past years before common stockholders receive anything. If dividends have been paid in all previous years, then only the current 5% must be paid to preferred stockholders. But if dividends on preferred stock were not paid in full in prior years, the cumulative deficiency must be paid before common stockholders receive anything.

With respect to the cumulative feature, it is important to repeat that companies are not required to pay dividends. Any past unpaid dividends are called **dividends in arrears**. Because they do not have to be paid unless dividends are declared in the future, dividends in arrears do not represent actual liabilities and thus are not recorded in the accounts. Instead, they are reported in the notes to the financial statements.

To illustrate the distribution of dividends for cumulative preferred stock, we will assume that the Boston Lakers Basketball Team has not paid any dividends for the last two years but has declared a dividend in the current year. The Lakers must pay $6,000 in dividends to preferred stockholders before they can give anything to the common stockholders. The calculation is as follows:

Dividends in arrears, 2 years	$4,000
Current dividend preference	
($40 × 0.05 × 1,000 shares)	2,000
Total	$6,000

Therefore, if the Lakers pay only $5,000 in dividends (Case 3), preferred stockholders will receive all the dividends, common stockholders will receive nothing, and there will still be dividends in arrears of $1,000 the next year. If $11,000 in dividends are paid (Case 4), preferred stockholders will receive $6,000, and common stockholders will receive $5,000.

The entries to record the declaration and payment of dividends in Case 4 are:

Date of Declaration

Dividends, Preferred Stock	6,000	
Dividends, Common Stock	5,000	
Dividends Payable		11,000
Declared dividends on preferred and common stock.		

Date of Payment

Dividends Payable	11,000	
Cash		11,000
Paid dividends on preferred and common stock.		

CONSTRAINTS ON PAYMENT OF CASH DIVIDENDS   Earlier in this section, the question was asked whether a company should pay cash dividends. A related question is: Can the company legally pay cash dividends? To illustrate, consider the following exaggerated scenario. Tricky Company obtains a corporate charter, borrows $1 million from Naïve Bank, pays out a $1 million cash dividend to the stockholders, and all the stockholders disappear to the Bahamas. Is this a legal possibility? No, it isn't, because the corporate right to declare cash dividends is

---

cumulative-dividend preference The right of preferred stockholders to receive current dividends plus all dividends in arrears before common stockholders receive any dividends.

dividends in arrears Missed dividends for past years that preferred stockholders have a right to receive under the cumulative-dividend preference if and when dividends are declared.

regulated by state law in order to protect creditors. The right to declare cash dividends is often linked to a company's Retained Earnings balance.

f y i

Delaware has a reputation for having the least restrictive dividend laws. This is one reason many of the major U.S. companies are incorporated in the state of Delaware.

In many states, a company is not allowed to pay cash dividends in an amount that would cause the retained earnings balance to be negative. Thus, if the retained earnings balance of the Boston Lakers were $8,500, the $11,000 dividend in Case 4 discussed above could not be paid, even if the Lakers had the available cash to make the payment. The incorporation laws in many states are less restrictive and allow the payment of cash dividends in excess of the retained earnings balance if, for example, current earnings are strong or the market value of the assets is high.

Frequently, lenders do not rely on state incorporation laws to protect them from excess cash dividend payments by corporations to which they lend money. Instead, the loan contract itself includes restrictions on the payment of cash dividends during the period that the loan is outstanding. In this way, lenders are able to prevent cash that should be used to repay loans from being paid to stockholders as dividends.

Dividend Payout Ratio

dividend payout ratio A measure of the percentage of earnings paid out in dividends; computed by dividing cash dividends by net income.

A ratio of interest to stockholders is the **dividend payout ratio**. This ratio indicates the percentage of net income paid out during the year in the form of cash dividends and is computed as follows:

$$\text{Dividend payout ratio} = \frac{\text{Cash dividends}}{\text{Net income}}$$

Dividend payout ratio values for Dow Jones, Microsoft, and **GENERAL ELECTRIC** for 1999 are computed below. The numbers are in millions.

	Dow Jones	Microsoft	General Electric
Cash dividends	$87	$28	$4,786
Net income	$272	$7,785	$10,717
Dividend payout ratio	32.0%	0.4%	44.7%

Both Dow Jones and General Electric pay out between 30 and 50% of their annual income as dividends, a normal level for large U.S. corporations. Microsoft's low dividend payout ratio is indicative of a rapidly expanding company. In fact, all of the Microsoft cash dividends are preferred stock dividends; as mentioned earlier, Microsoft has never paid any cash dividends to its common stockholders.

to summarize

The retained earnings account reflects the total undistributed earnings of a business since incorporation. It is increased by net income and decreased by dividends, net losses, and some treasury stock transactions. The important dates associated with a cash dividend are the date of declaration, the date of record, and the payment date. Preferred stockholders can be granted a current and a cumulative preference for dividends over the rights of common stockholders. In some states, the payment of cash dividends is limited to an amount not to exceed the existing Retained Earnings balance. The dividend payout ratio (cash dividends divided by net income) reveals the percentage of net income that is paid out as cash dividends.

5

Describe the purpose of reporting comprehensive income in the equity section of the balance sheet, and prepare a statement of stockholders' equity.

OTHER EQUITY ITEMS

In addition to the two major categories of contributed capital and retained earnings, the equity section of a balance sheet often includes a number of miscellaneous items. These items are gains or losses that bypass the income statement when they are recognized. A further discussion of these items is given below.

Equity Items That Bypass the Income Statement

Since 1980, the equity sections of U.S. balance sheets have begun to fill up with a strange collection of items, each the subject of an accounting controversy. Two of these items are summarized below:

- *Foreign currency translation adjustment.* The foreign currency translation adjustment arises from the change in the equity of foreign subsidiaries (as measured in terms of U.S. dollars) that occurs as a result of changes in foreign currency exchange rates. For example, if the Japanese yen weakens relative to the U.S. dollar, the equity of Japanese subsidiaries of U.S. firms will decrease, in dollar terms. Before 1981, these changes were recognized as losses or gains on the income statement. Multinational firms disliked this treatment because it added volatility to reported earnings. The FASB changed the accounting rule, and now these changes are reported as direct adjustments to equity on the balance sheet, insulating the income statement from this aspect of foreign currency fluctuations.
- *Unrealized gains and losses on available-for-sale securities.* As will be explained in Chapter 12, available-for-sale securities are securities that a company purchased without intending to resell them immediately but also not necessarily planning to hold them forever. When the FASB was considering requiring securities to be reported at their market values on the balance sheet, companies complained about the income volatility that would be caused by recognizing these changes as gains or losses on the income statement. The FASB made the standard more acceptable to businesses by allowing unrealized gains and losses on available-for-sale securities to bypass the income statement and go straight to the equity section of the balance sheet.

The hodgepodge of direct equity adjustments described above is conceptually unsatisfying. These adjustments have arisen on a case-by-case basis as part of the FASB's effort to establish accounting standards that are accepted by the business community. As mentioned, many businesspeople are opposed to including these categories on the income statement because, they say, the income statement would become cluttered with gains and losses from market value changes, distracting from the purpose of the income statement, which is to focus on reporting profits from the activities of the business. The compromise that allows market values in the balance sheet while keeping the income statement uncluttered is the creation of a separate category of equity called **accumulated other comprehensive income**. Accumulated other comprehensive income is composed of certain market-related gains and losses that are not included in the computation of net income. It is important to remember that accumulated other comprehensive income is not income at all, but an equity category that summarizes the changes in equity that result during the period from market-related increases and decreases in the reported values of assets and liabilities. The reporting of accumulated other comprehensive income equity is illustrated in the 1999 equity section of **DOW JONES & COMPANY**, shown in Exhibit 11-7.

A **statement of comprehensive income** provides a place, outside the regular income statement, for reporting all the unrealized gains and losses that are reported as equity adjustments. The appeal of comprehensive income is that this approach preserves the traditional income statement (calming the fears of the business community) but allows unrealized gains and losses to be reported. In essence, comprehensive income makes it possible to recognize unrealized gains and losses so that current market values can be reported on the balance sheet without having those unrealized gains and losses affect the income statement.

The statement of comprehensive income is very new; U.S. companies have been required to present it starting December 31, 1998. Dow Jones &

accumulated other comprehensive income Certain market-related gains and losses that are not included in the computation of net income; for example, foreign currency translation adjustments and unrealized gains or losses on investments.

statement of comprehensive income A statement outlining the changes in accumulated comprehensive income that arose during the period.

Which will have a greater impact on a company's stock price: net income of $100 million or a $100 million unrealized gain from a change in exchange rates or securities prices? Explain your answer.

exhibit 11-7   Equity Section for Dow Jones & Company

Dow Jones & Company's Equity Section
(amounts in millions of dollars)

	1999	1998
Common stocks		
Common stock, par value $1 per share	$ 81,004	$ 80,899
Class B common stock, convertible, par value $1 per share . . .	21,177	21,282
	$ 102,181	$102,181
Additional paid-in capital.	137,487	137,479
Retained earnings	809,517	624,239
Accumulated other comprehensive income:		
Unrealized (loss) gain on investments	(941)	35,775
Cumulative translation adjustment.	(1,257)	38
	$1,046,987	$899,712
Less treasury stock	493,497	390,372
Total stockholders' equity	$ 553,490	$509,340

Company's comprehensive income presentation for 1999 is shown in Exhibit 11-8. Note that net income is one component in the computation of comprehensive income. For Dow Jones, 1997 was a particularly bad year, with each of the three reported elements of comprehensive income being negative. By the way, the large loss reported by Dow Jones in 1997 resulted from a $1 billion restructuring charge.

Statement of Stockholders' Equity

statement of stockholders' equity A financial statement that reports all changes in stockholders' equity.

Companies that have numerous changes in their stockholders' equity accounts during the year usually include a **statement of stockholders' equity** (also called a statement of changes in stockholders' equity) with their financial statements. This statement reconciles the beginning and ending balances for all stockholders' equity accounts reported on the balance sheet.

An illustrative statement of stockholders' equity from the 1999 annual report of Dow Jones & Company is presented in Exhibit 11-9. Note the following items in the statement:

- As mentioned earlier in the chapter, Dow Jones has two classes of common stock. Class B common shares with a par value of $105,000 were converted into ordinary common shares during the year.
- Dow Jones both bought and sold treasury shares during the year. The $4,539,000 decrease in Additional Paid-In Capital from treasury stock sales indicates that these treasury shares were resold for less than the $43,604,000 Dow Jones spent to repurchase them.

exhibit 11-8   Statement of Comprehensive Income for Dow Jones & Company

(in thousands)	1999	1998	1997
Net income (loss)	$272,429	$ 8,362	$(802,132)
Unrealized gain (loss) on investments.	2,124	32,379	(8,957)
Foreign currency translation adjustments	(1,295)	555	(3,644)
Other	(38,840)	9,023	—
Comprehensive income	$234,418	$50,319	$(814,733)

exhibit 11-9   Statement of Stockholders' Equity for Dow Jones & Company

CONSOLIDATED STATEMENT OF STOCKHOLDERS' EQUITY
Dow Jones & Company, Inc.
For the Year Ended December 31, 1999
(amounts in thousands of U.S. dollars)

	Common Stock	Class B Common Stock	Additional Paid-In Capital	Retained Earnings	Accumulated Other Comprehensive Income	Treasury Stock	Total
Balance, December 31, 1998	$80,899	$21,282	$137,479	$624,239	$35,813	$(390,372)	$509,340
Net income—1999.				272,429			$272,429
Unrealized gain on investments .					2,124		2,124
Translation adjustment					(1,295)		(1,295)
Other					(38,840)		(38,840)
Comprehensive income							$234,418
Dividends, $0.96 per share				(87,151)			(87,151)
Conversion of class B common stock into common stock.	105	(105)					
Other equity changes			4,547				4,547
Sales under stock compensation plans.			(4,539)			43,604	39,065
Purchase of treasury stock						(146,729)	(146,729)
Balance, December 31, 1999	$81,004	$21,177	$137,487	$809,517	$(2,198)	$(493,497)	$553,490

The last column in the statement reflects the total beginning and ending stockholders' equity account balances and all increases and decreases. Both the individual account balances and total Stockholders' Equity at December 31, 1999, are reported on the balance sheet of Dow Jones & Company.

to summarize

Accumulated other comprehensive income is not income at all, but an equity category that summarizes the effect on equity of certain market-related gains and losses. Two examples of items giving rise to accumulated other comprehensive income are market fluctuations in the value of some investment securities and changes in the value of assets and liabilities held by foreign subsidiaries that are caused by exchange rate changes. A statement of stockholders' equity summarizes the changes affecting all the different categories of equity during the year.

Three topics related to equity financing need additional explanation. These topics are stock dividends and stock splits, prior-period adjustments, and accounting for equity financing in proprietorships and partnerships.

6

Account for stock dividends
and distinguish them from
stock splits.

stock dividend A pro rata
distribution of additional
shares of stock to stock-
holders.

ACCOUNTING FOR STOCK DIVIDENDS

Corporations sometimes distribute additional shares of their own stock to stockholders instead of paying a cash dividend. These **stock dividends** must be distributed to each stockholder in proportion to the number of shares held. For example, if a company issues a 10% stock dividend, each stockholder will receive one additional share for every 10 shares owned.

There is considerable disagreement as to whether stockholders receive anything of value from a stock dividend. Certainly, they do not receive corporate assets, as with a cash dividend. Nor does any stockholder own a larger percentage of the corporation after the stock dividend than before, because each stockholder receives a pro rata share of the stock issued. In fact, one way to view a stock dividend is that the company has just cut the total ownership up into smaller pieces, with each stockholder owning proportionately more pieces, and nothing has really changed.

Those who argue that stock dividends have value to stockholders point out that companies frequently maintain the same level of cash dividends per share after the stock dividend as before. Accordingly, a stock dividend is an indirect method of increasing the amount of total cash dividends to be received in the future by each stockholder.

Stock dividends are also sometimes used to mollify investors and lull them into thinking that a company is maintaining its record of paying dividends when, in fact, it is not. Corporations that issue dividends each year do not want to miss a year, so for them a stock dividend can be a useful substitute for cash when poor financial circumstances make payment of cash dividends difficult. It isn't clear whether investors are actually fooled by this tactic.

To illustrate the accounting for a stock dividend and to keep the example simple, we will assume that the stockholders' equity of the Boston Lakers Basketball Team is:

Common stock ($1 par value, 10,000 shares issued and outstanding)	$ 10,000
Paid-in capital in excess of par	40,000
Retained earnings	80,000
Total stockholders' equity	$130,000

If a 10% stock dividend is declared and issued when the stock's current market price is $70, the entry to record the stock dividend is:

Retained Earnings (1,000 shares × $70)	70,000	
Common Stock (1,000 shares × $1 par)		1,000
Paid-In Capital in Excess of Par, Common Stock		69,000
Declared and issued a 10% common stock dividend.		

---

business environment essay

Do You Want a Stock Tip? The conventional wisdom is that the announcement of a stock split is good news. Academic research has confirmed this—a company's share value goes up an average of 3% in the one or two days after a 2-for-1 split announcement appears in *The Wall Street Journal*. But for most of us, this market reaction to the split news is too fast to allow us to make any money. By the time we learn about the split announcement and buy the shares, the share price will have already increased.

All is not lost, however. Additional academic research suggests that the share values of splitting firms continue to go up for at least a year after the split announcement. In fact, if you buy the shares of a company one week after that company announces a stock split, you will earn, on average, an extra 7.9% on your investment during the following year. This extra 7.9%

STOP & THINK Look at the Boston Lakers example and explain how the accounting rules discourage companies from declaring small stock dividends on a regular basis.

Because the dividend was 10% and there were previously 10,000 common shares outstanding, 1,000 additional shares were issued for the dividend. The accounting rules dictate that when a "small" stock dividend is issued, the market value of the newly issued shares is transferred out of Retained Earnings, just as if that same amount had been paid out in cash. If a stock dividend is relatively large, the accounting rules state that only the par value of the newly issued shares is to be transferred out of Retained Earnings. A small stock dividend is one that is less than 25%.

To illustrate the accounting for a large stock dividend, we assume the same stockholders' equity for the Boston Lakers Basketball Team, except that the stock dividend is now 30%. The entry is:

Retained Earnings...	3,000	
Common Stock (3,000 shares × $1 par).....................		3,000
Declared and issued a 30% common stock dividend		
(10,000 shares × 0.30 = 3,000 shares).		

The impact of the 10 and 30% stock dividends on the Boston Lakers' stockholders' equity is detailed below:

	Before Stock Dividend	With 10% Stock Dividend	With 30% Stock Dividend
Common stock, $1 par value	$ 10,000	$ 11,000	$ 13,000
Paid-in capital in excess of par............	40,000	109,000	40,000
Retained earnings	80,000	10,000	77,000
Total stockholders' equity	$130,000	$130,000	$130,000

Note that a stock dividend does not change the total amount of stockholders' equity, regardless of the size of the dividend. The only effect is to reallocate some of the stockholders' equity into different categories.

Stock Splits

Many investors, particularly individuals with limited amounts to invest, will not purchase stocks with high market prices per share. For example, consider the case of BERKSHIRE HATH-

is over and above what you would have earned if you had invested in a similar company that had not announced a stock split.

Before you run off to buy *The Wall Street Journal* or subscribe to an online service that will alert you to stock split announcements, here are two more pieces of advice. First, always be suspicious of unsolicited stock tips (such as the one just given). You should ask yourself: "If this is such a good idea, why hasn't the person who told me about it become rich?" Second,

always remember that academic research is a good thing to keep professors occupied during their spare time but is a notoriously unreliable (and unprofitable) basis for investment strategy.

Source: David L. Ikenberry, Graeme Rankine, and Earl K. Stice, "What Do Stock Splits Really Signal?" *Journal of Financial and Quantitative Analysis*, September 1996, pp. 357–375.

stock split The replacement of outstanding shares of stock with a greater number of new shares.

AWAY, which will be spotlighted in Chapter 12 and is the holding company controlled by Warren Buffett (one of the richest people in the United States). In October 2000, the shares of Berkshire Hathaway were selling for over $58,000 per share! At that price, not many of us can own even one share. To encourage more investors to buy their stocks, companies sometimes enact a **stock split**, replacing the outstanding shares with a larger number of new shares that sell at a lower price per share. MICROSOFT, for example, has split its stock eight times in order to bring down the price per share. Because of these splits, a single original share of Microsoft stock is now the equivalent (as of October 2000) of 144 shares.

In essence, the difference between a stock dividend and a stock split is that a stock split is usually bigger. Whereas a stock dividend might increase the number of shares outstanding by 10 or 25%, a stock split is likely to increase the number of shares outstanding by 50% (3-for-2 stock split), by 100% (2-for-1 stock split), or more. Actually, there is no clear distinction between a stock split and a stock dividend. For example, there are 50% stock dividends and there are also 5-for-4 stock splits.

From an accounting standpoint, stock splits are accounted for in one of two ways. The most common way is to simply account for the stock split as if it were a large stock dividend. Thus, a 2-for-1 stock split would be accounted for as a 100% stock dividend with the par value of the newly created shares transferred from Retained Earnings. Alternatively, a stock split can be accounted for by reducing the par value of all outstanding shares. For a 2-for-1 stock split accounted for in this way, the par value is halved and the number of shares is doubled. Thus, the total par value of stock outstanding is unchanged. For example, a firm with 20,000 shares of $10 par-value common stock outstanding may reduce the par value to $5 and increase the number of shares outstanding to 40,000. No journal entry is needed to account for a stock split in this way; the company merely makes note of the fact that the par value and number of shares outstanding have changed.

to summarize

Stock dividends are distributions of additional stock to stockholders. Although a stock dividend does not increase a stockholder's percentage of ownership in a corporation, the additional stock may provide the expectation of increased future cash dividends. With small stock dividends, Retained Earnings is debited at the stock's market value; with large stock dividends (25% or more), Retained Earnings is debited at the stock's par value. A stock split is also an increase in the number of shares outstanding. Generally, stock splits are authorized so that companies can attract more investors with a lower market price per share. A stock split can be accounted for as a large stock dividend or by lowering the par value of each share.

7

Explain prior-period adjustments and prepare a statement of retained earnings.

prior-period adjustments Adjustments made directly to Retained Earnings in order to correct errors in the financial statements of prior periods.

PRIOR-PERIOD ADJUSTMENTS

In the first part of this chapter, it was shown that profits and losses, dividends, and certain treasury stock transactions affect retained earnings. In addition to these three events, there is one other type of event that affects retained earnings directly. This category includes adjustments to restate the net income of prior periods; these are called, appropriately, **prior-period adjustments**. Prior-period adjustments are relatively infrequent. In addition to some technical adjustments involving taxes and bonds, which are beyond the scope of this book, the main event that qualifies as a prior-period adjustment is the correction of an error in previous financial statements, such as an error in accounting for revenues or expenses of a previous period. In accounting for prior-period adjustments, Retained Earnings is increased or decreased directly because the net income for the years affected by the adjustments has already been closed to the retained earnings account.

exhibit 11-10   Statement of Retained Earnings for Boston Lakers

Boston Lakers Basketball Team Statement of Retained Earnings For the Year Ended December 31, 2003		
Retained earnings, January 1, 2003		$300,000
Prior-period adjustment:		
Deduct adjustment for 2002 inventory correction		(25,000)
Balance as restated		$275,000
Net income for 2003.		50,000
Less dividends declared in 2003:		
Preferred stock	$10,000	
Common stock	12,000	(22,000)
Retained earnings, December 31, 2003		$303,000

statement of retained earnings A report that shows the changes in the retained earnings account during a period of time.

Prior-period adjustments (if there are any) and dividends are usually disclosed in a **statement of retained earnings**. Exhibit 11-10 shows how the Boston Lakers Basketball Team might present a statement of retained earnings, using arbitrary numbers.

to summarize

In addition to net income, dividends, and certain treasury stock transactions, retained earnings can also be either increased or decreased by prior-period adjustments, which do not occur often. Prior-period adjustments usually involve corrections of errors in previous financial statements. Prior-period adjustments are disclosed in a statement of retained earnings.

8
Understand basic proprietorship and partnership accounting.

capital account An account in which a proprietor's or partner's interest in a firm is recorded; it is increased by owner investments and net income and decreased by withdrawals and net losses.

drawings account The account used to reflect periodic withdrawals of earnings by the owner (proprietor) or owners (partners) of a proprietorship or partnership.

PROPRIETORSHIP AND PARTNERSHIP ACCOUNTING

Because the majority of businesses organized in the United States are proprietorships and partnerships, it is important to understand the accounting for equity financing in these types of businesses.

The difference between accounting for proprietorships and partnerships and accounting for a corporation is the owners' equity accounts. In a corporation, owners' equity is divided into contributed capital and retained earnings (and some other equity items, as explained earlier in the chapter), with each of these categories possibly having several different accounts. In proprietorships and partnerships, all owners' equity transactions are recorded in only two accounts, **Capital** and **Drawings**.

Accounting for Equity Financing in a Proprietorship

To illustrate the accounting for the owner's equity of a proprietorship, we will assume that Megan Wilkes decides to start a small, independent real estate brokerage business. On January 1, 2003, she deposits $40,000 into a bank account to finance the business. The entry to record the $40,000 deposit is:

Cash...	40,000	
Megan Wilkes, Capital....................................		40,000
Invested $40,000 to start a real estate business.		

Once the business is established, the entries to account for the purchase of assets, the payment of business expenses, and the receipt of revenues are similar to those for corporations. There is one exception, however. Whereas in a corporation salaries paid to management are accounted for as expenses, in a proprietorship the salary paid to the owner is a distribution of earnings. The managers of a corporation are considered to be employees, even if they are also stockholders in the company. The owners of a corporation receive dividends, which are deducted directly from Retained Earnings. In a proprietorship, the owner receives no dividends, so any "drawing out" of funds is considered to be a distribution to the owner. Hence, the name "drawings" account. If Megan Wilkes decides to withdraw $650 cash for personal use or as salary, the entry is:

Megan Wilkes, Drawings.......................................	650	
Cash...		650
Withdrew $650 for personal use.		

The account Megan Wilkes, Drawings is similar to a dividends account in a corporation: at year-end, it is closed to the owner's equity account, Megan Wilkes, Capital.

Assuming that Megan Wilkes withdrew only $650 during the year, the closing entry to eliminate the balance in the drawings account is:

Megan Wilkes, Capital..	650	
Megan Wilkes, Drawings.......................................		650
To close the drawings account for the year.		

If we also assume revenues of $100,000 and expenses of $86,000, Megan Wilkes's closing entry for net income is:

Revenues (individual revenue accounts).....................	100,000	
Expenses (individual expense accounts)....................		86,000
Megan Wilkes, Capital....................................		14,000
To close net income for the year to the owner's capital account.		

From the preceding two entries, we see that Megan Wilkes's capital account has increased by $13,350 since January 1. Adding this amount to her original contribution results in a $53,350 balance at year-end, as the following statement of owner's capital shows:

Megan Wilkes
Statement of Owner's Capital
For the Year Ending December 31, 2003

Megan Wilkes, capital, January 1, 2003..............................	$40,000
Add net income..	14,000
Total..	$54,000
Less withdrawals..	(650)
Megan Wilkes, capital, December 31, 2003..........................	$53,350

The owner's equity section of Megan Wilkes's balance sheet would have only one item:

Megan Wilkes, capital $53,350

Accounting for Equity Financing in a Partnership

Like a proprietorship, a partnership differs from a corporation primarily in accounting for owners' equity. That is, a partnership has only two types of owners' equity accounts, Capital and Drawings. Whereas a proprietorship has only one of each type of account, a partnership maintains separate capital and drawings accounts for each partner.

FORMING A PARTNERSHIP   To illustrate the accounting for the formation of a partnership, assume that Dr. Mary Adams and Dr. Jim Bell decide to form a partnership on January 1, 2003. Their partnership agreement specifies that Dr. Adams will contribute land valued at $30,000, a building valued at $50,000, and $10,000 cash to the business and that Dr. Bell will contribute medical equipment valued at $40,000 plus $50,000 cash. The entry to record the capital contributions of the two partners is:

Cash	60,000	
Equipment	40,000	
Land	30,000	
Building	50,000	
Adams, Capital		90,000
Bell, Capital		90,000
To record the investments of Adams and Bell in a partnership.		

The valuation of noncash assets invested in a business is one of the most difficult tasks in accounting for the formation of a partnership. Generally, the fair market values on the date of transfer should be used, but these values must be agreed upon by all partners. For example, if the assets contributed by either Bell or Adams had been used in another business prior to the partnership, the values assigned to them for the partnership might be quite different from the amounts that were being carried on the previous business's books. Although the equipment invested by Bell may have had a book value of only $30,000, or the land and building invested by Adams may have cost only $15,000 several years ago, it is only fair to give each partner credit for the current market values of the assets at the time they are transferred to the partnership.

PARTNERS' DRAWINGS ACCOUNTS   As mentioned previously, in a corporation the managers are employees, so their salaries are accounted for as expenses; the stockholders are the owners, and distributions to them are in the form of dividends. In a partnership the managers are usually the owners, and any amounts they withdraw, either as salary or as a distribution of profits, are debited to their drawings accounts, which eventually reduces the capital accounts. Each partner has a drawings account in which his or her withdrawals are recorded for the year. For example, assume that sufficient income was earned during the year and that Adams withdrew $70,000 and Bell withdrew $55,000 as salary for the year. The entry is:

Adams, Drawings	70,000	
Bell, Drawings	55,000	
Cash		125,000
To record cash taken from the partnership as salary.		

Note that any salaries paid to employees who are not partners are expenses of the business.

If Adams or Bell had withdrawn funds, for example, for living expenses, that amount would also be debited to the drawings account. At year-end, the debits in the drawings accounts are totaled, and the accounts are closed to the partners' capital accounts. Assuming that the total in each drawings account was the salary, the entry to close the drawings accounts for the year is:

Adams, Capital...	70,000	
Bell, Capital	55,000	
Adams, Drawings		70,000
Bell, Drawings.......................................		55,000
To close the drawings accounts for the year.		

statement of partners' capital A partnership report showing the changes in the capital balances; similar to a statement of retained earnings for a corporation.

THE STATEMENT OF PARTNERS' CAPITAL   Because most partners want an explanation of how their capital accounts change from year to year, a **statement of partners' capital** is usually prepared. This statement, which is similar to a retained earnings statement for a corporation, lists the beginning Capital balances, additional investments, profits or losses from operations, withdrawals, and each partner's ending Capital balance. For example, given the preceding information and assuming that the Adams and Bell partnership had a 2003 profit of $140,000, the statement of partners' capital for the year ended December 31, 2003, would be as shown in Exhibit 11-11. Note that the partnership agreement specifies that Adams is to receive 60% of the profits and Bell is to receive 40%.

exhibit 11-11   Statement of Partners' Capital

Adams and Bell Partnership
Statement of Partners' Capital
For the Year Ended December 31, 2003

	Dr. Adams	Dr. Bell	Total
Investments, January 1, 2003..............	$ 90,000	$ 90,000	$180,000
Add net income for 2003.................	84,000	56,000	140,000
Subtotal	$174,000	$146,000	$320,000
Less withdrawals during 2003.............	(70,000)	(55,000)	(125,000)
Capital balances, December 31, 2003........	$104,000	$ 91,000	$195,000

to summarize

The assets and liabilities of a proprietorship are accounted for in the same way as they are in a corporation, but equity is handled differently. Whereas the accounting for corporate equity may involve several accounts, the accounting for proprietorship equity requires only two accounts, Drawings and Capital. The drawings account is used for recording withdrawals of funds by the owner. It is closed to the capital account at year-end. The capital account is increased when capital is invested in the business and when profits are earned; it is decreased when cash or other assets are withdrawn from the business or when losses occur. The basic elements in accounting for the owners' equity of a partnership are (1) accounting for investments by the partners, (2) recording withdrawals of assets by the partners, (3) closing the drawings accounts, and (4) preparing a statement of partners' capital. Investments by owners are usually recorded at the fair market value and are credited to the owners' capital balances. Owners' withdrawals of cash, inventory, and other business assets are recorded in drawings accounts, which are closed to the capital accounts at year-end. There is one capital and one drawings account for each partner. A statement of partners' capital reconciles the beginning and ending capital balances by adding any profits and additional investments to the beginning capital balances and subtracting any losses and withdrawals.

review of learning objectives

1 **Distinguish between debt and equity financing, and describe the advantages and disadvantages of organizing a business as a proprietorship or a partnership.** Borrowing money imposes a legal obligation to repay the amount borrowed, plus interest. Receiving investment funds does not obligate the company to repay investors. Investors stand to lose their investments if the company does poorly, but they also stand to share in the wealth if the company does well. Proprietorships are owned by one person; partnerships are owned by two or more persons or entities. Partnerships and proprietorships share three characteristics: (1) ease of formation, (2) limited life, and (3) unlimited liability.

2 **Describe the basic characteristics of a corporation and the nature of common and preferred stock.** A corporation is a business entity that is legally separate from its owners and is chartered by a state. It is independently taxed, and it can incur debts, conduct business, own property, and enter into contracts. Among the benefits of the corporate form of business are that ownership interests are easily transferred and that the liability of the owners is limited to the amount of their investment. Common stockholders are the true owners of a corporation. They have the right to vote in corporate matters and own all corporate assets that are left after the claims of others have been satisfied. Preferred stockholders are entitled to receive their full cash dividend payments before any dividends can be paid to common stockholders. Preferred stockholders are entitled to a fixed amount of the corporate assets, and that amount does not increase when the company is successful.

3 **Account for the issuance and repurchase of common and preferred stock.** Stock that is issued often has a par value associated with each share. This par value is a legal technicality and represents the minimum amount that must be invested. When stock is issued in exchange for a noncash item, the transaction is recorded at the market value of the noncash item. Repurchased stock is called treasury stock. When treasury stock is purchased by a corporation, it is accounted for at cost and deducted from total stockholders' equity as a contra-equity account.

4 **Understand the factors that affect retained earnings, describe the factors determining whether a company can and should pay cash dividends, and account for cash dividends.** Retained earnings is increased by net income and

is decreased by a net loss, by dividends, and by some treasury stock transactions. Corporations usually distribute cash dividends to their owners. The three important dates in accounting for cash dividends are the declaration date, the date of record, and the payment date. Dividends are not a liability until they are declared. If a company has common and preferred stock, the allocation of dividends between the two types of stock depends on the dividend preferences of the preferred stock. According to the incorporation laws in some states, the ability of a company to pay cash dividends can be restricted by the balance in Retained Earnings. In addition, private lending agreements sometimes constrain a company's ability to pay cash dividends. The dividend payout ratio, which is cash dividends divided by net income, reveals what percentage of a company's income it is paying out in dividends.

5 **Describe the purpose of reporting comprehensive income in the equity section of the balance sheet, and prepare a statement of stockholders' equity.** The accumulated amount of comprehensive income is reported in the equity section of the balance sheet. Comprehensive income items result from changes in market values of certain assets and liabilities. Comprehensive income is not income in the traditional sense but instead represents unrealized gains and losses that are excluded from the income statement. The statement of stockholders' equity summarizes the changes in each equity category during a year.

expanded material

6 **Account for stock dividends and distinguish them from stock splits.** Stock dividends and stock splits involve dividing the ownership of the corporation into smaller pieces but giving shareholders proportionately more of these smaller pieces. Generally speaking, stock dividends are smaller than stock splits. A small stock dividend is one that is less than 25% and is accounted for by transferring the market value of the newly created shares out of Retained Earnings. With a large stock dividend, only the par value of the new shares is transferred. A stock split can be accounted for as a large stock dividend or by decreasing the par value of the shares.

7 **Explain prior-period adjustments and prepare a statement of retained earnings.** Prior-period adjustments are adjustments to restate net income of prior periods. The most common prior-period adjustments stem from past accounting errors that have been discovered in the current period. Because past periods' net income has already been closed to Retained Earnings, the corrections are made directly to the retained earnings account. Companies often include a statement of retained earnings with their financial statements. A statement of retained earnings reconciles the ending retained earnings balance with beginning retained earnings.

8 Understand basic proprietorship and partnership accounting. There are two owner's equity accounts in a proprietorship: a capital account and a drawings account.

The capital account is increased by owner contributions and profits and decreased by owner withdrawals and losses. Events commonly accounted for in a partnership are investments by owners, withdrawals by partners, and allocation of partnership profits and losses. Investments and withdrawals by partners are treated in the same way as they are in a proprietorship. That is, investments increase the partners' Capital balances, and withdrawals decrease the partners' Capital balances. A statement of partners' capital is usually prepared at year end. This statement reconciles the ending Capital balances with the beginning Capital balances by adding profits and additional investments and deducting losses and partner withdrawals.

key terms and concepts

accumulated other comprehensive income 529

board of directors 517

cash dividend 524

common stock 518

contributed capital 520

convertible preferred stock 519

corporation 515

cumulative-dividend preference 527

current-dividend preference 526

date of record 525

declaration date 525

dividend payment date 525

dividend payout ratio 528

dividends 524

dividends in arrears 527

limited liability 515

par value 520

partnership 514

preferred stock 518

proprietorship 514

prospectus 517

retained earnings 524

statement of comprehensive income 529

statement of stockholders' equity 530

stockholders 517

treasury stock 521

expanded material

capital account 535

drawings account 535

prior-period adjustments 534

statement of partners' capital 538

statement of retained earnings 535

stock dividend 532

stock split 534

review problem

Stockholders' Equity

Clarke Corporation was organized during 1973. At the end of 2003, the equity section of the balance sheet was:

Contributed capital:

Preferred stock (8%, $30 par, 6,000 shares authorized, 5,000 shares issued and outstanding)	$150,000
Common stock ($5 par, 50,000 shares authorized, 20,000 shares issued, 17,000 shares outstanding)	100,000
Paid-in capital in excess of par, common stock	80,000
Total contributed capital	$330,000
Retained earnings	140,000
Total contributed capital plus retained earnings	$470,000
Less treasury stock (3,000 shares of common stock at cost, $10 per share)	(30,000)
Total stockholders' equity	$440,000

During 2003, the following stockholders' equity transactions occurred in chronological sequence:

a. Issued 800 shares of common stock at $11 per share.
b. Reissued 1,200 shares of treasury stock at $12 per share.
c. Issued 300 shares of preferred stock at $33 per share.
d. Reissued 400 shares of treasury stock at $9 per share.
e. Declared and paid a dividend large enough to meet the current-dividend preference on the preferred stock and to pay the common stockholders $1.50 per share.
f. Net income for 2003 was $70,000, which included $400,000 of revenues and $330,000 of expenses.
g. Closed the dividends accounts for 2003.

Required:
1. Journalize the transactions.
2. Set up T-accounts with beginning balances and post the journal entries to the T-accounts, adding any necessary new accounts. (Assume a beginning balance of $20,000 for the cash account.)
3. Prepare the stockholders' equity section of the balance sheet as of December 31, 2003.

Solution

1. Journalize the Transactions

a.
Cash	8,800	
Common Stock		4,000
Paid-In Capital in Excess of Par, Common Stock		4,800
Issued 800 shares of common stock at $11 per share.		

Cash received is $11 × 800 shares; common stock is par value times the number of shares ($5 × 800); paid-in capital is the excess.

b.
Cash	14,400	
Treasury Stock		12,000
Paid-In Capital, Treasury Stock		2,400
Reissued 1,200 shares of treasury stock at $12 per share.		

Cash is $12 × 1,200 shares; treasury stock is the cost times the number of shares sold ($10 × 1,200 shares); paid-in capital is the excess.

c.
Cash	9,900	
Preferred Stock		9,000
Paid-In Capital in Excess of Par, Preferred Stock		900
Issued 300 shares of preferred stock at $33 per share.		

Cash is $33 × 300 shares; preferred stock is par value times the number of shares issued ($30 × 300); paid-in capital is the excess.

d.
Cash	3,600	
Paid-In Capital, Treasury Stock	400	
Treasury Stock		4,000
Reissued 400 shares of treasury stock at $9 per share.		

Cash is $9 × 400 shares; treasury stock is the cost times the number of shares sold ($10 × 400); paid-in capital is decreased for the difference. If no Paid-In Capital, Treasury Stock balance had existed, Retained Earnings would have been debited.

e.
Dividends, Preferred Stock	12,720	
Dividends, Common Stock	29,100	
Cash		41,820
Declared and paid cash dividend.		

Calculations:

Preferred Stock	Number of Shares	Par-Value Amount
Original balance	5,000	$150,000
Entry (c)	300	9,000
Total	5,300	$159,000
		× 0.08
		$ 12,720

Common Stock	Number of Shares
Original balance (excludes treasury stock)	17,000
Entry (a)	800
Entry (b)	1,200
Entry (d)	400
Total	19,400 shares
	× $1.50
	$29,100
Total preferred stock dividend	$12,720
Total common stock dividend	29,100
Total dividend	$41,820

f.	Revenues (individual revenue accounts)	400,000	
	Expenses (individual expense accounts)		330,000
	Retained Earnings		70,000
	To close net income to Retained Earnings.		
g.	Retained Earnings	41,820	
	Dividends, Preferred Stock		12,720
	Dividends, Common Stock		29,100
	To close the dividends accounts for 2003.		

2. Set Up T-Accounts and Post to the Accounts

Cash				Preferred Stock				Paid-In Capital in Excess of Par, Preferred Stock		
Beg.					Beg.				(c)	900
Bal.	20,000	(e)	41,820		Bal.	150,000				
(a)	8,800				(c)	9,000			Bal.	900
(b)	14,400				Bal.	159,000				
(c)	9,900									
(d)	3,600									
Bal.	14,880									

Common Stock				Paid-In Capital in Excess of Par, Common Stock				Treasury Stock		
	Beg.				Beg.			Beg.	(b)	12,000
	Bal.	100,000			Bal.	80,000		Bal. 30,000	(d)	4,000
	(a)	4,000			(a)	4,800		Bal. 14,000		
	Bal.	104,000			Bal.	84,800				

Paid-In Capital, Treasury Stock		
(d) 400	(b) 2,400	
	Bal. 2,000	

Retained Earnings		
(g) 41,820	Beg. Bal. 140,000	
	(f) 70,000	
	Bal. 168,180	

Dividends, Preferred Stock		
(e) 12,720	(g) 12,720	
Bal. 0		

Dividends, Common Stock		
(e) 29,100	(g) 29,100	
Bal. 0		

Revenues		
(f) 400,000	Beg. Bal. 400,000	
	Bal. 0	

Expenses		
Beg. Bal. 330,000	(f) 330,000	
Bal. 0		

3. Prepare Stockholders' Equity Section of the Balance Sheet

Clarke Corporation
Partial Balance Sheet
December 31, 2003

Stockholders' Equity

Contributed Capital:
Preferred stock (8%, $30 par, 6,000 shares authorized,
  5,300 shares issued and outstanding) $159,000
Common stock ($5 par, 50,000 shares authorized,
  20,800 shares issued, 19,400 outstanding) 104,000
Paid-in capital in excess of par, preferred stock 900
Paid-in capital in excess of par, common stock 84,800
Paid-in capital, treasury stock 2,000
  Total contributed capital $350,700
Retained earnings 168,180
  Total contributed capital plus retained earnings $518,880
Less treasury stock (1,400 shares of common stock at cost, $10 per share) .... (14,000)
  Total stockholders' equity $504,880

Transaction	Common Stock Issued	Common Stock Authorized	Treasury Stock
Number of shares originally issued	20,000	50,000	3,000
Entry (a)	800		
Entry (b)			(1,200)
Entry (d)			(400)
Total	20,800	50,000	1,400

discussion questions

1. What are the primary differences between debt financing and equity financing?
2. What are the major differences between a partnership and a corporation?
3. How is a proprietorship or partnership established?
4. Does the death of a partner legally terminate a partnership? If so, does it mean that the partnership must cease operating?

5. Are partners legally liable for the actions of other partners? Explain.

6. In which type of business entity do all owners have limited liability?

7. In what way are corporate profits subject to double taxation?

8. How do common and preferred stock differ?

9. What is the purpose of having a par value for stock?

10. Why would a company repurchase its own shares of stock that it had previously issued?

11. Is treasury stock an asset? If not, why not?

12. How is treasury stock usually accounted for?

13. In what way does the stockholders' equity section of a balance sheet identify the sources of the assets?

14. What factors affect the retained earnings balance of a corporation?

15. Is it possible for a firm to have a large Retained Earnings balance and no cash? Explain.

16. When is a company legally barred from paying cash dividends?

17. Why should a potential common stockholder carefully examine the dividend preferences of a company's preferred stock?

18. The dividend payout ratio for Deedle Company is 40%. What does this mean?

19. What is accumulated other comprehensive income? Why was this concept adopted by accounting standard-setters?

20. Give two examples of other equity items (items that bypass the income statement and go directly to the equity section of the balance sheet).

expanded material

21. Does a stock dividend have value to stockholders? Explain.

22. What is the difference between large and small stock dividends?

23. Why are prior-period adjustments entered directly into Retained Earnings instead of being reflected on the income statement?

24. Is the payment of salary to a proprietor an expense that would be deducted on a proprietorship's income statement? Explain.

25. In a corporation, contributions by owners and accumulated earnings of the business are separated into contributed capital and retained earnings accounts. Are earnings and contributions separated into different accounts in a partnership? Explain.

discussion cases

CASE 11-1

DOES STOCKHOLDERS' EQUITY TELL THE REAL STORY?

Last year, Shades International (a hypothetical company) invented the famous Shades Sunglasses that are widely popular around the world and especially in Japan and the Far East. Citizens of these countries love the new-age sunglasses and are buying them as fast as they can. Shades International owns the patent but contracts out to other companies to manufacture the glasses. Shades International also leases its research and development facility, the only building it occupies. Royalties from the glasses exceeded $10 million last year and are expected to increase dramatically this year. Selected data (in millions of dollars) from Shades International's financial statements are as follows:

Patent	$0.3
Other assets	0.9
Total liabilities	4.5
Total stockholders' equity	(3.3)

In the next two months, Shades International will be offering stock for sale to the public. Your friend is encouraging you to buy some of the stock. You are leery about the negative stockholders' equity balance. Is Shades International worth even considering as a possible investment?

CASE 11-2

TO PAY OR NOT TO PAY DIVIDENDS

Assume Lenny Company manufactures specialized computer peripheral parts such as speakers and modems. It is a new company that has been in operation for just two years. During those two years, Lenny Company's stock price has increased over 400%. Lenny Company does not pay dividends nor does the company plan to do so in the future. However, the company's stock seems to be heavily traded. Why do you think there is so much interest in buying Lenny Company's stock if stockholders do not receive dividends?

exercises

EXERCISE 11-1

ISSUANCE OF STOCK

Brockbank Corporation was organized on July 15, 2003. Record the journal entries for Brockbank to account for the following:

a. The state authorized 30,000 shares of 7% preferred stock ($20 par) and 100,000 shares of no-par common stock.
b. The company gave 6,000 shares of common stock to its attorney in return for her help in incorporating the business. Fees for this work are normally about $18,000. (Note: The debit is to Legal Expense.)
c. Brockbank Corporation gave 15,000 shares of common stock to an individual who contributed a building worth $50,000.
d. Brockbank Corporation issued 5,000 shares of preferred stock at $25 per share.
e. Peter Brockbank paid $70,000 cash for 30,000 shares of common stock.
f. Another individual donated a $15,000 machine and received 4,000 shares of common stock.
g. The attorney sold all her shares to her brother-in-law for $18,000.

EXERCISE 11-2

NO-PAR STOCK TRANSACTIONS

Parker Maintenance Corporation was organized in early 2003 with 40,000 shares of no-par common stock authorized. During 2003, the following transactions occurred:

a. Issued 17,000 shares of stock at $36 per share.
b. Issued another 2,400 shares of stock at $38 per share.
c. Issued 2,000 shares for a building appraised at $40,000.
d. Declared dividends of $1 per share.
e. Earned net income of $99,000 for the year, including $200,000 of revenues and $101,000 of expenses.
f. Closed the dividends accounts.

Given this information:

1. Journalize the transactions.
2. Present the stockholders' equity section of the balance sheet as it would appear on December 31, 2003.

EXERCISE 11-3

TREASURY STOCK TRANSACTIONS

Provide the necessary journal entries to record the following:

a. Fayette Corporation was granted a charter authorizing the issuance of 100,000 shares of $16 par-value common stock.
b. The company issued 40,000 shares of common stock at $20 per share.
c. The company reacquired 2,000 shares of its own stock at $22 per share, to be held in treasury.
d. Another 2,000 shares of stock were reacquired at $24 per share.
e. Of the shares reacquired in (c), 800 were reissued for $26 per share.
f. Of the shares reacquired in (d), 1,400 were reissued for $18 per share.
g. Given the preceding transactions, what is the balance in the treasury stock account?

EXERCISE 11-4

STOCK ISSUANCE AND CASH DIVIDENDS

Stillwater Corporation was organized in January 2003. The state authorized 100,000 shares of no-par common stock and 50,000 shares of 10%, $20 par, preferred stock. Record the following transactions that occurred in 2003:

a. Issued 10,000 shares of common stock at $30 per share.
b. Issued 2,000 shares of preferred stock for a building appraised at $60,000.
c. Declared a cash dividend sufficient to meet the current-dividend preference on preferred stock and pay common shareholders $2 per share.

EXERCISE 11-5

STOCK ISSUANCE, TREASURY STOCK, AND DIVIDENDS

On January 1, 2003, Abbott Corporation was granted a charter authorizing the following capital stock: common stock, $20 par, 100,000 shares; preferred stock, $10 par, 6%, 30,000 shares. Record the following 2003 transactions:

a. Issued 80,000 shares of common stock at $30 per share.
b. Issued 14,000 shares of preferred stock at $12 per share.
c. Bought back 5,000 shares of common stock at $40 per share.
d. Reissued 500 shares of treasury stock at $25 per share.
e. Declared cash dividends of $38,600 to be allocated between common and preferred stockholders. (The preferred stock, which has a current-dividend preference, is noncumulative.)
f. Paid dividends of $38,600.

EXERCISE 11-6

STOCK ISSUANCE, TREASURY STOCK, AND DIVIDENDS

On January 1, 2003, Snow Company was authorized to issue 100,000 shares of common stock, par value $10 per share and 10,000 shares of 8% preferred stock, par value $20 per share. Record the following transactions for 2003:

a. Issued 70,000 shares of common stock at $25 per share.
b. Issued 8,000 shares of preferred stock at $30 per share.
c. Reacquired 5,000 shares of common stock at $20 per share.
d. Reissued 2,000 shares of treasury stock for $46,000.
e. Declared a cash dividend sufficient to meet the current-dividend preference on preferred stock and pay common shareholders $1 per share.

EXERCISE 11-7

STOCK TRANSACTIONS AND DIVIDENDS

Marion Corporation was organized in January 2003. The state authorized 200,000 shares of no-par common stock and 100,000 shares of 10%, $10 par, preferred stock. Record the following transactions that occurred in 2003:

a. Issued 20,000 shares of common stock at $20 per share.
b. Issued 8,000 shares of preferred stock for a piece of land appraised at $90,000.
c. Declared a cash dividend sufficient to meet the current-dividend preference on preferred stock and paid common shareholders $1 per share.
d. How would your answer to (c) change if the dividend declared were not sufficient to meet the current-dividend preference on preferred stock?

EXERCISE 11-8

DIVIDEND CALCULATIONS

On January 1, 2003, Oldroyd Corporation had 130,000 shares of common stock issued and outstanding. During 2003, the following transactions occurred (in chronological order):

a. Oldroyd issued 10,000 new shares of common stock.
b. The company reacquired 2,000 shares of stock for use in its employee stock option plan.
c. At the end of the option period, 1,200 shares of treasury stock had been purchased by corporate officials.

Given this information, compute the following:

1. After the foregoing three transactions have occurred, what amount of dividends must Oldroyd Corporation declare in order to pay 50 cents per share? To pay $1 per share?

2. What is the dividend per share if $236,640 is paid?
3. If all 2,000 treasury shares had been purchased by corporate officials through the stock option plan, what would the dividends per share have been, again assuming $236,640 in dividends were paid? (Round to the nearest cent.)

EXERCISE 11-9

DIVIDEND CALCULATIONS

Stewart Corporation has the following stock outstanding:

Preferred stock (5%, $20 par value, 20,000 shares)	$400,000
Common stock ($5 par value, 80,000 shares)	400,000

For the two independent cases that follow, compute the amount of dividends that would be paid to preferred and common shareholders. Assume that total dividends paid are $86,000. No dividends have been paid for the past two years.

Case A, Preferred is noncumulative.
Case B, Preferred is cumulative.

EXERCISE 11-10

STOCK ISSUANCE, TREASURY STOCK, AND DIVIDENDS

During 2003, Doxey Corporation had the following transactions and related events:

Jan. 15   Issued 6,500 shares of common stock at par ($16 per share), bringing the total number of shares outstanding to 121,300.
Feb. 6   Declared a 50-cent-per-share dividend on common stock for stockholders of record on March 6.
Mar. 6   Date of record.
       8   Pedro Garcia, a prominent banker, purchased 20,000 shares of Doxey Corporation common stock from the company for $346,000.
Apr. 6   Paid dividends declared on February 6.
June 19   Reacquired 800 shares of common stock as treasury stock at a total cost of $9,350.
Sept. 6   Declared dividends of 55 cents per share to be paid to common stockholders of record on October 15, 2003.
Oct. 6   The Dow Jones Industrial Average plummeted 300 points, and Doxey's stock price fell $3 per share.
      15   Date of record.
Nov. 16   Paid dividends declared on September 6.
Dec. 15   Declared and paid a 6% cash dividend on 18,000 outstanding shares of preferred stock (par value $32).

Given this information:

1. Prepare the journal entries for these transactions.
2. What is the total amount of dividends paid to common and preferred stockholders during 2003?

EXERCISE 11-11

DIVIDEND PAYOUT RATIO

The following numbers are for three different companies:

	A	B	C
Total assets	$1,000	$2,500	$2,000
Cash dividends	50	200	400
Total liabilities	600	800	1,400
Net income	200	500	500

For each company, compute the dividend payout ratio.

Required:
1. Prepare the journal entries to record the 2003 transactions.
2. Prepare the stockholders' equity section of the balance sheet at December 31, 2003.
3. Prepare a statement of stockholders' equity for the year ended December 31, 2003.

PROBLEM 11-14

UNIFYING CONCEPTS: STOCKHOLDERS' EQUITY

Icon Corporation was organized during 2001. At the end of 2002, the equity section of its balance sheet appeared as follows:

Contributed capital:	
Preferred stock (6%, $20 par, 10,000 shares authorized, 5,000 shares issued and outstanding)	$100,000
Common stock ($10 par, 50,000 shares authorized, 11,000 shares issued, 10,000 outstanding)	110,000
Paid-in capital in excess of par, preferred stock	20,000
Total contributed capital	$230,000
Retained earnings	100,000
Total contributed capital plus retained earnings	$330,000
Less treasury stock (1,000 shares of common at cost)	(12,000)
Total stockholders' equity	$318,000

During 2003, the following stockholders' equity transactions occurred (in chronological sequence):

a. Issued 500 shares of common stock at $13 per share.
b. Reissued 500 shares of treasury stock at $13 per share.
c. Issued 1,000 shares of preferred stock at $25 per share.
d. Reissued 500 shares of treasury stock at $10 per share.
e. Declared a dividend large enough to meet the current-dividend preference of the preferred stock and to pay the common stockholders $2 per share. Dividends are recorded directly in the retained earnings account.
f. Closed net income of $65,000 to Retained Earnings. Revenues were $400,000; expenses were $335,000.

Required:
1. Journalize the transactions.
2. Prepare the stockholders' equity section of the balance sheet at December 31, 2003.

PROBLEM 11-15

COMPREHENSIVE INCOME

The following information relates to Pecos Yo Company:

Sales	$15,000
Cost of goods sold	6,000
Other operating expenses	2,500
Interest expense	400
Income tax expense	3,000

In addition, the following events occurred during the year:

a. Pecos Yo Company has an investment portfolio for long-term investment purposes. That portfolio decreased in value by $7,000 during the year.
b. Pecos Yo Company owns a substantial amount of land. During the year, the land increased in value by $11,000.
c. Pecos Yo Company has several foreign subsidiaries. The currencies in the countries where those subsidiaries are located declined in value (relative to the U.S. dollar) during the year. Accordingly, the computed value of the equity of those subsidiaries, in U.S. dollars, decreased by $5,000.

Required:
1. Compute Pecos Yo's comprehensive income for the year.
2. **Interpretive Question:** Is comprehensive income a good measure of the change in a company's value during the year?

PROBLEM 11-16

STOCKHOLDERS' EQUITY SECTION WITH SELECTED "OTHER INFORMATION"

The stockholders' equity section of Glory Company's balance sheet was as follows as of December 31, 2003, and December 31, 2002:

Glory Company
Stockholders' Equity Sections of Balance Sheet
December 31, 2003 and 2002
(in millions)

	2003	2002
Preferred stock	$ 21.4	$ 21.4
Common stock	48.4	43.2
Paid-in capital, various types	22.6	15.3
Retained earnings	51.8	41.2
Subtotal	$144.2	$121.1
Accumulated foreign currency translation adjustments	21.4	57.3
Net unrealized gains (losses) on investments in certain debt and equity securities	(46.4)	(8.8)
Total stockholders' equity	$119.2	$169.6

Required: Based on the stockholders' equity section for Glory Company, answer the following questions:

1. Do you believe Glory Company made a profit during the year 2003? Assuming that only net income and dividends changed the retained earnings balance from 2002 to 2003, by how much did net income exceed dividends?
2. What was the total amount of money raised during 2003 from the selling of stock? (Assume that only the selling of stock affected the contributed capital accounts.)
3. Did the market value of Glory Company's securities that affect the equity section increase or decrease in 2003? By how much?
4. **Interpretive Question:** The board of directors believes it should fire the current management of the company because total stockholders' equity decreased substantially. Do you agree? Why or why not?

expanded
material

PROBLEM 11-17

General Ledger Software

RECORDING STOCKHOLDERS' EQUITY TRANSACTIONS

The stockholders' equity section of Hathaway Corporation's December 31, 2002, balance sheet is as follows:

Stockholders' Equity

Contributed capital:

Preferred stock (5%, $25 par, 2,000 shares issued and outstanding)	$ 50,000
Common stock ($30 par, 10,000 shares issued and outstanding)	300,000
Paid-in capital in excess of par, preferred stock	10,000
Paid-in capital in excess of par, common stock	100,000
Total contributed capital	$460,000
Retained earnings	340,000
Total stockholders' equity	$800,000

During 2003, Hathaway Corporation had the following transactions:

Feb. 1 Paid a cash dividend of $3 per share on common stock. The dividend was declared December 31, 2002.

Mar. 15 Declared and issued a 19% common stock dividend. The market price of the stock on this date was $40 per share.

June 1 Reacquired 3,000 shares of common stock at $35 per share.

Sept. 1 Reissued 500 shares of treasury stock at $40 per share.

Nov. 15 Reissued 500 shares of treasury stock at $32 per share.

Required: Record the transactions.

PROBLEM 11-18   DIVIDEND TRANSACTIONS AND CALCULATIONS

As of December 31, 2002, First Corporation has 200,000 shares of $10 par-value common stock authorized, with 100,000 of these shares issued and outstanding.

Required:

1. Prepare journal entries to record the following 2003 transactions:

Jan. 1 Received authorization for 200,000 shares of 7%, cumulative preferred stock with a par value of $10.

2 Issued 10,000 shares of the preferred stock at $15 per share.

June 1 Reacquired 40% of the common stock outstanding for $18 per share.

2 Declared a cash dividend of $10,000. The date of record is June 15.

June 30 Paid the previously declared cash dividend of $10,000.

2. Determine the proper allocation to preferred and common stockholders of a $100,000 cash dividend declared on December 31, 2003. (This dividend is in addition to the June 2 dividend.)

3. **Interpretive Question:** Why didn't the preferred stockholders receive their current-dividend preference of $7,000 in part (2)?

PROBLEM 11-19   RECORDING DIVIDEND TRANSACTIONS AND REPORTING STOCKHOLDERS' EQUITY

Murtry, Inc., reported the following stockholders' equity balances in its June 30, 2002, balance sheet:

Preferred stock (6%, $100 par, cumulative; 20,000 shares authorized,	
6,000 shares issued and outstanding)	$ 600,000
Common stock ($20 par; 250,000 shares authorized,	
60,000 shares issued and outstanding)	1,200,000
Retained earnings	950,000

Required:

1. The following stockholders' equity transactions occurred (in the order presented) during the fiscal year ending June 30, 2003. Prepare the necessary journal entries to record the transactions.
   a. Murtry declared and issued a 5% dividend on common stock; the market value of the stock was $30 per share on the date of the dividend.
   b. A 50% stock dividend on common stock was declared and issued when the stock was trading at a market price of $40 per share.
   c. A cash dividend was declared at the end of the fiscal year. The common stockholders will receive 50 cents per share after the current and cumulative preference on the preferred stock is satisfied. Preferred stock dividends are one year in arrears.
2. Assuming Murtry's net income for the year ended June 30, 2003, is $310,000, prepare the stockholders' equity section of the June 30, 2003, balance sheet and a statement of stockholders' equity for the 2002–2003 fiscal year.
3. **Interpretive Question:** What is the effect on earnings per share when a company has a stock dividend or stock split?

PROBLEM 11-20

STATEMENT OF RETAINED EARNINGS AND STOCKHOLDERS' EQUITY

The following balances appear in the accounts of Iron Corporation as of December 31, 2003:

Retained earnings, January 1, 2003	$128,000
Prior-period adjustment (tax adjustment for 2001)	(57,000)
Net income for 2003	60,000
Preferred stock (7%, $12 par, 20,000 shares authorized, 5,000 shares issued and outstanding)	60,000
Common stock ($5 par, 100,000 shares authorized, 16,000 shares issued, 200 held as treasury stock)	80,000
Paid-in capital in excess of par, preferred stock	13,400
Paid-in capital in excess of par, common stock	42,800
Treasury stock	3,600
Cash dividends (declared during 2003)	10,000

Required:

1. Prepare the statement of retained earnings for Iron Corporation as of December 31, 2003.
2. Prepare the stockholders' equity section of Iron Corporation's balance sheet as of December 31, 2003.

PROBLEM 11-21

STATEMENT OF RETAINED EARNINGS

Marsh Corporation records show the following at December 31, 2003:

Extraordinary loss (net of tax)	$(50,000)
Cash dividends declared during 2003	30,000
Stock dividends issued during 2003	14,000
January 1, 2003, retained earnings balance	690,000
Prior-period adjustment (net of tax)	(36,000)
Net income before extraordinary items and taxes (assume a 40% tax rate)	160,000

Required: Prepare a 2003 statement of retained earnings.

PROBLEM 11-22

ACCOUNTING FOR A PROPRIETORSHIP

On January 1, 2003, Pat Larsen decided to open the Donut Shop. Pat deposited $40,000 of her own money in a company bank account and obtained a $30,000 loan from a local bank. During its first year of operation, the shop had net income of $84,000, which included $150,000 of revenues and $66,000 of expenses. Pat withdrew a lump sum of $48,000 from the business that year to cover personal living expenses.

Required:

1. Prepare journal entries to record:
   a. Pat's original contribution to the firm.
   b. The bank loan.
   c. Pat's withdrawal for her living expenses.
   d. Any closing entries required at year-end.
2. Prepare a statement of owner's capital for 2003.
3. **Interpretive Question:** How would the accounting for the transactions in part (1) be different if Pat's business were a corporation?

PROBLEM 11-23

PARTNERSHIP ACCOUNTING

On January 1, 2003, Reed and Bailey established a partnership to sell fruit.

a. Reed invested $42,000 cash in the partnership, and Bailey invested $20,000 cash and a building valued at $25,000.
b. Reed invested another $6,000 cash. Bailey donated a truck valued at $7,000.
c. Reed withdrew $11,000 cash, and Bailey withdrew $6,300 cash.
d. A fire destroyed half of the building donated by Bailey. There was no insurance on the building. The partners share profits and losses equally.

e. Reed and Bailey agree to admit a third partner on March 1 of the next year. This partner, Kiefer, promises to invest $50,000 cash.

Required:

1. Journalize the transactions.
2. Journalize the closing entries. Assume revenues totaled $50,000 and expenses totaled $31,000.
3. Compute each partner's capital balance at the end of 2003.
4. **Interpretive Question:** What is the relationship between the amount of capital contributed by each owner and the way profits are to be allocated?

competency enhancement opportunities

▶ Analyzing Real Company Information
▶ International Case
▶ Ethics Case
▶ Writing Assignment

▶ The Debate
▶ Cumulative Spreadsheet Project
▶ Internet Search

The following additional assignments provide opportunities for students to develop critical thinking, ethical perspectives, oral and written communication skills, experience with electronic research, and teamwork through group and business activities.

▶ ANALYZING REAL COMPANY INFORMATION

• Analyzing 11-1 (Microsoft)

The 1999 annual report for MICROSOFT is included in Appendix A. Microsoft's stockholders' equity statements provide details of equity transactions of the company during the 1999 fiscal year. Locate the statements and consider the following questions:

1. What was the major reason that stockholders' equity increased for the year?
2. How much did common stockholders receive in dividends during the year? How much did preferred stockholders receive?
3. Did Microsoft issue more shares than it repurchased during the year or vice versa? How can you tell? (HINT: You should look in the notes to the statements to answer this question.)

• Analyzing 11-2 (Wal-Mart Stores, Inc.)

WAL-MART has a simple, straightforward statement of shareholders' equity. That statement for the years 1998 and 1999 is reproduced on the top of the next page.

Consolidated Statements of Shareholders' Equity

(Amounts in millions except per share data)	Number of Shares	Common Stock	Capital in Excess of Par Value	Retained Earnings	Other Accumulated Comprehensive Income	Total
Balance—January 31, 1998	2,241	$224	$585	$18,167	$(473)	$18,503
Net income				4,430		4,430
Cash dividends ($0.16 per share)				(693)		(693)
Foreign currency translation adjustment					(36)	(36)
Purchase of company stock	(21)	(2)	(37)	(1,163)		(1,202)
Two-for-one stock split	2,224	223	(223)			—
Other	4		110			110
Balance—January 31, 1999	4,448	445	435	20,741	(509)	21,112
Net income				5,377		5,377
Cash dividends ($0.20 per share)				(890)		(890)
Foreign currency translation adjustment					54	54
Purchase of company stock	(2)		(2)	(99)		(101)
Other	11	1	281			282
Balance—January 31, 2000	4,457	$446	$714	$25,129	$(455)	$25,834

1. Based on the dividends paid during each year, how many shares of stock were outstanding when the dividends were paid?
2. Why isn't the number of shares receiving dividends exactly the same as the number of shares outstanding on January 31 of each year as indicated in the statement?
3. Estimate Wal-Mart's dividend payout ratio for each year. (HINT: You will need to estimate an earnings-per-share figure given the available data.)

INTERNATIONAL CASE

• The EMI Group

The shareholders' equity section of the balance sheet of THE EMI GROUP, a company based in the United Kingdom, is reproduced below. Review this information and answer the questions below.

Balance Sheets
at 31 March 1999

	Group	
	1999 £m	Pro Forma 1998 £m
Capital and reserves		
Called-up share capital	110.2	110.1
Share premium reserve	441.2	439.0
Capital redemption reserve	495.8	495.8
Other reserves	636.9	786.3
Profit and loss reserve (including goodwill previously written off)	710.5	529.3
Equity shareholders' funds	**2,394.6**	**2,360.5**

Investments in Debt and Equity Securities

c h a p t e r

f12

learning objectives After studying this chapter, you should be able to:

1 Understand why companies invest in other companies.

2 Understand the different classifications for securities.

3 Account for the purchase, recognition of revenue, and sale of trading and available-for-sale securities.

4 Account for changes in the value of securities.

expanded material

5 Account for held-to-maturity securities.

6 Account for securities using the equity method.

Warren Buffett, who has been called "the world's greatest investor," has lived most of his life not far from the house in which he grew up in Omaha, Nebraska.[1] He attended the Wharton School at the University of Pennsylvania (but dropped out because he thought he wasn't learning anything); received a bachelor's degree from the University of Nebraska; applied for admission to do graduate work at Harvard but was rejected; and instead earned a master's degree in economics at Columbia.

Buffett began his professional career as a stock trader and eventually created an investment fund called the Buffett Partnership, which earned a 32% average annual return over its life from 1956 to 1969. Buffett also began purchasing shares in a small textile manufacturer called BERKSHIRE HATHAWAY. His first 2,000 shares of Berkshire Hathaway stock cost $7.50 per share (plus $0.10 per share in commissions). Buffett transformed Berkshire Hathaway from a textile manufacturer into a holding company that invests in the stock of other companies. A selection of the companies controlled by Berkshire Hathaway, along with some of Berkshire Hathaway's major investments, is shown in Exhibit 12-1.

How has Berkshire Hathaway's stock performed under Warren Buffett's leader-

setting the stage

---

exhibit 12-1   Berkshire Hathaway's Operations and Investments

Companies Owned by Berkshire Hathaway*

	Industry
GEICO	Property and casualty insurance
FlightSafety International	Aviation training
See's Candies	Candy
Kirby	Vacuum cleaners
Nebraska Furniture Mart, R.C. Willey, Star Furniture, and Jordan's Furniture	Home furnishings
The Buffalo News	Newspaper publishing
Dexter Shoe Company, H.H. Brown Shoe Company, and Lowell Shoe, Inc.	Shoes
Helzberg Diamond Shops and Borsheim's	Retail jewelry stores
International Dairy Queen	Fast food and dairy desserts
Orange Julius	Blended fruit drinks

Companies in Which Berkshire Hathaway Has Invested*

	Ownership Percentage
American Express Company	11.3%
The Coca-Cola Company	8.1%
M&T Bank	6.5%
Freddie Mac	8.6%
The Gillette Company	9.0%
The Washington Post Company	18.3%
Wells Fargo & Company	3.6%

*This information is as of the end of 1999.

---

1 Janet Lowe, *Warren Buffett Speaks: Wit and Wisdom from the World's Greatest Investor* (New York: John Wiley & Sons, 1997).

exhibit 12-6   Time Line of Business Issues Associated with Buying and Selling Investment Securities

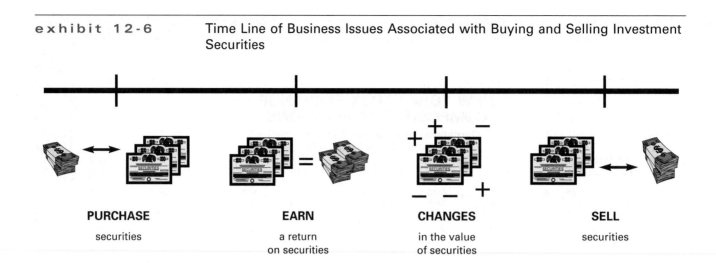

PURCHASE	EARN	CHANGES	SELL
securities	a return on securities	in the value of securities	securities

To illustrate the accounting for securities, we will use the following information throughout the chapter. On July 1, 2002, Far Side, Inc. purchased the following securities:

Security	Type	Classification	Cost (including Broker's Fees)
1	Debt	Trading	$ 5,000
2	Equity	Trading	27,500
3	Debt	Available-for-sale	17,000
4	Equity	Available-for-sale	9,200

The initial entry to record the investments is as follows:

Investment in Trading Securities...........................	32,500	
Investment in Available-for-Sale Securities	26,200	
Cash		58,700

Though investments in securities are all recorded at cost, each of the four classifications of securities is accounted for differently subsequent to purchase. As a result, separate accounts are used to record the initial purchase. Management purchased Securities 1 and 2 with the intent of earning a return on the investment and selling the securities should the need for cash arise. Therefore, those securities are classified as "trading." Securities 3 and 4 were also purchased to earn a return on excess cash, but management has classified them as "available-for-sale." While the journal entry illustrated above combines all securities of the same classification into one account, subsidiary records will be kept for each individual security purchased.

Accounting for the Return Earned on an Investment

When a firm invests in the debt or equity of another firm with the intent of earning a return on its investment, how that return is accounted for varies depending on the classification of the investment. Recall from Chapter 10 that when debt securities are sold, a premium or discount can arise as a result of differences between the stated rate of interest and the market rate of interest. The resulting premium or discount must then be amortized over the life of the investment, thereby affecting the amount of interest expense recorded by the issuer. Theoretically, the purchaser of that debt security must also account for the difference between the purchase price and the eventual maturity value. In the discussion that follows, however, we are assuming that the time for which the investor anticipates holding debt securities classified as "trading" or as "available-for-sale" is not long enough for any amortization of premium or discount to materially affect interest expense. Amortization of premiums and discounts on debt securities is illustrated for "held-to-maturity" securities in the expanded material section of this chapter.

With this caveat in mind, the accounting for dividends and interest received on trading and available-for-sale securities becomes relatively straightforward. Cash received relating to interest and dividends is credited to Interest Revenue and Dividend Revenue, respectively. Interest earned but not yet received or dividends that have been declared but not paid are also recorded as revenue with a corresponding receivable. Continuing our example, interest and dividends received during 2002 relating to Far Side's securities investments were as follows:

<table>
<tr><td colspan="3" style="background:#000;color:#fff">fyi</td></tr>
</table>

BERKSHIRE HATHAWAY reported interest, dividends, and other investment income earned of $1.4 billion during 1999.

Security	Interest	Dividends
1	$225	
2		$825
3	850	
4		644

The appropriate journal entry to record the receipt of interest and dividends is:

Cash...	2,544	
Interest Revenue		1,075
Dividend Revenue		1,469

Accounting for the Sale of Securities

Suppose that Far Side sells all of its investment in Security 2 for $28,450 on October 31, 2002. As Security 2 was purchased for $27,500, the security has increased in value and that increase must be recorded. The journal entry to record the sale is:

Cash...	28,450	
Investment in Trading Securities		27,500
Realized Gain on Sale of Trading Securities.................		950

If Security 2 had been sold for less then $27,500, a loss would have been recorded. If a broker's fee had been charged on the transaction, the fee would reduce the amount of cash received and decrease the gain recognized. If the broker's fee exceeded $950, a loss would be recorded on the books of the seller.

At the end of the accounting period, any gain or loss on the sale of securities must be included on the income statement. In the above example, the "Realized Gain on Sale of Trading Securities" would be included with Other Revenues and Expenses on the income statement. Note the term *realized*. **Realized gains and losses** indicate that an arm's-length transaction has occurred and that the securities have actually been sold. This distinction is important because in the next section we focus on accounting for unrealized gains and losses—those gains and losses that occur while a security is still being held and no arm's-length transaction has taken place.

realized gains and losses
Gains and losses resulting from the **sale** of securities in an arm's-**length** transaction.

On its statement of cash flows, BERKSHIRE HATHAWAY reported proceeds of $8,864 million from the sale of debt securities and equity securities. On its income statement, the company reported net realized gains of $1,365 million from the sale of securities. With this information, we can compute the historical cost of the securities sold during the period. Proceeds of $8,864 million less a gain of $1,365 million indicate that the cost of the securities was $7,499 million. A summary journal entry indicating the effects of these transactions for Berkshire Hathaway is as follows:

Cash	8,864	
Available-for-Sale Securities................................		7,499
Realized Gain on Sale of Securities		1,365

and the English word *sonny*; it was given to a small transistor radio sold by the company in the United States, starting in 1954. The radio was so popular that the entire company changed its name to Sony in 1958.

In its 2000 annual report, Sony included the note to its financial statements shown below.

(10) Marketable securities and securities investments

	Yen in millions							
	March 31, 1999				March 31, 2000			
	Cost	Gross unrealized gains	Gross unrealized losses	Fair value	Cost	Gross unrealized gains	Gross unrealized losses	Fair value
Available-for-sale:								
Debt securities	¥746,005	¥36,632	¥12,187	¥770,450	¥739,563	¥ 40,646	¥7,268	¥772,941
Equity securities	57,712	13,774	3,156	68,330	55,321	66,905	2,594	119,632
Total	¥803,717	¥50,406	¥15,343	¥838,780	¥794,884	¥107,551	¥9,862	¥892,573

	Dollars in millions			
	March 31, 2000			
	Cost	Gross unrealized gains	Gross unrealized losses	Fair value
Available-for-sale:				
Debt securities.	$6,977	$ 384	$69	$7,292
Equity securities.	522	631	24	1,129
Total.	$7,499	$1,015	$93	$8,421

1. In the notes to its English-language financial statements, Sony states that those statements "conform with accounting principles generally accepted in the United States." However, Sony's official accounting records are maintained using Japanese accounting principles. Why would Sony go to the trouble of preparing a separate set of English-language financial statements using U.S. accounting principles?

2. Assuming that approximately the same available-for-sale securities were on hand in both 1999 and 2000, how well did Sony's investments perform in 2000?

3. What journal entries did Sony make during the year to record the revaluation of available-for-sale securities? Use only the total amounts (that is, don't use the separate amounts for debt and equity securities), and ignore the fact that securities were bought and sold during the year.

▶ **ETHICS CASE**

• Is It OK to Strategically Classify Securities?
You have recently been hired as a staff assistant in the office of the chairman of the board of directors of Clefton, Inc. Because you have some background in accounting, the chairman has asked you to review the preliminary financial statements that have been prepared by the company's accounting staff. After

the financial statements are approved by the chairman of the board, they will be audited by external auditors. This is the first year that Clefton has had its financial statements audited by external auditors.

In examining the financial statement note on investment securities, you notice that all of the securities that had unrealized gains for the year have been classified as trading, whereas all of the securities that had unrealized losses have been classified as available-for-sale. You realize that this has the impact of placing all the gains on the income statement and hiding all the losses in the equity section of the balance sheet. You call the chief accountant who confirms that the securities are not classified until the end of the year and that the classification depends on whether a particular security has experienced a gain or a loss during the year. The chief accountant states that this policy was adopted, with the approval of the chairman of the board, in order to maximize the reported net income of the company. The chief accountant tells you that investment security classification is based on how management intends to use those securities; therefore, management is free to classify the securities in any way it wishes.

You are uncomfortable with this investment security classification strategy. You are also dismayed that the chief accountant and the chairman of the board seem to have agreed on this scheme to maximize reported income. You are also worried about what the external auditors will do when they find out about this classification scheme. You have been asked to report to the chairman of the board this afternoon to give your summary of the status of the preliminary financial statements. What should you do?

▶ WRITING ASSIGNMENT

• *Why Doesn't the Gain Go on the Income Statement?*

You are the controller for Chong Lai Company. You just received a very strongly worded e-mail message from the president of the company. The president has learned that a $627,000 gain on a stock investment made by the company last year will not be reported in the income statement because you have classified the security as available-for-sale. With the gain, the company would report a record profit for the year. Without the gain, profits are actually down slightly from the year before. The president wants an explanation—*now*.

It has been your policy for the past several years to routinely classify all investments as available-for-sale. Your company is not in the business of actively buying and selling stocks and bonds. Instead, all investments are made to strengthen relationships with either suppliers or major customers. As such, your practice is to buy securities and hold them for several years.

Write a one-page memo to the president explaining the rationale behind your policy of security classification.

▶ THE DEBATE

• *Market Values Do Not Belong in the Financial Statements!*

Accounting traditionalists opposed the move to report investment securities in the balance sheet at their current market value. These traditionalists complain that inclusion of market values reduces the reliability of the financial statements and introduces an unnecessary amount of variability in the reported numbers. On the other hand, supporters of reporting market values claim that market values are extremely relevant and, for investment securities traded on active markets, are reliable as well.

Divide your group into two teams.

- One team represents "Market Value." Prepare a two-minute oral presentation arguing that the market value of investment securities should be reported in the balance sheet. To do otherwise is to make the statements an out-of-date curiosity rather than a useful tool.
- The other team represents "Historical Cost." Prepare a two-minute oral presentation arguing for a return to strict historical cost in the balance sheet.

▶ **CUMULATIVE SPREADSHEET PROJECT**

This spreadsheet assignment is a continuation of the spreadsheet assignments given in earlier chapters. If you completed those spreadsheets, you have a head start on this one.

This assignment is based on the spreadsheet prepared in part (1) of the spreadsheet assignment for Chapter 9. Review that assignment for a summary of the assumptions made in preparing a forecasted balance sheet, income statement, and statement of cash flows for 2003 for Handyman Company. Using those financial statements, complete the following exercise.

Handyman has decided that, in 2003, it will create an available-for-sale investment portfolio. Handyman plans to invest $20 million in a variety of stocks and bonds. (Recall that the numbers in the Handyman spreadsheet are in millions.) As of the end of 2002, Handyman has no investment portfolio. Adapt your spreadsheet to include this expected $20 million investment portfolio as a current asset in 2003. Ignore the possibility of any interest, dividends, gains, or losses on this portfolio. Answer the following questions:

1. With the assumptions built into your spreadsheet, where will Handyman get the $20 million in funding necessary to acquire these investment securities?
2. Where in the statement of cash flows did you put the cash outflow associated with the acquisition of these investment securities? Explain your placement.

▶ **INTERNET SEARCH**

• Berkshire Hathaway

The history of BERKSHIRE HATHAWAY was outlined at the beginning of this chapter. Access Berkshire Hathaway's Web site at http://www.berkshirehathaway.com. Sometimes Web addresses change, so if this address doesn't work, access the Web site for this textbook (http://albrecht.swcollege.com) for an updated link. Once you've gained access to the site, answer the following questions:

1. Berkshire Hathaway can be described as primarily a holding company, which is a company that has no real operations of its own but instead holds ownership shares of other companies. Berkshire Hathaway's Web site offers links to a number of the subsidiaries that it holds. What are some of these subsidiaries?
2. Warren Buffett writes the best "Chairman's Letters to Shareholders" in corporate America. A historical collection of these letters is included in Berkshire Hathaway's Web site. Look at the 1994 letter and find out whom Warren Buffett quoted on the dangers of hard work.
3. Berkshire Hathaway has two classes of common stock. What does the Web site say about the difference between them?
4. Berkshire Hathaway is constantly making new investments. Search the Web site for recent news releases and identify the most recent investments.

comprehensive problem 9-12

165000

Hannah Company started business on January 1, 2002. The following transactions and events occurred in 2002 and 2003. For simplicity, information for sales, inventory purchases, collections on account, and payments on account is given in summary form at the end of each year.

2002

Jan.	1	Issued 100,000 shares of $1-par common stock to investors at $20 per share.
	1	Purchased a building for $550,000. The building has a 25-year expected useful life and a $50,000 expected salvage value. Hannah uses the straight-line method of depreciation.
	1	Leased equipment under a five-year lease. The five lease payments of $30,000 each are to be made on December 31 of each year. The cash price of the equipment is $113,724. This lease is accounted for as a capital lease with an implicit interest rate of 10%. The equipment has a five-year useful life and zero expected salvage value; Hannah uses straight-line depreciation with all of its equipment.
Feb.	1	Borrowed $1.5 million from Burtone Bank. The loan bears an 11% annual interest rate. Interest is to be paid each year on February 1. The principal on the loan will be repaid in four years.
Mar.	1	Purchased 40,000 shares of Larry Company for $35 per share. Hannah classifies this as an investment in trading securities. These securities are reported as a current asset.
July	15	Purchased 50,000 shares of Frances Ann Company for $21 per share. Hannah classifies this as an investment in available-for-sale securities. These securities are reported as a long-term asset.
Nov.	17	Declared a cash dividend of $0.25 per share, payable on January 15, 2003.
Dec.	31	Made the lease payment.
	31	The Larry Company shares had a market value of $30 per share. The Frances Ann Company shares had a market value of $27 per share.

Summary

a. Sales for the year (all on credit) totaled $800,000. The cost of inventory sold was $350,000.
b. Cash collections on credit sales for the year were $370,000.
c. Inventory costing $420,000 was purchased on account. (Hannah Company uses the perpetual inventory method.)
d. Payments on account totaled $400,000.

2003

Jan.	1	Issued $500,000 in bonds at par value. The bonds have a stated interest rate of 8%, payable semiannually on July 1 and January 1.
	1	The estimated useful life and salvage value for the building were changed. It is now estimated that the building has a remaining life (as of January 1, 2003) of 20 years. Also, it is now estimated that the building will have no salvage value. These changes in estimate are to take effect for the year 2003 and subsequent years.
	15	Paid the cash dividend declared in November 2002.
Feb.	1	Hannah Company repurchased 10,000 shares of its own common stock to be held as treasury stock. The price paid was $37 per share.
	1	Paid the interest on the loan from Burtone Bank.
Apr.	10	Sold all 40,000 shares of the Larry Company stock. The shares were sold for $28 per share.
July	1	Paid the interest on the bonds.
Oct.	1	Retired the bonds that were issued on January 1. Hannah had to pay $470,000 to retire the bonds. This amount included interest that had accrued since July 1.
Nov	20	Declared a cash dividend of $0.40 per share. The dividend applies only to outstanding shares, not to treasury shares.

Dec. 31   Made the lease payment.

31   After recording depreciation expense for the year, the building was evaluated for possible impairment. The building is expected to generate cash flows of $20,000 per year for its 19-year remaining life. The building has a current market value of $325,000.

31   The Frances Ann Company shares had a market value of $18 per share.

Summary

a. Sales for the year (all on credit) totaled $1.7 million. The cost of inventory sold was $800,000.

b. Cash collections on credit sales for the year were $1.43 million.

c. Inventory costing $900,000 was purchased on account.

d. Payments on account totaled $880,000.

Required:

1. Prepare all journal entries to record the information for 2002. Also prepare any necessary adjusting entries.

2. Prepare a trial balance as of December 31, 2002. There is no need to show your ledger T-accounts; however, preparing and posting to T-accounts may aid in the preparation of the trial balance.

3. Prepare an income statement for the year ended December 31, 2002, and a balance sheet as of December 31, 2002.

4. Prepare all journal entries to record the information for 2003. Also prepare any necessary adjusting entries.

5. Prepare a trial balance as of December 31, 2003. (As you compute the amounts to include in the trial balance, don't forget the beginning balances left over from 2002.)

6. Prepare an income statement for the year ended December 31, 2003, and a balance sheet as of December 31, 2003.

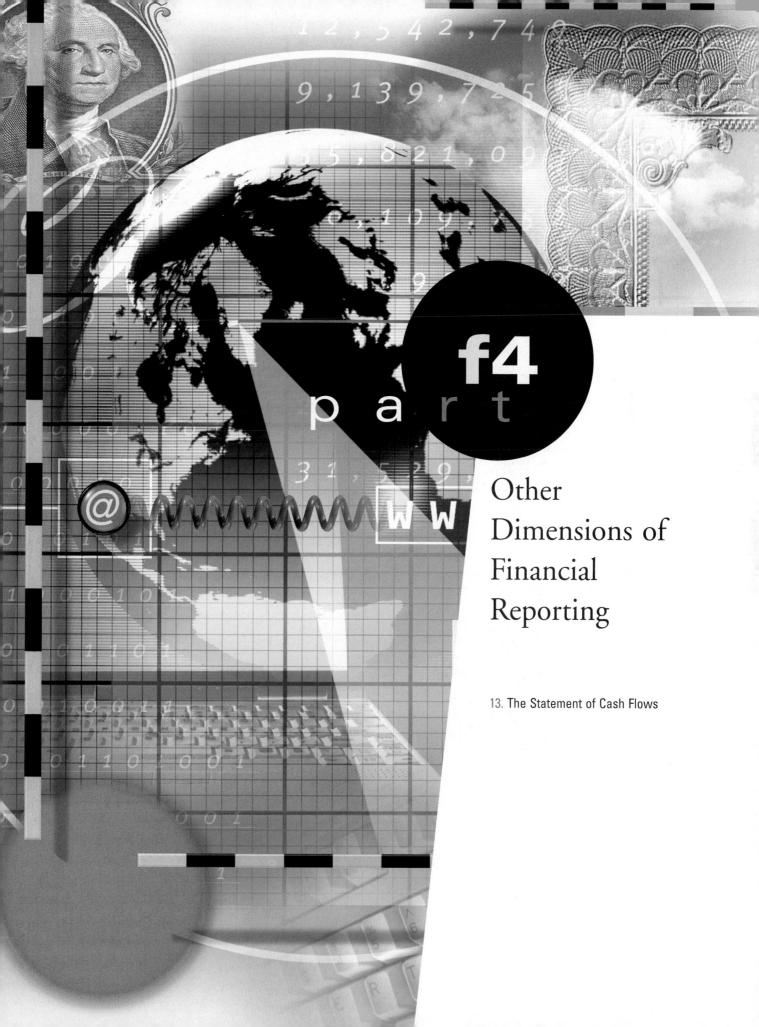

part f4

Other
Dimensions of
Financial
Reporting

The Statement of Cash Flows

chapter **f13**

learning objectives After studying this chapter, you should be able to:

1 Understand the purpose of a statement of cash flows.

2 Recognize the different types of information reported in the statement of cash flows.

3 Prepare a simple statement of cash flows.

4 Analyze financial statements to prepare a statement of cash flows.

5 Use information from the statement of cash flows to make decisions.

HOME DEPOT is the leading retailer in the "do-it-yourself" home handyman market. In January 2000, Home Depot had 913 stores in the United States, five Canadian provinces, and Chile. With each store averaging 108,000 square feet (and an additional 24,000 square feet in the outside garden center), a lot of shelf space is filled with paint, lumber, hardware, and plumbing fixtures. If plumbing fixtures don't seem very exciting to you, consider this: Home Depot is the 22nd largest company in the United States (in terms of market value), with a 2000 market value of $122.9 billion.[1] And if lumber and hardware seem obsolete in this high-tech world, consider that, for the past 10 years, Home Depot's earnings per share (EPS) have grown an average of 30.4% per year, close to the 32.2% annual growth in EPS experienced by high-flying INTEL during the same period. In fiscal 1999, Home Depot's sales reached $38.4 billion.[2]

But Home Depot's prospects weren't always so rosy. Back in 1985, when sales were only $700 million, Home Depot experienced cash flow problems, in large part due to rapid increases in the level of inventory. Part of this inventory increase was the natural result of Home Depot's expansion. But Home Depot stores were also starting to fill up with excess inventory because of lax inventory management. In 1983, the average Home Depot store contained enough inventory to support average sales for 75 days. By 1985, the number of days' sales in inventory had increased to 83 days. Combined with Home Depot's rapid growth, this inventory inefficiency caused total inventory to increase by $69 million in 1985, and this increase in inventory was instrumental in Home Depot's negative cash from operations of $43 million. Concerns about this declining profitability and negative cash flow caused Home Depot's stock value to take a dive in 1985, and the beginning of 1986 found Home Depot wondering where it would find the investors and creditors to finance its aggressive expansion plans. Exhibit 13-1 summarizes the differences between Home Depot's reported net income and the company's cash flow from operations for the fiscal years 1984 through 1986 as well as the company's recent performance.

Home Depot's current success is the result of an incredible operating cash flow turnaround that the company pulled off in fiscal 1987. Operating income almost tripled compared to fiscal 1986, and net income increased from $8.2 million to $23.9 million. A computerized inventory management program was instituted, and the number of days' sales in inventory dropped to 80 days. Improved profitability and more efficient management of inventory combined to transform the negative $43 million operating cash flow in fiscal 1986 into positive cash from operations of $66 million in fiscal 1987.

setting the stage

---

exhibit 13-1   Home Depot's Net Income and Cash Flows from Operations

	Fiscal Year Ended		
(in thousands)	February 2, 1986	February 3, 1985	January 29, 1984
Net earnings	$ 8,219	$14,122	$ 10,261
Net cash provided by operations	(43,120)	(3,056)	(10,574)

	Fiscal Year Ended		
(in thousands)	January 30, 2000	January 31, 1999	February 1, 1998
Net earnings	$2,320,000	$1,614,000	$1,160,000
Net cash provided by operations	2,446,000	1,917,000	1,029,000

---

1 See the Fortune 500 listing at http://www.fortune.com.
2 January 30, 2000, 10-K filing of The Home Depot, Inc.

In this chapter, we will study the statement of cash flows. You will learn that this statement provides one of the earliest warning signs of cash concerns of the type experienced by Home Depot. The statement of cash flows alerts financial statement readers to increases and decreases in cash as well as to the reasons and trends for the changes.

In today's business environment, it is not enough simply to monitor earnings and earnings per share measurements. An entity's financial position and especially its inflows and outflows of cash are also critical to its financial success.

The three primary financial statements were introduced and illustrated in Chapter 2. In subsequent chapters, we examined in detail the components of the balance sheet and income statement. For our discussion of the statement of cash flows, we will first describe the purpose and general format of a statement of cash flows. We will then show how easy it is to prepare a statement of cash flows if detailed cash flow information is available. A statement of cash flows can also be prepared based on an analysis of balance sheet and income statement accounts. We will also distinguish between the direct and indirect methods of reporting operating cash flows and discuss the usefulness of the statement of cash flows. Finally, we will explain how the statement of cash flows can be used to make investment and lending decisions.

1

Understand the purpose of a statement of cash flows.

statement of cash flows
The financial statement that shows an entity's cash inflows (receipts) and outflows (payments) during a period of time.

WHAT'S THE PURPOSE OF A STATEMENT OF CASH FLOWS?

The **statement of cash flows**, as its name implies, summarizes a company's cash flows for a period of time. It provides answers to such questions as, "Where did our money come from?" and "Where did our money go?" The statement of cash flows explains how a company's cash was generated during the period and how that cash was used.

You might think that the statement of cash flows is a replacement for the income statement, but the two statements have two different objectives. The income statement, as you know, measures the results of operations for a period of time. Net income is the accountant's best estimate at reflecting a company's economic performance for a period. The income statement provides details as to how the retained earnings account changes during a period and ties together, in part, the owners' equity sections of comparative balance sheets.

The statement of cash flows, on the other hand, provides details as to how the cash account changed during a period. The statement of cash flows reports the period's transactions and events in terms of their impact on cash. In Chapter 4, we compared the cash-basis and accrual-basis methods of measuring income and explained why accrual-basis income is considered a better measure of periodic income. The statement of cash flows provides important information from a cash-basis perspective that complements the income statement and balance sheet, thus providing a more complete picture of a company's operations and financial position. It is important to note that the statement of cash flows does not include any transactions or accounts that are not already reflected in the balance sheet or the income statement. Rather, the statement of cash flows simply provides information relating to the cash flow effects of those transactions.

Users of financial statements, particularly investors and creditors, need information about a company's cash flows in order to evaluate the company's ability to generate positive net cash flows in the future to meet its obligations and to pay dividends. In some cases, careful analysis of cash flows can provide early warning of impending financial problems, as was the case with HOME DEPOT.

Before moving on, it is important to reiterate that the statement of cash flows does not replace the income statement. The income statement summarizes the results of a company's operations, whereas the statement of cash flows summarizes a company's inflows and outflows of cash. Information contained in the income statement can be used to facilitate the preparation of a statement of cash flows; information in the statement of cash flows sheds some light on the company's ability to generate income in the future. The statement of cash flows and the income statement provide complementary information about different aspects of a business.

to summarize

The statement of cash flows, one of the three primary financial statements, provides information about the cash receipts and payments of an entity during a period. It provides important information that complements the income statement and balance sheet.

2

Recognize the different types of information reported in the statement of cash flows.

cash equivalents Short-term, highly liquid investments that can easily be converted into cash.

net work

Speaking of cash, what is the largest denomination ever printed by the U.S. Treasury Department? Go to http://www.ustreas.gov/currency to find out.

operating activities Transactions and events that enter into the determination of net income.

WHAT INFORMATION IS REPORTED IN THE STATEMENT OF CASH FLOWS?

Accounting standards include specific requirements for the reporting of cash flows. The general format for a statement of cash flows, with details and dollar amounts omitted, is presented in Exhibit 13-2. As illustrated, the inflows and outflows of cash must be divided into three main categories: operating activities, investing activities, and financing activities. Further, the statement of cash flows is presented in a manner that reconciles the beginning and ending balances of cash and cash equivalents. **Cash equivalents** are short-term, highly liquid investments that can easily be converted into cash. Generally, only investments with maturities of three months or less qualify as cash equivalents. Examples are U.S. Treasury bills, money market funds, and commercial paper (short-term debt issued by corporations). In this chapter, as is common in practice, the term *cash* will be used to include cash and cash equivalents.

Major Classifications of Cash Flows

Exhibit 13-3 shows the three main categories of cash inflows and outflows—operating, investing, and financing. Exhibit 13-4 summarizes the specific activities included in each category. Beginning with operating activities, each of the cash flow categories will be explained. We will also discuss the reporting of significant noncash transactions and events.

OPERATING ACTIVITIES **Operating activities** include those transactions and events that enter into the determination of net income. Cash receipts from the sale of goods or services are the major cash inflows for most businesses. Other inflows are cash receipts for interest revenue, dividend revenue, and similar items. Major outflows of cash are for the purchase of inventory and for the payment of wages, taxes, interest, utilities, rent, and similar expenses. As we will explain later, the amount of cash provided by (or used in) operating activities is a key figure and should be highlighted on the statement of cash flows.

Note that our focus in analyzing operating activities is to determine cash flows from operations. An analysis is required to convert income from an accrual-basis to a cash-basis number.

exhibit 13-2 General Format for a Statement of Cash Flows

Cash provided by (used in):	
Operating activities	$XXX
Investing activities.	XXX
Financing activities	XXX
Net increase (decrease) in cash and cash equivalents.	$XXX
Cash and cash equivalents at beginning of year.	XXX
Cash and cash equivalents at end of year.	$XXX

exhibit 13-3   The Flow of Cash

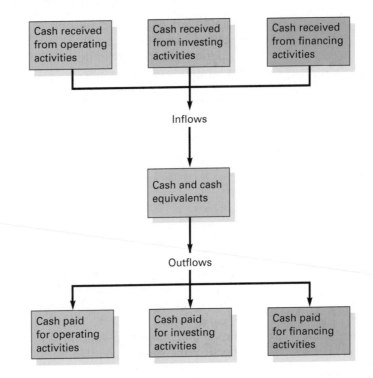

To do this, we begin with the net income figure, remove all items relating to investing activities (such as depreciation and gains/losses on the sale of equipment) and financing activities (such as gains/losses on retirement of debt), and then adjust for changes in those current assets and current liabilities that involve cash and relate to operations (which are most of the current assets and current liabilities).

Operating activities, including the sale of goods, help determine net income and are reported on the statement of cash flows.

exhibit 13-4   Major Classifications of Cash Flows

Operating Activities
Cash receipts from:
  Sale of goods or services
  Interest revenue
  Dividend revenue
  Sale of investments in trading securities
Cash payments to:
  Suppliers for inventory purchases
  Employees for services
  Governments for taxes
  Lenders for interest expense
  Brokers for purchase of trading securities
  Others for other expenses (e.g., utilities, rent)

Investing Activities
Cash receipts from:
  Sale of property, plant, and equipment
  Sale of a business segment
  Sale of investments in securities other than trading securities
  Collection of principal on loans made to other entities
Cash payments to:
  Purchase property, plant, and equipment
  Purchase debt or equity securities of other entities (other than trading securities)
  Make loans to other entities

Financing Activities
Cash receipts from:
  Issuance of own stock
  Borrowing (e.g., bonds, notes, mortgages)
Cash payments to:
  Stockholders as dividends
  Repay principal amounts borrowed
  Repurchase an entity's own stock (treasury stock)

investing activities Transactions and events that involve the purchase and sale of securities (excluding cash equivalents), property, plant, equipment, and other assets not generally held for resale, and the making and collecting of loans.

fyi

The purchase and sale of trading securities is classified as an operating activity.

financing activities Transactions and events whereby resources are obtained from, or repaid to, owners (equity financing) and creditors (debt financing).

INVESTING ACTIVITIES   Transactions and events that involve the purchase and sale of securities (other than trading securities), property, buildings, equipment, and other assets not generally held for resale, and the making and collecting of loans are classified as **investing activities**. These activities occur regularly and result in cash inflows and outflows. They are not classified under operating activities because they relate only indirectly to the entity's central, ongoing operations, which usually involve the sale of goods or services.

The analysis of investing activities involves identifying those accounts on the balance sheet relating to investments (typically long-term asset accounts) and then explaining how those accounts changed and how those changes affected the cash flows for the period.

FINANCING ACTIVITIES   **Financing activities** include transactions and events whereby resources are obtained from or paid to owners (equity financing) and creditors (debt financing). Dividend payments, for example, fit this definition. As noted earlier, the receipt of dividends and interest and the payment of interest are classified under operating activities sim-

business environment essay

The W. T. Grant Company's Negative Cash Flows Perhaps the most famous case highlighting the deficiencies of accrual-basis net income was that of the W. T. GRANT COMPANY. In 1906, William T. Grant opened his first 25-cent store in Lynn, Massachusetts. Twenty-two years later, stock of the W. T. Grant Company was offered for sale to the public. By 1953, the company had expanded to include over 500 stores, and the expansion continued into the 1960s. In 1969 alone, 410 new stores were opened. In 1973, the company's stock was selling at nearly 20 times earnings and peaked at $70⅝ per share. As late as September 1974, a group of banks loaned the company $600 million.

A careful analysis of W. T. Grant's financial statements, however, would have indicated that although the company was reporting profits through 1974, cash flows from operations were almost always negative from 1966 to 1975. Once the market realized the magnitude of W. T. Grant's cash flow problems, it reacted quickly. In December 1974, the company's stock was trading at $2 per share. The company closed 107 stores and laid off 7,000 employees in September 1975. On October 2, 1975, the nation's largest retailer filed for protection under Chapter 11 of the National Bankruptcy

Act. Only four months later, the creditors' committee voted for liquidation, and W. T. Grant ceased to exist.

Why didn't creditors and stockholders see W. T. Grant's impending problems sooner? As the chart shows, net income and working capital provided by operations were of little help in predicting W. T. Grant's problems, but a careful analysis of the company's cash flows would have revealed the problems as much as a decade before the collapse.

How could this happen? Oddly enough, firms were not required to provide investors and creditors with information about cash flows until 1987. Prior to that time, companies prepared a statement of changes in financial position, which measured changes in current assets and current liabilities. This statement of changes in financial position provided information that, if not carefully interpreted, could lead one to believe that a buildup of inventory and receivables was as good as money in the bank (as was the case with W. T. Grant).

The requirement of a statement of cash flows eliminated many of the alternatives used by companies to detail their liquidity position. Now, under generally accepted accounting principles, companies must disclose their liquidity position in terms of cash. Had this standard been applied to W. T. Grant, the negative cash flows from operations would have been highlighted and easily detected.

---

ply because they are reported as a part of income on the income statement. The receipt or payment of the principal amount borrowed or repaid (but not the interest) is considered a financing activity.

Analyzing the cash flow effects of financing activities involves identifying those accounts relating to financing (typically long-term debt and common stock) and explaining how changes in those accounts affected the company's cash flows. Exhibit 13-5 summarizes the activities reflected on the statement of cash flows and indicates how the balance sheet and income statement accounts relate to the various activities.

Noncash Investing and Financing Activities

Some investing and financing activities do not affect cash. For example, equipment may be purchased with a note payable, or land may be acquired by issuing stock. These noncash transactions are not reported in the statement of cash flows. However, if a company has significant noncash financing and investing activities, they should be disclosed in a separate schedule or in a narrative explanation. The disclosures may be presented below the statement of cash flows or in the notes to the financial statements.

Financial History of the W. T. Grant Company 1966–1975

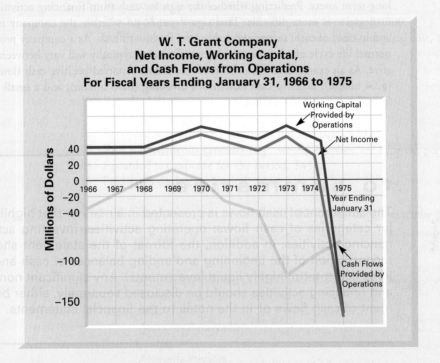

W. T. Grant Company
Net Income, Working Capital,
and Cash Flows from Operations
For Fiscal Years Ending January 31, 1966 to 1975

exhibit 13-5   How Balance Sheet and Income Statement Accounts Relate to the Statement of Cash Flows

Cash Flow Activity	Related Balance Sheet and Income Statement Accounts	Examples	Chapters in Which Accounts Were Covered
Operating	All income statement accounts **except** those income statement items relating to:	Sales, Cost of Goods Sold, Salaries Expense, etc.	Chs. 6–8
	• Investing	Depreciation, Gains/Losses on Sale of Equipment	Ch. 9
	• Financing	Gains/Losses on Retirement of Debt	Ch. 10
	Current assets	Accounts Receivable	Ch. 6
		Inventory	Ch. 7
	Current liabilities	Accounts Payable	Ch. 7
Investing	Long-term assets	Property, Plant, and Equipment	Ch. 9
	Long-term investments	Available-for-Sale and Held-to-Maturity Securities	Ch. 12
Financing	Long-term debt	Bonds and Mortgages	Ch. 10
	Stockholders' equity (except for	Common Stock	Ch. 11
	net income in Retained Earnings)	Dividends	Ch. 11

The Statement of Cash Flows—A Historical Perspective The statement of cash flows is a relatively new financial statement. In 1987, the Financial Accounting Standards Board (FASB) issued an accounting standard, FASB Statement No. 95, requiring that the statement of cash flows be presented as one of the three primary financial statements. Previously, companies had been required to present a statement of changes in financial position, often called the funds statement. In 1971, APB Opinion No. 19 made the funds statement a required financial statement although many companies had begun reporting funds flow information several years earlier. The funds statement provided useful information, but it had several limitations. First, APB Opinion No. 19 allowed considerable flexibility in how funds could be defined and how they were reported on the statement. As a result, many companies reported on a working-capital basis (current assets minus current liabilities), whereas others reported on a cash basis or some other basis. Further, in each case, the individual company selected its own format. This inconsistency across companies made comparisons difficult.

Second, the funds statement, even when prepared on a cash basis, did not provide a complete and clear

When these journal entries are posted, the following trial balance results:

Silmaril, Inc.
Trial Balance
December 31, 2002

	Debit	Credit
Cash	$ 1,430	
Accounts Receivable	2,000	
Inventory	1,800	
Property, Plant, and Equipment	4,500	
Accumulated Depreciation		$ 900
Accounts Payable		1,500
Interest Payable		20
Taxes Payable		50
Long-Term Debt		2,000
Common Stock		1,450
Retained Earnings		2,560
Sales		13,500
Gain on Sale of Equipment		100
Cost of Goods Sold	8,000	
Depreciation Expense	500	
Interest Expense	200	
Tax Expense	450	
Miscellaneous Expenses	3,200	
Totals	$22,080	$22,080

To this point, this is all a review—journalizing transactions, posting journal entries, and preparing a trial balance. From this trial balance, we can easily prepare an income statement

picture of a company's ability to generate positive cash flows. One reason is that APB Opinion No. 19 required that all investing and financing activities be reported in the statement, even those that did not affect cash or working capital. Another problem was that the funds statement usually included two sections— sources (inflows) and uses (outflows) of funds. Thus, the amount of working capital or cash provided or used by each major type of activity (operating, investing, and financing) was not identified.

The limitations of the funds statement often made it difficult to assess a company's ability to generate sufficient cash. Some companies were able to report favorable earnings in the income statement, even

while experiencing serious cash flow problems that were not readily apparent from the information reported in the funds statement. For example, ENDO-LASE, a distributor of medical lasers, reported a 200% increase in sales in one year. Unfortunately, due to poor collection performance, receivables increased at an even faster rate than sales, and much of the reported increase in revenues took the form of IOUs. When many of these receivables were determined to be uncollectible, Endo-Lase had to restate its previously reported earnings. So, although reported earnings appeared strong, Endo-Lase's cash flows were actually negative, and eventually the company had to file for bankruptcy protection.

and a balance sheet; but our objective here is to prepare a statement of cash flows. With information from the Cash T-account, we can prepare a statement of cash flows. The Cash T-account would contain the following information (journal entry reference numbers are in parentheses):

Cash

Beg. Bal.	300		
(2)	14,000	(5)	8,100
(7)	500	(6)	1,700
(9)	450	(8)	200
		(11)	180
		(13)	3,200
		(15)	440
End. Bal.	1,430		

Our task at this point is simply to categorize each cash inflow and outflow as an operating, investing, or financing activity. The inflows and outflows break down as follows:

Operating Activities:

Collections on account (2)...............................			$14,000
Payments for inventory (5)............................	$ 8,100		
Payments for miscellaneous expenses (13)............	3,200		
Payment for interest (11).............................	180		
Payment for taxes (15)...............................	440	(11,920)	
Cash flows from operating activities...................			$ 2,080

Investing Activities:

Sold equipment (7)...................................	$ 500		
Purchased equipment (6).............................	(1,700)		
Cash flows from investing activities..................		(1,200)	

for $450. If something out of the ordinary happened in the common stock account (like the retirement of stock), that information would generally be available in the notes to the financial statements and would be used to modify the analysis.

As an illustration of this type of complexity, consider Silmaril's property, plant, and equipment (PP&E) account. First of all, the PP&E account is associated with what type of cash flow activity?

Investing. Increases in property, plant, and equipment correspond to purchases of PP&E, and decreases relate to the sale of PP&E. Because the sale of PP&E is typically an out-of-the-ordinary type of transaction, we could look at the notes to the financial statements for information relating to any sales. In the case of Silmaril, Inc., we find that equipment costing $1,200, with accumulated depreciation of $800, was sold for $500. Based on this information, and using information from the comparative balance sheets, we can infer the purchases made during the period as follows:

Property, Plant, and Equipment

Beg. Bal.	4,000		
Purchases	?	Sold	1,200
End. Bal.	4,500		

How much PP&E was purchased during the period? The only amount that will reconcile the PP&E account is $1,700. The journal entry would have been a debit to PP&E and a credit to Cash. Again, we find that we don't need the details of the cash account to be able to infer the cash inflows and outflows for the company. Our knowledge of double-entry accounting allows us to do a little detective work and infer what went on in the cash account.

A Six-Step Process for Preparing a Statement of Cash Flows

Is there a systematic method for analyzing the income statement and comparative balance sheets to prepare a statement of cash flows? Yes, the following six-step process can be used in preparing a statement of cash flows:

1. Compute the change in the cash and cash-equivalent accounts for the period of the statement. Seldom is one handed a check figure in real life, but such is the case when preparing a statement of cash flows. The statement of cash flows is not complete until you have explained the change from the beginning balance in the cash account to the balance at year-end.

2. Convert the income statement from an accrual-basis to a cash-basis summary of operations. This is done in three steps: (1) eliminate from the income statement those expenses that do not involve cash (such **noncash items** would include depreciation expense that does not involve an outflow of cash in the current period even though income was reduced); (2) eliminate from the income statement the effects of nonoperating activity items (such items include gains and losses on the sale of long-term assets and gains and losses associated with the retirement of debt); and (3) identify those current asset and current liability accounts associated with the income statement accounts, and adjust those income statement accounts for the changes in the associated current assets and current liabilities. For example, Sales will be adjusted for the change between the beginning and ending balance in Accounts Receivable to derive the cash collections for the period. The final result will be cash flows from operating activities.

3. Analyze the long-term assets to identify the cash flow effects of investing activities. Changes in property, plant, and equipment and in long-term investments may indicate that cash has either been spent or been received.

noncash items Items included in the determination of net income on an accrual basis that do not affect cash; for example, depreciation and amortization.

 Why must gains (losses) on the sale of equipment be subtracted (added) when computing cash flows from operations?

4. Analyze the long-term debt and stockholders' equity accounts to determine the cash flow effects of any financing transactions. These transactions could be borrowing or repaying debt, issuing or buying back stock, or paying dividends.

5. Prepare a formal statement of cash flows by classifying all cash inflows and outflows according to operating, investing, and financing activities. The net cash flows provided by (used in) each of the three main activities of an entity should be highlighted. The net cash flows amount for the period is then added (subtracted) from the beginning Cash balance to report the ending Cash balance.

6. Report any significant investing or financing transactions that did not involve cash in a narrative explanation or in a separate schedule to the statement of cash flows. This would include such transactions as the purchase of land by issuing stock or the retirement of bonds by issuing stock.

An Illustration of the Six-Step Process

We will illustrate this six-step process for preparing the statement of cash flows using the information from the Silmaril, Inc., example presented earlier. Remember that in this case we are assuming that we do not have access to the detailed cash flow information. Thus, we are going to have to make inferences about cash flows by examining all other balance sheet and income statement accounts other than the cash account.

STEP 1. COMPUTE THE CHANGE IN THE CASH AND CASH-EQUIVALENT ACCOUNTS FOR THE PERIOD OF THE STATEMENT Recall that Silmaril began the year with a Cash balance of $300 and ended with a Cash balance of $1,430. Thus, our objective in preparing the statement of cash flows is to explain why the cash account changed by $1,130 during the year.

STEP 2. CONVERT THE INCOME STATEMENT FROM AN ACCRUAL BASIS TO A CASH BASIS From the trial balance prepared at the end of the year, we can prepare the following income statement for Silmaril, Inc.:

Sales	$13,500
Cost of goods sold	8,000
Gross margin	$ 5,500
Miscellaneous expenses	3,200
Depreciation expense	500
Income from operations	$ 1,800
Interest expense	(200)
Gain on sale of equipment	100
Income before taxes	$ 1,700
Tax expense	450
Net income	$ 1,250

Our objective at this point is to convert the income statement to cash flows from operations. Recall that this involves three steps: (1) eliminating expenses not involving cash, (2) eliminating the effects of nonoperating activities, and (3) adjusting the remaining figures from an accrual basis to a cash basis. We will use a work sheet to track the adjustments that will be made. The first two adjustments involve removing depreciation expense (because it does not involve an outflow of cash) and eliminating the gain on the sale of the equipment (because the sale of equipment is an investing activity, the effect of which will be disclosed in the investing activities section of the statement). The following work sheet reflects these adjustments:

c. The forecasted amount of inventory in 2004 is determined using the forecasted value for the number of days' sales in inventory (computed using the end-of-period Inventory balance). The number of days' sales in inventory for 2004 is expected to be 107.6 days. This is from the *Chapter 7 spreadsheet*.

d. The forecasted amount of accounts payable in 2004 is determined using the forecasted value of the number of days' purchases in accounts payable (computed using the end-of-period Accounts Payable balance). The number of days' purchases in accounts payable for 2004 is expected to be 48.34 days. This is from the *Chapter 7 spreadsheet*.

Clearly state any additional assumptions that you make.

2. Repeat (1), with the following changes in assumptions:
   a. The average collection period is expected to be 9.06 days with days' sales in inventory remaining at 107.6 days and days' purchases in payables remaining at 48.34 days.
   b. The average collection period is expected to be 20 days with days' sales in inventory remaining at 107.6 days and days' purchases in payables remaining at 48.34 days.
   c. Days' sales in inventory are expected to be 66.2 days with the average collection period remaining at 14.08 days and days' purchases in payables remaining at 48.34 days.
   d. Days' sales in inventory are expected to be 150 days with the average collection period remaining at 14.08 days and days' purchases in payables remaining at 48.34 days.

3. Comment on the forecasted values of cash from operating activities in 2004 under each of the scenarios given in (2).

▶ **INTERNET SEARCH**

• Home Depot
Access **HOME DEPOT**'s Web site at http://www.homedepot.com. Sometimes Web addresses change, so if this address does not work, access the Web site for this textbook (http://albrecht.swcollege.com) for an updated link.

Once you've gained access to the site, answer the following questions:

1. Locate Home Depot's services site and determine how many different ways Home Depot can help you finance your home improvement plans.
2. Home Depot is highly supportive of various community efforts. Use its Web site to identify the community activities that Home Depot sponsors or is associated with.
3. Home Depot's Web site also includes a number of calculators designed to help buyers determine how much of a given item they need to purchase. Access the calculator for ceramic tile and determine how many tiles you would have to purchase if the room is 10 feet by 20 feet, the surface tiles are 12 inches by 12 inches, and the border tiles are 6 inches by 6 inches.
4. Find Home Depot's most recent set of financial statements. In its statement of cash flows, does Home Depot use the direct method or the indirect method in reporting cash from operating activities?

5. In the most recent year, which is greater—Home Depot's net income or its cash flows from operating activities?

6. Did Home Depot pay any cash dividends in the most recent year?

appendix a

MICROSOFT CORPORATION
1999 ANNUAL REPORT

FINANCIAL HIGHLIGHTS

msft In millions, except earnings per share

Year Ended June 30	1995	1996	1997	1998	1999
Revenue	$6,075	$9,050	$11,936	$15,262	$19,747
Net income	1,453	2,195	3,454	4,490	7,785
Diluted earnings per share[1]	0.29	0.43	0.66	0.84	1.42
Cash and short-term investments	4,750	6,940	8,966	13,927	17,236
Total assets	7,210	10,093	14,387	22,357	37,156
Stockholders' equity	5,333	6,908	10,777	16,627	28,438

1 Diluted earnings per share have been restated to reflect a two-for-one stock split in March 1999.

FELLOW SHAREHOLDERS

> Microsoft continued to perform strongly in 1999. Our customers count on us to provide great software that helps them communicate more effectively, work more productively, learn more creatively, and make the most of their leisure time. We worked hard to meet those needs and to set the standard for features, functionality, simplicity, and seamless integration with the Internet in all of our products. The result was remarkable growth and record revenue.

In the years ahead, we will see accelerating change in the software industry, as the computing needs of our customers start to move beyond the PC into a "PC-Plus" world. The PC will undoubtedly remain at the heart of computing at home, work, and school, but it will be joined by numerous new intelligent devices and appliances, from handheld computers and auto PCs to Internet-enabled cellular phones. More software will be delivered over the Internet, and the boundary between online services and software products will blur. The Internet will continue to change everything by offering a level of connectivity that was unimaginable only a few years ago — and every home, business, and school will want to be hooked up to that incredible global database.

Microsoft's vision is to empower people through great software — any time, any place, and on any device. That means helping companies build friction-free knowledge-management systems, so information flows effortlessly through their businesses, and to implement flawless e-commerce operations. It means helping developers create great Web-enabled products for a wide range of devices. It means making PCs simpler and more reliable. It means helping consumers transform the Internet into their own "personal Internet" — a resource that learns from them over time and empowers them with all of the information they need, while protecting their privacy. Everything we do focuses on allowing people and organizations to create and manage their information.

BUILT AROUND YOU

> In a world of increasing technological complexity, one of our primary goals must be to make our products easier and more effective for customers to use. In part, this entails developing simpler interfaces, natural-language processing, and voice control to help hide the underlying complexity from users. We're working hard to achieve those breakthroughs. But it also means getting closer to our customers and working harder to understand their needs. We must help customers integrate technology by learning about how they work, how information flows through their organization, what they'll need in the future — and about where we're succeeding or failing. Customer-centric thinking must permeate everything we do.

Our growth is always forcing us to look at the best way to stay close to our customers and respond to their needs. This year we organized the company so that its structure is customer-based rather than product-based. The leaders of each of Microsoft's newly defined divisions now have end-to-end management accountability in their respective customer segments. Guided by the company's overall vision, they have total responsibility for setting a clear mission and priorities for their division, including all product planning and marketing strategies. The divisional leaders also have freedom to form business relationships both inside and outside Microsoft — freedom to work with the parties they need to do the best job for their customers.

Microsoft's mission has always been to connect customers with the information they need. But today there is more information to connect with than ever before, stored in more places than ever before, and accessible in more ways than ever before. By refocusing totally on offering customers what they want rather than what technology can provide, we will help them succeed in the PC-Plus world. We will also build a solid foundation for Microsoft well into the 21st century.

MANAGING KNOWLEDGE

> An organization's most valuable asset is its knowledge base. It is also the hardest to manage. For the majority of knowledge workers, getting the information they need is still more difficult than it should be. Mostly, it involves creating and distributing paper documents or telephoning and meeting with fellow employees. New digital approaches enabled by our software will make knowledge workers far more efficient.

With its Web-based collaboration tools, Microsoft® Office 2000 is already a powerful component of a knowledge management solution. In the coming year, we will augment it with several other key initiatives. Windows® 2000 Active Directory™ service will simplify administration and make it easier for knowledge workers to find resources throughout their organization. Future versions of Microsoft Exchange will offer both a platform for unified messaging and our Web Store technology, creating a powerful, centralized communications and knowledge management solution. In the future, we plan to introduce document library and search server technology that will help companies leverage their knowledge bases. Because 50% of work is now done in teams — compared with only 20% a decade ago — we have added team productivity features to the BackOffice® family and other products. And to help organizations realize the dream of a paperless office, our ClearType technology offers on-screen resolution and readability that equals or exceeds that of paper.

To help knowledge workers access information more efficiently, we're also developing what we call a digital dashboard. The digital dashboard is a customized Office 2000 solution that pulls together all of the information that is important to you — regardless of whether it's on your PC, corporate network, or the Internet — and makes it available in one place. A digital dashboard helps you manage and prioritize messages, tasks, information, meetings — in fact, whatever you want. It also gives you access to all of the analytical tools you need to process your data. And it makes all of this available wherever you are, whether on your handheld computer, PC, or smart telephone. The digital dashboard will bring the concept of empowerment any time, any place, and on any device even closer to reality.

CONNECTING EVERYWHERE

> Microsoft's fundamental vision for Windows is one of total scalability — from embedded operating systems in smart devices such as thermostats and light switches, through Windows CE on handheld PCs, and Web-enabled telephones, to the largest mission-critical server farms. Windows 2000, SQL Server™ 7.0, and the next version of Exchange will take our high-end scalability and around-the-clock availability

far beyond what was thought possible just five years ago, and we expect to make even greater progress in the years ahead. A key to this is using Windows 2000 breakthrough load-balancing to provide scaling and reliability beyond that of the most expensive systems of the past. Web sites can use Windows to easily add capacity and avoid having a single point of failure. The Windows 2000 load-balancing technology automatically redirects tasks to the server that is operating under the least load.

A core requirement of knowledge workers is access to their information wherever they are. Our IntelliMirror™ technology in Windows 2000 will help make that possible, by transparently and automatically backing up and synchronizing your data so that it is available on PCs or intelligent devices.

Your handheld computer, Web-enabled telephone, and PC will synchronize with each other wirelessly and automatically, whether you are in your office or on the road. At Microsoft, some of our employees already use Windows 2000 with a wireless network. When they walk into a meeting room, their laptop is automatically recognized and a "virtual workgroup" of everyone in the room is created. Wireless networks will transform the workplace.

Ubiquitous connectivity will also revolutionize the home, enabling consumers to leverage the power and richness of the PC on any intelligent device, thanks to fast, low-cost wireless networks that will make high-quality audio and video available in every room. For example, our Windows Media™ audio player downloads music twice as fast as previous formats, has double the storage capacity, and offers powerful anti-piracy protection. We're also evolving the WebTV Network™ service, which today has more than 800,000 subscribers, with on-demand programming, personalized viewing, more Web-enhanced content, great games, and powerful communications for the whole family. We aim to help millions of Americans enjoy the digital lifestyle at home as well as at work with exciting offerings such as the CarPoint™ online automotive service, HomeAdvisor™ online real estate service, MoneyCentral™ personal finance service, plus the MSN™ Hotmail Web-based e-mail service, which now has more than 40 million members.

EXPANDING BANDWIDTH

> Microsoft's vision of empowering people through great software — any time, any place, and on any device — depends on helping consumers and businesses advance from today's narrow-band world into a broadband future. Even now, the majority of consumers — along with many small and medium-sized businesses — still access the Internet via their regular telephone lines. The result is that the rich world of real-time interactivity remains a dream for most consumers, while many businesses are reluctant to put videoconferencing or multimedia on their networks, because they fear it will crowd out transaction traffic and other high-priority communications.

Our core strategy here is to make investments that will accelerate the deployment of high-speed broadband networks and to collaborate on the technology that will make interactive services for consumers and businesses run seamlessly across these networks. To that end, we are working with companies that will play a leading role in making broadband Internet and multimedia access widely available. We are enthusiastic about the many technologies that will deliver this, which is why we continue to invest in various infrastructures such as wired and wireless telecommunications, cable, and interactive television. Some of our exciting relationships include AT&T, Nextel Communications, NTL, Rogers Communications, WirelessKnowledge, Concentric Networks, Wink Communications, and more.

THE PC-PLUS ERA

> The enduring popularity of the PC — more than 100 million should be sold worldwide this year — is amazing, but not surprising. In a single, economical package, the PC offers individual students, knowledge workers, and consumers the kind of computing power that was found only in corporate computing departments just a decade ago. Whether you want to communicate, learn, work, or play, the PC can enrich and improve the experience.

In the new millennium, the remarkable power and flexibility of the PC will be available wherever it is needed. The PC-Plus era will be about connectivity, scalability, and simplicity. It will be an era when people are at the center, where technology is a natural extension of the way consumers and businesses think about themselves and their interactions with others. The combination of experience, resources, and research that is unique to Microsoft puts us in a strong position to transform this vision into reality.

We are investing heavily in the future — from world-class customer support to the $3.8 billion we plan to spend in fiscal 2000 on research and development for the products of tomorrow. There is, however, no guarantee of success. Competition continues to intensify, and regulatory pressures are unlikely to ease. Although global PC sales have proved remarkably robust, some slowdown is likely in the coming year. And as Microsoft's business becomes more complex, the strategic challenges and risks we face grow exponentially.

I remain optimistic, because the new opportunities for great software products are still incredible. I appreciate the unwavering support and trust of our shareholders and customers as Microsoft enters the 21st century.

Bill Gates

Bill Gates

offered to customers acquiring product from one channel but not the other. Upon adoption of this new rule in the fourth quarter of fiscal 1999, the percentages of the total arrangement treated as unearned decreased. This change in the timing of revenue recognition reduced the amount of Microsoft Windows and Microsoft Office sales treated as unearned and increased the amount of revenue recognized upon shipment. Additionally, as part of the Company's long range planning process and a review of product shipment cycles, it was determined that the life cycle of Windows should be extended from two years to three years. The net impact of these changes was to increase reported revenue $80 million in the fourth quarter of 1999.

BUSINESS DIVISIONS   >   Microsoft has three major segments: Windows Platforms; Productivity Applications and Developer; and Consumer, Commerce, and Other.

> WINDOWS PLATFORMS revenue was $4.92 billion, $6.28 billion, and $8.50 billion in 1997, 1998, and 1999. Platform revenue is primarily licenses of PC operating systems and business and enterprise server systems with client/server, Internet, and intranet architectures.

The Company's principal PC operating systems are Windows 95, Windows 98, and Windows NT® Workstation. Windows 95 was released in August 1995, while its successor, Windows 98, became available at the end of fiscal 1998. Windows NT Workstation version 4.0 was released in fiscal 1997. Although the growth rate of new PC shipments slowed, PC operating systems contributed to revenue growth as shipments of new PCs preinstalled with such systems increased during the three-year period. Additionally, increased penetration of the higher value Windows NT Workstation led to growth in all three years.

WINDOWS PLATFORMS
REVENUE

In billions

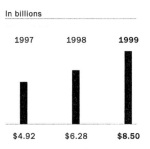

1997	1998	**1999**
$4.92	$6.28	**$8.50**

Windows NT Server is a comprehensive business and enterprise server operating system, combining application, file and print, communication, and Web services. Windows NT Server version 4.0 was released in fiscal 1997. Revenue from Windows NT Server increased strongly during each of the three years due to greater corporate demand, particularly for intranet computing solutions.

> PRODUCTIVITY APPLICATIONS AND DEVELOPER revenue was $5.62 billion, $7.04 billion, and $8.82 billion in 1997, 1998, and 1999. Products include primarily desktop applications, server applications, and software developer tools.

Microsoft Office integrated suites, including the Standard, Small Business, Professional, and Premium Editions, are the Company's principal desktop applications and a key driver of revenue growth. Microsoft Office 97 was released in fiscal 1997 and Microsoft Office 2000 was released at the end of fiscal 1999. The primary programs in Microsoft Office are the word processor Microsoft Word, Microsoft Excel spreadsheet, and Microsoft Outlook® messaging and collaboration client. Various versions of Office, which are available for the Windows and Macintosh operating systems, also include Microsoft Access database management program, Microsoft

PRODUCTIVITY APPLICATIONS
AND DEVELOPER REVENUE

In billions

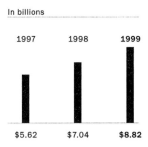

1997	1998	**1999**
$5.62	$7.04	**$8.82**

PowerPoint® presentation graphics program, Microsoft FrontPage® Web site creation and management program, or other programs. Revenue from stand-alone versions of Microsoft Excel, Word, and PowerPoint continued to decrease as the sales mix shifted to integrated product suites.

Server applications, based on Microsoft Windows NT Server, offer an enterprise-wide distributed client/server, Internet, and intranet environment. Products include Microsoft Exchange Server, Microsoft SQL Server, and other server applications in the Microsoft BackOffice family of products. Microsoft Exchange is an enterprise messaging and collaboration server while Microsoft SQL Server is a scalable database and data warehouse platform. Revenue from these products increased strongly over the three-year period, albeit with slowing growth rates in 1998 and 1999.

Independent software vendors, corporate developers, and solutions developers license tools such as the Microsoft Visual Studio® development system, which includes the Microsoft Visual Basic® development system, to develop software for the Windows operating systems and the Internet. Revenue from developer products increased moderately in 1997, was flat in 1998, and increased strongly in 1999.

Although revenue was not significant, preinstallations of Windows CE by OEMs on intelligent devices were strong in 1998 and 1999.

> CONSUMER, COMMERCE, AND OTHER revenue was $1.40 billion, $1.94 billion, and $2.43 billion in 1997, 1998, and 1999. This category of product revenue includes learning and entertainment software; PC input devices; training and certification fees; consulting; and the online services. The Company's Internet services include the MSN portal, MSN access, WebTV®, and vertical properties such as MSN Hotmail Web-based e-mail service, Expedia.com™ travel site, CarPoint car buying site, and MoneyCentral personal finance site.

Learning and entertainment revenue was relatively flat in all three years. Mouse, gaming device, and keyboard sales increased in 1997 and 1998, but were steady in 1999. Training and certification fees from system integrators, along with consulting services to large enterprise customers and technology solution providers, increased strongly in all three years. Revenue from MSN Internet access fees and WebTV services increased due to higher subscriber levels. Advertising revenue, although relatively small in amount, increased exceptionally well in 1999 for the online portal and vertical properties.

CONSUMER, COMMERCE, AND OTHER REVENUE

In billions

1997	1998	1999
$1.40	$1.94	**$2.43**

SALES CHANNELS > Microsoft distributes its products primarily through OEM licenses, organizational licenses, and retail packaged products. OEM channel revenue represents license fees from original equipment manufacturers who preinstall Microsoft products, primarily on PCs. Microsoft has three major geographic sales and marketing organizations: the South Pacific and Americas Region; the Europe, Middle East, and Africa Region; and the Asia Region. Sales of organizational licenses and packaged products via these channels are primarily to and through distributors and resellers.

OEM channel revenue was $3.49 billion in 1997, $4.72 billion in 1998, and $6.40 billion in 1999. The primary source of OEM revenue is the licensing of desktop operating systems, and OEM revenue is highly dependent on PC shipment volume. Growth was also enhanced by increased penetration of higher-value Windows NT Workstation licenses.

Revenue in the South Pacific and Americas Region was $4.39 billion, $5.57 billion, and $7.25 billion in 1997, 1998, and 1999. Revenue in the Europe, Middle East, and Africa Region was $2.77 billion, $3.50 billion, and $4.33 billion for the three years. Growth rates have been lower in Europe than in other geographic areas due to higher existing market shares and a faster shift to licensing programs. Asia Region revenue was $1.29 billion in 1997, $1.48 billion in 1998, and $1.78 billion in 1999. After strong growth in prior years, revenue was relatively flat in Japan and Southeast Asia in 1998 and the first half of fiscal 1999 due to economic issues and weak currencies.

The Company's operating results are affected by foreign exchange rates. Approximately 32%, 32%, and 29% of the Company's revenue was collected in foreign currencies during 1997, 1998, and 1999. Since a portion of local currency revenue is hedged and much of the Company's international manufacturing costs and operating expenses are also incurred in local currencies, the impact of exchange rates is partially mitigated.

OPERATING EXPENSES

> Microsoft encourages broad-based employee ownership of Microsoft stock through an employee stock option (ESO) program in which most employees are eligible to participate. Historically, exercise prices of grants of ESOs were struck at the lowest price in the 30 days following July 1 for annual grants and the 30 days after the start date for new employees. In connection with this practice, which is no longer employed, a charge of $217 million was recorded in the fourth quarter for fiscal 1999 compensation expense, calculated under the provisions of Accounting Principles Board Opinion 25 (APB 25). Charges related to ESO compensation were reflected in 1999 operating expenses as follows (in millions):

Cost of revenue	$ 44
Research and development	105
Sales and marketing	46
General and administrative	22
Total	$217

> COST OF REVENUE   Cost of revenue as a percent of revenue was 18.2% in 1997, 16.1% in 1998, and 14.3% in 1999. The percentage decreases resulted primarily from the trend in mix shift to OEM and organizational licenses. The decrease was also due to the shifts in mix to CD-ROMs (which carry lower cost of goods than disks) and higher-margin Windows NT Server, other servers, and client access licenses in the BackOffice product family. Additionally, cost of revenue in 1999 was positively impacted by a reduction in estimates of obsolete inventory and other manufacturing costs of $67 million. As discussed above, the Company's business model continues to evolve toward licensing from sales of packaged products through distribution channels. Consequently, risks associated with manufacturing and holding physical product have declined.

> RESEARCH AND DEVELOPMENT   Microsoft continued to invest heavily in the future by funding research and development (R&D). Expense increases in 1997, 1998, and 1999 resulted primarily from development staff headcount growth in many areas, particularly Windows platforms, including PC operating systems, servers, and Internet and intranet technologies. R&D costs also increased for productivity applications, development tools, and online services.

In 1998, the Company acquired WebTV Networks, Inc., an online service that enables consumers to experience the Internet through their televisions via set-top terminals. Microsoft paid $425 million in stock and cash. The accompanying income statement reflects a one-time write-off of in-process technologies under development by WebTV Networks of $296 million.

> SALES AND MARKETING   The increase in the absolute dollar amount of sales and marketing expenses in the three-year period was due primarily to expanded product-specific marketing programs, such as Office 97 in 1997, Windows 98 in 1998, and Office 2000 in 1999. Sales and marketing costs as a percentage of revenue decreased primarily due to moderate headcount growth. Microsoft brand advertising expenses rose slightly in 1998, but declined in 1999.

> GENERAL AND ADMINISTRATIVE   Increases in general and administrative expenses were attributable to higher legal fees, litigation costs, and growth in the number of people and computer systems necessary to support overall increases in the scope of the Company's operations.

> OTHER EXPENSES   Other expenses include the recognition of Microsoft's share of joint venture activities, including DreamWorks Interactive and the MSNBC entities.

INVESTMENT INCOME, GAIN ON SALE, AND INCOME TAXES

> Investment income increased primarily as a result of a larger investment portfolio generated by cash from operations in 1997, 1998, and 1999, coupled with realized gains from the sale of certain bond and equity securities in 1999.

In fiscal 1999, Microsoft sold its Softimage, Inc. subsidiary to Avid Technology, Inc. for a pretax gain of $160 million.

The effective income tax rate was 35.0% in 1997. The effective income tax rate increased to 36.9% in 1998 due to the nondeductible write-off of WebTV in-process technologies. Excluding the impact of the gain on the sale of Softimage, Inc., the effective tax rate for fiscal 1999 was 35.0%.

NET INCOME

> Net income as a percent of revenue increased in 1997, 1998, and 1999 due primarily to the lower relative cost of revenue and sales and marketing expenses, combined with greater investment income.

FINANCIAL CONDITION

> The Company's cash and short-term investment portfolio totaled $17.24 billion at June 30, 1999. The portfolio is diversified among security types, industries, and individual issuers. Microsoft's investments are generally liquid and investment grade. The portfolio is invested predominantly in U.S. dollar denominated securities, but also includes foreign currency positions in anticipation of continued international expansion. The portfolio is primarily invested in short-term securities to minimize interest rate risk and facilitate rapid deployment in the event of immediate cash needs.

Microsoft also invests in equities, primarily strategic technology companies. The Company has made large-scale investments in access providers, including cable, telephony, and wireless communications companies. During 1999, the Company purchased $5.0 billion of AT&T convertible preferred securities and warrants, $600 million of Nextel Communications, Inc. common stock, $500 million of NTL, Inc. convertible preferred stock, $330 million of United Pan-Europe Communications common stock, and $200 million of Qwest Communications International Inc. common stock. In connection with AT&T's proposed merger with MediaOne Group, Inc., the Company agreed to acquire MediaOne's interest in Telewest Communications plc, a leading provider of cable television and residential and business cable telephony services in the United Kingdom, subject to certain regulatory approvals and other conditions. During 1997, Microsoft purchased $1.0 billion of Special Class A common stock and convertible preferred stock of Comcast Corporation. Microsoft also owns an interest in MCI WorldCom, Inc.

Microsoft and National Broadcasting Company (NBC) operate two MSNBC joint ventures: a 24-hour cable news and information channel, and an interactive online news service. Microsoft is paying $220 million over a five-year period that ends in 2001 for its interest in the cable venture and one-half of the operational funding of both joint ventures. Microsoft guarantees a portion of MSNBC debt.

Microsoft has no material long-term debt and has $100 million of standby multicurrency lines of credit to support foreign currency hedging and cash management. Stockholders' equity at June 30, 1999 was $28.44 billion.

Microsoft will continue to invest in sales, marketing, and product support infrastructure. Additionally, research and development activities will include investments in existing and advanced areas of technology, including using cash to acquire technology. Additions to property and equipment will continue, including new facilities and computer systems for R&D, sales and marketing, support, and administrative staff. Commitments for constructing new buildings were $275 million on June 30, 1999. Cash will also be used to fund ventures and other strategic opportunities.

In addition, cash will be used to repurchase common stock to provide shares for employee stock option and purchase plans. The buyback program has not kept pace with employee stock option grants or exercises. Beginning in fiscal 1990, Microsoft has repurchased 710 million common shares while 1.79 billion shares were issued under the Company's employee stock option and purchase plans. The market value of all outstanding stock options was $69 billion as of June 30, 1999. Microsoft enhances its repurchase program by selling put warrants. During December 1996, Microsoft issued 12.5 million shares of 2.75% convertible exchangeable preferred stock. Net proceeds of $980 million were used to repurchase common shares. In December 1999, each preferred share is convertible into common shares or an equivalent amount of cash determined by a formula that provides a floor price of $79.875 and a cap of $102.24 per preferred share, equivalent to $19.97 and $25.56 per common share.

Management believes existing cash and short-term investments together with funds generated from operations will be sufficient to meet operating requirements for the next 12 months. The Company's cash and short-term investments are available for strategic investments, mergers and acquisitions, other potential large-scale cash needs that may arise, and to fund an increased stock buyback program over historical levels to reduce the dilutive impact of the Company's employee stock option and purchase programs.

Microsoft has not paid cash dividends on its common stock. The preferred stock pays $2.196 per annum per share.

ISSUES AND UNCERTAINTIES

> While Microsoft management is optimistic about the Company's long-term prospects, the following issues and uncertainties, among others, should be considered in evaluating its growth outlook.

> RAPID TECHNOLOGICAL CHANGE AND COMPETITION   Rapid change, uncertainty due to new and emerging technologies, and fierce competition characterize the PC software industry. The pace of change continues to accelerate, including "open source" software, new computing devices, new microprocessor architectures, the Internet, and Web-based computing models.

> FUTURE INITIATIVES   The Company continues to expand its efforts to provide and support mission-critical systems to large enterprises. Microsoft is also developing a Windows Web-centric platform and simpler and new natural interfaces for PC users. Additionally, Microsoft is committed to providing technologies, operating systems, and online services for all types of computing devices, including PCs, televisions, and intelligent appliances. Future revenue from these initiatives may not duplicate historical revenue growth rates.

> PC GROWTH RATES   The underlying PC unit growth rate and percentage of new PCs acquired as replacement units directly impact the Company's software revenue growth. Additionally, inexpensive PCs and specialty devices create less demand for Microsoft software than traditional PCs. The PC shipment growth rate may continue to decrease, the replacement rate may continue to increase, and limited-use PC growth may increase, reducing future software revenue opportunity.

> PRODUCT SHIP SCHEDULES   Potential delays in new product releases, including seminal products such as Windows 2000, could dampen revenue growth rates and cause operational inefficiencies that impact manufacturing and distribution logistics and relationships with customers, OEMs, and independent software vendors.

> CUSTOMER ACCEPTANCE   While the Company performs extensive usability and beta testing of new products, user acceptance and corporate penetration rates ultimately dictate the success of development and marketing efforts.

> PRICES   Future product prices may decrease from historical levels, depending on competitive market and cost factors. European and Asian software prices vary by country and are generally higher than in the United States to cover localization costs and higher costs of distribution. Increased global license agreements, European monetary unification, or other factors could erode such price uplifts in the future.

> SATURATION   Product upgrades, which enable users to upgrade from earlier versions of the Company's products or from competitors' products, have lower prices and margins than new products. Also, penetration of the Company's desktop applications into large organizations is becoming saturated. These factors are likely to depress future desktop applications revenue growth.

> ORGANIZATIONAL LICENSES   Average revenue per unit from organizational license programs is lower than average revenue per unit from retail versions shipped through the finished goods channels. Unit sales under licensing programs may continue to increase.

> EARNINGS PROCESS   An increasingly higher percentage of the Company's revenue is subject to ratable recognition, which impacts the timing of revenue and earnings recognition. This policy may be required for additional products, depending on specific license terms and conditions. Also, maintenance and other subscription programs may continue to increase in popularity, particularly with organizations.

> CHANNEL MIX   Average revenue per license is lower from OEM licenses than from retail versions, reflecting the relatively lower direct costs of operations in the OEM channel. An increasingly higher percentage of revenue was achieved through the OEM channel during 1998 and 1999.

> COST OF REVENUE   Decreases in cost of revenue as a percentage of revenue in 1998 and 1999 were due to general shifts from packaged products to OEM and organizational licenses, from lower-margin products to higher-margin products, and from disks to CD-ROMs. These shifts may not continue. Direct costs of product support; services such as consulting and training and certification of system integrators; and online operations comprise the majority of cost of revenue and are not likely to decrease. The trend of declining cost of revenue as a percentage of revenue is unlikely to continue in 2000.

> EMPLOYEE COMPENSATION   Microsoft employees currently receive salaries, incentive bonuses, other benefits, and stock options. Fiscal 2000 salaries will be enhanced, with the mid-point salary range raised from the 50th to the 65th percentile of competitive positions. Additionally, new government regulations, poor stock price performance, or other factors could diminish the value of the option program to current and prospective employees and force the Company into more of a cash compensation model. Had the Company paid employees in cash the equivalent of the Black-Scholes value of options vested in 1997, 1998, and 1999, the incremental pretax expense would have been approximately $620 million, $850 million, and $1.10 billion.

> LONG-TERM R&D INVESTMENT CYCLE   Developing and localizing software is expensive, and the investment in product development often involves a long payback cycle. The Company plans to continue significant investments in software research and development, including online initiatives. Significant revenue from these product opportunities is not anticipated for a number of years. Total spending for R&D in 2000 will increase over spending in 1999.

> SALES AND MARKETING INVESTMENTS   The Company's plans for 2000 include accelerated investments in its sales groups, customer satisfaction, and marketing activities.

> INTERNATIONAL OPERATIONS   Much of the Company's operations are conducted outside of the United States, and a large percentage of sales, costs of manufacturing, and marketing is transacted in local currencies. As a result, the Company's international results of operations are subject to local economic environments and foreign exchange rate fluctuations.

> MARKET RISK   The Company is exposed to foreign currency, interest rate, and equity price risks. A portion of these risks is hedged, but fluctuations could impact the Company's results of operations and financial position. The Company hedges the exposure of accounts receivable and a portion of anticipated revenue to foreign currency fluctuations, primarily with option contracts. The Company monitors its foreign currency exposures daily to ensure the overall effectiveness of its foreign currency hedge positions. Principal currencies hedged include the Japanese yen, British pound, German mark, French franc, and Canadian dollar. Fixed income securities are subject to interest rate risk. The portfolio is diversified and consists primarily of investment grade securities to minimize credit risk. The Company routinely hedges its exposure to interest rate risk with options in the event of a catastrophic increase in interest rates. Many securities held in the Company's equity and other investments portfolio are subject to equity price risk. The Company hedges its equity price risk on certain highly volatile equity securities with options.

The Company used a value-at-risk (VAR) model to estimate and quantify its market risks. The VAR model is not intended to represent actual losses in fair value, but is used as a risk estimation and management tool. Assumptions applied to the VAR model at June 30, 1999 include the following: normal market conditions; Monte Carlo modeling with 10,000 simulated market price paths; a 97.5% confidence interval; and a 20-day estimated loss in fair value for each market risk category. Accordingly, 97.5% of the time the estimated 20-day loss in fair value would be nominal for foreign currency denominated investments and accounts receivable, and would not exceed $95 million for interest-sensitive investments or $1.38 billion for equity securities.

Previously, the Company used a sensitivity analysis to estimate interest rate and equity price risk. A 10% increase in interest rates would have reduced the carrying value of interest-sensitive securities by $128 million and $101 million at June 30, 1998 and 1999. A 10% decrease in market values would have reduced the carrying value of the Company's equity securities by $300 million and $1.37 billion at June 30, 1998 and 1999.

> INTELLECTUAL PROPERTY RIGHTS   Microsoft diligently defends its intellectual property rights, but unlicensed copying of software represents a loss of revenue to the Company. While this adversely affects U.S. revenue, revenue loss is even more significant outside of the United States, particularly in countries where laws are less protective of intellectual property rights. Throughout the world, Microsoft actively educates consumers on the benefits of licensing genuine products and educates lawmakers on the advantages of a business climate where intellectual property rights are protected. However, continued efforts may not affect revenue positively.

> LITIGATION   Litigation regarding intellectual property rights, patents, and copyrights occurs in the PC software industry. In addition, there are government regulation and investigation risks along with other general corporate legal risks.

> YEAR 2000   The Year 2000 presents potential concerns for business and consumer computing. In addition to the well-known calculation problems with the use of 2-digit date formats as the year changes from 1999 to 2000, the Year 2000 is a special case leap year and in many organizations using older technology, dates were used for special programmatic functions. The problem exists for many kinds of software and hardware, including mainframes, mini computers, PCs, and embedded systems. The consequences of this issue may include systems failures and business process interruption.

Microsoft has tested more than 3,000 versions/languages of its products. The vast majority of these tested products are Year 2000 compliant, as defined by Microsoft. There are a small number of older products that are identified as being non-compliant, and Microsoft will provide recommendations regarding these products. Not all versions of products or all products will be tested. All Year 2000 software updates, resources, and tools are available to customers at no charge from the Microsoft Year 2000 Portal Page or Microsoft Year 2000 Resource CD.

Current information needed to evaluate the impact of the Year 2000 on organizational and home computing environments is available at the Microsoft Year 2000 Portal Page (www.microsoft.com/year2000) and the Microsoft Year 2000 Resource CD, which is released on a quarterly basis. The Web site and Microsoft Year 2000 Resource CD detail specific Year 2000 information concerning Microsoft products and technologies for large organizations. The detailed information available on the Web site and Microsoft Year 2000 Resource CD is presented to assist information technology (IT) professionals in planning their transition to the Year 2000. The Microsoft Year 2000 Portal Page also contains information for small business and home PC users, including in-depth product information, answers to frequently asked questions, and links to the other Year 2000 sites.

Variability of definitions of "compliance" with the Year 2000 and of different combinations of software, firmware, and hardware will likely lead to lawsuits against the Company. The outcome of such lawsuits and the impact on the Company are not estimable at this time.

The Year 2000 issue also affects the Company's internal systems, including IT and non-IT systems. Microsoft has assessed the readiness of its mission-critical systems for handling the Year 2000. Although testing and remediation of all systems have not been completed, management currently believes that all mission-critical systems will be compliant by the Year 2000 and that the cost to address the issues is not material. Nevertheless, Microsoft is creating contingency plans for certain internal systems.

Microsoft is addressing the effect this issue will have on its third-party supply chain and has undertaken steps to formulate a system of working with key third parties to understand their ability to continue providing services and products through the change to 2000. Microsoft is working directly with its key vendors, distributors, and resellers to avoid material business interruptions in 2000. Contingency plans are being developed where practicable for these key third parties.

Resolving Year 2000 issues is a worldwide phenomenon that is absorbing a substantial portion of IT budgets and attention. Certain industry analysts believe the Year 2000 issue will accelerate the trend toward distributed PC-based systems from mainframe systems, while others believe a majority of IT resources will be devoted to fixing older mainframe software in lieu of large-scale transitions to systems based on software such as that developed by Microsoft. The impact of the Year 2000 on future Microsoft revenue is difficult to discern, but it is a risk to be considered in evaluating the future growth of the Company.

> FUTURE GROWTH RATE   The revenue growth rate in 2000 may not approach the level attained in prior years. As discussed previously, operating expenses are expected to increase in 2000. Because of the fixed nature of a significant portion of such expenses, coupled with the possibility of slower revenue growth, operating margins in 2000 may decrease from those in 1999.

CASH FLOWS STATEMENTS

msft In millions

Year Ended June 30	1997	1998	1999
Operations			
Net income	$ 3,454	$ 4,490	$ 7,785
Depreciation and amortization	557	1,024	1,010
Write-off of acquired in-process technology	–	296	–
Gain on sale of Softimage, Inc.	–	–	(160)
Unearned revenue	1,601	3,268	5,877
Recognition of unearned revenue from prior periods	(743)	(1,798)	(4,526)
Other current liabilities	321	208	966
Accounts receivable	(336)	(520)	(687)
Other current assets	(165)	(88)	(235)
Net cash from operations	4,689	6,880	10,030
Financing			
Common stock issued	744	959	1,350
Common stock repurchased	(3,101)	(2,468)	(2,950)
Put warrant proceeds	95	538	766
Preferred stock issued	980	–	–
Preferred stock dividends	(15)	(28)	(28)
Stock option income tax benefits	796	1,553	3,107
Net cash from (used for) financing	(501)	554	2,245
Investing			
Additions to property and equipment	(499)	(656)	(583)
Cash portion of WebTV purchase price	–	(190)	–
Cash proceeds from sale of Softimage, Inc.	–	–	79
Purchases of investments	(18,216)	(19,114)	(36,441)
Maturities of investments	1,874	1,890	4,674
Sales of investments	13,752	10,798	21,080
Net cash used for investing	(3,089)	(7,272)	(11,191)
Net change in cash and equivalents	1,099	162	1,084
Effect of exchange rates on cash and equivalents	6	(29)	52
Cash and equivalents, beginning of year	2,601	3,706	3,839
Cash and equivalents, end of year	3,706	3,839	4,975
Short-term investments	5,260	10,088	12,261
Cash and short-term investments	$ 8,966	$ 13,927	$ 17,236

See accompanying notes.

BALANCE SHEETS

msft In millions

June 30	1998	1999
Assets		
Current assets:		
Cash and short-term investments	$13,927	**$17,236**
Accounts receivable	1,460	**2,245**
Other	502	**752**
Total current assets	15,889	**20,233**
Property and equipment	1,505	**1,611**
Equity and other investments	4,703	**14,372**
Other assets	260	**940**
Total assets	$22,357	**$37,156**
Liabilities and stockholders' equity		
Current liabilities:		
Accounts payable	$ 759	**$ 874**
Accrued compensation	359	**396**
Income taxes payable	915	**1,607**
Unearned revenue	2,888	**4,239**
Other	809	**1,602**
Total current liabilities	5,730	**8,718**
Commitments and contingencies		
Stockholders' equity:		
Convertible preferred stock – shares authorized 100; shares issued and outstanding 13	980	**980**
Common stock and paid-in capital – shares authorized 12,000; shares issued and outstanding 4,940 and 5,109	8,025	**13,844**
Retained earnings, including other comprehensive income of $666 and $1,787	7,622	**13,614**
Total stockholders' equity	16,627	**28,438**
Total liabilities and stockholders' equity	$22,357	**$37,156**

See accompanying notes.

STOCKHOLDERS' EQUITY STATEMENTS

msft In millions

Year Ended June 30	1997	1998	1999
Convertible preferred stock			
Balance, beginning of year	–	$ 980	$ 980
Convertible preferred stock issued	$ 980	–	–
Balance, end of year	980	980	980
Common stock and paid-in capital			
Balance, beginning of year	2,924	4,509	8,025
Common stock issued	744	1,262	2,338
Common stock repurchased	(91)	(165)	(64)
Structured repurchases price differential	–	328	(328)
Proceeds from sale of put warrants	95	538	766
Reclassification of put warrant obligation	45	–	–
Stock option income tax benefits	792	1,553	3,107
Balance, end of year	4,509	8,025	13,844
Retained earnings			
Balance, beginning of year	3,984	5,288	7,622
Net income	3,454	4,490	7,785
Other comprehensive income:			
Net unrealized investment gains	280	627	1,052
Translation adjustments and other	5	(124)	69
Comprehensive income	3,739	4,993	8,906
Preferred stock dividends	(15)	(28)	(28)
Common stock repurchased	(3,010)	(2,631)	(2,886)
Reclassification of put warrant obligation	590	–	–
Balance, end of year	5,288	7,622	13,614
Total stockholders' equity	$10,777	$16,627	$28,438

See accompanying notes.

NOTES TO FINANCIAL STATEMENTS

msft ACCOUNTING POLICIES

> ACCOUNTING PRINCIPLES   The financial statements and accompanying notes are prepared in accordance with generally accepted accounting principles.

> PRINCIPLES OF CONSOLIDATION   The financial statements include the accounts of Microsoft and its subsidiaries. Significant intercompany transactions and balances have been eliminated. Investments in 50% owned joint ventures are accounted for using the equity method; the Company's share of joint ventures' activities is reflected in other expenses.

> ESTIMATES AND ASSUMPTIONS   Preparing financial statements requires management to make estimates and assumptions that affect the reported amounts of assets, liabilities, revenue, and expenses. Examples include provisions for returns and bad debts and the length of product life cycles and buildings' lives. Actual results may differ from these estimates.

> FOREIGN CURRENCIES   Assets and liabilities recorded in foreign currencies are translated at the exchange rate on the balance sheet date. Translation adjustments resulting from this process are charged or credited to other comprehensive income. Revenue and expenses are translated at average rates of exchange prevailing during the year. Gains and losses on foreign currency transactions are included in other expenses.

> REVENUE RECOGNITION   Revenue is recognized when earned. The Company's revenue recognition policies are in compliance with all applicable accounting regulations, including American Institute of Certified Public Accountants (AICPA) Statement of Position (SOP) 97-2, *Software Revenue Recognition*, and SOP 98-9, *Modification of SOP 97-2, With Respect to Certain Transactions*. Revenue from products licensed to original equipment manufacturers is recorded when OEMs ship licensed products while revenue from certain license programs is recorded when the software has been delivered and the customer is invoiced. Revenue from packaged product sales to and through distributors and resellers is recorded when related products are shipped. Maintenance and subscription revenue is recognized ratably over the contract period. Revenue attributable to undelivered elements, including technical support and Internet browser technologies, is based on the average sales price of those elements and is recognized ratably on a straight-line basis over the product's life cycle. When the revenue recognition criteria required for distributor and reseller arrangements are not met, revenue is recognized as payments are received. Costs related to insignificant obligations, which include telephone support for certain products, are accrued. Provisions are recorded for returns and bad debts.

> COST OF REVENUE   Cost of revenue includes direct costs to produce and distribute product and direct costs to provide online services, consulting, product support, and training and certification of system integrators.

> RESEARCH AND DEVELOPMENT   Research and development costs are expensed as incurred. Statement of Financial Accounting Standards (SFAS) 86, *Accounting for the Costs of Computer Software to Be Sold, Leased, or Otherwise Marketed*, does not materially affect the Company.

> INCOME TAXES   Income tax expense includes U.S. and international income taxes, plus the provision for U.S. taxes on undistributed earnings of international subsidiaries. Certain items of income and expense are not reported in tax returns and financial statements in the same year. The tax effect of this difference is reported as deferred income taxes. Tax credits are accounted for as a reduction of tax expense in the year in which the credits reduce taxes payable.

NOTES continued

> STOCK SPLIT   During March 1999, outstanding shares of common stock were split two-for-one. All share and per share amounts have been restated.

> FINANCIAL INSTRUMENTS   The Company considers all liquid interest-earning investments with a maturity of three months or less at the date of purchase to be cash equivalents. Short-term investments generally mature between three months and six years from the purchase date. All cash and short-term investments are classified as available for sale and are recorded at market using the specific identification method; unrealized gains and losses are reflected in other comprehensive income. Cost approximates market for all classifications of cash and short-term investments; realized and unrealized gains and losses were not material.

Equity and other investments include debt and equity instruments. Debt securities and publicly traded equity securities are classified as available for sale and are recorded at market using the specific identification method. Unrealized gains and losses are reflected in other comprehensive income. All other investments, excluding joint venture arrangements, are recorded at cost.

Derivative financial instruments are used to hedge certain investments, international revenue, accounts receivable, and interest rate risks, and are, therefore, held primarily for purposes other than trading. These instruments may involve elements of credit and market risk in excess of the amounts recognized in the financial statements. The Company monitors its positions and the credit quality of counter parties, consisting primarily of major financial institutions, and does not anticipate nonperformance by any counter party.

During June 1999, the Financial Accounting Standards Board (FASB) issued SFAS 137, *Accounting for Derivative Instruments and Hedging Activities – Deferral of the Effective Date of FASB Statement 133*. The Statement defers the effective date of SFAS 133 to fiscal 2001. Management is evaluating SFAS 133 and does not believe that adoption of the Statement will have a material impact on its financial statements.

> PROPERTY AND EQUIPMENT   Property and equipment is stated at cost and depreciated using the straight-line method over the shorter of the estimated life of the asset or the lease term, ranging from one to 15 years.

> RECLASSIFICATIONS   The Company changed the way it reports revenue and costs associated with product support, consulting, MSN Internet access, and certification and training of system integrators. Amounts received from customers for these activities have been classified as revenue in a manner more consistent with Microsoft's primary businesses. Direct costs of these activities are classified as cost of revenue. Prior financial statements have been reclassified for consistent presentation. Certain other reclassifications have also been made for consistent presentation.

UNEARNED REVENUE

> A portion of Microsoft's revenue is earned ratably over the product life cycle or, in the case of subscriptions, over the period of the license agreement.

End users receive certain elements of the Company's products over a period of time. These elements include browser technologies and technical support. Consequently, Microsoft's earned revenue reflects the recognition of the fair value of these elements over the product's life cycle. Upon adoption of SOP 98-9 during the fourth quarter of fiscal 1999, the Company was required to change the methodology

NOTES continued

of attributing the fair value to undelivered elements. The percentages of undelivered elements in relation to the total arrangement decreased, reducing the amount of Windows and Office revenue treated as unearned, and increasing the amount of revenue recognized upon shipment. The percentage of revenue recognized ratably decreased from a range of 20% to 35% to a range of approximately 15% to 25% of Windows desktop operating systems. For desktop applications, the percentage decreased from approximately 20% to a range of approximately 10% to 20%. The ranges depend on the terms and conditions of the license and prices of the elements. The impact on fiscal 1999 was to increase reported revenue $170 million. In addition, the Company extended the life cycle of Windows from two to three years based upon management's review of product shipment cycles. The impact on fiscal 1999 was to decrease reported revenue $90 million. Product life cycles are currently estimated at 18 months for desktop applications. The Company also sells subscriptions to certain products via maintenance and certain organizational license agreements. At June 30, 1999, Windows platforms products unearned revenue was $2.17 billion and unearned revenue associated with productivity applications and developer products totaled $1.96 billion. Unearned revenue for other miscellaneous programs totaled $116 million at June 30, 1999.

FINANCIAL RISKS

> The Company's cash and short-term investment portfolio is diversified and consists primarily of investment grade securities. Investments are held with high-quality financial institutions, government and government agencies, and corporations, thereby reducing credit risk concentrations. Interest rate fluctuations impact the carrying value of the portfolio. The Company routinely hedges the portfolio's return with options in the event of a catastrophic increase in interest rates. At June 30, 1999, the notional amount of the options outstanding was $4.0 billion. The fair value and premiums paid for the options were not material. Much of the Company's equity security portfolio is highly volatile, so certain positions are hedged.

Finished goods sales to international customers in Europe, Japan, Canada, and Australia are primarily billed in local currencies. Payment cycles are relatively short, generally less than 90 days. Certain international manufacturing and operational costs are disbursed in local currencies. Local currency cash balances in excess of short-term operating needs are generally converted into U.S. dollar cash and short-term investments on receipt. Although foreign exchange rate fluctuations generally do not create a risk of material balance sheet gains or losses, the Company hedges a portion of accounts receivable balances denominated in local currencies, primarily with purchased options. At June 30, 1999, the notional amount of options outstanding was $662 million. The fair value and premiums paid for the options were not material.

Foreign exchange rates affect the translated results of operations of the Company's foreign subsidiaries. The Company hedges a portion of planned international revenue with purchased options. The notional amount of the options outstanding at June 30, 1999 was $2.25 billion. The fair value and premiums paid for the options were not material.

At June 30, 1998 and 1999, approximately 40% and 50% of accounts receivable represented amounts due from 10 customers. One customer accounted for approximately 12%, 8%, and 11% of revenue in 1997, 1998, and 1999.

Microsoft lends certain fixed income and equity securities to enhance investment income. Adequate collateral and/or security interest is determined based upon the underlying security and the credit worthiness of the borrower.

NOTES continued (in millions)

CASH AND SHORT-TERM INVESTMENTS

June 30	1998	1999
Cash and equivalents:		
Cash	$ 195	$ 635
Commercial paper	2,771	3,805
Certificates of deposit	419	522
Money market preferreds	454	13
Cash and equivalents	3,839	4,975
Short-term investments:		
Commercial paper	868	1,026
U.S. government and agency securities	3,511	3,592
Corporate notes and bonds	3,998	6,996
Municipal securities	1,361	247
Certificates of deposit	350	400
Short-term investments	10,088	12,261
Cash and short-term investments	$13,927	$17,236

PROPERTY AND EQUIPMENT

June 30	1998	1999
Land	$ 183	$ 158
Buildings	1,259	1,347
Computer equipment	1,182	1,433
Other	428	578
Property and equipment – at cost	3,052	3,516
Accumulated depreciation	(1,547)	(1,905)
Property and equipment – net	$ 1,505	$ 1,611

During 1997, 1998, and 1999, depreciation expense, of which the majority related to computer equipment, was $353 million, $528 million, and $483 million; disposals were not material.

NOTES continued (in millions)

EQUITY AND OTHER INVESTMENTS

June 30, 1999	Cost Basis	Net Unrealized Gains	Recorded Basis
Debt securities recorded at market, maturing:			
Within one year	$ 682	$ 8	$ 690
Between 10 and 15 years	533	(3)	530
Beyond 15 years (AT&T)	4,731	347	5,078
Debt securities recorded at market	5,946	352	6,298
Equity securities recorded at market:			
Comcast Corporation common stock	500	1,394	1,894
MCI Worldcom, Inc. common stock	14	1,088	1,102
Other	849	1,102	1,951
Unrealized hedge loss	–	(785)	(785)
Equity securities recorded at market	1,363	2,799	4,162
Equity securities and instruments recorded at cost:			
Nextel Communications, Inc. common stock	600	–	600
Comcast Corporation convertible preferred stock	555	–	555
NTL, Inc. convertible preferred stock	511	–	511
Other	2,179	–	2,179
Equity securities and instruments recorded at cost	3,845	–	3,845
Other investments	67	–	67
Equity and other investments	$11,221	$3,151	$14,372

Debt securities include corporate and government notes and bonds and derivative securities. Debt securities maturing beyond 15 years are composed entirely of AT&T 5% convertible preferred debt with a contractual maturity of 30 years. The debt is convertible into AT&T common stock on or after December 1, 2000, or may be redeemed by AT&T upon satisfaction of certain conditions on or after June 1, 2002. Unrealized gains on equity securities recorded at market were $1.4 billion on June 30, 1998. Equity securities and instruments recorded at cost include primarily preferred stock, common stock, and warrants that are restricted or not publicly traded. At June 30, 1998 and 1999, the estimated fair value of these investments was $2.4 billion and $6.1 billion, based on publicly available market information or other estimates determined by management. The Company hedges the risk of significant market declines on certain highly volatile equity securities with options. The options are recorded at market, consistent with the underlying equity securities. At June 30, 1999, the notional amount of the options outstanding was $2.1 billion; the fair value was $1.0 billion; and premiums paid for the options were not material. Realized gains and losses of equity and other investments in 1997 and 1998 were not material; realized gains were $623 million and losses were not material in 1999.

NOTES continued (in millions)

INCOME TAXES

> The provision for income taxes consisted of:

Year Ended June 30	1997	1998	1999
Current taxes:			
U.S. and state	$1,710	$2,518	$4,027
International	412	526	281
Current taxes	2,122	3,044	4,308
Deferred taxes	(262)	(417)	(202)
Provision for income taxes	$1,860	$2,627	$4,106

U.S. and international components of income before income taxes were:

Year Ended June 30	1997	1998	1999
U.S.	$3,775	$5,072	$10,649
International	1,539	2,045	1,242
Income before income taxes	$5,314	$7,117	$11,891

The effective income tax rate was 35.0% in 1997 and increased to 36.9% in 1998 due to the non-deductible write-off of WebTV in-process technologies. In 1999, the effective tax rate was 35.0%, excluding the impact of the gain on the sale of Softimage, Inc. The components of the differences between the U.S. statutory tax rate and the Company's effective tax rate were not significant.

Income taxes payable were:

June 30	1998	1999
Deferred income tax assets:		
Revenue items	$ 713	$ 1,145
Expense items	613	648
Deferred income tax assets	1,326	1,793
Deferred income tax liabilities:		
Unrealized gain on investments	(479)	(1,046)
International earnings	(373)	(647)
Other	(26)	(16)
Deferred income tax liabilities	(878)	(1,709)
Current income tax liabilities	(1,363)	(1,691)
Income taxes payable	$ (915)	$(1,607)

Income taxes have been settled with the Internal Revenue Service (IRS) for all years through 1989. The IRS has assessed taxes for 1990 and 1991, which the Company is contesting in U.S. Tax Court. The IRS is examining the Company's U.S. income tax returns for 1992 through 1994. Management believes any related adjustments that might be required will not be material to the financial statements. Income taxes paid were $1.1 billion in 1997, $1.1 billion in 1998, and $874 million in 1999.

NOTES continued (in millions)

CONVERTIBLE PREFERRED STOCK

> During 1996, Microsoft issued 12.5 million shares of 2.75% convertible exchangeable principal-protected preferred stock. Dividends are payable quarterly in arrears. Preferred stockholders have preference over common stockholders in dividends and liquidation rights. In December 1999, each preferred share is convertible into common shares or an equivalent amount of cash determined by a formula that provides a floor price of $79.875 and a cap of $102.24 per preferred share, equivalent to $19.97 and $25.56 per common share. Net proceeds of $980 million were used to repurchase common shares.

COMMON STOCK

> ISSUED AND OUTSTANDING   Shares of common stock outstanding were as follows:

Year Ended June 30	1997	1998	1999
Balance, beginning of year	4,776	4,816	4,940
Issued	188	202	213
Repurchased	(148)	(78)	(44)
Balance, end of year	4,816	4,940	5,109

> REPURCHASE PROGRAM   The Company repurchases its common stock in the open market to provide shares for issuing to employees under stock option and stock purchase plans. The Company's Board of Directors authorized continuation of this program in 2000.

During 1998, the Company executed two forward settlement structured repurchase agreements with an independent third party totaling 42 million shares of stock and paid cash for a portion of the purchase price. In 1999, the Company settled the agreements by returning 28 million shares of stock, based upon the stock price on the date of settlement. The timing and method of settlement were at the discretion of the Company. The differential between the cash paid and the price of Microsoft common stock on the date of the agreement was originally reflected in common stock and paid-in capital.

PUT WARRANTS

> To enhance its stock repurchase program, Microsoft sells put warrants to independent third parties. These put warrants entitle the holders to sell shares of Microsoft common stock to the Company on certain dates at specified prices. On June 30, 1999, 163 million warrants were outstanding with strike prices ranging from $59 to $65 per share. The put warrants expire between September 1999 and March 2002. The outstanding put warrants permit a net-share settlement at the Company's option and do not result in a put warrant liability on the balance sheet.

EMPLOYEE STOCK AND SAVINGS PLANS

> EMPLOYEE STOCK PURCHASE PLAN   The Company has an employee stock purchase plan for all eligible employees. Under the plan, shares of the Company's common stock may be purchased at six-month intervals at 85% of the lower of the fair market value on the first or the last day of each six-month period. Employees may purchase shares having a value not exceeding 10% of their gross compensation during an offering period. During 1997, 1998, and 1999, employees purchased

NOTES continued (in millions, except per share amounts)

5.6 million, 4.4 million, and 2.7 million shares at average prices of $14.91, $27.21, and $52.59 per share. At June 30, 1999, 70.9 million shares were reserved for future issuance.

> SAVINGS PLAN   The Company has a savings plan, which qualifies under Section 401(k) of the Internal Revenue Code. Participating employees may contribute up to 15% of their pretax salary, but not more than statutory limits. The Company contributes fifty cents for each dollar a participant contributes, with a maximum contribution of 3% of a participant's earnings. Matching contributions were $28 million, $39 million, and $49 million in 1997, 1998, and 1999.

> STOCK OPTION PLANS   The Company has stock option plans for directors, officers, and employees, which provide for nonqualified and incentive stock options. Options granted prior to 1995 generally vest over four and one-half years and expire 10 years from the date of grant. Options granted during and after 1995 generally vest over four and one-half years and expire seven years from the date of grant, while certain options vest over seven and one-half years and expire after 10 years. At June 30, 1999, options for 406 million shares were vested and 998 million shares were available for future grants under the plans.

Stock options outstanding were as follows:

| | Shares | Price per Share | |
		Range	Weighted Average
Balance, June 30, 1996	952	$ 0.28 – $14.74	$ 5.52
Granted	220	13.83 – 29.80	14.58
Exercised	(180)	0.28 – 14.74	3.32
Canceled	(36)	4.25 – 24.29	9.71
Balance, June 30, 1997	956	0.56 – 29.80	7.86
Granted	138	16.56 – 43.63	31.28
Exercised	(176)	0.56 – 31.24	4.64
Canceled	(25)	4.25 – 41.94	14.69
Balance, June 30, 1998	893	0.56 – 43.63	11.94
Granted	78	45.59 – 83.28	54.62
Exercised	(175)	0.56 – 53.63	6.29
Canceled	(30)	4.25 – 74.28	21.06
Balance, June 30, 1999	766	0.56 – 83.28	17.28

For various price ranges, weighted average characteristics of outstanding stock options at June 30, 1999 were as follows:

| Range of Exercise Prices | Outstanding Options | | | Exercisable Options | |
	Shares	Remaining Life (Years)	Weighted Average Price	Shares	Weighted Average Price
$ 0.56 –$ 5.97	242	2.9	$ 4.31	230	$ 4.24
5.98 – 13.62	158	3.9	10.85	89	10.62
13.63 – 29.80	173	4.7	14.92	66	14.67
29.81 – 43.62	117	5.5	32.06	21	31.83
43.63 – 83.28	76	6.2	55.04	–	–

NOTES continued (in millions, except per share amounts)

The Company follows Accounting Principles Board Opinion 25, *Accounting for Stock Issued to Employees,* to account for stock option and employee stock purchase plans. Historically, exercise prices of grants of ESOs were struck at the lowest price in the 30 days following July 1 for annual grants and the 30 days after the start date for new employees. In connection with this practice, which is no longer employed, a charge of $217 million was recorded in the fourth quarter for fiscal 1999 compensation expense.

An alternative method of accounting for stock options is SFAS 123, *Accounting for Stock-Based Compensation.* Under SFAS 123, employee stock options are valued at grant date using the Black-Scholes valuation model, and compensation cost is recognized ratably over the vesting period. Had compensation cost for the Company's stock option and employee stock purchase plans been determined based on the Black-Scholes value at the grant dates for awards, pro forma income statements for 1997, 1998, and 1999 would have been as follows:

Year Ended June 30	1997		1998		1999	
	Reported	Pro forma	Reported	Pro forma	Reported	Pro forma
Revenue	$11,936	$11,936	$15,262	$15,262	$19,747	$19,747
Operating expenses:						
Cost of revenue	2,170	2,290	2,460	2,628	2,814	3,024
Research and development	1,863	2,168	2,601	3,023	2,970	3,504
Acquired in-process technology	–	–	296	296	–	–
Sales and marketing	2,411	2,539	2,828	3,003	3,231	3,448
General and administrative	362	424	433	520	689	822
Other expenses	259	259	230	230	115	115
Total operating expenses	7,065	7,680	8,848	9,700	9,819	10,913
Operating income	4,871	4,256	6,414	5,562	9,928	8,834
Investment income	443	443	703	703	1,803	1,803
Gain on sale of Softimage, Inc.	–	–	–	–	160	160
Income before income taxes	5,314	4,699	7,117	6,265	11,891	10,797
Provision for income taxes	1,860	1,646	2,627	2,325	4,106	3,723
Net income	3,454	3,053	4,490	3,940	7,785	7,074
Preferred stock dividends	15	15	28	28	28	28
Net income available for common shareholders	$ 3,439	$ 3,038	$ 4,462	$ 3,912	$ 7,757	$ 7,046
Diluted earnings per share	$ 0.66	$ 0.58	$ 0.84	$ 0.73	$ 1.42	$ 1.29

The pro forma disclosures in the previous table include the amortization of the fair value of all options vested during 1997, 1998, and 1999, regardless of the grant date. If only options granted after 1996 were valued, as prescribed by SFAS 123, pro forma net income would have been $3,179 million, $4,019 million, and $7,109 million, and earnings per share would have been $0.61, $0.75, and $1.30 for 1997, 1998, and 1999.

The weighted average Black-Scholes value of options granted under the stock option plans during 1997, 1998, and 1999 was $5.86, $11.81, and $20.90. Value was estimated using an expected life of five years, no dividends, volatility of .32 in 1999 and 1998 and .30 in 1997, and risk-free interest rates of 6.5%, 5.7%, and 4.9% in 1997, 1998, and 1999.

NOTES continued (in millions, except per share amounts)

EARNINGS PER SHARE

> Basic earnings per share is computed on the basis of the weighted average number of common shares outstanding. Diluted earnings per share is computed on the basis of the weighted average number of common shares outstanding plus the effect of outstanding preferred shares using the "if-converted" method, assumed net-share settlement of common stock structured repurchases, and outstanding stock options using the "treasury stock" method.

The components of basic and diluted earnings per share were as follows:

Year Ended June 30	1997	1998	1999
Net income	$3,454	$4,490	$7,785
Preferred stock dividends	15	28	28
Net income available for common shareholders	$3,439	$4,462	$7,757
Weighted average outstanding shares of common stock	4,782	4,864	5,028
Dilutive effect of:			
Common stock under structured repurchases	–	6	13
Preferred stock	26	34	16
Employee stock options	436	458	425
Common stock and common stock equivalents	5,244	5,362	5,482
Earnings per share:			
Basic	$ 0.72	$ 0.92	$ 1.54
Diluted	$ 0.66	$ 0.84	$ 1.42

OPERATIONAL TRANSACTIONS

> In August 1997, Microsoft acquired WebTV Networks, Inc., an online service that enables consumers to experience the Internet through their televisions via set-top terminals based on proprietary technologies. A director of the Company owned 10% of WebTV. Microsoft paid $425 million in stock and cash for WebTV. The Company recorded an in-process technologies write-off of $296 million in the first quarter of fiscal 1998.

In August 1998, the Company sold a wholly-owned subsidiary, Softimage, Inc. to Avid Technology, Inc. and recorded a pretax gain of $160 million. As part of a transitional service agreement, Microsoft agreed to make certain development tools and management systems available to Avid for use in the Softimage, Inc. business.

In November 1998, Microsoft acquired LinkExchange, Inc., a leading provider of online marketing services to Web site owners and small and medium-sized businesses. Microsoft paid $265 million in stock. During fiscal 1999, Microsoft also acquired several other entities primarily providing online technologies and services. The Company did not record significant in-process technology write-offs in connection with these transactions.

In July 1999, Ticketmaster Online CitySearch, Inc. agreed to purchase certain online properties of Sidewalk in exchange for stock and warrants at a price to be determined upon closing.

NOTES continued

COMMITMENTS

> The Company has operating leases for most U.S. and international sales and support offices and certain equipment. Rental expense for operating leases was $92 million, $95 million, and $135 million in 1997, 1998, and 1999. Future minimum rental commitments under noncancelable leases, in millions of dollars, are: 2000, $133; 2001, $121; 2002, $97; 2003, $83; 2004, $75; and thereafter, $194.

In connection with the Company's communications infrastructure and the operation of online services, Microsoft has certain communication usage commitments. Future related minimum commitments, in millions of dollars, are: 2000, $125 and 2001, $22. Also, Microsoft has committed to certain volumes of outsourced telephone support and manufacturing of packaged product and has committed $275 million for constructing new buildings.

During 1996, Microsoft and National Broadcasting Company (NBC) established two MSNBC joint ventures: a 24-hour cable news and information channel and an interactive online news service. Microsoft agreed to pay $220 million over a five-year period for its interest in the cable venture, to pay one-half of operational funding of both joint ventures for a multiyear period, and to guarantee a portion of MSNBC debt.

CONTINGENCIES

> On October 7, 1997, Sun Microsystems, Inc. brought suit against Microsoft in the U.S. District Court for the Northern District of California. Sun's complaint alleges several claims against Microsoft, all related to the parties' relationship under a March 11, 1996 Technology License and Distribution Agreement (Agreement) concerning certain Java programming language technology. The Complaint seeks: a preliminary and permanent injunction against Microsoft distributing certain products with the Java Compatibility logo, and against distributing Internet Explorer 4.0 browser technology unless certain alleged obligations are met; an order compelling Microsoft to perform certain alleged obligations; an accounting; termination of the Agreement; and an award of damages, including compensatory, exemplary, and punitive damages, and liquidated damages of $35 million for the alleged source code disclosure.

On March 24, 1998, the court entered an order enjoining Microsoft from using the Java Compatibility logo on Internet Explorer 4.0 and the Microsoft Software Developers Kit (SDK) for Java 2.0. Microsoft has taken steps to fully comply with the order.

On November 17, 1998, the court entered an order granting Sun's request for a preliminary injunction, holding that Sun had established a likelihood of success on its copyright infringement claims, because Microsoft's use of Sun's technology in its products was beyond the scope of the parties' license agreement. The court ordered Microsoft to make certain changes in its products that include Sun's Java technology and to make certain changes in its Java software development tools. The court also enjoined Microsoft from entering into any licensing agreements that were conditioned on exclusive use of Microsoft's Java Virtual Machine. Microsoft appealed that ruling to the 9th Circuit on December 16, 1998. Oral argument on that appeal was held on June 16, 1999. In the interim, Microsoft is complying with the ruling and has not sought a stay of the injunction pending appeal. On December 18, 1998, Microsoft filed a motion requesting an extension of the 90-day compliance period for certain Microsoft products, which was granted in part in January 1999. Microsoft filed a motion on February 5, 1999, seeking clarification of the court's order that Microsoft would not be prevented from engaging in independent development of Java technology under the order. The court granted that motion. On July 23, 1999 the court also granted Microsoft's motion to increase the bond on the preliminary injunction from $15 million to $35 million.

NOTES continued

On January 22, 1999, Microsoft and Sun filed a series of summary judgment motions regarding the interpretation of the contract and other issues. On May 20, 1999, the court issued tentative rulings on three of the motions. In the preliminary rulings, the court (1) granted Sun's motion for summary judgment that prior versions of Internet Explorer 4.0, Windows 98, Windows NT, Visual J++® 6.0 development system, and the SDK for Java infringe Sun's copyrights, because they contain Sun's program code but do not pass Sun's compatibility tests and, therefore, Microsoft's use of Sun's technology is outside the scope of the Agreement and unlicensed; (2) granted Microsoft's motion that the Agreement authorizes Microsoft to distribute independently developed Java technology that is not subject to the compatibility obligations in the Agreement; and (3) denied Sun's motion for summary judgment on the meaning of certain provisions of the Agreement, tentatively adopting Microsoft's interpretation that Sun is required to deliver certain new Java technology, called "Supplemental Java Classes," in working order on Microsoft's then existing and commercially distributed virtual machine. On June 24, 1999, the court heard oral argument on the three tentative rulings. No final orders have been issued. At the hearing, the court also directed the parties to identify other pending summary judgment motions that the court should next consider. There are no other hearing or trial dates set.

On May 18, 1998, the Antitrust Division of the U.S. Department of Justice (DOJ) and a group of 20 state Attorneys General filed two antitrust cases against Microsoft in the U.S. District Court for the District of Columbia. The DOJ complaint alleges violations of Sections 1 and 2 of the Sherman Act. The DOJ complaint seeks declaratory relief as to the violations it asserts and preliminary and permanent injunctive relief regarding: the inclusion of Internet browsing software (or other software products) as part of Windows; the terms of agreements regarding non-Microsoft Internet browsing software (or other software products); taking or threatening "action adverse" in consequence of a person's failure to license or distribute Microsoft Internet browsing software (or other software product) or distributing competing products or cooperating with the government; and restrictions on the screens, boot-up sequence, or functions of Microsoft's operating system products. The state Attorneys General allege largely the same claims and various pendent state claims. The states seek declaratory relief and preliminary and permanent injunctive relief similar to that sought by the DOJ, together with statutory penalties under the state law claims. The foregoing description is qualified in its entirety by reference to the full text of the complaints and other papers on file in those actions, case numbers 98-1232 and 98-1233.

On May 22, 1998, Judge Jackson consolidated the two actions. The judge granted Microsoft's motion for summary judgment as to the states' monopoly leverage claim and permitted the remaining claims to proceed to trial. Trial began on October 19, 1998. Microsoft believes the claims are without merit and is defending against them vigorously. In other ongoing investigations, the DOJ and several state Attorneys General have requested information from Microsoft concerning various issues.

Caldera, Inc. filed a lawsuit against Microsoft in July 1996. It alleges Sherman Act violations relating to Microsoft licensing practices of the MS-DOS® operating system and Windows in the late 80s and early 90s — essentially the same complaints that resulted in the 1994 DOJ consent decree. Caldera claims to own the rights of Novell, Inc. and Digital Research, Inc. relating to DR-DOS and Novell DOS products. It also asserts a claim that Windows 95 is a technological tie of Windows and MS-DOS. Trial is scheduled for January 2000. Some partial summary judgment motions are pending. Microsoft believes the claims are without merit and is vigorously defending the case.

The Securities and Exchange Commission is conducting a non-public investigation into the Company's accounting reserve practices. Microsoft is also subject to various legal proceedings and claims that arise in the ordinary course of business.

Management currently believes that resolving these matters will not have a material adverse impact on the Company's financial position or its results of operations.

NOTES continued (in millions)

SEGMENT INFORMATION

Year Ended June 30	Windows Platforms	Productivity Applications and Developer	Consumer, Commerce, and Other	Reconciling Amounts	Consolidated
1997					
Revenue	$5,213	$5,992	$ 1,129	$ (398)	$11,936
1998					
Revenue	$6,236	$7,458	$ 1,765	$ (197)	$15,262
Operating income	3,661	4,824	(1,050)	(1,021)	6,414
1999					
Revenue	$8,590	$8,686	$ 1,784	$ 687	$ 19,747
Operating income	6,007	5,568	(1,072)	(575)	9,928

The Company's organizational structure and fundamental approach to business reflect the needs of its customers. As such, Microsoft has three major segments: Windows Platforms; Productivity Applications and Developer; and Consumer, Commerce, and Other. Windows Platforms includes the Business and Enterprise Division, which is primarily responsible for Windows NT and developing Windows 2000. Windows Platforms also includes the Consumer Windows Division, which oversees Windows 98 and Windows 95. Productivity Applications and Developer includes the Business Productivity Division, which is responsible for developing and marketing desktop applications, server applications, and developer tools. Consumer, Commerce, and Other products and services include primarily learning, entertainment, and PC input device products; WebTV and PC online access; and portal and other Internet services. Assets of the segment groups are not relevant for management of the businesses nor for disclosure. In addition, it is not practicable to discern operating income for 1997 for the above segments due to previous internal reorganizations.

Segment information is presented in accordance with SFAS 131, *Disclosures about Segments of an Enterprise and Related Information*. This standard is based on a management approach, which requires segmentation based upon the Company's internal organization and disclosure of revenue and operating income based upon internal accounting methods. The Company's financial reporting systems present various data for management to run the business, including profit and loss statements (P&Ls) prepared on a basis not consistent with generally accepted accounting principles. Reconciling items include certain elements of unearned revenue, the treatment of certain channel inventory amounts and estimates, and revenue from product support, consulting, and training and certification of system integrators. Additionally, the internal P&Ls use accelerated methods of depreciation and amortization, but do not reflect the charge for the ESO exercise price methodology previously employed by the Company.

Revenue attributable to U.S. operations includes shipments to customers in the United States, licensing to OEMs and certain multinational organizations, and exports of finished goods primarily to Asia, Latin America, and Canada. Revenue from U.S. operations totaled $7.8 billion, $10.1 billion, and $13.7 billion in 1997, 1998, and 1999. Revenue from outside the United States, excluding licensing to OEMs and certain multinational organizations and U.S. exports, totaled $4.1 billion, $5.2 billion, and $6.0 billion in 1997, 1998, and 1999.

Long-lived assets totaled $1.2 billion and $1.5 billion in the United States in 1998 and 1999 and $287 million and $154 million in other countries in 1998 and 1999.

QUARTERLY INFORMATION (in millions, except per share amounts, unaudited)

	Quarter Ended				
	Sept. 30	Dec. 31	Mar. 31	June 30	Year
1997					
Revenue	$2,405	$2,808	$3,365	$3,358	$11,936
Gross profit	1,923	2,250	2,782	2,811	9,766
Net income	614	741	1,042	1,057	3,454
Basic earnings per share	0.13	0.15	0.22	0.22	0.72
Diluted earnings per share	0.12	0.14	0.20	0.20	0.66
Common stock price per share:					
High	17.33	21.54	25.88	33.74	33.74
Low	13.44	16.36	20.19	22.44	13.44
1998					
Revenue	$3,334	$3,792	$3,984	$4,152	$15,262
Gross profit	2,800	3,179	3,344	3,479	12,802
Net income	663	1,133	1,337	1,357	4,490
Basic earnings per share	0.14	0.24	0.27	0.27	0.92
Diluted earnings per share	0.13	0.21	0.25	0.25	0.84
Common stock price per share:					
High	37.69	36.66	45.47	54.28	54.28
Low	30.82	29.50	31.10	40.94	29.50
1999					
Revenue	$4,193	$5,195	$4,595	$5,764	$19,747
Gross profit	3,544	4,407	3,887	5,095	16,933
Net income	1,683	1,983	1,917	2,202	7,785
Basic earnings per share	0.34	0.40	0.38	0.43	1.54
Diluted earnings per share	0.31	0.36	0.35	0.40	1.42
Common stock price per share:					
High	59.81	72.00	94.63	95.63	95.63
Low	47.25	48.13	68.00	75.50	47.25

The Company's common stock is traded on The Nasdaq Stock Market under the symbol MSFT. On July 31, 1999, there were 92,169 registered holders of record of the Company's common stock. The Company has not paid cash dividends on its common stock.

REPORTS OF MANAGEMENT AND INDEPENDENT AUDITORS

Management is responsible for preparing the Company's financial statements and the other information that appears in this annual report. Management believes that the financial statements fairly reflect the form and substance of transactions and reasonably present the Company's financial condition and results of operations in conformity with generally accepted accounting principles. Management has included in the Company's financial statements amounts that are based on estimates and judgments, which it believes are reasonable under the circumstances.

The Company maintains a system of internal accounting policies, procedures, and controls intended to provide reasonable assurance, at appropriate cost, that transactions are executed in accordance with Company authorization and are properly recorded and reported in the financial statements, and that assets are adequately safeguarded.

Deloitte & Touche LLP audits the Company's financial statements in accordance with generally accepted auditing standards and provides an objective, independent review of the Company's internal controls and the fairness of its reported financial condition and results of operations.

The Microsoft Board of Directors has an Audit Committee composed of nonmanagement Directors. The Committee meets with financial management, internal auditors, and the independent auditors to review internal accounting controls and accounting, auditing, and financial reporting matters.

Gregory B. Maffei
Senior Vice President, Finance and Administration; Chief Financial Officer

To the Board of Directors and Stockholders of Microsoft Corporation:

We have audited the accompanying balance sheets of Microsoft Corporation and subsidiaries as of June 30, 1998 and 1999, and the related statements of income, cash flows, and stockholders' equity for each of the three years ended June 30, 1999, appearing on pages 17 and 27 through 42. These financial statements are the responsibility of the Company's management. Our responsibility is to express an opinion on these financial statements based on our audits.

We conducted our audits in accordance with generally accepted auditing standards. Those standards require that we plan and perform the audit to obtain reasonable assurance about whether the financial statements are free of material misstatement. An audit includes examining, on a test basis, evidence supporting the amounts and disclosures in the financial statements. An audit also includes assessing the accounting principles used and significant estimates made by management, as well as evaluating the overall financial statement presentation. We believe that our audits provide a reasonable basis for our opinion.

In our opinion, such financial statements present fairly, in all material respects, the financial position of Microsoft Corporation and subsidiaries as of June 30, 1998 and 1999, and the results of their operations and their cash flows for each of the three years ended June 30, 1999 in conformity with generally accepted accounting principles.

Deloitte & Touche LLP
Seattle, Washington
July 19, 1999

DIRECTORS AND OFFICERS

DIRECTORS

William H. Gates, III
Chairman of the Board;
Chief Executive Officer,
Microsoft Corporation

Paul G. Allen
Chairman of the Board,
Vulcan Northwest Inc.

Jill Barad
President and
Chief Executive Officer,
Mattel, Inc.

Richard A. Hackborn
Chairman-Elect of the Board,
Hewlett-Packard Company

David F. Marquardt
General Partner,
August Capital and
Technology Venture Investors

Wm. G. Reed, Jr.
Chairman of the Board,
Simpson Investment
Company (retired)

Jon A. Shirley
President and
Chief Operating Officer,
Microsoft Corporation
(retired)

EXECUTIVE OFFICERS

William H. Gates, III
Chairman of the Board;
Chief Executive Officer

Steven A. Ballmer
President

Robert J. Herbold
Executive Vice President;
Chief Operating Officer

Frank M. (Pete) Higgins
Group Vice President
(on leave)

Paul A. Maritz
Group Vice President,
Developer

Jeffrey S. Raikes
Group Vice President,
Sales and Support

James E. Allchin
Senior Vice President,
Platforms

Orlando Ayala Lozano
Senior Vice President,
South Pacific and Americas

Joachim Kempin
Senior Vice President,
OEM Sales

Michel Lacombe
Senior Vice President;
President, Microsoft
Europe, Middle East,
and Africa

Gregory B. Maffei
Senior Vice President,
Finance and Administration;
Chief Financial Officer

Robert L. Muglia
Senior Vice President,
Business Productivity

Craig Mundie
Senior Vice President,
Consumer Strategy

William H. Neukom
Senior Vice President,
Law and Corporate
Affairs; Secretary

Bernard P. Vergnes
Senior Vice President;
Chairman, Microsoft
Europe, Middle East,
and Africa

VICE PRESIDENTS

Robert J. Bach
Home and Retail

Dick Brass
eMerging Technologies

Brad Chase
Consumer and Commerce

Frank M. Clegg
Central United States
and Canada

David Cole
Consumer Windows

John G. Connors
Enterprise

Jean-Philippe Courtois
Customer Marketing

Jon DeVaan
Consumer and Commerce

Richard R. Devenuti
Information Technology;
Chief Information Officer

Richard W. Fade
OEM Multinational Accounts

Dianne Gregg
Eastern United States

Paul H. Gross
Server Applications

William V. Henningsgaard
Western United States
and South Pacific

Laura Jennings
Planning

Kevin Johnson
Product Support Services

Pieter Knook
Asia

Harel Kodesh
Productivity Appliances

Thomas Koll
Network Solutions

Bruce A. Leak
WebTV

John Leftwich
Europe, Middle East,
and Africa Marketing

Lewis Levin
TransPoint

Moshe Lichtman
Consumer and Commerce,
International

Nick N. MacPhee
Operations

Mich Mathews
Corporate Communications

Robert L. McDowell
Enterprise Business
Relationships

Tod Nielsen
Developer Marketing

Umberto Paolucci
Europe, Middle East,
and Africa

Richard F. Rashid
Research

Darryl E. Rubin
Software Strategy

Stephen A. Schiro
Home and Retail Sales

Steven J. Sinofsky
Office

Charles Stevens
Business Solutions

Rick Thompson
Hardware

Rich Tong
Business Audience
Management

Brian Valentine
Business and Enterprise

David Vaskevitch
Distributed Applications
Platform

Henry P. Vigil
Consumer Strategy
and Partnerships

Christopher L. Williams
Human Resources

Deborah N. Willingham
Business and
Enterprise Marketing

glossary

A

Account. An accounting record in which the results of transactions are accumulated; shows increases, decreases, and a balance.

Accounting. A system for providing quantitative, financial information about economic entities that is useful for making sound economic decisions. Accounting is often called the "language of business" because it provides the means of recording and communicating business activities and the results of those activities.

Accounting cycle. The procedure for analyzing, recording, classifying, summarizing, and reporting the transactions of a business.

Accounting equation. An algebraic equation that expresses the relationship between assets (resources), liabilities (obligations), and owners' equity (net assets, or the residual interest in a business after all liabilities have been met): Assets = Liabilities + Owners' equity.

Accounting model. The basic accounting assumptions, concepts, principles, and procedures that determine the manner of recording, measuring, and reporting a company's transactions.

Accounting system. The procedures and processes used by a business to analyze transactions, handle routine bookkeeping tasks, and structure information so it can be used to evaluate the performance and health of the business.

Accounts receivable. A current asset representing money due for services performed or merchandise sold on credit.

Accounts receivable turnover. A measure used to indicate how fast a company collects its receivables; computed by dividing sales by average accounts receivable.

Accrual-basis accounting. A system of accounting in which revenues and expenses are recorded as they are earned and incurred, not necessarily when cash is received or paid.

Accumulated other comprehensive income. Certain market-related gains and losses that are not included in the computation of net income; for example, foreign currency translation adjustments and unrealized gains or losses on investments.

Adjusting entries. Entries required at the end of each accounting period to recognize, on an accrual basis, revenues and expenses for the period and to report proper amounts for asset, liability, and owners' equity accounts.

Aging accounts receivable. The process of categorizing each account receivable by the number of days it has been outstanding.

Allowance for bad debts. A contra account, deducted from accounts receivable, that shows the estimated losses from uncollectible accounts.

Allowance method. The recording of estimated losses due to uncollectible accounts as expenses during the period in which the sales occurred.

American Institute of Certified Public Accountants (AICPA). The national organization of CPAs in the United States.

Amortization. The process of cost allocation that assigns the original cost of an intangible asset to the periods benefited.

Annual report. A document that summarizes the results of operations and financial status of a company for the past year and outlines plans for the future.

Annuity. A series of equal amounts to be received or paid at the end of equal time intervals.

Arm's-length transactions. Business dealings between independent and rational parties who are looking out for their own interests.

Articulation. The interrelationships among the financial statements.

Asset turnover. A measure of company efficiency, computed by dividing revenue by total assets.

Assets. Economic resources that are owned or controlled by a company.

Assets-to-equity ratio. A measure of the number of dollars of assets a company is able to acquire using each dollar of equity; calculated by dividing assets by equity.

Audit committee. Members of a company's board of directors who are responsible for dealing with the external and internal auditors.

Audit report. A report issued by an independent CPA that expresses an opinion about whether the financial statements fairly present a company's financial position, operating results, and cash flows in accordance with generally accepted accounting principles.

Available-for-sale securities. Debt and equity securities not classified as trading, held-to-maturity, or equity method securities.

Average collection period. A measure of the average number of days it takes to collect a credit sale; computed by dividing 365 days by the accounts receivable turnover.

Average cost. An inventory cost flow assumption whereby cost of goods sold and the cost of ending inventory are determined by using an average cost of all merchandise available for sale during the period.

B

Bad debt. An uncollectible account receivable.

Bad debt expense. An account that represents the portion of the current period's credit sales that are estimated to be uncollectible.

Balance sheet (statement of financial position). The financial statement that reports a company's assets, liabilities, and owners' equity at a particular date.

Bank reconciliation. The process of systematically comparing the cash balance as reported by the bank with the cash balance on the company's books and explaining any differences.

Basket purchase. The purchase of two or more assets acquired together at a single price.

Board of directors. Individuals elected by the stockholders to govern a corporation.

Bond. A contract between a borrower and a lender in which the borrower promises to pay a specified rate of interest for each period the bond is outstanding and repay the principal at the maturity date.

Bond carrying value. The face value of bonds minus the unamortized discount or plus the unamortized premium.

Bond discount. The difference between the face value and the sales price when bonds are sold below their face value.

Bond indenture. A contract between a bond issuer and a bond purchaser that specifies the terms of a bond.

Bond maturity date. The date at which a bond principal or face amount becomes payable.

Bond premium. The difference between the face value and the sales price when bonds are sold above their face value.

Bonus. Additional compensation, beyond the regular compensation, that is paid to employees if certain objectives are achieved.

Book value. The value of a company as measured by the amount of owners' equity; that is, assets less liabilities.

Bookkeeping. The preservation of a systematic, quantitative record of an activity.

Business. An organization operated with the objective of making a profit from the sale of goods or services.

Business documents. Records of transactions used as the basis for recording accounting entries; include invoices, check stubs, receipts, and similar business papers.

C

Calendar year. An entity's reporting year, covering 12 months and ending on December 31.

Callable bonds. Bonds for which the issuer reserves the right to pay the obligation before its maturity date.

Capital account. An account in which a proprietor's or partner's interest in a firm is recorded; it is increased by owner investments and net income and decreased by withdrawals and net losses.

Capital budgeting. Systematic planning for long-term investments in operating assets.

Capital lease. A leasing transaction that is recorded as a purchase by the lessee.

Capital stock. The portion of a corporation's owners' equity contributed by owners in exchange for shares of stock.

Capitalized interest. Interest that is recorded as part of the cost of a self-constructed asset.

Cash. Coins, currency, money orders, checks, and funds on deposit with financial institutions; the most liquid of assets.

Cash disbursements journal. A special journal in which all cash paid out for supplies, merchandise, salaries, and other items is recorded.

Cash dividend. A cash distribution of earnings to stockholders.

Cash equivalents. Short-term, highly liquid investments that can be converted easily into cash.

Cash receipts journal. A special journal in which all cash received, from sales, interest, rent, or other sources, is recorded.

Cash-basis accounting. A system of accounting in which transactions are recorded and revenues and expenses are recognized only when cash is received or paid.

Ceiling. The maximum market amount at which inventory can be carried on the books; equal to net realizable value.

Certified Public Accountant (CPA). A special designation given to an accountant who has passed a national uniform examination and has met other certifying requirements.

Chart of accounts. A systematic listing of all accounts used by a company.

Classified balance sheet. A balance sheet in which assets and liabilities are subdivided into current and long-term categories.

Closing entries. Entries that reduce all nominal, or temporary, accounts to a zero balance at the end of each accounting period, transferring their preclosing balances to a permanent balance sheet account.

Common stock. The most frequently issued class of stock; usually it provides a voting right but is secondary to preferred stock in dividend and liquidation rights.

Common-size financial statements. Financial statements achieved by dividing all financial statement numbers by total revenues for the year.

Comparative financial statements. Financial statements in which data for two or more years are shown together.

Compound journal entry. A journal entry that involves more than one debit or more than one credit or both.

Compounding period. The period of time for which interest is computed.

Comprehensive income. A measure of the overall change in a company's wealth during a period; consists of net income plus changes in wealth resulting from changes in investment values and exchange rates.

Consignment. An arrangement whereby merchandise owned by one party, the consignor, is sold by another party, the consignee, usually on a commission basis.

Consolidated financial statements. Statements that report the combined operating results, financial position, and cash flows of two or more legally separate but affiliated companies as if they were one economic entity.

Contingency. Circumstances involving potential losses that will not be resolved until some future event occurs.

Contra account. An account that is offset or deducted from another account.

Contributed capital. The portion of owners' equity contributed by investors (the owners) in exchange for shares of stock.

Control account. A summary account in the general ledger that is supported by detailed individual accounts in a subsidiary ledger.

Control activities (procedures). Policies and procedures used by management to meet its objectives; generally divided into adequate segregation of duties, proper procedures for authorization of transactions and activities, adequate documents and records, physical control over assets and records, and independent checks on performance.

Control environment. The actions, policies, and procedures that reflect the overall attitudes of top management, the directors, and the owners about control and its importance to the entity.

Convertible bonds. Bonds that can be traded for, or converted to, other securities after a specified period of time.

Convertible preferred stock. Preferred stock that can be converted to common stock at a specified conversion rate.

Corporation. A legal entity chartered by a state; ownership is represented by transferable shares of stock.

Cost of goods available for sale. The cost of all merchandise available for sale during the period; equal to the sum of beginning inventory and net purchases.

Cost of goods sold. The expenses incurred to purchase or manufacture the merchandise sold during a period.

Cost principle. The idea that transactions are recorded at their historical costs or exchange prices at the transaction date.

Coupon bonds. Unregistered bonds for which owners receive periodic interest payments by clipping a coupon from the bond and sending it to the issuer as evidence of ownership.

Credit. An entry on the right side of a T-account.

Cumulative-dividend preference. The right of preferred stockholders to receive current dividends plus all dividends in arrears before common stockholders receive any dividends.

Current assets. Cash and other assets that can be easily converted to cash within a year.

Current (working capital) ratio. A measure of the liquidity of a business; equal to current assets divided by current liabilities.

Current-dividend preference. The right of preferred stockholders to receive current dividends before common stockholders receive dividends.

D

Date of record. The date selected by a corporation's board of directors on which the stockholders of record are identified as those who will receive dividends.

Debentures (unsecured bonds). Bonds for which no collateral has been pledged.

Debit. An entry on the left side of a T-account.

Debt ratio. A measure of leverage, computed by dividing total liabilities by total assets.

Debt securities. Financial instruments issued by a company that carry with them a promise of interest payments and the repayment of principal.

Debt-to-equity ratio. The number of dollars of borrowed funds for every dollar invested by owners; computed as total liabilities divided by total equity.

Declaration date. The date on which a corporation's board of directors formally decides to pay a dividend to stockholders.

Declining-balance depreciation method. An accelerated depreciation method in which an asset's book value is multiplied by a constant depreciation rate (such as double the straight-line percentage, in the case of double-declining-balance).

Defined benefit plan. A pension plan under which the employer defines the amount that retiring employees will receive and contributes enough to the pension fund to pay that amount.

Defined contribution plan. A pension plan under which the employer contributes a defined amount to the pension fund; after retirement, the employees receive the amount contributed plus whatever it has earned.

Depletion. The process of cost allocation that assigns the original cost of a natural resource to the periods benefited.

Depreciation. The process of cost allocation that assigns the original cost of plant and equipment to the periods benefited.

Direct method. A method of reporting net cash flows from operations that shows the major classes of cash receipts and payments for a period of time.

Direct write-off method. The recording of actual losses from uncollectible accounts as expenses during the period in which accounts receivable are determined to be uncollectible.

Discounting a note receivable. The process of the payee's selling notes to a financial institution for less than the maturity value.

Dividend payment date. The date on which a corporation pays dividends to its stockholders.

Dividend payout ratio. A measure of the percentage of earnings paid out in dividends; computed by dividing cash dividends by net income.

Dividends. Distributions to the owners (stockholders) of a corporation.

Dividends in arrears. Missed dividends for past years that preferred stockholders have a right to receive under the cumulative-dividend preference if and when dividends are declared.

Double-entry accounting. A system of recording transactions in a way that maintains the equality of the accounting equation.

Drawings account. The account used to reflect periodic withdrawals of earnings by the owner (proprietor) or owners (partners) of a proprietorship or partnership.

Dupont framework. A systematic approach for breaking down return on equity into three ratios: profit margin, asset turnover, and assets-to-equity ratio.

E

Earnings (loss) per share (EPS). The amount of net income (earnings) related to each share of stock; computed by dividing net income by the number of shares of stock outstanding during the period.

Effective-interest amortization. A method of systematically writing off a bond premium or discount that takes into consideration the time value of money and results in an equal rate of amortization for each period.

Employee stock options. Rights given to employees to purchase shares of stock of a company at a predetermined price.

Entity. An organizational unit (a person, partnership, or corporation) for which accounting records are kept and about which accounting reports are prepared.

Environmental liabilities. Obligations incurred because of damage done to the environment.

Equity method. Method used to account for an investment in the stock of another company when significant influence can be imposed (presumed to exist when 20 to 50 percent of the outstanding voting stock is owned).

Equity securities (stock). Shares of ownership in a corporation that can change significantly in value and that provide for a return to investors in the form of dividends.

Expenses. Costs incurred in the normal course of business to generate revenues.

External auditors. Independent CPAs who are retained by organizations to perform audits of financial statements.

Extraordinary items. Nonoperating gains and losses that are unusual in nature, infrequent in occurrence, and material in amount.

F

FIFO (first in, first out). An inventory cost flow whereby the first goods purchased are assumed to be the first goods sold so that the ending inventory consists of the most recently purchased goods.

Financial accounting. The area of accounting concerned with reporting financial information to interested external parties.

Financial Accounting Standards Board (FASB). The private organization responsible for establishing the standards for financial accounting and reporting in the United States.

Financial ratios. Ratios that show relationships between financial statement amounts.

Financial statement analysis. Examining both the relationships among financial statement amounts and the trends in those numbers over time.

Financial statements. Reports such as the balance sheet, income statement, and statement of cash flows, which summarize the financial status and results of operations of a business entity.

Financing activities. Activities whereby cash is obtained from or repaid to owners and creditors.

Finished goods. Manufactured products ready for sale.

Fiscal year. An entity's reporting year, covering a 12-month accounting period.

Fixed asset turnover. The number of dollars in sales generated by each dollar of fixed assets; computed as sales divided by property, plant, and equipment.

Floor. The minimum market amount at which inventory can be carried on the books; equal to net realizable value minus a normal profit.

FOB (free on board) destination. A business term meaning that the seller of merchandise bears the shipping costs and maintains ownership until the merchandise is delivered to the buyer.

FOB (free on board) shipping point. A business term meaning that the buyer of merchandise bears the shipping costs and acquires ownership at the point of shipment.

Foreign Corrupt Practices Act (FCPA). Legislation requiring any company that has publicly traded stock to maintain records that accurately and fairly represent the company's transactions; additionally, requires any publicly traded company to have an adequate system of internal accounting controls.

Foreign currency transaction. A sale in which the price is denominated in a currency other than the currency of the seller's home country.

Franchise. An entity that has been licensed to sell the product of a manufacturer or to offer a particular service in a given area.

G

Gains (losses). Money made or lost on activities outside the normal operation of a company.

Generally accepted accounting principles (GAAP). Authoritative guidelines that define accounting practice at a particular time.

Generally accepted auditing standards (GAAS). Auditing standards developed by the AICPA.

Going concern assumption. The idea that an accounting entity will have a continuing existence for the foreseeable future.

Goodwill. An intangible asset that exists when a business is valued at more than the fair market value of its net assets, usually due to strategic location, reputation, good customer relations, or similar factors; equal to the excess of the purchase price over the fair market value of the net assets purchased.

Gross margin method. A procedure for estimating the amount of ending inventory; the historical relationship of cost of goods sold to sales revenue is used in computing ending inventory.

Gross profit (gross margin). The excess of net sales revenue over the cost of goods sold.

Gross sales. Total recorded sales before deducting any sales discounts or sales returns and allowances.

H

Held-to-maturity security. A debt security purchased by an investor with the intent of holding the security until it matures.

Historical cost. The dollar amount originally exchanged in an arm's-length transaction; an amount assumed to reflect the fair market value of an item at the transaction date.

I

Impairment. A decline in the value of a long-term operating asset.

Income statement (statement of earnings). The financial statement that reports the amount of net income earned by a company during a period.

Independent checks. Procedures for continual internal verification of other controls.

Indirect method. A method of reporting net cash flows from operations that involves converting accrual-basis net income to a cash basis.

Intangible assets. Long-lived assets without physical substance that are used in business, such as licenses, patents, franchises, and goodwill.

Interest rate. The cost of using money, expressed as an annual percentage.

Internal auditors. An independent group of experts (in controls, accounting, and operations) who monitor operating results and financial records, evaluate internal controls, assist with increasing the efficiency and effectiveness of operations, and detect fraud.

Internal control structure. Safeguards in the form of policies and procedures established to provide management with reasonable assurance that the objectives of an entity will be achieved.

Internal Revenue Service (IRS). A government agency that prescribes the rules and regulations that govern the collection of tax revenues in the United States.

International Accounting Standards Board (IASB). The committee formed in 1973 to develop worldwide accounting standards.

Inventory. Goods held for resale.

Inventory shrinkage. The amount of inventory that is lost, stolen, or spoiled during a period; determined by comparing perpetual inventory records to the physical count of inventory.

Inventory turnover. A measure of the efficiency with which inventory is managed; computed by dividing cost of goods sold by average inventory for a period.

Investing activities. Activities associated with buying and selling long-term assets.

J

Journal. An accounting record in which transactions are first entered; provides a chronological record of all business activities.

Journal entry. A recording of a transaction where debits equal credits; usually includes a date and an explanation of the transaction.

Journalizing. Recording transactions in a journal.

Junk bonds. Bonds issued by companies in weak financial condition with large amounts of debt already outstanding; these bonds yield high rates of return because of high risk.

L

Lease. A contract that specifies the terms under which the owner of an asset (the lessor) agrees to transfer the right to use the asset to another party (the lessee).

Ledger. A book of accounts in which data from transactions recorded in journals are posted and thereby summarized.

Lessee. The party that is granted the right to use property under the terms of a lease.

Lessor. The owner of property that is leased (rented) to another party.

Liabilities. Obligations to pay cash, transfer other assets, or provide services to someone else.

License. The right to perform certain activities, generally granted by a governmental agency.

LIFO (last in, first out). An inventory cost flow whereby the last goods purchased are assumed to be the first goods sold so that the ending inventory consists of the first goods purchased.

Limited liability. The legal protection given stockholders whereby they are responsible for the debts and obligations of a corporation only to the extent of their capital contributions.

Liquidity. The ability of a company to pay its debts in the short run.

Long-term assets. Assets that a company needs in order to operate its business over an extended period of time.

Long-term liabilities. Debts or other obligations that will not be paid within one year.

Long-term operating assets. Assets expected to be held and used over the course of several years to facilitate operating activities.

Lower-of-cost-or-market (LCM) rule. A basis for valuing inventory at the lower of original cost or current market value.

M

Maker. A person (entity) who signs a note to borrow money and who assumes responsibility to pay the note at maturity.

Management accounting. The area of accounting concerned with providing internal financial reports to assist management in making decisions.

Market Adjustment—Trading Securities. An account used to track the difference between the historical cost and the market value of a company's portfolio of trading securities.

Market rate (effective rate or yield rate) of interest. The actual interest rate earned or paid on a bond investment.

Market value. The value of a company as measured by the number of shares of stock outstanding multiplied by the current market price of the stock; the current value of a business.

Matching principle. The concept that all costs and expenses incurred in generating revenues must be recognized in the same reporting period as the related revenues.

Maturity date. The date on which a note or other obligation becomes due.

Maturity value. The amount of an obligation to be collected or paid at maturity; equal to principal plus any interest.

Monetary measurement. The idea that money, as the common medium of exchange, is the accounting unit of measurement, and that only economic activities measurable in monetary terms are included in the accounting model.

Mortgage amortization schedule. A schedule that shows the breakdown between interest and principal for each payment over the life of a mortgage.

Mortgage payable. A written promise to pay a stated amount of money at one or more specified future dates; a mortgage is secured by the pledging of certain assets, usually real estate, as collateral.

N

Natural resources. Assets that are physically consumed or waste away, such as oil, minerals, gravel, and timber.

Net assets. The owner's equity of a business; equal to total assets minus total liabilities.

Net income (net loss). An overall measure of the performance of a company; equal to revenues minus expenses for the period.

Net purchases. The net cost of inventory purchased during a period, after adding the cost of freight in and subtracting returns and discounts.

Net realizable value. The selling price of an item less reasonable selling costs.

Net realizable value of accounts receivable. The net amount that would be received if all receivables considered collectible were collected; equal to total accounts receivable less the allowance for bad debts.

Net sales. Gross sales less sales discounts and sales returns and allowances.

Nominal accounts. Accounts that are closed to a zero balance at the end of each accounting period; temporary accounts generally appearing on the income statement.

Noncash items. Items included in the determination of net income on an accrual basis that do not affect cash; examples are depreciation and amortization.

Noncash transactions. Investing and financing activities that do not affect cash; if significant, they are disclosed below the statement of cash flows or in the notes to the financial statements.

Nonprofit organization. An entity without a profit objective, oriented toward providing services efficiently and effectively.

Note receivable. A claim against a debtor, evidenced by an unconditional written promise to pay a certain sum of money on or before a specified future date.

Notes to the financial statements. Explanatory information considered an integral part of the financial statements.

NSF (not sufficient funds) check. A check that is not honored by a bank because of insufficient cash in the check writer's account.

Number of days' purchases in accounts payable. A measure of how well operating cash flow is being managed; computed by dividing total inventory purchases by average accounts payable and then dividing 365 days by the result.

Number of days' sales in inventory. An alternative measure of how well inventory is being managed; computed by dividing 365 days by the inventory turnover ratio.

O

Operating activities. Activities that are part of the day-to-day business of a company.

Operating lease. A simple rental agreement.

Organizational structure. Lines of authority and responsibility.

Other revenues and expenses. Items incurred or earned from activities that are outside, or peripheral to, the normal operations of a firm.

Owners' equity. The ownership interest in the net assets of an entity; equals total assets minus total liabilities.

P

Par value. A nominal value assigned to and printed on the face of each share of a corporation's stock.

Partnership. An association of two or more individuals or organizations to carry on economic activity.

Patent. An exclusive right granted for 17 years by the federal government to manufacture and sell an invention.

Payee. The person (entity) to whom payment on a note is to be made.

Pension. An agreement between an employer and employees that provides for benefits upon retirement.

Periodic inventory system. A system of accounting for inventory in which cost of goods sold is determined and inventory is adjusted at the end of the accounting period, not when merchandise is purchased or sold.

Perpetual inventory system. A system of accounting for inventory in which detailed records of the number of units and the cost of each purchase and sales transaction are prepared throughout the accounting period.

Physical safeguards. Physical precautions used to protect assets and records, such as locks on doors, fireproof vaults, password verification, and security guards.

Post-closing trial balance. A listing of all real account balances after the closing process has been completed; provides a means of testing whether total debits equal total credits for all real accounts prior to beginning a new accounting cycle.

Postemployment benefits. Benefits paid to employees who have been laid off or terminated.

Posting. The process of transferring amounts from the journal to the ledger.

Preferred stock. A class of stock that usually provides dividend and liquidation preferences over common stock.

Prepaid expenses. Payments made in advance for items normally charged to expense.

Present value of $1. The value today of $1 to be received or paid at some future date given a specified interest rate.

Present value of an annuity. The value today of a series of equally spaced, equal-amount payments to be made or received in the future given a specified interest rate.

Price-earnings (P/E) ratio. A measure of growth potential, earnings stability, and management capabilities; computed by dividing market price per share by earnings per share.

Primary financial statements. The balance sheet, income statement, and statement of cash flows, used by external groups to assess a company's economic standing.

Principal (face value or maturity value). The amount that will be paid on a note or other obligation at the maturity date.

Prior-period adjustments. Adjustments made directly to Retained Earnings in order to correct errors in the financial statements of prior periods.

Profit margin. A measure of the number of pennies in profit generated from each dollar of revenue; calculated by dividing net income by revenue.

Property, plant, and equipment. Tangible, long-lived assets acquired for use in business operations; includes land, buildings, machinery, equipment, and furniture.

Proprietorship. A business owned by one person.

Prospectus. Report provided to potential investors that presents a company's financial statements and explains its business plan, sources of financing, and significant risks.

Purchases journal. A special journal in which credit purchases are recorded.

R

Raw materials. Materials purchased for use in manufacturing products.

Real accounts. Accounts that are not closed to a zero balance at the end of each accounting period; permanent accounts appearing on the balance sheet.

Realized gains and losses. Gains and losses resulting from the sale of securities in an arm's-length transaction.

Receivables. Claims for money, goods, or services.

Registered bonds. Bonds for which the names and addresses of the bondholders are kept on file by the issuing company.

Retained earnings. The amount of accumulated earnings of the business that have not been distributed to owners.

Return on equity. A measure of the amount of profit earned per dollar of investment, computed by dividing net income by equity.

Return on sales. A measure of the amount of profit earned per dollar of sales, computed by dividing net income by sales.

Revenue. Increase in a company's resources from the sale of goods or services.

Revenue recognition. The process of recording revenue in the accounting records; occurs after (1) the work has been substantially completed and (2) cash collection is reasonably assured.

Revenue recognition principle. The idea that revenues should be recorded when (1) the earnings process has been substantially completed and (2) cash has either been collected or collectibility is reasonably assured.

S

Sales discount. A reduction in the selling price that is allowed if payment is received within a specified period.

Sales journal. A special journal in which credit sales are recorded.

Sales returns and allowances. A contra-revenue account in which the return of, or allowance for reduction in the price of, merchandise previously sold is recorded.

Sales tax payable. Money collected from customers for sales taxes that must be remitted to local governments and other taxing authorities.

Salvage value. The amount expected to be received when an asset is sold at the end of its useful life.

Secured bonds. Bonds for which assets have been pledged in order to guarantee repayment.

Securities and Exchange Commission (SEC). The government body responsible for regulating the financial reporting practices of most publicly owned corporations in connection with the buying and selling of stocks and bonds.

Segregation of duties. A strategy to provide an internal check on performance through separation of authorization of transactions from custody of related assets; separation of operational

responsibilities from record-keeping responsibilities; and separation of custody of assets from accounting personnel.

Separate entity concept. The idea that the activities of an entity are to be separated from those of the individual owners.

Serial bonds. Bonds that mature in a series of installments at specified future dates.

Social security (FICA) taxes. Federal insurance contributions act taxes imposed on employee and employer; used mainly to provide retirement benefits.

Special journal. A book of original entry for recording similar transactions that occur frequently.

Specific identification. A method of valuing inventory and determining cost of goods sold whereby the actual costs of specific inventory items are assigned to them.

Stated rate of interest. The rate of interest printed on the bond.

Statement of cash flows. The financial statement that shows an entity's cash inflows (receipts) and outflows (payments) during a period of time.

Statement of comprehensive income. A statement outlining the changes in accumulated comprehensive income that arose during the period.

Statement of partners' capital. A partnership report showing the changes in the capital balances; similar to a statement of retained earnings for a corporation.

Statement of retained earnings. A report that shows the changes in the retained earnings account during a period of time.

Statement of stockholders' equity. A financial statement that reports all changes in stockholders' equity.

Stock dividend. A pro rata distribution of additional shares of stock to stockholders.

Stock split. The replacement of outstanding shares of stock with a greater number of new shares.

Stockholders (shareholders). The owners of a corporation.

Stockholders' equity. The owners' equity section of a corporate balance sheet.

Straight-line amortization. A method of systematically writing off a bond discount or premium in equal amounts each period until maturity.

Straight-line depreciation method. The depreciation method in which the cost of an asset is allocated equally over the periods of an asset's estimated useful life.

Subsidiary ledger. A grouping of individual accounts that in total equal the balance of a control account in the general ledger.

Sum-of-the-years'-digits depreciation method. The accelerated depreciation method in which a constant balance (cost minus salvage value) is multiplied by a declining depreciation rate.

T

T-account. A simplified depiction of an account in the form of a letter T.

Term bonds. Bonds that mature in one single sum at a specified future date.

Time period concept. The idea that the life of a business is divided into distinct and relatively short time periods so that accounting information can be timely.

Time value of money. The concept that a dollar received now is worth more than a dollar received far in the future.

Times interest earned. A measure of a borrower's ability to make required interest payments; computed as income before interest and taxes divided by annual interest expense.

Trading securities. Debt and equity securities purchased with the intent of selling them should the need for cash arise or to realize short-term gains.

Transactions. Exchange of goods or services between entities (whether individuals, businesses, or other organizations), as well as other events having an economic impact on a business.

Treasury stock. Issued stock that has subsequently been reacquired by the corporation.

Trial balance. A listing of all account balances; provides a means of testing whether total debits equal total credits for all accounts.

U

Unearned revenues. Cash amounts received before they have been earned.

Units-of-production method. The depreciation method in which the cost of an asset is allocated to each period on the basis of the productive output or use of the asset during the period.

Unrealized gains and losses. Gains and losses resulting from changes in the value of securities that are still being held.

Unrecorded liabilities. Expenses incurred during a period that have not been recorded by the end of that period.

Unrecorded receivables. Revenues earned during a period that have not been recorded by the end of that period.

W

Work in p
   ductic
Work she
   mariz

6-8   (1) Bad debt expense = $7,000
6-10   (2) Ending Accounts Receivable = $1,340,000
6-12   (3) Net Accounts Receivable = $149,010
6-14   2003 Debit to Bad Debt Expense = $60,000
6-16   (1) Boulder, Inc. average collection period for Year 3 = 118 days
6-18   N/A
6-20   (2) Debit to Estimated Liability for Service = $675
6-22   (2) Debit to Miscellaneous Expenses = $50
6-24   12/1 Debit to Cash = $13,041
6-26   10/1 Credit to Interest Revenue = $732
6-28   (1) Debit to Cash (Japanese yen) = $10,000

Problems

6-2   N/A
6-4   N/A
6-6   (2) (a) Net sales = $1,570,000
6-8   (2) Debit to Bad Debt Expense = $63,500
6-10   (1) Debit to Bad Debt Expense = $65,600
6-12   N/A
6-14   (1) Suspected stolen = $28,453
6-16   (3) Debit to Cash = 25,462

CHAPTER 7

Exercises

7-2   6/30 Debit to Sales Returns = $16,000
7-4   Debit to Inventory Shrinkage = $28,000
7-6   Debit to Cost of Goods Sold = $244,000
7-8   Carter Co. Cost of goods sold = $43,100
7-10   Credit to Inventory = $12.25
7-12   N/A
7-14   (b) Ending inventory LIFO = $59,700
7-16   (1) (a) Gross margin = $35,000
7-18   (5) Credit to Inventory = $100
7-20   (1) Gross margin = $160,000
7-22   Gross margin = $600,000

Problems

7-2   (2) (j) Debit to Sales Returns = $630
7-4   (10) Gross margin = $675
7-6   (2) Ending inventory LIFO = $42,000
7-8   (1) Net Purchases = $79,600
7-10   (1) 2003 Correct gross margin = $14,700
7-12   (1) (a) Gross margin = $9,336

CHAPTER 8

Exercises

8-2   (2) Credit to Bonus Payable = $24,000
8-4   N/A

8-6   (1) Pension = $55,000
8-8   (2) Debit to Property Tax Expense = $3,800
8-10   (2) Income Tax Expense = $200,000
8-12   N/A
8-14   Gross margin = $124,938

Problems

8-2   (2) Cash paid to employees = $15,193
8-4   (1) Pension expense = $350
8-6   (3) 2003 Deferred tax liability = $0
8-8   (10) Net sales revenue = $35,000

CHAPTER 9

Exercises

9-2   (1) Debit to Machine = $11,850
9-4   (1) Credit to Cash = $115,000
9-6   Building = $654,800
9-8   (1) (b) 2003 Depreciation expense = $3,375
9-10   (1) Credit to Cash = $47,100
9-12   Credit to Land = $160,000
9-14   (1) Credit to Gain on Sale of Machine = $5,000
9-16   (3) Credit to Franchise = $25,000
9-18   Fixed asset turnover = 2.05
9-20   (1) Total cost = $12,350
9-22   (2) 2003 = $6,825
9-24   (4) Credit to Accumulated Depletion, Coal Mine = $100,000

Problems

9-2   N/A
9-4   (3) 1/2 Debit to Leased Computer = $238,820
9-6   (2) Alternative B = $42,150 per year
9-8   (2) Debit to Equipment = $45,000
9-10   (1) Credit to Cash = $114,000
9-12   (3) Debit to Depletion Expense = $180,000
9-14   (2) Credit to Goodwill = $750
9-16   (1) Fixed asset turnover = 3.08
9-18   (3) Depreciation = $50,400
9-20   (2) 2003 Depreciation expense = $3,500
9-22   (3) Uranium book value = $24,000

CHAPTER 10

Exercises

10-2   (4) $20,000
10-4   (1) Payment = $26,380
10-6   12/31/03 Credit to Cash = $1,250
10-8   (2) Total interest paid = $5,582
10-10   (2) Debit to Rent Expense = $4,141

10-12 Total issuance price = $51,675

10-14 (3) 4/1 Debit to Bond Interest Expense = $18,000

10-16 (1) Debt ratio = 55.6%

10-18 (1) (b) Debit to Premium on Bonds = $100

10-20 (4) Bonds Payable Carrying Value = $51,772

Problems

10-2 (2) (a) $32,210

10-4 1/1/03 Debit to Interest Payable = $1,295

10-6 (2) 12/31/03 Debit to Interest Expense = $1,998

10-8 (2) Debit to Leased Starship = $148,547

10-10 (4) 10/1/06 Credit to Gain on Bond Retirement = $5,000

10-12 Total current liabilities = $153,800

10-14 (1) Current ratio = 1.6

10-16 (2) (a) Credit to Discount on Bonds = $135

10-18 (1) Debit to Cash = $463,500

10-20 (2) Total interest expense = $24,759

10-22 (2) Total discount amortization = $8,844

10-24 (1) Issuance price of bonds = $467,664

CHAPTER 11

Exercises

11-2 (2) Retained earnings = $77,600

11-4 (c) Credit to Dividends Payable = $24,000

11-6 (e) Credit to Dividends Payable = $79,800

11-8 (3) $1.69 per share

11-10 (2) Total dividends paid = $172,485

11-12 (2) $8.43 per share

11-14 Comprehensive income = $9,000

11-16 (c) Debit to Retained Earnings = $750,000

11-18 (2) Retained earnings = $144,000

11-20 Retained earnings, 12/31/03 = $78,000

11-22 (2) Total investments = $100,500

Problems

11-2 (2) Total contributed capital = $1,802,200

11-4 (2) Total stockholders' equity = $398,175

11-6 (3) Total preferred stock dividends = $64,000

11-8 (1) (a) Dividend payout ratio = 0.40

11-10 (1) (c) $9,000

11-12 (2) Total contributed capital = $791,500

11-14 (2) Total stockholders' equity = $395,800

11-16 (3) Decrease = $37.6 million

11-18 (2) Total dividends = $110,000

11-20 (2) Total contributed capital = $196,200

11-22 (2) Pat Larsen, capital, 12/31/03 = $76,000

CHAPTER 12

Exercises

12-2 12/31 Credit to Unrealized Gain on Trading Securities—Income = $1,560

12-4 12/31/03 Debit to Unrealized Increase/Decrease in Value of Available-for-Sale Securities—Equity = $27,500

12-6 Debit to Investment in Trading Securities = $20,500

12-8 Debit to Market Adjustment—Available-for-Sale Securities = $100

12-10 Credit to Cash = $24,700

12-12 (2) Total present value = $113,592

12-14 (1) 12/31 Debit to Bond Interest Receivable = $1,500

12-16 Total amount of amortization = $1,706

12-18 (2) Credit to Dividend Revenue = $3,000

Problems

12-2 (1) Unrealized gain/loss for 2002 = $68,000 loss

12-4 8/31 Debit to Realized Loss on Sale of Trading Securities = $28,000

12-6 12/31/03 Credit to Market Adjustment—Available-for-Sale Securities = $1,680

12-8 (3) Debit to Realized Loss on Sale of Available-for-Sale Securities = $8,000

12-10 (2) 12/31 Credit to Market Adjustment—Available-for-Sale Securities = $15,000

12-12 (1) 10/1/03 Credit to Investment in Held-to-Maturity Securities = $43.60

12-14 (2) Total interest revenue = $10,123

12-16 (2) 12/31/03 Credit to Investment in Equity Method Securities to record dividends from Essem = $15,000

12-18 (1) (a) 12/1/02 Credit to Dividend Revenue = $6,250

12-20 (2) Balance sheet—Investment in equity method securities = $645,450

CHAPTER 13

Exercises

13-2 N/A

13-4 (1) (d) Credit to Interest Revenue = $1,500

13-6 (1) Cash collected from customers = $223,000

13-8 Net cash flows provided by operations = $21,700

13-10 Net cash flows provided by operating activities = $161,600

13-12 Net cash flows provided by operating activities = $243,000

13-14 Net cash flows by operating activities = $116,000

13-16 Net cash flows used in investing activities = ($60,000)

13-18 N/A

Problems

13-2 (2) Net increase in cash = $22,300

13-4 (1) Net cash flows provided by operating activities = $13,000

13-6 (1) Net cash flows from operations = $15,490

13-8 Net income = $95,000

13-10 (1) Net cash flows from operating activities = $580

13-12 (1) Cash paid for taxes = $8,400

indexes

SUBJECT INDEX

indexes

INTERNET INDEX*

*Note: These Web site addresses may also be accessed at **http://albrecht.swcollege.com**